# COPYRIGHT AND PIRACY

An understanding of the changing nature of the law and practice of copyright infringement is a task too big for lawyers alone; it requires additional inputs from economists, historians, technologists, sociologists, cultural theorists and criminologists. Where is the boundary to be drawn between (illegal) imitation and (legal) inspiration? Is the answer different for creators, artists and experts from different disciplines or fields? How have concepts of copyright infringement altered over time and how do such changes relate – if at all – to the cultural norms operating among creators in different fields? With such an approach, one might perhaps begin to address the vital and overarching question of whether strong copyright laws, rigorously enforced, impede rather than promote creativity. And what can be done to avoid any such adverse consequences, while maintaining the effectiveness of copyright as an incentive mechanism for those who need it?

LIONEL BENTLY is Herchel Smith Professor of Intellectual Property Law, Director of the Centre for Intellectual Property and Information Law, and Professorial Fellow at Emmanuel College, University of Cambridge.

JENNIFER DAVIS is Herchel Smith College Lecturer in Intellectual Property Law and a member of the Centre for Intellectual Property and Information Law, University of Cambridge. She is also a Fellow of Wolfson College, Cambridge.

JANE C. GINSBURG is Morton L. Janklow Professor of Literary and Artistic Property Law, and Director of the Kernochan Center for Law, Media and the Arts, at the Columbia University School of Law. She is also an Honorary Fellow of Emmanuel College, University of Cambridge.

# COPYRIGHT AND PIRACY: AN INTERDISCIPLINARY CRITIQUE

Edited by

LIONEL BENTLY,

JENNIFER DAVIS

and

JANE C. GINSBURG

CAMBRIDGE UNIVERSITY PRESS
Cambridge, New York, Melbourne, Madrid, Cape Town, Singapore,
São Paulo, Delhi, Dubai, Tokyo, Mexico City

Cambridge University Press
The Edinburgh Building, Cambridge CB2 8RU, UK

Published in the United States of America by Cambridge University Press, New York

www.cambridge.org
Information on this title: www.cambridge.org/9780521193436

© Cambridge University Press 2010

First published 2010

Printed in the United Kingdom at the University Press, Cambridge

*A catalogue record for this publication is available from the British Library*

ISBN 978-0-521-19343-6 Hardback

# CONTENTS

# NOTES ON THE CONTRIBUTORS

JONATHAN ALDRED

Fellow of Emmanuel College and a Newton Trust Lecturer in the Department of Land Economy, both at the University of Cambridge. An economist by training, his research interests are now inter-disciplinary, spanning economics, philosophy, law and political theory. He has particular interests in the philosophical foundations of welfare economics and economic theories of rational choice. Recent publications have focused on the scope and limitations of using monetary measures to value environmental impacts and public policy outcomes. Dr Aldred is currently working on an introductory book on the ethical assumptions behind popular economic arguments, *Ethical Economics*.

ISABELLA ALEXANDER

Newton Trust Lecturer in the Faculty of Law, University of Cambridge and Beachcroft LLP Fellow in Law and Director of Studies in Law at Robinson College, Cambridge. Her research interests lie in intellectual property law and legal history. She is the author of *Copyright and the Public Interest in the Nineteenth Century*.

TANYA APLIN

Reader in Intellectual Property Law at the School of Law, King's College London. She teaches courses on UK copyright law, international and comparative copyright law, patent law, trade marks and passing off, and legal regulation of the cultural industries. Dr Aplin has written extensively on copyright law, particularly in relation to digital technologies, as well as on the protection of confidential information. Her publications include: *Copyright Law in the Digital Society: The Challenges of Multimedia* (2005); *Intellectual Property: Text, Cases, and Materials* (2009).

ANNE BARRON

Reader in Law at London School of Economics and Political Science, where she specializes in intellectual property law (in particular copyright law) and legal and social theory. Currently working on a book that aims to map the contemporary field of theoretical inquiry in relation to the institution of copyright.

PAUL CLOUGH

Lecturer in Information Systems in the Department of Information Studies, University of Sheffield (UK). He received his B.Eng. from the University of York in computer science while also working for British Telecommunications plc as a software engineer. He received his Ph.D. from the Department of Computer Science, University of Sheffield, and has since worked as a researcher on a range of language-engineering and information access projects. Clough is member of the Information Retrieval (IR) group and his core research interests are information retrieval (geographical IR, multimedia IR and evaluation), computational text analysis (plagiarism detection, authorship attribution and creating corpora) and human–computer interaction. He has over seventy peer-reviewed publications in his research area and a US patent for an information management system.

JON CROWCROFT

Marconi Professor of Networked Systems in the Computer Laboratory, of the University of Cambridge. Prior to that he was Professor of Networked Systems at University College London in the Computer Science Department. He is a Fellow of: the ACM; the British Computer Society; the IET; the Royal Academy of Engineering; and the IEEE. He was a member of the IAB 96–02, and went to the first 50 IETF meetings; was general chair for the ACM SIGCOMM 95–99; is recipient of Sigcomm Lifetime Achievement Award in 2009. He has supervised twenty-five Ph.D. students to completion and has published five books and around 150 papers.

JENNIFER DAVIS

Herchel Smith College Lecturer in Intellectual Property Law and a member of the Centre for Intellectual Property and Information Law, University of Cambridge. She is also a Fellow of Wolfson College, Cambridge. She is the author of *Intellectual Property Law* (2008) and with Tanya Aplin, *Intellectual Property: Text, Cases, and Materials*

(2009). Together with Lionel Bently and Jane Ginsburg, she edited the first book in this series: *Trade Marks and Brands: An Interdisciplinary Critique* (2008). She has a particular interest in trade mark law and unfair competition and has published extensively on these topics. Before joining the Faculty of Law, Dr Davis practised as a lawyer specializing in intellectual property litigation.

GRAEME B. DINWOODIE

Professor of Intellectual Property and Information Technology Law at the University of Oxford, Director of the Oxford Intellectual Property Research Centre and a Professorial Fellow of St. Peter's College. Prior to taking up the IP Chair at Oxford, Professor Dinwoodie was a Professor of Law and Director of the Program in Intellectual Property Law at the Chicago-Kent College of Law. He is the author of several casebooks and numerous articles on various aspects of intellectual property law. Professor Dinwoodie holds a first-class LLB (Hons.) degree from the University of Glasgow, an LLM from Harvard Law School, and a JSD from Columbia Law School.

ALAN DURANT

Professor of Communication at Middlesex University Business School, London, and the author of *Meaning in the Media: Discourse, Controversy and Debate* (2010). His earlier publications include a number of textbooks on English language and literature as well as the textbook *Language and Media*, co-written with Marina Lambrou (2009). Other studies include: *Conditions of Music* (1984) and (ed. with Nigel Fabb, Derek Attridge and Colin MacCabe) *The Linguistics of Writing* (1987).

LORAINE GELSTHORPE

University Reader in Criminology and Criminal Justice at the Institute of Criminology, University of Cambridge and a psychoanalytic psychotherapist (UKCP registered). She is also chair of the Cambridge Socio-legal Group (an interdisciplinary initiative) and chair of the British Society of Criminology's Ethics Committee. She has published widely and internationally on a range of matters in the fields of youth justice, community penalties, and, in particular, women, crime and criminal justice. She recently published *The Handbook of Probation* (ed. with Rod Morgan, 2007).

JANE C. GINSBURG

Morton L. Janklow Professor of Literary and Artistic Property Law and Co-Director of the Kernochan Center for Law, Media and the Arts. Teaches legal methods, copyright law, and trade marks law at Columbia Law School. Has taught French and US copyright law and US legal methods and contracts law at the University of Paris and other French universities. During the 2004–5 academic year held the Arthur L. Goodhart Chair of Legal Science at the University of Cambridge.

Publications: co-author (with Sam Ricketon), *International Copyright and Neighbouring Rights: The Berne Convention and Beyond* (2006); (with Robert P. Merges) *Foundations of Intellectual Property* (2004) and (with Rochelle Dreyfuss) *Intellectual Property Stories* (2005). With Professors Dreyfuss and François Dessemontet, Co-Reporter for the American Law Institute project entitled *Intellectual Property: Principles Governing Jurisdiction, Choice of Law and Judgments in Transnational Disputes* (2008), *Legal Methods: Cases and Materials* (3d edn, 2008); *Cases and Materials on Copyright* (with Gorman, 7th edn, 2006 and 2010 suppl.) and *Trademark and Unfair Competition Law* (with Litman and Kevlin, 4th edn, 2007 and 2010 suppl.), as well as a variety of law review articles. Co-editor (with Lionel Bently and Jennifer Davis) of *Trade Marks and Brands: An Interdisciplinary Critique* (2008).

JONATHAN GRIFFITHS

Senior Lecturer, Queen Mary, University of London. Specializes in intellectual property law (particularly copyright law) and information law. Mr Griffiths is a solicitor and teaches intellectual property law, international and comparative copyright law and the law of torts. He has published widely on the relationships between intellectual property, free speech and access to information, and is currently engaged in research on the three-step test in copyright law and on the impact of the Human Rights Act 1998 on trade mark law. Since 2008, a senior fellow of Melbourne Law School, University of Melbourne.

Publications include: *Blackstone's Guide to the Freedom of Information Act 2000* (with John Wadham and Kelly Harris, 3rd edn, 2007); *Copyright and Free Speech: International and Comparative Perspectives* (ed. with U. Suthersanen, 2005).

NICK GROOM

Professor, Department of English, University of Exeter. His work investigates questions of authenticity and the emergence of national and regional identities, particularly in the eighteenth and early nineteenth centuries. Following predominantly literary critical studies, his work has become more emphatically interdisciplinary. An interest in national identity and culture has inspired further research into the relationship of culture variously with the past, with noise and with the landscape; currently working on a history of representations of the British environment and the problems of sustainability. Professor Groom has frequently appeared on radio and television and is a regular reviewer for the *Independent*. He teaches literature and culture from Shakespeare to the present day, and runs option courses on national identity, literature and the environment, and erotic literature.

Publications include: *The Making of Percy's Reliques* (1999), editions of Thomas Percy's collection of ballads and associated Arthurian texts; *Thomas Chatterton and Romantic Culture* (1999); *The Forger's Shadow* (2002); and *The Union Jack: The Story of the British Flag* (2006).

ADRIAN JOHNS

Professor of History and Chair of the Committee on Conceptual and Historical Studies of Science at the University of Chicago. Educated at the University of Cambridge, he has also taught at the California Institute of Technology and the University of California, San Diego. He is the author of *The Nature of the Book* (1998); *Piracy: The Intellectual Property Wars from Gutenberg to Gates* (2010); and *Death of a Pirate: British Broadcasting and the Origins of the Information Age* (forthcoming, scheduled for late 2010).

DAVID LEFRANC

A French lawyer specializing in intellectual property. He obtained his doctorate in law in 2003 . His thesis, under the direction of Professor Henri-Jacques Lucas, addressed the legal consequences of fame in copyright and trade mark law and rights of personality. Following six years of university teaching, David Lefranc became an *avocat*. He continues his research through the publication of numerous articles. He also contributes to one of the LexisNexis legal encyclopaedias. David Lefranc is also interested in literary history, and has published a study of the Dada movement in Paris. A participant in the defence of intellectual property, he is a member of the French national group

ALAI (Association Littéraire et Artistique Internationale). In addition, he is the president of the Association pour le Droit de la Création Intellectuelle, whose website he manages (www.ip-sharing.com). David Lefranc also composes electronic music and designs websites.

### DANIEL McCLEAN

An independent art curator and lawyer, specializing in art law. He is currently advising Seth Siegelaub's Stichting Egress Foundation in the Netherlands, on the creation of an art law centre and is curating an exhibition related to copyright with the Danish artist group, Superflex at the Van Abbemuseum, Eindhoven. He has commissioned and edited two publications examining the relationship between art and law: *Dear Images: Art, Copyright and Culture* (2002); *The Trials of Art* (2007).

### SÉBASTIEN ODDOS

A dual-qualified lawyer in France (*avocat*) and in England (solicitor). His experience is in private practice in Paris (2000–3) and London (2006–9). His main focus is intellectual property law and information technology law from transactional and litigation standpoints. More recently he served as UK Corporate Counsel for Sybase, a US software publisher for the financial services industry. He has an LL.M. from Columbia Law School; Master's degrees in intellectual property law from King's College, London (LL.M.) and from the University of Poitiers, France. He also holds a Master's in corporate law from the University of Paris XI and HEC Business School and a BA in economics and finance from Sciences Po Paris.

### JOHNSON OKPALUBA

Visiting lecturer at King's College London, where he gained his Ph.D. for his thesis entitled 'Digitisation, culture and copyright law: digital sampling, a case study'. Dr Okpaluba also lectures at Pepperdine University on the International Copyright and Entertainment course. As a lawyer in private practice, he advises recording artists, songwriters, producers and managers on all aspects of the music industry and also advises clients on intellectual property matters.

### SHIRA PERLMUTTER

Executive Vice President for Global Legal Policy at the International Federation of the Phonographic Industry (IFPI). She leads the department that develops and coordinates IFPI's positions for improving the legal framework under which record producers operate worldwide, in particular with respect to copyright and related rights. Ms Perlmutter joined IFPI from Time Warner, where she held the position of Vice President and Associate General Counsel for Intellectual Property Policy. She previously worked at the World Intellectual Property Organization (WIPO) in Geneva, as a consultant on the copyright issues involved in electronic commerce. From 1995 to 1999, she was Associate Register for Policy and International Affairs at the US Copyright Office. In that capacity, she advised Congress on and drafted portions of, the Digital Millennium Copyright Act of 1998, and prepared the Copyright Office's 1999 Report on Copyright and Digital Distance Education and its 1997 Report on Legal Protection for Databases. In 1996, Ms Perlmutter was a key member of the US delegation that negotiated the two WIPO Internet Treaties, and served as the expert on the copyright law of the US during the WTO TRIPs Council review of developed countries' copyright laws. From 1990 to 1995, Ms Perlmutter was a law professor at the Catholic University of America, teaching copyright law, trade marks and unfair competition, and international intellectual property law.

Publications include: co-author (with Graeme Dinwoodie and William O. Hennessey), *International Intellectual Property Law: Problems and Materials* (2002); numerous articles on copyright issues.

CATHERINE SEVILLE

University Lecturer in Law, Vice-Principal and Director of Studies in Law at Newnham College. First degrees in music and English led inexorably to an interest in copyright law. She has written two books on the history of copyright. Her research interests also include intellectual property law in the EU, and a book on this is forthcoming. Her most recent article is 'Authors as Copyright Campaigners: Mark Twain's Legacy' (2008). Provoked by the Google Library controversy, it considers the role and influence of authors and authors' organizations in copyright reform.

Publications include: *Literary Copyright Reform in Early Victorian England* (1999); *The Internationalisation of Copyright Law: Books, Buccaneers and the Black Flag in the Nineteenth Century* (2006).

JASON TOYNBEE

Senior Lecturer in Media Studies, the Open University. His research interests are in media and cultural production, and the way that it impacts on textual form and meaning. He argues for the prevalence of 'social authorship', whereby music makers are creative agents, yet are also enmeshed in social networks of collaboration, competition and economic exploitation. This has led to an interest in copyright and its economic function of specifying the cultural commodity which installs a regime of enforced originality. Dr Toynbee is also involved in a research project on British jazz completed in 2007 which explored authorship and cultural policy. He is currently researching 'Migrating Music' as part of the AHRC-funded project Tuning In Diasporic Contact Zones at BBC World Service. 'Migrating Music' is an international, collaborative inquiry into the socio-cultural implications of music and diaspora across the world.

Publications include: *Making Popular Music* (2000); *Bob Marley: Herald of the Postcolonial World?* (2008).

EDITORS' PREFACE

Copyright infringement has been high on the national, regional and international political agenda for some time. The creative industries – publishers, the film and music industries and broadcasters – have lobbied hard for improved mechanisms of enforcement and stronger penalties in the face of what they describe as rampant 'piracy' of their products. The UK government increased criminal penalties for copyright infringement in 2002 from a maximum of two years' imprisonment to a maximum of ten years, putting copyright infringement on a par with assault and other violent crimes. The French government in 2009 introduced a mechanism (dubbed 'graduated response') that would oblige Internet service providers (ISPs) to cut off (or reduce) Internet access for users implicated in peer-to-peer file sharing. This initiative has been imitated in the UK, where the Digital Economy Act 2010 provides a framework for imposing similar obligations on ISPs to impose 'technical restrictions' on the services offered to subscribers who appear to have been involved in repeated copyright infringements. In 2007, the US launched an action at the WTO, complaining that China had not complied with the TRIPs Agreement because the relevant Chinese laws set certain thresholds for prosecution of copyright piracy. New initiatives are being discussed in the EU, the US, Japan, Australia and several other nations for an 'Anti-Counterfeiting Trade Agreement'.

Although the question of copyright infringement has gained a great deal of political attention and is unquestionably controversial, academics have generally attended more to other questions, particularly, 'authorship'. But there is much valuable work that could be undertaken with a view to understanding the nature, causes and effects of infringement, the parallels and differences between the norms of copyright infringement and cultural and social norms, and, perhaps, more importantly, the nature and effects of different enforcement mechanisms. In this volume, we have sought to address some of the key questions which present themselves in any study of copyright infringement. Thus, we have asked why does infringement occur and who, precisely, is involved in such infringements? How is it detected? And what are the consequences of infringement, for both the creation and exploitation of copyright works? How, if at all, can such infringements be prevented in the light of new digital communications technologies? More generally, where is the boundary to be drawn between (illegal) imitation and (legal) inspiration? Is the answer different for creators, artists and experts from different disciplines or fields? How have concepts of copyright infringement altered over time and how do such changes relate, if at all, to the cultural norms operating among creators in different fields? What, if anything, are the practical implications of the use of the term 'piracy' rather than 'infringement' in relation to copyright works. Indeed, how should the significance of the rhetoric of 'piracy' be measured?

It is certainly the case that while plagiarism continues to garner moral opprobrium, its legal counterpart, copyright infringement, has become controversial both as a matter of legal doctrine, and of social ordering. The related concept of 'piracy' also appears to be losing rhetorical bite. There is no doubt that there is widespread disregard of copyright laws by the public at large, following the introduction of technology that enabled the public first to acquire and then to disseminate copies for free. This raises the wider question of whether laws against copyright infringement can maintain their normative appeal. It follows that in the face of oversimplified rhetoric demonizing 'copyright piracy' and its apparent lack of resonance among large sections of the general public, it is important for academic study to step back and take a deeper and more reflective approach. Such an understanding of the changing nature of the law – and practice – of copyright infringement is a task too big for lawyers alone. We take the view that it requires the multiple inputs of economists, historians, technologists, sociologists, cultural theorists and criminologists – as well as lawyers. With such an approach, one might perhaps begin to address the vital and overarching question of whether strong copyright laws, rigorously enforced, impede rather than promote creativity. And what can be done to avoid any such adverse consequences, while maintaining the effectiveness of copyright as an incentive mechanism for those who need it?

This volume is the second in a series of books offering multidisciplinary examinations and critiques of various issues concerning intellectual property. The previous volume in the series, *Trade Marks and Brands: An Interdisciplinary Critique* (2008), was the first sustained examination of trade marks and brands from a multiplicity of disciplines. Similarly, in this volume, we seek to offer a series of discrete chapters not from a single perspective but rather to pair lawyers and non- lawyers, so that each commentator will address and critique his or her counterpart's analysis from the viewpoint of their different disciplines. In contrast to most of the legal studies of copyright infringement, we have given prominence primarily to specialists from other disciplines who have in most cases authored the main chapters; lawyers have supplied most of the commentaries. We hope that this format will successfully highlight why interdisciplinary inquiries should be of interest and assistance to legal academics and practitioners. In addition, we believe the volume should prove of interest to academics in other disciplines whose modes of analysis are brought to bear on the issue of copyright infringement and piracy. For those who wish to explore further, an extensive bibliography collecting commentaries from all the fields here represented concludes the volume.

The chapters in this volume grew out of two successive workshops held at Emmanuel College, University of Cambridge, in July 2007 and July 2008. We are grateful to all the participants, including those who did not present papers, but whose questions and critiques helped the presenters to sharpen or rethink their arguments. We express our appreciation as well to the Master and Bursar of Emmanuel College for their support of this project. Both of the workshops were generously funded by the Herchel Smith bequest to Emmanuel College for the promotion of research into intellectual property law.

Lionel Bently
Jennifer Davis
Jane C. Ginsburg
Cambridge and New York, December 2009

# TABLE OF CASES

# TABLE OF STATUTES

# PART I

Introduction

1

# Inspiration or infringement: the plagiarist in court*

ISABELLA ALEXANDER

In Maurice Shadbolt's novel, *The House of Strife*, the protagonist Ferdinand Wildblood finds himself fleeing London for Blackguard Beach in New Zealand, in the year 1840. Wildblood's crime was plagiarism and the destination is more than ironic. As a hack writer, Wildblood had been asked to edit a manuscript by a man called James Dinwiddie which tells a blood-curdling tale of murder, mayhem, battle and bravery, lust and lasciviousness in the far-flung colony of New Zealand. Finding the writing style impenetrable and the storyline highly improbable, Wildblood rewrites the work, under the pseudonym of Henry Youngman. The story is a runaway success and Youngman becomes the toast of London. But Dinwiddie catches up with Wildblood and, in fear for his life, Wildblood jumps aboard the first ship for New Zealand. While in New Zealand, Wildblood becomes caught up in the Maori wars initiated by the young Maori chief, John, or Hone, Heke. After numerous hair-raising adventures, Wildblood returns to spend his twilight years in London. But at the point of finishing his first-hand, original, account of what will become known as the 'Flagstaff Wars', he is tracked down in his gentleman's club by Dinwiddie and meets his mysterious, uncertain, fate at the hands of his nemesis.

Wildblood has perpetrated a literary 'crime' against the 'original author', for which he pays dearly. In fiction, then, a rough justice is meted out against literary offenders. In real life too, plagiarists may be

---

* I am grateful to Lionel Bently for advice and helpful editorial input. In the inevitable state of hypersensitivity induced by writing about plagiarism, I acknowledge that this title is borrowed from Mark Rose, 'The Author in Court: *Pope* v. *Curll* (1741)', in M. Woodmansee and P. Jaszi (eds.), *The Construction of Authorship: Textual Appropriation in Law and Literature* (Durham, NC: Duke University Press, 1994), pp. 211–30.

punished by institutional sanctions or social stigma.[1] But what are their crimes precisely and, most pertinently for present purposes, can these wronged authors find redress in the law of copyright or, indeed, elsewhere in the law? The recent, high-profile case involving Dan Brown's bestselling novel *The Da Vinci Code*, shows that this will not always be possible.[2] This is because the law of copyright infringement does not map precisely onto the literary offence of plagiarism, despite the fact that both share a concern with 'originality'. However, while there has recently been valuable and fascinating interdisciplinary work on the relationship between originality in literature and law, less has been done on copyright infringement. This chapter sets out to examine the overlap and the lacunae between the plagiarism and infringement, as well as briefly considering two alternative legal actions that may also address some elements of the problem of plagiarism: the tort of passing off and the criminal offence of fraud. First, however, it is necessary to attempt the difficult task of pinning down the meaning of 'plagiarism'.

In her book *Pragmatic Plagiarism*, Marilyn Randall identifies plagiarism as a pragmatic, rather than a textual category, meaning it is 'principally determined by a wide variety of extra-textual criteria that constitute the aesthetic, institutional and cultural contexts of production and reception of the work'.[3] Thus, plagiarism is a judgement, made by a reader and, as such, works of plagiarism remain objects of controversy. Notwithstanding the difficulties inherent in identifying plagiarism, Randall argues that there is considerable historical consistency among definitions of plagiarism.[4] Taking her two exemplary definitions, one from the eighteenth century and one from the twentieth century, we can identify the following elements commonly considered to form the criteria of plagiarism: fraud, bad faith or covertness; copying, sometimes expressed as theft of another's property; claiming the work of another as one's own and thereby obtaining an unearned advantage (in the eighteenth-century definition characterized as claiming the honour due to another); and, making only small alterations, or not enhancing or improving the materials taken in any way. A further element in the

---

[1] See the examples of Raj Persaud and Jacob Epstein in Nick Groom's contribution to this volume (Chapter 14).
[2] *Baigent and Leigh* v. *Random House Group* [2007] EWCA Civ 247.
[3] Marilyn Randall, *Pragmatic Plagiarism: Authorship, Profit and Power* (University of Toronto Press, 2001), p. 4.
[4] *Ibid.*, pp. 15–16, 189.

eighteenth-century definition was lack of the talent to become an author.[5]

As Laurie Sterns has noted, 'The framework in which the law has found plagiarism to be most conveniently located is intellectual property law'.[6] In the United Kingdom, it is most usually found in the subcategory of copyright law. Indeed, in some cases, particularly older ones, the words 'plagiarism' and 'infringement' appear to be used interchangeably.[7] It is not surprising that copyright and plagiarism share certain characteristics. As discussed further below, plagiarism is frequently described in terms of theft, and the existence of theft presupposes the existence of property. Copyright law is that statutory instrument that creates a property in creative products, and so the two are closely related. However, it is important to bear in mind that concepts of plagiarism pre-dated the first copyright law in 1710. Moreover, the elements of copyright that developed following that first statutory enactment owed a considerable debt to practices relating to the regulation of the book trade in the seventeenth century and earlier.[8] Thus, while copyright law picks up some of the elements of plagiarism, it leaves others unaddressed and, at the same time, contains criteria that may make it difficult for those who believe they have been plagiarized to achieve legal outcomes with which they are satisfied.

The key similarity between the two concepts is the criteria of copying. A work that is identical or similar to an existing work, but was created without any knowledge of that work – in other words, the similarities are completely coincidental – will be neither a plagiarism nor a copyright infringement. However, in both cases, copying alone is not enough. In copyright, the copying must be done in relation to the whole work, or to a substantial part of it.[9] The question of what amounts to a 'substantial' part is not always straightforward; since 1836 the test has been one of not just quantity but also quality.[10] A court must therefore look not only at the amount that has been copied, but also at how important that part is to the work from which it was taken. A second core copyright doctrine is that the copying must occur in relation to expression, rather than ideas.

---

[5] *Ibid.*, pp. 17–18.
[6] Laurie Sterns, 'Copy Wrong: Plagiarism, Process, Property, and the Law', Cal. L. Rev., 80 (1992), 513, 522.
[7] E.g. *Tate* v. *Fullbrook* [1908] 1 KB 821; *Chatterton* v. *Cave* (1874–5) LR 10 CP 572.
[8] See Alexander in this volume, Chapter 15.
[9] Copyright, Designs and Patents Act 1988, s. 16(3).
[10] *Bramwell* v. *Halcomb* (1836) 3 My. & Cr. 737.

In the UK, this principle emerges from the common law but has also been adopted in a number of international and European instruments.[11] The devil of such a principle lies in its application to the details of particular cases and it is not always clear where 'idea' stops and 'expression' begins. As Judge Learned Hand famously said, 'nobody has ever been able to fix that boundary, and nobody ever can'.[12] The courts have accepted that 'non-literal copying', as it is called, may be infringement. Consequently, infringement is possible when the plot, incidents or themes of a story are copied, even if none of the same words are used, and also theoretically possible when a computer program is structured in a similar manner to another program (probably with a view to achieving a similar function), but no actual code is copied.[13]

Different courts have said different things about how to ascertain whether a case of non-literal copying amounts to infringement. In the most recent House of Lords' decision on the subject, *Designers' Guild* v. *Russell Williams*,[14] Lord Hoffmann attempted to bring some clarity to the idea–expression dichotomy by noting: 'Generally speaking, in cases of artistic copyright, the more abstract and simple the copied idea, the less likely it is to constitute a substantial part. Originality, in the sense of the contribution of the author's skill and labour, tends to lie in the detail with which the basic idea is presented. Copyright law protects foxes better than hedgehogs.'[15] Mark Chacksfield points out that it makes more sense to see this not as a direct reference to the Greek poet Archilocus' well-known quote – 'the fox knows many things but the hedgehog knows one big thing', but to Isaiah Berlin's essay on different types of historian.[16] Whatever the allusion, it may not get us much closer to clarifying the border between idea and expression. Indeed, it was upon this point that the two authors, Baigent and Leigh, failed in their legal action against Dan Brown in respect of their allegations that he had plagiarized their historical work, *Holy Blood Holy Grail*, in his bestselling novel *The Da Vinci Code*. Upholding the judgment of the court below,

---

[11] *Hollinrake* v. *Truswell* [1894] 3 Ch. 420. Agreement on Trade-Related Aspects of Intellectual Property 1994 (TRIPS Agreement), Art. 9(2) and WIPO Copyright Treaty 1996, Art. 2. See also European Council Directive 91/250/EEC of 14 May 1991 on the legal protection of computer programs, Art.1(2).
[12] *Nichols* v. *Universal Pictures* 45 F (2d) 119 (1930).
[13] See *John Richardson Computers Limited* v. *Flanders* [1993] FSR 497.
[14] [2001] 1 WLR 2416.   [15] *Ibid.*, 2423.
[16] M. Chacksfield, 'The Hedgehog and the Fox: A Substantial Part of the Law of Copyright', EIPR, 23(5) (2001), 259.

the Court of Appeal in this case held that although some elements had been copied they were 'of too high a level of generality and abstraction to qualify for copyright protection: they were ideas and not the expression of ideas'.[17]

The substantial-part rule and the idea–expression dichotomy are both indispensable elements of copyright infringement doctrine. However, the extent to which they are relevant to an assessment of plagiarism is less straightforward. Randall points out that the substantial-part rule might be inverted in cases of plagiarism: 'Since plagiarism depends on the reader's recognition of repeated discourse, the copying of a little known or obscure, that is, insignificant, source rather implies that the perpetrator counted on not being found out, which goes a long way to establishing fraudulent intent.'[18] For others, plagiarism is not a matter of degree and even the smallest copying counts as plagiarism.[19] In the case of the idea–expression dichotomy, plagiarist-hunters and accusers find themselves in similar difficulties to copyright claimants. While the various definitions of plagiarism, and its discourse as found in accusations and judgments, contains no such strictures on the copying of ideas, it will invariably be harder to prove plagiarism of an idea and, as Randall points out, 'many non-legal accusations of plagiarism have fallen into ridicule for the misapprehension of the fine distinction between an "idea" and its "expression"'.[20] In literary terms, some ideas are so well known, or commonplace, that they are incapable of being plagiarized, or so defenders against plagiarism argue.

Three further points of distinction between plagiarism and infringement also need to be made. First, there can be no copyright infringement of a work that is itself not protected by copyright. Works in which copyright has expired cannot be infringed but can be plagiarized. Second, some judgments of plagiarism make a distinction between, on the one hand, copying that improves or transforms the work, and, on the other hand, copying that involves no improvement. This differentiation is expressed by T. S. Eliot's famous claim: 'Immature poets imitate; mature poets steal; bad poets deface what they take, and good poets make it into something better, or at least something different.'[21] While

---

[17] *Baigent and Leigh* v. *Random House Group* [2007] EWCA Civ 247, para. 92.
[18] Randall, *Pragmatic Plagiarism*, p. 151.
[19] See *ibid.*, 150; Stearns, 'Copy Wrong', 528.     [20] Randall, *Pragmatic Plagiarism*, p. 147.
[21] T. S. Eliot, 'Philip Massinger', *The Sacred Wood: Essays on Poetry and Criticism* (4th edn, London: Methuen & Co., 1934).

such considerations did play a role in UK copyright law in the late eighteenth and early nineteenth centuries, it is no longer any defence to an infringement action to claim that a new or different work has been created.[22]

Third, the question of intention is irrelevant to a charge of copyright infringement, but its role in relation to plagiarism is less clear. Copyright infringement, in its civil form, is a strict liability offence. Despite some historical references to *animus furandi*,[23] the Copyright, Designs and Patents Act 1998 (CDPA), makes it clear that intention is not required.[24] Indeed, copyright infringement can even be carried out subconsciously, as long as there is a causal connection between the two works. While the defendant's denials that he consciously copied may be evidence which could rebut the suggestion of a causal connection, if there is sufficient objective similarity between the works then the court may draw the inference of a causal connection.[25] In the case of plagiarism, by contrast, Randall asserts, 'Identifying plagiarism entails ascribing to an agent a series of guilty or fraudulent intentions, the necessity to show intent, in order to establish guilt, or at least degrees of it, is by far the most important of all criteria for establishing plagiarism.'[26] Intention is relevant not just in the sense that the copying is deliberate, but also in terms of a further intention, sometimes referred to in the criminal law as an ulterior intent, to claim the credit by passing the work off as one's own. While some institutional statements explicitly include unintentional copying and non-attribution within their definition of plagiarism,[27] the centrality of the element of deceit or bad faith suggests that, at least outside the academic sphere (where, as Groom observes,[28] the concern is really with cheating rather than plagiarism in its literary or artistic context), intention should be key to a charge of plagiarism.

This brings us to a further element of plagiarism, that of incorrect attribution. This is something that can be recognized in copyright law, although not through the action for infringement of economic rights we have been discussing so far. The CDPA 1988 recognized several moral rights, giving effect to Article 6*bis* of the Berne Convention which

---

[22] See Chapter 15, also by Alexander, in this volume.
[23] E.g. *Cary* v. *Kearsley* (1802) 4 Esp. 168; *Lewis* v. *Fullarton* (1839) 2 Beav. 6.
[24] CDPA 1988, s. 16. See also *Baigent* v. *Random House* [2007] EWCA Civ 247, para. 95.
[25] *Francis Day & Hunter* v. *Bron* [1963] Ch. 587.
[26] Randall, *Pragmatic Plagiarism*, p. 126.
[27] See Groom, Chapter 14, and response of Alexander, Chapter 15, n. 41, in this volume.
[28] See Chapter 15, n. 42.

required member states to protect authors' rights of attribution and integrity. Thus, section 77 of the Act confers upon authors the right to be identified as the author of a work. This section could therefore be invoked by an author (or composer or artist) whose work has been plagiarized under the name of another author and this would be appropriate. Moral rights, despite their name, are not about morality but about protecting the non-economic interests of authors and other creators. The language of moral rights emerged in the copyright regimes of Continental Europe as an expression of the belief that an author's personality is an integral aspect of his work and that misuse of his work causes him personal, non-financial harm.[29] In this concern with the psychological aspects of the relationship between the author and his work, moral rights share a close affinity with the category of plagiarism. However, again, the right is hedged with numerous restrictions that mean it will not always be useful to punish plagiarists, the main restrictions being that the work in question must be published commercially and copies issued to the public, the author must have asserted the right before she or he can bring an action, and the right does not apply to anything done with the authority of the copyright owner if the work was produced in the course of employment.[30] The right also applies only so long as the work remains in copyright.

A final point to be made about the interaction between copyright and plagiarism is to note the existence of certain 'permitted acts' that will not amount to copyright infringement. Chapter 3 of the CDPA 1988 contains an extensive list of acts that are allowed by the statute, ranging from concessions to the visually impaired, through exceptions allowed for educational institutions and libraries to specific exceptions in relation to folksongs. The permitted acts are commonly referred to as exceptions or defences, and the most flexible of them are known as the fair dealing defences, and must be distinguished from the broader US defence of 'fair use'. In order to take advantage of one of the UK fair dealing defences, the use of the work must fall into a particular category. These are research or private study, reporting current events

---

[29] See J. Ginsburg, 'Moral Rights in a Common Law System', Ent. LR (1990), 121, 122. In Britain, the Fine Arts Copyright Act of 1862 protected artists against misrepresentations of a work's authorship, as well as protection against works being altered and resold, but these rights were not discussed or presented in the context of moral rights theory: see Elizabeth Adeney, *The Moral Rights of Authors and Performers: An International and Comparative Analysis* (Oxford University Press, 2006), pp. 371–2.

[30] CDPA 1988, ss. 77, 78, 79.

and criticism or review.[31] This means that, unlike in the US, there is no room for a defence of parody, or satire, in UK copyright law. Instead, these works will fall to be judged by the usual question of whether a substantial part has been taken and, if so, whether the criticism and review exception will apply.[32]

All three of the fair dealing categories have the same threshold requirement of 'fairness' – another somewhat vague concept in copyright law. Once again, different courts have said different things about what will count as 'fair' and, again, the decision is largely a matter of impression. Some relevant matters include the extent and number of quotations, the length or amount of what is taken, the purpose for which the extracts are used, particularly whether they are used in competition with the original work, and how the material was obtained. The statute specifically states that in order to take advantage of it, the work in question must be accompanied by a sufficient acknowledgement and, as noted above, one of the essential criteria of plagiarism is non-revelation of the original author. Thus, fair dealing could only be available as a defence to a plagiarist of anonymous works. However, even in such a case the element of 'fairness' is likely to prove a stumbling block to a would-be plagiarist, as the covert and deceptive act of a plagiarist in claiming authorship of such a work is unlikely to be considered 'fair'. In such a situation, it seems highly likely that the legal notion of fairness would give expression to the literary norms against plagiarism. A fourth defence is one that has been developed through the common law, and this is the power of the judges to refuse to enforce copyright on public policy grounds.[33] The existence and scope of this defence has been the subject of debate and contradictory judicial decisions in recent years, but most recently, in *Ashdown v. Telegraph Group*, the Court of Appeal affirmed the existence of the public interest defence.[34] Little guidance was given, however, as to when such a defence would operate. The Court noted that the circumstances in which it might operate are not capable of precise categorization, but indicated that it would succeed only in rare cases. Thus, this defence is similarly unlikely to be relevant in a case involving plagiarism.

This comparison between copyright infringement and plagiarism reveals that copyright law addresses only two aspects of plagiarism:

---

[31] *Ibid.*, ss. 29, 30.
[32] See Robert Burrell and Alison Coleman, *Copyright Exceptions: The Digital Impact* (Cambridge University Press, 2005), p. 50.
[33] CDPA 1988, s. 171(3)   [34] [2001] EWCA Civ 1142.

copying and failure to attribute authorship. And even in these areas the overlap is far from complete. As noted above, the regime of moral rights is in some ways a better fit for plagiarism, with its central concern for the relationship between author and work, but the limited way in which moral rights have been implemented in the UK means they may not always assist in bringing plagiarists to 'justice'. Although Randall refers to copyright as a 'subset' of plagiarism,[35] copyright and plagiarism are more like intersecting sets. Some acts will be copyright infringement or moral rights breaches but not plagiarism and vice versa.

Having looked at the advantages and disadvantages that copyright law offers for authors who believe they have been plagiarized, it is worth considering whether any other areas of intellectual property law can step into the breach. One possible candidate is the tort of passing off. The elements of this action are threefold: there must be goodwill, misrepresentation and damage.[36] The first criterion, goodwill, relates to trading goodwill and professional writers and other authors have been found by the courts to qualify in this respect.[37] The second criterion, misrepresentation, in its traditional formulation states that it must be such that it is likely to lead the public to believe that the goods or services offered by the claimant are those of the defendant. However, the courts have also recognized 'reverse passing off', that is, the misrepresentation that the goods of the defendant are those of the claimant.[38] This form of the action, although rarely used in practice, would be the most relevant to an author complaining of plagiarism. This point was made obliquely in the 1892 case of *Walter* v. *Steinkopf*,[39] which arose from *The Times'* complaint that the *St James' Gazette* was publishing a number of extracts from its articles. The allegation was one of copyright infringement, and the *Gazette* had identified the sources of its material but North J. observed, 'A man cannot justify the taking of what he has no right to take by stating whence he has taken it, though he may thereby avoid the additional dishonesty of passing off as the product of his own labour what is really cribbed from another.'[40] The third criterion is that the claimant must demonstrate that he has suffered, or is likely to suffer,

---

[35] Randall, *Pragmatic Plagiarism*, p. 16.
[36] *Reckitt & Colman Products Ltd* v. *Borden* [1990] 1 WLR, 491.
[37] See *Landa* v. *Greenberg* (1908) 24 TLR 441 (pen-name of Aunt Naomi), *Sweeney* v. *Macmillan Publishers Ltd* [2002] RPC 35 (James Joyce); *Archbold* v. *Sweet* (1832) 1 M. & Rob. 162; 5 Car. & P. 219 (barrister writing a legal textbook).
[38] *Bristol Conservatories* v. *Custom Built* [1989] RPC 455.
[39] [1892] 3 Ch. 489.   [40] *Ibid.*, 497.

damage resulting from the misrepresentation. The relevant type of damage in cases of plagiarism would be lost profits, or opportunities of profit.

The advantage of passing off as a possible legal avenue for the plagiarized author is that the first two elements of the action recognize three of the crucial elements of plagiarism: the importance of the original author's reputation (in passing off reconfigured in economic terms as goodwill), the false claims made by the plagiarism and the plagiarist's use of these claims to free-ride on the labour invested by the original author. Fraudulent intention is not, however, necessary in an action for passing off; the focus is rather on the effect of the representation on the relevant public. If a substantial number are deceived, then it will be misrepresentation. However, fraudulent intention will have a strong evidential value in proving that deception has occurred. Plagiarism and passing off are therefore not a perfect fit, as passing off covers neither the copying aspect nor the covert intention element of plagiarism. Moreover, other elements of passing off may limit its usefulness in respect of plagiarism. The misrepresentation must be 'material' for it to be actionable, and must influence the prospective customer.[41] As observed above, plagiarism covers insignificant and small copying, just as much as copying extensive or distinctive features of a work; in fact, the latter is more likely to result in detection and the former speaks to fraudulent intention. A second limitation, as noted by Jonathan Griffiths, is that an author who has assigned all interests in a work may lose his standing to bring an action in passing off, because goodwill is a commodity which can be traded.[42] However, Lionel Bently observes that an assignment of copyright is not necessarily an assignment of goodwill, where that goodwill relates more broadly to an author's reputation as a writer and may include a capacity to make money from book signings, television appearances, and so on, as well as the prices an author might demand for future copyrights.[43]

The areas of law examined so far have been civil law actions. Plagiarism, however, is commonly referred to in the language of crime. Indeed, the very word derives from the legal Latin term *plagium*, meaning the kidnapping of a slave, and when the poet Martial was first to use

---

[41] Christopher Wadlow, *The Law of Passing Off: Unfair Competition by Misrepresentation* (London: Sweet & Maxwell, 2004), p. 294. This point is also made by Jonathan Griffiths in 'Misattribution and Misrepresentation – The Claim for Reverse Passing Off as "Paternity" Right', IPQ, 34 (2006), 50–1. Griffiths' concern is largely with the opposite problem to plagiarism, i.e. misattribution rather than non-attribution.

[42] Griffiths, 'Misattribution and Misrepresentation', 48.    [43] Personal communication.

the word in the context of literature, he included a reference to theft.[44] The *Oxford English Dictionary Online* combines the civil and the criminal, defining plagiarism as 'The action or practice of taking someone else's work, idea, etc., and passing it off as one's own; literary theft'.[45] The protagonist in *The House of Strife*, referred to at the start of this chapter, finds himself obliquely accused by a literary critic of 'Theft, perhaps. Enthusiastic imitation. Bare-faced pastiche. Borrowed thoughts. Pilfered phrases. Purloined images. Erudite larceny. Not to speak of commonplace plagiarism.'[46]

Stuart P. Green investigates the possibility of using the law of theft to sanction plagiarism, but founders on the difficult doctrinal question of what constitutes the relevant 'property' that is being stolen, as well as the criterion of 'intention to deprive permanently'.[47] In the UK, this issue could be avoided by resorting to the new statutory offence of fraud. The Fraud Act 2006 makes it an offence to dishonestly make a false representation with the intention to make a gain for himself or cause a loss to another.[48] In plagiarism, the false representation would lie in the claim to be the author of the copied work, and the dishonesty in the deception thereby entailed. Following the *Ghosh* test, it seems likely that both the defendant and reasonable people would find this to be dishonest.[49] The representation can be express or implied[50] and the defendant must also know or have reason to believe that the representation is false and, as discussed above, this relates to the key criteria of bad faith in plagiarism.

The real difficulty with applying the fraud offence to plagiarism arises with the third criterion, as the gain or loss must be in terms of money or other property. While this might be made out in the case of a commercial production, it becomes more tangential in other fields, such as an academic publishing not for immediate gain but in the hope of eventual promotion and increased salary. Often, the direct intention of a plagiarist may be more to do with completing a task within a specified time frame,

---

[44] Randall, *Pragmatic Plagiarism*, p. 62

[45] www.dictionary.oed.com. For other examples of criminal metaphors, see Stuart P. Green, 'Plagiarism, Norms and the Limits of Theft Law: Some Observations on the Use of Criminal Sanctions in Enforcing Intellectual Property Rights', *Hastings Law Journal*, 54 (2002–3), 167 and accompanying notes.

[46] Maurice Shadbolt, *The New Zealand Wars Trilogy: The House of Strife* (Auckland, NZ: David Ling Publishing, 2005), p. 287.

[47] Green, 'Plagiarism, Norms'.   [48] Fraud Act 2006, s. 2.

[49] *R* v. *Ghosh* [1982] 3 WLR 110.   [50] Fraud Act 2006, ss. 2(2) (4).

or enhancing her own reputation, and any thoughts of pecuniary gain will be in the future and more a matter of desire than intention, while the effect of her actions on the author being plagiarized seem unlikely to enter her mind at all. However, the terms of the Act are broadly drawn and the question as to how remote the gain or loss must be to fall within it remains open.[51]

The main advantage of using the criminal offence of fraud to prosecute plagiarists is that it appears to address the central ethical wrong of plagiarism, which is the covert and deceptive use of another's work. It also addresses the issue of unearned advantage, but limits this to gain in property terms, rather than broader gains in terms of reputation and honour. A second attraction to using a criminal offence to punish plagiarism is that plagiarism is not just an ethical wrong but also, in the worlds of literature and art, considered an aesthetic wrong. As Macfarlane explains, 'Objections to [plagiarism] have tended to be either that it contravenes writerly honour code, or that as a compositional practice it does not result in good art.'[52] Once the nature of the wrong is identified in this way, it becomes clear that the harm is not just done to the author whose work has been plagiarized. The community as a whole suffers from such behaviour, whether it is the community of writers or artists, or the community of readers and viewers. It is the role of the criminal law to address such wrongs. Andrew Ashworth observes that 'The chief concern of the criminal law is to prohibit behaviour that represents a serious wrong against an individual or against some fundamental social value or institution.'[53]

It may be this underlying purpose of criminal law that explains the repeated use of its terms as metaphors in discussions of plagiarism. Similar tendencies can be observed in the law of copyright infringement, most notably in the use of the term 'piracy' to describe infringement generally. In a copyright case of 1880, James LJ coined the term 'literary larceny' to describe the case 'where a man pretending to be the author of a book illegitimately appropriates the fruit of a previous man's labour'.[54] This term was picked up by the influential treatise writer Augustine

---

[51] See comment of David Ormerod, 'The Fraud Act 2006 – Criminalising Lying?', Crim. LR [2007], 193, 203.

[52] Robert Macfarlane, *Original Copy: Plagiarism and Originality in Nineteenth-Century Literature* (Oxford University Press, 2007), p. 44.

[53] Andrew Ashworth, *Principles of Criminal Law* (6th edn, Oxford University Press, 2009), p. 1.

[54] *Dicks* v. *Yates* (1880–1) LR 18 Ch. D. 76, 90.

Birrell,[55] although the elision of theft and copyright law was hardly new to the late nineteenth century, and can now be heard every time one goes to the cinema or watches a rented DVD. Indeed, in calling for a law protecting authors and booksellers in 1709, Daniel Defoe asked rhetorically, 'Why have we Laws against House-breakers, High-way Robbers, Pick-Pockets, Ravishers of Women, and all Kinds of Open Violence [and yet no protection for the author]? When in this Case a Man has his Goods stolen, his Pocket Pick'd, his Estate ruin'd, his Prospect of Advantage ravish'd from him, after infinite Labour, Study, and Expence.'[56]

James LJ's definition of literary larceny could equally be a definition of plagiarism and brings us back to the point at which we started: the observation that plagiarism is most commonly addressed legally in the form of copyright law, a civil action. Copyright infringement can give rise to criminal proceedings and sanctions but this only occurs when infringement is carried out in a commercial context or 'to such an extent as to affect prejudicially the owner of the copyright'.[57] While plagiarism could amount to a criminal infringement, it will depend on the dealings with the plagiarizing work and not on the action of copying itself.

The prevalence of the language of the criminal law as used in relation to the civil offence of copyright has been noted before.[58] However, the observation that it shares this characteristic with accusations of plagiarism highlights a common perception that copyright infringement is about more than an economic dispute between two players, that there is an ethical element to such disputes and that there is the possibility for harm to the community as a whole. The language of theft can be cynically characterized as a rhetorical strategy used by interested parties, particularly large copyright-owning and exploiting corporations, seeking to enlarge their proprietary claims. However, for such a strategy to be effective it must also resonate with the human players. The shared use of such language in both plagiarism and copyright infringement cases reveals that it has such resonance and reminds us that copyright law is often more than just a contest between economic rivals. For the

---

[55] Augustine Birrell, *Seven Lectures on the Law and History of Copyright in Books* (London, Cassell & Co Ltd, 1899).
[56] Quoted in Mark Rose, *Authors and Owners: The Invention of Copyright* (Cambridge, MA: Harvard University Press, 1993), p. 37.
[57] CDPA 1988, s. 107(1).
[58] See discussion in Patricia Loughlan, '"You Wouldn't Steal a Car . . .": Intellectual Property and the Language of Theft', EIPR, 29 (2007), 401.

authors, artists and composers involved it raises issues relating to valid forms of creativity, authorial status and authorial identity – just as plagiarism does. In *The House of Strife*, the narrator Wildblood recounts the following conversation with the Maori warchief Heke:

> 'Storytellers are precious among men,' he informed me . . . 'That is a pleasure to hear,' I replied.'
> They keep treasure safe,' Heke explained.
> 'On one view of the matter,' I agreed.
> 'There is no other view,' he said forbiddingly. 'What are we, if not our stories?'
> I had to think.
> 'Have you found yours?'
> 'Perhaps in those of others,' I suggested.
> 'A man must have his own,' he argued. 'Otherwise he walks the world in a shadow.'[59]

[59] Shadbolt, *The House of Strife*, p. 65.

# PART II

History

# 2

# Nineteenth-century Anglo–US copyright relations: the language of piracy versus the moral high ground

CATHERINE SEVILLE

Piracy, Piracy, they cry'd aloud, What made you print my Copy, Sir, says one,
You're a meer Knave, 'tis very basely done.[1]

America did not grant international copyright until 1891. As a result, for most of the nineteenth century, foreign works could be published in America, freely and quite legally, without permission or payment. Given the immense size of the market at stake, it is small wonder that foreign authors and publishers protested. Dickens' notorious intervention in the campaign for international copyright is often presented as if it offered a synoptic view of a pitched battle between two sides; with the righteous British on one side of the Atlantic, and the piratical Americans on the other. Such an image offers a dangerously unfair and one-sided portrait. The true picture alters significantly during the nineteenth century. In particular, possession of the moral high ground does not rest unfailingly with the British. Both sides merit the 'pirate' badge, in different degrees at different times.[2]

America began the nineteenth century as a very young nation, as yet uncertain where independence from Britain would lead. Britain, similarly, had to come to terms with significant political changes affecting its sense of nationhood, and its relationships with other nations. The

---

[1] Edward ('Ned') Ward, 'A Journey to Hell, or, A Visit Paid to the Devil: A Poem' (Part I) (1700), II. vii. 14. An early example of the 'metaphor of counterfeit', noted by William St Clair, 'Metaphors of Intellectual Property', in R. Deazley et al. (eds.), *From Privilege to Property* (Cambridge: Open Book, 2010), pp. 369–95.
[2] William St Clair has noted the power of metaphors of intellectual property, and identifies the piracy metaphor as a common example from the end of the seventeenth century: 'Metaphors'.

influence of these wide questions can be seen in the debates regarding copyright. International copyright (or its absence) came to be perceived and portrayed as linked to a nation's sense of identity and moral standing. This chapter sketches the variations in the language of piracy as circumstances change through the century, and the debate progresses. What is revealed is an increasingly subtle and sensitive use of such language, as awareness of the complex issues underlying the international copyright question increases. By the end of the century, international copyright relations between Britain and America exhibit self-respect and mutual respect, as well as political realism.

## American copyright legislation: overview and context

The Declaration of Independence in 1776 transformed Britain's American Colonies into independent states 'absolved from all allegiance to the British Crown', giving them 'full power to levy war, conclude peace, contract alliances, establish commerce, and to do all other acts and things which independent states may of right do'. As far as copyright was concerned, the priority was domestic protection. The earliest American copyright laws were secured by the lexicographer Noah Webster, who travelled widely to lobby each individual state's legislature. Connecticut was the first to pass copyright legislation, in January 1783. By 1786 all of the original states of the Confederation except Delaware had enacted copyright legislation of some sort. Federal legislation came in 1790. The United States Constitution had granted Congress the power 'to promote the progress of science and useful arts, by securing for limited times to authors and inventors the exclusive right to their respective writings and discoveries'.[3] In May 1790 a bill was passed, giving copyright protection for a term of fourteen years, renewable for a further fourteen if the author was still living.[4] Protection was granted only to US citizens and residents.

Webster continued to believe that an original literary composition, being 'a species of property more peculiarly a man's own than any other', should be treated no differently from other personal property, and thus in principle perpetual.[5] His petition in favour of perpetual copyright was presented in the Senate in 1828. Acknowledging, however, that others

---

[3] Article I, Section 8, Paragraph 8.  [4] US Statutes at Large 124.
[5] Webster to John Pickering, December 1816: H. R. Warfel (ed.), *Letters of Noah Webster* (New York: Library Publishers, 1953), pp. 341–89, at p. 386.

had objections to a perpetual term, Webster also supported efforts towards a further extension of term. In 1831 the basic copyright term was increased to twenty-eight years, renewable for a further fourteen by the author's heirs.[6] Thus it remained for the remainder of the century.

Webster's concern for the protection of his own works should be seen against a background of his concern for the emerging American nation. In the first issues of *The American Magazine* (1797–8), he urged his countrymen towards cultural independence from Britain:

> Americans, unshackle your minds, and act like independent beings. You have been children long enough, subject to the control, and subservient to the interest of a haughty parent. You have now an interest of your own to augment and defend – You have an empire to raise and support by your exertions – and a national character to establish and extend by your wisdom and your virtues.[7]

Webster's now famous speller, grammar and reader were powerful tools for the creation of a single unified language in America, and he was conscious of their potential value.

It should be emphasised that at this time the American printing trade was still comparatively limited. America's first press was shipped from England, and set up in Cambridge, in the Massachusetts Bay Colony. The first work printed in America was the *Freeman's Oath* (1638). The wooden press itself was little changed from the mechanical screw press invented by Gutenberg in the 1450s. Printing was a skilled and labour-intensive process, resulting in perhaps 3,000 impressions a day at most. By the mid-eighteenth century there were 24 presses operating in the British colonies, and at least 1,200 titles had been printed. The focus was on government work, sermons, philosophy and science, rather than imaginative literature. Skilled and experienced labour was scarce, impacting on the quality of the output. Inevitably, many books were imported from Britain.

In the late-eighteenth century, printers in the United States began to look to reclaim the American market from British books and British publishers. The challenge was to match the British in quantity and quality, and to undercut them in price. Printers advertised their titles using patriotic appeals to support American manufacturing, and to advance democracy. One noteworthy contribution to this effort was Thomas Dobson's eighteen-volume reprint of the third edition of the

---

[6] US Statutes at Large 436.
[7] Noah Webster, 'On Education', *American Magazine* (December–May 1787), 22–374.

*Encyclopaedia Britannica* (itself published in Edinburgh from 1788 to 1797), with American additions and emendations. Begun in early December 1789 and completed in April 1798, Dobson's *Encyclopaedia*, as it came to be called, eventually included a supplement extending the work to twenty-one volumes – one more than the British original from which it descended. There were 16,650 letterpress pages in a quarto edition of 2,000 sets, closely printed in double columns, with 595 engraved copperplates. Marketed by subscription in direct competition with the *Britannica*, Dobson's advert promised (of necessity) that 'every part of the Work will be executed by American artists'. George Washington, Thomas Jefferson and Benjamin Franklin were among the 246 names on the original subscription list.

One element of the original *Britannica* which Dobson did not copy, of course, was its dedication to King George III; a figure heavily implicated in the American War of Independence, and hugely unpopular with the American public. Dobson's dedication was, 'To the Patrons of the Arts and Sciences; the promoters of useful and ornamental Literature in the United States of America, whose communications have enriched this extensive and important work; and by whose generous encouragement this arduous enterprise has been brought to its completion.' The word 'arduous' was no exaggeration. Dobson encountered many difficulties, including economic instability, inadequate distribution methods and episodes of yellow fever in his workforce. Although it made Dobson's reputation, and remains a milestone in American publishing history, it is not clear whether the *Encyclopaedia* was a financial success. Dobson was careful to enter all its volumes for copyright, but he was only briefly a pioneer in the market for encyclopaedias; rivals soon rushed to follow his example. The *Encyclopaedia* was not sold out even at the time of Dobson's death in 1823. Such rewards as there were from this sort of 'piracy' were uncertain and hard won.[8]

However, the technological environment in the printing trade was beginning to change. Production materials were becoming more plentiful, and manufacturing techniques improved fast. Although the hand press remained in widespread use, by the middle of the nineteenth century high-speed cylinder and rotary presses (and associated innovations) had transformed the printing industry. By the 1860s, a web rotary

---

[8] For more detail, see R. D. Arner, *Dobson's* Encyclopaedia: *The Publisher, Text, and Publication of America's first* Britannica, *1789–1803* (Philadelphia, PA: University of Pennsylvania Press, 1991).

press could print 10,000–12,000 double-sided sheets in an hour. The American population was growing rapidly, and literacy rates were extremely high.[9] America's economic position was powerful also. By 1860 per capita income in the United States was second only to Britain among the major world economies, and its GDP overtook Britain's at the end of the century. General industrial production rose sharply after the Civil War. Economic growth was rapid, and the publishing industry was quick to take advantage of improved conditions. Technological advances were quickly incorporated into book production, methods of distribution improved significantly, and postal rates were favourable. From 1845 until the panic of 1857 the book trade enjoyed a tremendous expansion. In the 1830s and early 1840s, American presses produced about 100 titles a year. By 1855 the number had leapt to almost 1,100. The value of the market ratcheted up in a similar way.[10] Reading had reached the masses, and cheap books were widely available. The standard price of a clothbound paperback, was 50c or 25c. From 1860 the 5c 'dime novel' flourished, distributed in massive editions from newsstands and dry goods stores, and shipped in barrels to soldiers during the Civil War.

It is against this backdrop that the various campaigns for American legislation on the subject of international copyright should be seen. The history may be very briefly summarised at this point. The first major initiative came from the British in 1837. Although several bills were introduced in Congress between 1837 and 1842, they all failed to pass. This was the campaign in which Dickens was implicated. In the early 1850s a draft international copyright treaty was signed, but did not pass Congress. Between 1868 and 1872, more bills were presented, but again did not pass. Between 1873 and 1878 there were further negotiations towards a treaty, which also failed. From 1884 onwards, however, steady pressure and a more pragmatic approach bore fruit, and the 1891 US Copyright Act was eventually passed, granting international copyright

---

[9] The 1850 census figures record that 90.4% of American adults over 20 could read and write. At the same period in England the comparable figure was perhaps 50–60%, and rates did not approach 100% until the end of the century. R. J. Zboray, *A Fictive People: Antebellum Economic Development and the American Reading Public* (New York and Oxford: Oxford University Press, 1993), p. 83. D. Vincent, *Literacy and Popular Culture* (Cambridge University Press, 1989), p. 22.

[10] In 1840 the value of books manufactured and sold in the United States was $5.5m. In 1850 it was $12.5m, and in 1856 it was $16 million. J. Tebbel, *A History of Book Publishing in the United States, Volume I: The Creation of an Industry 1630–1865* (New York and London: Bowker, 1975), p. 221.

subject to a manufacturing clause. The language of 'piracy' changes and develops, in response to these events.

## 'Piracy' as a synonym for 'infringement'

The American publisher Samuel Goodrich estimated that in 1820, 70 per cent of American book manufacture was the work of British authors (although this figure declined as the century progressed).[11] At this time, American printers who were first in the market with a particular title gained a real competitive advantage over their rivals, so were sometimes willing to pay for early sheets of works by the most popular British authors. Normally a fixed fee was offered, rather than a royalty, and the amounts did not approach what would have been offered for a copyright (if one had been available).[12] There are examples of this as early as 1817, and it continued until the passage of the 1891 Act, although it was by no means the usual practice. Many British authors were reprinted without their consent, and without any reward.

Sir Walter Scott was one of the lucky few whose works were particularly sought. In the early 1820s Carey & Lea of Philadelphia paid Scott's publisher to send them early sheets from Edinburgh immediately they were printed. Scott himself was aware of the discrepancy between his rates of pay in Britain and America, but was apparently grateful for the courtesy, rather than resentful at the absence of a right. In 1826, in an attempt to assist Scott with his serious financial troubles, James Fenimore Cooper suggested that Scott's forthcoming *Life of Napoleon* be copyrighted in the United States as the property of an American citizen. Scott was uneasy with this plan, but was prepared to convey to Carey 'the exclusive right of publishing' in America this and all his future works.[13] He told Cooper:

---

[11] S. G. Goodrich, *Recollections of a Lifetime*, 2 vols. (New York and Auburn: Miller, Orton and Mulligan, 1857), vol. II, pp. 388–91 and 552–3. The figures are necessarily very rough. Goodrich put the British share of American productions at around 60% in 1830, 45% in 1840, 30% in 1850 and under 20% by 1856.

[12] For example, in 1835 the Harpers made a formal agreement with the British author and politician Edward Bulwer-Lytton, to pay him £50 per volume for advance sheets of his highly popular novels. He was paid many times this for his British copyrights.

[13] S. Smiles, *A Publisher and His Friends: Memoir And Correspondence of the Late John Murray*, 2 vols. (London: Murray, 1891), vol. I, p. 27. A. J. Eaton, 'The American Movement for International Copyright, 1837–60', *Library Quarterly*, 11 (1945), 99. Scott to Cooper [?6] November 1826: Sir Walter Scott, *The Letters of Sir Walter Scott 1826–1828*, H. J. C. Grierson (ed.) (London: Constable, 1936), p. 122.

the literature of both countries must always remain a common property to both nor can anything tend better to support the mutual good understanding betwixt the kindred nations than the assimilation of their laws concerning literary property. At any rate if what I propose shall not be found of force to prevent piracy I cannot but think from the generosity and justice of American feeling that a considerable preference would be given in the market to the editions directly emanating from the publisher selected by the author and in the sale of which the author had some interest.[14]

Scott uses 'piracy' here in a neutral manner, consistent with its use in contemporary English legal treatises. An entire section of Robert Maugham's *Treatise on the Laws of Literary Property* (1828) is entitled 'Of Pirating Copyright', and the running header continues for over forty pages. 'Piracy' appears to carry no particular moral charge, and is used simply as a word meaning, 'infringement'. For example, Maugham writes:

> A fair and bona fide abridgment of any book, is considered a new work; and however it may injure the sale of the original, yet it is not deemed a piracy or violation of the author's copyright.[15]

Such usage is consistent with that found in *The Penny Cyclopaedia*, an encyclopaedia published for the Society for the Diffusion of Useful Knowledge by Charles Knight between 1833 and 1843. The entry on copyright was almost certainly written by Thomas Noon Talfourd, a famous campaigner for the rights of authors. The article was published in 1837, when Talfourd would have been deeply immersed in efforts to pass an ambitious copyright bill – including the provision of international copyright – through Parliament. As a barrister, he was well aware of the law. As an author, Talfourd was extremely protective of literary privileges, and alert for any encroachment. Yet Talfourd, too, uses 'piracy' interchangeably with 'infringement':

> The usual modes of legal proceeding to prevent or punish the infringement of copyright, or, as it is more usually termed, piracy, are by action for damages, or for the penalties given by the statute; or more commonly

---

[14] Scott to Cooper [?6] November 1826: *Letters*, 122. A fixed fee was the usual arrangement, though a 10% royalty was sometimes negotiated. Scott asked for half-profits, though proposed that the payments already made to his publisher for early sheets be deducted from his share.

[15] R. Maugham, *Treatise on the Laws of Literary Property* (London, 1828), p. 130. Compare the earlier hostile usage of John Fell, Bishop of Oxford (1674 and 1684), quoted in St Clair, 'Metaphors', 18.

still, by obtaining an injunction in equity to prohibit the unlawful publication, which affords immediate and summary redress.[16]

This is a straightforward, descriptive usage. Although piracy was clearly a
wrong, the word did not yet convey the strongly condemnatory moral
connotations which it later came to bear.

### 'Injury' to the British – early claims to the moral high ground

At precisely this time, the question of international copyright was a matter
of serious controversy in America, because of the London publishers,
Saunders & Otley. In an attempt to forestall the increasing number of
American reprints of the firm's works, in 1836 Frederick Saunders opened
a branch office in New York, intending to publish there and in London
simultaneously. The aim was to acquire copyright in both places, if possible,
and, if not, to be first in the market. Saunders met hostile and determined
opposition. His own workers were bribed, and the New York publishers
Harper & Bros., in particular, went to great lengths to drive Saunders out of
the market.[17] For example, when Saunders & Otley were promoting their
forthcoming *Memoirs of Prince Lucien Bonaparte*, they made much of the
fact that they had the author's exclusive authority to publish in England,
France and America (for what this was worth). Harper & Bros. immediately
announced that they had the same work in press and almost ready for
publication. Stung by this behaviour, Saunders printed an advertisement
detailing the facts, and inviting the public to judge the 'moral rectitude' of
the rival publication. The Harpers replied with a rather clumsy parody of the
Saunders advertisement, attempting to drive home the message that international copyright would raise the price of books.[18] Following this incident

---

[16] *The Penny Cyclopaedia*, vol. VIII ('Copyright') (London, 1837).

[17] For detail, see F. Saunders, *The Early History of the International Copyright in America*
(1888), *Saunders Mss.*, and largely reprinted in J. A. Rawley, 'An Early History of the
International Copyright Movement', *Library Quarterly*, 11 (1941), 202–6. A. L. Bader,
'Frederick Saunders and the Early History of the International Copyright Movement in
America', *Library Quarterly*, 8 (1938), 25–39. Saunders wrote: 'The NY publishing firm
of Harper & Bros got hold of proof sheets of our books; our own pressmen having been
tampered with; and published books, that were the property of S & O, several days sooner
than we could get them out ourselves. This action of the NY firm was widely announced
with placards proclaiming "Great American Enterprise"' (Frederick Saunders,
*Recollections* (1890), George Haven Putnam Papers, Manuscripts and Archives
Division, New York Public Library, Astor, Lenox and Tilden Foundations).

[18] Saunders' advertisement, *New York Evening Post*, 22 September 1836. Harpers' riposte,
*Morning Courier and New-York Enquirer*, 26 September 1836.

Saunders & Otley began to lobby strenuously for international copyright. A clear 'moral' thread runs through the language of this campaign.

One of Frederick Saunders' first steps was to draft a petition in favour of international copyright, which was signed by fifty-six British authors, and presented to Congress by Senator Henry Clay in February 1837. It asked that the British authors' 'right of property' should be protected,[19] and protested that, 'their works are published without any compensation being made to them for their copy-rights; that they are frequently altered and mutilated, so as to affect injuriously their reputations'. An influential British author notably absent from the list of signatories was William Wordsworth. Although strongly in favour of reciprocal copyright protection he refused to sign, because he 'thought it impolitic to speak of the American Publishers who had done what there was no law to prevent them doing, in such harsh and injurious terms'.[20] A Select Committee, chaired by Clay, was appointed to look into the question. It reported that 'justice' required protection for foreign authors, and Clay submitted a bill which would have extended copyright privileges to British and French authors on condition that their works were reprinted and published in the United States within a month of their appearance abroad. Although Clay introduced his bill several times between 1836 and 1842, it did not pass. The American publishing trade was well organised and effective in its opposition to it.

Dickens' intervention in this period of the international copyright debate is well known. One of the most popular authors in America, his works were reprinted in America in editions of hundreds of thousands. Early in 1842 he was in America for a lecture tour, and called for international copyright, '*firstly*, because it is justice; *secondly*, because without it you can never have, and keep, a literature of your own'.[21] The argument is thus grounded both on a moral appeal, and on an appeal to the self-interest of the American nation. The latter point echoes Noah Webster's 1797 plea for America to throw off the yoke of British culture.

---

[19] For wider reflection and examples, see St Clair's discussion of the property metaphor: 'property – landed, moveable and virtual' ('Metaphors', 21–31).

[20] Wordsworth to Crabb Robinson, 15 December 1837: Alan G. Hill (ed.), *The Letters of William and Dorothy Wordsworth*, 8 vols. (2nd edn, Oxford: Clarendon Press, 1967–93), vol. VI, p. 493. See also Henry Clay, *The Papers of Henry Clay*, Robert Seager II (ed.), 11 vols. (Lexington, KY: University of Kentucky Press, 1959–92), vol. IX, p. 22 (which has the text of the British petition).

[21] K. J. Fielding (ed.), *The Speeches of Charles Dickens: A Complete Edition* (Brighton: Harvester Wheatsheaf, 1988), pp. 17–22, at 21.

Several American authors had noted the difficulty of finding a publisher willing to pay for the copyright enjoyed by American citizens, particularly since tried-and-tested British authors were due no such payment.[22]

Some newspapers were highly critical of what they regarded as Dickens' impertinent interference. The *Hartford Daily Times* wrote, haughtily: 'It happens that we want no advice upon this subject, and it will be better for Mr Dickens, if he refrains from introducing the matter hereafter.' The *New World* attacked the remarks as 'in the worst taste possible'. The *New World* was one of the leading 'mammoth' weekly newspapers, with a national circulation. Its success lay in its ability to offer huge quantities of cheap print to its readers, and it regularly trawled the works of British authors for material. In 1841 it began reprinting entire books (not just instalments) in its newspaper format, as gifts for new subscribers. A normal edition was at least 10,000 copies. The *New World* attempted to turn the tables on Dickens, by arguing that it was the very absence of international copyright law to which he was indebted for his popularity, and boasting that it had sold thousands of copies of his works throughout America.[23] *Brother Jonathan*, the first of the mammoths, expressed pride in 'having first introduced into the cash newspapers the custom of reprinting [Dickens'] novels as they appeared in numbers'.[24]

Far from letting the matter drop, Dickens obtained letters of warm support from British authors, and a memorial to Congress, both of which were sent to the editors of four leading American newspapers.[25] Editorial reactions to the letters were at best mixed. Many were provoked by Thomas Carlyle's bald characterisation of the American position on copyright as theft from another nation:

> That thou belongest to a different "Nation" and canst steal without being certainly hanged for it, gives thee no permission to steal. Thou shalt not in

---

[22] Washington Irving observed that: 'the public complains of the price of my work – this is the disadvantage of coming in competition with those republished English works for which the Booksellers have not to pay anything to the authors. If the American public wish to have literature of their own they must consent to pay for the support of authors' (Irving to Henry Brevoort, 12 August 1819, *Letters*, Ralph M. Aderman *et al.* (eds.), 4 vols. (Boston: Twayne Publishers, 1978–1982), vol. I, p. 554).

[23] Madeline House *et al.* (eds.), *The Letters of Charles Dickens*, 12 vols. (Oxford: Clarendon Press, 1965–2002), vol. III, p. 60, n. 1.

[24] *Brother Jonathan*, 5 February 1842, 157.

[25] The memorial was not in fact presented to Congress. For text and signatories, see House *et al.*, *Letters*, vol. III, pp. 621–2.

any wise steal at all! So it is written down for Nations and for Men, in the Law Book of the Maker of this Universe.[26]

America was a nation where deep religious convictions were commonly held, and Carlyle's homily was certainly perceived as arrogant, high-handed and grossly insensitive. It also gave the American press an excuse to handle the issue without gloves. Dickens' private secretary during this trip, George Washington Putnam, wrote that a large number of publishers of very popular papers had 'lavished upon Mr Dickens abuse and insult without stint'.[27]

On his return home, Dickens published an account of his trip, *American Notes for General Circulation*. Although his picture of America was generally a favourable one, Dickens' merciless parodies of local habits and manners were not well received there. Like other British copyright works, *American Notes* was shipped to America on the *Great Western*, immediately it was published. The day after it arrived, several American newspapers reprinted it in its entirety, as an 'extra' number, priced at 12½ cents.[28] Subsequently, writing about the episode to an American author, Dickens used an extended piratical metaphor to encapsulate the issue.

> As to the Pirates, let them wave their black flag, and rob under it, and stab into the bargain, until the crack of doom. I should hardly be comfortable if they bought the right of blackguarding me in the Model Republic; but while they steal it, I am happy.[29]

Although his tone here is light, Dickens' words attempt to convey a disinterestedness which, perhaps, he did not really feel. Dickens found

---

[26] Carlyle to Dickens (26 March 1842): *ibid.*, p. 623.

[27] George Washington Putnam, unpublished ms entitled 'To the purchaser of the mss in the handwriting of Charles Dickens upon the subject of an "International Copyright Law"', dated 13 July 1886. *Berg Collection of English and American Literature*, New York Public Library, Astor, Lenox and Tilden Foundations. George W. Putnam (1812–96) was studying with the Boston artist, Francis Alexander, who painted Dickens' portrait during his visit. Dickens, overwhelmed with correspondence, asked Alexander to recommend a secretary, and Putnam was proposed. George W. Putnam should be distinguished from George Palmer Putnam (1814–72) and his son George Haven Putnam (1844–1930), both of whom were American publishers closely involved in the international copyright campaign.

[28] House *et al.*, *Letters*, vol. III, p. 346, n. 2. The *New World* printed an announcement that it had received *American Notes* at 8 p.m. on Sunday evening, and issued it as a 'double extra' at 1 p.m. on Monday, a mere 17 hours later. It claimed to have printed 24,000 copies in 24 hours, and to have orders for 100,000 copies.

[29] Dickens to William Hickling Prescott, 2 March 1843: *ibid.*, p. 457.

the whole affair a painful one, and he largely withdrew from the public campaign for international copyright. He did contribute to the more discreet treaty negotiations in the early 1850s. But he did not speak publicly on the subject during his second trip to America, in the winter of 1867.

### Copyright for foreigners: the position under British law

The status of foreigners who sought copyright in Britain was somewhat unclear at this time. It had been believed that first publication in Britain could secure copyright, but contradictory judicial decisions had left the matter uncertain. This was a matter of concern to British publishers such as John Murray and Richard Bentley, who had paid significant sums to popular American authors in the good faith belief that they were acquiring copyright in their works. In 1849 the music publisher Thomas Boosey lost an important case in the Court of Exchequer: *Boosey v. Purday*. Boosey had been assigned certain rights in Vincenzo Bellini's opera, *La Sonnambula*, composed in Milan. Although the arias were first published by Boosey in London, Chief Baron Pollock held that he had no copyright in them. In Pollock's view, the legislature legislated prima facie for its own subjects, and those (such as foreigners resident in Britain) owing obedience to its laws. Its object was not to encourage the importation of foreign works and their first publication in Britain, but to promote the cultivation of the intellect of its subjects. Foreign copyright was thus dependent on the foreign author's place of residence when the work was first published, and not on the place of first publication.[30]

This was a serious blow to British publishers who had paid for and issued American works, because unauthorised reprints were now legal publications, and (technically) not piracies. Nevertheless, Bentley referred to the reprinters as 'pirates', when relaying the decision to an American author on his list, Herman Melville:

> our sapient Sir Frederick Pollock with Justices Platt & Rolfe have decided that a foreigner has no copyright. This drivelling absurdity can scarcely be suffered to remain, I trust, but in the mean time this decision will expose publishers like myself, who am so largely engaged in this department of publishing to the risk of attack from any unprincipled persons who may choose to turn Pirate.[31]

---

[30] *Boosey v. Purday* (1849) 154 ER 1159.

[31] Bentley to Melville 20 June 1849: Herman Melville, *Correspondence*, Lynn Horth (ed.) (Evanston and Chicago, IL: Northwestern University Press, 1993), p. 596.

Reprinters rushed to take advantage of the decision, racing against each other to issue the complete works of the most saleable American authors. These were anxious times for the established publishers. An injunction was refused in Chancery in a case concerning Washington Irving's works, and Murray and Bentley had to decide whether or not to test their claims in the common law courts. It emerged during the hearing that Murray had paid Irving £10,000 during the course of their relationship. Although initially confident that the decision in *Boosey* v. *Purday* would be overturned, a year later, Bentley was wondering desperately whether the American Congress would offer a way out. He wrote to James Fenimore Cooper (another American author on his list):

> Almost every American book is now pirated by the infamous dealers in stolen goods here; and there literally appears to be no chance for an American book. Surely, surely it must be worth while to preserve this market for American literature, which could be done immediately by your Congress granting a similar right to us Britishers.[32]

It is worth emphasising that Bentley's anguish was caused by British pirates, not American. Here, 'piracy' has become a term of moral opprobrium, used to refer to an unauthorised though perfectly legally reprint. The unexpressed objection to such conduct is that, unlike the authorised publisher, the reprinter has not paid the author. When unpacked, the criticism is largely directed at the 'robbery' of the publisher, and the reprinter's unscrupulous conduct in printing the paid-for titles of his fellow publisher. In earlier times, 'the trade' would have used its concerted might to stamp out such behaviour. But the nature of the market had changed. There was little informal pressure that could be brought to bear on reprinters such as Bohn and Routledge, who sold popular titles in large, cheap editions, and did not much trouble themselves over the book trade's 'ethics'.

Nevertheless, reprinters were subject to the law, and in 1851, the decision in *Boosey* v. *Jefferys* appeared to settle the matter of foreign copyright against them. Lord Campbell, presiding in the Court of Exchequer Chamber, confirmed that, wherever a foreigner was residing, first publication in the United Kingdom made him 'an author within the meaning of our statutes for the encouragement of learning'.[33] Bentley wrote jubilantly to Cooper:

---

[32] Dated [1?] August 1850: James Fenimore Cooper, *Letters and Journals*, J. F. Beard (ed.), 6 vols. (Cambridge, MA: Harvard University Press, 1960–68), vol. VI, p. 178. The Chancery hearings were 7–8 August.

[33] *Boosey* v. *Jefferys* (1851) 155 ER 675.

> At last we have had a decision of the Question – whether a foreigner can hold Copyright – by the Lord Chief Justice and five other judges sitting in a court of Error, deciding this point affirmatively. I am therefore now proceeding against those who have interfered with the novels by you and published by me ... Not but that the pirates threaten to carry the matter to the court of last resort – The House of Lords – but we shall see whether they will like to spend more money.[34]

Although publishers such as Bentley were delighted with the decision, it dealt a serious if indirect blow to British authors. Once American authors could obtain copyright simply by first publication in the UK, there was very little practical incentive for America to grant copyright to British works. Any case would now have to be based on claims to justice, rather than on the demonstrable needs of American authors for reciprocal protection, and Congress (influenced by the American book trade) had seemed deaf to such claims in the past.

A public meeting was held, at the Hanover Square rooms, to promote the 'equitable adjustment of British and Foreign Copyright'. The meeting's organisers asserted that Lord Campbell's decision should be reversed, in the interests of British authors and publishers. There was opposition from those who thought that the British should do what was right, rather than adopting a position which they sought to denounce in others. The *Athenaeum* took this principled stance: 'The men who hold the right to pirate good under any circumstances, weaken the argument against piracy itself.'[35] Criticism was directed explicitly at the British reprinters who had 'invaded the supposed rights for which their professional brethren had paid large sums of money – that money going into the hands of those justly entitled'. The *Athenaeum* considered that such behaviour was not only dishonourable, but also had a deleterious effect on popular literature in Britain: the system of 'smuggling American literature and selling it at the lowest price' had driven original British works from the market.[36]

The Hanover Square meeting was chaired by Edward Bulwer-Lytton, a novelist who ranked with Dickens in terms of sales. Immensely popular in America, Bulwer-Lytton was one of the few British authors paid by American publishers for advance sheets. However, the sums were comparatively small, as compared to his payments for his British copyrights. He estimated that full American copyright would have brought him an

---

[34] 3 June 1851: Cooper, *Letters and Journals*, vol. VI, p. 274.
[35] *Athenaeum*, 5 July 1851.    [36] *Ibid.*

extra £60,000 during his writing career.[37] Soon afterwards Bulwer-Lytton was involved in a covert attempt to secure Anglo-American copyright by paying a lobbying group, known as 'The Organisation'. A fee of $60,000 was quoted, with $20,000 in cash needed as an advance. Bulwer-Lytton coordinated confidential approaches to leading British authors and publishers, and, after initial reluctance, a significant sum was raised. A draft treaty was agreed, but various reverses caused discussions to drag on well into 1854. Once American publishers got wind of the venture, opposition grew significantly. Although eventually the treaty was signed, it was never ratified.

Perhaps Congress might have taken a different view of the Treaty had it known that the British position on foreign copyright was to change yet again, only a couple of months later. *Jefferys* v. *Boosey* was appealed to the House of Lords, and the appeal was allowed.[38] It was held that only a *resident* alien would be covered by the statute, and thus the foreigner's residence at time of first publication became a crucial factor in determining whether copyright was obtained. Those already holding American copyrights were again upset, because the author's place of residence had not been a factor in their arrangements, and it was open season once more on American works. The *Athenaeum* maintained its righteous tone, while indicating that America's previous self-interestedness left it little room to complain of her treatment now:

> The appeal has been to the spirit of selfishness – and this very spirit is now about to turn against them. Their strong ground was – that the wrong was done on English – not on American writers. Now the wrong falls equally on both. The Pirate cause has therefore lost its mainstay.[39]

In fact, the impact of the House of Lords' decision was not as serious for American authors as at first seemed likely. The ruling bore harshly on existing agreements, but, for new works, arrangements could be made to ensure the American author's 'residence' in Britain during publication. The inconvenience was too minor to drive America into negotiating a treaty.

### America reclaims the initiative

It was not until after the Civil War that efforts towards international copyright, led by American authors and publishers, resumed. There was

---

[37] *The Question of Unreciprocated Foreign Copyright in Great Britain* (London: Bohn, 1851).
[38] *Jefferys* v. *Boosey* (1854) 10 ER 681; 4 HLC 815.    [39] *Athenaeum*, 14 October 1854.

a growing sense that America's position was not only harming American authors, but also depriving the American people of a literature of its own. In 1868 the American Copyright Association was founded, 'for the purpose of securing the rights of authors and publishers among the civilised nations of the earth'.[40] Reciprocal protection arrangements were envisaged, with trade interests demanding that foreign works should be wholly manufactured within the United States, and published by a US citizen. Senator Edwin D. Morgan of New York sought the views of the powerful local firm, Harper & Bros. They were quick to disclaim any selfish interest in opposing the passage of a law: 'As far as we are concerned personally, it will make little or no difference, whether there is or is not an International Copyright Law.'[41] And, responding to the assertion that a 'civilised' nation would grant copyright to all, they also emphasised (at some length) that America's position was fully defensible in moral terms:

> It should not be forgotten that by refusing an international copyright we do not inflict injustice or commit a wrong. Copyright is not anywhere admitted to be a natural right, else it would be wrong to limit it, as all nations (including the English) do. If the right of an author, or his assign, in his printed thought were, as is wrongly taken for granted by some, like the right of an owner to real estate, then England and all civilized States have done a gross wrong to the author in limiting that right to a term of years. They might as justly limit the terms of ownership in a house or ship to fourteen or twenty-eight years. It is clear, that Copyright is a gift; the duration and content of which, depends upon the giver (the Government) which asserts the right to look to the general interest in deciding for what length of time a copyright shall endure, and who shall participate in this privilege, whether citizens only, or citizens residents, or these and also foreigners, who may be excluded from this, as they are from other privileges, as from voting, owning land &c. This is held, in practice, in England as well as here. The question is to be regarded then, as one, not of right, but of a privilege, to be granted or with-held, or curtailed or limited, as the general interest demands.[42]

Unsurprisingly, a British proposal for a treaty giving reciprocal protection without a manufacturing clause was unequivocally rejected by

---

[40] Eventually signed by 153 people, the memorial was never presented to Congress, although it was published. An account of the proceedings was published in a pamphlet, 'International Copyright', issued by the Copyright Association for the Protection and Advancement of Literature and Art (New York, 1868).
[41] Harper & Bros., Franklin Square to Hon. E. D. Morgan, Washington, DC, 27 February 1868 (Morgan Library: Literary and Historical Manuscripts).
[42] *Ibid.*

American publishers. A number of bills were introduced in Congress between 1871 and 1874, but the issue continued to simmer without resolution.

The American book trade had managed to convey the impression that international copyright would be a lopsided transaction; a valuable gift to the British publishing trade at the expense of the ordinary American reader, with no perceptible recompense. In response, one tactic adopted by American advocates of international copyright was to show that the reality was that American interests were being injured by the prevailing situation. In 1877 the American author Brander Matthews wrote an article for the *Princeton Review*, 'American authors and British pirates'. American works which had appeared in British catalogues were listed, as were details of mutilations of American works by British publishers. Matthews observed: 'The British pirate is not at all inferior in enterprise to the American pirate, nor is he more infrequent.'[43] Matthews' aim was not so much to abuse the British for their behaviour, but rather to persuade his American readers that there was a genuine problem, which would be solved by the grant of reciprocal copyright. Ignoring Matthews' strategic purpose, Mark Twain sent the *Princeton Review* a characteristically immoderate letter of reaction:

> I think we are not in a good position to throw bricks at the English pirate. We haven't any to spare. We need them to throw at the American Congress; and at the American author, who neglects his great privileges and then tries to hunt up some way to throw the blame on the only nation in the world which is magnanimous enough to say to him: "While you are the guest of our laws and our flag, you shall not be robbed."[44]

Twain's point was that Americans *could* obtain copyright protection, if they visited the British Dominions at the time of publication of their works, and thus that America was in no position to assert moral superiority. However, as Matthews later observed, untried American authors would not necessarily be in a position to run up to Canada or down to Bermuda (as Twain habitually did) in order to secure British copyright.[45]

---

[43] Brander Matthews, 'American Authors and British Pirates', *Princeton Review*, 5(4) (1877), 201–12.

[44] *Princeton Review*, 5(5) (1887), 47–65.

[45] See also Brander Matthews, 'Memories of Mark Twain', in *The Tocsin of Revolt and Other Essays* (New York: Charles Scribner's Sons, 1922), pp. 255–9: 'What had aroused the sudden wrath which had blazed up in Mark's epistolary excoriation was my assertion that the British law could be improved, it being then perfectly satisfactory to Mark himself.'

What is notable is that the condemnation of the American position was now coming primarily from American campaigners. There was a belief that the strategy of denying copyright to foreigners, valuable though it might be to the publishing and printing trades, brought unwelcome consequences for American authors and the American reading public. The attitude of even the publishers was changing, as they came under pressure from conditions in the publishing market. The 1870s saw the explosion of cheap publishing in America. New publishing firms in the Midwest and elsewhere were competing fiercely for the business which the established Eastern firms had been accustomed to regard as their own. Paper prices had declined sharply, so large editions of paper-cover books could be produced cheaply, and then sold for little more than the cost of production. British works were an obvious target for the Western trade, and the Eastern firms felt the squeeze. Price-cutting and loss-leaders did little to discourage the new entrants into the market. Firms who had established relationships with British authors began to see advantage in an international copyright law, which would protect them from potentially ruinous competition at home. Even Harper & Bros. began to advocate an international copyright treaty, although insisting that a manufacturing clause was indispensable.

By the mid-1880s two alternative approaches had emerged. One, represented in the Hawley and Dorsheimer Bills, was to grant international copyright on the basis of reciprocity alone. The American [Authors] Copyright League (founded in 1883) supported this position, arguing that copyright should be available without condition, as a matter of principle. James Russell Lowell composed a quatrain which was to become the slogan of the authors' movement:

> In vain we call old notions fudge
> And bend our conscience to our dealing
> The Ten Commandments will not budge,
> And stealing *will* continue stealing.[46]

However, protectionists and others argued that trade interests necessitated a manufacturing clause. This alternative view was embodied in the Chace Bill, drafted by the Philadelphia publishers. It seemed virtually impossible that a bill granting simple reciprocal copyright would pass. The American Copyright League continued to advocate the Hawley Bill

---

[46] It was printed in facsimile in the *Century* (February 1886), and later reproduced in the Platt Committee's report.

nevertheless, producing a pamphlet urging its adoption 'solely for reasons which touch the honor and interests of the country'.[47]

Both bills were referred to the Committee on Patents, and testimony was taken on the whole subject in four public hearings in 1886. Many leading authors and publishers testified as to their support for international copyright, but the Committee also received petitions and statements of opposition from powerful trade groups all over the country. Mark Twain testified in favour of the Hawley Bill, but nevertheless spoke up for 'those persons who are called "pirates"', defending them from charges of 'dishonesty', reasoning that they were 'made pirate by the collusion of the United States government, which made them pirates and thieves'.[48] The Philadelphia printer and publisher Roger Sherman teased others for their hypocrisy in using the 'pirate' label, though good-humouredly consented to wear it himself. Sherman, following in Dobson's footsteps, was now the publisher of the *Encyclopaedia Britannica* in America. Asked if he paid *Britannica*'s authors anything he replied, unapologetically: 'No, sir; our encyclopaedia is a reprint. We are what these gentleman call "pirates" and I have got the black flag up now.'[49]

The Patents Committee was not prepared to view piracy so coolly, and backed an amended version of the Chace Bill. It was critical of the fact that:

> The United States alone, of all the great civilized nations which have made advances in literature, still refuses to recognize the principle of international comity as applied to the production of literary property.

However, the report also supported the 'safeguard' of a manufacturing clause. The more dogmatic members of the American Copyright League considered the manufacturing clause a violation of the author's property right, and it was characterised as 'dishonest' in a sharply critical piece in the *New York Tribune*.[50] Support for this position was dwindling, however. After a struggle for power, a more pragmatic group won control of

---

[47] International Copyright: Memorandum in behalf of Senate Bill No. 191 and H. R. Bill No. 2493 [c.1885].

[48] P. Fatout (ed.), *Mark Twain Speaking* (University of Iowa Press, 1976), pp. 206–9, at 208.

[49] Chace Report, 21 May 1886 (49th Congress, 1st session: Report No. 1188).

[50] 'A Publisher on Justice to Authors', *New York Tribune* 24 May 1886. Chace suspected that the piece was by E. C. Stedman, Vice-President of the American Copyright League. Support for the Chace report's approach, including the manufacturing clause, came from George Parsons Lathrop: 'Should foreign authors be protected?', *Forum*, 1 (1886), 495–500. Lathrop was one of the founders of the American Copyright League, but resigned in 1885 when its Executive Committee refused to endorse a manufacturing clause.

the Authors Copyright League (as the American Copyright League now became known), and a new executive committee was named. It was given full discretion to secure 'such enactment of International Copyright as might be found equitable and practicable'.[51] The Authors League then agreed to work in tandem with the newly formed American Publishers Copyright League, in support of the Chace Bill.

The Leagues understood that persuasive and sustained campaigning would be required, and organised themselves to undertake it. The fact that public opinion had been for so long against international copyright was one reason that the Leagues preferred legislation, which would be publicly debated, to a treaty. After a visit to the United States, W. G. Cavendish Bentinck, Private Secretary to the British Foreign Secretary, offered a first-hand account of the way the international copyright question was perceived there:

> The fundamental difficulty in America is a moral one. The system of piracy has been so long protected by their laws, and so many interests have strengthened under it, and the belief that it fosters cheap literature is so widespread, that it does not seem possible to accomplish anything without a radical change in the opinion of the country on these heads, and for this we must probably trust to long-continued discussion.[52]

It is hard to detect in these words any confidence that British hopes would be fulfilled. However, the Leagues were resourceful and imaginative in their efforts; lobbying Senators and Congressmen, organising authors' readings, mobilising public support with newspaper and magazine articles, and distributing open letters.[53] The Authors Copyright League regarded itself as a 'moral movement', so would not employ professional lobbyists, instead relying on personal approaches to Congressmen. Although someone was hired to report on the situation in Washington, he was fired when he employed a page of the House not

---

[51] *Publishers' Weekly*, 12 November 1887, 679.
[52] *National Archives* (FO 881/5651), Further Correspondence respecting International Copyright (1887), pp. 8–9.
[53] For example, the Executive Committee of American Copyright League sought 'from all citizens who desire the development of American literature and regard the good name of the American people, their personal and active aid in securing International Copyright'. It asked readers (not just authors) to join the League, sign a memorial for International Copyright, and to write to their Congressmen: 'An open letter to readers of books, address of the American Copyright League, January 1888'. One of those who responded was Frederick Saunders, now librarian of the Astor Library in New York, but formerly of Saunders & Otley, the London firm whose activities precipitated the first British campaign for international copyright in 1837 (see above): *Publishers' Weekly*, 30 June 1888.

merely to place the League's printed arguments on the desks of the Representatives, but to remove those of its opponents.[54]

One of the most remarkable events was not orchestrated by the League, at least not initially. In January 1888 the Presbyterian clergyman Henry van Dyke preached a sermon, 'The National Sin of Literary Piracy' in the Brick Church, New York. His concerns were 'the perversion of national taste and manners by the vast circulation of foreign books that are both cheap and bad', 'the partial atrophy of our native literature' and, above all, 'the weakening and degeneration of the popular conscience'.[55] He was uncompromising in his criticism of America's position with respect to international copyright:

> The sin lies in the stupefying fact that ours is the only civilized Christian country on the globe which deliberately and persistently denies to foreigners the same justice which it secures to its own citizens, and declares that the intellectual property of an alien shall be forfeited and confiscated the moment it touches our shore or crosses our border.

His text was *Ephesians* iv: 28: 'Let him that stole steal no more.' The League contacted van Dyke, and a month later he preached the sermon again in Washington. President Cleveland's wife was present at the New York Avenue Presbyterian Church to hear it, as were a number of Congressmen (all of whom had been sent a personal invitation). The sermon was published as a pamphlet and widely distributed.[56]

An account of the sermon appeared in the *Manufacturer and Builder*, an established magazine which described itself as 'a practical journal of industrial progress'. Its articles reflected that tag, and it regularly took notice of changes to patent law, actual or proposed. The need for international copyright was conceded in its notice, although objection was taken to the fact that foreign pirates had been spared criticism:

> the author preaches a vigorous sermon against what he is pleased to call our national sin of stealing the literary productions of foreigners, a state of things which will doubtless continue until an international copyright

---

[54] Robert Underwood Johnson, *Remembered Yesterdays* (London: Allen & Unwin, 1924), p. 265.

[55] St Clair notes the separation of the word 'pirate' from the practice on which it was metaphored, and characterises the image of piracy as 'literary knockabout': 'Metaphors', 20. But here, although van Dyke is not of course advocating that the criminal punishments for theft should be applied to the theft of intellectual property, he is nevertheless making a serious practical point about the moral consequences of this pattern of behaviour.

[56] Henry van Dyke, *The National Sin of Literary Piracy* (New York: Scribner's, 1888).

law shall be enacted. The enactment of such a law would meet the
approval of all fair-minded men. The reverend author's statement of
the case would, in our opinion, have been fairer had he taken the trouble
to show (which he could readily have done) that American authors are
made to suffer quite as severely by the license of foreign publishers as are
foreigners by the license of ours. Two wrongs do not, of course, make a
right; but it is scarcely fair to give to the American publisher the monopoly of the business of piracy, the profits of which are shared quite as
largely by foreigners.[57]

The qualification was a fair one, although the American publishing
market was vast, as compared to any foreign publishing market. As has
been discussed, Brander Matthews, in his *Princeton Review* article, had
been deliberately careful to demonstrate that there were faults on both
sides. The notice also displays an unwillingness to adopt van Dyke's
pulpit language of fire and brimstone. Nevertheless, his analysis is not
repudiated. What is significant is that a popular journal, with no particular brief for literary subject matter, considered that an international
copyright law was a reasonable thing for America to put in place.

Others were unafraid to adopt blunt language when advocating international copyright. The publisher Henry Holt (whose firm was known
for its quality European editions) published an article entitled, 'The recoil
of piracy'. He responded scathingly to the argument (advanced by Mark
Twain at the 1886 Patent Committee hearings) that reprinting was
defensible because it was legal under American law:

> The gentry who are accused of piracy indignantly repudiate the term,
> because their proceedings are within the law, that it, within the law of
> their own country. This identical answer, however, could have been made
> by the Algerines to Commodore Decatur. In Algiers piracy was within the
> law too. Great Britain might send a navy over here, as we sent one to
> Algiers, to stop proceedings which our own laws will not stop, and collect
> an indemnity for the millions of which a most important class of her
> citizens has been despoiled by the "industry" of a certain class of ours. Yet
> if she were to do so, we probably should answer, with many shrieks of the
> eagle, that we proposed to be governed by our own laws, and not by those
> of Great Britain.[58]

Commodore Decatur was an American naval officer notable for his
heroism in the Barbary Wars. The Barbary States of North Africa had
for centuries plundered seaborne commerce, demanding tribute money

[57] *Manufacturer and Builder* (April 1888), 94.
[58] Henry Holt, 'The Recoil of Piracy', *Forum*, 5 (1888), 27–37.

from foreigners who wished to trade in African ports, or sail through their territorial waters. Following the Declaration of Independence, American merchant ships no longer enjoyed British protection. Their ships were seized by Barbary pirates, and their crews enslaved. The United States at first agreed to pay substantial tribute, but balked when demands escalated. In 1801 the Pacha of Tripoli declared war on the United States, and Decatur was prominent in daring action against the pirates. America's firm approach brought it widespread respect as a nation, and established its reputation as a force to be reckoned with in international diplomacy. Holt's reference to Decatur would have evoked a powerful reaction in his American readers, giving considerable charge to his characterisation of a different kind of piracy. Holt argued that American policy had 'vitiated the people's reading' by affecting the quality of books available, and had 'done cruel injustice' to American authors and American literature. He regarded the assertion of national autonomy in this case as no more than an expedient façade concealing trade interests, and was quick to demolish it.

Holt's piece was forceful, arresting and influential. The striking image he had used reappeared in a Senate Committee report early the following year:

> It is time that the United States should cease to be the Barbary coast of literature, and that the people of the United States should cease to be the buccaneers of books.[59]

The Patents Committee had been considering a compromise bill, agreed by both Copyright Leagues and the typographical unions. In previous versions of the Chace Bill, the manufacturing clause required printing to be done in the United States, but permitted import of clichés of type or duplicates of the plates used in printing the original editions. From a publisher's point of view, dual typesetting was a futile and wasteful exercise likely to introduce errors into the text. However, the typographical unions were insistent that American typesetting was essential to protect trade interests. Recognising the power of the unions, the Leagues reluctantly acceded to their demands. From this point, all the interest groups worked together; although a great deal of lobbying work was still necessary, both at home and abroad. Knowing the likely reaction of British authors and publishers to the amended manufacturing clause, the Leagues explained and defended the compromise in twin letters to

---

[59] Senate Report No. 622, 50th Congress, 1st Session, p. 2 (1888).

the *Athenaeum*. They appealed to 'our English friends' to forbear from criticism while the bill was pending in Congress, 'as they cannot know the exigencies which have compelled modifications of the present measure'.[60]

## Moral courage[61]

The bill finally passed in March 1891. The immediate British reaction was one of amazement, though gratitude was tempered by uncertainty as to the practical effect of the manufacturing clause. Informed commentators expressed admiration for the manner in which the American campaigners had pursued their beliefs, while understanding the political obstacles they had faced. Sir Henry Bergne, an experienced negotiator who was Britain's representative at the Berne Convention negotiations, applauded the Americans' 'principles of high national morality', but acknowledged that they 'would have been powerless to pass this Act if the aid of the manufacturers on the ground of protection had not been secured'.[62]

What remains striking is the extent to which the American advocates of international copyright identified it as a matter of national significance, and linked it to national pride. The *Century Magazine* (one of the principal organs of the international copyright campaign) considered that the 1891 Act secured an 'incalculable' gain for 'American letters and American prestige'. Although the manufacturing clause was acknowledged to be a limitation on 'the ideal right of property', there was no need for national abasement or apology. What really mattered was the principle of the thing: 'Our law no longer tolerates the literary "pirate".'[63] This presentation of the 1891 Act expressed a pride and self-respect which seemed distinctively American.

America's stance on international copyright law remained essentially unchanged for a further century. Although the exercise is historiographically most unsound, it is tempting to wonder what Commodore

---

[60] *Athenaeum*, 3 March 1888.
[61] 'For every ten men who are willing to face the guns of an enemy there is only one willing to brave the disapproval of his fellow, the censure of his colleagues, the wrath of his society. Moral courage is a rarer commodity than bravery in battle or great intelligence' (Robert Kennedy, speech in Cape Town, 7 June 1966, *Oxford Dictionary of Quotations* (ed.) Elizabeth Knowles (Oxford University Press, 2004)).
[62] J. H. G. Bergne, 'Anglo-American Copyright', *Quarterly Review*, 172 (1891), 380–98.
[63] 'International Copyright Accomplished', *Century Magazine*, 42 (1891), 148.

Decatur, as a celebrated opponent of maritime pirates, would have thought of literary piracy. If he has been reported correctly, it seems most likely that he would have endorsed America's approach as expressed in the 1891 Act:

> Our country! In her intercourse with foreign nations, may she always be in the right; but our country, right or wrong.[64]

---

[64] Stephen Decatur, toast at dinner in his honour, Norfolk, VA, April 1816: *Oxford Dictionary of American Quotations* (eds.) Hugh Rawson and Margaret Miner (Oxford University Press, 2006).

# 3

# Language, practice, and history

ADRIAN JOHNS

Catherine Seville's chapter performs at least three major services for the historian of copyright. The first is to treat the British and American sides in the bitter struggles over transatlantic reprinting symmetrically. One would have thought that this would be an elementary requirement for any self-respecting historian, but in fact sympathetic attention to the case for reprinting has been scarce, particularly for the very period on which Seville focuses: that between the first organized campaign for an international copyright measure and the eventual adoption of a protocol in the 1890s. The second is to demonstrate that this conflict did change its character over time. What it meant to argue against – or, more interestingly, for – transatlantic reprinting was significantly different in 1790 from what it would be in 1890. And Seville shows, third, that these changes took place at a semantic level. The language of piracy itself took on different connotations, becoming more overtly moral as the debate intensified. In each respect, her chapter tackles a major problem that dogs the historiography of intellectual property: its tendency to presume a normative tone, its legal essentialism, and its neglect of the fine grain of cultural history.

None of these three services should be regarded as taking precedence over the others. They are interdependent. Their underlying thread, it seems to me, is an insistence that the meanings of actions and statements can only be appreciated in terms of their embedding in situations of practice, which have their own chronologies. For example, a history of the metaphor of piracy itself makes sense only if it draws attention to the shifting contexts of use in which that metaphor received its different meanings. The continuities and discontinuities of copyright history will therefore not always be evident from explicit changes in terminology. Sometimes existing terms will shift subtly (or dramatically) in their meanings, because their uses change. Implicit here is an agenda that goes beyond recommending a "linguistic turn," and suggests revisions in the history of intellectual property itself.

The passage that Seville uses as an epigraph serves to make the point well. Ned Ward's verse of course derives from a much earlier period than the debates that interest Seville, but that makes it all the more helpful to show just how context-specific the meanings of metaphors like "piracy" can be. To see what I mean, we should start by putting Ward's piracy victims in their place. That place is hell.

Ward was a brilliantly scabrous Tory observer of London life, helping to create the role of the hack poet in the first generation after 1688. His *Journey to Hell* parodies Dante's Underworld to articulate a typology of the presumptive professions of this fast-changing city, immersed in a financial and commercial revolution. Lawyers, physicians, priests, and poets all come under attack. Among them is a crowd of booksellers and printers too.[1] They are first heard complaining loudly about their mutual offence of "piracy." Ward thus puts piracy at the center of his acid portrait of the book trade of the end of the seventeenth century. Despite what at first glance looks like proof of the *longue durée* of the piratical metaphor, however, the term is in fact quite different in meaning from that which would echo around the Philadelphia and New York of the nineteenth century. It reflects very accurately a struggle that had raged in the book trades of London since the mid-seventeenth century, and was not yet at its climax.

Briefly, beginning long before the Civil War, a conflict had been brewing between the printers and booksellers of London. The printers saw themselves as master-craftsmen, and fondly recalled that in the sixteenth century they had dominated the ranks of the metropolitan book trade. But publishing booksellers (the term *publisher* had not yet taken on its modern connotation) were fast usurping that supremacy. This can be seen as typical of well-recognized changes under way in the period that were essential to the development of capitalism. It gave rise to persistent complaints by the printers about the moral perils implicit in replacing putatively honest craft skills with financial speculation. To their camp, the one represented certainty of value, in both moral and economic senses. The other amounted to uncertainty, risk, and an addiction to gambling. These complaints could be found in many arenas in the 1690s – that "age of projects," in which stockjobbing became the

---

[1] [E. Ward], *A Journey to Hell: Or, a Visit Paid to the Devil* (2nd edn, London: printed, and are to be sold by the Booksellers of London and Westminster, 1700), Part II, pp. 14–21.

standard point of reference for moral campaigns in all realms. But they took on a special character because of the centrality of publishing, printing, and bookselling to the public sphere that was so central a part of post-revolutionary England's image of itself. It is this that gives Ward's evocation of a piratical trade its point.

Ward portrays a horde of outraged specters – the booksellers – characterized by their familiarity only with the outward accoutrements of books, not their "contents." All of them are complaining of piracy at the hands of each other, because all are in fact guilty of it. Piracy seems to be their *modus operandi*. But some kinds of piracy stand out as worse for them than others. These booksellers are in "a great Contest" with "their Slaves," the printers, whom they single out for presuming to print "Copies for your selves, and fill the Town / Instead of ours, with Pamphlets of your own." The printers, these haughty booksellers complain, buy off "our" authors, when both craftsmen and writers should accede to the supremacy of the booksellers themselves. But this complaint does not go unanswered, for the printers reply in equally angry terms that the booksellers are delusional. It is the printer's craft that disperses "the labours of the Learn'd" and diffuses knowledge across the world. "We give new Light, Obscurities remove, / All Sciences preserve, the same improve." In earlier years, they point out, they were the ones who sustained the realm of print – and in those years the booksellers' ancestors had been mere hawkers, unpropertied and contemptible. In accord with standard early modern convictions, they had merited no representation in the early book trade's body politic. "No Copies cou'd ye buy, no Charter boast," the printers point out – the lack of property had coincided with institutional powerlessness. Now, however, "those good old Times are lost." Booksellers owned physical, personal, and literary properties alike. They had "Made Authors Hacknies, and the Press your Slaves."

At this point, Ward conjures a court to suppress the contest and pass judgment. The entire trade stands accused of inflaming the mob for the sake of profit. What could have been a rational public sphere had thus become a sphere of unreason: "the blind Crowd believing [the pamphlets] were misled, / And still were greater Fools the more they read." Civil war had been the inevitable consequence. It was as part of this that the stationers had begun invading each others' "Properties," their contempt for their own "Fraternity" corresponding to that for the broader commonwealth. Found guilty, they are condemned to stand beneath the poets and broil in a fire fueled by their endless hack verses, basted in authorial dung.

In the generation when Ward published this verse, *piracy* became the routine term within the London book trade to describe immoral practices, especially the reprinting of titles registered to another. While it can occasionally be found earlier than the Civil War – William St Clair gives a particularly good example from 1625 in his recent article about intellectual property metaphors – it only became a commonplace after the 1670s.[2] When it did, it was as part of this struggle over the moral constitution of the book trade itself, and in particular the relative places of financial speculation (publishing) and craft skill (printing). The clash found an even more specific focus in contests for the immensely valuable patent covering law books. This feud, which continued for decades, gave rise to high-flown arguments contending that printing itself should be regarded as the property of the crown by descent from its original introduction into England, which had supposedly been at the behest of the then king. On the other side, the booksellers claimed that this supposed history was false, and that the trade had always been a commercial enterprise; over time, it had become the livelihood – and hence, in their view, the property – of a community. They further urged the novel idea that their properties in titles, within this broader political economy, derived from the creative work of their authors. Each side accused the other of "piracy," and in the end the courts curtailed the production of law books in order to quash the controversy.[3] In short, every aspect of Ward's picturesque portrayal captured an element of this real conflict, the resolution of which was not yet clear. What piracy *was*, in the first generation when literary piracy was first regularly identified, incorporated those elements of conflict and community.

I dwell on Ward's verse partly to make the simple point that concepts – or metaphors, if one prefers – do indeed take their meanings from their uses, and that they therefore change in ways that may be hard to discern without contextual research. This matters because the meanings that result can then solidify and become lasting. But I want to draw attention to one aspect in particular of this process. At the end of the seventeenth century, Ward invoked not just the current state of the book trade, and not just its denizens' view of that state, but specifically their perception of its change over time. That is, the cry of "piracy" loosed by Ward's

---

[2] The example came in a complaint by the University of Cambridge against the London trade: see W. St Clair, 'Metaphors', p. 390.
[3] For this conflict, see A. Johns, *The Nature of the Book: Print and Knowledge in the Making* (University of Chicago Press, 1998), pp. 299–320, 326–43.

booksellers contained as a central component of its meaning a specifically *historical* account of practices. It was this historical character that
gave it its moral edge. And in this it seems to me to be representative of
piracy discourses in general. Whenever debates about intellectual piracy
have flared up in the centuries since 1700, they have typically – and
perhaps necessarily – drawn upon rival accounts of history. It is partly
this that would forestall any attempt to explain copyright, too, as simply
determined by the material practices of a given society. The concept of
piracy has always been shaped by perceptions of continuity and deviance.
It has always been to an important degree historiographic.

The most important piracy debate of the period between Ward and
Seville's nineteenth-century conflicts serves to reinforce this contention.
The long and complex arguments over Anglo-Scottish and Anglo-Irish
reprinting in the eighteenth century, culminating in the epochal case of
*Donaldson* v. *Becket* in 1774, involved sustained and profound engagement with historical questions. Their most prominent focus was on the
Glorious Revolution of 1688. That event, which so dominated
eighteenth-century political and economic sensibilities,[4] was central to
the literary property debates too, not least because rival interpretations of
its character determined whether the entire archival record dating from
earlier periods could be regarded as evidence at all. Were the Stationers'
Register entries of the early seventeenth century evidence of a long-
standing property right, or were they merely signs of Stuart tyranny?
Thus the Jacobite Thomas Carte claimed that the thousands of registra-
tions surviving from before 1688 were "clear Proof" of an authorial
property having existed from the outset: "I hardly think," Carte declared,
"there ever was a Book (unless of a seditious Nature) printed, till within
Forty Years past [that is, 1695], but ... the Property thereof was ascertained, and the sole Right of Printing it secured to the Proprietor by such
an Entry." In other words, a natural property right had obtained until the
Revolution, and the end of licensing, had thrown it into jeopardy. Only
since 1688 had the "Pyrating of Books" become "common."[5] On the
other side, Whig jurists would insist that good doctrines could never be
drawn from "so polluted a Fountain." Carte's whole list of precedents,

---

[4] S. Pincus, *1688: The First Modern Revolution* (New Haven, CT: Yale University Press,
2009), pp. 12–13.
[5] *A Second Letter from an Author to a Member of Parliament* (London: n.p., 23 April 1735).
The identification of Carte as author of the *Second Letter* is mine, and is subject to
correction.

one expostulated, formed "the History of *Despotism*, NOT of the *Common Law.*" Camden gave particularly short shrift to the pre-1688 record when *Donaldson* v. *Becket* came to the Lords, dismissing it outright as a "heterogeneous heap of rubbish."[6] Meanwhile, outside the legal realm, printers in their continuing revolt against the copy-owners' oligarchy continued to insist, as Ward's had, that Enlightenment was owed to their craft skills and fraternal spirit.[7] Advocates on all sides thus pursued the technicalities of conjectural, political, and natural history, seeking to define the relationship of authorship to civilization, knowledge, and the created world. Historical contentions became central to the question of literary property, and indeed to the moral constitution of print commerce. These efforts – not only arguments, but the evidence dug up to support them, and the methods developed to do so – would become a valuable trove for the debates over national and international copyright in the next century.

The question that this poses is that of what history of history, as it were, underpins the concept of piracy. We need to understand how changing approaches to the past impinged upon the concept of piracy and anti-piracy efforts, not least because it is already clear that those approaches did indeed change radically from the seventeenth century to the mid-nineteenth. For example, it is evident that Romantic convictions about the genealogy of creative authorship contributed substantially to bids to elevate copyright into a real property. But it may be that the clearest examples are actually to be found in the very international conflict that Seville describes. As she has revealed, the moral connotations of the term changed quite markedly in the mid-nineteenth century, as efforts to forge a transatlantic copyright agreement mounted. I suspect that a reason for this may lie in shifting historiographic sensibilities, and that these were registered in some of the major participants in that debate.

The example I would cite to support this is that of the most important single figure in the creation of the US publishing industry, the Irish émigré Mathew Carey. Carey's role in establishing a trade dedicated

---

[6] *Tonson* v. *Collins* (Trin. 1 Geo. III, KB, and Mich. 2 Geo. III, KB: 1 Black. W. 301, 322), 335; "Gentleman," *The cases of the appellants and respondents in the cause of literary property* (London: for J. Bew, W. Clarke, P. Brett. C. Wilkin, 1774), p. 8; *The pleadings of the counsel before the House of Lords, in the great cause concerning literary property* (London: for C. Wilkin, S. Axtell, J. Axtell, and J. Browne, [1774]), pp. 29–30.

[7] E.g., *The Speech of Mr. Jacob Ilive to his brethren the Master-Printers* (London: n.p. n.d. [1750]).

partly to transatlantic reprinting is very well known, as is his personal
dedication to a political economy of the "harmony of interests." His
hostility to what he thought of as the distinctively British doctrine of
free trade is also familiar.[8] But what is less widely appreciated is the
centrality to those convictions of Carey's views of history. As Seville
notes, the confrontation between the new United States and the Algerian
corsair society in the 1790s was a key episode here, and in fact it was
transforming for Carey himself, who wrote an interesting analysis that
condemned Algiers not for piracy but for monarchy.[9] But it was the
history of Ireland that really dominated his thoughts. And in particular,
it was the history of Ireland as refracted through the book trade of Ned
Ward's era.

After the War of 1812, as his Philadelphia publishing house developed
the practices that would define mid-century transatlantic reprinting,
Carey spent years hard at work on a book that he called *Vindiciae
Hibernicae*. It was long in the planning, but its proximate causes were
the debates over Catholic emancipation in Britain, and a novel called
*Mandeville* published in 1817 by the radical William Godwin. The novel,
which was immediately reprinted in both New York and Philadelphia,
resurrected an old narrative about a massacre of hundreds of thousands
of Protestants that had allegedly occurred in Ireland during the uprising
that had occurred there in 1641. In the 1640s and 1650s, belief in the
reality of this story had led directly both to the outbreak of the English
Civil War and, later, to Cromwell's devastating conquest of Ireland.
Carey produced an elaborate and outraged response. It was printed in
1819 in only 750 copies, 250 of which he distributed free to libraries,
reading rooms, and "enlightened individuals." Yet he himself consistently named this book – rather than, for example, the far better-known
*Olive Branch* – as the most important work of his life. Dedicated to
republicans and past Irish heroes, on its face it was about a long-past
incident, but in reality concerned an essential nexus linking trust, communication, and colonial power.

---

[8] For Carey, see A. Johns, *Piracy: The Intellectual Property Wars from Gutenberg to Gates*
(University of Chicago Press, 2010), pp. 179–211; T. Loughran, *The Republic in Print:
Print Culture in the Age of US Nation Building, 1770–1870* (New York: Columbia
University Press, 2007), pp. 15–21; and R. Remer, *Printers and Men of Capital:
Philadelphia Book Publishers in the New Republic* (Philadelphia: Pennsylvania
University Press, 1996), pp. 1–4, 57–65.
[9] M. Carey, *A Short Account of Algiers* (2nd edn Philadelphia, PA: for M. Carey, 1794).

The 1641 legend mattered because the incident had become a pivotal moment in the history of relations between England and Ireland. The rising was rumored to have had the complicity of Charles I, and had therefore become a major element in English revolutionaries' belief that the king had rounded on his own people. It had subsequently been made the warrant for the violent imposition of Protestant rule by Parliament, for real massacres by Cromwell's Ironsides at Drogheda and elsewhere, and for the wholesale expropriation of Irish land to English "adventurers." The Ascendancy of the eighteenth century – under which Carey had chafed in his youth – had rested directly on beliefs about the 1641 rising. And now it looked like those beliefs were going to be dragged out again. This was why Carey devoted himself to proving them false. They rested, he claimed, on "Fraud, Imposture, Bigotry, and Delusion." Carey further insisted that these were the same vices embraced in his own day by the British and, by extension, their free-trader allies. He called Ireland's continuing anti-Catholic laws the archetypal example of monarchy intruding on the rights of man – "as piratical a depredation of property," indeed, "as the annals of the world can produce." What sustained this piracy, he insisted, was public belief in the 1641 massacre – and that belief in turn rested on false printed reports. In short, a corrupt, monopoly-ridden culture of print in the London of the seventeenth and eighteenth centuries was to blame. But he himself was now able to unmask the deception thanks to the very different regime of print that Carey and his fellow citizens had created in the New World. "In the present state of printing," he crowed, with Americans enjoying "open, unreserved communication between nations," such "fraud and falsehood" could no longer prevail. Ireland had suffered for the lack of this kind of print culture; America benefited from its presence. In effect, Carey was claiming that his activities as the leading American publisher were of far more than economic or personal value: they stood to change the conditions of truth, and hence civilization, in the modern world. As he concluded, "What a lesson on history generally – but more especially on Irish history!"[10]

---

[10] M. Carey, *Vindiciae Hibernicae* (Philadelphia, PA: M. Carey and Son, 1819), sig. π2$^{r-v}$, pp. ix–x, xvi–vii, xx, xxvi, xxxii, 25–6, 28; M. Carey, *Autobiography* (New York: E. L. Schwaab, 1942), pp. 58–81. It is perhaps worth noting that recently historians have agreed that printers vied with each other in 1640s London to exaggerate reports from Ireland, but, *contra* Carey, this is now explained by their operating in a competitive and effectively deregulated realm. See E. Shagan, "Constructing Discord: Ideology, Propaganda, and English Responses to the Irish Rebellion in 1641," *Journal of British Studies*, 36 (1997), 4–34, and J. Cope, "The Experience of Survival during the 1641 Irish Rebellion," *Historical Journal*, 46 (2003), 295–316, esp. 296.

*Vindiciae Hibernicae* represented convictions that were absolutely central to Carey's understanding of himself, his practices, and the trade of which he was a pioneer. As is very well known, Carey devoted enormous effort to attempting to forge a common civility in the book trades of the new nation. Some at the time thought he was obsessed by this idea. He was the standard-bearer for separating publishing from printing and retail bookselling, and he was instrumental in expanding the horizons of American publishing beyond local populations to a national scale. In a bid to manage the conflicts over reprinting that inevitably resulted from that expansion, he worked hard to create some kind of modern counterpart to the old fraternal spirit referred to in Ward's poem. His trade would reprint internationally, but abjure domestic reprinting as "piratical." Carey's complex relations to practices that he and others called piratical emerged from passionately held convictions resting on historical grounds, which involved themes of imperialism, religious division, and Enlightenment ideals of public knowledge. His major effort to forge a practical morality of publishing in the United States was similarly historiographic. It involved attempting to create a booksellers' institution modeled on precedents drawn from both the old London Stationers' Company and the German book fairs of the sixteenth century. These represented two histories of moral commerce in the book trade, the one continuous and civic, the other periodic and (quasi-) national. It is plausible to suggest that his failure, and the subsequent fissiparous character of US publishing, resulted from the inconsistencies between those two histories.

We should be far more reticent than we have been, therefore, in assuming the meanings of terms like piracy to have persisted just because the words themselves did. What we need is a fully cultural history of their deployment and use. As yet, we understand far too little about when and how their practical meanings changed, why, and to what effect. My contention is that the role of specifically historical knowledge – and of the practices used to get that knowledge – will prove to have been central to the kind of transformation that Catherine Seville has so acutely noticed. And what goes for the concept of piracy should go for that of literary property too.

# PART III

Comparative Law

# 4

## The metamorphosis of *contrefaçon* in French copyright law*

DAVID LEFRANC

TRANSLATION FROM FRENCH BY

SÉBASTIEN ODDOS

In French copyright law, *contrefaçon* consists of the infringement of any of the author's rights. As the only basis for a remedy for the violation of French *droit d'auteur*, *contrefaçon* originally lacked a broad scope. The expansion of *contrefaçon* is a relatively recent development, which is now being challenged by offences committed by the general public.

In the past, the general public associated *contrefaçon* exclusively with the sale of counterfeit goods of luxury brands. The media regularly echoed this narrow interpretation. It is only recently that the *contrefaçon* of works of authorship has been in the media spotlight. The general public has grown increasingly aware that downloading movies or songs without authorization is illegal. In 2006, a large part of French public opinion demanded the freedom to download, in other words, the end of *contrefaçon* on the Internet – at least as applied to non-commercial users. In summary, because the public understands *contrefaçon* to entail the penalty of either a monetary fine or the threat of imprisonment, public opinion considers actions for *contrefaçon* to impede free access to culture and to marginalize young people. The concept of *contrefaçon* is clearly undergoing an unprecedented crisis of legitimacy. This phenomenon however appears specific to *droit d'auteur*. In contrast, the sanctions associated with trade mark and patent infringements are not being challenged; in fact the European Union does not hesitate to describe these infringements as a kind of international organized crime. History

---

* A prior version of this chapter was published in French as 'Les métamorphoses de la contrefaçon. Naissance – extension – scission', in *Propriétés Intellectuelles*, January 2009, 19–30.

might help us understand why *contrefaçon* is so contested when it comes to copyright. This chapter therefore will broadly survey the history of *contrefaçon* in French *droit d'auteur*.

Until now, historians of copyright have mainly focused on the notion of 'literary property'.[1] This was to be expected, considering the French interest in subjective rights. The French are indeed fascinated by the idea that the state delegates some power to citizens. The system of printing privileges epitomizes this trend. Reducing the history of *droit d'auteur* to its sole enforcement mechanisms does not equate with French legal tradition. The fact that French legal commentators display a relative lack of interest in *contrefaçon* is slightly surprising considering that this concept has survived throughout history from the time of privileges to the Internet era. Despite conflicting opinions,[2] the same cannot be said of the concept of '*auteur*', which only became central in French law after the Revolution. *Contrefaçon* is therefore a remnant of 'literary property' in today's *droit d'auteur*.

*Contrefaçon* primarily refers to an action for infringement of intellectual property. In the United Kingdom the Copyright, Designs and Patents Act 1988 uses the generic term infringement[3] to describe a breach of copyright. In contrast to *contrefaçon*, infringement is a transparent notion applying to numerous subjective rights. How then can we explain such dissimilarity between *contrefaçon* and infringement? A common law lawyer would probably question the need for a specific concept of *contrefaçon*. The justification may rest in that the notion of *contrefaçon* strengthens intellectual property. French law uses *contrefaçon* as a specific notion covering all breaches of intellectual property rights and copyright infringement in particular. In addition to being a civil tort, *contrefaçon* has another specific feature: it also constitutes a criminal offence. In practice the copyright owner needs to choose a legal ground for bringing an action against infringers. As a civil tort, *contrefaçon* is subject only to pecuniary sanctions. As a criminal offence, *contrefaçon* may impose on the infringer up to three years' imprisonment and a fine of €300,000.[4]

---

[1] L. Pfister, 'L'auteur, propriétaire de son œuvre?' (thesis, Université Robert Schuman, Strasbourg 1999); F. Rideau, *La formation du droit de la propriété littéraire en France et en Grande Bretagne* (Aix en Provence: Presses Universitaires d'Aix–Marseille, 2004).

[2] B. Edelman, *Le sacre de l'auteur* (Paris: Seuil, coll. Essai, 2004).

[3] Copyright, Designs and Patents Act 1988, ss. 16-27.

[4] Art. L. 335–2 of the French Code of Intellectual Property (FCIP): 'Any edition of writings, musical compositions, drawings, paintings or other printed or engraved production made in whole or in part regardless of the laws and regulations governing the ownership of

Common law lawyers are often surprised that *contrefaçon* may be equally subject to civil and criminal sanctions, without, for example, a higher burden of proof to establish the violation or a requirement of intent to profit. History provides a likely explanation: it is the analogy between authors' rights and property rights which has drawn *contrefaçon* closer to the criminal offence of theft. This approach, supported by the early nineteenth-century lawyer and treatise writer Philippe-Antoine Merlin in 1825,[5] has a much earlier origin. A decision by the King's Council of 27 February 1682 already treated *contrefaçons* as theft.[6] During the 1793 legislative debates, Hell declares that '*contrefaction is a genre of theft*',[7] while Lakanal denounces the damages inflicted by '*literary pirates*' malfeasance.[8] By comparison William St Clair has shown that in the United Kingdom the analogy with piracy is mainly used at a time of legal vacuum (1695–1710).[9] In his opinion, it is paradoxical that English lawyers never relied on the analogy between infringement and theft to justify the same sanction as theft.[10] In France the association of *contrefaçon* with theft is crucial in justifying imprisonment. This approach allowed certain late eighteenth-century and early nineteenth-century criminal courts (*tribunaux correctionnels*) to convict infringers before the French Criminal Code came into

authors shall constitute an infringement. Any infringement shall constitute an offence. Infringement in France of works published in France or abroad shall be liable to a three-year imprisonment and a fine of €300,000. The sale, exportation and importation of infringing works shall be subject to the same penalties. Where offences provided for by this Article are committed by an organized criminal group, the penalties will be increased to five-year imprisonment and a fine of €500,000.' L. 335–3 FCIP: 'Any reproduction, performance or dissemination of a work of the mind, by any means whatsoever, in violation of the author's rights as defined and regulated by law shall also constitute an infringement. The violation of any of the rights of an author of software as defined in Article L122–6 shall also constitute an infringement.'

5. Ph.-A. Merlin, '*Contrefaçon*', in *Répertoire universel et raisonné de jurisprudence* (Brussels: H. Tarlier, 1825) (available at: www.copyrighthistory.org/cgi-bin/kleioc/ 0010/exec/ausgabe/"f_1825").

6. *Ibid.*

7. C. Couhin, *La propriété industrielle, artistique et littéraire* (Paris: Librairie de la Société du Recueil Général des Lois et des Arrêts, Larose, 1894), vol. I, p. 68.

8. *Ibid.*, p. 173.

9. 'The language of stealing arrived in England quite suddenly at the end of the seventeenth century, and established itself as one of the main metaphors between the lapsing of the Licensing Act in 1695, after which, until the 1710 statute, there was no statutory basis for copyright' (St Clair, 'Metaphors', p. 387).

10. 'Until very recent years, even during the most authoritarian eras, nobody is recorded as suggesting that the penalties for theft should be applied to the money that publishers claimed had been "stolen" from them by infringement of copyright' (*ibid.*, 393.).

force.[11] Nowadays, penalization for *contrefaçon* is even favoured by European Union institutions. A draft directive indeed tries to impose penalties of imprisonment in the field of intellectual property generally.[12]

French *droit d'auteur* now defines *contrefaçon* as the infringement of an author's rights. Some of these rights, also called monopoly of exploitation or patrimonial rights, are economic in nature. It is well known that French *droit d'auteur* adopts a synthetic approach to economic rights.[13] The *droit d'auteur* usually prohibits any unauthorized reproduction or performance of a work of the mind (*œuvre de l'esprit*).[14] But *contrefaçon* does not only cover economic rights. A breach of an author's moral right will equally be considered as a *contrefaçon*. Hence a publisher who omits the name of an author could in theory face up to three years' imprisonment.[15] *Contrefaçon* is intended to punish all infringements of an author's (or his assignee's) interests. But, at the beginning, *contrefacon* grew up in relation to a very particular act in relation to literary works and carried not just civil but criminal penalties (1). At some point it became general to all types of works but this was at a time when infringers were generally seen to be commercial bodies or with commercial motives and the imposition of criminal penalties did not seem particularly problematic (2). Now that *contrefacon* is being applied to new media, that is the Internet, which involves private individuals, the criminal penalties seem inappropriate and oppressive to many and this is something the state now has to address (3).

## The birth of *contrefaçon*

### *The publishing paradigm*

In France, from the first privileges in the sixteenth century to the Copyright Act of 1957, *contrefaçon* has been literary property's specific sanction.

---

[11] Merlin, '*Contrefaçon*'.

[12] Amended Proposal for a Directive of the European Parliament and of the Council on Criminal Measures aimed at Ensuring the Enforcement of Intellectual Property Rights (COM (2006) 168 final 2005/0127 (COD)).

[13] Art. L. 122–1 FCIP: 'The right of exploitation belonging to the author shall comprise the right of performance and the right of reproduction.'

[14] Art. L. 122–4 FCIP: 'Any complete or partial performance or reproduction made without the consent of the author or of his successors in title or assigns shall be unlawful. The same shall apply to translation, adaptation or transformation, arrangement or reproduction by any technique or process whatsoever.'

[15] E. Dreyer, 'La protection pénale du droit moral de l'auteur' (*Communication Commerce Électronique*) (CCE), September 2007, chron. no. 20.

During this period, *contrefaçon* did not punish every infringement of authors' interests. Initially, it remained fundamentally associated with the world of publishing. Around 1750 the Encyclopaedists defined *contrefaçon* as a 'word relative to booksellers' which means 'the publishing [. . .] of a *contrefait* book', i.e. a book printed without authorization.[16] The term *contrefaçon* then appeared as a combination of two words separated by a hyphen. '*Contre-façon*' is primarily a '*façon*' (i.e. a way of making or crafting objects). In its strictest meaning *contrefaçon* depicts an object which has been crafted against the rules of the art. The reference to publishing (*édition* in French) should therefore be understood in this historical context. Publishing a book consists of manufacturing copies. The concept of *contrefaçon* which also stems from the publishing paradigm implies a material reproduction of works of authorship. It is well known that a paradigm consists of a certain representation of the world that structures thought. We believe that such a paradigm exists because at the time the manufacturing of copies was the main method of economic exploitation of works. The king's multiple attempts to regulate the publishing trade support this theory.

### The royal legislation

The Royal Declaration of 15 March 1777 protecting the books of the Academy of Engraving made *contrefaçon* subject to a fine. Most notably it also provided for the confiscation of counterfeit copies and the 'tools used to copy and print them'.[17] This latter sanction shows that *contrefaçon* was perceived as a manufacturing activity (within the publishing trade). The King's Council's Order 'on book *contrefaçons* [. . .]' is one of several statutes enacted on 30 August 1777. This Order focuses on the fate of illegal copies. After being seized and confiscated, the infringing copies were meant to be destroyed.[18] When the king decided to regulate the specific issue of music *contrefaçon*, he focused exclusively on printed sheet music. Article 1 of the King's Council's Order of 15 September

---

[16] A. Sauvy, 'Livres contrefaits et livres interdits', in R. Chartier and H.-J. Martin, *Histoire de l'édition française* (Paris: Fayard, 1990), vol. II, p. 129.

[17] Couhin, *La propriété industrielle*, vol. I, p. 163.

[18] E. Laboulaye and G. Guiffrey, *La propriété littéraire au XVIIIe siècle* (Paris: Librairie Louis Hachette, 1859), 149; A.-Ch. Renouard, *Traité des droits d'auteurs* (Paris: Jules Renouard et Cie, 1838–9), vol. I, 172; Couhin, *La propriété industrielle*, vol. I, p. 161.

$1786^{19}$ deals only with engravings and printed sheet music. Significantly, the regulatory regime regarding books is extended to music as well. A music tradesman is mainly a *'libraire'* (bookseller). Article 19 of the same Order should be read in light of this fact: 'It is forbidden for anybody, subject to a fee of three thousand livres, to *contrefaire* a piece of music'. *Contrefaçon* of musical works is therefore inextricable from the publishing paradigm.

## The revolutionary legislation

During the French Revolution, the meaning of *contrefaçon* did not evolve. It remained subject to the publishing paradigm. Changes occurred elsewhere, for example in the central role now played by the author. Regardless of its historical significance, the rise of the author does not affect the concept of *contrefaçon*. There is indeed great continuity in the way the French approached literary property in 1793 and with the predecessor regime of printing privileges. In his report to the Constituent Assembly, François Hell argued that 'freedom of the press, the sentry of freedom, pleads for [a law on literary property]'.[20] In protecting authors' property, the legislature sought to incentivize creativity and to acknowledge that *contrefaçon* disadvantages the printer of a work as much as the author. While literary property is above all considered as a means to fulfil the freedom of the press, *contrefaçon* remains the specific sanction of the regulatory framework regarding books. The Order of 19 and 24 July 1793, creating the first author-vested exclusive right of reproducing copies, does not free itself from the publishing paradigm. While the Order grants writers, composers and artists the exclusive right to sell and distribute their works,[21] it covers only the exploitation of printed or engraved works. A twenty-first-century lawyer would interpret this Order as regulating the reproduction rights of an author.[22] The 1793 Order highlights the specific features of *contrefaçon*. Inspired by past

---

[19] Decree of the King's Privy Council of State, which establishes a Stamp Office for Music. Of 15 September 1786, in Couhin, *La propriété industrielle*, vol. I, p. 163 (available at: www.copyrighthistory.org/cgi-bin/kleioc/0010/exec/ausgabe/%22f_1786%22).

[20] F. Hell, 'Rapport à l'Assemblée Constituante sur la propriété littéraire', in Couhin, *La propriété industrielle*, vol. I, p. 157 (available at: www.copyrighthistory.org/cgi-bin/kleioc/0010/exec/ausgabe/%22f_1791a%22).

[21] Law of 19 July 1793 in Couhin, *La propriété industrielle*, vol. I, p. 174; (available at: www.copyrighthistory.org/cgi-bin/kleioc/0010/exec/ausgabe/%22f_1793%22).

[22] A. Lucas and H.-J. Lucas, *Traité de la propriété littéraire et artistique* (Paris: Litec, 2006), paras. 8, 9.

royal orders, article 3 of the new statute created the ancestor of the contemporary *saisie-contrefaçon*, a special procedure which permits the confiscation of works which infringe copyright. Most notably, Article 6 required authors to deposit two copies of their work with the national library in order that they may be entitled to sue potential infringers. The Act of 5 February 1810 'regulating printers and booksellers' confirms that *contrefaçon* only covers printed materials. Clarifying the meaning of *contrefaçon*, articles 41 and 42 define it as 'a book printed without the author's consent and to his detriment'. In 1810, *contrefaçon* was therefore still understood as the unlawful production of a printed, tangible object. It is hardly surprising that the same year article 425 of the *Code Pénal* (Napoleonic Criminal Code) defines *contrefaçon* as 'every publication of writings, music composition, drawing, painting, or any other production, printed or engraved in full or in part, in breach of laws and regulations relative to authors' property'.[23] *Contrefaçon* was still equated with publication.

## *The commentators' approach*

It is also interesting to observe how treatise writers approached the topic of *contrefaçon*. At the time, these authors were almost all judges or legal practitioners. Given the small number of works dedicated to copyright law, it is certain that these authors' opinions would have been very influential. But, with respect to *contrefaçon*, early nineteenth-century commentators introduce no revolutionary concepts. Few contemporary commentators challenged the publishing paradigm. Throughout the nineteenth century they all acknowledged to some extent that *contrefaçon* was the specific sanction of literary property; i.e. *contrefaçon* was specifically designed to remedy violations of the exclusive right to print works. In 1825 Merlin wrote in his Directory that 'in booksellers' terms [*contrefaçon* ] is the kind of criminal offence against those who print a book to the author's detriment'.[24] The reference to books and to bookselling is still reminiscent of the 1750 *Encyclopedie*'s definition. In 1837 Adrien-Joseph Gastambide wrote in his treaty that *contrefaçon* describes the sanction of literary property.[25] The publication of a book without the author's authorization is sufficient for

---

[23] E. Pouillet, *Traité théorique et pratique de la propriété littéraire et artistique et du droit de représentation* (Paris: Imprimerie et Librairie Générale de Jurisprudence, 1908), p. 886.

[24] Merlin, *Contrefaçon*.

[25] A. Gastambide, *Traité théorique et pratique des contrefaçons en tous genres* (Paris: Legrand and Descauriet, 1837), para. 38.

*contrefaçon* to arise. *Contrefaçon* is therefore distinct from forgery, which aims at misleading the public. To prove *contrefaçon*, claimants do not need to give evidence of a risk of confusion. Claude Couhin wrote that the likelihood of confusion is 'only required for "distinctive signs", but not for works of authorship'.[26] Gastambide and Couhin thereby contribute to clarifying the meaning of *contrefaçon* in *droit d'auteur*, contrasting it with other branches of intellectual property. Étienne Blanc, a mid-nineteenth-century *avocat*, wrote another treaty on *contrefaçons*.[27] Aware of the poor quality of legislation at the time, he regretted the disaggregation of intellectual property rights. Well ahead of his time, Blanc dreams of an 'Intellectual Property Code' which would be a more efficient way to fight *contrefaçon*, 'this worm eating up industry'. Blanc does not however challenge the publishing paradigm. He highlights the 'movable' nature of literary property thereby showing the difficulty of disconnecting the right of property from books. Blanc defines *contrefaçon* as 'any infringement of the right to publish and sell'.[28] Finally, despite being one of the last of the nineteenth-century writers of a treaty on the subject, Eugène Pouillet can be described as 'reactionary' when he deals with *contrefaçon*. He defines it as the 'prohibited manufacture' of a book.[29] By doing so he stays in line with pre-revolutionary definitions. Overall, nineteenth-century commentators do not further develop the notion of *contrefaçon*. Most of these authors rely on the existing creative genres to organize the chapters of their legal treaties. This is why *contrefaçon* does not yet transcend the regulatory regime of publishing during this period.

## The unlawful performance

As part of the publishing paradigm, *contrefaçon* sanctions only the unlawful exploitation of works to the extent that they are reproduced in tangible copies. The notion of *contrefaçon* cannot be used when communication of the work to the public does not require tangible media. Until the Act of 11 March 1957, the infringement of performing rights was covered by a specific offence called *représentation illicite* (unlawful performance). This offence results from two revolutionary Orders of 13–19 January and 6 August 1791 which only refer to dramatic works (theatre and opera). Renouard writes that 'performance is a

---

[26] Couhin, *La propriété industrielle*, vol. II, p. 436.
[27] É. Blanc, *Traité de la contrefaçon en tous genres et de sa poursuite en justice*, Plon, 1855.
[28] *Ibid.*, p. 154.    [29] Pouillet, *Traité théorique et pratique*, p. 460.

method of publication and exploitation which is specific to dramatic works'.[30] In the language of the time, music is not 'performed' but 'executed'. By his strict interpretation of the Criminal Code, Renouard denied music composers a claim against the unauthorized performers of their works. In his opinion, composers' claims were to be limited to civil liability in tort. In practice, this limitation subjected composers to two disadvantages. On the one hand, unlike other creators, they had no criminal action. On the other hand, by proceeding before the civil courts, they incurred a higher burden of proof than other creators. A civil action is always easier when the civil tort corresponds to a criminally wrongful act. In order to prevail, authors of dramatic works could contend that the criminally sanctioned act of unauthorized performance corresponded to a tort. By contrast, in the absence of a formal legal prohibition, composers were obliged to convince judges why the unauthorized performance of their works was wrongful. Thus Renouard relied on the judges' ad hoc decision to protect (or not) musical works. At that time the law prohibited only the performance of dramatic works from living authors in public theatres without the authors' formal and written consent. In such cases the sanction was the confiscation of profits for the authors' benefit.[31] In devising the statute, the legislatures' goal was not to regulate authors' rights but rather to regulate live productions. Before the Revolution, by abusing its monopolistic position[32] as Paris' only theatre, the Comédie-Française obtained the rights to most plays. The revolutionary legislature hoped to terminate the Comédie-Française's privilege by permitting any citizen to set up a theatre, and granting authors the right to authorize the performance of their plays in other theatres. The performing right was indeed considered as a tool in the regulation of live theatrical productions. Significantly, only one-quarter of the famous *Le Chapelier* report accompanying the law on the regulation of theatres deals with 'authors' property',[33] an issue which caused no debate in parliament. Like the inclusion of literary property within the freedom of the press, the right of authors of dramatic works was subordinate to the freedom of theatres. The preparatory work for the January Order reveals an initial intention to regulate both the freedom of the press and the freedom of theatres under a unified statute. However, this intention was

---

[30] Renouard, *Traité des droits d'auteurs*, vol. II, para. 25.
[31] Couhin, *La propriété industrielle*, vol. I, p. 133.
[32] J. Boncompain, *La Révolution des auteurs* (Paris: Fayard, 2001), p. 43.
[33] Couhin, *La propriété industrielle*, vol. I, pp. 116–32.

abandoned,[34] thus showing the legislature's unambiguous aim was to address these two issues separately. This resulted in the 1791 Orders dealing with the offence of unlawful performance while the 1793 Order covered *contrefaçon*.

## The extension of *contrefaçon*

### From printing to reproducing

If *contrefaçon* has today become the general sanction of *droit d'auteur*, it is mainly because revolutionary legislation was synthesized by commentators and the French courts. Article 425 of the Criminal Code creates the criminal offence of *contrefaçon* in 1804 and is progressively interpreted more broadly as echoed by the commentators of the time. Étienne Blanc should be given credit for substituting the concept of reproduction[35] for the notion of publishing, thereby making *contrefaçon* the sanction for infringement of a reproduction right. The benefits of the word 'reproduction' reside in its power to set the exploitation act free from the printing technique. Contrary to the old 'right to print', the scope of the 'reproduction right' was applicable to new kinds of exploitation. It is mainly Couhin who developed the use of the concept of reproduction at the end of the nineteenth century. Commenting on article 3 of the 1793 Order he writes that 'the expression "every publication [. . .] printed or engraved" should be construed in its broadest meaning and should be understood as covering any reproduction regardless of its nature'.[36] Couhin thereby defines the 'offence of *contrefaçon* of works of the mind' as being 'any intentional infringement, consisting of a material reproduction of a work, infringing the author's exclusive right to sell, to allow the sale or to distribute this work'.[37] By doing so, he abstracts from the letter of the statute, to encapsulate the 'exclusive right to sell and to distribute' into a single 'reproduction' right. This doctrinal leap forward significantly broadens the definition of *contrefaçon*.

### Composers' problematic protection

The offence of unlawful performance undergoes a similar extension. Renouard first attempted to free performing rights from the regulatory framework of live performance. By doing so he challenges a bad

---

[34] Renouard, *Traité des droits d'auteurs*, vol. I, p. 307.     [35] Blanc, *Traité de la contrefaçon*.
[36] Couhin, *La propriété industrielle*, vol. II, p. 433.     [37] *Ibid.*, vol. II, pp. 435–6.

habit inherited from pre-revolutionary times, even if, at that time, the performing right would have covered nothing else but live performances. Curiously, Renouard did not propose extending the statute's protection to musical works. Gastambide, a contemporary of Renouard, acknowledged that article 428 of the Criminal Code 'mentions dramatic works; but not musical works'.[38] He suggested nonetheless that dramatic works should be defined as 'any work which can be performed in a theatre, including a musical work as well as a literary work'.[39] Gastambide defended this interpretation stressing that the 1791 Orders refer to all works which can be performed in public theatres. As 'any music is by nature a work susceptible of being performed in public, it is accordingly protected against unlawful performances under the Order of 19 January 1791'.[40] This interpretation prevailed in practice as epitomized by the foundation in 1851 of the SACEM,[41] a collective administration society, formed to manage composers' public performance rights. Article 4 states that the company's object is to defend the right to 'execute' literary and musical works. How could SACEM have been created if music 'execution' was not akin to performance? Couhin relied on this example to demonstrate the extension of performing rights. In his opinion, the scope of the 1791 Order was not limited to works created for theatres but also covered any work that was capable of being performed. The word 'performance' is therefore 'understood in its broadest meaning and should refer to any execution by voice, instruments or gestures'.[42]

*Impact of technological progress*

From the end of the nineteenth century, technological advances promoted new ways of exploiting works of the mind (1877: Edison's phonograph; 1895 Lumière's *cinématographe*; 1906: radio broadcast; 1940s: vinyl records and television). Initially, it appeared difficult to apply old revolutionary statutes to these new methods of communication. For example, in 1904 the Pau Court of Appeal held that the showing of a cinematographic movie was not a performance, because the exhibition of the film occurred through a purely mechanical process.[43] Nonetheless,

---

[38] Gastambide, *Traité théorique et pratique*, p. 28.    [39] *Ibid.*, para. 264.
[40] *Ibid.*, para. 266.
[41] Sociétés des Auteurs, Compositeurs et Éditeurs de Musique [Association of Composers and Music Publishers to Protect Copyright and Royalties].
[42] Couhin, *La propriété industrielle*, vol. II, p. 564.
[43] Quoted by Pouillet, *Traité théorique et pratique*, para. 747.

the development of new methods of communication progressively compelled courts to synthesize authors' rights. Thus, courts extended the concept of 'publishing' to the manufacturing of copies of sound recordings. On 10 November 1930 the Cour de cassation ruled that a 'phonographic reproduction, from its beginning to its end, can only be compared to an *édition* (i.e. the publishing of copies)'.[44] The reproduction right was thus extended beyond print to other tangible media. The concept of 'performance' underwent an even more dramatic evolution. The performing right came to encompass the performance of a recording in public (sound recording or movie) as well as to radio broadcasting.[45] From this moment on, the performing right is no longer limited to live productions.

### Connection between reproduction and performance

As the reproduction right and the performing right broaden in scope, they drift away from the original letter of the revolutionary statutes. Throughout the nineteenth century it was generally acknowledged that the reproduction and performance rights were both authors' rights, but dissimilarities subsisting in their legal regimes prevented the emergence of a common sanction. These differences disappear progressively throughout the century. Apart from the issue of criminal sanctions another difference arises in connection with the duration of rights. The 1791 Order protected the performing right during the author's lifetime and for five years after his death. The 1793 Order protected the reproduction right during the author's life and for ten years after his death. When article 39 of the Order of 5 February 1810, regulating the duration of the 'right of property',[46] extended the term of protection to cover the life of the author's widow, and accorded an additional twenty years of protection to the surviving children, the administrative Supreme Court (Conseil d'État) strongly emphasized that this extension applied only to the reproduction right. The Act of 8–19 April 1854, however, unified the duration of rights created under the 1791 and 1793 Orders, and added another ten years to the surviving children's rights.

---

[44] *Dalloz Périodique* (DP), 1932, 1, 29, note Nast; *Recueil Sirey* (S), 1931, 1, 161, note Lagarde.
[45] Desbois, *Le droit d'auteur*, Dalloz, 1950, no. 356, p. 388.
[46] Pouillet, *Traité théorique et pratique*, p. 885.

The obligation to deposit copies of the work with the national library provides another and more enduring example of the disparate treatment of the reproduction and performance rights. As we have seen, deposit was a prerequisite to any claim of *contrefaçon*. In contrast, the author was protected against unlawful performance without any formality. In a decision of 24 June 1852 the Cour de cassation clearly highlighted this difference.[47] For Pouillet, the requirement of a deposit was not well adapted to theatrical plays, as they may not always be published.[48] It was not until the Act of 29 May 1925 that the requirement of legal deposit as a prerequisite to sue disappeared and that both the reproduction rights and the performing rights became subject to a single regulatory framework. It then became possible to bring the two rights within a unified monopoly of use subject to a common sanction.

### *The victory of* contrefaçon

If *contrefaçon* has prevailed as a concept, it is not only because it is specific to intellectual property. It is mostly because *droit d'auteur*'s historical roots originated with the regulation of books and not with theatre. History explains why nineteenth-century commentators established a hierarchy between reproduction and performance. In their view, reproduction was the principal method of exploitation of works of authorship, whereas performance was considered ancillary. Couhin expressed this idea: 'productions of the mind all share a common method of communication: publishing, i.e. the multiplication of copies for "distribution and sale". In addition, performance is a method of communication specific to dramatic and musical works.'[49] This now-obsolete conception explains why, notwithstanding the separate regulation of the reproduction and performance rights, nineteenth-century French courts considered performance as a kind of reproduction. On 15 February 1822 the Paris Tribunal de police correctionnelle (regional criminal court for trial of misdemeanours) relied on the 1791 and 1793 Orders to find that 'performance should be understood as any means by which one reproduces a work before a public [which] encompasses both performed musical compositions and dramatic works reproduced by way

---

[47] Couhin, *La propriété industrielle*, vol. II, pp. 561–2, n. 895.
[48] Pouillet, *Traité théorique et pratique*, para. 833.
[49] Couhin, *La propriété industrielle*, vol. II, p. 557.

of recitation or live production'.[50] That is why Gastambide asserted in 1837 that unlawful performance '*results from* [. . .] *a reproduction*' which is just 'in fact another kind of *contrefaçon*'.[51] In effect, the term 'reproduction' received such a broad and general meaning that it became synonymous with communication to the public. On a more technical level Gastambide deduced that unlawful performances are subject to a similar legal test as *contrefaçon*. Quoting Gastambide, Couhin also considered that performance and publishing are 'two methods of reproduction'.[52] Pouillet wrote that 'performance means any reproduction of a work in public by way of speech or gestures'.[53] Pouillet reasoned that the rules applying to *contrefaçon* also extended to unlawful performances.[54] Because reproduction was considered the universal method of exploitation of works of authorship, unlawful performance therefore appeared as a neighbouring offence to *contrefaçon*. If *contrefaçon* becomes the general sanction of *droit d'auteur* this is indeed because performance has been absorbed by reproduction.

## The 1957 Act

For the first time the 1957 Act[55] formally consolidated authors' rights into a unified *droit d'auteur*. The 1957 law (which is still largely in effect) applied to all works of authorship regardless of their genre.[56] No distinction subsisted between dramatic works and other works. The Act granted the author a unified monopoly of exploitation. Where revolutionary legislation granted only distinct exclusive rights of variable scope, the new Act created 'a right of exploitation belonging to the author'[57] which encompasses the reproduction right[58] and the performing right.[59]

---

[50] A. F. Blanc and E. Vivien, *Traité de la législation des théatres* (Paris: Brissot-Thivars, 1830), p. 326.

[51] Gastambide, *Traité théorique et pratique*, para. 224.

[52] Couhin uses this expression while discussing the issue of the duration of rights: Couhin, *La propriété industrielle*, vol. II, p. 562.

[53] Pouillet, *Traité théorique et pratique*, para. 800, quoting Édouard Calmels, *De la propriéé et de la contrefaçon des œuvres de l'intelligence* (Paris: Cosse, 1856).

[54] *Ibid.*, para. 803.    [55] Loi no. 57–298, 11 March 1957, on literary and artistic property.

[56] Art. 2. – 'The provisions of this Code shall protect the rights of authors in all works of the mind, whatever their kind, form of expression, merit or purpose.'

[57] Art. 26.

[58] Art. 27 stipulates that 'performance shall consist in the communication of the work to the public by any process'.

[59] Art. 28 defines reproduction as 'the physical fixation of a work by any process'.

Reproduction and performance being two categories of the same monopoly, it became logical to provide for a single sanction, i.e. *contrefaçon*. The 1957 Act reworded article 426 of the Criminal Code. This change acknowledged the extension of *contrefaçon* now defined as 'any reproduction, performance, communication by whatever means, of a work of authorship in breach of the author's rights, as defined and regulated by laws'. As already foreseen by Renouard in 1839, *contrefaçon* became 'the legal notion covering any infringement of an author's rights'.[60] The leading mid-twentieth-century treatise writer, Henri Desbois welcomed this 'important innovation' which substitutes 'unity for diversity'.[61] Significantly, the reformulation of *contrefaçon* to cover *all* of the authors' rights meant that violations of the author's non-economic ('moral') rights also came under the umbrella of *contrefaçon*. Desbois, who had previously opposed the idea that an infringement of the moral right is also a *contrefaçon*,[62] subsequently approved this view.[63] As an advocate of 'personalism' he emphasized the legislators' will to grant a high level of protection to the author. Desbois also considered the wording of article 426 ('in breach of the author's rights') to be sufficiently broad to encompass the moral right.[64] Desbois' interpretation is nowadays followed by the Cour de cassation's criminal chamber.[65] As the moral right protects an author's reputation,[66] its criminal sanction is somehow surprising. It should indeed be stressed that, by contrast, the reputation of a business is not protected by *contrefaçon* under trade mark law but only by general remedies for civil torts.[67]

---

[60] '*Contrefaçon* est le nom légal des violations du droit d'auteur', Renouard, *Traité des droits d'auteurs*, vol. II, para. 4.

[61] H. Desbois, *Le droit d'auteur en France* (2nd edn, Paris: Dalloz, 1966), para.743.

[62] H. Desbois, *Le droit d'auteur en France* (1st edn, Paris: Dalloz, 1950), para.615.

[63] H. Desbois, *Le droit d'auteur en France*, 2nd edn, para. 746.

[64] Gavin, 'Vers une sanction pénale du droit moral', *Revue Internationale du Droit d'Auteur* (RIDA), 31 (April 1961), 3; A. Françon, 'Les sanctions pénales de la violation du droit moral', *Mélanges offerts à J.-J. Burst* (Paris: Litec, 1997) 171; E. Dreyer, 'La protection pénale du droit moral de l'auteur': CCE.

[65] The Cour de cassation is France's Supreme Court. Cass. crim., 13 December 1995, *Bouvier v. Gassigneul*: RIDA, July 1996, no. 196, 307 – Cass. crim., 24 September 1997: *Bulletin de la Cour de cassation, chambre criminelle* (*Bull. crim.*), no. 310, 1036; *Gazette du Palais* (*Gaz. Pal.*), 1998, jur. 529, note Leclerc.

[66] We do not share this interpretation of the moral right which comes from the Berne Convention; see in this respect, D. Lefranc, *La renommée en droit privé* (Paris: LGDJ, 2004), paras. 221–8.

[67] Art. L. 713–5 FCIP: 'Any person who uses a mark enjoying repute for goods or services that are not similar to those designated in the registration shall be liable under civil law if such use is likely to cause a prejudice to the owner of the mark or if such use constitutes unjustified exploitation of the mark.'

## A severing of *contrefaçon*?

### *The breaking up of* contrefaçon *by new media*

*Contrefaçon* reaches its apex after 1957. *Contrefaçon* now applies to all works, extends to all methods of exploitation and sanctions the infringement of all authors' rights without exception. *Contrefaçon*'s domination will however progressively be challenged and trigger a real backlash against *droit d'auteur*.[68] The reason is that technological advances have provoked an imbalance in the respective rights of copyright owners on the one hand, and the general public on the other. From 1870 to 1950 technological innovation led to new modes of disseminating works of authorship. New types of entrepreneurs appeared: record companies, radio broadcasters and movie producers. Each of these new methods of production and communication required massive investments, putting their exploitation beyond the reach of the general public. Until the mid-twentieth century the exploitation of works of authorship was, as a practical matter, reserved to professionals. Beginning in the 1940s, however, thanks to the emergence of new technologies for making analogue copies (photocopiers, audio and video tapes, etc.), the general public starts reproducing and distributing works of authorship. The participation of the public in acts of reproduction and dissemination introduces a new element: from the first privileges until the end of the twentieth century, the legislature has always considered the person exploiting the work to be a professional. Another, related, assumption was that acquiring means of reproducing required substantial economic investments and therefore was beyond the means of non-professionals.

Since the 1980s, right-owners began to challenge the manufacturers of copying machines for encouraging *contrefaçon* carried out by the public. The Cour de Cassation in 1984 ruled that photocopy centres are liable for *contrefaçons*.[69] It held that the person directly engaged in the *contrefaçon* was the copy shop; that the clients were not the copyists. The 1984 decision required the Cour de Cassation to interpret the private copying exception. In ruling that the person making the copy was the copy shop,

---

[68] C. Caron, 'Droit pénal de la contrefaçon. Bilan des acteurs sur le terrain', CCE, July–August 2006, chron. no. 1.

[69] Cass. 1^re civ., 7 mars 1984: RIDA, 1984/3, 151; *Semaine Juridique Générale* (JCP G), 1985, II, 20351, note Plaisant; *Revue trimestrielle de droit commercial* (RTD com.), 1984, 677, obs. Françon. See A. Lucas, 'Le droit d'auteur français à l'épreuve de la reprographie', JCP G, 1990, I, 3438.

and that the exception, being limited to the private use of individuals, therefore did not apply, the Court eluded the real problem: that individual users are in fact engaged in significant levels of copying. Similarly, rather than confronting the role of the individual *contrefacteur*, the legislature preferred to choose temporary solutions such as the 1985 private copy remuneration scheme[70] or ten years later, the compulsory licence covering the right of reprography.[71] The authorities are never keen to tackle the more global issue of *contrefaçon* carried out by the public.

The advent of digital copying in the 1990s delivered the last blow to the fragile legitimacy of *droit d'auteur*. Financial losses suffered by rightowners, and *contrefaçon* carried out by the public caused considerable damage to right-owners. Meanwhile the development of the Internet has made public commission of *contrefaçon* commonplace. Internet websites allow users to store unauthorized music files on their own servers. Courts can easily sanction them on the grounds of *contrefaçon*. French law has also established the liability of persons who create hypertext links to unlawful files.[72] By the same token, there has been little difficulty establishing a legal basis for the shutting-down of clandestine fora dedicated to piracy.[73] A further step is the appearance of file-sharing 'peer-to-peer' applications, which allow individuals to store files on their own computers. These networks allow users to make their own files available to others in addition to being allowed to access files stored on others' computers. Giving and taking are therefore closely intertwined. Many cases raised the delicate issue of contributory liability.[74] In all these instances right-owners prefer to sue professionals rather than private individuals. Nonetheless, public guilt, hitherto repressed, now becomes obvious. It is however no small thing to challenge individual misdemeanours which trigger disasters at a collective level. As to right-owners, they perceive each Internet user as a constitutive element of a human group

---

[70] Art. 31 and s., L. no. 85–660, 3 July 1985 (available at: www.legifrance.gouv.fr).

[71] L. no. 95–4, 3rd January 1995 (available at: www.legifrance.gouv.fr); this statute created art. L. 122–10 FCIP: 'The publication of a work shall imply assignment of the right of reprographic reproduction to a society governed by Title II of Book III and approved to such end by the Minister responsible for culture.'

[72] CA Paris, 24e ch., 4 December 2003: Juris-Data no. 235997.

[73] Tribunal correctionnel of Lille, 29 January 2004: unpublished.

[74] Tribunal correctionnel of Vannes, 29 April 2004: Juris-Data no. 239835; Tribunal correctionnel of Pontoise, 2 February 2005: Juris-Data no. 262938; J. Ginsburg and Y. Gaubiac, 'Contrefaçon, fourniture de moyens et faute: perspectives dans les systèmes de common law et civilistes à la suite des arrêts Grokster et Kazaa', RIDA, 2006, no. 207, 3.

which cuts into their profits. But pointing the finger at the public only increases public distaste for *droit d'auteur*. In this context the French Act of 1 August 2006,[75] which purports to update *droit d'auteur* for the digital age appears both late and premature: late because the current crisis could have been foreseen thirty years ago[76] and premature because no adequate solution is yet available.

### Life and fate of the compulsory licensing

Parliamentary debates began in December 2005. Many members of parliament see a compulsory licence as a possible solution to unlawful downloading. The underlying assumption is that once the licence is in place, any communication of a work over the Internet will have been authorized by law. The compulsory licence therefore sets aside any *contrefaçon* on the Internet in exchange for financial compensation. However, by excluding *contrefaçon* the compulsory licence would have transformed the legal issue of downloading into a purely economic issue. The licence also would have reinforced the contention that *droit d'auteur* is not an author's property right but is only a cultural tax. In a nutshell, this solution would have abandoned a liability-based system to focus instead on the idea of compensation. The temporary victory of compulsory licensing highlights the real issue of whether the *contrefaçon* paradigm can survive when unauthorized copying is carried out by the general public. Parliamentary debates have shown that *contrefaçon* lacks legitimacy when it is brought to bear against private individuals. This discomfort is even more obvious in France where an action for *contrefaçon* may seek both civil and criminal penalties.

### Life and fate of the 'sliding-scale response'

The French government, confronted with the knowledge that a compulsory licence would both violate international norms and undermine the EU's anti-piracy goal, reworked the bill to eliminate the compulsory licence. When parliamentary debates resumed on 7 March 2006 the minister of culture tried to justify his *'manœuvres'* by stating that 'all

---

[75] L. no. 2006–961, 1 August 2006 (available at: www.legifrance.gouv.fr).
[76] Mr Mathus expressly draws a parallel with reprography: JOAN SO 2005–6, 161[e] sitting, 7 March 2006, 1582 (both available at: www.assemblee-nationale.fr/12/dossiers/031206.asp).

individuals who contribute to [unlawful downloading] are not equally liable'.[77] According to him there are several distinct categories of offenders: the person who downloads for his/her personal use; the person who induces downloading, and the person who benefits from downloading. For the minister it is unthinkable that 'an Internet user who illegally downloads music files for his/her personal use could risk imprisonment:. Since all agreed that *contrefaçon* should not apply with regards to private individuals, the minister suggested a mechanism of 'sliding-scale sanctions' as an alternative to the compulsory licence. Parliament accordingly adopted a new article submitting peer-to-peer users to a fine[78] instead of the three years' imprisonment sanctioning *contrefaçon*. However, the Conseil constitutionnel (Constitutional Council) set aside the new draft,[79] holding that it breaches the principle of equality of citizens before the criminal law.[80] An Internet user posting on his blog a hyperlink which connects to a music file would have been subject to imprisonment, whereas somebody making thousands of songs available on a peer-to-peer network would have only been liable to pay a fine. The law was indeed flawed.

### The global issue of public offence

The idea of a 'sliding-scale response' was in itself satisfactory. The explanation of the French legislature's failure lies instead in its overly simplistic approach. Narrowing down the debate to the sole issue of Internet *contrefaçon* prevented France from enacting satisfactory laws. *Contrefaçon* carried out by the public is a general issue which should be considered beyond the existence of the Internet. It is time to acknowledge that due to its broad scope, the notion of *contrefaçon* is not adequate to cover offences committed by the public. History shows that the professional nature of infringers has always been taken for granted. Many reasons can explain this defect. First, until the 1980s the infringer is seen as a businessperson reaping the financial benefits from *contrefaçon*. The infringer is therefore implicitly associated with a professional

---

[77] *Ibid.*, 1578.
[78] TA no. 554, AN SO 2005–6, 21 March 2006, 'Projet de loi relatif au droit d'auteur et aux droits voisins dans la société de l'information'.
[79] Cons. cons. no. 2006–540 DC, 27 July 2006, 'Loi relative au droit d'auteur et aux droits voisins dans la société de l'information' (available at: www.assemblee-nationale.fr/12/dossiers/031206.asp).
[80] Cons. cons. 27 July 2006.

entrepreneur. Being taken for granted, the infringer's identity is an issue which is never raised. Second, the private copying exception[81] is supposed to exhaust all the legitimate goals of the general public. Beyond this exception, the law strictly forbids to take into account the particular situation of private individuals. Accordingly, courts rely on the assumption that the infringer is either acting in bad faith[82] or that his intention is irrelevant.[83] Nowadays there are two distinct categories of infringers: professional entrepreneurs and private individuals. Clarifying the situation implies that we should give up the notion of *contrefaçon* altogether to refer instead to the offence of the public.[84] As a consequence, a new lesser offence should be created specifically to address any infringement committed for personal purposes and on a non-commercial scale. No individual can reasonably be held responsible for mass piracy and the global damage it causes to copyright owners. Admittedly, this assumption would be difficult when applied as a practical solution, where one file posted by one individual may have travelled around the world. However, from a legal standpoint, each individual can only be liable for his or her own contribution to the general damage. In order to sanction piracy, it should therefore be necessary to strike numerous times but in a less drastic way.

## Life and fate of the HADOPI

After the statute of 1 August 2006 was invalidated by the Constitutional Council, the French government adopted a more cautious approach. It publicly consulted the main industry players before drafting a new bill. A report published in November 2007 suggested that cutting off individual users' Internet access would be an appropriate sanction. It also stressed that it was necessary to provide and develop lawful alternatives to counteract unlawful peer-to-peer copying. It further urged the improvement of public information about authors' rights. The French President supervised the signing of an inter-professional agreement on the same

---

[81] Art. L. 122–5 FCIP: 'Once a work has been disclosed, the author may not prohibit: [...] 2°. copies or reproductions reserved strictly for the private use of the copier and not intended for collective use [...]'.

[82] This is the case for criminal *contrefaçon*, Bouzat, 'La présomption de mauvaise foi en matière de contrefaçon de propriété littéraire et artistique': RIDA, (1972/3), 171.

[83] Cass. 1re civ., 6 June 1990: *Bulletin de la Cour de cassation, chambres civiles* (*Bull. civ.*), I, no. 144, 103.

[84] Mr Caron seems opposed to giving up the term 'contrefaçon': C. Caron, 'La loi du 1er août 2006 relative au droit d'auteur et aux droits voisins dans la société de l'information', CCE October 2006, chron. no. 22.

terms as the report and a statute (inspired by this agreement) was voted on 12 June 2009.[85] However, this approach had several downsides. This bill required Internet users to check that no infringement had been committed in relation to their Internet protocol (IP) addresses. If a given user ignored the new legal prescription, the HADOPI,[86] a new administrative authority, would send him/her a warning by email. In the event of any recurrence, this authority could cut off the alleged infringer's Internet access. While the statute's 'three-strikes' approach may have been more effective at stopping peer-to-peer piracy than suing private individuals, the statute presented a number of highly debatable aspects. First, the law's sanction (termination of service) could be imposed by an administrative authority without judicial intervention. Second, the new monitoring obligation (which would fall within the domain of consumer law) placed the file-sharing issue outside the realm of intellectual property law.[87] As the individual is only sanctioned for not having monitored his Internet access, the draft artificially cut the link between piracy and *contrefaçon*. Third, because the termination-of-service sanction that applied if the consumer failed to monitor his Internet usage did not supplant actions for *contrefaçon*, users remained (at least in theory) vulnerable to be sued on grounds of *contrefaçon* (and subject to sanctions for breach of their monitoring obligation). Thus, they had no guarantee that the three years' imprisonment sanction for *contrefaçon* would never apply to them. Fourth, the bill did not address the issue of anonymous peer-to-peer, the new generation of file-sharing networks which already allow users to remain anonymous and to hide their IP addresses.[88] Lastly, despite the law being named '*création et internet*', creators did not occupy the centre stage. They were not entitled to claim damages in the proceedings before the HADOPI and they were unlikely to be informed of the existence of any such procedures. In this respect, the law seemed to be the mark of a '*droit d'auteur*' without the '*auteur*'.[89] This imperfect system crumbled when the

---

[85] L. no. 2009–669, 12 June 2009, *favorisant la diffusion et la protection de la création sur internet*.

[86] Haute Autorité pour la Diffusion des Œuvres et la Protection des droits sur Internet [lit. high authority promoting the distribution and protection of creative works on the Internet].

[87] D. Lefranc, 'Le piratage déraciné', *Omnidroit newsletter*, 14 (27 August 2008), 2; D. 2008, 2087–8.

[88] D. Lefranc, 'Téléchargement illégal: que faire?', *Gaz. Pal.*, 119–20 (29–30 April 2009), 2.

[89] J. Ginsburg, 'L'avenir du droit d'auteur: un droit sans auteur?', CCE, May 2009, study no. 10.

Constitutional Council denied to the HADOPI the right to disconnect alleged infringers' Internet access. In its decision of 10 June 2009,[90] the Council held that only judges could impose such sanctions. More importantly, access to the Internet is now officially recognized as essential to guarantee citizens' freedom of speech and communication. Despite the partial invalidation of the bill in relation to HADOPI's punitive powers, the administrative authority retains its role as a pre-trial filter. Its existence is also validated by the Constitutional Council as being justified by the massive extent of piracy. After this episode, French copyright is 'back to square one'. The three years' imprisonment penalty remains the common sanction of *contrefaçon*.

## The paradoxical choice of criminal law

The French government could not stay passive after being 'slapped' twice on the piracy issue by the country's constitutional court. The minister of culture was dismissed and the 'case' was passed on to the ministry of justice. A renewed and shortened bill was then presented to parliament on 24 June 2009. This new draft gives back to judges the authority to sanction pirates, in particular the right to cut off their Internet access. But the special feature of this text is to confer this task, not on civil judges, but on the criminal courts. Non-French lawyers might be surprised at the apparent absurdity of this system. In France, right-holders bring the major copyright infringement cases before civil courts. In these cases, the infringers incur no risk of imprisonment. Why, then, ask the criminal courts to punish infractions committed by private individuals? The answer is purely practical. The French legislature directs recourse to criminal procedure because it is automatic. Once unlawful downloading is detected, it is up to the state to organize the prosecution. The procedure is entirely borne by the state, not by the right-holders. That is why, for practical reasons, illegal downloading cannot be punished by civil courts. Were that the case, the right-holders would be obliged to pay lawyers to initiate and pursue the trial. Thus, criminal law seems better adapted than civil law to address the phenomenon of mass infringement. This is why the judge who is in theory the less lenient (the criminal judge) is in charge of imposing the lightest punishments.

---

[90] Cons. cons. no. 2009–580 DC, 10 June 2009, '*Loi favorisant la diffusion et la protection de la création sur internet*' (available at: www.conseil-constitutionnel.fr/).

Fearing, however, that this approach could open the floodgates for cases that the criminal courts would be unable to manage, the bill states that piracy cases may be handled without a hearing. In the course of July 2009, parliament improved the draft further. The administrative authority HADOPI will, for instance, now have the obligation to inform copyright owners of the existence of procedures. The new bill places the author at centre stage of *droit d'auteur*, by giving back to him the right to claim damages as part of the criminal procedure. It also provides guarantees for individuals that only a judge can restrict their liberties, in particular in relation to cutting off their Internet access. By adopting this approach, the government seems to have learned from past mistakes. That is probably why the constitutional council in its decision of 22 October 2009 did not again condemn the latest version. A new law of 28 October 2009 thus has supplemented the prior text of 12 June 2009. The first cases arising under it were expected to be heard by criminal court judges in early 2010. The new statute, however, is still imperfect from a legal standpoint. In theory individuals still risk three years' imprisonment (maximum sanction). Second, the criterion which allows an infringer to benefit from a more favourable regime appears discriminatory. The new statute is indeed directly benefiting infringers over the Internet. This means that a very serious infringement could be subject to a more favourable regime depending on whether it was committed on the Internet. In our opinion, to determine whether the offence took place over the Internet should not be a valid criterion and the government should rather modulate the sanction depending on the person(s) being sued. Professionals should remain subject to the '*contrefaçon*' offence, whereas individuals should only have to pay a fine and/or when necessary have their Internet access disconnected.

### *European law and the 'commercial scale' criteria*

The severing of *contrefaçon* now appears unavoidable in light of recent EU law developments. The Directive of 29 April 2004 on the enforcement of intellectual property rights provides a more rigorous procedural regime for infringements 'on a commercial scale'.[91] The notion of 'commercial scale' is indeed still used in the draft directive on criminal

---

[91] This notion of commercial scale can be found at arts. 6, 8 and 9 of the Directive.

measures for the enforcement of intellectual property rights.[92] On 25 April 2007 the European Parliament approved a draft version which carefully defines intellectual property's specific criminal offence.[93] It states that contrefaçon should now be defined as any intentional infringement of intellectual property rights. The draft also emphasizes that 'infringement committed on a commercial scale' should be understood as meaning 'any infringement of an intellectual property right committed in pursuit of a direct pecuniary gain, with the exception of acts committed by individuals for their personal enjoyment and for non-lucrative purposes'. European legislators now seem favourable to the severing of contrefaçon. They think that it is indispensable to make a distinction between professional contrefaçon and offences committed by private individuals. In the future the notion of 'commercial scale' may serve to draw the line between 'contrefaçon' and the aforesaid lesser offence. We believe that only a severing of contrefaçon could safeguard droit d'auteur's future consistency.

## Grounds for leniency towards individuals

One may nonetheless inquire why private individuals should benefit from a new, lighter punishment. Legal, historical and political reasons may be offered. On the legal side, some assert that the infringements by private individuals are less significant than others. This is not persuasive. The particular problem with the Internet is that the harm caused by an act of uploading is very difficult to measure. Some private individuals do indeed share their files only with close friends. But this situation is rare. Many users do not control the circulation of their files. Most downloading sites are constructed specifically to ensure that users never acquire this control. Whether the matter concerns peer-to-peer networks, or clandestine fora, the ability to download files from other users is granted only on condition that the user makes his or her own files permanently available. The functioning of the Internet therefore makes it impossible to assert that downloading or uploading are benign infringements because they would cause only modest damage to rightholders.

---

[92] W. Bourdon, 'Le droit pénal est-il un instrument efficace face à la criminalisation croissante de la contrefaçon?', D. 2008, 729–34; see also, C. Caron, 'Vers un droit pénal communautaire de la contrefaçon', CCE June 2007, para. 6.

[93] See above n. 12.

On the historical front, it is very clear that *contrefaçon* was conceived to punish professional infringers. This focus was normal and obvious for centuries. That may be why lawyers never bothered to express it. In practice, the commercial goal of the infringer was never set out in the law as a condition for claiming *contrefaçon*. As a result, there is a paradox: *contrefaçon* has always been directed against professionals, but the law has always been addressed to all. History and law have not always followed the same path.

In fact, leniency toward private individuals is justifiable only as a political matter. One must be realistic: no individual has the means to repair the systemic damages that he may cause. If tomorrow it were decided to oblige individuals to pay right-holders damages proportionate to their lost profits, a political crisis would ensue because too many individuals would be bankrupted. In some countries, infringement trials already seemed a menace to society. And perhaps the pirates are right to remind us that the public cannot be blamed for technological advances. The vast majority of individuals have not programmed the file-sharing software that they use. The fact is that, in the technological arena, the public uses the tools that others invent for it. That is why it is necessary to pursue the managers of sharing sites and fora. Nonetheless, it is futile to fight against the offer of infringements if one does not also combat the demand. In fact, the actions against file-sharing sites is ultimately of limited interest. If one site is closed down in one country, another will appear in another country. It is necessary to roll out the big international guns to combat file-sharing sites efficiently. It seems at once more efficient and more reasonable to fight against public demand. France is not the only country to implement a policy of combating piracy by the general public. The patronage of illegal sites should therefore diminish.

This chapter has shown that it is time to respond to the essential question: can copyright law be brought to bear against the general public? The response is yes. That is why some punishment is indispensable. But for political reasons this punishment can only be limited in scope. Perhaps the public does not so much reject copyright as the severity of *contrefaçon*.

# 5

# A common lawyer's perspective
# on *contrefaçon*

JANE C. GINSBURG

*Contrefaçon* in French copyright law examines the scope of French copyright through the lens of remedies. *Contrefaçon* is the act to which certain civil and criminal sanctions attach. Viewed from this angle, the history of French copyright law tells a tale of the slow emergence of a unified concept of the wrongful act, covering not only the manufacturing of copies but also public performances, live and through transmissions. The emphasis on *contrefaçon* reveals the continuity of the revolutionary authors' right of 1793 with the *ancient régime* of printing regulation, with unauthorized production of physical copies of books remaining the essence of the reformulated wrongful act. By the same token, the early treatment of the playwright's exclusive right of public performance shows how far French law was from a general conceptualization of authors' rights. The regime of the performance right, introduced in 1791 as a coda to new regulation of theatres, long remained distinct from the reproduction right, particularly regarding its enforcement. Indeed, nineteenth-century legal commentators struggled to bring performance rights within the remedies for *contrefaçon* by recharacterizing a public performance as a kind of publication.[1]

The 1957 French copyright law, which finally replaced the 1791 and 1793 laws and their ensuing amendments and judicial interpretations, also finally synthesized authors' rights, with *contrefaçon* providing the all-purpose remedial structure. The story does not end there, however, for the pressures of recent technological developments now threaten the coherence of *contrefaçon*. Throughout the twentieth century, *contrefaçon* was able to absorb new technologies, as courts overcame their initial reluctance to conceptualize new modes of exploitation as coming within the ambit of reproduction or performance. But if the transition, for

---

[1] See Lefranc, Chapter 4 in this volume, pp. 55–79.

example, from live performance to transmissions of live – and then of recorded – performances may have been strenuous, the shift from analog to digital may prove even more profound. Not because of the medium per se, but because the medium enables end-users to accomplish copyright-implicating acts previously reserved to professional interme-diaries. Today's *contrefacteurs* are not just unauthorized publishers, producers, and commercial record and film pirates, but also individuals who copy and communicate works of authorship on a massive scale. The number of participants engaged in illegal file sharing in France at any given time has been estimated at 4.6 million.[2]

## Contrefaçon and the common law

*Contrefaçon* entails criminal as well as civil penalties, but the prospect of jailing or imposing substantial fines on individuals for private conduct in their homes enrages much of the French public, and therefore troubles French politicians. In 2006, the parliament enacted major reforms to the copyright law, including provisions substantially diminishing the liabi-lity of individuals for file sharing. But the Conseil constitutionnel struck down this splitting of *contrefaçon* on the ground that the divided struc-ture of sanctions violated the principle of equality of citizens before the criminal law.[3] Nonetheless, the impetus to treat end-users as a different class of *contrefacteurs* remains strong. Whatever the conceptual justifi-cations for distinguishing end-users from traditional commercial inter-mediaries (and these may be hotly debated), the political imperative portends a scission. Thus, the tortuous path of the HADOPI law, twice voted in 2009, which would create a new wrongful act of failure to supervise the use of the subscriber's Internet connection, and a new administrative authority initially empowered to terminate the subscri-ber's access to the Internet.[4] The law as initially passed created an alternative structure to actions for *contrefaçon*; indeed individual authors

[2] International Federation of the Phonographic Industry, 'Fact Sheet – Statistics on Internet Piracy in France' (at: www.ifpi.org/content/section_news/20041007j.html, last visited September 17, 2009).

[3] Conseil Constitutionnel decision no. 2006–540DC, July 27, 2006, Rec. p. 88, paras. 57, 59–61, 64–65 (available at: www.conseil-constitutionnel.fr/decision/2006/2006540/2006540dc.htm, last visited September 17, 2009).

[4] Conseil des Ministres, Diffusion et protection de la création sur internet, June 18, 2008 (available at: www.premier-ministre.gouv.fr/acteurs/gouvernement/conseils_ministres_35/conseil_ministres_18_juin_1346/diffusion_protection_creation_sur_60340.html, last visited September 17, 2009; summary).

did not have standing to initiate the termination process. The Conseil constitutionnel, however, struck down the centerpiece of the law, holding that the Constitution requires judicial rather than administrative process before access to the Internet may be terminated. The latest version reinstates judicial enforcement, via the criminal courts – a surprising enforcement choice to common lawyers, but understandable within the French judicial framework as David Lefranc explains. Whether or not the HADOPI law offers a successful or desirable response to end-user infringement, it illustrates acutely the tendency to disaggregate *contrefaçon*, or liability for copyright infringement.

David Lefranc suggests that this focus on remedies might seem a particularly common law approach, but, curiously, analysis of Anglo-American copyright law trains primarily on the articulation of exclusive rights. I have not found a nineteenth or early twentieth-century volume title equivalent to Gastambide's 1837 *Traité théorique et pratique des contrefaçons en tous genres* [Theoretical and practical treatise of infringements of all kinds],[5] though John Herbert Slater's 1884 primarily practical rather than theoretical handbook, *The Law Relating to Copyright and Trade Marks, Treated More Particularly with Reference to Infringement*, may come closest.[6] Later twentieth-century volumes with 'infringement' in the titles also appear to be practical manuals directed to the Bar.

Difficulties in drawing comparisons in fact begin with the terminology: there is no real English-language equivalent for *contrefaçon*, though we weakly translate it as 'infringement.' The literally closer term, 'counterfeit' will not do because it is at once too broad and too narrow. In usage since at least the sixteenth century, 'counterfeit' has generally (if now archaically) meant imitation, often tinged with falsity.[7] In the modern legal sense, at least in the US, 'counterfeit' refers to a particular form of copyright or especially trademark infringement, subject to special procedural rules for enforcement and enhanced criminal penalties.[8] So I will carry on with 'infringement' despite its incomplete correspondence to *contrefaçon*.

---

[5] J.-A. Gastambide, *Traité théorique et pratique des contrefaçons en tous genres* (Paris: Legrand et Descauriet, 1837).

[6] J. H. Slater, *The law relating to copyright and trade marks, treated more particularly with reference to infringement: forming a digest of the more important English and American decisions, together with the practice of the English courts and forms of informations, notices, pleadings and injunctions* (London: Stevens and Sons, 1884).

[7] See, e.g., W. Shakespeare, *Twelfth Night*, Oxford World's Classics (New York: Oxford University Press, 1994), act IV, sc. 2, 197 ('Feste: But tell me true, are you not mad indeed? Or do you but counterfeit?').

[8] See 18 USC ss. 2318–20 (2008).

Nineteenth-century Anglo-American legal commentators, and for that matter current expositors of positive law, call the violation of authors' rights 'infringement.' In the nineteenth century, it seems that this term was used interchangeably with 'piracy.'[9] (By contrast, one rarely encounters the term 'counterfeit.') Today, 'piracy' implies commercial reproduction (as in 'record piracy'), and accordingly carries a taint of moral opprobrium. Hence the rhetorically charged and, to many, highly contestable character of calling file-sharing 'piracy.'

This commentary will endeavor a parallel common law perspective on the consolidation and disaggregation of authors' rights under US copyright law. While rights rather than remedies will provide the focus for most of this overview, recent controversies concerning US remedies for infringement provide a counterexample to the current French urge to devise a separate regime for end-user non-commercial infringers. In the US, the imposition on non-commercial end-users of remedies initially – and allegedly better – conceived for redress of commercial infringements has sparked controversy with respect to the award of statutory damages under US copyright law. But, if some of the impetus for the current critique stems from concerns similar to those identified by David Lefranc, the ensuing calls for reducing the amount of damages the statute authorizes, or for more closely controlling the determination of the damages award, treat the file-sharing cases as an example of a broader problem of disproportionate remedies for infringement.[10] Ultimately, any impending disaggregation of US copyright emanates less from the fairly coherent (if contestable) remedial structure, than from the hyper-specificity with which Congress has increasingly tended to define the scope of exclusive rights and/or concomitant limitations.

## Broadening conceptions of exclusive rights

David Lefranc traces the separate origins and eventual regrouping of the reproduction and public performance rights in France. He emphasizes how the reproduction right was deeply rooted in the regulation of the

---

[9] See, e.g., *Baker v. Selden*, 101 US 99, 103 (1879) ('The very object of publishing a book on science or the useful arts is to communicate to the world the useful knowledge which it contains. But this object would be frustrated if the knowledge could not be used without incurring the guilt of piracy of the book').

[10] See, e.g., P. Samuelson and T. Wheatland, 'Statutory Damages in Copyright: A Remedy in Need of Reform' (2009) (available at: http://papers.ssrn.com/sol3/papers.cfm?abstract_id=1375604, last visited September 17, 2009).

printing trades. The close correspondence of authors' rights with the
production of physical copies of books persisted even in the US, despite
the absence of regulatory antecedents to the statutes governing the
Stationers Company. Thus, as defined in the first American treatise on
copyright, appearing ten years after Gastambide, George Ticknor Curtis'
1847 *A Treatise on the Law of Copyright*, 'the right to multiply copies of
whatever is written or printed . . . constitutes the whole claim of literary
property.'[11] Later on, after reviewing English copyright, and particularly
the laws establishing performance rights in musical and dramatic works,
Curtis observes that the same right does not exist in the US (at least not
with respect to published works; unpublished works being protected by
common law copyright, which did extend performance rights).[12] In
Britain, before the 1833 law on dramatic performance rights, the courts
declined to equate performance with publication. Where in France, this
equivalence afforded greater protection to performance rights, in
England the opposite characterization served the same end. By deeming
a publicly performed but unprinted play 'unpublished,' the courts pre-
served the theater producer's common law copyright claim against a rival
producer whose employee had memorized the plaintiff's play in performance, and then mounted a competing production of the same play.[13]

Throughout the nineteenth and twentieth centuries, copyright in
England and the US expanded through judicial interpretation or legislative enactment to cover new rights or new modes of exploitation, such as
the rights of adaptation,[14] and of musical and dramatic performing
rights,[15] including by transmission.[16] It would not be correct, however,
to say that the author's exclusive rights were synthesized to the extent
that they came to cover all manner of exploiting a work of authorship.
Despite the US 1976 Copyright Act's general efforts at synthesis, there
remain many gaps (for example, the public performance right in a sound
recording is restricted to digital transmissions,[17] and the exhaustion

---

[11] G. T. Curtis, *A Treatise on the Law of Copyright* (3rd ptg. 1847) (Clark, NJ: Lawbook
Exchange, 2005), p. 11.
[12] Ibid., p. 109.
[13] See, e.g., *Morris* v. *Kelly* (1820) 1 Jac. & W. 481, 37 Eng. Rep. 451 (Ch.); see also, for
common law performance right in the US, *Boucicault* v. *Fox*, 3 F. Cas. 977, 981
(CCSDNY 1862) (No. 1,691).
[14] US Copyright Act 1870, 16 Stat. 198 (translation and dramatization) (repealed 1909).
[15] US Copyright Act Amendment of 1856, 11 Stat. 138 (public performance) (repealed
1870).
[16] See, e.g., 17 USC s. 101 (2005) (definition of public performance by transmission).
[17] Ibid. s. 106(4)(6).

rule – called the 'first sale doctrine' in US case law – cuts off copyright control over subsequent sales of physical copies once the first authorized sale is made).[18] The UK Copyright, Designs and Patents Act 1988, as far as I can tell, forgoes even the pretense of synthesis, instead covering both the subject matter of copyright and the scope of exclusive rights in a series of specific dispositions (what the French would call 'pointillist' lawmaking).

In the US 1976 Copyright Act, new technologies furnished the impetus toward synthesis of the exclusive rights. Congress sought to create technology-neutral rules that would evolve with changed conditions.[19] Despite the goal to 'future-proof' the copyright law, the reality is only inconsistently encouraging. Congress did to some extent greet the advent of new technological modes of exploitation by expressing the exclusive rights at a high enough level of abstraction to permit the rights' effective future application.[20] Recourse to general principles is more likely to produce flexible laws than is legislation enmeshed in technological specificity.

The recent file-sharing litigations initiated by the Recording Industry Association of America (RIAA) against end-users illustrate the courts' pragmatic construction of the broadly worded rights: '(1) to reproduce the copyrighted work in copies or phonorecords [fixations of sound recordings]' and '(3) to distribute copies or phonorecords of the copyrighted work to the public by sale or other transfer of ownership, or by rental, lease, or lending.'[21] In these cases, the courts have sought to resolve whether a peer-to-peer (P2P) network user who designates for 'sharing' digital files containing mp3 format copies of recorded musical compositions is 'distributing' 'phonorecords' in violation of the sound-recording copyright owner's exclusive rights.[22] The US Copyright Act does not expressly include a 'making available' right, but the record companies contended that making digital files available from one's computer to other P2P users to copy into their computers constituted a 'distribution' even in the absence of proof that other users had in fact copied the files. The users resisted that characterization on the grounds (a) that a 'copy' or 'phonorecord' must be a tangible object, and therefore

---

[18]  Ibid. s. 109(a).

[19]  See, e.g., *ibid.* s. 102(a) (copyright subsists in works of authorship fixed in any tangible medium of expression 'now known or later developed').

[20]  See *ibid.* s. 106.    [21]  17 USC s. 106(1) (3).

[22]  See, e.g., *London-Sire Records* v. *Does*, 542 F. Supp. 2d 153 (D. Mass. 2008); *Elektra Entm't Group* v. *Barker*, 551 F. Supp. 2d 234 (SDNY 2008).

cannot be a digital file, and (b) that a 'copy' or 'phonorecord' has not been 'distributed' unless the person effecting the copy's distribution parts with its physical possession. Because digital dissemination leaves the sender's file in her computer, no matter how many recipients there may be, the distribution right must be limited to traditional physical objects.

These contentions would make the Copyright Act largely inapplicable to digital media, which seems an improbable result given Congress' awareness in 1976 that it was legislating at the advent of the computer age. Nonetheless, an inapt text can undermine whatever intent one might impute to the lawmakers. In the most rigorously reasoned opinion yet to address these issues, *London-Sire Records* v. *Does*,[23] the District of Massachusetts examined the statutory definition of 'phonorecord' as a 'material object ... in which sounds, other than those accompanying a motion picture or other audiovisual work, are fixed by any method now known or later developed, and from which the sounds can be perceived, reproduced, or otherwise communicated, either directly or with the aid of a machine or device.'[24] The court emphasized that:

> [A]ny object in which a sound recording can be fixed is a 'material object.' That includes the electronic files at issue here. When a user on a peer-to-peer network downloads a song from another user, he receives into his computer a digital sequence representing the sound recording. That sequence is magnetically encoded on a segment of his hard disk (or likewise written on other media.) ...With the right hardware and software, the downloader can use the magnetic sequence to reproduce the sound recording. The electronic file (or, perhaps more accurately, the appropriate segment of the hard disk) is therefore a 'phonorecord' within the meaning of the statute.[25]

With respect to whether a 'phonorecord' (or, for that matter, a copy) cannot be 'distributed' unless its distributor divests herself of its possession, the court declined to interpret 'or other transfer of ownership' as limiting the distribution right to 'hand-to-hand' transfers of physical objects:

> First, while the statute requires that distribution be of 'material objects,' there is no reason to limit 'distribution' to processes in which a material object exists throughout the entire transaction – as opposed to a transaction in which a material object is created elsewhere at its finish. Second, while the statute addresses ownership, it is the newly minted ownership

---

[23] Above n. 22.   [24] 17 USC s. 101.   [25] *London-Sire*, 542 F. Supp. 2d at 171.

rights held by the transferee that concern it, not whether the transferor gives up his own ... [T]he Court concludes that an electronic file transfer can constitute a 'transfer of ownership' as that term is used in § 106(3) ... Congress wrote § 106(3) to reach the 'unauthorized public distribution of copies or phonorecords that were unlawfully made.' House Report at 62, reprinted in 1976 U.S.C.C.A.N. at 5676. That certainly includes situations where, as here, an 'original copy' is read at point A and duplicated elsewhere at point B. Since the focus of § 106(3) is the ability of the author to control the market, it is concerned with the ability of a transferor to create ownership in someone else – not the transferor's ability simultaneously to retain his own ownership.[26]

The record company also argued that, even without a 'making available' right *in haec verba*, the distribution right could be read to cover not only digital transmissions actually effected, but also the offering to transmit a digital file, without proof of actual receipt. The *London-Sire* court stopped short of equating the statutory distribution right with the mere *offer* to distribute (i.e., making available for copying) the file to any P2P user who requested a file. This reluctance could have been fatal to the copyright owner's claim, because proof of actual unauthorized receipt by another Internet user may be very difficult to establish. But in an ingenious procedural twist, the court held that once the defendants were found to have put in place all the elements leading to the conclusion of the digital transaction, save the actual third-party download, then actual distribution would be presumed, thus shifting to the defendants the burden of proving that no one in fact copied from the defendants' 'shared' files. The court's analysis thus shows that the generally open-ended text of § 106(1) and (3) of the 1976 Act is capable of adaptation to new modes of exploitation, albeit with a little help from creative judges.[27]

### Pressures toward and resistance to disaggregation

Unfortunately, while in most instances § 106 of the Copyright Act's statement of exclusive rights is very inclusive, the law's articulation of ever more excruciatingly detailed exceptions disaggregates the regime of exclusive rights into a series of excessively complex and often incomprehensible sub-regimes resisting any unifying rationale. This profusion of verbiage precedes digital media; for example, the original 1976 Act

---

[26] *Ibid.* at 173–4.
[27] But see *Cartoon Network LP v. CSC Holdings, Inc.*, 536 F.3d 121 (2d Cir. 2008) (interpreting definition of fixation to exclude transient digital copies).

included detailed special regimes for cable retransmissions, public broadcasting, and jukebox public performances.[28] But creating newer carve-outs for certain digital exploiters has not staunched legislative logorrhea. On the contrary, in addition to bringing us overly specific exceptions, Congress has since 1995 also initiated new rights both within copyright,[29] and 'para-copyright' rights alongside copyright.[30]

Lefranc attributes the current or impending scission of *contrefaçon* to end-user activity. Even if end-users are now capable of causing as much economic harm as professional infringers, the system is reluctant to impose the same sanctions. Hence the ongoing attempts in France to limit the liability of end-users while purporting to protect the exclusive rights of authors. The advent of the infringing end-user exerts pressure on the remedial scheme of US copyright law as well. On the one hand, and in contrast to the current evolution in France, Congress in 1997 unambiguously encompassed non-professionals within the zone of criminal liability. In the 'No Electronic Theft Act' Congress amended the provision of the Copyright Act that imposes criminal penalties in order to extend liability to non-commercial actors who willfully 'reproduce[e] or distribut[e], including by electronic means, during any 180-day period, of 1 or more copies or phonorecords of 1 or more copyrighted works, which have a total retail value of more than $1000.'[31] Thus, individual end-users who in any six-month period post or download large quantities of third-parties' commercially valuable copyrighted material (i.e., the average computer-equipped teenager?) could at least in theory be subject to prosecution notwithstanding these individuals' lack of commercial motivation (other than to acquire vast volumes of works without paying for them).[32] While there appear to have been no criminal charges pressed against individual file-sharers (teenage or otherwise), the 'No Electronic Theft Act' illustrates legislative disinclination towards a

---

[28] See 17 USC ss. 111, 118, 116.

[29] See *ibid*. ss. 106(6), 114(d)–(j) (digital performance right in sound recordings).

[30] See *ibid*. ss. 1201, 1202 (technological protection measures; copyright management information). The expression 'para-copyright' appears to have originated with D. Nimmer, 'A Riff on Fair Use in the Digital Millennium Copyright Act,' *University of Pennsylvania Law Review*, 148 (2000), 673–742, 686, n. 66.

[31] 17 USC s. 506(a)(1)(B) (2008) (formerly 17 USC s. 506(a)(2)), as amended by the No Electronic Theft Act, Pub. L. No. 105–147, 111 Stat. 2678 (1997).

[32] In the context of assessing the first fair use factor (nature of the use, including whether commercial) the *Napster* court suggested that this kind of end-user conduct could not properly be deemed 'non commercial.' *A&M Records, Inc.* v. *Napster, Inc.*, 239 F.3d 1004, 1015 (9th Cir. 2001).

two-track copyright enforcement regime, in which end-users would ride the weaker rail.

On the other hand, the recent imposition of very large awards of statutory damages against individual file-sharers has sparked debate about the proportionality of the remedy to the harm.[33] Because the Copyright Act authorizes courts to award up to $150,000 per work willfully infringed,[34] proportionality concerns may be particularly acute when the defendants are individual file-sharers. The statute does not generally exempt non-commercial users from liability for statutory damages; on the contrary, it directs courts to remit statutory damages in the case of certain unintentional infringements by non-profit educational institutions, libraries and archives, and public broadcasters. The specificity with which Congress treated certain non-commercial infringements suggests no disposition to reduce statutory damages for all non-commercial, or even individual, actors. Accordingly, at least one court has rejected attempts to read a non-commercial actor exception into the statutory damages provision.[35] Nonetheless, while the file-sharing cases afford a perhaps extreme example of draconian damage awards, criticism of statutory damages goes well beyond the file-sharing context. Indeed, the most complete study to date of the problem, while highly critical of both the statutory provision and of many of the awards of damages made under it, devotes relatively little attention to the particular plight of non-commercial defendants.[36]

## Conclusion

The apparition of the end-user in the large-scale commission of infringing acts raises the question whether current copyright norms can respond to end-user behavior. But, at least as a matter of US copyright law, I suspect the emergence of the consumer-as-massive-infringer is more a symptom than a cause of any disaggregation of copyright. The

---

[33] See, e.g., J. C. Barker, Note, 'Grossly Excessive Penalties in the Battle Against Illegal File-Sharing: The Troubling Effects of Aggregating Minimum Statutory Damages for Copyright Infringement,' *Texas Law Review*, 83 (2004), 525–60; see also S. Berg, 'Remedying the Statutory Damages Remedy for Secondary Copyright Infringement Liability: Balancing Copyright and Innovation in the Digital Age,' *Journal of the Copyright Society of the USA*, 56 (2009), 265–333; B. Evanson, Note, 'Due Process in Statutory Damages,' *Georgetown Journal of Law and Public Policy*, 3 (2005), 601–38.

[34] 17 USC s. 504(c)(2).

[35] See, e.g., *Capitol Records* v. *Alaujan*, 626 F. Supp. 2d 152 (D. Mass. 2009).

[36] See Samuelson and Wheatland, 'Statutory Damages'.

cause derives from a legislative technique that responds point by point to new technological challenges, filling gaps or resolving ambiguities (and just as often introducing new ones). Add the pressure of powerful interest groups, and laws 'made-to-order' for the relevant lobbies (whether representing copyright owners or technological entrepreneurs) result. These texts, which more resemble contracts between private parties than laws of general application, tend to be ill-suited to the needs and aspirations of those not represented in the bargaining process that yielded such insalubrious sausages as § 1201 of the US Copyright Act (on technological protection measures).[37] Indeed, in the long run these hyper-detailed texts may not even well serve their sponsors. As a general matter, recourse to the legislature every time a new technology threatens the economic balance between copyright owners and users (professional or otherwise), risks producing laws both excessively complex and remarkably short-lived. Whether the copyright system is grounded in the civil[38] or the common law, we might all be better off were we to leave to the courts the specific application of grand norms (including contrefaçon) to the particular problems new technologies may generate.

[37] For fuller development of this argument in connection with the 1976 Copyright Act, see J. Litman, *Digital Copyright* (Amherst, NY: Prometheus, 2001), pp. 22–34, 51–3.

[38] For a civilian's critique of unwise technology impelled intellectual property legislation, see V. Di Cataldo, 'Nuove tecnologie e nuovi problemi – Chi inventa le nuove regole e come?,' in S. Rossi and C. Storti (eds.), *Le matrici del diritto commerciale tra storia e tendenze evolutive* (Insubria University Press, 2009), pp. 147–8.

# PART IV

Economics

# 6

# Copyright infringement, 'free-riding' and the lifeworld

## Introduction

There is now a voluminous international literature on copyright law, policy and theory. Yet despite its apparent diversity, much of this commentary (particularly the very large proportion that emanates from authors based in the United States) is underpinned by the same unquestioned assumption: that some version of economic efficiency – the achievement of which involves balancing the social costs of activities (such as creating cultural artefacts and controlling how these are used) against the benefits of those activities – is the crucial, if not the only, criterion for evaluating both the copyright system and the field that it regulates.[1] Commentators may have different understandings of how costs and benefits should be measured, and of how private costs and benefits can be made to match up with social costs and benefits, but the idea that a cost–benefit equation is the acid test of defensible analysis and policy in this area is rarely challenged.[2] Among the more

* Law Department, London School of Economics. I am grateful to Brett Frischmann and Mark Lemley for engaging generously with an earlier draft of this chapter, and I owe a large debt to Carsten Gerner-Beuerle for invaluable comments on that draft. Any remaining confusions or misconceptions are mine alone.
[1] For an analysis of the concepts of economic efficiency at play in the law and economics literature generally, see N. Mercuro and S. G. Medema, *Economics and the Law* (Princeton University Press, 2nd edn, 2006), esp. pp. 20–32; 68–93.
[2] Wendy Gordon has recently noted that '[t]he most profitable lines of analysis for copyright . . . have been drawn from economics, where the most influential writing has so far come out of the United States' (W. Gordon, 'Intellectual Property', in P. Cane and M. Tushnet (eds.), *The Oxford Handbook of Legal Studies* (Oxford University Press, 2003), pp. 617–46, 624).

overtly committed of law-and-economics (L&E) scholars, this general idea tends to be invoked in relation to a cluster of rather more technical categories of economic analysis, and some of these – notably the concepts of public good and externality – are particularly relevant to the project of explaining, and prescribing for, copyright law in economic terms. Very briefly, the premise of this project is that information 'goods' are often difficult and expensive to create; yet once produced, they tend towards the condition of public goods – they are non-rivalrous in consumption, and relatively non-excludable.[3] In so far as they remain in that condition, they are easily reused by others apart from their originators, and it is difficult if not impossible to enforce payment for acts of reuse. The immediate result is 'free-riding': the obtaining of benefits from these goods by those who have not shared in the cost of producing them. The ultimate result is under-production,[4] because the inability to enforce payment for the use of these goods acts as a disincentive to their production in the first place.

Adherents to the framework of L&E agree that the solution to this problem is to institute rights of private property in relation to these goods, although there is considerable disagreement as to how and to what extent this should occur. A property right is a mechanism (though not necessarily a legal mechanism)[5] by which a would-be non-payer can be denied use of the goods to which the right pertains unless the right-holder's price is paid. Instituting property rights thus enables the internalization – within a market in valued uses of valued goods – of

---

[3] A public good is centrally characterized by the attribute that one person's use of it does not interfere with any other person's use of it and, relatedly, that it is not exhausted by use. Public goods often, though not always, possess a second feature that distinguishes them from private goods: it is difficult to exclude those who do not pay to use them from the benefits of so doing. Frequently cited examples of such 'pure' public goods (possessing both characteristics) would include lighthouses and public defence.

[4] Goods are under-produced in this sense when they are not produced even though, once produced, they would be worth more to consumers than the cost of producing them.

[5] For economists of property rights, the latter could simply be factual capacities to enjoy assets, as distinct from government-sanctioned privileges. Thus, '[w]here a person is capable of effectively creating exclusive control over some resource, he has the equivalent of an exclusive right, by whatever name his situation goes. Exclusivity is sufficient for simulating an exclusive right' (E. Mackaay, 'Economic Incentives in Markets for Information and Innovation', *Harvard Journal of Law and Public Policy* (1990), 867, 875). See further e.g. J. Umbeck, 'Might Makes Rights: A Theory of the Foundation and Initial Distribution of Property Rights', *Economic Inquiry*, 19 (1981), 38; Y. Barzel, *Economic Analysis of Property Rights* (Cambridge University Press, 1989), ch. 1.

'external'[6] benefits formerly accruing to users.[7] A copyright is a legally enforceable property right that is vested in the first instance in the originator of certain categories of information good ('works'), and subsists in relation to them. It gives to the originator exclusive legal control over certain acts in relation to the work – *not* acts of use as such, but only certain acts of replication and repetition (in what follows I shall use the term 'copying' to encompass both acts of replication and repetition). 'A' copyright is thus in fact a bundle of discrete rights, each relating to a different act. To be effective, the rights in the bundle must be enforced through the courts, which can either enjoin unauthorized uses or award monetary damages when infringements cannot be enjoined. The economic logic of this structure can be represented as organized around the assumption that information goods – as public goods – are exceptionally easy to replicate and to repeat. If the originator is unable to invoke a legal right to prevent the copying of his or her work, competitors have an

---

[6] In general, externalities are social consequences of action – whether harmful or beneficial – that are not registered, or not fully registered, by the actor; while internalization is a process of bringing the consequences of action to bear in some way on the actor that caused them. Welfare economists argue that the market is in general the most effective system for internalizing externalities, because it subjects action consequences to a pricing mechanism that causes actors to count their monetary costs or benefits. (Moreover, where the social costs or benefits entailed by an action are priced in this way, actors are given reliable signals as to what kind of conduct to engage in and what to avoid: the market thereby deploys the price mechanism to efficiently coordinate productive activities and allocate society's scarce resources to their most valued uses.) As Wendy Gordon has pointed out, 'most of IP law is concerned with internalizing positive externalities: when someone copies or adapts a book or invention without paying the originator, the benefit remains "external" to the originator and is thus unlikely to affect her incentives. When IP [law] requires the copier or adaptor to pay, part of the benefit is "internalized" to the originator' ('Intellectual Property', p. 622).

[7] A user in this context could be one whose use of the good is merely consumptive, or one whose use involves the production of another instantiation of the good for consumption by others. In relation to the latter, something like Richard Watt's distinction between information goods and what he calls 'delivery' goods or services is useful (R. Watt, *Copyright and Economic Theory* (Cheltenham: Edward Elgar, 2000), p. 4). A delivery good is a physical artefact (such as a book) in which information is relatively durably instantiated; a delivery service (such as a lecture) communicates information while leaving no physical trace after the delivery has been completed. Uses of information that involve conveying it to others necessarily involve embedding it in one or other of these modes of delivery. In the absence of property rights in information, its public good characteristics entail that anyone other than its originator can embed it in new delivery goods and services and sell these at a price that does not reflect the investment incurred by the originator in generating the information. This ability to undersell the originator in markets for delivery goods and services in turn enables this category of non-paying user to compete profitably with the originator in these markets.

incentive to make replications and repetitions available to consumers by means, respectively, of delivery goods (e.g. books) and services (e.g. film showings) incorporating these as long as the market price for these delivery goods and services is greater than the marginal cost of producing them (e.g. the cost of printing each additional copy of a book). Consequently, the market price for these goods and services will be driven down to the marginal cost of production. However in that event, the originator of the work – or the investor who has paid for the right to produce commodities incorporating that work – will be unable to price its own delivery goods and services at a level yielding an adequate return on the investment in the work.[8] (In a competitive market, the market price will be that of the lowest-cost producer, and copiers of works will face lower average production costs than investors in works, if only because copiers do not have to pay for the use of the work.) As a result, those who would have invested in works may turn to other activities that are better recompensed, even though social welfare[9] would have been better served by their investing in creating and/or disseminating works.

Viewed from an economic perspective, the function of copyright law is to deal with this problem. As currently organized, it does so by vesting in the 'author'[10] of a work an array of transferable[11] rights to control certain acts of copying: all kinds of reproduction (including adaptation) of the work, various forms of distribution (including commercial sales and rentals, and institutionalized lending) of the work, and all kinds of public communication (including public performance and electronic

---

[8] Private goods are produced efficiently when the value consumers place on the last unit of the good to be produced equals the cost of producing that unit (its marginal cost).

[9] Social welfare is generally defined in the L&E literature as the sum of all individual utilities.

[10] The authors that UK law recognizes as copyright owners are not simply individuals, nor is the authorial effort rewarded by the law confined to intellectual effort alone: corporate enterprises whose organizational and financial inputs yield films, sound recordings, broadcasts and publications (sometimes referred to as 'entrepreneurial' works to distinguish them from the 'authorial' literary, dramatic, musical and artistic works produced by merely intellectual investment) are also defined as authors by virtue of these inputs; and an employer who employs a human author to create an authorial work will generally be regarded as the first owner of any copyright in it: Copyright, Designs and Patents Act 1988, ss. 9–11.

[11] In practice, of course, the copyrights in works that have commercial value generally are transferred to commercial intermediaries – e.g. publishers and producers of various kinds – who expect to profit from their own investment in acquiring rights to works and then embedding these in delivery goods and services which can be sold to consumers.

transmission) of the work. These controls extend to non-literal as well as literal copies, and more generally to copies that replicate or repeat less than the whole of the work.[12] The UK's Copyright, Designs and Patents Act 1988 thus provides that anyone who does any of the acts restricted to the copyright owner to the whole of a protected work, or any substantial part of it, infringes copyright in the work unless some defence or exception applies. (The most well known of the available defences in the UK context are those which excuse 'fair dealing' with a work for the purposes of non-commercial research and private study, criticism or review of that or another work, and news reporting.) Liability for these acts of 'primary' infringement is strict in the sense that no knowledge of any wrongdoing needs to be shown. However, the Act also imposes liability on those who have materially contributed to the doing of these acts by others or have dealt commercially with infringing copies made by others, though generally[13] only where such contribution or dealing is accompanied by actual or constructive knowledge of the infringing act. In sum, whether copyright in a given copyright work has been infringed depends on: (a) whether the statutory list of restricted acts extends to the act carried out by the alleged infringer; (b) if so, whether that act has been done to the whole of the work or a substantial part of it; and (c) if so, whether a defence or exception applies. Further, (d) copyright in the work may in some circumstances be invoked to prevent not only acts of primary infringement carried out directly in relation to the work, but also further acts carried out in relation to some act of primary infringement.

Acts of copyright infringement can be redescribed in economic terms as acts of free-riding[14] and, as such, condemned as socially harmful as well as unlawful. (For the economist of copyright law, 'piracy' – the focus of this book – is merely a morally charged but, in economic terms, meaningless label for a species of free-riding.) The real power of the economic analysis of copyright law, however, resides in its claim to be able to judge whether any given copyright system – as a particular configuration of legally instituted property rights in information – is

---

[12] As a legal matter, a copyright work is conceived of as extending well beyond a notional 'surface' (e.g. the sequence of words appearing on the pages of a book) to deeper 'layers of abstraction' (including e.g. the plot of a novel) underlying or structuring that surface. Thus non-literal copies of a work may infringe copyright in that work.

[13] s. 16(3) CDPA imposes strict liability for 'authorising' the carrying out of one of the acts exclusively reserved to the copyright owner without the latter's permission.

[14] '[C]opyright is only valid against those who "free-ride", and not against fully independent creators' (Gordon, 'Intellectual Property', p. 630).

*itself* efficient. Where it is judged not to be, acts involving *no* infringe-ment of copyright under the current law can nonetheless be declared harmful acts of free-riding that call for some process of internalization. The expansion of copyright in recent years – transforming activities previously deemed lawful into acts of copyright infringement that can be legally enjoined – is attributed by some commentators to the pressure exerted by precisely this kind of argument.[15] The argument proceeds, it is said, from the idea that externalities amount to a market failure requiring correction, and this in turn is said to be the organizing idea of a new, but currently dominant, school of economic theorizing about copyright which is quite distinct from the standard economic analysis of the institution.

According to the standard analysis – what Glynn Lunney has termed 'copyright's incentives-access paradigm'[16] – an efficient regime of copy-right protection is a 'balanced' regime that limits the unpaid use of information goods just enough to ensure the right level of incentive to motivate their production at a socially optimal level. The newer frame-work, described by Mark Lemley as an 'absolute protection' or 'full value' view of intellectual property, is said to be defined by a strong normative commitment to the internalization of *all* externalities arising from the use of information:[17] it holds that legally instituted rights of private property should ideally extend to every valued use of information, such that users would be required by law to pay the owner's price for any such use except in atypical instances of unavoidable market failure. It is this view, so it is claimed, which has legitimated the steady expansion in the scope of copyright at national, regional and international levels along each of the four axes identified above: the range of acts restricted to the copyright owner has widened, the range of circumstances in which secondary liability will be found has also widened, the likelihood that courts will find partial or non-literal takings 'substantial' (and so infringing) has increased, and the reach of defences and exceptions has narrowed. Meanwhile, recent legal initiatives have given copyright owners new rights – variously dubbed 'para-copyrights' or 'digital'

---

[15] See e.g. N. W. Netanel, 'Copyright and a Democratic Civil Society', 106 (1996), *Yale Law Journal*, 283; M. A. Lemley, 'Property, Intellectual Property, and Free Riding', *Texas Law Review*, 83 (2005), 1031; B. M. Frischmann, 'Evaluating the Demsetzian Trend in Copyright Law', *Review of Law and Economics*, 3(3) (2007), 649.

[16] G. S. Lunney, 'Reexamining Copyright's Incentives-Access Paradigm', *Vanderbilt Law Review*, 49(3) (1996), 483.

[17] Lemley, 'Property'.

rights – oriented towards preventing the circumvention of digital rights management (DRM) systems applied to copyright material. DRM systems enable right-owners to *physically* limit access to, and regulate use or reuse of, any information (including information taking the form of a copyright work) that exists in a digitized form. These mechanisms can thus enable a kind of control that goes well beyond copyright in so far as it regulates access to and use of digitized material in general (whether protected by copyright or not) as opposed to particular acts of copying carried out in relation to copyright works. In this way, DRM permits a form of control in relation to intangible information roughly equivalent to that achieved by fences, locks or guards in relation to tangibles. Considered in relation to the absolute protection model of copyright, DRM seems a major step towards the actualization of this model.

This chapter is animated by the conviction that too much has been made of the distinction between the incentives-access and absolute protection approaches to copyright. Ultimately, my aim here is to show that these have much more in common than is generally perceived, and that the debate over which should have priority in determining the contours of copyright policy distracts attention from a more fundamental issue – the hegemony of economic analysis generally in organizing the conceptual and normative universe of US-based legal scholars working in this area. That said, most of the chapter is oriented towards attending to the features that are said to distinguish the absolute protection paradigm from the incentives-access paradigm, and to the efforts of critical economists of IP law such as Mark Lemley and Brett Frischmann to retrieve and advance versions of the latter with a view to counteracting the disadvantages for society they believe are associated with the former. Sections 1 and 2 below accordingly consider how 'incentives-access' and 'absolute protection' have been constructed *as* two distinct frameworks within the field of copyright-law-and-economics by scholars working in this field. Section 1 briefly considers the incentives-access paradigm. Section 2 considers the absolute protection paradigm, chiefly from the perspective of the critical accounts of it that Lemley and Frischmann have offered. Both of these critics are convinced of this paradigm's distinctness from the traditional incentives-access rationale for copyright. Both aim to regenerate a version of the incentives-access rationale to counteract the absolute protection approach. Both believe that the latter is largely responsible for the expansion in copyright's scope in recent years, an expansion they are concerned to reverse or at least suspend. And both appear to agree that Harold Demsetz's economic theory of property rights provides the normative foundation for the absolute protection approach.

Section 3 focuses on interrogating these critics' conception of the normative questions at stake in the 'incentives-access versus absolute protection' debate, and to this end it investigates the core premises of Demsetz's theory. What I aim to uncover here is the fundamental unity that underlies the apparent divide separating the incentives-access approach from its supposed rival. Briefly put, what the two paradigms share is a particular vision of the social order and of the nature of social interaction – a vision that animates economic theory generally, whatever its particular applications.[18] At root, economic theory advances a model of society as constituted by individual actors whose actions are governed solely by the urge to maximize their utilities; and it conceives of social coordination as emerging from the competitive exchanges of these actors, typically mediated by the price mechanism in the context of a market that has been institutionalized via property rights, contracts and monetary transfers.[19] 'Utility' here is inferred from the choices actors make in ranking their wants in order of preference and calculating how to deploy their scarce means to satisfy these preferences.[20] Utility is thus claimed to be an objective measure of satisfaction that abstracts from (what to the economist appear as) the many subjective and incommensurable ends that motivate individuals to act. It is objective, so it is said,

---

[18] For an illuminating elaboration of the core premises of modern economics, see D. Slater and F. Tonkiss, *Market Society: Markets and Modern Social Theory* (Cambridge: Polity, 2001), ch. 2.

[19] It is important to point out that, for economic theory, the market is fundamentally a device for representing social interaction. Of course the term 'market' also describes the mechanisms by which some forms of this interaction are institutionalized through the commercial exchange of goods or services between buyers and sellers. However it is the former, more general, meaning that enables economic theory to explain behaviour which is not so institutionalized, as well as that which is. The market in this general sense is the conceptual space within which purposively acting agents are represented as ranking their wants, calculating the resources available to them to realize their wants, identifying other actors whose cooperation is necessary to the realization of their wants, and exchanging resources (which could include time, energy, attention, emotional commitment, and so forth) with such others so that the mutual realization of wants can be achieved at least cost. I argue here that practitioners of both the incentives-access and the absolute protection approaches to copyright are committed to the view that this general idea of the market *accurately* represents social relations – that is, they agree that the market's logic of calculation and exchange fully characterizes interaction between persons – even as they disagree about the proper reach of markets in the narrower sense.

[20] Slater and Tonkiss, *Market Society*, p. 48. See also J. O'Neill, *The Market: Ethics, Knowledge and Politics* (London: Routledge, 1998), ch. 3.

because it refers only to what is objectively observable: the preferences revealed by market behaviour. In facilitating the satisfaction of a multitude of these 'revealed preferences' through a network of competitive exchanges mediated by price, the market is supposed to reconcile individual self-interest with social welfare mechanically, as it were, and without embedding within itself any particular conception of what is normatively (or cognitively, or aesthetically) valuable.

Yet while ostensibly only a technical design for the allocation of scarce resources, the idea of the market in economic theory is also a particular representation of social relations as competitive interactions between atomized, purposively rational agents. Further, this idea has influenced how normative questions of all kinds – and not simply questions of efficient resource allocation – are addressed in societies whose modes of social exchange are in fact dominated by the calculative strategies associated with the market.[21] In particular, economic theory's privileging of choice, competition and the price mechanism reflects its positive evaluation not only of the economic functions these serve but also the norms they presuppose: a norm of freedom as individual liberty to rank and pursue given wants, a norm of equality that refers to the processes rather than the outcomes of this pursuit, and a norm of rationality as the calculation of the least costly means of this pursuit. The reasons why individuals want what they want are irrelevant from this perspective (economic theory does not aspire to explain how preferences are formed), as are the questions of whether and under what conditions those reasons could be intersubjectively shared: as far as economic theory is concerned, there is no dimension of meaning or value that is not reducible, in the end, to the private calculations of individuals.

When applied to the field regulated by copyright law, economic theory produces a peculiar picture of the social relations and dynamics that it finds there. From its perspective, the emanations of language and art are so many units of 'information' that can be reified as objects of property rights and allocated to 'innovators' as if created from nothing; while communicative interactions are reduced to exchange relations between producers and consumers of information goods. Moreover, the reasons why producers supply, and consumers demand, information goods are peripheral to a properly economic explanation of these behaviours. For example, the writer who churns out formulaic potboilers for no

---

[21] See generally J. G. Carrier, 'Introduction', in J. G. Carrier (ed.), *Meanings of the Market: The Free Market in Western Culture* (Oxford: Berg, 1997).

other reason than to pay her rent is indistinguishable – *qua* economic actor – from the journalist who seeks through her works to enrich political debate, the scholar who advances a theory in the hope of convincing others of its explanatory power, or the poet who endeavours through words to transfigure others' imaginative horizons. By the same token, the reasons motivating the various forms of engagement that these works invite among readers cannot be differentiated either. From the vantage point of economic theory, all economic actors are presumed to choose between different action possibilities with a view only to maximizing their utilities. The choice of each actor is based on a ranking of preferences that must be taken by the theorist to be exogenously given: the ranking reflects only a calculation of the relative costs and benefits to the actor of satisfying them. Copyright's role here is simply to steer action involving the production of information by influencing the cost–benefit calculations engaged in by information producers. It achieves this by enabling uses of that information to be controlled and so priced, thereby also influencing the cost–benefit calculations of information consumers. The only issue dividing economists of copyright from each other is which uses should be capable of being controlled/priced by the right-owner: absolute protection theorists tend towards the view that all uses fall unto this category; incentives-access theorists distinguish between uses the control of which would affect the right-owner's calculations *ex ante*, and those that would not, and recommend that copyright protection should extend to the former category only.

Commentators such as Lemley and Frischmann – practitioners of L&E who are nonetheless critical of some of the latter's applications – condemn the absolute protection approach to this issue. For these commentators, many uses of information that proponents of absolute protection would argue ought to be deemed infringements of copyright if the right-owner's price is not paid involve 'innovation spillovers' (uncompensated benefits generated by the activity of producing information) that should not be capable of being legally enjoined. While sympathetic to the impulse underlying this position – a concern to resist the seemingly relentless expansion of copyright towards the horizon of absolute right-holder control of all uses of copyright material – I argue that the lingering adherence of these critics to economic theory, and thus to the representations and norms that are presupposed by economic theory, has stymied their well-meaning efforts to account for the social value of 'information' in terms distinct from the merely economic measure of price. In Section 4 I consider the framework that, separately and together, they have advanced as an antidote to the absolute protection paradigm. I argue that their position – which effectively reinvents the idea of a balance between incentives and access as the key to an efficient copyright system – is in fact remarkably close to the neoclassical property rights theory of Harold Demsetz, so much so that their critique of the absolute protection paradigm becomes in the end an endorsement of the latter's core premises. I further argue that to the extent that Lemley and Frischmann try to eschew these premises while remaining wedded to law and economics – as when they invoke social benefits of free-riding that *in principle* cannot be internalized to market exchanges – their position reduces to the recommendation that certain socially valued uses of information goods ought to be priced at zero. Although it is not at all clear that purely economic considerations lead them to this conclusion, their position nonetheless precludes any analysis of whether the logic of pricing itself (whether at zero or not) *already* misrepresents the social significance of the very communicative interactions (occurring in contexts such as education and political discourse) that they want to facilitate. Drawing on the social theory of Jürgen Habermas, my own conclusion claims that these kinds of interactions simply exceed economic theory's field of vision altogether, and that the blindness of law and economics to the limitations of its own categories seriously compromises its capacity to explain what is at stake in the attempt to transform copyright protection into absolute protection.

## The 'incentives-access' paradigm

This way of thinking (which has a long history within copyright discourse, even if it has not always been articulated in the technical language of modern economics)[22] is structured by the idea that copyright is itself attended by two kinds of social cost, associated with the lost access to information resources that right-owners' powers of exclusion in respect of them entail. First, copyright can equip right-owners with a degree of monopoly power in markets for delivery goods and services incorporating exact replications or repetitions of their works. The greater the number of modes of delivering a work that copyright law places within the right-owner's control, the more competitors are impeded from embedding the same work in new delivery goods and services of their

---

[22] J. Ginsburg 'A Tale of Two Copyrights: Literary Property in Revolutionary France and America', *Tulane Law Review*, 46 (1990), 991.

own devising. This may in turn insulate right-owners from effective price competition in markets for delivery goods and services: when would-be competitors are prevented from marketing perfect substitutes[23] for authorized goods and services, supracompetitive prices[24] can be charged to consumers of these. Whatever about the regressive distributional consequences of this kind of 'overpricing'[25] – which welfare economics tends not to register as a social cost[26] – one upshot is undeniably relevant to the assessment of aggregate social welfare: lost sales to those consumers who are unwilling or unable to pay the supracompetitive prices, but would have been willing to pay competitive prices. As far as these consumers are concerned, copyright – in the absence of perfect price discrimination[27] – imposes 'deadweight loss'. To understand why this is so, it is necessary to recall that copyright works are non-rivalrous in consumption, and that because of this, the consumption of a work by 'low-paying' users at the competitive price would not be at the expense of others who valued it more – all could consume it simultaneously without interfering with each other's consumption. It follows that the exclusion of these low-value users represents a permanent social loss.[28]

The second cost the incentives-access paradigm identifies as imposed by copyright concerns second-generation creators, as distinct from

---

[23] Perfect substitutes are identical to the authorized goods and services in all respects that affect consumer preferences (Gordon, 'Intellectual Property', p. 641). Exact, and in some circumstances even inexact, copies of copyright works will fall into this category.

[24] Supracompetitive prices are prices in excess of the marginal costs of delivery goods and services.

[25] Consumers who remain willing to purchase the work at its higher, more monopolistic price must pay more for the work than they would have had to pay in a more competitive market, and this transfers to the right-owner (as a monopoly profit or rent) resources that would otherwise have remained with them as 'consumer surplus' (the amount by which consumers benefit by being able to purchase a product for a price that is less than they are willing to pay).

[26] 'Assuming we value the welfare of both consumers and authors equally, this is simply a wealth transfer and is welfare-neutral' (M. J. Sag, 'Beyond Abstraction: the Law and Economics of Copyright Scope and Doctrinal Efficiency', *Tulane Law Review*, 81 (2006), 187, 196).

[27] Gordon, 'Intellectual Property', pp. 642–3. Price discrimination involves charging different prices, reflecting different levels of willingness to pay, for the same uses.

[28] Sag, 'Beyond Abstraction', 196. Wendy Gordon has pointed out that the label 'deadweight loss' is inappropriately applied to lost access to works that would not have come into existence without copyright. Properly speaking, then, deadweight losses can only arise in relation to a particular work when the level of copyright protection available for it is beyond that necessary to call forth the work in the first place ('Authors, Publishers and Public Goods', *Loyola of Los Angeles Law Review*, 36 (2002) 139, 195).

passive consumers. Copyright – the very mechanism that should stimulate the production of information goods – can itself limit their production. In particular, to the extent that copyright hinders follow-on creators from taking elements from protected works and building upon these to create new ('derivative') works, it necessarily raises the costs faced by these subsequent innovators: they must find the right-owner and negotiate and pay for licences to use these elements; and this may be impossible.

All this suggests that information markets exhibit a tension between efficiency in production and efficiency in consumption, or between dynamic and static efficiency.[29] Proponents of the incentives-access model regard the challenge this presents as one of balancing the copyright system's dynamic benefits against its static costs. They acknowledge that potential producers of information have an incentive to invest in production only if they can appropriate at least some of the value that users of information place on what they produce; and they recognize that if the ability to capture this value is non-existent, socially optimal levels of information production may not be achieved. *Some* producer controls over the copying activities of others are therefore regarded within this paradigm as necessary to incentivize the right level of production, but it is also recognized that these controls should be limited. As far as *exact* copying is concerned, the limit is reached where further producer control over what others may do with exact copies generates no additional incentive to create, and discourages production of new delivery goods and services costing less to produce than the price consumers would be willing to pay for them.[30] As far as *inexact* copies of protected works are concerned, the paradigm acknowledges that the law must enable some of these to be controlled by the right-owner if the protection it provides is to be meaningful as an incentive. However it also recognizes that the more instantiations of the work in new formats the right-owner can veto, and the deeper copyright penetrates into the sub-surface of a work (reaching elements within the work that second comers may wish to use), the more the law approaches the point where the social benefit of the added incentive it provides is outweighed by the social cost of new production foregone.

---

[29] Sag, 'Beyond Abstraction', 196–7.

[30] An example of a limit recognized in copyright law is the exhaustion doctrine, which restricts copyright owners to controlling the first entry onto the market of delivery goods incorporating copies of their works: subsequent sales of these goods cannot be controlled.

At a very general theoretical level, the difference between the absolute protection and incentives-access models is that while the latter identifies the lost free access associated with a copyright system as a cost of the system, and only measures the benefits accruing from the degree to which the system incentivizes the *initial* creation of information goods, the former sees free access (i.e. access unimpeded by others' property rights) to these goods as itself imposing social costs, and emphasizes additional benefits of the copyright system not registered by the incentives-access model: copyright's incentivization of efficient use and development of information goods *after* they have been created. Consequently, each model produces a different answer to the cost–benefit calculation that is the hallmark of any economic analysis of copyright law. More particularly, each produces a different answer to the question of what activities should be regarded as infringing the copyright in any given work. Since the incentives-access model puts a positive value on free access to a work, it considers the erosion of this freedom as a cost associated with any expansion in the scope of copyright in it; meanwhile, it only registers as a benefit to be weighed against this cost any increase the expansion will bring to the incentives available for the production of works of that kind. This, then, is an approach that looks with suspicion at claims for broad copyrights, both where these claims are advanced in individual cases (when the issues are whether the defendant has carried out one of the acts restricted to the copyright owner to the whole or a substantial part of a work and if so, whether his/her activity is covered by an exception to copyright protection), and where they are advanced in the legislative arena (when the issues are whether new rights should be added to the copyright bundle or whether new exceptions to existing rights should be recognized).

Proponents of the absolute protection model, as we shall see, are troubled by none of these concerns. Simply put, their argument is that access is not in fact 'lost' as copyright expands, because as copyright expands access is *organized*, efficiently, through the private initiatives of right-owners and would-be users – initiatives that would include not only licensing, but also other mechanisms (such as voluntary donations to the public domain).[31] Efficient private ordering ensures access – albeit at the right-owner's price, if any – and in so doing it also ensures that the

---

[31] See e.g. R. P. Merges, 'A New Dynamism in the Public Domain', *University of Chicago Law Review*, 71 (2004), 183; R. P. Wagner, 'Information Wants to be Free: IP and the Mythologies of Control', *Columbia Law Review*, 103 (2003), 995.

emergent future value of works is properly managed and fully 'mined': right-owners who cannot themselves develop the potential embedded in their works (e.g. by producing derivatives of these, or reformatting them) can nonetheless license others who are better placed to do so, thereby coordinating the investment necessary to maximize the work's value. Efficient private ordering in turn depends on the right-owner's willingness to license and ability to engage in price discrimination. But once all this is in place, copyright can 'facilitate market transactions that transfer information assets to their highest valued uses'.[32]

## The 'absolute protection' paradigm

Neil Netanel offered a prescient analysis of this position as long ago as 1996, when in 'Copyright and a Democratic Civil Society'[33] he problematized the expansion in copyright's length, breadth and depth that was already gathering pace in the US at that time. Netanel isolated, as one of the major factors behind this expansion, 'a blend of neoclassical and new institutional economic property theory'[34] that he dubbed 'neoclassicism' and attributed to key L&E scholars such as Paul Goldstein, Richard Epstein and Frank Easterbrook. Emphasizing that this approach was conceptually distinct from the more traditional 'economic incentive' rationale for copyright, Netanel explained that on the neoclassicist view, the essential function of copyright is to enable copyright owners to 'realize the full profit potential for their works in the market' (because only then will creative works '[m]ove to their highest socially valued uses');[35] that it is more likely to achieve this the more it approximates to an ideal property rights regime; and that such a regime has four key characteristics. First, it is universal, which in the context of a copyright regime means that every valued use of every work covered by the regime should be included within the scope of the right-owner's rights, and that the law should allow right-owners free rein to appropriate the value of these uses by whatever means necessary, including refusals to licence and discriminatory pricing. Second, ownership of the rights made available by the regime should be concentrated in a single person so that transaction costs can be minimized in the management of the resources

---

[32] W. J. Gordon and R. G. Bone, 'Copyright', in B. Bouckaert and G. Degeest (eds.), *Encyclopedia of Law and Economics*, vol. 2 (Cheltenham: Edward Elgar, 2000), pp. 189–223, 194.
[33] Netanel, 'Copyright'.  [34] *Ibid.*, 306.  [35] *Ibid.*, 309.

(works, in the copyright context) covered by it. (Of course efficient management may involve permitting others who are better placed to develop the work's potential to use it in one of the ways reserved to the right-owner; and this in turn will necessarily involve some transaction costs. However, on the neoclassicist view, concentration minimizes these because would-be users can avoid having to deal with *multiple* owners of different rights in the same work.) Third, the rights made available by the regime should be exclusive, which in the context of the copyright regime means that they should equip the right-owner with an absolute power of veto over others' use of the work, such that users must contract with the right-owner for the uses they want and in each case pay an agreed price: only in situations where voluntary exchange is, and will remain, impossible should these rights be limited by mechanisms such as compulsory licences and copyright exceptions. Finally, rights made available by the regime should be fully transferable, such that they may be readily moved to the highest-value users.[36]

Essentially, the ideas animating this picture of copyright as a species of property are that consumer preferences should ultimately direct investment in the production and management of works; that consumer preferences are best signalled through the market's price mechanism; and that copyright law's 'reification of claims to market potential'[37] enables markets in desired uses of works to form and operate efficiently. Netanel's article identified as the crucial assumption embedded in this understanding of the institution of copyright that the institution gives to the right-owner a power, not so much over *previously* committed investment in information goods, as over the value accruing from these goods in the future.[38] Whereas the former premise implies that the owner of copyright in a work should have sufficient control over the work to enable the initial investment in producing it to be recouped, the latter implies that the copyright should be broad enough to enable appropriation of the emergent value of the work over time. This conception of what is at stake in the shift within the economic analysis of copyright law – from traditional incentive theory to the newer property rights

---

[36] *Ibid.*, 314–21.    [37] *Ibid.*, 312.

[38] Hence Netanel cited Edmund Kitch as one of the key architects of the absolute protection approach to IPRs, because Kitch analogized patent rights to prospecting rights in mineral-rich lands: E. W. Kitch, 'The Nature and Function of the Patent System', *Journal of Law and Economics*, 20 (1977), 265. For another early characterization of the absolute protection position, see J. Cohen, 'Lochner in Cyberspace: The New Economic Orthodoxy of Rights Management', *Michigan Law Review*, 97 (1998), 462.

paradigm – has also been advanced more recently, in a sustained way over numerous articles, by Mark Lemley. A consistent theme of Lemley's work in this area has been that the newer paradigm recommends the elimination of all free-riding on (or the internalization of all positive externalities generated by) intellectual creations as an end in itself, but that this position is inconsistent with the realisation of an efficient copyright system, for three reasons: '(1) there is no need to fully internalize benefits in intellectual property; (2) efforts to capture positive externalities may actually reduce them, leaving everyone worse off; and (3) the effort to capture such externalities invites rent-seeking.'[39]

Most (though not all) of Lemley's work on this theme is firmly situated within the discipline of L&E: it is best described as an internal critique of one application of L&E by a committed practitioner of L&E. In this work Lemley's essential point is that the absolute protection paradigm cannot deliver an efficient intellectual property system: that it fails *as* an economic analysis of intellectual property law rather than *because* it is an economic analysis of intellectual property law. He distinguishes between two variants of what he calls the 'ex post' justification for very broad intellectual property rights (ex post because it focuses on how IPRs incentivize the management or control of works that have already been created):

> One form . . . argues that intellectual property protection is necessary to encourage the intellectual property owner to make some further investment in the improvement, maintenance, or commercialization of the product. Another strand argues that such protection is necessary to prevent a sort of "tragedy of the commons" in which the new idea will be overused.[40]

The key to the appeal of both variants, he argues, is the too-easy analogy between intellectual property and tangible property on which each depends.[41] The first variant analogizes IPRs to ownership rights in respect of tangible things, but suggests that rights in intellectual creations should be such as to enable *all* the social benefits generated by these creations to be internalized, even though neither the economic theory nor the law of tangible property sanctions this in relation to tangibles.

[39] Lemley, 'Property', 1032.
[40] M. A. Lemley, 'Ex Ante versus Ex Post Justifications for Intellectual Property', *University of Chicago Law Review*, 71 (2004), 129, 130.
[41] Lemley, 'Property'.

The second variant analogizes intellectual creations to tangible things and suggests that IPRs are necessary to prevent their overuse, even though intellectual creations – unlike tangible things – are inexhaustible: the intellectual commons is *not* subject to the tragedy that afflicts open-access tangible resources, because information cannot be depleted by overuse. Lemley insists that although the resources invested in producing information goods are indeed finite, the waste of these resources is guarded against by giving producers a limited right of exclusion, adequate to 'permit [them] to make enough money to cover their costs, including a reasonable return on fixed-cost investment'[42] but no more. It follows, in his view, that absolute protection would impose unnecessary social costs for no additional social benefits: the full value idea, in other words, fails to connect the right to capture this value to the social benefit of having intellectual property rights in the first place, which is that of incentivizing the production of information.[43]

For Lemley, overbroad rights simply transfer wealth from users to right-owners for no good economic reason. They impose added costs on society in the form of deadweight losses for consumers, impediments to follow-on creation, the waste associated with rent-seeking, the administrative costs associated with enforcing IPRs, and the costs to society arising from over-investment in activities likely to attract IPRs.[44] Their supposed benefits depend on the assumption that these rights will indeed be efficiently managed by their owners. However this assumption is unwarranted: there is no guarantee that those who happen to be designated in law as right-owners will in fact appreciate the value of the works they control and act effectively to exploit this value; and there are several reasons to doubt that efficient licensing will solve this problem.[45] In this connection, Lemley notes that despite its ostensible privileging of the market as a resource allocation mechanism, the 'ex post' justification for very broad IPRs is in fact profoundly anti-market in that it favours central (albeit private) control rather than free competition: 'the ex

---

[42] *Ibid.*    [43] *Ibid.*, 1057.    [44] *Ibid.*, 1058–64.
[45] M. A. Lemley, 'The Economics of Improvement in Intellectual Property Law', *Texas Law Review*, 75 (1997), 989: 'Problems of imperfect information, transaction costs, strategic behavior, and market power [which may incentivise the right-owner to refuse to deal with market actors that might compete with it] all impose barriers to the hypothetical efficient license' (*ibid.*, 1048–72). See also M. A. Lemley, 'Romantic Authorship and the Rhetoric of Property', *Texas Law Review*, 75 (1997), 873, 903 and B. M. Frischmann and M. A. Lemley, 'Spillovers', *Columbia Law Review*, 257 (2007), 277–8.

post justifications, in other words, seem to depend on private ordering without relying on market ordering'.[46]

The above summary of Lemley's position is drawn from a series of articles in which he makes no distinction between copyright and other areas of intellectual property law whose purpose is the furtherance of innovation. However his sometime co-author, Brett Frischmann, has pursued similar themes in the particular context of copyright law – arguing, indeed, that 'copyright ... is the intellectual property system that ought to be the least private-property-like'.[47] In 'Evaluating the Demsetzian Trend in Copyright Law' Frischmann insists (echoing Lemley) that '[c]opyright is a system that is designed to both internalize and to promote externalities'.[48] Externalities, he argues, 'do not necessarily distort incentives, or more generally, the market allocation of resources:'[49] externalities are ubiquitous in society, and many externalities are in fact irrelevant to decisions about whether or not to invest in the activities that led to their production. Consequently, intervention to eliminate irrelevant externalities cannot be justified on efficiency grounds; and externalities to the copyright system that do not undermine incentives to invest in the creation, development and dissemination of protected works are irrelevant in this sense. Copyright thus rightly promotes externalities (or free-riding) by leaving many uses of works (or elements of works) in the public domain, and by deploying 'muddy', context-specific doctrines such as fair use/dealing or substantiality to determine whether works have been unlawfully copied.

It is not clear from Frischmann's analysis where the dividing line is to be drawn between incentive-relevant and incentive-irrelevant externalities: the most he will grant is that both externalities and property rights have the *potential* to distort the market's allocation of resources, which Frischmann seems at this point in his argument to acknowledge as the benchmark of a socially optimal allocation.[50] Externalities have this potential where they are indeed incentive-relevant; property rights however also have this potential because instituting them may involve government intervention where a more welfare-enhancing private solution to a genuine free-riding problem might have been found. As for the

---

[46] 'Ex Ante', 148.   [47] Frischmann, 'Evaluating the Demsetzian Trend', 653.   [48] *Ibid.*
[49] *Ibid.*, 663.
[50] *Ibid.* Subsequently, however, he contends that 'the market may fail to allocate resources efficiently in cases where consumers' willingness to pay understates societal demand' (*ibid.*, 665).

neoclassical argument that propertization is nonetheless to be favoured because efficient licensing will ensure use of propertized information goods at socially optimal levels, Frischmann's position is that this is implausible. His central argument in this connection is that 'purchasers'/licensees' willingness to pay for access and use rights will not adequately reflect *social* demand in market transactions'.[51] Such a deficit will occur when a purchaser/licensee uses a work as an input to 'socially valued productive activities:'[52] Frischmann cites as examples education, community development, democratic discourse and political participation. Willingness to pay reflects only private demand – the value the purchaser or licensee expects to realize from the use – and so takes no account of the wider 'social' value that others apart from the purchaser/licensee might realize from the use. Given this gap between private and social value, the institution of copyright should be designed so as to leave such uses in the public domain.

From these observations about both the supply and demand sides of the market for copyright-protected information, Frischmann concludes that:

> (1) externalities do not necessarily or generally distort the allocation of resources by the market; (2) the market may fail to allocate resources efficiently in cases where consumers' willingness to pay understates societal demand; and (3) ... even where externalities distort market allocation, such distortions may be social welfare enhancing.[53]

Now Frischmann's category of the 'incentive-irrelevant externality' clearly implies that there are forms of social action that are not (or not completely) motivated by *monetary* incentives. Authorial production falls into this category of action that benefits others, but is performed without the expectation of remuneration from (all of) those others: authors will continue to 'supply' regardless of whether they are able to capture the full social value of their products (i.e. extract payment for all the ways in which their creations inform, teach and engage audiences). Frischmann also acknowledges that social 'demand' for these uses can never be reflected adequately in monetary transactions between right-holders and purchasers/licensees of use rights. In short, Frischmann recognizes that the 'information' incentivized by the copyright system necessarily generates social value that is not, and could not be, fully reflected in the prices that could be charged for it; and, in particular,

---

[51] *Ibid.*, emphasis added.    [52] *Ibid.*, 670.    [53] *Ibid.*, 665.

that communicative exchange between authors and audiences could never be reducible to monetary exchange. However he offers no alternative theoretical framework that could account for the non-market dimension of copyright law otherwise than in terms of the categories invoked to account for its market dimension – supply, demand, incentive, externality, (zero) pricing, and so on. He acknowledges the claim of many critics of copyright expansionism that the latter phenomenon has been bound up with 'an over-reliance on economic theory'[54] in making sense of the copyright system, and notes the insistence of these critics that copyright is more than an economic system because it implicates 'various public policies and values that are not well explained or theorized within economic theory'.[55] Yet having acknowledged this he simply equivocates, claiming that his own position 'fits somewhere between'[56] these critical stances and the cautious balancing of the (economic) costs of the copyright system against its (economic) benefits that is characteristic of traditional L&E. Nonetheless, his qualms at least seem infectious, for in a recent article co-written with Frischmann, Lemley seems to relinquish his own earlier certainties about economic theory by situating himself somewhere in this middle ground alongside his co-author. The implications of this will be explored further in section 4 below. First, however, I examine Lemley and Frischmann's shared debt to Harold Demsetz, a figure whose staunch attachment to economic theory has remained unquestioned over many decades, and is reaffirmed in his recent reply to Frischmann in the *Review of Law and Economics*.[57]

## Two paradigms, one foundation

Crucial to an understanding of both Lemley and Frischmann's critiques of the absolute protection paradigm is an appreciation of their relation to Demsetz's theory of property rights, first advanced in an article published in 1967.[58] Lemley and Frischmann each consider this article

---

[54] *Ibid.*, 661.
[55] *Ibid.*, 662. Frischmann has in mind commentators such as Yochai Benkler, James Boyle, Julie Cohen, Terry Fisher, Lawrence Lessig and Neil Netanel, who try to combine economic analysis with other forms of theorizing that account for the non-economic values also served by copyright law.
[56] *Ibid.*
[57] H. Demsetz, 'Frischmann's View of "Toward a Theory of Property Rights"', *Review of Law and Economics*, 4(1) (2008), 127.
[58] H. Demsetz, 'Toward a Theory of Property Rights', *American Economic Review*, 57(2) (1967), 347.

to be a canonical text in the absolute protection literature, because it fostered the notion that his economic theory of property rights could be applied in the same way to information as to land. However, as I argue below, it is impossible to attribute to Demsetz unqualified support for the total privatization of information. In fact, Demsetz's position is far closer to that of Lemley and Frischmann than either seems willing to admit. Like them, he is committed to the view that open-access arrangements for information resources can in some circumstances be efficient.[59] More fundamentally, Demsetz's theories of rational action and of society are shared by Lemley and Frischmann. That is, even as they take issue with the policy prescriptions linked with the absolute protection approach to copyright, these critics retain Demsetz's commitment to the presupposi-tions of economic theory more generally. As we shall see, this blunts the critical edge of the conceptual tools they invoke to contest the absolute protection approach, and limits their ability to devise real alternatives to that approach.

The immediate focus of Demsetz's analysis in the 1967 essay is on the emergence of private property rights in land among certain groups of indigenous people in parts of North America in the early eighteenth century, but the most abstract statement of its central thesis is as follows: 'property rights develop to internalize externalities when the gains of internalization become larger than the cost of internalization'[60] – typically because technological change or the opening of new markets raises the value of a resource to such an extent that it becomes cost-effective to internalize costs that were previously experienced as extern-alities. Although Demsetz mentioned intellectual property rights only in passing, he appeared to endorse the notion that changes to their structure could be explained in the same way as changes to property rights in land.[61] As far as copyright is concerned, Demsetz's analysis can therefore

---

[59] Demsetz, 'Frischmann's View', 130.

[60] Demsetz, 'Toward a Theory', 350. As Merrill has helpfully pointed out, Demsetz actually identified three distinct kinds of externality that could be internalized by means of property rights: the external benefits that arise from investments in open-access resources, the external costs that arise from dissipation of open-access resources, and the external costs that arise from transacting over the use of open-access resources (T. W. Merrill, 'The Demsetz Thesis and the Evolution of Property Rights', *Journal of Legal Studies*, 31 (2002), 331).

[61] Towards the end of his essay, Demsetz suggests that the externality issues that arise in relation to open-access 'ideas' are 'closely analogous to those which arise in the land ownership example' ('Toward a Theory', 359), and thus can be dealt with by the same means: internalisation via property rights in 'ideas'.

be taken as suggesting that an expansion in its scope might be expected to occur when new information and communications technologies raise the value of existing information goods by facilitating new means of access to and enjoyment of them, and lowering fencing and transaction costs in relation to them. This enhanced value leads to modifications in property rights[62] to enable the appropriation of that value by the creators of these resources as long as the social cost of controlling the new uses is exceeded by the social benefit of doing so.

There is no shortage of copyright-law-and-economics scholarship exhibiting a broadly Demsetzian approach to the phenomenon of copyright expansion: indeed it has become a commonplace of this scholarship that the scope of copyright has in fact expanded to enable the internalization to the copyright owner of the beneficial effects of using information goods as the value of information goods has increased and technologies and markets have emerged to make internalization seem more beneficial.[63] Hence Brett Frischmann has asserted that as a method of predicting where copyright law is currently heading, the Demsetzian approach 'hardly seems controversial'.[64] However Frischmann insists that Demsetz's essay has also been read by some L&E scholars (whether or not Demsetz intended this reading) as carrying a strong normative message: that the continual evolution of private property rights towards a condition of complete security, absolute breadth/depth, perfect definition and full exchangeability is *desirable*. In an article recently co-written with Frischmann, Mark Lemley lends his support to this claim.[65] The preoccupation of these scholars, then, has been with the normative thesis

---

[62] These could be achieved by means of self-help fencing measures such as encryption, social norms-based property systems, copyright reforms, legal prohibitions on the circumvention of self-help fencing measures, or all of these.

[63] See in particular R. P. Merges 'One Hundred Years of Solicitude', *California Law Review*, 88 (2000), 2187 and B. Depoorter, 'The Several Lives of Mickey Mouse: The Expanding Boundaries of Intellectual Property Law', *Virginia Journal of Law and Technology*, 9(4) (2004), 14–15. Some of Wendy Gordon's work also fits into this category: see esp. W. J. Gordon, 'Introduction', in W. J. Gordon and R. Watt (eds.), *The Economics of Copyright* (Cheltenham: Edward Elgar, 2003). Gordon does not cite Demsetz here, but her account is consistent with his analysis.

[64] Frischmann, 'Evaluating the Demsetzian Trend', 651.

[65] Frischmann and Lemley, 'Spillovers', 265–6. Here again, though, there is an acknowledgement that this normative 'Demsetzian' theory was not necessarily Demsetz's own position. See also Lemley, 'Ex Ante', 148, n. 74, arguing that the assumption of absolute protection theorists that information goods would not be produced at socially optimal levels unless their full social value could be captured by their producers 'is an unwarranted extension of Harold Demsetz's argument that property rights limit the creation of

that – rightly or wrongly – has been attributed to Harold Demsetz, for it
is this thesis that in their view legitimates the continuing expansion of
copyright's scope towards the horizon of full ownership of creative
works. Their concern is to contest this normative argument for enabling
the private appropriation of a given work's full value, and to show why a
more modest copyright regime is preferable. In Section 4 I consider how
they prosecute this task.

In what remains of this section, however, I examine Demsetz's recent
clarification of what his original essay was intended to say. This foregrounds a quite different dimension to Demsetz's analysis than the
normative thesis that concerns Lemley and Frischmann – his *descriptive*
claims, together with the normative vision of society and rationality that
is implied by these claims. It will be shown in Section 4 that these claims
and this vision are also presupposed in the work of Lemley and
Frischmann in so far as they join Demsetz in adopting the premises of
economic theory, and that this limits their ability to justify restrictions on
the scope of copyright. However the first step towards clearing the way
for a consideration of these issues is to dispense with the suggestion that
the normative thesis Frischmann and Lemley describe as 'Demsetzian' is
necessarily embedded in or implied by Demsetz's theory of property
rights.

In a recent rejoinder to Frischmann's attack on 'his' normative thesis,
Demsetz himself has definitively refuted this suggestion.[66] In particular,
he contests the reading of his article that yields this normative thesis, a
reading in which private property rights figure as 'natural' results of a
spontaneous evolutionary process. It is not surprising that Demsetz
has distanced himself from this reading, because it is clearly impossible
to argue that property rights emerge spontaneously; and indeed on
Demsetz's own account they necessarily originate with a positive decision to stake a claim to a valuable resource and to back this claim with
the assertion of a power to exclude, followed if necessary by practices of
exclusion. Demsetz's analysis implies that, far from being natural,
private property is thoroughly bound up with power and actual or
potential resistance to power.[67] Further, where the power to exclude is

---

uncompensated externalities ... Demsetz did not argue that all externalities must be
internalized.'
[66] Demsetz, 'Frischmann's View'.
[67] S. Banner, 'Transitions Between Property Regimes', *Journal of Legal Studies*, 31 (2002),
359 (powerful groups who have most to gain from introducing or extending property
rights are likely to push the propertization process forward).

legally endorsed, the decision to endorse it is invariably itself preceded by a decision to pursue that endorsement. Again, these initiatives of claiming and granting legal rights cannot possibly be regarded as occurring 'spontaneously' (although L&E scholars of all stripes certainly seem attracted to the notion that one form of law making – common law adjudication – somehow adapts legal norms 'organically' to social norms emerging spontaneously from human interaction).[68] Demsetz in his recent work makes clear that he intends to argue only that 'a cost–benefit calculus will drive *legislation* toward (or away from) privatization' in those areas of property law that – like copyright law – are products of legislation.[69] Further, the parenthetical words in this formulation drive home his point that 'communal rights are the more efficient social arrangement under some circumstances'.[70] Thus although there has been a general historical trend towards the institutionalization of private property regimes, evidence of a contrary movement – from private property to open access – in some contexts (including that of copyright) can, he insists, be accommodated by his theory:

> When the costs of preventing involuntary takings rise, as they have during the last decade in regard to computerized music downloading and computer disk copying, society shifts to greater tolerance of communal rights in the use of the involved resources, at least until cheaper methods of monitoring involuntarily arranged "takings" arise. All this is in accord with the theory of institutional change discussed in "Toward a Theory [of Property Rights]" ...[71]

Yet despite these disavowals and clarifications, certain unproblematized assumptions are nonetheless embedded in Demsetz's analysis. The analysis implies that the taint of merely individual interest and decision that motivates the emergence and development (or not) of private property rights is ultimately negated by the *social* welfare gains that attend these rights (or their absence) *by virtue of* their origins in

---

[68] See e.g. T. Palmer, 'Intellectual Property: A Non-Posnerian Law and Economics Approach', *Hamline Law Review* (1989), 261. Although Palmer distinguishes his position from Richard Posner's, Posner himself also privileges common law decision making as more likely than legislation to lead to efficient regimes of intellectual property rights (W. M. Landes and R. A. Posner, *The Economic Structure of Intellectual Property Law* (Cambridge, MA: Harvard University Press, 2003), p. 417), though he adopts a very broad understanding of the 'common law' as referring 'not only to judge-created bodies of law but also to judge-created doctrines that fill gaps or resolve ambiguities in statutes or constitutions' (*ibid.*, p. 417, n. 25).

[69] Demsetz, 'Frischmann's View', 129 (emphasis added).     [70] *Ibid.*, 130.     [71] *Ibid.*, 131.

individual interests and decisions. As far as Demsetz is concerned, this in turn entails only uncontroversial descriptive claims: that society is constituted by private parties;[72] that, collectively, these parties 'positively value efficiency'[73] and strive (though not necessarily consciously)[74] to maximize social welfare; that social welfare is the aggregate of individual utilities; and that the aggregation of these utilities is achieved by the market. (For Demsetz, there is no social phenomenon that lies outside the market: even that which appears as the market's outside is in truth a product of the market considered as a mechanism for achieving efficiency. 'Just as the market dictates that there will be no good X if the cost of producing X exceeds what people are willing to pay for it, so *the market dictates that there will be no market* if the cost of producing the market exceeds what people are willing to pay for it.'[75] Thus 'efficiency [can] be gained in some instances by not having markets'.)[76] Even if Demsetz is right about the purely descriptive character of these claims – and in so far as they describe an ideal market order that cannot be achieved in practice,[77] they are in fact highly *pre*scriptive in nature – they are not as modest or uncontroversial as he seems to think, for they advance an eminently contestable theory of social interaction. It is difficult to ignore the implications that arise from Demsetz's identification of the private individual as the fundamental unit of his analysis, and his singling out of efficiency – the achievement of given ends at least cost – as that which individuals 'value' (whatever particular ends they may value). The implications are that the liberty of individuals to pursue their own wants is the normative foundation of social life; that the pursuit of these wants by the most effective means is the essence of rational individual action; and that price is the necessary mechanism by which individual liberties can be made compatible with social order (prices being market-generated regulatory signals that coordinate utility-maximizing actions). Here the methodological individualism which is the hallmark of economic theorizing shades into a utilitarian liberalism that produces a very powerful normative message indeed – albeit one that is so taken for granted by both Demsetz and his interlocutors as to escape thematization by any of them.

---

[72]  *Ibid.*, 132.    [73]  *Ibid.*, 128.    [74]  Demsetz, 'Toward a Theory', 350.
[75]  Demsetz, 'Frischmann's View', 132 (emphasis added). See n. 19 above for an explanation of the dual significance of the category of 'the market' within economic theory.
[76]  Demsetz, 'Frischmann's View', 130, n. 3.    [77]  Slater and Tonkiss, *Market Society*, ch. 5.

## Beyond Demsetz? Copyright infringement as 'good' free-riding

Mark Lemley engages explicitly with none of these dimensions of Demsetz's thought, focusing instead on attacking the pro-propertization thesis that he characterizes as 'Demsetzian'. Yet in so far as he defends economic theory as the appropriate framework for prosecuting his case against the absolute propertization of information, Lemley's critique of 'Demsetzianiam' is simultaneously an implied endorsement of Demsetz's social theory and his utilitarian–liberal philosophy of action. Occasionally this endorsement of the premises of economic theory has been explicit: thus in 'Property, Intellectual Property and Free-Riding', Lemley insists that despite its inability to give one right answer to the question of how much IP protection is socially optimal, the economic analysis of intellectual property law still offers an objectivity and a determinacy that is missing from non-economic discourses that proceed from 'nonutilitarian first principles'.[78] Here too he suggests that it is simply not worth discussing any value other than efficiency when evaluating the intellectual property system.[79]

Elsewhere, however, Lemley seems less sure about precisely this point. In a more recent article, co-written with Brett Frischmann, he appears to insist upon the *limits* of efficiency analysis in understanding how the use of information resources ought to be regulated. In 'Spillovers' Frischmann and Lemley argue that the market mechanism may systematically under-record 'societal demand' (as distinct from private demand measured by willingness to pay) for access to and use of – among other information goods – copyright works. Likening information in this respect to other intangible 'infrastructural resources' such as education, they claim that some uses of these resources may be socially desirable, and yet *prevented* if the attempt is made to internalize them to market exchanges underpinned by property rights. This argument entails that property rights and contractual arrangements *cannot and should not* internalize all the social benefits of using information. Acknowledging that 'the conventional law and economics thinking about externalities is that they are a bad thing, a market failure in need of correction',[80] Frischmann and Lemley argue that this thinking is flawed in relation to what they call 'innovation spillovers': uncompensated benefits generated by the activity of producing information. They propose a new theory that

---

[78] Lemley, 'Property', 1065.   [79] *Ibid.*, n. 135.   [80] Lemley, 'Spillovers', 299.

can account for both the need to incentivize this activity and the need
to make room for innovation spillovers that are good for society: 'infrastructure theory gives us powerful demand-side reasons for incorporating and sustaining commons within IP rights systems, and therefore for
refusing to try to achieve full internalization of spillovers ... IP is [best
regarded as] a mixed system of private rights and commons – a semi-
commons – designed to generate both incentives and externalities'.[81]

Yet it is not entirely clear what is new about this new theory. On one
level, it can be read as a conventional economic theory of property
rights – a Demsetzian theory, in fact – adjusted to account for the
peculiarities of information as an inexhaustible and infinitely shareable
resource. These peculiarities, Frischmann and Lemley seem to be suggesting (in a thoroughly Demsetzian vein), mean that 'even where internalizing externalities increases incentives to invest, the social costs of
relying on property rights to do so still may exceed the benefits'.[82] Where
this is the case, property rights in information must be 'balanced' by
commons (open access) arrangements to yield the incentives-access
equilibrium reminiscent of traditional copyright-law-and-economics.
So far, so familiar. But at least their position is consistent when read in
this way: it is recognizably, as they say, an 'economic theory ... [of] IP'[83]
even if not the 'alternative' economic theory they would like it to be.
However another way of interpreting their argument is that positive
externalities arising from the use of information ought not to be internalized because society would be worse off, *in some sense that cannot be
grasped using a cost–benefit equation*, if they were.[84] This reading suggests itself where the authors discuss the socially valuable spillovers
enabled by the intellectual 'commons' maintained by copyright law,
comprising e.g. general ideas, facts and excepted uses. 'Creating and
consuming creative expression of different types develops human capital,
educates, and socializes in a manner that benefits not only creators
and consumers but also nonparticipants.'[85] Many exemplary excepted

---

[81] *Ibid.*, 282.    [82] *Ibid.*, 258.    [83] *Ibid.*, 257 (emphasis added).

[84] John P. Duffy also notes this conflict between Demsetz's theory and Lemley's view that
there is no need to fully internalize benefits arising from the use of information:
'Demsetz's theory views external harms and benefits as always providing a potential
justification (subject to cost considerations) for the extension of property rights;
Lemley's theory of intellectual property posits some natural stopping point beyond
which the existence of external benefits provide no justification for more property rights'
('Intellectual Property Isolationism and the Average Cost Thesis', *Texas Law Review*, 83
(2005), 1077, 1077).

[85] Lemley, 'Spillovers', 285.

uses – such as fair uses for educational or critical purposes – are attended by these kinds of benefit.[86] Moreover:

> observing and measuring these spillover benefits is probably an impossible task. That is our point, in fact. As a society, on the whole, we recognize the value of active, widespread participation in these types of activities, and we know that creative expression is essential to participation. Thus, we encourage common access to and use of expression for these types of activities. Doing so provides a justification for a fair use doctrine based on public benefit . . . [87]

But what kind of public benefit is this, exactly? From the perspective of economic theory, it may only be represented as the aggregate of the benefits accruing to *individuals* as the consequence of 'creating and consuming . . . expression of different types'. Further, although theoretically conceivable as such an aggregate, it cannot in practice be grasped as such: 'observing and measuring [it] . . . is probably an impossible task'. Yet if this is so, the conclusion that immediately suggests itself is that economic theory, even on its own terms, *fails* to take account of the social benefits of human expression and communication, and cannot explain why 'as a society . . . we recognize' these benefits and encourage the activities that give rise to them. It would seem, then, that economic theory's own inadequacies as a framework for thinking about the social meaning of expression and communication necessarily propel the theorist beyond economic theory.

In his sole-authored 'Evaluating the Demsetzian Trend in Copyright Law', considered in section 2 above, Frischmann seems to recognize this, although he stops well short of a repudiation of economic theory and has little to say about what a movement beyond it would entail. Indeed on one level, his point here seems straightforwardly Demsetzian: balancing incentives and access within the copyright system is appropriate because the '"ancillary" social value'[88] generated by using works for purposes related to education, community development, democratic discourse, political participation, and the like cannot realistically be internalized due to 'collective action problems, imperfect information, transaction costs, and the diffuseness of [its] distribution'.[89] In other words, Frischmann's argument here seems to be that subjecting these uses to rights of private property would be *inefficient*, because any incentive-relevant gains achieved by subjecting them to the price mechanism

---

[86] *Ibid.*, 288–9.   [87] *Ibid.*, 289.   [88] Frischmann, 'Evaluating the Demsetzian Trend', 670.
[89] *Ibid.*, 664.

would be outweighed by the cost of internalization.[90] Yet he seems also to regard these kinds of uses as posing a problem that cannot be addressed in the language of economic analysis at all. Their full social value is 'difficult to quantify'.[91] Moreover, in encouraging these uses by leaving them in the public domain, copyright law rightly pursues goals and expresses values that are other than economic. Frischmann claims that '[r]eframing copyright in this manner helps bridge the gap between economic and "noneconomic" theories of intellectual property and begins to lay the foundation for a different way of conceptualizing and evolving copyright law'.[92] But does it? Ultimately Frischmann offers no theory of the 'noneconomic' dimension of copyright, and gives no account of the 'ancillary social value' the production of which copyright is supposed to encourage except the simple assertion that this ancillary value is 'well recognized as reflected in our society's long-standing normative commitments'.[93] Indeed in the end, having hinted at the limits of economics, he simply reverts to the claim that 'there are strong *economic* reasons to question the Demsetzian [by which he means the propertization] impulse in copyright law' and that a limited, 'leaky' copyright system 'can be an attractive and viable allocation system for nonrival resources, such as intellectual resources, provided that we can overcome supply-side problems and create sufficient incentives to provide the resources in the first place'.[94]

It is tempting to conclude this discussion with the suggestion that the only normative thesis that can be attributed to Harold Demsetz is one that Mark Lemley and Brett Frischmann in fact share, and indeed must share if they are to remain – as they claim – committed to an economic analysis of copyright in some form. Essentially, either they are doing economic analysis – in which case everything they want to say about the proper design of the copyright system must be said in terms consistent with economic analysis[95] – or they are not, in which case their argument

---

[90] This indeed is Sag's interpretation of Frischmann's argument: see 'Beyond Abstraction', 211–12.
[91] Frischmann, 'Evaluating the Demsetzian Trend', 670.      [92] *Ibid.*, 672.      [93] *Ibid.*, 670.
[94] *Ibid.*, 673.
[95] In a telling rejoinder to Frischmann's critique of this theory, Demsetz has recently rebuked Frischmann for failing to recognize this. Demsetz insists that persistent externalities can always be recharacterized as products of the market, not as indicators of the market's limits ('Toward a Theory', 132). Equally, the social demand understated by consumers' willingness to pay for using information can be recharacterized as a set of private demands awaiting market representation once the benefit of propertizing those uses exceeds the cost (*ibid.*). Finally, Demsetz regards it as simply meaningless to say that

rests on a different foundation which they neither fully reveal, nor appropriately justify. Yet they try both to do economic analysis and not do it at the same time, on the ground that its limitations need to be cured by adding a supplement drawn from elsewhere – 'our society's long-standing normative commitments' (or some undisclosed 'nonutilitarian first principle' to which they are personally committed). Unfortunately this strategy leads only to a kind of paralysis: an acknowledged inability to use economic theory to explain or account for the social value of human expression and communication, coupled with an acknowledged unwillingness to abandon economic theory in favour of an alternative approach that could make better sense both of these processes and of copyright law's role in relation to them.

## Conclusion: thinking otherwise about 'free-riding'

Lemley and Frischmann are right to criticize the absolute protection paradigm, but in the end it is hard to believe that their critique(s) could have much critical purchase on the paradigm. Their shared difficulty lies in their unwillingness to leave law and economics behind when taking on the latter's most bullish representative in the field of copyright – neoclassical property rights theory – and their consequent inability to offer a comprehensive analysis of the social significance of copyright law, and in particular its infringement norms. This in turn, I suggest in conclusion, is bound up with their failure to produce a satisfactory account of copyright law's relation to what Jürgen Habermas calls the 'lifeworld'[96] – the web of intersubjectively produced interpretive, evaluative and expressive frameworks that both enable what we experience as facts, norms and personal identities and make it

there is something called a societal benefit or cost that is separable from private benefits and costs without relinquishing the fundamental premise of modern economics, which is that 'social cost and social benefit are, respectively, summations of privately borne cost benefits [*sic*]' (*ibid.*).

[96] J. Habermas, *The Theory of Communicative Action*, vol. 2 (Cambridge: Polity Press, 1987). Very briefly, Habermas represents modern society as constituted by two distinct spheres – 'lifeworld' and 'system' – each of which exemplifies a different form of rationality (communicative and instrumental-strategic rationality respectively). For Habermas, the lifeworld has priority over the system (which comprises the subsystems of state–administration and economy): the system is embedded in and indeed parasitic on the lifeworld (*ibid.*, 154). Yet the lifeworld is threatened by the seemingly inexorable encroachments of the system, and law is implicated in this process of 'colonisation' (but cf. n. 99 below.)

possible to renew or to question these.[97] From the perspective made available by L&E, the lifeworld is invisible except as an environment for economic activity. Moreover, the intersubjectively generated meanings it enables appear, from this perspective, as an undifferentiated collection of discrete 'information resources', distinguishable from society's tangible resources chiefly in that it is relatively difficult to monetize them. Other equally reductive representations of the activities regulated by copyright law are linked with this one. The reasons motivating efforts to renew or alter the lifeworld's repository of meanings in the process of producing or engaging with copyright works (e.g. concerns to advance knowledge in a particular field, to promote more legitimate political arrangements, or to achieve authentic self-expression) are reduced to nothing other than exogenous individual 'preferences'. Social benefits of these efforts that are difficult to price (e.g. scientific progress, a more vibrant public sphere) are reduced to 'spillover' effects of individuals' purposively rational decisions that ought to be priced – ironically enough – at zero.[98] The symbolic reproduction of society is reduced to a mere by-product of its material reproduction. And as a consequence of these representations of copyright law's domain, copyright law itself is reduced to nothing more than a 'steering medium' in Habermas' sense of that term.[99]

[97] Habermas claims that modern subjects are capable of recognizing three distinct 'worlds' as components of any action situation – an objective world of existing states of affairs, a social world of norm-guided interactions and a subjective world of inner experience (see e.g. J. Habermas, 'Remarks on the Concept of Communicative Action', in G. Seebass and R. Tuomela (eds.), *Social Action* (Dordrecht: Kluwer, 1985), pp. 161–4). Corresponding to these worlds are three distinct criteria of 'validity' – truth, rightness and authenticity – by reference to which cognitive, normative and expressive utterances are rendered rationally acceptable to others. The lifeworld is the indispensable 'horizon-forming context' (*ibid.* 165) of communication within these recognized worlds: a set of taken-for-granted background assumptions that 'does not stand at our disposition, inasmuch as we cannot make it conscious and place it in doubt as we please' (*ibid.*). Economic theory by contrast posits purposively acting, self-contained agents who only relate to one world – an objectively existing state of affairs – and for whom everything in that world can be objectified and instrumentalized. Economic theory cannot therefore grasp either the complexity of modern action orientations, or the role of intersubjectively produced meanings (the whole repository of socially validated facts, norms and identities) in both enabling and circumscribing action.

[98] See e.g. B. M. Frischmann, 'Speech, Spillovers, and the First Amendment', *University of Chicago Legal Forum* (2008), 301 (arguing that the guarantee of freedom of speech under the US Constitution 'functions as a spillover-promoting institution that sustains a spillover-rich [information] environment' (*ibid.* 302)).

[99] In *The Theory of Communicative Action* Habermas theorizes law as simultaneously a 'steering medium' – constituting the subsystems of administration and economy and (along with the media of power and money) directing their development – and an

Considered in relation to the increasing complexity of the modern economic 'system' (in Habermas' sense), copyright law's evolution has indeed been organized around the function of augmenting the support available for the commercial production, distribution and consumption of 'information'. But considered in relation to the lifeworld, copyright law also reflects intersubjectively shared norms – notably the norms of communicative freedom and equality of participation in the process of cultural transmission. These norms are given a binding form in what Lemley and Frischmann refer to as the 'commons' aspects of copyright law (e.g. its defences and exceptions), but also in, for example, its provision for authors' moral rights and (where these exist) its mechanisms for compensating authors for their unequal bargaining power relative to commercial investors. Such doctrines – which together form a regime of cultural rights within copyright law – reflect norms that are legal 'institutions' in Habermas' sense. Together, they have helped to defend the lifeworld against the encroachments of the system – the very encroachments that copyright law in its guise of steering medium has itself encouraged – by facilitating the discussion and critique of the products of the culture industry, and forms of cultural production that defy the latter's logic. Yet this defence does not depend purely on legal

'institution', reflecting and giving binding force to norms developed informally in the lifeworld. Hence law is *both* a medium of the lifeworld's 'colonisation' *and* a mechanism for its defence and invigoration (*ibid.*, 356–73). Here, too, Habermas characterizes new social movements – not courts or legislatures – as the real engines of resistance to colonization and the most effective laboratories for the development of new institutions that could contain this threat. Habermas' conception of what is entailed by law's existence as a 'medium' shifts in his subsequent work, notably *Between Facts and Norms* (Cambridge: Polity 1996), his major work on legal and political theory. Here he disavows the institution–medium distinction (see *ibid.*, 562, n. 48), and dismisses as 'rash' (*ibid.*, 416) the conclusions he had previously reached about the colonizing impact of the legal medium on the communicative structures of informally organized social domains. Yet despite this shift in his position, it is clear that something like the medium–institution distinction reappears in Habermas' legal theory as a distinction between uses of the legal medium that are dictated simply by the functional imperatives of the system or 'the factual strength of privileged interests' (*ibid.*, 150), and those that are communicatively rational (i.e. supported by reasons that are acceptable to all and decided upon in such a way that the basic rights of citizens are specified and realised). Moreover Habermas continues to link free-floating discursive processes in the informal public spheres of the lifeworld with the formal decision-making institutions of the state, although he now foregrounds law and legal procedures rather more than social movements: law, he now argues, is the crucial 'transformer' that converts the 'communicative power' generated by discursive processes in the lifeworld into the 'administrative power' of the state, and this in turn enables communicative power to determine, or at least influence, the direction of both the state and the economy.

institutions. It also depends on practices of resistance to system encroachments: indeed informally recognized norms can become legally institutionalized only to the extent that these practices mobilize decisions within the political system that have legal force. Copyright law is more vulnerable to resistance than most legal regimes: infringements are relatively difficult to police and effective policing inevitably conflicts with well-established expectations of privacy and personal freedom. Hence even where copyright law has categorized activities as unlawful – such as photocopying entire books for personal study or uploading others' music to social networking websites in acts of self-expression – these prohibitions have been widely flouted, and without attracting moral condemnation.[100]

L&E cannot account for these doctrines and practices except via an impoverished language of 'commons' and 'free-riding' that wholly misses their point. Far from diagnosing and curing this deficiency, Lemley and Frischmann's criticisms of the absolute protection paradigm simply exemplify it. The only way out of the impasse towards which their approach leads, it seems to me, is to contest the implicit claim of economic theory to be a comprehensive theory of society and rational action. Hence (although space does not permit this project to be advanced very far here) I end this chapter by proposing Jürgen Habermas' social theory as an alternative framework in relation to which critics of copyright expansionism might fruitfully orient ourselves in the future. This is for four main reasons. First, Habermas' two-tiered conception of modern society as constituted by the distinct spheres of system and lifeworld yields a rigorous conceptualization of the tension between the economic and the non-economic realms – a tension that Lemley and Frischmann hint at but cannot adequately explain. Second, Habermas' distinction between law as steering medium and as institution better accounts for these commentators' own intuitions about copyright law: that it both serves an economic function (by underpinning investments) and reflects non-economic norms (e.g. by enabling critical debate). Third, Habermas' evolutionary conception of society – his understanding of society as subject to historical change, and his conviction that there is a logic to that process of change – illuminates the historicity of copyright law (and law in general) in interesting ways. In particular, it explains both the possibility and the necessity of seeing

---

[100] See generally J. Tehranian, 'Infringement Nation: Copyright Reform and the Law/Norm Gap', *Utah Law Review*, 3 (2007), 537.

copyright expansionism – and the resistances to it – in the context of broader societal tendencies, not as discrete phenomena that could be evaluated in relation to an idea of 'the market' as an unquestionable given of social life. Fourth, this evolutionary conception of society affords a new perspective on contemporary practices of copyright infringement: it brings these practices into view as aspects of a diffuse social movement to defend the lifeworld against an historical process – the 'colonisation' of the lifeworld by the system – that Habermas (plausibly, it seems to me) regards as pathological. In other words, Habermas' social theory enables us to take seriously the possibility that, in some instances at least, copyright infringement is not just unlawful behaviour, or a form of 'free-riding' on the investments of others; rather, it may be oriented towards reclaiming processes of cultural transmission, social integration and socialization from the systemic logic to which intellectual property law (among other forces) subjects them, and so serve to advance social emancipation.

I am far from suggesting here that every aspect of copyright law and the domain that it regulates could be adequately explained in Habermasian terms, not least because the blind spots within Habermas' own conceptions of society[101] and rational action[102] are problematic in their turn. What I am suggesting is that the hegemony of economic analysis within scholarly commentary on copyright law can only be effectively challenged from the perspective of a critical theory of society; and that Habermas' version of critical theory seems a particularly illuminating basis from which to address the very concern that Mark Lemley and Brett Frischmann espouse – to counteract the threat to society represented by relentlessly spreading commodification processes, including copyright expansionism.

---

[101] For example, A. Honneth, *Critique of Power* (Cambridge, MA: MIT Press, 1991) argues persuasively that Habermas hypostatizes the system as an arena of 'norm-free sociality' and the lifeworld as an arena of 'power-free communication'.

[102] See e.g. P. Duvenage, *Habermas and Aesthetics* (Cambridge: Polity, 2003); N. Kompridis, *Critique and Disclosure* (Cambridge, MA: MIT Press, 2006).

# 7

# Copyright and the limits of law-and-economics analysis

JONATHAN ALDRED

## Introduction: the law-and-economics of copyright

Anne Barron's chapter offers a provocative and insightful discussion of the law-and-economics (L&E) perspective on copyright law.[1] Although I am an economist, I largely share her views on the limits of L&E analysis in this field. I also share her concerns about the expansionist tendencies of some contemporary copyright regimes. Therefore I see my main role in what follows as attempting to elaborate and extend her critique, particularly of the so-called 'absolute protection paradigm'. However, in the nature of a scholarly commentary, I begin by noting two points of disagreement, even though they are of minor importance compared to our shared concerns about L&E as an engine of copyright expansionism.

Although L&E analysis of copyright is problematic, Barron wrongly assumes her objections extend to economics more generally, and therefore concludes that Frischmann and Lemley's critique of the absolute protection paradigm fails. She complains about their 'lingering adherence' to economic theory, and seems to imply Frischmann goes astray because 'he stops short of a wholesale rejection of economic theory'.[2] What kind of economic theory does Barron have in mind for wholesale rejection? Barron only goes into details in a passage outlining a 'vision of the social order . . . that animates economic theory'.[3] Her summary of mainstream neo-classical economics is accurate, although many contemporary economists do not share this perspective. But even among those who do,

---

[1] Anne Barron, Chapter 6 'Copyright Infringement, "Free-Riding" and the Lifeworld', in this volume.
[2] Barron, 'Copyright Infringement', pp. 102 and 121 respectively.
[3] *Ibid.*, p. 100.

few would recognize the *normative* status Barron attributes to economic theory. Economists study markets and the price mechanism, but outside Chicago they do not regard them as inherently desirable institutions which should ideally spread to all areas of social life. Rather, the mainstream view is roughly 'markets have many drawbacks, but on balance are often, but not always, the least bad allocation mechanism'. Relatedly, most economists recognize ideas of 'freedom to', not just the 'freedom from' norm ascribed to them by Barron. Much of economics is concerned with defining and measuring (in) equality of outcome,[4] so again Barron's 'norm of equality that refers to the processes rather than the outcomes' is misapplied.

Put another way, there are many different theoretical perspectives in economics, and some of them are less vulnerable to Barron's criticisms than others. One theoretical perspective can of course be used to critique another: thus Frischmann and Lemley can use economic concepts and modes of analysis to critique the absolute protection paradigm without contradicting themselves. They are using one kind of economic analysis to question another. Similarly, insofar as Frischmann and Lemley share similar analytical starting points to Demsetz, that does not invalidate their critique of the absolute protection paradigm, because Demsetz's writings provide no support for that paradigm, as Barron rightly emphasizes. Frischmann and Lemley's analysis should be regarded as an internal critique of absolute protection, 'internal' in the sense of leaving the presuppositions of mainstream L&E unquestioned. Unlike Barron, I believe their critique essentially succeeds, and an internal critique is well worth having, although I agree that they are much less successful in developing an alternative perspective on copyright which rejects those presuppositions. However, I disagree with Barron's diagnosis: it is not necessary to abandon economics altogether in order to make progress here, as I hope to show in the following sections.

My second disagreement concerns the presentation of the 'absolute protection paradigm'. As Barron and others have characterized it,[5] the paradigm appears, at least at first glance to someone new to the literature, as a fully fledged, well-defined, alternative analysis of copyright to the 'incentives-access paradigm'. Critics have explicitly associated the

---

[4] For example, there is a large literature concerned with measuring the Gini coefficient of economic outcomes such as income or wealth (the Gini coefficient is a measure of statistical dispersion showing how far a distribution deviates from perfect equality).

[5] Prominent critics include Frischmann, Lemley and Netanel.

absolute protection paradigm with the work of scholars such as Goldstein, Easterbrook, Epstein, Merges and Posner.[6] I find this presentation of the absolute protection paradigm misleading, although I am new to this literature, and my reading during the preparation of this chapter has necessarily been selective. While some scholars, such as Goldstein and Epstein, may take the extreme view of copyright represented by the absolute protection paradigm, others, including Landes, Merges and Posner appear to take a more nuanced view. Accordingly, some of the attributions made by critics of the absolute protection paradigm appear misplaced. For example, in support of his claim that the absolute protection paradigm seeks to universalize property rights, Netanel begins his subsection on universality by writing: 'Given the inherent inefficiency of the public domain in the neoclassical scheme, neoclassicists posit that, ideally, *all* scarce resources should be owned, or ownable, by someone.'[7] Netanel references the fourth edition of Posner's *Economic Analysis of Law*. But Posner writes:

> Ideally *all* land should be owned by someone, to prevent the congestion externalities that we discussed in connection with the natural pasture from arising. But . . . there is no parallel problem concerning information and expression. A's use of some piece of information will not make it more costly for B to use the same information.[8]

In the sixth edition he adds the following sentence immediately after the previous one:

> Information, broadly defined to include symbolic and expressive goods, is an example of what economists call a "public good." A public good is a good that can be consumed without reducing any other person's consumption of it.[9]

It is hard to conclude that Posner believes that *all* information goods should be owned, even 'ideally'. Similarly, while Frischmann refers to 'Demsetz's view that efficiency requires privatization of valuable resources',[10] Demsetz makes no general presumption in favour of

---

[6] Barron, 'Copyright Infringement', p. 106 mentions Merges and cites N. W. Netanel, 'Copyright and a Democratic Civil Society', *Yale Law Journal*, 106(2) (1996), 283–387, referring to Goldstein, Epstein and Easterbrook.

[7] Netanel, 'Copyright', 314, emphasis added.

[8] R. Posner, *Economic Analysis of Law* (4th edn, Boston, MA: Little, Brown, 1992), p. 41.

[9] R. Posner, *Economic Analysis of Law* (6th edn, New York: Aspen, 2002), p. 41.

[10] B. Frischmann, 'Evaluating the Demsetzian Trend in Copyright Law', *Review of Law and Economics*, 3(3) (2007), 649–77, 654, n. 14.

privatization, a point recognized by Barron (and more recently by Frischmann).[11] In short, the 'absolute protection paradigm', at least in the strong sense that Frischmann, Lemley (sometimes) and Netanel appear to invoke, may have few supporters. Instead, I find L&E scholars including Landes, Merges and Posner operating essentially within the incentives-access paradigm, but appending to it various *ad hoc* economistic arguments. These scattered arguments, often barely more than remarks, generally imply an extension of copyright protection compared to that entailed by incentives-access considerations alone, but not always. Sometimes they imply the opposite. For example, the fair use doctrine allows book reviewers to review books, and people to time-shift TV programmes for private viewing, without seeking permission from the copyright holder. Posner favours these restrictions of copyright, on the grounds that the copyright owner will benefit.[12] And Merges worries about intellectual property law's 'built-in distributional bias' in favour of creators.[13] It is hardly surprising that L&E scholars espousing a strong version of the absolute protection paradigm are uncommon, because as will be explained below, the economic arguments to support it are wildly implausible.

Nevertheless, my disagreement with Barron here is not a large one, for several reasons. First, she recognizes that the absolute protection paradigm barely has an independent existence from its incentives-access counterpart.[14] Second, as Barron points out, there is evidence of the courts, especially in the US, adopting an 'absolute protection' approach, stretching L&E arguments beyond what their authors intended. More precisely, the courts appear to assign rights to the creator as a kind of default, in the absence of strong reasons to do otherwise, and justify their decisions by vague appeal to 'absolute protection' arguments. Third, as already noted, there are various *ad hoc* economistic arguments in circulation which favour extending copyright protection in particular cases. Thus it is well worth examining the absolute protection paradigm in more detail, providing care is taken to avoid attacking straw men. The absolute protection paradigm is best understood in contrast to the basic efficiency argument at the heart of the incentives-access paradigm, so

---

[11] Barron, 'Copyright Infringement', p. 117.
[12] Posner, *Economic Analysis of Law*, 6th edn, 42.
[13] R. Merges, 'Of Property Rules, Coase, and Intellectual Property', *Columbia Law Review*, 94 (1994), 2655–95, 2661.
[14] Barron, 'Copyright Infringement', p. 99: 'too much has been made of the distinction between the incentives-access and absolute protection approaches'.

that will be briefly reviewed in the next section. The absolute protection paradigm is the subject of section 3, leading to a discussion of the limits of economic analysis in section 4. Section 5 concludes with some remarks on Barron's move beyond economics to a Habermasian analysis.

## The incentives-access paradigm

Demsetz states at the end of his seminal article that 'All problems of externalities [including copyright] are closely analogous to those which arise in the land ownership example. The relevant variables are identical.'[15] Demsetz makes a fundamental error here which appears to have passed unmentioned in the commentaries on his article, although Lemley points out the error elsewhere.[16] There is a crucial distinction between information and goods such as land; it is the one stated in the quotation from Posner above. While excessive use of unprivatized land leads to a 'tragedy of the commons', there is no problem of excessive use of information.[17] Since information is a public good, A's use of it imposes no cost – negative externality – on B. The absence of negative externalities implies that once the information exists, the only cost of making it available to someone is the cost of producing the delivery good in which it resides. Books are relatively cheap to manufacture, CDs and DVDs cheaper still, and downloadable electronic information is almost costless. In other words, the marginal cost of producing most delivery goods is very low, sometimes almost zero. The key condition for a (Pareto) efficient level of production is that price equals marginal cost. Hence, unless the price is very low, in some cases zero, an efficient level of production of the good will not be achieved. Unfortunately this basic efficiency analysis is 'static': it takes various parameters as fixed, exogenously determined, including production possibilities. But whether it is even possible to produce a delivery good depends on whether the information has been created. This in turn depends, in the standard analysis,

---

[15] H. Demsetz, 'Towards a Theory of Property Rights', *American Economic Review*, 57(2) (1967), 347–59, 359.

[16] Barron, 'Copyright Infringement', p. 110: 'the intellectual commons is *not* subject to the tragedy that afflicts open-access tangible resources'.

[17] In the limit, there could be a problem of excessive creation of derivative works – how many *Harry Potter* sequels can anyone stand? But this limit is hard to identify. For example, in terms of willingness-to-pay, the *n*th *Harry Potter* sequel would most likely still have value, even for large *n*. I thank Jane Ginsburg for suggesting this point, and this example.

on the financial incentives facing the creator. A higher price may be required to generate a financial return to the creator to give him sufficient incentive to create the information in the first place. Thus the essential trade-off between incentives and access arises. Higher prices bring higher incentives, but reduced access.

Although this analysis will doubtless be familiar, it is worth adding some further clarifications. To begin with, we can easily dismiss nebulous talk of 'resources going to their most highly valued use': the marginal cost of producing the information good is approximately zero, because few resources are needed to produce it. Enough resources need to go to the most highly valued use to permit an efficient level of output (where price equals marginal cost), but no more. Even if the information good is very highly valued, it should attract few resources, because the production costs are so low.

Much of the L&E literature draws a sharp distinction between 'optimal creation' and 'optimal use' of information, treating them as independent.[18] This is misleading (aside from the misleading use of 'optimal' to denote 'efficient'). There is no such thing as optimal creation of information in isolation, independent of use or access, because, at least in mainstream economics, information has no value unless it can be accessed. In a regime of perpetual copyright, the copyright holder in an old jazz recording may decide for misanthropic or other non-financial reasons not to allow another party to develop a much improved remastered version of the original recording. Then the efficient level of investment in creating new information – remastering the original – would be zero: it would be wasteful to do otherwise, even though many jazz enthusiasts might be willing to pay a high price for such a recording were it made available. It might seem helpful to preserve a hypothetical notion of efficient creation, at least as a theoretical benchmark. This would be the efficient level of creation assuming, hypothetically, that any created information would be available to users, whenever the amount they are willing to pay covers the production costs – that is, the efficient level of creation, assuming the price equals marginal cost condition will be satisfied for the book, recording or download conveying the information. But this is not a useful theoretical benchmark because it is not possible using theory alone to measure, or even characterize in broad terms, society's total willingness to pay for the information at stake. Once we

---

[18] S. Shavell, *Foundations of Economic Analysis of Law* (Cambridge, MA: Harvard University Press, 2004) is a very clear textbook treatment.

return to reality, it is in principle possible to measure this total willingness to pay, but only after answering the 'willingness to pay for what?' question by specifying in detail the rights of access to the information. Willingness to pay (WTP) cannot be measured in isolation without assuming a particular access regime.

## The absolute protection paradigm

Noting the caveats outlined above regarding the coherence of the absolute protection paradigm, Goldstein offers the strongest statement I have come across:

> The logic of property rights dictates their extension into every corner in which people derive enjoyment and value from literary and artistic works. To stop short of these ends would deprive producers of the signals of consumer preference that trigger and direct their investments.[19]

This view is clearly inspired by Demsetz and Coase, even though both would reject Goldstein's extreme conclusion. A familiar implication of Coase is that *who* receives the property rights is irrelevant to efficiency objectives; as long as they are clearly assigned, then an efficient outcome will result (subject to stringent assumptions about transactions costs, bargaining problems, etc.). The most sensible reconstruction of the absolute protection paradigm that I can envisage begins with this insight, and advocates allocating all rights to creators, on the grounds that this will maximize their incentives to create. At first glance this might seem a plausible argument. But this is not the standard Coasean situation of 'internalizing externalities': as already noted, we are not interested in achieving an efficient level of information creation, insofar as that can be defined. Creation without access has little if any value in L&E properly applied, and the extensive copyright granted by the absolute protection paradigm creates a monopoly which generally leads to insufficient access, since the monopoly price exceeds marginal cost. So the urge to allocate all rights to creators is deeply implausible, because the trade-off between incentives and access is generally unavoidable.

However, there is an important exception to this general result. Perfect price discrimination, once just a theoretical curiosity, now

---

[19] P. Goldstein, *Copyright's Highway: From Gutenberg to the Celestial Jukebox* (2nd edn, Stanford: Stanford Law and Politics, 2003), p. 146.

seems feasible, at least in the market for electronic downloads. Digital rights management (DRM) systems make it possible to imagine a supplier of downloadable information achieving near perfect price discrimination, through an array of carefully structured licensing agreements, each one offering slightly different access conditions, at a different price. Thus every consumer willing to pay at least the marginal cost will be catered for, ensuring efficiency; the 'marginal price' still equals marginal cost, it is just that consumers willing to pay more face a higher price. Under perfect price discrimination, then, all rights could be assigned to the creator, and yet efficient access where price equals marginal cost is still achieved.

This analysis might appear to suggest that, at least in the market for electronic downloads, the absolute protection paradigm can be interpreted as a legitimate rival to the incentives-access paradigm. But that would greatly overstate its relevance, because even under near perfect price discrimination, the trade-off between incentives and access remains central. To see this, assume for the moment that near perfect price discrimination exists in the market for the information good. The following question must still be answered: does extending copyright as far as absolute protection advocates recommend increase incentives to create over what they would be under a weaker copyright regime? If not, there is no obvious benefit from more extensive copyright. By assumption, there is no loss either, because perfect price discrimination ensures efficient access. However, in reality, matters are more complex. First, *reducing* the reach of copyright may increase returns to the creator, and thus desirable incentives to create. In static analysis, perfect price discrimination maximizes profits, so returns cannot be improved, but this assumes preferences are fixed. Reality is dynamic and preferences change: by reducing the extent of copyright, more people may come to want the information contained in the delivery good. For example, if some types of performance of a song lose copyright protection, they are likely to be performed more often, thus more people hear the song, probably leading to higher demand for copyrighted recordings of the song, and so increasing revenue to the creator. This 'sampling effect' does not depend on copyright having expired. Free samples may be licensed by right-owners as a way of stimulating demand. This has become much more common now that downloads make it possible to offer free information at almost zero marginal cost to the creator. Right-owners who make free downloads available presumably believe that they stand to benefit in the long run. Whether free downloads do in fact stimulate demand for future delivery goods, or simply displace it, remains highly controversial.[20]

Second, some consumers of information will themselves be creators of new delivery goods which build on the original information. Obviously, the incentives of these 'second-round' creators will be reduced under the extensive copyright regime of the absolute protection paradigm.

Third, in reality, it is highly unlikely that near perfect price discrimination will be achievable. It requires that the creator knows not just consumers' total WTP for the delivery good, but the distribution of WTP values, so that the creator knows how much to charge each consumer to extract the full surplus. The plausibility of every creator possessing this perfect knowledge is further reduced in light of the fact that some consumers are simultaneously second-round creators: to know *their* maximum WTP, the initial creator must be able to forecast demand perfectly for future, second-round delivery goods. The total WTP for these second-round delivery goods would in turn depend on demand for third-round goods, and so on. If at any stage present or prospective future creators undervalue their returns, then they will not buy the information in a world of perfect price discrimination, resulting in a large efficiency loss. An efficient outcome obtains only if all creators, in all rounds, know all WTP values. Moreover, these values are inter-dependent: in general, demand for the first-round good will be affected by the demand for second-round goods, both positively (sampling effects) and negatively (substitution effects). And demand is generally hard to forecast for all these delivery goods because they are usually in some sense novel – distinct from previously existing goods. All these considerations suggest that, even in a world of DRM, perfect price discrimination is likely to be extremely rare. Once price discrimination falls short of perfection, then reducing the extent of copyright protection will widen access and avoid efficiency losses; it will not harm incentives either, since the extent of copyright protection under an absolute protection regime is likely to be more than that required to maximize incentives.

---

[20] The study by F. Oberholzer, and K. Strumpf, 'The Effect of File Sharing on Record Sales: An Empirical Analysis', *Journal of Political Economy*, 115 (2007), 1–42, has received much attention for its empirical evidence suggesting that file-sharing had no adverse impact on record sales. The authors have, however, been criticized for not disclosing the data on which they base their conclusions.

Fourth, distributional considerations rightly matter to almost all policy makers, even if, for some, they only enter as secondary considerations once the primary efficiency objective has been met. Suppose again that near perfect price discrimination ensures efficiency. If some extension in the scope of copyright does not further increase (or reduce) incentives to create, then the impact appears purely distributional, that is, a wealth transfer to the creator from those who would wish to use the information, in which wealth losses for the latter are exactly matched by wealth gains for the creator. However this is a spurious interpretation: the distributional impact is typically not the 'neutral' transfer implied here. The reasons go beyond the confines of the absolute protection paradigm, so discussion is postponed till the next section.

I have dwelt at length on the case of near perfect price discrimination because I can find no other defensible rationale for the absolute protection paradigm. But even here, the balance between incentives and access still drives the analysis. The absolute protection paradigm is redundant.

The argument that creators should be given all rights over the *ex post* value accruing from created works, because they are best placed to maximize it, can be dismissed more quickly. Barron interprets Lemley's criticism astutely here: 'the *ex post* justification for very broad IPRs is in fact profoundly "anti-market" in that it favours central (albeit private) control rather than free competition'. The following rhetorical suggestion may help draw out the force of this point. A textbook market-based solution would involve allocating rights over *ex post* value to the party likely to maximize it, as measured by a market test – the party willing to pay the most for the rights. That is, the rights should be auctioned to the highest bidder (what to do with the money handed over by the winner is of no concern within mainstream L&E, providing it is not spent in a way which distorts the incentives of bidders in the first place). There is no reason to expect that creators would always win such an auction.

## The limits of economic analysis

Perhaps the most obvious limitation of mainstream economic analysis applied to copyright issues is its simplistic understanding of the motives of creators. The implicit presumption is that strong copyright protection increases the incentive to create, by increasing the financial return available to the creator. This presumption is a corollary of a more basic assumption in economics, that people respond positively to financial incentives. But there is now powerful evidence from recent research in behavioural economics (complementing earlier work by psychologists) that this assumption is often falsified.[21] Financial incentives may have little effect on behaviour, or even be counterproductive, leading individuals to cease or reduce certain activities once financial rewards are attached to them. These responses are especially apparent in the workplace. There is a large body of both econometric and anecdotal evidence that in their working lives, individuals' motives are complex and money is only one influence among many.[22] It is notoriously difficult to establish a clear link between effort and financial reward. Probably the most unambiguous 'stylized fact' is that financial rewards have a much lower incentive effect in some occupations (e.g. nursing) than others (e.g. banking). This appears partly due to self-selection: nurses have already chosen an occupation where the financial rewards are known to be poor, so they are unlikely to be highly motivated by such rewards. Against this background, it is hardly surprising that creators may be relatively uninfluenced by financial incentives, because the typical financial rewards for writers, musicians and other creators are known to be low. And financial incentives can be counterproductive if the agent perceives them as a tool to manipulate the agent's behaviour. In a copyright context, a similar phenomenon appears at work when musicians release their recordings online for free, to avoid various forms of control by recording companies.

As well as assuming that people are substantially motivated by money, mainstream economic analysis typically assumes that individuals can switch occupations relatively easily. This leads to the free labour market for creators implicitly underpinning L&E analysis: as the rewards to specific forms of creative activity fall, fewer workers undertake that activity. Novelists stop writing novels and switch to writing MBA textbooks (or vice versa); or they stop writing altogether and become hedge fund managers. Of course, labour economics recognizes that certain jobs require specific skills or training, but the analysis is rudimentary, representing these skills as bits of human capital to be 'bolted on' as necessary.

---

[21] For surveys of the psychological and related behavioural economics literature, see, respectively, E. Deci, R. Koestner and R. Ryan, 'A Meta-Analytic Review of Experiments Examining the Effect of Extrinsic Rewards on Intrinsic Motivation', *Psychological Bulletin*, 125(3) (1999), 627–68; B. Frey, and R. Jegen, 'Motivation Crowding Theory', *Journal of Economic Surveys*, 15(5) (2001), 589–611.

[22] For example, an overview of the economic issues concerning non-monetary motivation in the public sector can be found in A. Dixit, 'Incentives and Organizations in the Public Sector', *Journal of Human Resources*, 37 (2002), 696–727.

The possibility that some people, because of their particular skills and interests, are effectively tied to particular jobs (in labour economics jargon, the labour market is not just 'imperfect' but 'strongly segmented') receives scant attention. But it is directly relevant here. Financial incentives to encourage specific forms of creative activity may be less effective because creators cannot change their behaviour in response. So if the nature or extent of copyright protection is reduced, novelists will not switch from writing novels to textbooks, nor will they switch occupations and become hedge fund managers.

There is a more general point here: mainstream economics lacks institutional detail. Gordon inadvertently gives another example by asserting that 'the label "deadweight loss" is inappropriately applied to lost access to works that would not have come into existence without copyright'.[23] Gordon's point may be correct, but there is nothing in mainstream economics to support or reject it. Economic theory simply lacks this level of institutional detail.

I turn now to the measurement of the value of information in terms of willingness to pay (WTP) for delivery goods. WTP is not an *ex ante* measure of value but, at best, a measure of subjective preference once the information is already in the marketplace and its characteristics are to some extent known to consumers. The presumption of much L&E analysis that creators will undertake optimal investment decisions, investing time and other resources on the basis of an accurate forecast of future returns (future consumers' WTP), is a highly unrealistic basis for law making. Demand for an as yet uncreated information good is notoriously hard to forecast in creative industries: it often depends on the novelty, originality and distinctiveness of the good, rendering demand for 'similar' existing information goods an unreliable guide; the exact nature of the good may be unknown, even to the creator, until its creation is complete; most of the final return from an information good may be due not to the good itself but to second-round delivery goods and other spin-off products, linked to the original in complex ways. A single ground-breaking work by creator C may have low value in terms of WTP because it is too unfamiliar to consumers, but its creation may be an essential step in the process of establishing an entirely new genre of creative work, with potentially enormous returns to C and profitable new creative opportunities for others. This point links to one made earlier: mainstream economics takes the preferences upon which WTP

---

[23] Cited by Barron, 'Copyright Infringement', n. 27.

valuations are based as fixed, determined exogenously to the analysis. In contrast, a striking feature of many information goods is their ability to *transform* preferences, not merely satisfy them, so that the same consumer's *ex post* WTP valuation of the good may be very different from her *ex ante* valuation. The consumer's preferences for related goods may be transformed too, further undermining the reliability of *ex ante* WTP valuations as a guide to the (social) welfare generated by a particular information good. Arguably, some goods have predictably more transformative potential than others. Shakespeare can be transformative, but not Dan Brown.

If these latter remarks appear dangerously elitist, or at least lack the normative neutrality of the market, it is notable that 'objectivist' claims about value *also* arise in the writings of L&E scholars ostensibly committed to that neutrality. Shavell provides a piracy-related example, describing the efforts of software owners to prevent their software from copying or other acts of 'piracy' as 'socially wasteful'.[24] But this description cannot be justified without an objectivist judgement that some activities are more valuable than others, a judgement which goes beyond WTP accounts of value. The software owner would be willing to pay for software security measures, just in the way that a bicycle owner is willing to pay for a bike lock. Some economists regard all such security expenditure as 'socially wasteful'; one implication of this view is that security expenditure has no positive value, and therefore should not be included in GDP. This perspective may be persuasive, but it is not mainstream economics, and it is unlikely that L&E scholars can easily embrace it. Their view traditionally owes more to Chicago economics: *de gustibus non est disputandum*.[25]

Barron gives another example of objectivist talk, citing Gordon defining perfect substitutes as goods which are 'identical . . . in all respects that affect consumer preferences'.[26] But the standard definition of perfect substitutes in economics makes no identity claim; goods are perfect substitutes if and only if the consumer is willing to exchange one for another at a constant rate. The goods could have very different physical properties and functions. One attempt to reconcile the ordinary meaning of 'substitute' with the standard definition in economics involves

---

[24] Shavell, *Foundations*, p. 149.
[25] G. Stigler and G. Becker, 'De Gustibus Non Est Disputandum', *American Economic Review*, 67 (1977), 76–90.
[26] Barron, 'Copyright Infringement', n. 23.

specifying *characteristics* for each good. For goods to be substitutes, a consumer's subjective preferences over their characteristics must satisfy certain conditions, but the characteristics themselves remain 'objective' – defined exogenously by the analyst.[27] The broader lesson is that economics has little to say, especially on normative matters such as law making, unless 'objective' elements are introduced into the analysis. Since these elements are unavoidable, a more radical analysis – such as one which distinguishes between information goods according to their potential for transforming preferences – should not be dismissed merely because it eschews subjectivism.

These hints of 'objective' notions of welfare lurking behind WTP measures remind us that as well as its measurement problems, WTP is not the theoretically correct measure of welfare in any case. The difficulties emerge particularly clearly once we turn to distributional issues.

A common assumption in the mainstream L&E of intellectual property is that outcomes essentially involving the transfer of £x from one party to another are 'purely distributional' and have no normative significance – or at least, they have neutral significance as far as economic analysis is concerned.[28] But these wealth-neutral transfers are generally *not* welfare-neutral transfers. The gain in welfare by one party will not exactly match the loss incurred by another. The overall effect may be an increase in total welfare or a reduction; either way, the effect is not 'purely distributional' but has efficiency implications, following the common L&E practice of defining efficiency in terms of social welfare maximization. Wealth-neutral transfers are not welfare-neutral because money has a different value to different people. Typically, a marginal unit of money is worth more to the poor than the rich, so a wealth-neutral transfer from rich to poor is likely to increase total welfare while a transfer in the other direction will reduce it. A wealth-neutral transfer of information from consumers to creators may do either, although in particular cases the effect is more predictable. The creator may be a very rich author or musician, gaining relatively little additional welfare from extra wealth. More generally, whenever changes in copyright law tend to concentrate ownership in fewer hands, then, *ceteris paribus*, total welfare

---

[27] K. Lancaster, *Consumer Demand: A New Approach* (New York: Columbia University Press, 1971).

[28] Barron, 'Copyright Infringement', n. 26, cites Sag making this presumption: M. Sag, 'Beyond Abstraction: the Law and Economics of Copyright Scope and Doctrinal Efficiency', *Tulane Law Review*, 81 (2006), 187–250.

is likely to fall even if the wealth effects are neutral. WTP and other monetary measures of welfare obscure the fact that so-called purely distributional, wealth-neutral transfers have efficiency implications.

The broader lesson is that the utilitarian 'social welfare maximization' of L&E supports much more egalitarian distributional outcomes than many supporters and critics appear to realize, *provided that* social welfare is explicitly maximized, not wealth. In general, social welfare maximization implies wealth transfers from rich to poor, so it favours copyright regimes which have that effect, not 'absolute protection' regimes which do the opposite. Put another way, the absolute protection paradigm cannot reach the conclusions it does based on social welfare maximization alone. One explanation may be the confusion just mentioned, treating WTP as if it measured welfare directly, but it is hard to resist Merges' observation that there is also 'built-in distributional bias' in favour of creators.

## Conclusion: beyond economic analysis?

In light of her findings regarding the limits of economic analysis, Barron turns to a Habermasian framework. I am in substantial agreement with her arguments here – specifically, the aim to protect a sphere of life (the 'lifeworld' or the 'public sphere') from colonization by market values and practices. Overbroad copyright regimes threaten the public sphere by privatizing expressions of ideas, knowledge or culture: these regimes effectively turn ideas into private property, subjecting them to market values and practices. In particular, their value is now measured in monetary terms, by WTP in the market. In contrast, in the public sphere, value is built on judgements which are assessed not in monetary terms, but in terms of the reasons and arguments which support them. The Habermasian perspective is helpful, but alone, it does not provide the basis for a robust critique of overbroad copyright regimes in practice. Behind any such critique must stand a substantive account of the values at stake; in contrast, 'Habermas's emphasis is entirely on the procedures' [which characterize the public sphere vis-à-vis the market].[29] A procedural account of value is not enough. In order to identify to what extent

---

[29] A. Barron, 'What Economic Analysis Doesn't Get: Copyright Infringement, "Externalities" and the Lifeworld', paper presented at a workshop, Emmanuel College, Cambridge, UK, 1 July 2008, p. 28. [This chapter is an earlier version of Barron's chapter in this volume].

expressive works are to be kept outside the market, a substantive account of value is unavoidable. For example, some Aristotelian or perfectionist accounts of value sketch out an 'objective list' of capabilities and needs which are necessary for a flourishing life. Since education and cultural understanding are typically central to these lists, a likely implication is that all humans need access to works which convey the core ideas and stories emerging from millennia of accumulated human knowledge and experience. Copyright regimes should not be allowed to restrict access unduly. Of course, piecemeal developments in copyright law making need not proceed on the basis of a fully developed substantive account of value, but the essential point remains: attempts to roll back overbroad copyright regimes cannot proceed without substantive value commitments.

A similar point can be seen from another direction. Barron is right to emphasize that a key claim shared by critics of expansionist tendencies in copyright is that some values should not be expressed in monetary terms. But it is not enough to sketch an alternative discourse in which values are expressed and contested by means of reasoned argument. Economists have powerful, well-rehearsed arguments in favour of expressing values in monetary terms whenever possible. If some ideas or expressive works are to be kept outside the market, these arguments must be tackled directly, probably on a case-by-case basis.

Despite endorsing most of Barron's remarks concerning the limits of economics, and adding a few further limitations of my own, I would urge caution before abandoning or going 'beyond' economic analysis altogether. To begin with, since most of the current debate about copyright revolves around L&E reasoning, critics need an economistic bridge into that debate. Second, much L&E reasoning relies on a distinctive and controversial interpretation of many economic concepts and theories. It cannot be justified by appeal to mainstream economics, and one need not go beyond mainstream economics in order to reject it. For example, although Demsetz implies otherwise,[30] nothing in mainstream economics requires that social welfare be the sum of each individual's welfare. As any good textbook will state, social welfare is usually defined to respond positively to increases in individual welfare, but the link need be no closer. It concedes too much to regard copyright arguments built on L&E analysis as emerging from settled economic science.

---

[30] See Barron, 'Copyright Infringement', n. 95.

Finally, I see the important lesson as not so much one about the limits of economic analysis in general, but about the limits of mainstream economic thinking. Critics of expansionist tendencies in copyright will find too many friends in economics, outside the mainstream, so they should not abandon it altogether. For example, Bruno Frey and others have examined why monetary incentives can be counterproductive, and in doing so helped to shed light on how expressing value in monetary terms is not merely a neutral act of scientific measurement, but a social act whose meaning can threaten our moral convictions. Amartya Sen has extended welfare economics to include values such as freedom which are central to debates about copyright; and brought welfare economics into contact with a (broadly Aristotelian) substantive account of value, some form of which I have argued is essential to any defence of the public sphere.

In short, while L&E is fundamentally flawed as a perspective on copyright, and mainstream economics is little better, there are rich intellectual resources elsewhere in economics which could help protect a sphere of creative expression from ever-greater encroachment by copyright.

# PART V

Linguistics

# 8

# 'Substantial similarity of expression' in copyright infringement actions: a linguistic perspective

ALAN DURANT

## Non-literal copying and literary copyright

Commenting on the resemblance between two designs with similar patterns of stripes and flowers in *Designers' Guild*, Lord Hoffmann explains how there can still be infringement without literal copying. He points out that:

> The original elements in the plot of a play or a novel may be a substantial part, so that copyright may be infringed by a work which does not reproduce a single sentence of the original. If one asks what is being protected in such a case, it is difficult to give any answer except that it is an idea expressed in the copyright work.[1]

'It is difficult', says Lord Hoffmann, 'to give any answer'. The answer he does give (that the idea is 'expressed' in the copyright work) neatly encapsulates the challenge presented by what is called the 'idea–expression dichotomy' in copyright law. That dichotomy, visited and revisited from different points of view in judicial statements and in the academic literature, forms the main topic of this chapter. My aim is to consider whether linguistic description can add anything to its clarification.

The basic distinction between 'ideas' and 'expression' can be simply stated: ideas are not protected (and so cannot be monopolised by a

---

[1] Lord Hoffmann in the House of Lords, in *Designers' Guild* v. *Russell Williams* (*Textiles*) *Ltd* [2001] FSR 11 at [24], and quoted in Jennifer Davis, *Intellectual Property Law* (Oxford University Press, 2008), p. 48. The design alleged to have been copied *from* was called Ixia, and consisted of vertical stripes of alternating colours with scattered flowers; the design alleged to have been a copy was called Marguerite. The Court of Appeal upheld the decision against the complainant, that the copied elements were not a substantial part of the original design.

copyright holder, remaining available for everyone to use) but the specific *expression* of an idea is.[2] This is an established concept of Anglo-American copyright law, based on the contribution made by public communications to the 'marketplace of ideas'. The distinction is also central to modern copyright law internationally, enshrined both in Article 9(2) of TRIPS 1994 and Article 2 of the WIPO Copyright Treaty 1996 (WCT).[3] The distinction is intuitive. There are ideas that it is relevant and socially advantageous for anyone to be able to apply, discuss and evaluate; this requires that, once published, ideas should circulate freely beyond the specific works in which they originate. On the other hand, creators of ideas need an incentive to develop and publicise them; so the fruits of their labour need to be protected, if creators are to have a means of exploiting what they create and of preventing copying or extensive derivation by others. Public access to ideas, combined with protection of specific forms of the expression of ideas, offers a way to encourage creators without compromising the interest of society at large.[4]

The assumed benefit of the expression–ideas dichotomy in literary copyright lies, then, in a balance it achieves between the protection offered to an author's labour, skill and judgement and the public interest in dissemination and circulation of ideas. Close interconnectedness or even merger between an 'idea' and how it is 'expressed', on the other hand, would challenge the contrast between the two sides of the

---

[2] For exposition of the core expression–ideas distinction, see J. Davis, *Intellectual Property Law* (3rd edn, Oxford University Press, 2008), pp. 27–8 and 47–50.

[3] On TRIPs and WIPO, see Hector MacQueen *et al.*, *Contemporary Intellectual Property: Law and Policy* (Oxford University Press, 2008), pp. 20–9, and Tanya Aplin and Jennifer Davis, *Intellectual Property Law: Text, Cases, and Materials* (Oxford University Press, 2009), pp. 47–50. It is these international provisions which are referred to in Lord Justice Jacob6s comment that: 'When I say well-known [about the dichotomy between an idea and its expression] I mean not just known to copyright lawyers of one country but well known all over the world. Recital 15 refers to the protection of the expression of ideas as being "in accordance with the legislation and jurisprudence of the member states and the international copyright conventions" and is clearly a reference to this dichotomy. The agreement on Trade-related Aspects of Intellectual Property Rights (TRIPs) likewise recognises this dichotomy, see particularly Article 9 (2)' (*Nova Productions Ltd* v. *Mazooma Games Ltd* [2007] RPC 25, at para. 31).

[4] For description of the utilitarian 'reward theory' of intellectual property, see H. MacQueen *et al.*, *Contemporary Intellectual Property* (Oxford University Press, 2009), pp. 7–15. An extract (from E. C. Hettinger) critiquing the incentive view, along with discussion, can be found in T. Aplin and J. Davis, *Intellectual Property Law: Text, Cases, and Materials* (Oxford University Press, 2009), pp. 9–12.

dichotomy in respect of labour, skill or judgement. A lifetime's labour, as well as considerable cost, may be involved in developing an 'idea' (which is *not* protected) as much as in composing a work in a distinctive form of expression (which *is*). So the distinction between ideas and expression becomes all the more important, in that only one specialised kind of effort and skill is protected: the form of discourse labour expended in *conveying* ideas while still being distinguishable from the ideas that are conveyed.

Lord Hoffmann's formulation also draws attention to a further consideration that complicates the expression–ideas dichotomy: that infringement only occurs if what is taken without licence represents, if not the whole, then at least a 'substantial' part of the earlier author's endeavour in creating the work.[5] Substantiality is inherent in 'original elements', no matter how many or how few, how big or how small. But while size may not matter, the substantial part must be 'original' in at least the minimal sense associated with the effort of selection, arrangement and composition that converts ideas into expression (or as is sometimes said, 'reduces' ideas to expression). What is conveyed must not be what Mr Justice Wills, in *Kenrick* v. *Lawrence* (1890), called 'the common property of all the world'.[6] The 'substantial' element of a work must also be judged in terms of cumulative effect, across the whole work, and qualitatively rather than in terms of amount. Qualitative considerations extend not only to formal characteristics (above the level of incidental style or technique) but also to social impact (what the matter of consequence was to users of the original work). One result of these finer points is that what is substantial may sometimes closely *resemble* an idea, even if for legal purposes it isn't one.

Why is there no more direct route through the complexity inherent in the expression–ideas dichotomy? Any plausible response must start with a larger context. It has long been recognised (not only in copyright law but also in other fields concerned with texts and communication, including aesthetics, rhetoric and philology) that kinds of copying exist besides direct reproduction from one work to another. There is edited copying, for instance (or copying with 'colourable alteration' or modification, such as added material, omitted material, rearranged material, transposed material and abbreviated material). There is adaptation and imitation of many different kinds and degrees. And there is fully 'non-literal'

---

[5] Copyright Designs and Patents Act (CDPA) 1988, s. 16(3)(a).
[6] *Kenrick & Co* v. *Lawrence & Co* [1890] LR 25 QBD 99; 38 WR 779.

copying. The last of these, as Lord Hoffmann points out, need not reproduce wording at all (wording in the case of literary copyright; equivalently precise visual design in the case of artistic copyright). Rather, such copying presents an assemblage of material that has the overall 'look and feel' of some earlier treatment of essentially the same idea or ideas. 'Non-literal copying' is problematic because the new presentation is not the idea 'itself', in a form that is *not* expression or is *beyond* expression ('expression' being the legal name for individual treatment of an idea). For the purpose of copyright law, reproduction of the mode of presentation of an idea sticks too closely to its source material and, because it still reflects qualities of expression, is held to have made illegitimate use of an earlier author's skill and labour in creating the composition that has been copied. Only beyond all the various kinds of copying indicated above is there engagement with an idea *itself*, treated in a new way that does not encroach on the earlier creator's formulation.

Because different kinds of copying exist in which the derived text is similar but not identical to an original, a spectrum or scale of copying is needed: from direct, copy-and-paste, 'slavish' reproduction, through various kinds of adaptation or imitation, to legitimate influence and inspiration. Whether or not an idea, as presented, is sufficiently detailed to be protected in copyright law (rather than being abstract or generalised like a nugget of information or a convention that is publicly available as raw material for elaboration) is a question of degree and a matter for the court to determine in trying the facts of a particular case.

The gradation of different kinds of copying is fuzzy, however. Beyond the legal field, difficulty may even be exacerbated by statements about the expression–ideas distinction such as Judge Learned Hand's often approvingly cited view from 1930 that 'Nobody has ever been able to fix that boundary and nobody ever can',[7] or Mr Justice Laddie's more recent statement that, 'Although describing what is at too high a level of

---

[7] The whole passage from Judge Learned Hand in which this quotation occurs is interesting for its insight into copying of theme or treatment. Wherever the line is drawn between expression and idea, it is suggested, will seem arbitrary, as can be illustrated through the example of protection of a play: 'Upon any work, and especially upon a play, a great number of patterns of increasing generality will fit equally well, as more and more of the incident is left out. The last may perhaps be no more than the most general statement of what the play is about, and at times may consist of only its title; but there is a point in this series of abstractions where they are no longer protected, since otherwise the playwright could prevent the use of his ideas, to which, apart from their expression, his property is never extended' (*Nichols* v. *Universal Pictures Co* [1930] F 2nd 119, 212 (2nd Cir), quoted

abstraction to be protected may be difficult, like the elephant, you recognise it when you see it.'[8] These are robust legal judgments. But they appear unconcerned to describe the aspects of discourse structure on which judgements about language use, including these judgements, inevitably rely.

Could it be helpful for the 'recognisable elephant' view of the boundary between similarity of expression and abstract ideas to engage more closely with technical accounts of linguistic discourse structure, in a way that would not be thought unusual or unnecessary if proposed in relation to musical composition or software design? There is reason to think it might. We live in a media-saturated environment, in which nearly everyone has not only conscious but also subliminal awareness of particular books, films, poster images, tunes, computer software and game screens. We typically draw on a mental reservoir of conventional images, idioms, styles and quotations whose exact provenance is often unknown and in some cases probably unknowable. Actively drawing on such material in communicating – in the form of unacknowledged quotation, allusion or mimicry – is for most people an integral part of their day-to-day communicative repertoire. A descriptively clear boundary between echoing, on the one hand, and actionable infringement, on the other, is desirable if people are to fit copyright awareness into a coherent overall view of their experience and knowledge.

## Linguistics and copyright

I want to suggest that impressions of similarity of expression, including in relation to non-literal copying, can be clarified by describing features of discourse organisation that give rise to them. Such description, I suggest, may also help our understanding of the degree of 'abstraction' and 'generality' that signals the boundary between treatment, or architecture, and ideas.

Linguistic insights will be central to my discussion. So it is worth contrasting at the outset the overall approach adopted in linguistic investigation with the rather different way that language questions arise in copyright.

Linguistics, we might begin by saying, is typically interested in analysing language *forms* (e.g. the sounds used in speech, word forms and their inflection, patterns created by lexical items, grammatical constraints on

by Mr Justice Laddie in *IPC Media Ltd* v. *Highbury Publishing Ltd* [2004] EWHC 2985, at [14] and by Davis, *Intellectual Property Law*, p. 48).

[8] *IPC Media Ltd* v. *Highbury Publishing Ltd* [2004] EWHC 2985, at [15].

word order, etc). If we start with this assumption, however, we must soon acknowledge a complementary interest: an interest in how language serves a variety of communicative *functions*. As well as investigating forms, linguistics also investigates how language is used to persuade, to report events or processes occurring in different places and at earlier times (as well as counterfactual states of affairs), to model possible worlds, and to establish and maintain interpersonal contact in face-to-face interaction. Each of these areas of interest has a historical dimension (concerned with language change, including borrowing during earlier periods from other languages) and also a variation dimension (concerned with regional and social differences in how language is used). Form and function work together. A particular linguistic act (e.g. asking permission or bringing a meeting to an end) is typically achieved through use of relatively predictable forms. In a given instance, evidence from those linguistic forms serves as a guide to communicative function; it also points towards linguistic knowledge shared by language users, who have a communicative 'competence' that they deploy in selecting appropriate forms from an available range and in interpreting linguistic forms used by others.[9] Users of a language know how forms combine, broadly how communication functions, and which forms of expression are routine, which are unusual, and which are new.

This is all rather different from how language matters in copyright. Language questions in copyright generally concern what the complainant must show in order to succeed in preventing infringement, whether for financial reasons or in order to control the impact and use of the discourse she or he has produced. The allegedly infringing work must:

- Involve *expression*, not ideas (i.e. there must be copying of some individual, distinctive treatment of (unprotected) subject matter).
- Be copied from a *work* (cf. the *de minimis* rule, which prevents short texts such as single-word names, taglines or headlines from qualifying for copyright protection);[10] to constitute a 'work', the language used

---

[9] Dell Hymes's concept of 'communicative competence' is outlined in Dell Hymes, *Foundations in Sociolinguistics: An Ethnographic Approach* (University of Philadelphia Press, 1977).

[10] '*De minimis*' refers to the exclusion from protection of single-word names, taglines or similarly 'minimal' material. See for example *Exxon Corporation* v. *Exxon Insurance* [1982] Ch. 119 (CA) for arguments in relation to the single word 'Exxon', and further discussion in MacQueen *et al.*, *Contemporary Intellectual Property*, pp. 60–1; Davis, *Intellectual Property Law*, pp. 25–6.

must exhibit some degree of unity and reflect labour in selection and transformation of relevant source materials.

- Be *similar* to an antecedent/senior work in which the claimant has the relevant property right.
- Be *copied*: in many cases, the causal link of copying will be inferred from a combination of access plus similarity beyond what could have occurred by chance. Copying may take the form of exact reproduction, non-literal copying or even subconscious copying;[11] whatever form it takes, such copying will be demonstrated initially through evidence of similarity of expression.
- Involve a *degree of* similarity that is substantial; how 'much' has been taken will be judged in terms of its salience in the alleged source text, not just by amount.
- Be *beyond the scope of permitted acts* (such as criticism, review and reporting of current events) which make up the 'fair dealing' defence. Permitted acts provide a defence that the amount of material taken was permissible in the circumstances; such acts will typically be reflected in textual markers indicating function (such as criticism) as well as by context.[12]

Each of these considerations calls for practical judgements about language, to the extent that degree of similarity between the allegedly infringing work and the allegedly copied work (as well as the function or significance of any such copying) is inferred from the form of the respective works. One fundamental difference, however, between judgements made about language in copyright and investigation of language in linguistics is that observations made about language in copyright take on their significance only when linked to legally relevant findings of fact in the particular case.

## Can linguistics offer anything to copyright?

Given the differences I have outlined, it is sensible to ask what, if anything, linguistics might offer to legal understandings of copying or of the boundary between expression and ideas. You might expect that linguistic insights *should* be useful, since analysing language patterns is largely

[11] Davis, *Intellectual Property Law*, 44–5. On subconscious copying, see the extensive arguments in *Francis, Day and Hunter Ltd* v. *Bron* [1963] Ch. 587.
[12] CDPA 1988, ss. 28–76. For discussion, see MacQueen *et al.*, *Contemporary Intellectual Property*, pp. 164–81; Davis, *Intellectual Property Law*, pp. 56–64.

what linguistics does. Linguistics might offer literary copyright what software engineers bring to copyright discussion of the structure of computer programmes, or what a musicologist brings to discussion of the structure of a musical composition. As Paul Clough shows (in Chapter 12 of this volume), modern computational approaches to textual similarity (e.g. for use in investigating plagiarism) have massively extended the potential for comparing texts. Word forms, collocations and word-strings of chosen length can all now be counted far more easily than previously, and the results subjected to statistical tests.[13] Overall impressions of relative similarity, essential in proof of copying, seem exactly the kinds of intuition that linguistics is well placed to clarify and support with detailed evidence.

Things are not so straightforward, however, even where comparison is made simply in order to identify verbatim or so-called 'language' copying. Comparative analysis of two allegedly similar texts would typically show up only what *was* chosen. Such analysis is less suited to showing what *could have been* chosen, which may also be significant and might need to be shown to the court: was there, for example, another available way of expressing 'the same idea' that differs from the form of expression used in the antecedent text? Comparative textual analysis would not normally be much concerned with what is *usually* chosen, either: is some aspect of the text, as presented, merely commonly available or stock material rather than a distinctive form of presentation? If linguistic description had nothing to say about either of *these* considerations, it would be seriously limited in its usefulness within copyright litigation. Its analyses would offer an alternative (though arguably less accessible) metalanguage for describing copying. But linguistic analysis would be unlikely to contribute much to assessing what makes a given section of a work or stretch of wording 'substantial' in copyright terms, or what constitutes similarity *beyond* copied verbal forms in the vital area of treatment and architecture. Other kinds of linguistic analysis, beyond identification of formal similarity, are needed if linguistic approaches are to illuminate the problem of non-literal copying with which this chapter began.

## A basic picture: chain and choice

Subject to the qualifications just made, linguistic approaches can be useful in clarifying how close, numerous or extensive the similarities

---

[13] See Paul Clough's contribution to this volume (Chapter 12).

are between two works. Creative verbal production can be viewed, for example (and has been viewed this way in some grammatical models) as a complex process of 'chain and choice'. In a more technical vocabulary, traceable to the founding linguistic work of Ferdinand de Saussure,[14] such models involve series of paradigmatic selections, combined syntagmatically. Linguistic models developed from Saussure combine a notion of selection (the paradigmatic or 'vertical' axis) with a notion of combination (the syntagmatic or 'horizontal' axis), and offer a descriptively more precise parallel to copyright's notion of 'selection and arrangement'.

The principle of selection and combination has been applied to most if not all aspects of language organisation (e.g. in the systemic–functional approach developed by Michael Halliday).[15] The same principle has been extended to description of other kinds of text, reflecting Saussure's wished-for development of a general science of signs, or semiology.[16] The basic structuralist approach of describing levels and units of selection and combination can be brought to bear in investigating, for instance, different kinds of conversational move (pre-request, uptake, request, response, etc.); episodes in a narrative (disruption to family or social order, journey, setbacks, meeting with helper, reversal, resolution, etc.); style of clothing (head covering, garment covering torso, shoes, etc.); menus in restaurants (starter, main course, dessert); and many other kinds of textual system.[17] The approach in each case starts from the premise that producing discourse involves choosing between conventional alternatives within different signifying sub-systems, and combining such choices in distinctive ways. Together, any series of discourse

---

[14] Ferdinand de Saussure, *Course in General Linguistics*, trans. and annot. Roy Harris (London: Duckworth, 1983).

[15] A succinct, early statement of this position is Halliday's, 'grammar is based on the notion of choice. The speaker of a language, like a person engaging in any kind of culturally determined behaviour, can be regarded as carrying out, simultaneously and successively, a number of distinct choices. At any given moment, in the environment of the selections made up to that time, a certain range of further choices is available. It is the system that formalizes the notion of choice in language' (see, 'A Brief Sketch of Systemic Grammar', in M. A. K. Halliday, *System and Function in Language* (Oxford University Press, 1976), p. 3). See also M. A. K. Halliday, *An Introduction to Functional Grammar* (Hodder Arnold, 2004), or any of Halliday's more recent publications on systemic grammar.

[16] For Saussure's statement of his ambition that a new science of semiology, wider than linguistics, should be developed, see Saussure, *Course in General Linguistics*, pp. 15–16.

[17] Each of these fields of inquiry has been extensively investigated in literary, cultural and anthropological versions of structuralism, often following a methodological lead provided by the early work of Claude Lévi-Strauss and Roland Barthes.

choices serves a particular communicative function, because of the defining pattern they produce. Conventions that create the communicative capability associated with chain and choice vary in precision and normativity across different subsystems and text-types. They also remain more controversial in some fields than others. For its own core areas, it should also be said, linguistics has over the last half-century largely moved beyond left-to-right ordering of choices towards more complex, non-linear notions of structure.[18]

The basic structuralist insight remains useful in considering copyright, however, because choice and combination are processes that make it possible to analyse relative similarity of expression in ways that have affinities with copyright law's own vocabulary. In a Saussurean framework novelty of expression is understood through the distinction made between 'langue' (the public symbolic code or system, or reservoir of alternatives from which selection is made) and 'parole' (particular utterances articulated from that symbolic code through selection and combination).[19] Formally speaking, to produce a novel utterance – and so be creative linguistically – is to make choices in successive slots, leading cumulatively to some distinctive, overall communicative combination. Allowing for the complication that linguistic structure is in fact more complex than such linear ordering, the operation of chain and choice begins to describe the practical 'labour' or 'endeavour' of discourse production that permits expression of ideas.

The notion of choice and combination can be refined. As a stretch of discourse progresses, each choice is affected by previous choices as well as by the purpose and context of the communication. The linguist Roman Jakobson influentially showed how aesthetic effects, for example, are created in such series of choices in formulating his concept of a 'poetic function' in language that is to be found not only in poetry but also, to different extents, in language use generally.[20] A simple prediction

---

[18] The most well-known statement of the need to develop levels of representation and shift away from simple left–right ordering in grammatical structure is Chomsky's account, early in *Syntactic Structures* (The Hague: Mouton, 1957), of the difference between finite state, phrase structure, and transformational grammars, see esp. pp. 18–25.

[19] For 'langue' and 'parole', see Saussure, *Course in General Linguistics*, pp. 13–15.

[20] Roman Jakobson, 'Closing Statement: Linguistics and Poetics', in T. Sebeok (ed.), *Style in Language* (Cambridge, MA: MIT Press, 1960), pp. 350–77. One example given by Jakobson is that of the 1950s presidential campaign badge 'I like Ike', where the second and third words have been chosen so that, as well as fulfilling grammatical and semantic requirements (which alternative words might have done equally well), they also create a rhyme with the first word.

with potential interest for the copying question in copyright law may now be made: that repeated or cumulative coincidence of choices between two utterances or texts is less likely as they become longer. A more interesting prediction also follows: that similarity is less likely again where identical choices have been made at different discourse levels (e.g. an identical sequence of topics combines with overlap at the level of sentence construction and at the level of word selection). This narrower prediction needs to be qualified. Much of our everyday conversation and routine production of written discourse is formulaic, and so repetitive. Some social situations call for verbal rituals that are repeated verbatim or which use quite restrictive templates for improvisation. Such ritualised behaviour increases the likelihood of items, including clusters of items, being repeated between utterances or texts. With most kinds of text likely to become the focus of copyright litigation, however, formulaic usage is unlikely to weaken the prediction of cumulative divergence: the longer the verbal text, the smaller the likelihood of successive identical choices being made coincidentally, especially at different discourse levels, and the stronger the warrant for a causal inference of copying if two texts resemble one another.

Push this view of discourse a step further. Consider how, if an 'expression of ideas' is to convey what it seeks to express, its originality in doing so must be carved out of symbolic codes which are *already there*. No utterance or written work is wholly new. The available symbolic codes form what barristers and judges call the 'building blocks' of discourse. We might nevertheless ask how these 'building blocks' are put to use in building something. In order to communicate successfully, a communicator starts with his or her audience's expectations (an idea sometimes called the principle of 'recipient design' in text composition). Familiar ideas, words and ways of viewing a topic are presented as an initial reference or take-off point – as a kind of given information – and used as the foundation for extrapolating something new. Copyright law reflects this view in seeing textual originality as an investment of 'work', in the effort or labour–process sense, that adds value to existing raw materials through the communicator's labour of selection and combination, resulting in composition of a 'work' in the related, intellectual product sense.

## Similarity at different levels

When infringement is alleged, the relationship between language forms in question is a three-way relationship. There is the senior (alleged source) work; there is the allegedly derived (infringing) work; and there are norms of discursive practice traceable to wider usage. This last category is essential in determining how far the cumulatively chosen features of any textual version are novel or 'original'.

Texts can proceed in a number of different ways. They can use available 'building blocks' in a distinctive manner to create some new arrangement; alternatively, they can reinforce an established arrangement of formal elements by simply repeating that arrangement in a given context (as with formulaic usage); or else – most interesting but also problematic for copyright – they can use an existing arrangement of language forms for a new purpose or to communicate something original in a new context.

Over time, any kind of individual innovation in language use (and so 'originality') can become familiar, and may be adopted by others and so become conventional. In this way, originality of expression contributes to language change, including meaning change. In effect, it donates value to the inherited stock of the language. In infringement cases, by contrast, what is in question is a different relationship between inherited, symbolic forms ('building blocks') and particular arrangements of them ('works'): a relationship in which the new use is considered to have taken material which has *not* been donated in this way.[21] The allegedly infringing text is not merely similar to the language all around it. It has gone beyond drawing on raw materials and is claimed to have appropriated a specific arrangement of those raw materials, not adding to but becoming a potential substitute for or rival to that arrangement of materials, for instance in commercial or reputational terms.

How can different degrees of similarity between source work, allegedly infringing work, and language use more widely be assessed? The framework I have sketched so far should make it possible to be more specific. Selecting one form, for instance, involves *not* selecting others. So we can begin to appreciate the likelihood of similarity between two works in some given respect by considering not only what is put in but also what is left out. This can be illuminating if we remember that the pools from which choices are made in different discourse subsystems differ in size: 26 letters in English; 40 or so phonemes; a countable number of pronouns, tenses or determiners; an open class of a million or more lexical items; an investigable number of ways of structuring stories, telling jokes, or narrating some specific sequence of events. Choosing in some pools offers more scope than in others.

---

[21] For extensive discussion of the idea of an intellectual 'commons', or public resource of ideas and symbolic material, see James Boyle, *The Public Domain: Enclosing the Commons of the Mind* (New Haven, CT: Yale University Press, 2008).

Below, I illustrate the significance for copyright of different kinds of discourse choice. Generally – subject to my qualification about formulaic expression above – similarity of choices in restricted fields (e.g. between alternative pronouns) may be considerable while still warranting no more than a weak inference of copying. Similarity of choices in open-class, large fields, on the other hand, may suggest greater likelihood of copying because such similarity is less likely to have occurred by coincidence. This basic principle applies not only where particular word choices are in question, but also (if an overall 'chain and choice' model of composition is adopted) in other aspects of discourse structure, including where likeness must be established conceptually rather than with a highlighter pen, because overlap consists of organisation and 'treatment' rather than exact reproduction of wording.

Consider each of the following aspects of discourse structure, starting with typographical design and ending with questions of theme and genre. For each, I describe briefly the nature of compositional choices in question and indicate areas of copyright law to which the aspect of discourse structure seems relevant.

## Design

At one end of a continuum of verbal copying there is copying of features of design and layout. Such features include typeface, font, point size, number of columns and typical paragraph length. We can say that this is the 'end' of the continuum for literary copyright because there is a boundary here between language structure and physical presentation of language. That boundary is significant because texts can have multiple copyrights, and typographical features enjoy a different copyright from the (coexisting) literary copyright in the same work.[22] As Mr Justice Laddie emphasised in *IPC* v. *Highbury*,[23] typographical features should be kept distinct in analysis from other aspects of similarity (including incidental aspects of a work's style or technique, which are not protected by copyright)[24] in order to avoid confusion as to what any particular, claimed copyright protects and what it does not.

---

[22] CDPA 1988, ss. 1 (1) (c) and 8 (1).
[23] *IPC* v. *Highbury* [2004] EWHC 2985, at [23] (Laddie J.).
[24] A case commonly used to illustrate this point is *Norowzian* v. *Arks Ltd* (*No. 2*) [1999] FSR 394; [2000] FSR 363 (CA). A film entitled *Joy* depicted a man dancing to music by employing the filmic technique of 'jump-cutting'. Although a striking resemblance to the techniques used in *Joy* was found in a later advertisement for Guinness, no copyright was

Typography and design matter in relation to copyright infringement because texts can take on an appearance which goes beyond following an established, general style and begins to imitate another particular work to an impermissible extent. Execution of any given design depends on available technologies, function, and circumstances of reception, as well as on convention and creativity; so evaluating originality of layout must disentangle originality from both the conventions and the conditions of production.[25] Layout is still a semiotic system overall, however. So a text's physical appearance reflects judgement and expertise. It may use indentation of different kinds, or avoid use of upper-case characters; or it may number each paragraph of copy, or enter text in a stamp-like text box, or present each sentence as a new bullet point.

The case of *IPC* v. *Highbury* was concerned with design practice and conventions in the magazine industry, especially styles adopted for magazine covers. Frequent reference was made at trial to the so-called 'hotspot' area of cover images, as well as to cover lines and straplines. The claimants argued that copyright subsisted in design elements they had used in a series of covers rather than (or not only) in one particular cover. Rejecting the view that copyright can be held in this way in isolated textual features, Mr Justice Laddie stated that, 'Copyright is not associated with individual elements: copyright is not a legal millefeuilles with layers of different artistic copyrights. There is only one artistic copyright asserted for each cover and article, namely that in the cover or article as a whole.'[26] In design as with verbal text, copyright is accordingly not a matter of habitual choices but a composite effect produced for a given work by an accumulation of and interaction between choices. Evidence of similarity may be presented as a list of features, and such a list may be useful in the same way that evidence of software code can be helpful in software infringement cases. But it is overall impression or impact, rather than the precise detail of the copying, that is decisive.

A considerable amount of discussion in *IPC* v. *Highbury* was concerned with evaluating the impact of fonts such as Tranquillity Roman (a serif font), Stones Serif (a sans serif font) and Rotis Sans Serif (Bastardised). The contribution made by each font to a section of text depended on both the range of alternatives available and how commonly

---

held to subsist in this aspect of style (and no particular similarity was found in the dance movements themselves).

[25] For discussion of the semiotic properties and effects of fonts, see Alan Durant and Marina Lambrou, *Language and Media* (London: Routledge, 2009), pp. 63–7.

[26] *IPC* v. *Highbury* [2004] EWHC 2985, at [24] (Laddie J.).

each was in use in other magazines. Experts advised (in the judge's view sometimes but not always helpfully)[27] on what constituted routine practice in magazine cover layout at the time of publication of the covers under discussion. Of special interest was the range of dingbats used (or small symbols employed in conjunction with text and headlines to create lists, like bullet points). The court addressed the question of how commonly particular dingbats are used and so how far in a given text they amount to a design convention rather than an original aspect of expression. One of the experts suggested during cross-examination, and the court echoed the perception in different terms in its judgment, that many of the contested features of the magazine covers complained of in this case were 'bog standard design work'.[28]

### Word choice

Moving 'up' a level of discourse organisation, patterns can be found in the word tokens used in a work.[29] Words can be counted, their distribution through a text mapped, and (if required) their frequency compared with frequency of use in a reference corpus of texts in the same field or about the same topic.[30]

The probability of exactly the same words being chosen in two different texts is much less with open-class items (nouns, verbs, adjectives, etc.) than with closed-class terms (e.g. pronouns). This will be the case even where the forms used refer to a single, common topic. This difference of relative likelihood constrains what kinds of claim in relation to copying it is sensible to make. It would not be sensible, for example, to suggest that frequent use of 'I' in one autobiography shows copying from

[27] As well as on occasion criticising the expert evidence given in this case, Mr Justice Laddie offered a more positive comment on the usefulness of experts: 'Sometimes the court will benefit from tutoring from experts to appreciate the similarities and differences between the claimant's and defendant's work and to appreciate better how those in the art design the type of works with which the action is concerned. They can also give valuable evidence of what are common design techniques in the trade' (*IPC* v. *Highbury* [2004] EWHC 2985, at [40]).

[28] *Ibid.*, at [54].

[29] On the distinction between word tokens and lexemes, see for example Howard Jackson, *Lexicography: An Introduction* (London: Routledge, 2002), pp. 1–20.

[30] For an outline of corpus linguistics with useful discussion of lexicography, see Douglas Biber, Susan Conrad and Randi Reppen, *Corpus Linguistics: Investigating Language Structure and Use* (Cambridge University Press, 1998). A detailed account of corpus approaches to word use and meaning is Michael Stubbs, *Words and Phrases: Corpus Studies of Lexical Semantics* (Oxford: Blackwell, 2002).

another particular autobiography, unless there is something further to be observed (e.g. if 'I' collocated throughout the autobiography with 'myself', or failed to agree with its dependent verb form, or only occurred in the second half of sentences or the second half of the book). With open-class items choice is still constrained by semantic field (i.e. by what the text is about), and so by the range of other words available to express the same and related ideas, or to represent the same topic, though the power of this constraint is offset by alternative wording facilitated by synonyms and cognates. Vocabulary resources will vary between semantic fields. But networks of related words make it likely that alternative resources will normally exist for expressing any given idea.

The issue of how *far* ideas can be put into other words was tested in evidence in *Ravenscroft v. Herbert and New English Library Ltd.*[31] The case concerned a novel *Spear of Destiny* about the fate of a spear said to have pierced the side of Christ. A number of sections of the novel were alleged to have been copied from an earlier work of non-fiction written by the claimant, which detailed the history of the spear (part of the Habsburg treasure on display in the Hofburg Museum in Vienna).[32] The defendant accepted that he had used historical facts contained in the complainant's work but maintained that this use was of ideas rather than expression, and that his purpose in repeating such ideas was not to copy but to add 'an air of credence' to his own novel.

During cross-examination, the question of how far you can say the same thing in different words was put directly to the author of the allegedly infringing work. Mr Justice Brightman, summarising this probing, felt that the discussion had taken the following form:

> Where the defendant concedes that the language is the same his answer is: 'Of course they would be identical words; we are saying the same thing'; or: 'would you think there is another way of putting that?'; or: 'I put the same facts down, they have got to appear similar.' Similarly, where the defendant is asked whether he agrees that there is a remarkable similarity in the words, his answer is: 'Of course there is, they are saying exactly the same thing'. When asked whether the words are almost identical, the defendant answers, 'they were saying exactly what needed to be said.' [33]

These statements made by the author of *Spear of Destiny* may be interpreted as putting forward the view, sometimes held, that to convey the same ideas *requires* the same words. On this interpretation, the author of

---

[31] *Ravenscroft* v. *Herbert and New English Library Ltd* [1980] RPC 193.
[32] See Davis, *Intellectual Property Law*, pp. 48–9.    [33] *Ravenscroft* v. *Herbert*, 201–2.

*Spear of Destiny* appears simply not to acknowledge scope for synonyms, paraphrase, summary or other kinds of restatement that distinguish ideas from their form of expression. His claim that ideas dictate expression was not however something that the court was willing to accept. To subscribe to a notion that each idea requires particular words for its expression would undermine the expression–ideas dichotomy, which as we have seen is central to copyright protectability.

## Figurative language

Remaining at the level of word choice, further questions arise in relation to figurative language, especially metaphor. Such language seems as if it should contribute something distinctive, even essential, to a work. But this is not always the case.

Metaphors (and other figurative language) are commonly believed to convey new and striking meanings. They are often valued as 'poetic' and 'original'. This view, traceable at least to Aristotle, sees non-literal language as a decorative addition to 'ordinary' language: a departure from ordinary language that is detected as abnormal by the reader or hearer. A different processing strategy is often thought to be used by the interpreter, who rejects a nonsensical 'surface' interpretation and creates an alternative interpretation on the assumption that communicators try to make sense, even where a satisfactory or relevant interpretation can only be achieved if conventional constraints on interpretation are overridden.[34]

Undoubtedly many metaphorical expressions do carry condensed and highly charged meanings. In some circumstances, accordingly, figurative choices may contribute disproportionately to the impact and memorability of a work. If a verbal image is paraphrased it may also be that impact is lost, hence why it is often thought impossible to paraphrase metaphors. Many metaphors are nevertheless not original in this way. Instead, they are 'metaphors we live by' (the title of George Lakoff and

---

[34] An especially clear introduction to metaphor is provided in John I. Saeed, *Semantics* (Oxford: Blackwell, 1997), pp. 302–8. A more detailed account designed to engage with theoretical issues in cognitive semantics is William Croft and Alan Cruse, *Cognitive Linguistics* (Cambridge University Press, 2004), pp. 193–221. For discussion of how interpreters endeavour to make sense, see Dan Sperber and Deirdre Wilson, *Relevance: Communication and Cognition* (2nd edn, Oxford: Blackwell, 1995) and Raymond Gibbs, *Intentions in the Experience of Meaning* (Cambridge University Press, 1999).

Mark Johnson's celebrated study of this topic).[35] Lakoff and Johnson identify clusters of metaphoric use and give each cluster a label, such as 'Time is money' or 'Argument is war'. Examples of metaphorical expressions related to 'Time is money', for example, include 'you're wasting my time', 'this gadget will save you hours' and 'how do you spend your time'.[36] Such metaphors exhibit systematic features. They are conventional rather than novel; yet rather than being fossilised, they can be elaborated in various directions by fresh twists to the conceptualisation they are based on. They are structures rather than one-off coinages: source and target domains are linked by a network of connections (e.g. with 'life is a journey', the mapping of likeness encompasses departure, routes, obstacles, guides, progress and arrival). Everyday metaphors are also directional and asymmetric (e.g. life is commonly viewed as a journey, with a setting-out, changes of direction and a destination; but it is unusual to present a journey metaphorically in terms of a life, for example by seeing arrival at a destination as a kind of dying). Finally, such metaphors tend towards abstractness: a concrete source is typically used to describe an abstract target (e.g. the everyday experience of physically moving about offers a basis for characterising processes such as birth and death, ageing, organising a career, etc.).

For Lakoff and Johnson, what makes such metaphors interesting ultimately is that they are less a property of individual linguistic expressions than of conceptual domains. They allow human beings to understand one idea or domain of experience in terms of another, especially by being grounded, or 'embodied', in our physical experience and orientation in space. Metaphorical discourse is accordingly not an isolated stylistic effect but an integral feature of human categorisation, ubiquitous in ordinary language and with no principled distinction between what is literal and what is non-literal. In this respect, metaphor occupies the crucial border zone between conceptualisation and linguistic representation, and is on the cusp between expression and ideas.

Some metaphors, it is worth noting, lie midway between the general 'embodied' basis of human experience and creative or poetic inspiration.

[35] George Lakoff and Mark Johnson, *Metaphors We Live By* (University of Chicago Press, 1980).

[36] Lakoff and Johnson, *Metaphors We Live By*, p. 7. Among Lakoff and Johnson's other well-known examples are the metaphorical clusters 'Happy is up; sad is down' (high spirits, lift spirits, spirits rose; feeling down, felt low, fell into a depression, spirits sank); 'Wealth is a hidden object'; 'Significant is big'; and 'The mind is a machine'. Each can be exemplified by numerous metaphorical expressions.

They are socially constructed in and for a given cultural formation, as specific ways in which that society conceives some particular idea, experience, or topic. Such metaphorical clusters are often called 'frames' (e.g. 'the mind is a computer', 'Nature is a nurturing goddess', 'adopting ideas is a marketplace'). Highlighting how such frames can have implications for social action as well as belief, in his more recent book *Don't Think of an Elephant: Know Your Values and Frame the Debate* Lakoff analyses the metaphorical equation 'tax reduction is a kind of relief', a frame he points out is usually condensed into the nominalised expression 'tax relief'.[37] Elsewhere, the series of metaphorical patterns used in 500 years of conceptualising copyright has itself been examined by William St Clair as an overlapping and changing mix of imagery, including 'commonwealth', 'body', 'garden', 'piracy' and 'property'.[38] 'Cultural' metaphors of this kind illustrate further the complexity of the division of labour between particular speakers or writers and the common language they inherit. Images of 'piracy' in writing about copyright, for instance, may be highly evocative. Any 'new' exemplar along such lines, however (e.g. taking 'a Jack Sparrow approach to research publication'), has been endowed with much of its communicative value prior to being coined. So while metaphor is usually treated as a highly original aspect of expression, it may equally draw on cultural tradition or give new form to some basic building block of thought. Similarity between two works in terms of their figurative use of language may provide strong, but in other cases misleading, evidence for a causal inference of copying.

### Sentence structure

Sentence structure is a further step 'up' in terms of level of textual organisation. Words collocate (or have a tendency to co-occur in predictable phrases). They also tend to be organised in certain kinds of word order (hence grammatical 'rewrite rules' that reformulate sentences into constituents and the relationship between them: S → NP VP; VP → V NP, etc.). By means of alternative constructions (such as active–passive

---

[37] *Don't Think of an Elephant: Know Your Values and Frame the Debate* (Vermont, VT: Chelsea Green Publishers, 2004). Lakoff moves from describing metaphorical frames of this kind to investigating techniques for 'reframing', often by systematic use of alternative metaphors, within contemporary political and commercial discourse.

[38] William St Clair, 'Metaphors of Intellectual Property'. Unpublished paper presented at 'Inspiration, Innovation, or Infringement: multidisciplinary perspectives on privacy and copyright', a Seminar held at Emmanuel College, University of Cambridge, 1 July 2008.

constructions, interrogative formation, and so on), meaning relations are packaged differently, including in some cases in order to express what might be considered equivalent propositions (or nuggets of 'information' or 'ideas'). As with synonyms and cognates in vocabulary, ideas may be presented in related but not identical ways: similar but not the same, with nuances of expression tailored to functional goals. Optional elements such as adverbials can be added to core sentence structures; and elements can be moved to different positions, subject to grammatical constraints. Particular grammatical constructions and ordering of optional sentential elements create emphasis, visualise events or situations from different points of view, treat information as given or new, and direct the flow of a text in new directions or with particular emphasis. At this level of structure, choices are sometimes motivated rather than arbitrary. For example, events are typically narrated in chronological order, with temporal and causal relations inferred from coordinated, sequential statements (e.g. 'she went skiing and broke her leg' suggests that the leg was broken both while and as a result of skiing).[39] Striking or new sentence constructions stand out to the extent that they differ from expected patterns.

Similarity of grammatical structure may be a useful indicator of copying. Because a sentence contains a string of words, and strings of sentences contain further strings of words, the cumulative effect of choice will show more clearly than for example with recurrent sound segments in the speech stream, which are usually only noticed when foregrounded in verse, proverbs or jokes. But copying is not the only possibility. Patterning of choices at sentential level also contributes to discourse register, which is achieved by choices being made consistently in order to fit or shape a perceived social situation.[40] Over the course of a work by one author, however, consistently made choices begin to create a personal compositional style: an authorial thumbprint (sometimes known as an idiolect) of the kind analysed in literary stylistics (e.g. the contrasting styles of Ernest Hemingway and Henry James) or in forensic linguistics (e.g. the style of authentic sections of a police witness statement or a serial killer's cryptic messages to the press). Analysis of the relative frequency of particular linguistic choices can help in judging how likely it is that

---

[39] For discussion, see Stephen Levinson, *Pragmatics* (Cambridge University Press, 1983), pp. 98–9.
[40] For a highly accessible introduction to the concept of register, see Aileen Bloomer *et al.*, *Introducing Language in Use: A Coursebook* (London: Routledge, 2005).

two authors might each have independently used a particular word, collocation, or grammatical construction.[41]

## Speech acts and discourse moves

'Up' one level again, and we can see patterning at the level of acts or moves that language performs: requesting, inviting, advising, questioning, warning or announcing a verdict. While the variety of such acts can be obscured in stretches of narrative or textual exposition by our tendency to read quickly for meaning, such acts form distinctive sequences (e.g. a welcome may precede an announcement, which may be followed by a warning and then a request; or a promise may be followed by a series of assertions, followed in turn by a statement of thanks or a question or invitation). Such sequences are partly conventional and partly original; the balance between the two depends on the situation and on the speaker or writer's purpose. Note, however, that a given speech act can be achieved by *alternative wordings*. Such acts are a matter of function rather than of unique, prescribed forms that can have attention drawn to them with a highlighter pen. Speech acts become 'visible' only when you categorise the various forms through which they can be realised. The number of alternative exponents for a particular speech act or discourse move is not fixed, but there do exist conventional, canonical forms as well as indirect forms of realisation.

Patterns of speech acts in texts are relevant to copyright because, while there is some degree of formulaic repetition in how people interact, choice in sequence of speech acts (and whether to use direct or indirect, or neutral, boosted or mitigated forms of such acts) is an important aspect of presenting some given content. At a certain threshold of similarity between two texts, the likelihood of a particular sequence of speech act choices having been arrived at independently all but vanishes, with the result that speech act analysis may be helpful in assessing copying. Overlap in order of speech acts, and the distinctiveness of a given sequence by comparison with reference norms (e.g. from other

---

[41] For a general introduction to attribution of authorship, see Harold Love, *Attributing Authorship: An Introduction* (Cambridge University Press, 2002); for historical application of electronic methods of attribution, see for example Jonathan Hope, *The Authorship of Shakespeare's Plays: A Socio-linguistic Study* (Cambridge University Press, 2008). Forensic applications are outlined, with extensive illustration, in Malcolm Coulthard and Alison Johnson, *An Introduction to Forensic Linguistics: Language in Evidence* (London: Routledge, 2007).

texts of the same general kind) may significantly strengthen or weaken an inference of copying even where few (or perhaps even no) identical words are used.

## Themes

'Above' the level of speech acts and moves are to be found a given text's themes. Theme is generally thought to lie on the ideas rather than expression side of the expression–ideas boundary. Developing this view in *Kenrick v. Lawrence*, which concerned similar graphic representations of a hand in a box, Justice Wills stated that 'Choice of subject is not likely to confer copyright'. In *IPC v. Highbury* Mr Justice Laddie elaborates the same point more vividly: 'The law of copyright has never gone as far as to protect general themes, styles or ideas. Monet, like those before him, acquired no right to prevent others from painting flowers or even water lilies . . .'[42]

Like other discourse features, however, theme is not straightforward in relation to the expression–ideas dichotomy. Typical themes include subjects (e.g. a particular sitter for portraits, life in a particular town, water lilies) but also concepts or propositions (e.g. generosity, the harshness of life in the tropics, how rarely good triumphs over evil). Given such variation in level of abstraction in specifying theme, it is not always clear what the theme (or themes) of a particular text is (or are). The very formulation 'theme or themes' opens up a related question: whether there will only be one theme for a given text, or perhaps many. The notion of theme can also be applied with varying scope: it can refer either to the main topic of a single work or to an insistent concern in a series of works (e.g. when used to describe how Monet painted ten canvasses of his Giverny pond in different light conditions, then painted a similar series representing the play of light on poplars, haystacks and the façade of Rouen Cathedral).

Despite apparent synonymy between 'theme', 'topic', 'subject' and 'subject matter', we might question whether these concepts are equivalent either in general use or when invoked in copyright. How far is

---

[42] *IPC v. Highbury* [2004] EWHC 2985, at [14]. The other side of the picture is that, as Laddie J. points out earlier in his judgment, 'If an author puts sufficient relevant artistic effort into producing a drawing or other artistic work from known ingredients, it will be protected by copyright. Monet was, no doubt, not the first artist to paint water lilies, but his paintings of them were protected by copyright' (at [9]).

'theme', for example, something inherent in a text and how far is it something constructed by inference from a text's words, its hierarchy of related propositions, and stated or implied events (i.e. something partly produced *for* the text by its readers' contribution of further labour in interpretation)? Monet's water lilies, to continue with this example, are the subject matter of a number of his paintings. But other possible themes in, of, or for those same paintings coexist at a more abstract level and seem arguably as descriptive: the transcendent power of vision; how what you observe interacts with your inner vision, etc. Similarly, if we ask what the theme of the story Little Red Riding Hood is, a number of possibilities emerge rather than one ready-made answer: the danger presented by outsiders, risks associated with travelling alone, the importance of obedience, conventional gender roles. This is not unimportant, because if theme is to some extent derived from discourse on the basis of how propositions are linked, how points or events are sequenced, and how contrasts are foregrounded, then what we call 'theme' may be associated as much with the arrangement of ideas, and so with expression, as with ideas themselves.

In considering the architecture of literary works for copyright purposes, it may therefore be important to distinguish 'theme' as what a text is about (its subject matter, not protectable) from theme as something inferred from the combination of defining discourse features. Any such arrangement of discourse features might still be questioned as to how conventional it is, or even how inevitable given the subject matter (or 'theme' in the other sense). With incidents and events, for example, chronological order seems insufficient as a criterion of originality (it is simply how things happen). Point of view, connotation, attitude towards the subject and unusual sequence may all be more important indicators.

In copyright, one common illustration of difficulties in this area is that of a courting couple sitting at a stile; another is that of the Manhattan skyline.[43] Each is recognisable as a 'theme' in the sense of subject matter.

---

[43] *Hanfstaengl* v. *Baines and Co* [1895] AC 20 (HL), discussed in Davis, *Intellectual Property Law*, p. 32. Pictorial composition also contributed to theme or subject matter in *Baumann* v. *Fussell* [1978] RPC 485 (CA). The case concerned a painting based on a photograph of two cocks fighting. The likeness between painting and photograph was found, however, not to be sufficient for an infringement action to succeed; rather, the degree of resemblance was considered to lie somewhere 'betwixt and between' the case of a photographed event as simply something taking place in front of the camera and a crafted arrangement set up by the photographer in order to appear particularly harmonious or aesthetically pleasing.

But each may be clothed in detail of pictorial composition, gesture, and lighting, all of which introduce elements of treatment. Without detail, 'theme' remains a matter of ideas and convention. Add detail, and new thoughts can emerge where meaningful choices are made between alternative styles or emphases (e.g. in posture, clothing, and lighting with the courting couple; in camera angle or colour tinting with the Manhattan skyline). Context is also significant. A courting couple on a bench within a story might situate that couple as a trope or motif[44] signifying personal closeness in an alienating society or symbolising a particular rite of passage; the Manhattan skyline might signify a city at rest (in the manner of Wordsworth's, 'On Westminster Bridge') or convey the idea that a big city can be aesthetically pleasing or that all human life is to be found on its streets. Theme functions as an aspect of treatment to the extent that depiction of subject matter *creates* ideas rather than reflecting them, and where the precise idea conveyed is only inferable from the detail of its treatment.

Finally, it is worth noting that thematic material can draw on conventional symbolic imagery. For instance a verbal or visual representation of the sun can signify power; the couple on the bench can symbolise the human family; lilies can signify purity or, when displayed at a funeral, a return to innocence at death. In such instances, theme functions in ways resembling metaphor as described above. In some cases, the symbolism will seem striking and original; in others, it may be the usual way in which an abstract concept is grasped; and in other cases again, it may be conventional and meaning-laden for a given period or style but susceptible to historical changes of meaning. Where such symbolism is involved, deciding whether thematic material is original or conventional may come down to how far the symbolic devices in question reflect what is known as genre.

## Genre

Lastly in my rapid run up the discourse structure ladder, there are general ideas that can be represented in many different ways but for which there

---

[44] Clarifying the boundary between theme as subject matter and theme as treatment may be helped by considering the whole cluster of terms concerned with this aspect of discourse structure, including 'trope' and 'motif'. While such terms are sometimes used interchangeably, it is arguable that 'theme' points more towards the 'ideas' side of the ideas–expression boundary while 'motif' and 'trope', which to many people appear synonymous, have more the characteristics of 'expression'.

already exist *conventions* of treatment: a kind of architecture that surely qualifies as expression in a formal sense but which is conventional rather than original.

One work in a given genre (a timetable, company website, news report, horse race photo finish, yodel, twelve-bar blues, novel, haiku or sonnet) may resemble another particular work, and so be copied. Or both works may depict common subject matter and so resemble one another at the level of their general topic or idea rather than in terms of their expression. Or both may reflect generic conventions. A sonnet need not be a copy of another particular sonnet simply because both deal with the pain of love or have fourteen lines and a volta between line eight and line nine. Each may draw on thematic conventions of the form (e.g. love or separation) and/or on the form's expressive conventions (e.g. fourteen lines and one of several variant rhyme schemes). Genre is conventional treatment or execution. It guides choice of formal elements, thematic concerns and stance towards the chosen subject matter. Jealousy, betrayal and bereavement (which are general themes or topics) are typically depicted differently in crime fiction from how they are represented in a criminal prosecution or tabloid story, or in different kinds of song (which are different genres).

Plot in fiction provides a related illustration. Echoing earlier statements along similar lines, the critic Christopher Brooker has suggested that there are only seven basic plots: overcoming the monster; rags to riches; the quest; voyage and return; comedy; tragedy; rebirth.[45] Plot in this view is a vehicle that allows more specific ideas to be conveyed; it is the degree of specification in narration that differentiates one realisation of a given plot type from another and confers its originality. Incidents, characters and events in plots can all be described as patterns of selection and combination at different levels of representation, in the manner pioneered by Vladimir Propp in his account of the 'morphology' of Russian folktales (and taken up in more recent work in the field of narratology).[46] Plots involve a combination of generic elements (such as the functions performed by the story's dramatis personae) with

---

[45] Christopher Brooker, *The Seven Basic Plots: Why We Tell Stories* (London: Continuum, 2005).

[46] Propp's study was based on a corpus of Russian folk stories, from which he constructed 'a description of the tale according to its component parts and the relationship of these components to each other and to the whole'; see Vladimir Propp, *The Morphology of the Folktale* (Austin: University of Texas Press, 1968), p. 19.

original details, and so blend earlier labour with the skill and labour expended by an individual author.

## Three examples

To relate the different levels of discourse structure I have described more closely to issues in literary copyright, I propose now to consider three brief illustrations. My examples are not aimed at technical legal points but serve rather to illustrate how describing discourse organisation may help to sharpen focus on issues in the border zone between what counts as ideas and what counts as expression.

### 'Shall I compare thee to a summer's day'

Shakespeare's 'Sonnet 18', with its famous opening line 'Shall I compare thee to a summer's day', was published in 1609. The sonnet is not in copyright, though particular editions in which it appears (such as the Arden or Stephen Booth's outstanding Yale edition) are.[47] Even if one or more specific sources were found for 'Sonnet 18', Shakespeare would have been unlikely to feel troubled, given the extent of his versification elsewhere of published histories and the generally different climate of originality and imitation of the period.[48]

'Shall I compare thee to a summer's day' is (or is part of) a 'work': it reflects an investment of labour and skill in composition that results in what is generally perceived as a unified expressive artefact. We might nevertheless just pause over what that work is. Is it the single sonnet? Or, given potential uncertainty about exactly what constitutes a text series, a compilation: the sonnet sequence? Shakespeare's 154 sonnets are usually, though not always, attributed to the same author, Shakespeare; and certain unifying features of style and topic are interwoven throughout. But the sonnets were not, as far as we know, published in the order intended, if indeed there was an intended order. So if the sonnets are considered a series, it is possible (in fact it is likely) that it was someone

---

[47] Katherine Duncan-Jones (ed.), *Shakespeare's Sonnets* (Arden) (3rd edn, London: Thomson Learning, 2010); Stephen Booth (ed.), *Shakespeare's Sonnets* (New Haven, CT: Yale University Press, 1977).

[48] In fact the final two sonnets (nos. 153 and 154) do appear to have been closely modelled on a particular Greek epigram, and most of the sonnets show distinct echoes of Ovid's *Metamorphoses* XV in addition to their more general debt to Petrarch. See notes and commentary provided in Booth, *Shakespeare's Sonnets*.

other than Shakespeare who exercised the labour, skill and judgement which resulted in their now celebrated, enigmatic sequence.

The opening line of 'Sonnet 18' itself, 'Shall I compare thee to a summer's day', is not only one of the best-known lines of English poetry; for most people, it is the only line of the sonnet, or of Shakespeare's whole sonnet sequence (or perhaps of poetry as a whole), that they know. The line appears accordingly to make a substantial contribution to the overall work if judged qualitatively, at least if considered now (reflecting incidentally how time-sensitive such impressions may be). The impact of the line seems disproportionate to quantity either in the individual sonnet (one line out of fourteen) or in the sonnet sequence (one line out of somewhere over 2,000).

What does Shakespeare's line consist of in terms of the discourse levels outlined above? And can analysing its composition help us understand what makes it 'original'?[49] The iambic pentameter, for example, was common property rather than Shakespeare's invention. As an abstract system of rhythmic possibilities, the metre was used by English writers before Shakespeare, having developed over generations not without labour on the part of those who wrote in it. Shakespeare adapted the metre, though in ways that a hypothetical (and anachronistic) copyright action would need to call on expert evidence to establish, rather than relying on its own impressions.[50]

The words that make up the line were part of the public resource of the English language of the period. Some linguistic choices Shakespeare makes are from closed classes ('I', 'thee', 'shall'), others are from open-classes ('compare', 'summer', 'day'). Note that at least one choice brought with it a frame of dependent choices: 'compare' calls for arguments involving the person who compares and two or more things being compared; and with 'compare' the preposition 'to' (or 'with') is highly likely to co-occur. In a line with only eight words, this is a lot of constraint on choice.

If we move 'up' a level, we see that the words of Shakespeare's line are also constrained in their word order. Some fit together into phrases, including 'a summer's day', a phrase commonly in use before

---

[49] For students of literature, co-author Nigel Fabb and I explored the 'originality' of this line (in a stronger, literary sense of 'original') in an earlier work, *Literary Studies in Action* (London: Routledge, 1990).

[50] For exposition of the difference between rhythm, metre and metrical variation, see Derek Attridge, *The Rhythms of English Poetry* (London: Longman 1982). On Shakespeare and the iambic pentameter in particular, see Nigel Fabb, *Linguistics and Literature* (Oxford: Blackwell, 1997), esp. 37–55.

Shakespeare and certainly not original to him. The poet's ordering of words follows grammatical conventions (he couldn't write 'Shall summer's I thee compare day a to', though nearly four centuries later e.e.cummings would write 'anyone lived in a pretty how town').[51] Constraints on word order are superimposed on those of metre: Shakespeare creates something distinctive within what was already linguistically available by combining word choice and sentence structure with metrical pattern. For someone else to create a line simultaneously similar at these three levels would go beyond coincidence.

'Up' another level, and a further choice is made in the opening words 'shall I'. These simulate a speech act of asking for permission or alternatively speculating about making a comparison ('what if I . . .'). Was *this* choice 'original', or a copy from a particular source or adoption of literary convention? The answer is to be found not by comparing the phrasing with any single alleged source but by interpreting evidence as to what was common and what was unusual in terms of the speech acts with which sonnets begin.

A thematic comparison is also made in the line, between the addressee and some assumed (i.e. conventional) characteristics of a particular type of day. Those characteristics are contrasted throughout the sonnet in an (also conventional) opposition between things of lasting duration and things that are changeable: a traditional topos of permanent beauty and mutability that Shakespeare didn't invent either. The opening line in fact plays on a proverbial comparative formula, 'as good as one shall see in a summer's day', meaning 'as good as the best there is'. Shakespeare didn't invent that proverb either. But he did combine the topos with the proverbial expression, and both of these with his preferred sentence construction, word choice, and metrical pattern. Finally, we might note that the sonnet form or genre in which this line fulfils its role of being a first line is massively conventional, with its own fascinating history of imitation and borrowing.[52]

[51] e. e.cummings, *Complete Poems, 1904–1962* (New York: Norton, 1994).

[52] See for example Michael Spiller, *The Development of the Sonnet: An Introduction* (London: Routledge, 1992). Spiller points out that between 1530 and 1650, some 3,000 writers in Western Europe produced a combined output of about 200,000 sonnets, and that the list of sonneteers during the period includes almost everyone known as a poet, yet after that period (or even the shorter high period of activity in Britain, 1580–1600), few sonnets were written until the nineteenth century Romantic revival of the form. A significant proportion of sonnets within that overall number were produced as a form of dedication at the beginning or end of volumes of theology or law, or some other

This (still greatly simplified) example illustrates, I hope, how even the line of English literature perhaps most glorified for its poetic creativity is not purely 'original' but *is* nevertheless 'original' in the sense required for copyright: that of selection and arrangement of raw materials or ingredients assembled in a distinctive way. Its debt to existing symbolic resources is not just a result of the fact that the sonnet is a pre-Romantic composition. Something similar could be shown of almost any line of *modern* poetry, and (at greater length) of most kinds of discourse. Although the point is commonly made that a major historical shift took place as regards attitudes towards originality and copying between the Renaissance and the Romantic period, the process of cumulative 'value chain' creation out of symbolic resources is similar between the two periods. The earlier labour of discursive invention in this case was performed both by some other writers we could track down and name and by innumerable other, anonymous users of the language in earlier periods and contemporaneous with Shakespeare.

### Roger Shuy: fighting over words

The text-type chosen for my second brief example is very different: not an almost universally celebrated sonnet but a book and a pamphlet which each explain how drivers can get more miles per gallon from their petrol. The one-page pamphlet, called 'Savin' Gas Is Easy', was alleged to have been copied from the book, Robert Sikorsky's *How to Get More Miles per Gallon*. The US applied linguist Roger Shuy, who has given expert evidence in many criminal and civil cases, prepared an opinion for the case (which in fact did not reach court and so Shuy's evidence was never tested).[53] What makes Shuy's draft evidence of interest nevertheless is its illustration of the possibility of linguistic evidence as to non-literal copying.

Shuy starts by pointing out that inconsequential changes to texts are often made precisely in an effort to mitigate the risk of alleged copyright infringement. From a linguistic perspective, he observes, 'Minor variations can include changes to punctuation, use of synonyms, deletions, shortened words, within otherwise identical syntactic constructions.'[54]

---

unliterary subject, with spiritual and moral sonnets, occasional sonnets, and love sonnets dividing the remaining number roughly equally between them (*ibid.*, 83).

[53] Roger Shuy, *Fighting over Words: Language and Civil Law Cases* (Oxford University Press, 2008), pp. 133–41.

[54] *Ibid.*, p. 135.

Such variation is important to note even where 'non-literal' kinds of copying seem more significant, because they help to build up a picture of simultaneous similarity at different discourse levels. In his evidence Shuy accordingly draws attention to synonym substitutions, deletions and grammatical variations.

What is new in Shuy's approach, however, is his proposal that aspects of discourse further *up* the scale of textual organisation, such as the sequence of speech acts, can also provide evidence of similarity of expression. He claims that higher-level features of discourse:

> can help to define 'expression' in a way that is different from merely comparing word choices or phrasing. 'Expression' here is used to include the choices of speech acts used and the way they are sequenced in texts [. . .] In the past, the expression value of copyright law has tended to focus primarily on comparing similar vocabulary and expressions.[55]

In the case in question, Shuy argues that the main change made in the pamphlet in terms of speech acts was to switch 'offering advice' into 'directives', with the exception of one tip which was changed into a warning. While such changes collectively bring about a shift towards an abbreviated pamphlet style, and so may contribute to a change of audience and function, they make little change to textual architecture in the sense of a distinctive selection and arrangement of material. The systematic nature and direction of the changes suggests rather a kind of textual reverse engineering: a process of working backwards from the book, as source, to the conventionally different requirements of a pamphlet containing the same material.

Alongside speech acts, Shuy suggests that topic sequence provides a further way of determining whether one text has borrowed its organizational structure from another. He shows how it is possible to describe precisely how far the presentation of topics is similar. While there is some degree of convention in how topics are presented for a given purpose (e.g. in a political campaign address, an advert or a vote of thanks), topic order reflects strategy and is therefore a feature of textual selection and arrangement. To Shuy's knowledge, the extent to which topic sequencing can serve as an indicator of possible copyright infringement had never been tested, and he concludes his analysis with the comment that his 'effort to recognise and use additional levels of language, judgement about the acceptability of the sequence of discourse topics, and speech acts, will need to be tested in court at some other

---

[55] *Ibid.*, p. 140.

time'.[56] The published summary of his proposed evidence is a helpful example of what such evidence might look like.

### Originality in The Da Vinci Code

My third example concerns the challenge of evaluating whether a 'theme' or even 'Central Theme' in one work had been copied from another, an issue which became central to the English case of *Baigent* v. *The Random House Group Ltd.* In this case, elements of Dan Brown's novel *The Da Vinci Code*, published in 2003, were alleged to have been copied from the 'Central Theme' of a work called *The Holy Blood and the Holy Grail* (HBHG), written by the claimants and described by them as 'a work of historical conjecture'.[57]

In their pleadings, the claimants contended that *The Da Vinci Code* had infringed their work not by verbatim copying but by taking what they presented (after a number of amendments during proceedings) as fifteen central thematic elements: a series of (in some cases lengthy) propositions including the suggestion that Jesus married Mary Magdalene and had children; that the bloodline of Jesus could be traced through a French royal dynasty; and that the bloodline extended into a family network containing Leonardo da Vinci, Botticelli and Sir Isaac Newton. The author of *The Da Vinci Code* acknowledged that there had been some local language copying and accepted that he had drawn on HBHG as one source in conjunction with others. Whether there had been copying of textual architecture, in allegedly copying the claimed 'Central Theme' of the earlier work, became as a result a major question for the court to examine.

In the Court of Appeal, four tests were laid out as thresholds in relation to copying. With regard to copying of thematic material, two were particularly relevant: whether what was copied was on the copyright side of the line between ideas and expression; and whether any copied material which did qualify as expression amounted to a substantial part of the alleged source work.[58] Both tests depend on assessment of how far thematic material constitutes treatment and architecture and how far it counts as unprotected ideas and facts.

---

[56] *Ibid.*, p. 141.
[57] *Baigent* v. *The Random House Group Ltd* [2006] EWHC 719; [2006] EMLR 16 FSR 24.
[58] *Ibid.*, at [7].

In analysing thematic material, the court looked first at whether the relevant material did in fact exist in both works. At first instance Judge Peter Smith concluded that some of the elements (numbered as 10, 11 and 13 out of 15) could not be found in *The Da Vinci Code* at all, and element 14 out of 15 could not be found in HBHG. To have been copied from one work to the other, he surmised, relevant thematic material needed at least to exist in both works, a question on which linguistics might provide further relevant evidence.

Reaffirming that ideas cannot be protected, only how 'effort, time and skill had been invested in reducing available facts, ideas and theories into material form such as words, signs and symbols',[59] the Court of Appeal emphasised that the appellants needed to demonstrate that there was 'a putting together of facts, themes and ideas by them, as a result of their efforts, and that it was this that Mr Brown had copied'.[60] This require-ment amounted to showing that the 15 points of the Central Theme were presented in HBHG in a way that differentiated them from the mass of other material in the book, and that a reader would recognise those 15 points *as* HBHG's Central Theme. On this issue, the court cross-examined the first appellant but his evidence was found to be 'lamentably inadequate'.[61] However, the appellants maintained at appeal that it was for the court to decide what constitutes the book's central theme rather than relying on an account given by one of its authors.

The historical dimension of the two works in this case raised further problems, including whether there were common facts reported in each work that either or both authors had drawn from other, common sources. Even if it was the alleged source of copied material that led the defendant to read and then draw on earlier source material, this would not constitute infringement. Dan Brown claimed to have relied, in addi-tion to working with HBHG, on another work called *The Templar Revelations*, and also claimed (though this was not fully accepted by the court) that an early synopsis he had written contained the contested thematic elements even before he had had an opportunity to familiarise himself with the claimants' work.[62] A further problem concerned the chronological presentation of the fifteen themes claimed as constituting

---

[59] *Ibid.*, at [H26] and [141].   [60] *Ibid.*, at [H11].   [61] *Ibid.*, at [H7].
[62] *Ibid.*, at [15]. As in related cases (such as *Pike* v. *Nicholas* [1869–70] 5 Ch App 251; *Harman Pictures* v. *Osborne and others* [1967] 1 WLR 723, and *Warwick Film Productions Ltd* v. *Eisinger and others* [1969] 1 Ch 508), latitude was given in relation to use of historical sources, though such latitude is limited by protection afforded to the expressive potential of interpretive and speculative accounts of history. Cf. Mr Justice

the architectural structure. As this order is effectively a 'default' order of presentation, it appeared too general and at too low a level of 'extraction from available source materials' to justify protection against copying.[63] The court, upheld by the Court of Appeal, took the view that what had been taken amounted to ideas rather than expression and consisted of historical theories, general arguments, hypotheses, themes and generalised propositions at too high a level of abstraction to qualify for copyright protection. It was also held that the 'Central Theme', as alleged, did not constitute a substantial part of the claimants' work; its elements were viewed instead as a selection of features put together as 'a mere litigation construct'.

What is notable about the judgment in *Baigent* v. *The Random House Group Ltd* is that, while detailed exposition is presented of the plot of *The Da Vinci Code*, little guidance is offered as to *how* the assessment of non-literal copying was made. The decision itself is unequivocal:

> The claimed central elements did not contain detailed similarities of language or architectural similarities in the detailed treatment or development of the collection or arrangement of incidents, situations, characters and narrative, such as was normally found in cases of infringement of literary or dramatic copyright. The 11 aspects of the central theme in *Da Vinci Code* were differently expressed, collected, selected, arranged and narrated.[64]

In addition, the central theme was 'not a theme of HBHG at all', but rather 'no more than a selection of features collated for forensic purposes rather than emerging from a fair reading of the book as a whole'.[65]

It remains uncertain, however, what sort of evidence of 'detail', 'development', 'collection', etc. *would* have been sufficient to support a view that there was relevant architecture or structure to the combination of elements relied on; or what would have rendered thematic elements 'of a sufficiently developed character to constitute a substantial part of the source work'; or more generally how a line can be drawn in a principled or insightful way between 'an assortment of items of historical fact and

---

Brightman in *Ravenscroft* v. *Herbert and New English Library Ltd* [1980] RPC 193: 'The author of a historical work must, I think, have attributed to him an intention that the information thereby imparted may be used by the reader, because knowledge would become sterile if it could not be applied. Therefore, it seems to me reasonable to suppose that the law of copyright will allow wider use to be made of a historical work than of a novel so that knowledge can be built upon knowledge.'
[63] *Baigent* v. *The Random House* [2007] FSR 24, at [H11].   [64] *Ibid.*, at [H37].
[65] *Ibid.*, at [H42].

information, virtual history, events, incidents, theories, arguments and propositions' and elements of the same kind which are not 'an assortment' but lock together in a sufficiently distinctive interaction to constitute a central theme. In copyright law, such questions are a matter of judgement rather than analysis. An authoritative assessment is made taking all relevant particulars into account rather than matching discourse evidence in particular to criteria governing how the process of 'work' undertaken by an author or editor is reflected in features of the product 'work' that results.

### Ideas and ways of expressing them

Most of what I have said so far starts with verbal copying and moves up a scale of discourse organisation, first towards indirect ways of formulating ideas and then towards (unprotectable) general ideas. If words are copied directly from a literary work, the copier is likely to be easily caught because those words will be traceable by eye or by means of plagiarism software. The copied words can be highlighted on the script and stand as potential evidence of copying. If a text's architecture is copied, on the other hand, it is more difficult to be precise about what exactly has been copied. Evidence of similarity depends on descriptive or theoretical constructs rather than being directly visible on the page; similarity must be argued rather than observed.

Not unreasonably, treatment of similarity of expression adopted in copyright takes exact replication as effectively its canonical case. Nonliteral copying is the oblique case, each example of which is interpreted in applying the law by weighing up the facts and reflecting the overall aims of copyright: protecting an author's labour and skill; providing an incentive to future creators; avoiding monopolies in relation to ideas; and so on. This raises an intriguing question. Would the expression–ideas dichotomy look different if instead of starting with exact copying and moving upwards towards non-literal copying, we started with ideas and looked 'downwards', at how (as Lord Hoffmann put it, in *Designers' Guild*) ideas are 'expressed in the copyright work'? Would such a reversal of direction, which captures the notion of ideas being 'reduced to expression' but seems in other ways to conflict with a norm of what 'copying' involves, lead to different comments from a linguistic perspective than those I have made so far?

What is meant by 'ideas' in copyright law, we should note straightaway, may not be any more straightforward than what is meant by 'expression'. In *LB Plastics Ltd* v. *Swish Products Ltd*, for example, Lord Hailsham draws attention to a basic difficulty with the expression–ideas dichotomy: that, 'as the late Professor Joad used to observe, it all depends on what you mean by ideas'.[66] Several complications with the notion of 'idea' in copyright stand out particularly.

One complication arises if we ask whether a published work really does convey a single 'idea', or some small and determinate number of distinct ideas (an overall message, or something a text grammarian might designate as its macro-proposition).[67] We might wonder, alternatively, whether what is conveyed is more likely to be an indeterminate number of interlocking meanings, constructed by us in response to signification by the work at a number of different levels.[68] Such multiple ideas might not be easy to disentangle one from another in any given case, and some might be read into the work rather than lifted from the page; but from such a mesh of ideas an overall macro-proposition (or kind of top-level précis) might well be constructed in the process of interpretation. If we pursue this second view, which is not at odds with current understandings of communication and comprehension,[69] then ideas expressed in a work might need to be thought of more as something constructed by the reader from the particular configuration of discourse material than something fixed or ready-made associated with the work. Ideas would emerge from, rather than contrast with, expression, except at a level of generality at which a mostly, but by no means consistently, uncontroversial overall 'point' of the discourse might be stated – more easily for

---

[66] Lord Hailsham of St Marylebone, *LB Plastics Ltd* v. *Swish Products Ltd* [1979] RPC 551, 629. 'The late Professor Joad' was a philosophy professor famous for his appearances on a BBC TV programme called 'The Brains Trust' in which his comments typically began with the phrase, 'It all depends on . . .'.

[67] An early study of the relation between psychological patterning and text structure is Teun van Dijk, *Text and Context: Explorations in the Semantics and Pragmatics of Discourse* (London: Longman, 1977); a more developed approach is that advanced by van Dijk's former co-author, the psychologist Walter Kintsch, *Comprehension: A Paradigm for Cognition* (Cambridge University Press, 1998). A pioneering collection of experimental studies of reading investigating textual 'model-building' is Charles Weaver, Suzanne Mannes and Charles Fletcher (eds.), *Discourse Comprehension: Essays in Honor of Walter Kintsch* (Hillsdale, NJ: Lawrence Erlbaum, 1995).

[68] On analysing meaning in discourse, with illustration from a number of fields of media law, see Alan Durant, *Meaning in the Media: Discourse, Controversy, Debate* (Cambridge University Press, 2010).

[69] See references above, in n. 67. For an accessible and fascinating introduction to reading and reading skills, see Maryanne Wolf, *Proust and the Squid: The Story and Science of the Reading Brain* (New York: HarperCollins, 2007).

some kinds of discourse (e.g. a timetable, news item or magazine feature) than for others (e.g. a poem or work of conceptual art).

The different emphasis in understanding what a communicated idea might be suggested here is not in itself a problem for copyright. For example, Judge Learned Hand's characterisation of ideas in a play (referred to above) distinguished between generality and specificity of ideas, as does Lord Hoffmann's discussion in *Designers' Guild*;[70] and in a treatment of essentially the same issue (and reaching ultimately a similar conclusion), Mr Justice Pritchard in *Plix Products* v. *Frank M. Winstone* draws a distinction between two *kinds* of idea, in an effort to reconcile two positions on copyright that are sometimes opposed in a conflict he considers 'more apparent than real'. 'If there is any conflict', he suggests, 'it can be resolved by an analysis of the concept of ideas'.[71]

*Plix Products* v. *Frank M. Winstone* concerned the design of mini kiwi fruit pockets used in packaging. But Mr Justice Pritchard's discussion ranges across a number of fundamental copyright issues. The two contending views he believes can be reconciled are, first, the view that copyright *does* sometimes extend into ideas, and second, the view that copyright *never* extends to ideas and always remains restricted to their expression. The seed of reconciliation, he argues, lies in the notion that what are sometimes misconceived as general ideas are in fact expressions of ideas. Mr Justice Pritchard's formulation merits attention partly because of a useful term he introduces ('constructive ideas') that seems nevertheless not to have found favour in subsequent judgments.

One type of idea, Mr Justice Prichard argues, is what he calls the 'general idea or basic concept of the work', such as unrequited love, a dog listening to a gramophone, or indeed a kiwi fruit pocket pack. Even if reduced to some tangible form, such basic ideas (which can nevertheless in some cases be 'complex') cannot be monopolised; they will always remain 'a mere idea'. The second kind of idea is one transformed in the process of its expression by the addition of detail, ornamentation and further complexity. For a novelist, such an idea requires characters, dialogue and plot; for a visual artist, it might require a particular tilt of the dog's head, or perspective and lighting. Ideas of this second kind require skill, knowledge and research, and merit copyright protection. So far, the distinction sounds familiar, and is amply in evidence in cases referred to above. What makes Mr Justice Prichard's contribution unusual is the directness of his acknowledgement that both kinds of ideas

---

[70] See above.   [71] *Plix Products* v. *Frank M. Winstone* [1986] FSR 92.

start in the head and draw on the imagination, such that expression in the relevant sense is itself a matter of 'ideas'. What seems more useful, as a result, is some set of distinctions *within* the notion of an idea rather than a polarity (or dichotomy) between idea and expression. Mr Justice Pritchard goes on to introduce his notion of 'constructive ideas', in contrast with general ideas, to denote those ideas that have undergone the development of conceptual material that takes place in the process of expression, and which therefore merit copyright protection. As with other characterisations of the expression–ideas dichotomy, the precise boundary between general concept and 'constructive idea' is not defined, and remains a matter of interpretation (based on 'degree') rather than a firm category boundary. Typical differences are not pursued, either, between basic concepts, thoughts that take the form of propositions built out of combined basic concepts, images which depict exemplars of concepts, and so on; and the relationship between an idea as an individually conceived thought, on the one hand, and 'information' as publicly available data of the kind found in a timetable or list of addresses, on the other, remains slightly unclear.

Copyright law is not a psychology class, however, and it is perfectly possible that the distinctions drawn by Mr Justice Pritchard and others are well suited to the wider purpose. But there is a further, wider issue to contend with. Beyond the conceptual complexity of 'idea', there is a difficulty associated with the varied forms of its expression: that 'idea', like other terminology in legal use, functions differently in copyright depending on the context in which and purpose for which it is used. On one understanding, the notion of an 'idea' signifies only the horizon of what matters as regards the expression–ideas dichotomy: i.e. that expression is protected and falls within the scope of copyright law, whereas ideas are over that horizon and cannot be protected. In this context, 'idea' is a kind or type, in contrast with (for example) 'object', 'substance' or 'expression'. All 'ideas', on this interpretation, are in some sense equivalent: what matters about them is their category rather than their content, such that if something is an 'idea' (a general idea) rather than expression (a 'constructive idea') then what is important about it is merely that copying will not be actionable.

The expression–ideas dichotomy interacts with what makes a borrowing substantial, however, and this introduces a complication into this formalistic understanding. Part of what gives significance to a work, for users, is the work's social *functioning* (e.g. what it is about the work that is perceived to be significant). This quality, which is another kind of 'proposition' (a big idea, or the point of the work), may also be relevant in weighing up whether infringement has taken place. Such an idea must have content, rather than being simply a limit category, if it is to confer substantiality. Yet perceived significance is not an inherent element in or property of the work. Rather, it is a relation between work and audience, and so a matter of the use of the work rather than of its form. The big idea of the work, in effect the essence of substantiality as a qualitative concept, is not a general idea nor purely an expressed idea but a perceived idea, an attribution on the part of users of that work. Ascertaining what idea or ideas may be conveyed by the work, accordingly, needs to pick its way through different ideas of 'idea' as well as to police a broad category boundary.

### From direct copying, through substantial taking, to use

Do the complications I have outlined with the notion of 'ideas' in copyright affect the comments I made above about my three brief examples? Beginning an analysis with language copying and moving up through different kinds of indirect copying seems a logical approach to analysis, given that copying is what is fundamentally at stake. Language copying is evidently copying of expression; and while architecture may not be visible, it is a protected 'essence' of the work. Starting with ideas, on the other hand, then moving 'down' through various levels of expression, seems counter-intuitive, at least in common cases of reproduction. It prioritises communicative import and value rather than the root problem: copying. Analysis following such a trajectory is likely to pull away from the question of whether there has been copying towards consideration of what would constitute a 'substantial' borrowing, seduced by a perception that resemblance is less striking where material, even very similar material, is expressed in a new genre, for a new purpose, or to a new audience. Differences between the two kinds of analysis may be illuminating, if only because, depending on the direction of analysis, the capacious meaning in copyright of 'substantial' (as some blend of amount, distinctiveness and what matters about a work to its users) will be diffracted through a different prism.

### *'Substantial' similarity*

The 'substantial part' in question in copyright analysis is a quality of (or judgement made about) the work copied *from*. Although dissenting views are sometimes unsuccessfully canvassed, substantiality has in principle nothing to do with the allegedly infringing work. Questions as to salience or significance in relation to the allegedly infringing work – such as what makes that new work distinctive for *its* audience, or whether it is functioning as a criticism, parody or pastiche of the copied text – are questions of fair dealing exceptions rather than of substantiality, or of fair use in jurisdictions where this defence is available.[72]

Is this restriction on substantiality watertight, however? It is, where 'substantial' borrowing means amount. It can also be, where 'substantial' borrowing means architecture, viewed as selection and arrangement: a distinctive arrangement can be identified in the work borrowed from and then checked for (as in *Baigent*) to see whether it exists similarly in the allegedly infringing work. Where what has allegedly been taken is some more general point or significance expressed by the architecture of the work, however, then evidence as to copying is likely to be found only at the level of a similarly abstract point or significance expressed by the copying work, rather than in chunks of words on the page or some calculable syntax of elements. Establishing whether what has been taken is substantial in such cases – substantial now at its most qualitative – calls for criteria of similarity of communicative purpose and effect (i.e. functional similarity) alongside the more established categories of formal similarity. As noted above, linguistic form and function work together, so this should not be surprising. But linguistic form, I also pointed out, underdetermines function, in that one form can serve different functions and one function can be realised by alternative forms. As a result, judging what is a 'substantial' taking, beyond amount of wording or selection and arrangement of identifiable discourse material, is an interpretive activity rather than a matter of observation. This is why an appeal to different kinds of discourse 'use', fair or otherwise, may

---

[72] E.g. as provided by the US Copyright Act 1976, s. 107. A striking illustration of the distinction between substantiality and exceptions, in light of my arguments below, is to be found in *Williamson Music* v. *Pearson* [1987] FSR 97. The case concerned a television advertisement for a bus company which set out to parody the lyrics and music of 'There's Nothing like a Dame' from the musical *South Pacific*. Baker J. reviewed the grounds on which parody is given extra licence because of the need to conjure up the work being parodied, contrasting the view taken by McNair J. in *Joy Music Ltd* v. *Sunday Pictorial Newspapers* [1960] 2 QB6 with the view taken by Falconer J. in *Schweppes* v. *Wellingtons Limited* [1984] FSR 210. Following extensive exposition of arguments in favour of greater licence, Baker J. returned to the acid test: whether there has been reproduction in the defendant's work of a substantial part of the claimant's work.

begin to creep into analysis of what is substantial even where copying rather than use is the issue and no 'fair use' defence is available.

Reversing the order or direction of analysis of similarity may offer new insights in this context. Starting with language copying, and moving up through discourse levels towards ideas, anchors itself in highlighted text and traceable arrangements of thematic material. Inevitably such analysis will begin to fall short on explicitness, when what makes similarity substantial is considered to be something more abstract. Starting with interpretive questions about ideas and their circulation, on the other hand, then working down through a text's different levels of discourse organisation tracking details of formulation, is likely to be eloquent on the imputed significance of similarity, and on claims in relation to exceptions, but can only present evidence in support or rebuttal of other, less indirect and more mechanical kinds of copying.

## Three examples revisited

Some of the tensions identified in the previous section can be illustrated by briefly revisiting my three examples in this wider context.

With 'Sonnet 18', the overall 'idea' conveyed by the sonnet (something about mutability and permanence) was and remains commonplace, especially by comparison with Shakespeare's inventiveness at 'lower' levels of discourse organisation. An idea of this general kind would not be protectable if original, nor an infringement if taken from someone else. The sonnet's overall 'idea', accordingly, seems less important than its rhetorical profusion of insights at other discourse levels: conceits, parallelisms, paradoxes, antitheses and other poetic effects. These clearly fall within Mr Justice Pritchard's second category of ideas: 'constructive ideas' (or detailed ideas which emerge from specific forms of expression). A high degree of imitation and allusion in a work functioning in this way seems to add to rather than detract from its aesthetic and social value. For a reader's perception to shift from aesthetic appreciation to perceived freeloading, market substitution or rivalrous competition with some other specific work, echoic material would need to conjure up one or a small number of sources in a sustained way and at different levels, without at the same time conjuring up any original purpose such as comment, critique or pastiche. Even extensive similarity, if shown, invites being construed as inspiration, homage, satire or some other kind of meaningful dialogue with – and so addition to – the work or works borrowed from, rather than being damaging to the earlier

author.[73] Viewing a high degree of intertextuality of this kind enthusias-
tically nevertheless appears to condone a high degree of copying as a fair
use of earlier works, presumably because of beneficial effects created
by the *new* work somehow trumping the earlier authors' entitlement in
relation to their work, without which the later work would not exist.
Some degree of legitimacy for borrowing of this kind might be found in
an accepted aesthetic that sonnets (and implicitly many other kinds of art
work), both in Shakespeare's time and now, are enriched in communicative value by their engagement with conventions of the genre in which
they are written, including with influential precedents or authorities in
that genre, and that the new works in turn enrich the overall intellectual
environment.

In contrast with my sonnet example, the informational purpose of the
petrol consumption book and pamphlet implies social benefits associated
with information disseminated (i.e. with facts and ideas), rather than
with other kinds of meaning. In information genres discourse typically
succeeds to the extent that information is conveyed clearly or appropriately, rather than because of how aesthetically pleasing it is; the social
value of a work lies in fitness for purpose of the mode of exposition
employed. The most salient similarities and differences between an
allegedly copied and copying work, from this point of view, would be
those associated with recipient design (e.g. simplicity and accessibility of
composition, mode of address and overall register), since these characteristics might legitimise some degree of borrowing as a fair use in a
publication in a new medium or addressing a different readership. Again,
however, such commentary risks shifting emphasis away from copying –
with its short-circuiting of effort on the part of the infringing author
(who acquires material with the least possible labour) – towards social
benefits of the derived work. As with the sonnet example, such a shift

---

[73] A related point – though with the fundamental proviso that the inspiring work was out of
copyright – is made in Andrew Gowers' 2006 review of intellectual property, as part of an
argument for benefits associated with a US-style fair use exception (and accompanied by
a sidebar heading 'Exceptions can create value'): '"Fair uses" of copyright can create
economic value without damaging the interests of copyright owners. As well as being
more flexible, the exception can be interpreted more broadly. The film *West Side Story*,
which grossed $43.7 million ($39.9 million when adjusted for inflation), may be considered a reworking of *Romeo and Juliet*, which is out of copyright. This figure indicates
that works which build on others can be extremely valuable, and also are not necessarily
substitutes for the original work – indeed, it is not the case that *West Side Story* has made
*Romeo and Juliet* less popular or less commercially successful' (*Gowers Review of
Intellectual Property* (HM Treasury on behalf of HMSO, 2006), s. 4.70, p. 62).

exacerbates tension in the balance copyright must achieve between protecting the earlier author's expenditure of labour and skill (and so willingness to engage in equivalent labour in future) and social interest in the potential value of the infringing work that results from any copying.

In *Baigent* v. *The Random House*, my third example, what was decisive was whether the ideas of the pleaded Central Theme had been linked together in HBHG in a sufficiently distinctive manner. Copying such an arrangement would undoubtedly give a later author an unfair advantage by comparison with having to collate, synthesise and compose equivalent material independently. The purpose and effect of Dan Brown's inclusion of elements from the earlier work, however, if such material had been found to be substantial and to consist of 'constructive' rather than general ideas, might still be construed in a number of ways: as freeloading on existing material; as an effort to build credibility by means of echoic language; as demonstration of general inspiration; as encouragement to readers to follow up relevant sources; etc. To the extent that the claimed 'central' ideas did reappear, they appeared in a work of fiction rather than of speculative history, addressed to a different audience with different expectations, in a different style, and fostering a different kind of reading experience. Borrowing, if it occurred, would not have been substantial in the infringing work but – essentially for English law – could have been substantial in HBHG as the source work (and so might have constituted infringement despite the novelist's other creative labour, which would have been irrelevant). Once more a tension is accentuated here between copyright's protection of capital invested by the earlier author, in the form of a property right, and a social policy of cultivating a marketplace of ideas enriched by publications that nevertheless achieve some of their effect by referring to earlier works through varying degrees of resemblance.

The central tension running through these revised accounts of my three earlier examples is addressed in copyright law not in terms of substantiality but, to the extent that it is felt necessary, by means of the scope of exceptions (e.g. in relation to criticism and review, reporting of current events, parody, caricature, and burlesque). Where a relevant exception applies, the value created by the mental labour of an otherwise infringing author, in subjecting what is taken to revision and alteration so as to produce an original work of the specified kind, is held to outweigh benefits otherwise conferred by copyright in the earlier work.

None of the relevant exceptions applies in any of my three examples. The exceptions are exceptional because, in specified cases (and not in others), conjuring up an earlier work is recognised as essential if the criticism, or parody or pastiche is to be effective. In such circumstances, authors are allowed extra latitude, though that latitude can be exceeded where what is taken is held to be more than needed to recall the earlier work sufficiently, or where insufficient effort is made to supplement the original, resulting in an effect more like reproduction than comment. With categories of discourse purpose not deemed exceptional, protection of the original author's investment of skill and judgement prevails over unlicensed later use, and less direct methods of referring to the earlier work (e.g. by means of paraphrase) have to be adopted. It might be argued, given my arguments above, that other categories of work and other discourse purposes besides those specified as exceptions might invite similar latitude, either by treatment as additional exceptions or by means of a wider 'use' defence.[74] Such categories of work might include for instance compositions in all those genres in which credibility with an audience depends on an author's conversancy with – without critical dissection of – the relevant precedents, authorities and field-leaders.

## Linguistic and conceptual representation

To complete my account of the expression–ideas dichotomy as viewed from a linguistic perspective, complications with the two terms need to be placed in a more theoretical context of approaches to language and mind. Some of the difficulties raised above as regards how far expression and ideas are intertwined, for instance, follow fairly clearly from a fundamental issue to do with language and thought touched on either unwittingly or opportunistically by the author of *Spear of Destiny* in *Ravenscroft v. Herbert and New English Library Ltd*: the problem of how much separation exists in the relationship between linguistic representation (expression) and conceptual representation (ideas).

Put simply, the issue is this.[75] People are able to speak and understand a language or languages, so they must have some mental representation

---

[74] EC Directive 2001/28/EC, Art. 5 (3), 2001 (implemented 2003) allows member states, if they wish to, to create a 'use' exception for the purposes of caricature, parody or pastiche. There is no reference to other purposes. For discussion, see MacQueen *et al.*, *Contemporary Intellectual Property*, p. 136.

[75] My description at this point closely follows the succinct account given by Jans Nuyts and Eric Pedersen in their editorial introduction to *Language and Conceptualization* (Cambridge University Press, 1997). The editors outline the basic problem as follows: 'Linguistic representation is some kind of systematic, structural patterning at different

of linguistic knowledge that allows them to do this. Equally, people acquire, store and transmit information about the world not only through language but also in other forms of behaviour. That information is used in planning, reasoning, problem-solving and in performing many kinds of intentional actions in a systematic way in many different environments. So they must also have some mental representation of knowledge about the world, or conceptual knowledge. Are these two kinds of representation identical, or do they differ? And if they differ, what relationship holds between the two?

As might be expected, this question is central to a great deal of work in linguistics, psychology and philosophy. Such work has developed in many different traditions, however, and would not offer copyright scholars a coherent viewpoint even if they were to seek one there. One view, now considered overstated, is that language is the principal or only tool of thought (i.e. that thinking happens in language, with no gap at all between idea and expression): in this view, expression *is* the thought. Synonymy or paraphrase are at best an approximation. At the other end of a spectrum of views, language and thought are considered fully separate, linked by an arbitrary mapping system which allows translation of information from one format into the other. This view implies considerable latitude for reformulation and alternative expression of ideas. Between these two positions are to be found a range of views, which, broadly paralleling my alternative directions of text analysis above, can be roughly divided into those which see conceptualisation as derivative from or heavily influenced by language and those which view conceptualisation as primary and language as derived from or based on it.[76] In cognitive science, for example, recent discussion has tended towards a 'universalist' position: that there is a medium-independent 'language of thought' into which different forms of input representation, including verbal and visual representation, are converted mentally.[77] A

levels of organisation: sound, word structure, sentence structure, text structure. Such systematic structure can be observed in language behaviour. Conceptual representation is less clear: what are concepts, what do they look like, how do they relate to one another, how are they organised in relation to each other? Sometimes conceptual representations are taken to be propositional or proposition-like systems, on other occasions image-based systems, and in some cases mixed systems' (*ibid.*, p. 2).

[76] *Ibid.*, pp. 1–7.

[77] Debates over the 'language of thought' hypothesis are largely concerned with the degree of the mind's 'modularity', and often take the form of responses to Jerry Fodor's *The Modularity of Mind* (Cambridge, MA: MIT Press, 1983). A wide-ranging collection of essays on mental representation is Stephen Stich and Ted Warfield (eds.), *Mental Representation: A Reader* (Oxford: Blackwell, 1994). An accessible introduction to the

fundamentally contrasting view of symbolisation, however, exemplified by Lacanian psychoanalysis, holds that thought emerges only after differentiation has been made possible by a series of stages of infantile development which introduce difference through entry into language slightly (or sometimes very) differently into individual life histories, with long-term effects on adult subjectivity.[78] A different view again, with some implications similar to those of the Lacanian psychoanalytic view of difference, is that of cultural relativity of conceptualisation inspired by the work of Sapir and Whorf.[79] In this view, originally based on comparison between European and American Indian languages, the verbal distinctions available within a given language are its categories for thinking (a hypothesis often simplistically discussed by reference to the example of different languages having a different number of words for snow and referred to in shorthand as the proposition that language 'determines' thought).

Investigating how concepts relate to words, and how more complex ideas relate to expression, is inevitably made more difficult by the fact that access to conceptual structures is only ever indirect. Concepts never reveal themselves at the observable surface of human behaviour. Evidence for and against each of the positions referred to above, perhaps unsurprisingly as a result, is inconclusive. What is clear, though, is that for everyday purposes 'the same idea' is effable, or expressible, in different words even if circumlocution may be needed in order to achieve this. To paraphrase or state something differently may always be arguably to express a slightly different idea, rather like words tracking an original in a translation into another language. But the resources of language allow ideas to be expressed in variant forms, hence the complexity of the ideas–expression dichotomy as worked through in any given case.

Because copyright law is concerned to balance social interests and responsibilities and to resolve disputes, however, rather than to explore

issues at word level is Jean Aitchison, *Words in the Mind: An Introduction to the Mental Lexicon* (Oxford: Blackwell, 1994).

[78] See Jacques Lacan, *Four Fundamental Concepts of Psycho-analysis*, trans. Alan Sheridan (London: Hogarth Press and the Institute of Psycho-analysis, 1977).

[79] For an overview, see John Gumperz and Stephen Levinson, 'Introduction: Linguistic Relativity Re-examined', in Gumperz and Levinson (eds.), *Rethinking Linguistic Relativity* (Cambridge University Press, 1996). The origins and subsequent history of the hypothesis generally known as the Sapir–Whorf hypothesis are complicated, and involve not only all the celebrated words for snow, or Sapir and Whorf themselves (separately and together) but numerous antecedents including the eighteenth-century linguist and philosopher Wilhelm von Humboldt and the nineteenth-century anthropologist Franz Boas.

theoretical arguments about ideas and expression, much of the theoretical investigation that takes place into the nature of ideas and expression goes far beyond what is ever likely to be helpful. For copyright law to become engrossed in theoretical speculation in this area would be potentially to undermine rather than enrich litigation as a process, by raising extraneous, expensive and time-consuming arguments including disputes over versions of text analysis software and the status of particular linguistic categories. The result is nevertheless a slightly unsettled position. Copyright law promulgates a dichotomy whose effectiveness depends on the confidence with which the courts apply it. Yet those same courts must apply the dichotomy in a manner that appears wary of interrogation of the terms in which it is expressed and the ideas it purports to be about.

## Conclusions

What follows from the points I have made? First, I should caution against attributing two conclusions I do not wish to draw. I am not urging that in copyright actions the parties should undertake detailed linguistic analysis of the contested works. This needs clarification. There is no reason *not* to take advantage of automation in searching for language copying, if that is found to be convenient. But there would be dangers in presenting and testing findings of linguistic analysis, even where admissible, in a manner that complicates the central questions of fact and issues of social policy that copyright litigation needs to address. Nor am I proposing adoption of linguistic terminology in preference to more everyday language about similarity of expression, even though such language ranges from precisely defined legal categories through to vague impressions about how discourse is organised and achieves its effects.

Neither of these conclusions would be appropriate. But there may still be a practical implication. For anyone who wishes to write and publish it is understandable, and may sometimes be essential, to build on published works and ideas (hence provision made in copyright for permitted acts listed as fair dealing exceptions in English law and 'fair use' defences in some other jurisdictions). For an author who wishes to express ideas that have already been published in a particular form but who is made anxious about or wishes to mitigate the risk of infringement, the challenge is an open-ended one of expressive technique: of reworking an original into a new treatment by some combination of local rewriting (effectively with the aid of a thesaurus), incorporating stylistic variation, and repackaging information in a new overall discourse architecture with a different network of connections between component ideas in order demonstrably not to have taken more material from any source than can be justified. Communicating the earlier work's *ideas* by such means is consistent with the commitment in copyright law to a marketplace of ideas. But because of uncertainties at the border between expression and ideas, a court might still find the resulting, altered material too close to an original. For an author working with source texts, therefore, expressive technique involves second-guessing how *much* re-presentation is needed to capture ideas referred to sufficiently precisely without 'overborrowing'.[80] If the boundary in relation to non-literal copying is unclear, there will be a chilling effect imposed by the implied threat of legal action.

For a rights-holder, a different problem arises as a result of lack of clarity about the boundary between expression and ideas: how much protection will be available to 'treatment' of ideas when material is transferred or adapted across platforms and non-literal copying is more likely than exact replication. Commercial protection of such material (e.g. material created to carry across from novel to film to computer game) increasingly requires a notion of textual 'content' at the very border between expression and ideas: a notion that must encompass whatever is meant by expression (though not in a way that is reducible to one particular medium, such as its language); at the same time, a notion that must not be so abstract as to be subsumed in the category of unprotectable ideas. Protecting 'an idea expressed in the copyright work', as Lord Hoffmann puts it, is inevitably in such circumstances largely a matter of discourse organisation. Yet discourse organisation seems the least clearly articulated aspect of what copyright law protects. From both a writer's and a text user's perspective, therefore – even if not from the vantage point of a trial judge – discourse organisation may seem at present less the kind of elephant that Mr Justice Laddie says it is easy to recognise than potentially copyright's elephant in the room.

---

[80] The suggestive word 'overborrowing' is used by Davis in her gloss on the position put forward by Lord Justice Jacobs in *Ibcos Computers Ltd* v. *Barclays Mercantile Highland Finance Ltd* [1994]. See Davis, *Intellectual Property Law*, p. 73.

# 9

# Refining notions of idea and expression through linguistic analysis

GRAEME B. DINWOODIE

## Introduction

The distinction between unprotectable ideas and copyrighted expression is one of the most fundamental principles of copyright law.[1] It is a ubiquitous principle of national copyright law, and may even be the international ceiling on the subject matter capable of protection under national law.[2] But no principle has been so frequently repeated and yet so badly understood. Indeed, commentators and courts have not been slow to comment on how difficult it is to grasp the distinction between idea and expression – or, perhaps more accurately, how difficult it is to articulate the distinction, or to draw it in practice.[3]

---

[1] See *L. B. (Plastics)* v. *Swish Products* [1979] FSR 145, 160 (HL); *Harper & Row Publishers, Inc.* v. *Nation Enterprises*, 471 US 539, 547 (1985); 17 USC s. 102(b) ('In no case does copyright protection for an original work of authorship extend to any idea, procedure, process, system, method of operation, concept, principle, or discovery, regardless of the form in which it is described, explained, illustrated, or embodied in such work'). Of course, this bright line can quickly dissolve. See, e.g., *Ibcos Computers* v. *Barclays Mercantile Highland Finance* [1994] FSR 275 (Jacob J.) ('United Kingdom copyright cannot prevent the copying of a mere general idea but can protect the copying of a detailed "idea"'); *Kregos* v. *Associated Press*, 937 F2d. 700, 706 (2d Cir. 1984) (suggesting a distinction between what the Court of Appeal for the Second Circuit later described as hard ideas and soft ideas).

[2] See Agreement on Trade-Related Aspects of Intellectual Property Rights, 15 Apr. 1994, Marrakesh Agreement Establishing the World Trade Organization, Annex 1C, Legal Instruments – Results of the Uruguay Round, 33 ILM 1125 (1994) (hereafter TRIPs Agreement), art. 9(2); WIPO Copyright Treaty, opened for signature 20 Dec. 1996, S. Treaty Doc. No. 105–17 (1997), art. 2; *Nova Products* v. *Mazooma Games Ltd* [2007] RPC 25 [at 37] (Jacob LJ) (discussing relevance of provisions in TRIPs).

[3] See *L. B. (Plastics)* v. *Swish Products* [1979] FSR 145, 160 (HL) (Lord Hailsham) (commenting that 'it all depends on what you mean by ideas'); *Nichols* v. *Universal Pictures*, 45 F.2d 119, 121 (2d Cir. 1930) ('Nobody has ever been able to fix that boundary and nobody ever can').

Some of the most intractable problems in applying the distinction (and hence of making overall determinations of infringement) have arisen in the context of applying copyright law to new technologies.[4] Protection of software, in particular, has generated difficult decisions for courts seeking to sustain and apply the distinction.[5] This is in part because computer programs 'hover more closely to the elusive boundary line between idea and expression'[6] and hence repeatedly test the resilience of the distinction. Likewise, musical copyright cases, even more so of late, have presented courts with similarly hard questions (possibly because of a felt lack of judicial expertise, and perhaps also with an eye to the 'functional' aspects of certain parts of the musical work).[7] In both types of cases, courts as a result appear more comfortable with an expansive role for expert testimony to aid judicial resolution of the dispute.[8]

The implication is that the principle is more intuitive, and perhaps less troubling for courts to apply, in the case of traditional literary works.[9] However, in his contribution to this volume (Chapter 8), Alan Durant demonstrates that our understanding of the distinction between idea and expression in the context of literary works is far from perfect and could be enriched by drawing on a number of insights from other fields, and in particular from linguistic theory.[10] In this brief response, I consider whether and how a fuller understanding of those features might be accommodated in the adjudication of legal disputes about copyright infringement.

---

[4] See the contributions by Crowcroft (Chapter 10) and Davis (Chapter 11) in this volume.

[5] See, e.g., *Whelan Assocs. v. Jaslow Dental Lab., Inc.* 797 F.2d 1222 (3d Cir. 1986); *Computer Associates Int'l v. Altai, Inc.*, 982 F.2d 693 (2d Cir. 1992); *Ibcos Computers v. Barclays Mercantile Highland Finance* [1994] FSR 275 (Jacob J.).

[6] See *Lotus v. Borland Int'l, Inc.*, 49 F.3d 807, 819–20 (1st Cir. 1995) (Boudin J., concurring).

[7] See Sergiu Gherman, 'Harmony and Its Functionality: A Gloss on the Substantial Similarity Test in Music Copyrights', Fordham Intell. Prop. Media & Ent. LJ, 19 (2009), 483 (discussing functional aspects of musical works). Litigation of the infringement question in the case of musical works of course goes back much further. See, e.g., *Arnstein v. Porter*, 154 F.2d 464 (2d Cir. 1951).

[8] See Miah Rosenberg, 'Note, Do You Hear What I Hear? Expert Testimony in Music Infringement Cases in the Ninth Circuit', UC Davis L. Rev., 39 (2006), 1669, 1675–76 (noting relevance of type of work and citing cases).

[9] See *Stromback v. New Line Cinemas*, 384 F.3d 283, 295 (6th Cir. 2004) (noting that expert testimony not generally necessary in the case of traditional literary works).

[10] See Durant, Chapter 8, in this volume, p. 151.

## Analysing infringement

Durant discusses many features of discourse that seem salient to the legal distinction between the categories of 'expression' and 'ideas.' For purposes of this brief comment, I focus on three aspects of his discussion: (a) those aspects of discourse organisation that copyright law already appears to accommodate, perhaps validating existing legal doctrine; (b) areas of legal doctrine that instinctively make assumptions about literary works that may be insufficiently nuanced; (c) aspects of discourse organisation that do not typically appear in legal discussions about copyright infringement involving works of literature, but which do inform discussion of copyright infringement involving other works such as computer programs.[11] Because Durant takes as his focus questions of copyright *infringement*, I shall first address relevant legal doctrine on infringement in both the United States and the United Kingdom.[12]

## The United States

In the United States, a plaintiff (after having shown ownership of a valid copyright and possibly some procedural prerequisites, such as registration of the copyright claimed to be infringed) can establish a prima facie case of infringement by showing that: (a) the defendant copied from the plaintiff's work; and (b) that such appropriation was improper.[13]

---

[11] I use the term 'work of literature' here simply to distinguish more conventional literary works from works such as computer programs that are deemed to be literary works, although clearly different in kind from the traditional category. See TRIPs Agreement, art. 10(1): 'Computer programs, whether in source or object code, shall be protected as literary works under the Berne Convention.' I do not mean to invoke a concept of literary quality.

[12] The distinction between idea and expression can also be addressed in considering the subsistence of copyright. When litigated in this context, the question quickly becomes entangled with other relevant thresholds such as originality. That is, does the work for which protection is sought display original expression? Yet, the exclusion of protection of ideas applies apart from the question of originality. It may be that the originality threshold seeks to exclude from protection matters too trivial for protection, while the idea–expression doctrine applies because some things are too important to protect through exclusive rights.

[13] See *Gaste* v. *Kaiserman*, 863 F.2d 861 (2d Cir. 1988); *Arnstein* v. *Porter*, 154 F.2d 464, 468–9 (2d Cir. 1951). The precise doctrinal contours vary from circuit to circuit in part because the standards have been developed almost entirely by courts free from legislative intervention. The Ninth Circuit employs a test that perhaps most dramatically departs from this formulation, at least in language if not in operation. See, e.g., *Brown Bag Software* v. *Symantec Corp.*, 960 F.2d 1465, 1475 (9th Cir. 1992) (discussing extrinsic and intrinsic elements of the test that map perhaps imperfectly to the prevailing test in other circuits).

The first question is essentially a factual determination, involving proof of access to the plaintiff's work as well as the extent of similarities. The second question contains factual components, but at bottom is a legal determination about the appropriate scope of copyright protection.[14] It is sometimes expressed in language suggestive of a purely empirical assessment,[15] but such language is simply the vehicle for legal policy determinations.[16]

Each question deals differently with the distinction between idea and expression. In proving copying, similarity of ideas (or indeed any other non-protectable matter) might still contribute to the plaintiff meeting its evidentiary burden. Hence, Alan Latman helpfully described the similarities relevant to this question as 'probative' similarities.[17] These help to

---

[14] See David Nimmer, 'Access Denied', Utah L. Rev. (2007)769, 770 ('copying . . . in turn subdivides into two components: copying as a factual matter and copying as a legal matter: the latter is also known as "substantial similarity"'); cf. Jane C. Ginsburg, 'No "Sweat?" Copyright and Other Protection of Works of Information After *Feist* v. *Rural Telephone*', Colum. L. Rev., 92 (1992), 338, 346 (discussing idea–expression distinction); L. Bently and B. Sherman, *Intellectual Property Law* (3rd edn, Oxford University Press, 2009) (discussing UK law, and noting that 'the exclusion of ideas from the scope of protection is an important judicial technique that is used to reconcile the divergent interests of copyright owners against the interests of users, creators and the public more generally'). The tension between these two propositions is shown in judicial deliberations about the availability of summary judgment on the question of substantial similarity. See Daniel A. Wanat, 'Copyright Law: Infringement of Musical Works and the Appropriateness of Summary Judgment under Federal Rules of Civil Procedure, Rule 56 (c)', U. Memph. L. Rev., 39 (2009), 1037.

[15] See *Peter Pan Fabrics* v. *Martin Weiner Corp.*, 274 F.2d 487, 489 (2d Cir. 1960) (asking whether 'the ordinary observer, unless he set out to detect the disparities, would be disposed to overlook them and regard their aesthetic appeal as the same'); *Positive Black Talk Inc.* v. *Cash Money Records*, 394 F.3d 357, 374 (5th Cir. 2004) (substantial similarity is a jury question). Compare *Designers' Guild* v. *Russell Williams (Textiles)*, [2001] 1 All ER 700 (HL) and *Baigent* v. *Random House* [2007] FSR 24.

[16] The use of such doctrinal tests serves at least two purposes. First, to the extent that civil juries might make such determinations in US courts where the plaintiff is seeking remedies at law, such as damages, it operationalises the question for lay persons. Cf. *Société Technique de Pulverisation Step* v. *Emson Europe Ltd* [1993] RPC 513, 519 (CA) (Hoffmann LJ) (suggesting that use of legal fictions such as whether an alleged inventive concept under patent law is something which would have been obvious at the priority date to a skilled man, aware of what was known or used at the time and of common general knowledge in the art but lacking in inventive imagination 'may have seemed a folksy way of explaining the law to a jury' but that reliance on the legal test in the statute was preferable). Second, and relatedly, masking policy determinations as empirical assessments might be thought by some to confer greater legitimacy on the decisions rendered. This latter supposed justification (or explanation) implicates more fundamental principles of legal philosophy that transcend copyright law.

[17] See Alan Latman, '"Probative" Similarity as Proof of Copying: Toward Dispelling Some Myths in Copyright Infringement', Colum. L. Rev., 90 (1990), 1187.

prove the plaintiff's case, but such a finding does not necessarily suggest plaintiff's ownership of exclusive rights in the subject matter the similarity of which proved copying.

The second question – whether any appropriation was improper – requires courts to determine whether there is substantial similarity of protected expression. At first blush, this would seem a more attractive point at which to make use of the insights provided by linguistics. Similarity of ideas is insufficient to sustain an infringement claim; thus the distinction between ideas and expression that Durant seeks to illuminate is facially significant. However, ironically, although expert evidence is favoured in determining whether the defendant had copied from the plaintiff's work, US courts do not typically admit expert evidence on the second question of whether appropriation has been improper (subject to exceptions discussed below).[18]

## The United Kingdom

In the United Kingdom, a copyright claimant must make similar showings,[19] though the doctrinal elements are differently stated (and, where phrased similarly, may sometimes be deceptively similar).[20] Thus, a claimant must show that: (a) the defendant's work was derived from the claimant's work; and (b) the alleged infringing act was carried out in relation to the work or a substantial part thereof.[21] As under US law, the first element ('derivation') is a factual question, requiring the claimant to prove a causal link between its work and the allegedly infringing use. And, as under US law, this element can be proved by reference to similarity of any type, even if the similarity consists of subject matter

---

[18] Durant also discusses the 'substantiality' of any similarity. This too involves a qualitative policy assessment. Durant argues (in discussing UK law) that such qualitative assessments are an appropriate point at which expert evidence might assist the courts. In many respects, the questions that a court is asking in determining 'substantiality' echo those that might enrich an understanding of the distinction between idea and expression. As a result, it may make sense to adopt the same approach to expert evidence on the two questions. But cf. below the text accompanying nn. 39–42 (discussing policy dimension to second question).

[19] In both the United States and the United Kingdom, the plaintiff must also show that the defendant engaged in an act that is reserved exclusively for the copyright owner. See, e.g., 17 USC s. 106 (US); Copyright, Designs and Patents Act 1988, ss. 16–27 (UK).

[20] See *Ibcos Computers* v. *Barclays Mercantile Highland Finance* [1994] FSR 275, 289 (Jacob J.) (noting dangers of assuming that concepts bearing the same label in US and UK copyright law could be applied in identical fashion).

[21] Copyright, Designs and Patents Act 1988, s. 16(3) (UK) (substantial part element).

that would not of itself be protected by copyright.[22] The second question (substantiality) replicates the 'improper appropriation' question asked under US law, although it may embody a greater number of legal judgments or policy values[23] because UK copyright law lacks the type of flexible defences to infringement found in US fair use doctrine.[24] As a result, analysis of substantiality in the United Kingdom may arguably involve even more complex judgments than required of US courts in assessing improper appropriation. However, it is unarguable that an important aspect of the judgment in either jurisdiction is the refusal to grant protection to ideas. Thus, the basic structure of infringement analysis in the United Kingdom does not depart radically from that found in the United States.

## Concordance between legal and linguistic analyses

From this summary, it can be seen that the legal distinction between idea and expression is important in different ways for different parts of the infringement analysis. Durant's chapter offers a description of the work, developed using insights from other fields, that is far more complex than typically found in legal opinions. In this part of my response, I consider whether that description corroborates the heuristics used by courts in assessing copyright infringement, and whether it suggests any changes courts might adopt.

### Validation of legal analysis

In several respects, the picture that Durant paints confirms assumptions on which courts operate. Generally, Durant's insights may prove useful in proving copying (in US terminology) or establishing the causal connection between the plaintiff's and defendant's work (as we might express the same issue in the United Kingdom). If one viewed his

---

[22] Cf. *Billhofer Maschinenfabrik GmbH* v. *Dixon & Co.* [1990] FSR 105, 123 (Hoffmann J.) (noting potential relevance of unprotected or trivial matter).

[23] See *Designers' Guild* v. *Russell Williams* (*Textiles*) [2001] 1 All ER 700 (HL) (substantiality is a mixed question of fact and law).

[24] Compare 17 USC s. 107 (US) with Copyright, Designs and Patents Act 1988, ss. 29–30 (UK); see generally Aplin and Davis, *Intellectual Property Law* (noting and describing difference); see also Nimmer, 'Access Denied', 770 (noting that the appropriate balance in copyright law can be secured via defences to infringement or the rules for establishing a prima facie case of copying and substantial similarity).

explanation as simply exploring the fixed categories of 'idea' and 'expression', this potential contribution may not be apparent. The basic question being asked by courts determining 'copying' or 'causation' is apparently uninformed by whether we classify an aspect of a work as 'idea' or 'expression'. The focus on *any probative* similarity might be thought, in both the United States and the United Kingdom, to render the idea–expression distinction irrelevant; similarity (plus access) is paramount in judicial analysis.

However, as Durant demonstrates, understanding the process by which a literary work is constructed more generally helps to determine whether the defendant's explanations of original creation ring true. It may well be that drawing the *legal* categories of 'idea' and 'expression' with certainty is not relevant, but considering the 'language patterns' that Durant discusses will undoubtedly aid the questions of proof. Indeed, on *factual* questions typified by inquiries into copying or causation, courts already make substantial use of expert evidence.[25]

When we compare Durant's narrative with the ways that the courts have fleshed out the copying or derivation question, we find that considerations typically taken into account by courts are consistent with how linguistics would regard the works in question. As a result, the insights from linguistics can help to establish and corroborate such factual findings. For example, in rebutting the inference of copying that might flow from similarities between the defendant's work and that of the plaintiff, a defendant might point to a common source for both works that would provide an alternative explanation other than copying. Durant explains that linguistic analysis of works likewise recognises that the relationship between two works need to be understood in the context of a broader discourse: 'There is the senior (alleged source) work; there is the allegedly derived (infringing) work; and there are norms of discursive practice traceable to wider usage which are essential in determining how far the cumulatively chosen features of any textual version are novel or "original"'.[26]

### Enriching legal analysis

This is not to say that all forms of legal analysis probing the distinction between idea and expression comport with the linguistic understanding

---

[25] See *Arnstein* v. *Porter*, 154 F.2d 464 (2d Cir. 1951)
[26] See Durant, above, n. 10, pp. 157–8; see also *IPC Media Ltd.* v. *Highbury Publishing* [2004] EWHC 2985, at 43 (Ch. D.) (noting value of experts in identifying common ideas in the field).

set out by Durant. If one reads legal scholarship or judicial opinions, one would come to at least two conclusions about the relationship between idea and expression that Durant's analysis might call into question.

First, legal scholars and courts talk of the relationship between idea and expression in terms that suggest a linear development, from general to specific, from unprotected to protected, from abstract theme to literal text. This comes through in the directional language often deployed by courts and scholars in describing the relationship.[27] Indeed, courts often talk in terms that are almost chronological: an author has an idea, and that idea is then clothed with expression.

Yet, in describing that same line from a linguistic perspective, Durant talks about a distinction between 'information' and 'representation'.[28] 'Information' is commonly treated as ideas or nuggets of content that exist beyond how they are shaped by specific forms of their representation. That would connote what copyright law calls ideas. 'Representation' comes closer to the expression of an idea. But Durant explains how an 'idea' is represented is widely recognised as significantly shaping how any idea is understood. That is, expression may in fact be the seed which gives life to the idea; language may determine thought.[29]

To some extent, the description of this *relationship* might parallel what US copyright law calls the merger doctrine, where the intertwining of the idea and the expression is such that copyright law will not protect the expression lest it offers protection to ideas. But Durant's analysis suggests an inversion of how lawyers see the relationship between ideas and expression, that denying protection to representation may be important to serve the objectives that the legal distinction between idea and expression purports to further. This should perhaps make copyright law more cautious in assuming that the text in a literary work is the purest form of independent expression, warranting more ready protection.

A second feature of the legal analysis of the relationship between idea and expression that Durant's discussion calls into question is the assumption that the relationship is a binary one: there is a line, a boundary. Indeed, one often hears the idea–expression relationship described as a dichotomy. Of course, this might simply be the result of the binary nature of the legal questions. Is the subject matter protected? Has the defendant engaged in infringement? And to be sure courts are

---

[27] See, e.g., *Nash* v. *CBS, Inc.*, 899 F.2d 1537, 1540 (7th Cir. 1990) (talking in terms of setting the level of protected abstraction 'high' or 'low').
[28] See Durant, above, n. 10, p. 166.     [29] *Ibid.*

aware that the dynamic is complicated. As Learned Hand warned, 'Nobody has ever been able to fix that boundary [between ideas and expression] and nobody ever can.'[30] Or, as Judge Easterbook said in *Nash v. CBS*, we have to muddle through, at least aware of the consequences of moving the line between up or down.[31]

But Durant explains that we can inject far more complexity into our understanding of literary works.[32] To sharpen analytic focus on blurred degrees of similarity and difference between literary works, he identifies different *levels* of textual organisation at which patterns of similarity and difference are woven together need to be identified: features of design and layout; patterns of word tokens; sentence structure; grammatical constructions; topic organisation and sequencing, themes or general ideas.[33] Importantly, at *each* of these levels of abstraction, Durant identifies features of a work that may cohere more with the legal category of idea, and other aspects more redolent of what the law calls expression.

Of course, such an approach to the legal question is not absent from judicial decisions. For example, Judge Learned Hand famously explained in *Nichols* that:

> Upon any work, and especially upon a play, a great number of patterns of increasing generality will fit equally well, as more and more of the incident is left out. The last may perhaps be no more than the most general statement of what the play is about, and at times may consist of only its title; but there is a point in this series of abstractions where they are no longer protected, since otherwise the playwright could prevent the use of his ideas, to which, apart from their expression, his property is never extended.[34]

In later cases, most notably in the software context, courts have relied on this explanation (tendered in the context of literary works) to endorse a

---

[30] *Nichols v. Universal Pictures*, 45 F.2d 119, 121 (2d Cir. 1930).

[31] See *Nash v. CBS, Inc.*, 899 F.2d 1537, 1541 (7th Cir. 1990) ('This single rule must achieve as much as possible of these inconsistent demands. Neither Congress nor the courts has the information that would allow it to determine which is best. Both institutions must muddle through, using not a fixed rule but a sense of the consequences of moving dramatically in either direction').

[32] See Durant, above, n. 10, p. 181. ('One complication arises if we ask whether a published work really does convey a single "idea", or some small and determinate number of distinct ideas (an overall message, or something a text grammarian might designate as its macro-proposition'); p. 183 ('What seems more useful, as a result, is some set of distinctions *within* the notion of an idea rather than a polarity (or dichotomy) between idea and expression').

[33] See Durant, above, n. 10, pp. 157–72.

[34] *Nichols v. Universal Pictures*, 45 F.2d 119, 121 (2d Cir. 1930).

more nuanced approach to ascertaining the protected parts of a work. For example, in *Computer Associates* v. *Altai* the Court of Appeals for the Second Circuit considered whether to follow the then-prevailing precedent on the scope of protection for computer programs (*Whelan*). The Court declined to follow *Whelan* because:

> [T]he crucial flaw in [*Whelan's*] reasoning is that it assumes that only one 'idea,' in copyright law terms, underlies any computer program, and that once a separable idea can be identified, everything else must be expression...This criticism focuses not upon the program's ultimate purpose but upon the reality of its structural design. [A] computer program's ultimate function or purpose is the composite result of interacting subroutines. Since each subroutine is itself a program, and thus, may be said to have its own 'idea,' *Whelan's* general formulation that a program's overall purpose equates with the program's idea is descriptively inadequate.[35]

Although the *Altai* court criticised *Whelan* as relying 'too heavily on metaphysical distinctions and ... not plac[ing] enough emphasis on practical considerations', the conception of the work upon which it acted was in fact grounded in a real understanding of the nature of computer programs. And that understanding had been developed in part by use of a court-appointed expert. (Indeed, courts deciding cases of alleged infringement of software have frequently had regard to expert testimony.)

Courts deciding questions of substantial similarity in software cases applying *Altai* have thus, in determining whether there is substantial similarity of protected expression, examined the work at issue at each level of abstraction to determine whether the features for which protection is sought constitutes an idea or is otherwise unprotectable. Durant's careful description of the organisation of literary works suggests the opportunity for delineating a scope of copyright protection mapped more closely to non-legal understandings of the expressive parts of a work.

### Literary works as less intuitive subjects of analysis

But should courts seize this opportunity? The question implicates two considerations that are often considered as one. First, what is the role for expert evidence in pursuing the second analysis relevant to infringement,

---

[35] *Computer Associates* v. *Altai, Inc.*, 982 F.2d 693, 706 (2d Cir. 2002).

namely, improper appropriation (or, in UK terms, substantiality)? Might we make greater use of experts in developing more refined analytic techniques for separating ideas and expression? Judge Learned Hand was extremely sceptical of the use of experts. Thus, while he was willing to tolerate such evidence as an aid in proving copying, the question of substantial similarity or improper appropriation remained an impressionistic one.[36]

Since *Nichols*, US courts have begun to make more widespread use of expert evidence.[37] The most frequent use remains in connection with the first question, of copying or derivation. However, in the context of certain classes of works (such as software or those works intended for a specialised audience), courts have also become willing to use experts to assist in questions of substantial similarity.[38] This has occurred in areas where courts have felt less comfortable about making assessments about the nature of the works at issue; courts, who work daily with words, perhaps instinctively believe they understand the nature of literary works. Durant's analysis suggests, however, that such judicial analysis is incomplete.

Of course, this proposition does not mean that courts should without question accept the evidence of experts. And Durant acknowledges as much.[39] Admitting the evidence of experts changes the nature and costs of the litigation process.[40] And, as noted above, the question of improper

---

[36] See *Nichols* v. *Universal Pictures*, 45 F.2d 119, 120 (2d Cir. 1930) ('We cannot approve the length of the record, which was due chiefly to the use of expert witnesses . . . We hope that in this class of cases such evidence may in the future be entirely excluded, and the case confined to the actual issues; that is, whether the copyrighted work was original, and whether the defendant copied it, so far as the supposed infringement is identical').

[37] The UK courts have also been willing to admit expert testimony. See, e.g., *Designers' Guild* v. *Russell Williams (Textiles)* [2001] 1 All ER 700 (HL); *Cantor Fitzgerald Int'l* v. *Tradition (UK)*, 2000 RPC 95. For example, courts have been particularly deferential to expert evidence from musicologists when deciding whether a contribution is significant enough to give rise to joint authorship. See L. Bently, 'Authorship of Popular Music in UK Copyright Law', *Information, Communication and Society*, 12 (2009), 179, 192–4. If such evidence is relevant to establish 'substantiality' for co-authorship, it could well be relevant to substantiality in infringement. Of course, the mix of law and fact in determining 'substantiality' may vary from one context to the other. See below text accompanying nn. 39–40

[38] See, e.g., *Dawson* v. *Hinshaw Music Inc.*, 905 F.2d 731 (4th Cir. 1990); *Computer Associates* v. *Altai, Inc.*, 982 F.2d 693 (2d Cir. 2002).

[39] See Durant, above, n. 10, p. 192.

[40] See *Procter & Gamble Co* v. *Reckitt Benckiser (UK) Ltd* [2007] EWCA Civ 936 (suggesting a limited role for expert evidence in deciding of similarity of designs, in part in response to concerns over costs of litigation). Moreover, some scholars have argued that

appropriation or substantial similarity involves more than mimicking reality. It embodies a wide range of policy choices, perhaps even more so in the United Kingdom than in the United States.[41] As Jane Ginsburg said several years ago, idea and expression are not to be understood by courts as epistemological concepts, but as efforts to draw a line that allows appropriate levels of competition. 'In copyright law, an "idea" is not an epistemological concept, but a legal conclusion prompted by notions – often unarticulated and unproven – of appropriate competition.'[42]

Rather, this suggests simply that the line drawn between judicial approaches to literary works, on the one hand, and other works such as computer programs might be reconsidered. When software was brought within the copyright fold, the treatment of computer programs was analogised to literary works.[43] Perhaps the time has come for literary works to learn the lessons of software, aided by expert analysis of the type offered by Durant.

A second, related, question prompted by Durant's insights is whether (through the use of expert evidence or otherwise), courts should dissect works to identify component protectable parts. This is an analytically distinct question, but it tends to get wrapped up in choices about the admissibility of expert evidence because experts facilitate this type of analysis.[44] As seen in the different scope of protection offered works by courts engaged in dissection, on the one hand, and courts pursuing an impressionistic analysis, on the other, dissection tends to lead (inappropriately) to a more cramped scope of rights.[45] But there is no logical reason why courts cannot have their eyes opened up to the more complex organisation of literary works, while being reminded that protection may properly extend to an original, expressive combination of otherwise unprotectable parts.

reliance on such experts introduces some qualitative biases that are implicit in the ideology and methodology of classical musicology. See Bently, 'Authorship', 192–4 (discussing expert evidence on the question of substantiality of contributions relevant to co-authorship status).

[41] See above text accompanying n. 24; Bently and Sherman, *Intellectual Property*, p. 181.

[42] See Ginsburg, 'No "Sweat?"', 346.

[43] See National Commission on New Technological Uses of Copyrighted Works (CONTU).

[44] See *Designers' Guild* v. *Russell Williams (Textiles)* [2001] 1 All ER 700 (HL); *Apple Computer, Inc.* v. *Microsoft Corp.*, 35 F.3d 1435, 1442 (9th Cir. 1994).

[45] See *Designers' Guild* v. *Russell Williams (Textiles)* [2001] 1 All ER 700 (HL) (criticising Court of Appeal's dissection of work because it 'dealt with the copied features piecemeal instead of considering . . . their cumulative effect').

## Conclusion

The choices about whether and how to incorporate the expertise of linguistic analysis into adjudication of questions of copyright infringement implicate broader questions about the structure of copyright litigation (and indeed of the scope of copyright protection). However, awareness of that expertise is valuable. It confirms that judicial exploration of a distinction long thought fundamental to the field does not deviate that far from the reality of how literary works are constructed and understood. Moreover, and perhaps more importantly, it makes the choices confronting copyright law genuine ones.

# PART VI

Computer software

# 10

## Copyright, piracy and software

JON CROWCROFT

Software is the output of creative efforts by programmers, which differs in a number of ways from other protected works. In this chapter, I will discuss the technical and cultural differences between software and other works that may be protected by copyright or intellectual property more generally, and will thereby endeavour to demonstrate that concepts of infringement which may apply to other works do not readily transpose to software.

I try to show those characteristics of software which differ significantly from other works sufficiently to justify at least a significant review of the types and scope of protection that should be provided legally, economically and technologically. Most of these differences in characteristics are quantitative, and can be captured in the idea that software has transient value, and is always evolving to improve based on past use, and to meet new needs of old and new users. This impermanence means that software is almost always a 'work-in-progress', rather than a finished product. The process of that progress may be more important (in terms of creativity, invested effort and value, worth protecting) than any particular 'snapshot' of the software at any particular moment. Against this background, novel approaches to ownership and enforcement have emerged, such as open source, as well as copyleft. These have been accompanied by novel business models for recovering costs and making money from the generation of software goods and services.

The bulk of the chapter is devoted to explaining in more detail the salient characteristics of software and the process of its production, its distribution and its protection, or otherwise, and the businesses that surround this. Subsequently, I look at new and old models of intellectual property in the software industry. Then I will take a brief look at the significance of software piracy, followed by a brief look at technological approaches to enforcement. Finally, I conclude with a brief discussion of the relative cost and value invested in these processes that might be worth protection by legal, technical or economic means.

## Computer programs as 'works'

In this section I describe how programs are 'created' and how that act of 'creation' and the finished result differs from other copyright works.

Software is the general term that applies to computer programs. A computer program is a collection of code which instructs hardware, and possibly other software, to carry out some task. Tasks that a computer may carry out include mathematical computations (e.g. find the average of a list of numbers), graphical rendering (e.g. draw a picture of a sphere reflecting light from a nearby lamp), text processing (store a document typed by a human user, and check the English spelling and grammar), and so on. Hardware is the term used to describe the electronic machine that stores information in memory, or on long-term storage hardware such as disks and executes programs that are also stored on the computer. Information can be both data provided by the user and programs; computer hardware does not distinguish.

Software is generally divided into applications and systems. Applications are used to carry out tasks that the human user wants, while systems programs support these tasks by implementing various administrative duties necessary for the ease of programming the hardware, and for the longer term maintenance of information resources such as documents or databases stored on a computer's disks or other media.

## *Writing and using software*

Software is composed by programmers, who usually write code in high-level languages which look something like natural languages. Computer hardware 'runs' binary executable instructions which are usually very long lists of very simple steps (e.g. add x to y, or move z to w, or display q, or 'if the answer is zero, stop'). Thus programs usually have (at least) two forms: so called source code, and executable objects. Source code is what programmers work with. Executable objects are what are stored and executed by the hardware. Programs to convert software from source form to executable form are called compilers or interpreters. It is sometimes possible to take the executable form and 'de-compile' it into the source form.

## Abstraction and modularization

Software often interacts with other software. Applications interact with systems software to make use of computer resources such as storage and network hardware. This allows the programmer writing an application to ignore the details, since the programmer writing the system has already hidden the solution in their system software. This process of hiding details can be referred to as 'abstraction'. The task of dividing a program into different components is known as modularization. This allows groups of programmers to work separately to produce large complex systems and applications, more quickly than an individual could achieve.

## The art of computer programming

Writing software, programming the computer, is both an art and a skill. The skills to program take years to acquire, usually with formal training and qualifications, although not always. There are many good amateur programmers. There is a wide range of innate ability[1] in programmers in terms of productivity and quality of output, and it is hard to identify who will (or even is) better out of any group. Some people never manage to comprehend programming. Even among experts, the range many be as much as hundreds of times productivity between fastest and slowest, and between most high quality and least. Quality of production is not well correlated with speed.[2]

The software engineering profession requires programmers to continually update their skills, or else an ever increasing demand for young new software creators will not be met.

Education in computer science generally has to deliver both knowledge and skills. At some level, a programmer resembles a musician who plays and composes. This is very different from the novelist or the artist. However, unlike most authors and artists, the programmer is also required to have strong scientific/mathematical skills too. The good programmer is rare and in high demand. Part of the training of programmers, whether in school or

---

[1] R. Bornat and S. Dehnadi, 'Mental Models, Consistency and Programming Aptitude', *Proceedings of the Tenth Conference on Australasian Computing Education*, 78 (2008), 53–61.

[2] N. Nagappan *et al.*, 'The Influence of Organizational Structure on Software Quality: An Empirical Case Study', ICSE (2008), 521–30.

in work, necessarily then involves experience with working with (either debugging or upgrading) other programmers' code. Much software is written then in a research and educational setting, in addition to much in a purely commercial setting. Software can migrate between these settings.

## Source and executable code

Software is an artefact that is relatively new compared with books and music, or even film. Although programming has been discussed since the time of Ada Lovelace, who described the process when writing how to use Babbage's Difference Engine,[3] the business of programming is really something that emerged in the last thirty years. Some people refer to the profession as software engineering.

As discussed above, software has at least two forms: the source form, which is used by programmers; and the binary form executed by computers. Programmers use tools much like authors of books or papers use, such as word processors, to edit and create their software code.

## Software maintenance

It is very rare that the source code of a program is written and delivered to the users, and then never looked at again. The bulk of software requires maintenance and frequently is subject to requests from users for enhancements. Software maintenance is required for at least two reasons. First, programs are rarely perfect, and often contain 'bugs'. A bug is something that may not be fatal for the usefulness of a program, but simply means that from time to time it doesn't do precisely what the user wanted. In a book, the analogy would be a spelling or grammatical error, which could be repaired by issuing a new edition of the book. A more fatal error might involve a critical error in the plot of a book. In a program, this might be the situation where the program 'crashes' and loses user data. Bugs are fixed by programmers identifying the error and changing the code and releasing a new version of the program. In addition, a program might need to be used by someone who has

---

[3] The Difference Engine was a machine conceived by Charles Babbage in 1822 for the computation of tables of logarithmic and trigonometric functions. A working model can be seen in the British Science Museum. See also School of Mathematics and Statistics, University of St Andrews, *The MacTutor History of Mathematics Archive* (1998) (at: www-gap.dcs.st-and.ac.uk/~history/Mathematicians/Babbage.html, accessed June 14, 2006).

bought a new computer or upgraded the systems software on his or her computer so that it is no longer 'compatible' with the older program.

Second, programs are often delivered that work as expected, but then the users decide that they need some new feature. Examples might be a calculator that works out an average that the user would now also like to work out the median; another example would be a word-processing application that is used to spell-check in English, but now the user demands that it spell-check in American English and British English separately. Such modifications are known as 'features'.

Programmers require access to the source code and the ability to understand how to modify it to repair defects ('fix bugs') and add enhancements ('features'). Authors rarely make significant alterations to novels or even poems once written. Indeed, the new editions often simply fix errata reported by readers or the proofreader employed by a publisher. On the other hand, musicians performing live may often alter the piece they are playing, whether in jazz or folk. Classical composers often adapt a piece for the available orchestra.

### Substitute products

In many walks of life, there is a range of products that are said by economists to be substitutes for one another. Thus there is competition for consumers for things like cars or fridges. Each is functionally equivalent, although there may be differences in price and performance. In computers, there is some competition in hardware, although there is a dominant chip manufacturer in Intel. In the software side of the business, there is also a dominant manufacturer, in Microsoft. However, in both cases there are alternative products: AMD make Intel clone chips, but ARM, for example, make completely different chips; and instead of Windows, one can use the Apple operating system or Linux; and instead of Microsoft Word, one could use one of many other word processor products (e.g. LaTeX), or Firefox instead of Internet Explorer. This is obviously not the case with creative works in the world of music, film, games and books, where a product by one artist is not perfectly substituted by the work by another: I cannot be expected to buy the cheaper Mozart instead of the more expensive Eminem, even though in some purely technical sense (rather than merely aesthetic) they are identical. We will see that this matters very much when some of the competing products are 'open source' and some are proprietary.

## Component markets

As discussed above, while programs exist as separate artefacts, they are of little use without a computer to run them, and usually they interact with other programs on the computer. When I buy a book, I do not need to buy anything else to enjoy reading it. On the other hand, if I buy a CD or download an MP3, I need a CD player with an amplifier and speakers or MP3 player with headphones to listen to the music. Hence computer programs exist in a component market. They are typically dependent on both the hardware and the systems software. Programmers need to be experts at understanding both of these other systems, although they may not need to modify them (since they are potentially insulated by abstraction and modularization).

## Substitution and components and open systems

A computer user wants a software application. An application runs on an operating system. The application and operating system have been built (compiled) for a particular hardware platform. Thus it may not be trivial to substitute one component for another unless there is some level of compatibility.

Open systems are defined by the business world to allow levels of compatibility. Thus AMD and Intel processors are compatible hardware and allow the same operating systems and applications to run 'transparently'. This entails using open interfaces (between the application and the operating system, one talks about application programming interfaces or APIs). Operating systems allow the same application to run. There are clearly different cost barriers to move from one component product to another depending on whether a platform for that component is open or at least compatible.[4]

The deliberate use of obfuscation or secrecy about interfaces, or rapid changes in interface between different versions of operating system or hardware is also a controversial tactic employed by some software businesses to create barriers to other businesses competing in offering compatible components.[5]

---

[4] A.S. Tanenbaum *et al.*, 'Guidelines for Software Portability', *Software: Practice and Experience*, 8(6) (1978), 681–98.
[5] See, for example, S.K. Udupa *et al.*, 'Deobfuscation: Reverse Engineering Obfuscated Code', 12th Working Conference on Reverse Engineering, 7–11 Nov. 2005, ISSN: 1095–1350.

## Networked economics

A large fraction of computer hardware in the world today is connected to the Internet. On the order of 1 billion PCs and 4 billion cellular telephones form part of a communications system which links programs together and allows the rapid movement of information between systems at very low cost. This adds a level of complexity to the 'component market' discussed above.

Some programs depend for their usefulness on programs on another computer. This split between programs may be structured in the form of a customer and provider (usually known as client–server), or a more equal footing (peer-to-peer). In general there is asymmetry in the roles of programs as there is asymmetry in the roles of information flow. If I use a computer program to access information on another computer, I typically use a client program (e.g. a web browser), while the other computer uses a server program (e.g. a web server). The latter program may be part of a much more complex system since an information provider (Amazon, Google, YouTube, Facebook, Internet banking, online travel agencies, oil field production monitoring, etc.) may have very large amounts of information. Such organizations are very big customers for complex software, or else they create their own. The software that the client/customer uses may be simpler (and therefore cheaper to produce and maintain). This has led to a common practice of giving away the client component of such a system, whether it is the browser itself (e.g. Firefox) or plug-in programs for the browser. The business model that has evolved in such a world depends on various ways of recovering costs from the service (advertising, subscription, or charging for items downloaded) rather than charging for software. This has often led to open-sourcing of the software, even for the more complex server side, since there is no need to recover software production costs directly by selling and protecting code, and since this may lead to free bug fixes from the community of skilled programmers who use such applications.

A related model for software is that it is written in a way that is specific to particular hardware. In this case, the consumer buys the hardware with the software (and upgrades) bundled in the price. It might be hard to see how software piracy could happen in this case, and yet it does, but requires a lot of resources – essentially, the pirate needs to produce the hardware too! Many consumer electronic devices contain software, which is provided bundled with the hardware, but some highly priced systems, such as Internet routers, are often delivered with software which is then updated 'for free' as part of the hardware price.

In the past, software for mobile phones was sold with the software bundled. Increasingly, as phones become closer to general purpose computers, software is distributed from third parties. Indeed, the iPhone, Google's Android phone and Windows Mobile phones are all based on the model of Apple, Linux and Microsoft's software businesses, with online distribution of applications. The other major players (Symbian and RIM's Blackberry phones) are similar. In this new world, software copying is easy and one assumes that breaches of copyright and piracy are following similar trends to those in the traditional computer marketplace. However, restrictions on which applications can be downloaded and run on some of these devices are sometimes imposed by network service providers. (Working around these restrictions is known as 'jailbreaking', and often breaches an end-user license agreement, either with the device hardware or software vendor, or the service provider.)[6]

Software is now a component in many other artefacts in the world, ranging from consumer electronics and cars, through to televisions and kitchen appliances. In most of these areas, software is closely tied to a very specific piece of hardware and is known as 'embedded', and is rarely the subject of worries about copyright or piracy.

## Pace of change

Software is not only a relatively recent advent in the world. It is also the product of an extremely fast evolving technology. Computer science and engineering researchers have sustained a doubling of performance and productivity every year or so in almost every dimension of the discipline for around three decades. Moore's law[7] described how the hardware complexity of a computer chip doubled in performance each year, but the same is also approximately true of the disk storage, network performance and programming productivity. To put this in perspective, this is an improvement of one thousand times in ten years or one million times

---

[6] See for example the 'Unofficial Apple Site' report at: www.tuaw.com/2009/02/13/apple-says-jailbreaking-is-illegal/.

[7] Originally, Gordon Moore of Intel wrote this in his article in a 1965 issue of *Electronics Magazine*, which is hard to locate. A good modern reference is online at: http://en.wikipedia.org/wiki/Moore's_law.

in twenty years. This rate of change rests on continual innovation. Hence the computer hardware, including information processing, storage and networks, and computer software (including source programming languages and low level machine code) are quite different from those twenty years ago.

## Hardware is also software

Increasingly, in recent years, hardware is not as immutable as it once was. At the lowest level, hardware is reconfigurable. Hardware is also specified by designers using software (specialized programming languages such as Verilog, allow one to write specifications that are compiled into hardware, but also allow verification of the hardware before expensive production processes are begun). This means that any intellectual property rules about software may also apply to hardware.

The flexibility that software specification brings means that there is a massive acceleration in the production of new hardware, which leads to a very rapid 'upgrade' lifecycle in computers. The new versions of older computer lines may not always be completely compatible with their ancestors, which means that users will need to carry out software upgrades when they buy newer hardware.

The existence of the Internet has eased this process, since software can be downloaded on a new machine, subject to checks on licenses and relevant payment. Software might also be open source, or specific to a particular machine's hardware configuration, and updates included in the price. At the same time, the increasing use of the network for routine software distribution and update has made access to illicit copies of software ever easier. Until recently, technology was not widely deployed to check whether a particular piece of software was licensed to run on a particular piece of hardware. Digital rights technology has emerged to make such checks, but, to date, there is little real enforcement. Partly this is because many enforcement technologies put up barriers to entry for any software, including open source which recovers its production costs in other ways. This is because many rights enforcement technologies are draconian in their implementation, only permitting the installation of software from known or approved sources. This results in a 'lock-in' effect, which may not be intentional, but is a common side effect of the way a license check can be implemented in its simplest form. There are few incentives for companies building such monolithic rights-management systems to make them more complex in ways which would allow free products from other (possibly competing) organizations to be installed that do not infringe any licenses.

## Intellectual property and software

Early communities in programming were established around various positions on whether software should be the subject of copyright or patent protection for those who wished to make a business out of being programmers or owners of programs.[8]

The general consensus seems to be that the core of programs (algorithms) are sufficiently similar to mathematical expressions that the application of copyright protection might not be appropriate. Copyright will not protect the core innovation (an algorithm) if it is of such widespread use, and yet there are many potentially useful algorithms, that the entire creation of useful software would be hopelessly deadlocked if the core building blocks were tied up in such protection.

However, there are at least three very different views on how to apply copyright protection, which rest very much in a debate about the productivity and inventiveness of the programming communities. The first approach is a simple classical approach to copyright protection, typically taken by large computer software companies such as Microsoft. Here the source code has in the past been a closely guarded secret, revealed only to employees. Compiled (i.e. executable programs) are licensed to customers to use. The licence may be time limited, although usually it is only practically limited by the lifetime of the hardware the user has to run it on. Various techniques exist to allow large organizations to license multiple copies. Organizations wishing to extend the software are at arm's length and work with abstract interfaces to the software. Occasionally, the source code might be also licensed for very large fees, compared with acquiring the right to merely 'use' a program.[9]

---

[8] The most extensive discussion of the applicability or otherwise of patent or copyright protection is in J. H. Reichman, 'A Manifesto Concerning the Legal Protection of Computer Programs', *Columbia Law Review*, 94 (1994), 2308–31 (available at: http://eprints.law.duke.edu/896/). In this paper, the authors propose the notion of most software as 'industrial design' is fairly correct – software is both a 'text' and a 'machine' – any novelty in the machine (i.e. an algorithm) is really discovery, in the same sense as mathematical progress. Novelty abounds in the text, but is mostly superficial. This is consistent with my discussion of the computer program as a work.

[9] John Gillespie-Brown writes online advice on software licensing, and his company represents a fairly standard set of solutions (at: www.nalpeiron.com/).

The second and third approaches are usually known as the open source community viewpoints. There are two very divergent models here. The most extreme position is represented by the Free Software Foundation's Gnu General Public License (GPL).[10] Here the model was to protect code written by programmers to ensure that it remained in the public domain. The GPL is generally regarded as 'viral' in the sense that if I were a programmer working on some other software, and were to include any aspect of code that had been subject to the GPL, my code would be 'infected by', or would 'inherit' the GPL model of ownership, which is to say that I would be obliged to put my new code too into the public domain. Ironically, there have been many occurrences of computer science researchers in the academic community moving into the commercial world, and finding themselves not allowed to look at their own 'GPL'ed' code from the past. This is policy, for example, for employees of Microsoft.

The less extreme view is typified by the Creative Commons, but probably emerged much earlier. I would identify this with the UC Berkeley release of their variant of the Unix Operating System, but crucially, with US government funding (from DARPA) of the Internet Protocol Suite back in 1982.[11] The license used for such software is now frequently used by programmers who release their code, but have no wish to prevent for-profit exploitation by others. The so-called Berkeley Software Distribution (BSD) license[12] is widely used and some significant software systems in commercial use today are based on code that was written in the open-source community and released under such a license. Companies such as Sun Microsystems, Citrix, IBM and others have made public that they have products based on BSD-licensed code.

This software allowed computers anywhere to connect to each other. The software was made available in source form to anyone with no restrictions and many successful companies were then built on top of the modifications to that software (Sun, Cisco, et al.). Even now small pieces of code (e.g. mysql) are crucial to companies like IMDB, Facebook and Amazon.

The large body of open-source software is also an educational resource of some value. Its existence allows a large body of programmers to learn

---

[10] See www.gnu.org/licenses/gpl-3.0.txt.
[11] This is documented in the Internet Society's online history of the development of the Internet (at: www.isoc.org/internet/history/brief.shtml).
[12] See www.opensource.org/licenses/bsd-license.php.

from examples, but also to learn familiarity with systems that they can later extend, either for the research and education community, or else for profit.

There is an ongoing debate in policy and economics science about this. A very good background reference is Eric S Raymond's 'The Cathedral and the Bazaar'.[13] This paper discussed the difference between the closed proprietary production of software systems (the Cathedral) and the open-source community (the Bazaar). There is a finer distinction made within the open-source community itself between the GPL and the BSD license models,[14] with GPL proponents claiming that the so-called copy-left provided by GPL creates a stronger protection for the open-source developer, since it requires other developers to continue to contribute their changes under the same license. By contrast, developers basing code on the BSD model can diverge, and not commit their changes back to the original release in the public domain. There is no empirical evidence I can find in favour of the GPL argument that it increases the amount of open-source contribution compared with the non-copyleft open-source approach.

How could there be any business based on the open-source models? There certainly are successful businesses that produce code subject to the BSD open-source models, and even the GPL. The companies Red Hat and Citrix both make good money from maintaining and enhancing software. One claim is that by maintaining software in the public domain, a large body of programmers in the academic and research community will continue to contribute to that software. Indeed there is evidence that some companies will also allow employees to contribute as well as using that software. In the world of literature and TV, this phenomenon also exists, and is known as fan-contributed literature,[15] and has similar tensions.

A claim that this leads to higher productivity and reliability in software (less bugs) is the subject of ongoing debate. Professor Ross Anderson has compared open source and commercial software from the robustness

[13] Available online at: www.catb.org/~esr/writings/cathedral-bazaar/.
[14] www.gnu.org/philosophy/bsd.html.
[15] An excellent study of this, is: K. F. Lawrence, 'The web of community trust – amateur fiction online: a case study in community focused design for the semantic web' (Ph.D. thesis, University of Southampton, 2007) available from Southampton University's eprint service (at http://eprints.ecs.soton.ac.uk/14704/).

perspective and concluded that the important thing is that the approaches are in the same ballpark.[16]

A more complex claim to evaluate is that the overall levels of innovation in the sector are higher among the open-source programmers than among the proprietary closed communities. Since the groups are not completely distinct (programmers employed by proprietary software producers by day may be contributing to open-source projects by night), but also have different emphasis in other social matters, it is very hard to make any plausible comparison.

It is not apparent how traditional models of copyright ever made sense for software. Copyright concerns the expression of an idea not the idea itself – in software, any program in any language that implements the same thing is what is known as 'Turing equivalent'[17] – indeed, the Church–Turing thesis (from the 1930s) makes strong statements about the equivalence of all computer programs. Thus there is potentially a mechanical translation from any form to any other (indeed, compilation, decompilation, disassembly, are just special cases of this). The creative act (if there is one) is in coming up with novel data structures and algorithms. However, algorithms are in essence equations. They express a relation between input and output (a function) and so are really mathematical discoveries. Algorithms are certainly not engineering artefacts[18] in the sense of mechanical inventions.

Luckily for the software business, there are numerous useful algorithms published, although the level of effort in thinking up new algorithms is very much like that of solving new mathematical problems. On the other hand, for many useful tasks that programs have to perform,

---

[16] R. J. Anderson, 'Security in Open Versus Closed Systems – The Dance of Boltzmann, Coase and Moore', presented at Open Source Software Economics (available at: www.cl. cam.ac.uk/~rja14/Papers/toulouse.pdf).

[17] Turing defines the necessary and sufficient features of a system (language and machine) to support the full generality of computation – i.e. to do anything any other computational engine could do. This is an immensely powerful result since it applies to something so flexible and generally applicable as computing. An analogy would be if in pharmaceutical work, someone found a panacea, literally a drug that could transform into any and all other drugs, or a machine for making any and all drugs. A. M. Turing, 'On Computable Numbers, with an Application to the *Entscheidungsproblem*', *Proceedings of the London Mathematical Society*, 2 (1937), 42, 230–65 (available online at: www. turingarchive.org/browse.php/B/12).

[18] Early work on expressing algorithms includes David Hilbert's definition of the 'decision problem', which places the concept squarely in the realm of mathematics, discussed in A. Martin, *The Undecidable, Basic Papers on Undecidable Propositions, Unsolvable Problems And Computable Functions* (New York: Raven Press, 1965).

there is usually an algorithm for the core ('machine-like') component. The programmer has to realize which algorithm is applicable, and might do so using design patterns, or just informal experience.

On the other hand, there is also a reasonable level of skill in coding a program (the text) in a given language, and paying attention to many details of the specific environment that the software is to be used in. In some sense, this part of software production is really a design problem, and therefore a craft. Later in the lifetime of a program, there may be a higher level of skill in maintaining (fixing and enhancing) a program.

When we set programming coursework in computer science classes, there is often quite a lot of similarity in solutions, but the similarities do not necessarily denote infringement – provided there's no causal path. In this respect, software does not differ from plagiarism detection for other works of authorship – correlation does not prove causation – not even when the works show common mistakes. Once a program gets sufficiently complicated, there's a lot of bookkeeping in it, and this is often going to differ in many minor details (although not in semantics). This is often where you see plagiarism, and in the education business, we have, and use programs to detect plagiarism that rely on converting things into a canonical form – any residual differences or similarities are strong hints that copying may have happened.[19]

It would be interesting to use plagiarism detection programs in looking for evidence of copyright theft/infringement.[20] As far as I can ascertain, this has not been done to date.

Programs can be used in a number of ways that may differ from the number of (sensible) uses of other protected works. As well as the need to maintain a program and therefore have access to both source and tools to compile and test a program, it may be necessary to debug a running program. To this end, you need to record a program as it is running and then replay it. Should this not be a different right to that of copying a program and reusing it?

Indeed, this ability to improve (or repair) a program is part of the investment made by the original production team. It is generally much easier for someone involved in the project that created a program in the

---

[19] See Paul Clough's contribution to this volume (Chapter 12, 'Measuring Text Reuse in the News Industry').

[20] I'm reminded of the Borges story where someone lives a better life than a famous author, and then writes an exact 'copy' of the same novel, but critics deem it superior as the relationship between auteur and object are more elegant, in J. L. Borges, 'Pierre Menard, Author of the Quixote', in *Labyrinths* (London: Penguin Classics, 2000).

first place, to maintain or enhance the program. This seems to reflect some idea that copyright protects the financial investment, an investment mainly made in the programmers' minds who wrote the original system, not in the code per se.

It seems to me that a simple analysis of the process of creating and maintaining a program illustrates that there are more stakeholders than with other protected works, as well as more uses. Users almost always buy or rent 'binary' programs rather than source code, whereas with other media, the user acquires a right to the source, in general (i.e. the text of a book). This means that the skills in the software are by default hidden, whereas the skills of Vikram Seth or Arnold Schoenberg or Damien Hirst are all entirely visible and freely available to the student. Why is software nonetheless regarded as a similar property?

It behoves us to ask then, how do I judge the effort in creating a software work? What is the investment in each stage of development of software, and what therefore the appropriate level of protection for that stage and for its uses.

## Piracy and infringement

There are two separate faces of software piracy, because software has two crucially different forms, as discussed above where I have described the difference between the source code of a program (the text) and the executable or compiled form of the program (the machine).

First, people may take copies of binaries (executable programs) because they want a backup or secure copy or perhaps because they are lazy and just want the software on several of their own computers, and sometimes, in a large organization, one could imagine doing this wholesale to save money (i.e. serious infringement).

I cannot find reliable evidence that there is much 'wholesale' piracy at the level of video piracy, i.e. criminals making bulk copies of DVDs for profit.[21] I believe that this is because much software today is frequently bundled with specific hardware, e.g. Windows on a PC; Apple software

---

[21] In the case of some popular commercial software, in some parts of the world, there may be many individual illegal copies, but since the cost of copying is virtually zero, this is unsurprising. It is analogous to the many copies of popular music on file-sharing systems, and does not indicate that there is a large-scale, centralized organized criminal activity involved in this distribution.

on an iPhone; networking software on a Cisco router; indeed, even updates are most frequently 'free' to the user who has paid for the hardware and its original software release.[22]

Second, users take copies of source code because they are too lazy to figure out how to do it themselves: this is common at the personal level in students – plagiarism of programs in computing courses is a well-known problem: this is just plain laziness.

Laziness aside, and more interestingly, there is an important behavioural, or social norm, that is regarded as normal and acceptable in a large part of the software creation business, which is 'reuse'. In the software engineering industry, a business might start from someone else's source code for two very different motives. One, because the existing software captures an important solution to the requirements (i.e. someone did something creative in figuring out the problem, mapping out a solution and coding it); two, because existing software is 'mature' – i.e. has had a lot of skill and time expended on debugging it.

One interesting recent comment by Professor Bjarne Stroustrup of Texas A&M University and creator of the widely used programming language C++ is that he 'based it on C because then he knew it started from something that solved a lot of peoples' problems'[23] – this is a typical (positive) attitude to reuse of ideas in computer science.

Another hint that we are in a world of different social norms comes from the open-source movement, which is strongly motivated by addressing both of these last two motives so that the whole community of stakeholders moves continually forward – reuse both of creative solutions and also of the maturity of working code. Thus, it is easy to see that there are strong technical and economic reasons to reuse working solutions, and there is a strong cultural bias towards making this acceptable – however, it does not follow that the bulk coping of executable/binary programs is acceptable.

Even if software engineers do not condone bulk copying, that does not mean that it does not occur. Software piracy in the sense of copyright

---

[22] One caveat here is that the companies selling bundled software with updates together with hardware often introduce steep price rises for software, when the hardware to which it pertains is reaching some 'obsolescent' age, determined when the cost of upgrade to new hardware might be lower for both company and bulk of users than maintaining legacy hardware base and its software. This is not quite the same as the classic automotive industry historical 'built-in obsolescence' strategy to maintain high profits in the 1950s in the USA.

[23] http://talks.cam.ac.uk/show/archive/18612.

infringement by individuals is rife. Of course, one can only steal software if it is not open source (although passing off GPL'ed code as proprietary would amount to passing off). However, the most widely used operating system, Microsoft Windows and applications (Microsoft Office) are proprietary. It is estimated that there are cases where the majority of copies being run in certain countries are illegal – e.g. China running four times as many 'illegal' copies as 'legal'.[24] Some of this piracy stems from the business culture in different jurisdictions. China was not a member of the World Trade Organization (WTO) until relatively recently; as a result there was a common view, in China that copying software was not infringement. Now that China has acceded to international norms requiring copyright protection for software, commercial and individual behaviour may be changing. Other countries which were outside of the WTO in the past had a similar pattern of behaviour.

However it is also the case that in countries where copyright and other IP are generally respected, at least for some kinds of works, the behaviour of a large fraction of the community with respect to software is generally not in line with law. Thus in North America and Europe, there is wide disregard for copyright for software both in large corporations, where frequently, many illegal copies of commercial software are run, but also among the younger part of the population, where a commonly expressed view is that software is far too expensive, and that large software companies profiteer from near monopoly positions.[25] This attitude overlaps with common youthful behaviour with regards to music copyright, where online sharing of music via P2P and other mechanisms is rife. There are some differences in the music and computer software worlds however.

First, the charges for music on old media and online are seen by some as too similar to justify them, and DRM technology applied to music is sometimes draconian (although changing rapidly right now as the majority of users appear no longer to use traditional media such as CDs or even vinyl). Second, in the software world, the user community has an alternative (for example, OpenOffice is freely available) and so do not have to break the law to make use of computers or information in most formats. The distinction between different media is also becoming blurred: computer games are partly software, but often contain

---

[24] According to www.ifact-gc.org/.
[25] For example, the EU ruling on antitrust against Microsoft is widely reported (e.g. at http://news.bbc.co.uk/1/hi/business/6998272.stm).

significant audio, video and graphic art. At one extreme, a game like Lego's add-on to Activision's Guitar Hero includes all of these and a patented children's building-block game.

The most common acts of copyright infringement are the making of unlicensed copies. Typically, since copying may be allowed in some circumstances (fair reuse, or backup is allowed in some countries), it can be simply confusion on the part of the user. In other cases, it may be culturally acceptable even if it is infringement. Downright piracy, the act of selling unauthorized copies for profit, as opposed to individual copying, seems to be relatively rare in the software business all around the world. However, as with film and music, it is very hard to get any good estimates of either practice, or the levels of lost (or gained) revenues these practices entail.

Another problem specific to software is that of reverse engineering. In most of the world, the core algorithms of a program are not protected. Thus if a competing organization can infer what these algorithms are, they may be able to construct a competing product without infringing any intellectual property rights. This is known as reverse engineering and is quite common practice. In some cases, the reverse engineering process involves 'disassembling' or 'decompiling' a running program. In communications systems, this also entails decoding messages sent between computers. There are many cases where this is a completely legitimate exercise that is required to make one component of a system work with the others, where lamentably, documentation of the way to interwork may be inadequate. At another extreme, software engineers have looked at detailed documentation and inferred how a program works from that. In some administrations, this is viewed as a breach of copyright since the detailed documentation is in some senses equivalent to the actual program source code, and therefore covered by property rights. A useful analogy here is to think about academic definitions of plagiarism. A clear distinction is made between quotation of work with accreditation, and unattributed use of material. In software production, innovation would proceed more rapidly if one could refine and extend other works (with attribution, and without restriction). An open-source system such as the BSD license does this, although the GPL does not.

Having laid the ground work for what software is, we are now perhaps in a position to see how it differs from books, film, music and other works in terms of copyright and piracy. In particular, we shall look at software copyright enforcement, piracy detection, related technology and law.

## Licences

### Software protection, technology and law

Software creators use technology as well as legal means to protect their products.[26] Two common techniques to prevent reverse engineering (or even downright theft) are obfuscation and encryption. Both techniques are designed to raise the cost to the copier. Obfuscation is not terribly effective since it simply involves rewriting released code automatically in some way to create less humanly readable code. The process can be reversed. Encryption is more useful since the released code requires a key to be useable, and the code that decrypts the rest of the code may be created in some way to render it hard to access, perhaps requiring specialized hardware, e.g. an add-on dongle, or a trusted platform module (TPM) on the main processor, which then uses the key to allow the program to run. TPMs are increasingly common on many newer microprocessor chips.

This latter protection requires an adjunct system to distribute keys to allow users to run programs. Such a system is usually a large part of any digital rights management (DRM) technology. Just as the programs themselves can be reverse engineered, and potentially therefore copied or altered (or exploited through protection vulnerabilities), a DRM system itself can also can be subverted. In the end, there is a circular dependence between the law and the technology. To protect the DRM systems themselves, legal mechanisms were brought to bear, and led to the USA creating the Digital Millennium Copyright Act (DMCA), to bring legal sanctions against people undermining DRM technology. This act was designed to apply to all DRM, not just that technology used for computer software. Some communities view this act as untenable since it could prevent legitimate research in computer security (e.g. even the legitimate uncovering of flaws in a DRM system). Key distribution systems are also frequently vulnerable to human error.

---

[26] As discussed above, most software is subject to license agreements, even when those are open source. The end-user license agreement (EULA), comes in many forms. Indeed one common complaint by the public is that the typical EULA is simply far too long and complex for the average person to understand, or have the time even to read. Whether a license explicitly allows lending software or giving a copy to friends or swapping software or making a backup are all matters that vary.

*Detection technology*

Another aspect of copyright enforcement entails the detection of
unauthorized copies of a program being used. To this end, several
operating systems vendors have looked at monitoring all software activity on a computer, and reporting the use of well-known programs
(perhaps by their 'signature' in terms of program size and behaviour).
This relies on network connectivity, in the same way that software
distribution does. Such network connectivity is a benefit to the user
and only the sophisticated user would figure out how to retain the useful
side but block the usage reporting. However, privacy laws in many parts
of the world may conflict with this approach. Indeed, there are also
reported cases of false positive detection of unauthorized program use
leading to inappropriate instruction by legal organizations.

Finally, one can track the movement of copies of software (and other
media types) through the use of ingenious marking schemes that embed
patterns of data in programs or other content – techniques such as
steganographic marking and digital watermarking can lead to finding
the origin of a particular copy of a program, thus allowing one to find the
source of a leak. This may create disincentives to users to give copies to
their friends, since they may get caught.

## Conclusion

To conclude, the use of IP rights to bring legal protection for software has
a cost. Software has a set of costs associated with its production which
are different from other media and hence, in a system of checks and
balances for supporting protection of IP, bears thinking about differently. Creators spend as much or more time maintaining and enhancing
software as they do in its original creation. Software needs hardware,
often very specific hardware, to be useful. Practitioners need access to
principles and examples of software to continue to innovate. The relative
costs of these states are very different, and very different from the
equivalent phases in production and maintenance and use of other
media, notably music, novels and films. Software is itself a tool used to
provide a technical means for protection of IP for software and for most
other types of creative output.

At any given moment, a snapshot of a piece of software is only a tiny
part of the value chain associated with its production, maintenance,
enhancement, distribution, and use. The software is in many mutable

forms, and in a continual state of flux. The transience of the technology as seen by each stakeholder, and the impermanence of any particular instance are not properly reflected in the legal, economic and technical means currently employed to try to protect the various stakeholders' rights. Indeed, I claim that the definitions of those rights as I perceive them from the CDPA, and as applied in various cases do not precisely cover all the possible actions that might be considered, nor does the law capture real costs and values of this entirely new type of property. As a result, the software industry has evolved new models such as open source and copyleft, and new business models (bundling software and updates with specific hardware) to avoid these problems.

11

# Of plots, puddings and draught-excluders: the law as it applies to the infringement of computer programs

JENNIFER DAVIS

In his contribution to this volume (Chapter 10), Jon Crowcroft raises a number of concerns, widely shared among those who create software, regarding the legal protection afforded to computer programs. Most notably, there is broad apprehension that the protection afforded to computer programs (or software) under the law of copyright is deficient, for at least two key reasons. First, it fails adequately to protect the creative effort which is embodied in software from those who would seek to exploit it. Second, it signally fails to prevent the 'piracy' of software. These two concerns, although both relate to perceived free-riding on the creative effort of the software programmer, are not the same. In the first instance, it is argued by Crowcroft and others,[1] that software is unlike other works protected by copyright and that the law does not protect those aspects of software which entail the most creative effort. As a result, such effort may be unjustly but nonetheless legally appropriated. Second, there is a general perception that for a number of reasons, it is far easier illegitimately to copy and distribute software than it is other sorts of copyright works. This chapter looks at each of these concerns and goes on to ask whether, as Crowcroft and others have advocated, software deserves new *sui generis* legal protection apart from that afforded to it under the law of copyright.

## Software does not equate with other copyright works

According to Crowcroft, software significantly departs from other copy-right works in a number of ways which lead to its being under-protected

---

[1] Crowcroft, Chapter 10 in this volume, 'Copyright, Piracy and Software', above p. 209.

against legitimate copying. Most notably, as Crowcroft describes it, writing software and programming a computer are both an art and a skill. The art is involved with creating the algorithm and designing the software so that it will capture both the problem and the solution at hand; by contrast, the craft relates to the tasks of coding or perhaps debugging the software once the problem–solution has been arrived at or formatting the software.[2] The investment of both intellectual and financial resources generally goes into the former and not the latter.[3] Second, software has 'transient value'. That is most software is not a one-off finished product. It is constantly being improved, debugged, or adapted for new purposes. All of these acts involve effort and add value to the software, but it is argued that the present copyright regime is not designed to adequately recognise and reward this particular type of effort.[4] This section will concentrate on the issue of whether copyright law adequately protects the creative effort which is embodied in a computer program. In the context of British law, this debate has been framed around the difference between the idea and the expression of that idea.

*Software and the idea–expression*
*dichotomy in copyright*

A computer program is identified as a literary work under s. 3 (1)(b) of the Copyright, Designs and Patent Act (CDPA) 1988.[5] It is recognised as

---

[2] *Ibid.*, p. 211.

[3] Three other differences between software and other copyright works identified by Crowcroft are that: (a) software exists in a component market; (b) it may be dependent upon either hardware or other systems software to function; and (c) some software may work only if it interacts with other software on another computer, for example as is the case with Internet banking.

[4] The fact that software is frequently updated was considered in *Ibcos Computers Ltd v. Barclays Mercantile Highland Finance Ltd* [1994] FSR 275, at 287. Jacob J. noted that this problem was 'not unique to computer programs' but also applied to 'directories such as telephone books'. And, one might add, textbooks and particularly law textbooks, where the subject matter might be subject to rapid change. It can, of course, be argued that since the decision in *Ibcos*, directories will now be protected by the *sui generis* database right. This right arises from the Directive 96/9/EC of the European Parliament and of the Council of 11 March 1996 on the legal protection of databases.

[5] The Directive on the legal protection of computer programs (Council Directive 91/250/EEC of 14 May 1991) (OJ L122/42) harmonised the protection of computer programs across the EU. It is sometimes referred to as the 'Software Directive', but is not limited in its application to computer programs embodied in software. The Directive required member states to protect a computer program by copyright as a literary work

a fundamental characteristic of British copyright law that copyright protects the expression of and not the ideas embodied in a work and this is as true for computer programs as for all literary works. This principle is also recognised in relation to computer programs from a broader European perspective. Thus, according to the EU Computer Program Directive, protection should not be accorded to 'the ideas and principles which underlie any element of a computer program' (art. 1 (2)).[6] Furthermore, 'to the extent that logic, algorithms and programming languages comprise ideas and principles' these are also not protected.[7] If Crowcroft is right and software is not sufficiently protected by copyright, it follows that one reason for this is that the distinction between an idea which is not protected by copyright and the expression of the idea which is has been wrongly drawn both by statute and by the courts in cases concerning copyright infringement.

There is no argument that copyright will protect the source or object code in which a program is expressed from literal copying of a substantial part.[8] It will also protect against infringement through an unauthorised arrangement or altered version of a program or a translation into another computer language.[9] The key area of contention is the extent to which copyright could or indeed should go further to protect what many, including Crowcroft, sees as the truly creative and original aspect of software: that is its problem–solution approach rather than the mere skill which is embodied in writing the code in which the program is expressed or its structure. Here the determinative factor is not statute law, but rather judicial decision making. It follows that it is worth considering the major English cases concerned with copyright infringement and the idea–expression dichotomy in order to judge whether it is true that the latter has been protected at the expense of the former.

---

in situations where the program is original in the sense that it constitutes the author's own intellectual creation (art. 1(3)). The Directive has been codified and is now Directive 2009/24/EC. For a general discussion of the Directive, see T. Aplin, *Copyright Law in the Digital Society: The Challenges of Multimedia* (Oxford: Hart, 2005).

[6]  This distinction does not have statutory status in the United Kingdom but is understood to be the case. For a general discussion of the idea–expression dichotomy see, L. Bently and B. Sherman, *Intellectual Property* (3rd edn, Oxford University Press, 2009), pp. 182–5. For further analysis and criticism of the ideas–expression dichotomy in UK copyright law, see P. Masiyakurima, 'The Futility of the Idea/Expression Dichotomy in UK Copyright', ICC (2007), 548.

[7]  See recital 11 of Directive 2009/24/EC.

[8]  *Ibcos Computers Ltd* v. *Barclays Mercantile Highland Finance Ltd* [1994] FSR, at 296.

[9]  Section 3(3)(ab) Copyright Designs and Patents Act (CDPA) 1988.

These three cases are: *Ibcos* v. *Barclays*, *Navitaire* v. *Easyjet*[10] and *Nova* v. *Mazooma*.[11]

The earliest of the three cases, *Ibcos*, has generally been understood to have taken a generous attitude to protecting against what is termed the 'non-literal' copying of software.[12] The case concerned the literal copying of a computer program through 'disk-to-disk copying' by the defendant. But in this case, the court went further and found that the defendant had also copied both the design features of the original program (what is frequently described as its 'look and feel') and also the program structure, that is the particular arrangement of the individual programs which went to make up the overall program.[13] Jacob J., as he then was, identified the latter as an original compilation and hence protected by copyright. He noted that in protecting these elements, he was following precedent which acknowledged that while copyright protection did not extend to general ideas it might cover 'detailed ideas' which had attracted skill, labour and judgement.[14] For example, in relation to a literary work, he noted: 'the taking of a plot (i.e. the "idea") of a novel or play can certainly infringe – if that plot is a substantial part of the copyright work.'[15]

In addition, Jacob J. also found that a program might be protected by copyright even if it were purely functional and even if that function could be achieved in only one or 'a limited number of ways'.[16] This is an important observation in relation to computer programs in particular since most are, by their nature, functional. According to Jacob J. what

---

[10] *Navitaire* v. *Easyjet Airline Co.* [2006] RPC 3.

[11] *Nova Productions Ltd* v. *Mazooma Games Ltd & others* [2007] RPC 25.

[12] See for example, M. Heritage, 'The End of "Look And Feel" and the Invasion of the Little Green Men? UK Copyright and Patent Protection for Software After 2005', CTLR (2006), 67.

[13] It is generally accepted that the concept of 'look and feel' was first introduced into UK software cases in *John Richardson Computers Ltd* v. *Flanders* [1993] FSR 497, as suggested by R. Arnold, 'Infringement of Copyright in Computer Software by Non-Textual Copying: First Decision at Trial by an English Court', EIPR [1993], 250. The term has a longer history in US cases relating to the infringement of copyright in computer programs. An overview of the history of the protection afforded to the 'look and feel' of a computer program is set out by P. Samuelson in 'Why Copyright Law Excludes Systems and Processes from the Scope of Its Protection', Tex. L. Rev., 85 (2006–7), 1921, 1961–73. Briefly, she suggests that in early cases such as *Whelan Associates Inc* v. *Jaslow Dental Laboratory Inc.*, 797 F. 2d 1222, 230 USPQ 481 (3d Cir. 1986) the look and feel of computer programs were given substantive protection, but this protection was whittled down in *Computer Associates* v. *Altai* (1992) 982 F.2d. 693 (2nd Cir.) and subsequent cases. See n. 17 below.

[14] *Ibcos Computers Ltd* v. *Barclays Mercantile Highland Finance Ltd* [1994] FSR, at 302.

[15] *Ibid.*, at 296.   [16] *Ibid.*, at 290.

was key was not to confuse the idea with its expression, which, although it might in fact be the only way or the best way to express that idea, was nonetheless entitled to copyright protection.[17]

The arguably generous protection offered to computer programs in *Ibcos* was, to a certain extent clawed back in *Navitaire*, a judgment which was confirmed by Jacob LJ, himself, in the later case of *Nova* v. *Mazooma*. Crucially, *Navitaire* differed from *Ibcos* because in *Navitaire* the defendant did not have access to the original program, so there could be no question of literal copying. The question then raised in *Navitaire* was whether something other than the code might be protected against copying, a question which as we have seen had apparently been answered positively in *Ibcos*. Here the claimants had designed an online booking system (OpenRes) for the defendant airlines. Subsequently, the defendant designed its own online booking system (eRes) which was intended to have the same 'look and feel' as OpenRes. The three areas of non-textual copying that the claimants alleged were the 'look and feel' of the program, its user command structure and certain display screens. The claimant succeeded on the latter claim as the court treated these as artistic works protected by copyright. But it failed on the first two. The user commands were not capable of copyright protection under the *de minimis* principle.[18] Nor was the collection of commands protectable as a compilation as there was no author and no overall design to create a compilation, but rather it was equivalent to a computer language which is not itself protected by copyright.[19] Finally, the question arose as to whether copyright should protect the 'look and feel' of the program. In *Ibcos*, it appeared that it might do so, in the sense that copyright might protect an idea if it was sufficiently detailed. Pumfrey J. disagreed. He chose to differentiate a computer program from other copyright works,

---

[17] Arguably, this distinguished the English approach from the abstraction–filtration approach which had been adopted in the US, most notably in *Computer Associates* v. *Altai* and had been adopted by Ferris J. in *Richardson* v. *Flanders*. As described by Jacob J. in *Ibcos* the abstraction–filtration approach seeks to identify a core of protectable expression, in the process excluding from consideration: '(a) elements dictated by efficiency; (b) elements dictated by external factors and (c) elements taken from the public domain.' Jacob J. took the view that this approach was 'not helpful in English law' (*ibid.*, at 302). *Ibcos* was followed in *Cantor Fitzgerald International* v. *Tradition UK Ltd* [2000] RPC 95.

[18] *Navitaire* v. *Easyjet Airline Co.* [2006] RPC, at 79. Copyright will not protect single words as a literary work, *Exxon Corpn* v. *Exxon Insurance Consultants International Ltd* [1982] Ch. 119.

[19] *Navitaire* v. *Easyjet Airline Co.* [2006] RPC, at 88.

because, 'two completely different computer programs can produce an identical result . . . at any level of abstraction'. And this was the case even if the author of one had had no access to the other except for its results. This differentiated a computer program from a book with a plot as did the fact that a computer program, like a book of instructions, has 'no theme, no events, and does not have a narrative flow'.[20] This was not to say that the ideas behind the program did not involve considerable skill, labour and judgement. Rather, it was not the relevant skill, labour and judgement.[21] According to Pumfrey J., a better analogy for a computer program was not a plot but a pudding.[22] He noted:[23]

> Take the example of a chef who invents a new pudding. After a lot of work he gets a satisfactory result, and, thereafter, his puddings are always made using his written recipe, undoubtedly a literary work. Along comes a competitor who likes the pudding and resolves to make it himself. Ultimately, after much culinary labour, he succeeds in emulating the earlier result, and he records his recipe. Is the later recipe an infringement of the earlier, as the end result, the plot and purpose of both (the pudding) is the same? I believe the answer is no.

The principles enunciated in *Navitaire* were endorsed by Jacob LJ in the Court of Appeal in *Nova* v. *Mazooma*. He, in turn offering his own contestant for most apt metaphor, compared a computer program not to a plot or a pudding but to a draught-excluder.[24] The claimant produced a computer game based on pool as did the defendant. In most respects the games were quite different, but there were some common features, apart from their subject matter, including, for example, the ideas of a rotary controller and of synchronising the pulsing power meter with a pulsing cue, which the claimant maintained had been copied by the defendant. Once again, it was crucial that the defendant had not had access to the code of the original game. Jacob LJ endorsed the finding of the High Court that there had been no copyright infringement

---

[20] *Ibid.*, at 125.

[21] Pumfrey J. cites Lord Hoffmann in *Designers' Guild Ltd* v. *Russell Williams (Textiles) Ltd (No. 2)* [2001] FSR 11, at 27.

[22] The issues relating to copyright protection of recipes and computer programs is discussed by T.S.L. Cheng, in 'Copyright Protection of Haute Cuisine: Recipe for Disaster?', EIPR [2008], 93.

[23] *Navitaire* v. *Easyjet Airline Co.* [2006] RPC, at 127.

[24] The draught-excluder metaphor derives from *Kleeneze Ltd and another* v. *DRG (UK) Ltd and another* [1984] FSR 399 which concerned the idea–expression dichotomy in relation to a design for letterbox draught excluders and was cited by Lord Hoffmann in *Designers' Guild*.

because the defendants had copied the claimants' ideas, not their expression.[25] In particular, he did not accept the argument that software is different from other copyright works in that ideas are the 'building blocks' of a computer program.[26] For his part, Jacob LJ believed that in this case, and with respect to computer programs more generally:

> The nature of the work is a computer program having all the necessary coding to function. The general idea is only faintly related to that – no different from the relationship of the general idea of a plastic letter-box draught excluder to the artistic works consisting of the drawings for a particular excluder . . .Not all the skill which goes into a copyright work is protected – the obvious example being the skill involved in creating an invention which is then described in a literary work. An idea consisting of a combination of ideas is still just an idea. That is as true for ideas in a computer program as for any other copyright work.[27]

He concluded that what had been taken by the defendant did not amount to a substantial part of the claimant's program, as it did not constitute the taking of a substantial part of the skill and effort which had been expended on the program.[28]

## The idea–expression dichotomy and other copyright works

Are critics correct that the courts have been discriminatory in the copyright protection they have afforded to computer programs as opposed to other copyright works? It is argued here that that they have not.[29] In particular, it is submitted that copyright should be understood not to protect that which is the most original or creative, since it is certainly possible that even very general ideas might be both. Rather, it is intended to protect the expression of that creativity from illegitimate

---

[25] The court also considered and rejected the claim that a series of graphic frames which showed the movement of the cue and balls should be protected beyond the protection afforded to a single frame as an artistic work.

[26] This was the argument of counsel for the claimant (*Nova Productions Ltd* v. *Mazooma Games Ltd & others* [2007] RPC 25, at 32).

[27] *Ibid.*, at 35. The claimant also failed to persuade the court that copying the ideas in the preparatory design works for computer programs was an infringement. Jacob LJ held that as with any other copyright work, what was protected in the preparatory works was the expression not the ideas (*ibid.*, at 49). See recital 7 of the Software Directive.

[28] *Ibid.*, at 45.

[29] And this is the view taken by other commentators. See, for example, S. Miles and E. Stoker, '*Nova Productions Limited* v. *Mazooma Games Ltd*', Ent. LR (2006), 181 and S. Stokes, 'The Development of UK Software Copyright Law: From *John Richardson Computers* to *Navitaire*', CTLR, 11(7) (2005), 129.

appropriation provided that the expression is itself original, in the sense of not copied from elsewhere. It is further submitted that given both an idea and its expression might embody creativity, what distinguishes expression from the simple idea, in the eyes of the court, is that the latter (the idea) may involve skill and effort which may be appropriated legitimately. In contrast, it is the skill and effort in expressing ideas rather than some more general notion of skill and effort which copyright protects. The exercise for the courts, in relation not only to software but also to literary and other works more generally, has been to draw the line between ideas, which may in themselves be creative, and their expression, which need not necessarily be creative but will nonetheless embody the relevant skill and effort. As explained by Lord Hoffmann in *Designers' Guild:*[30] 'Originality, in the sense of the contribution of the author's skill and labour, tends to lie in the detail with which the basic idea is presented. Copyright law protects foxes better than hedgehogs.'

While it is necessary to locate the line between idea and expression in all infringement cases involving non-literal copying, the critical issue is whether software is particularly disadvantaged in this regard because, as Crowcroft argues, the expression of the ideas is in general the least creative element of such a work: a craft rather than an art? But it is certainly the case that in many other situations involving copyright-protected works the expression constitutes the least creative element. Consider, for example, *The Da Vinci Code*[31] by Dan Brown. Although this is one of the bestselling books of all time, even its most fervent admirers would not maintain that its prose was anything other than workmanlike. The author (and his publisher) were sued by two historians who claimed that the central theme of Brown's book was based on historical research and theories which they had published in an earlier volume, *Holy Blood, Holy Grail,* and which included the startling claim that Jesus had married Mary Magdalene and had had children.[32] Brown admitted to copying this and other 'ideas' published by the claimants but the Court of Appeal did not find infringement. The claimants' ideas were too 'generalised' to constitute a substantial part of their own oeuvre and hence had not been illegitimately appropriated, in a copyright sense, by

[30] *Designers' Guild Ltd* v. *Russell Williams (Textiles) Ltd (No. 2)* [2001] FSR 11, at 2423. This case concerned an artistic work, but was cited as applicable to computer programs by Pumfrey J. in *Navitaire,* at 128.
[31] Dan Brown, *The Da Vinci Code* (New York: Doubleday, 2003).
[32] *Baigent* v. *Random House Group Ltd* [2007] FSR 24.

Brown. Furthermore, there were no similarities of language or architectural similarities between the two books. It was acknowledged by the
Court that the historical research undertaken by the claimants and the
conclusions that they had reached entailed both 'skill and effort'. But this
was not the relevant skill and effort for copyright purposes.[33] They were
the hedgehogs not the foxes. Conversely, it is undoubtedly the case that
were a third party to appropriate the mundane prose in which these
original ideas had been expressed by Brown, or indeed the developed plot
of his novel, this would almost certainly amount to infringement. In sum,
the fact that copyright may protect the banal at the expense of the truly
original is not unique to software.

## Should software be protected by a *sui generis* right?

Crowcroft and others view software as a new form of 'creative and
inventive work'. From this viewpoint, it follows that copyright is not
the appropriate legal regime for protecting software and that it deserves[34]
its own *sui generis* right.[35] One basis of this claim, as was noted above,
rests on the fact that, as Crowcroft argues, the creative element of a
computer program is always embodied in its idea, rather than its expression. We have already suggested that this may also be true, for other sorts

---

[33] *Ibid.*, at 155–6.

[34] Interestingly, in his chapter, Crowcroft rests his appeal for greater protection for
computer programs not primarily on moral arguments but rather on more utilitarian
concerns regarding the optimum protection needed to ensure continued innovation.
While there seems to be no reason why contrasting 'moral' justifications for copyright,
such as 'rights'-based justifications (which broadly argue that an individual has a right to
the fruits of his labour) should not apply as much to computer programs as to other types
of work, such justifications do not seem to be generally employed by those who are
concerned with the protection of computer programs. For a general overview of these
arguments in relation to copyright, see G. Davies, *Copyright and the Public Interest*
(London: Sweet & Maxwell, 2002). For a more focused discussion of justifications in
relation to digital works, see Aplin, *Copyright Law*, ch. 1.

[35] There has been a long and ongoing debate as to whether software should be protected by
patent law which cannot be canvassed here. It remains the case that in the UK, software will
not be patentable unless it has a technical effect. Hence, in the foreseeable future, patent
protection is unlikely to fill the lacuna in the protection afforded to software against copying
which Crowcroft identifies in copyright law. For a summary of the position, see Aplin and
Davis, *Intellectual Property*, pp. 705–13. See also, A. Christie, 'Designing Appropriate
Protection For Computer Programs', EIPR (1994), 11, G. Ghidini and E. Arezzo, 'Patent
and Copyright Paradigms vis-à-vis Derivative Innovation: The Case of Computer Program',
IIC, 2 (2005), 159–278 and M. Heritage, 'The End of "Look And Feel"'.

of works.[36] But Crowcroft also identifies two other key reasons for drawing this conclusion, both of which relate to the ease with which a computer program might be copied and distributed. First, any piece of software might be the perfect equivalent of another piece of software without in any way being a copy of the latter's code or architecture (which might be protected by copyright). As Crowcroft explains it, a computer program in any language, even though not copied from an earlier piece of software, but which performs an identical function (as in *Navitaire*), constitutes a 'Turing equivalent'.[37] From this perspective, copyright does not simply under-protect the creative elements of software from copying, it is unable to provide an adequate level of protection. Second, because software is distributed primarily on the Internet and because its functions can be reproduced simply by copying either its source or its object codes, it can be easily copied and distributed illegitimately. Let us consider each of these points in turn.

### *Copyright cannot adequately protect the investment in software*

Elsewhere it has been argued that the ease with which it is possible to produce a computer program which has identical functions to an earlier program, without reproducing the latter's text, may lead to market failure, in particular making it difficult for small and start-up companies both to enter the market and to prosper. Thus innovative software once placed on the market may have no time to recoup the initial investment made in its development before functionally equivalent software, without the same sunk costs, undercuts its market. Furthermore, because software is continually subject to incremental change, this latter software may be better than the original innovative product, but still not as expensive to develop.[38] One suggestion has been therefore that a legal

---

[36] It may have been the case that for most artistic works, in the past, creativity lay largely in the expression of the idea, but this is certainly not the case today. Conceptual art is an obvious example. As early as 1917, Marcel Duchamp, signed a urinal, 'R. Mutt' and exhibited it as a work of art. It was one of what he referred to as 'Readymades', which also included a bicycle wheel and other found objects. According to Duchamp, 'The creative act is not performed by the artist alone; the spectator brings the work in contact with the external world by deciphering and interpreting its inner qualifications and thus adds his contribution to the creative act' (quoted by R. Lebel, in *Marcel Duchamp* (New York: Grove Press, New York, 1959), pp. 77–8).

[37] See Crowcroft, 'Copyright, Piracy and Software'.

[38] P. Samuelson, R. Davis, M. D. Kapor and J. H. Reichman, 'A Manifesto Concerning the Legal Protection of Computer Programs', Columbia L. Rev., 94 (1994), 2308, 2357–64.

regime should be developed which offers innovative software artificial lead time in which to recoup sunk costs before substitutable products enter the market.[39] It is possible to take issue with this approach on two counts. First, since both these arguments were tendered in 1994, and as Crowcroft acknowledges, there has continued to be a tremendous rate of innovation in software development.[40] It is true that Microsoft and other relatively large companies have come to dominate the software market. But it is also true that this may be the result of seeking network efficiency, so software may work best when it is maximally compatible with other software.[41] Furthermore, the consolidation of certain industries has been a characteristic of late twentieth-century capitalism. Returning to the pudding analogy, the confectionary industry has seen massive concentration in a small number of large multinationals, and there seems no reason why the software industry should be protected from similar developments.[42] However, it is also notable, again as Crowcroft makes clear, that much of this innovation has originated, not from large multinationals, but from programmers developing software collaboratively using open-source models, in both a commercial and non-commercial context.[43]

### Software is exceptionally easy to 'pirate'

Second, software is said to display its 'know how on its face', and hence to be easily reproduced.[44] Certainly, such a characteristic ensures that it cannot be protected as a trade secret and we have already seen that copyright may offer it scant protection. Indeed, this characteristic of

---

[39] J. H. Reichman, 'Legal Hybrids between Patent and Copyright Paradigms', Colum. L. Rev., 94 (1994), 2434, 2506.

[40] He writes: 'Computer science and engineering researchers have sustained a doubling of performance and productivity every year or so in almost every dimension of the discipline for around three decades' (Crowcroft, p. 216).

[41] I am grateful to Dr M. Nabar for making this point. See A. Gupta, 'Are Open Standards a Prerequisite to Open Source? A Perspective in Light of Technical and Legal Developments', CTLR, 15(1) (2009), 3.

[42] Thus in 2005, US multinational Kraft bought the European operations of United Biscuits (http://news.bbc.co.uk/1/hi/business/6083282.stm, accessed 4 October 2009). It bought Cadburys. Cadburys and Kraft are placed second and fifth in terms of world confectionery sales (*Guardian*, 7 September 2009). Another multinational, Premier Foods, took over Rank Hovis McDougall in 2007, and now controls, as well as 'Hovis', a large number of major confectionery brands, including cake and pudding brands, such as 'Mr. Kipling' and 'Gateaux'.

[43] Crowcroft, 'Copyright, Piracy and Software', p. 22.

[44] Reichman, 'Legal Hybrids', 2511.

software contributes to the ease with which it might be reproduced without copying the code in which the program is expressed. But once again, is software unique in this regard? One obvious response to this argument would lie in Pumfrey's pudding metaphor. Puddings too might be reverse engineered and Turing equivalents reproduced without infringement. But the Internet also ensures that what had previously been non-substitutable copyright works, for all practical purposes, have now gone the way of software. In a sense it is in the nature of all copyright works, books, pictures, music and films, to display their know-how on their face. It is true that another novel about the progeny of Jesus and Mary Magdalene would not be a Turing equivalent of the *Da Vinci Code* if it did not copy the novel's expression, that is its words, sentence structure or phrases, or indeed its architecture.[45] However, what differentiated software from other copyright works in the pre-digital age, was the ease with which it might be not only literally copied but also be open to having a perfect substitute provided through the elaboration of its ideas without the reproduction of the expression of those ideas. Such a difference may no longer be so profound. In the digital age, the wide-scale piracy of all sorts of copyright works means that they have, in a sense, become substitutable for themselves. It is possible for the film, *The Da Vinci Code* to be copied easily on the Internet, and an infinite number of perfect substitutes for the original film produced and the same is, of course, true for recorded music and for books.

### Software and a sui generis right

It may appear, therefore, that arguments which seek to assert that computer programs are sufficiently different from other copyright works such that they deserve a new *sui generis* form of protection are not particularly convincing. Ironically, the strongest counter-argument to this stance, made clear in Crowcroft's article, is that such *sui generis* rights have in fact emerged in relation to computer programs, in the form of the GPL (general public licence) and the Creative Commons, both of which Crowcroft describes in some detail. Neither of these *sui generis*

---

[45] There is an illuminating and detailed discussion of the ideas–expression dichotomy as it relates to *The Da Vinci Code*, and more generally, in Alan Durant's contribution to this volume: see Chapter 8 "'Substantial Similarity of Expression" in Copyright Infringement Actions: A Linguistic Perspective'.

regimes give 'stronger' protection[46] to proprietary computer software, in the sense for example of protecting the lead time for a new program to enable its creator to recover sunk costs. But neither, do they abandon copyright altogether. In the case of the GLP, computer programmers assert copyright in their creations, but also license their programs so that others are guaranteed the freedom to copy, adapt or distribute it.

Conversely, under the Creative Commons approach, most specifically under the BSD[47] model, programmers may retain the rights to their improvements and successful, business models have been built on its foundations. As one observer points out, this latter model, 'depends heavily on copyright law to effectuate it'.[48] Furthermore, as Crowcroft admits, there is as yet no conclusive evidence as to whether these models contribute to higher productivity or to the production of more reliable software.[49] Nonetheless, the open-source approaches do appear to introduce new models of protection which cover some of the major concerns about software protection, which were noted at the start of this chapter, including the importance to computer programs of continuous updating, adaptation and improvement by a multiplicity authors.

Once again there is, however, a caveat. There are now a growing number of instances in which the Internet is employed, in much the same way as computer programmers use the GPL or the Creative Commons models, to create, adapt or improve a variety of copyright works. Most notable of course is Wikipedia, but Crowcroft also rightly refers to fan-contributed literature, otherwise known as 'fan fiction'. Recently, the pop group, the Black Eyed Peas, released an album which was made available for fans to remix over the Internet. According to one report, 'The Black Eyed Peas anticipate a future in which albums are

---

[46] Although, as Crowcroft, 'Copyright, Piracy and Software', points out at p. 219, the GPL gives 'stronger' protection but to the public domain, since improvements to existing programs created under a GPL cannot be appropriated by any individual. From this viewpoint, it might be more accurate to describe the GPL as a *sui generis* mode of exploitation and marketing.

[47] BSD stands for Berkeley Software Distribution (www.freebsd.org/).

[48] H. Meeker, 'Origins and Development of Open Source and GPL Licensing', CTLR (2008), 42. She argues that drawing a dichotomy between proprietary and non-proprietary software is, in any event, misleading. In the open-source community, proprietary software refers to software distributed in its binary code only and not its source code (thus, the source code is protected, as she notes, much like a trade secret) whereas Creative Commons software publishes the source code. But both are equally protective in relation to copyright.

[49] Crowcroft 'Copyright, Piracy and Software', p. 220.

fluid, download-only constructions that will be regularly supplemented by new mixes of every track' while, on the album itself, a voice announces, 'There is no longer a physical record store.'[50] All of these new forms of creativity were, of course, made possible by the Internet. From this viewpoint, computer programs do not appear to be unique. Rather we might conclude that computer programmers were 'early adopters' – which given their particular line of work is perhaps scarcely surprising.

---

[50] C. Sullivan, 'The Black Eyed Peas: The E.N.D.', *Guardian*, 5 June 2009. It might be argued that Wikipedia's contributors do not acquire new proprietary rights from their contributions, but the same is presumably not true of fan fiction. Each new story will carry with it a new copyright.

# PART VII

Information studies

# 12

# Measuring text reuse in the news industry

PAUL CLOUGH*

## Introduction

The activity of text reuse describes the situation in which pre-existing written material is *consciously* used again during the creation of a new text or version.[1] This might include the reuse of an entire document (e.g. in the case of duplicate web pages), or smaller segments (e.g. chunks, paragraphs and sentences) from one or more existing texts. From the author's perspective, the process of reuse involves 'finding the relevant material, modifying it as needed and stitching the pieces together'.[2] This may involve a process of text rewriting (or editing), with the author reusing existing material with (or without) permission from the owner. From the reader's perspective, text reuse can be cast as a problem of text analysis or attribution:[3] given two texts is it possible to determine, within an acceptable degree of probability, whether one text is derived from the other? Identifying text reuse can be difficult due to the degree of textual transformation that can occur, from simple cut-and-paste reuse to more complex cases involving paraphrasing and summarisation making the revised version appear very different to the original text. One might add to this that recent advances in technology are also making the activity of

* This work was made possible by the following: Yorick Wilks, Robert Gaizauskas, Ted Dunning, Jonathan Foster, Scott Piao, John Arundel, the Press Association and the UK EPSRC. I also thank Tanya Aplin and Jennifer Davis for their insightful comments on previous versions of this chapter.
[1] More details about my work on text reuse can be found in: P. D. Clough and R. Gaizauskas, 'Corpora and Text Re-use', in A. Lüdeling and M. Kytö (eds.), *Corpus Linguistics: An International Handbook* (Berlin: Mouton de Gruyter, 2009), pp. 1249–71 and P. D. Clough, 'Measuring text reuse' (Ph.D. thesis, University of Sheffield, 2003).
[2] D. Levy, 'Document Re-Use and Document Systems', *Electronic Publishing*, 6(4) (1993), 339–48, 339.
[3] Wilks discusses further problems of text attribution in this article: Y. Wilks, 'On the Ownership of Text', *Computers and the Humanities*, 38(2) (2004), 115–27.

text reuse easier. For example, the search engine Google indexes and makes easily accessible billions of web pages on a diverse range of topics and in many different languages. Being able to discover such documents may promote their use as a basis for new texts. Word processors have also become more sophisticated, enabling users to easily cut and paste, merge and reformat existing texts from a variety of sources into a new document.

Between 1999 and 2002 the UK Engineering and Physical Sciences Research Council (EPSRC) funded the MEasuring TExt Reuse (METER) project,[4] an investigation of text reuse within the British press. The project aimed to develop and evaluate various computational approaches for analysing and quantifying text reuse. Previous work had already highlighted the existence of text reuse in the news industry,[5] but the METER project aimed at assessing the effectiveness of automated approaches for identifying text reuse. Being able to measure text reuse reliably and accurately is of great commercial interest to news agencies. Given the important role that they play in the news industry, accurately measuring text reuse could have the following practical benefits: enable the news agency to charge customers on a pay-per-usage basis rather than a flat fee (more competitive and fairer); detect copies of newswire copy on the Internet or within some other set of electronic documents held external to the news agency; identify material no customers are using and hence eliminate redundant or unnecessary services; help establish trends and patterns about reuse by paying customers; and, enable them to determine the amount of self-reuse (i.e. re-duplication of the same text). This chapter summarises recent work at studying text reuse in the news. Section 2 describes the general practices of producing newspaper articles, with a particular focus on the activity of text reuse. Section 3 describes the METER project, including manual analysis carried out to investigate text reuse, the creation of a corpus to develop and evaluate automated methods of detecting text reuse in the news domain,

---

[4] P. D. Clough, R. Gaizauskas, S. L. Piao and Y. Wilks, 'Measuring Text Re-use', in *Proceedings of the 40th Anniversary Meeting for the Association for Computational Linguistics ACL'02* (Philadelphia, USA, 2002), pp. 152–9.

[5] The following include discussions of text reuse in the news: A. Bell, *The Language of News Media* (Oxford: Blackwell, 1991); A. Bell, 'Text, Time and Technology in News English', in S. Goodman and D. Graddol (eds.), *Redesigning English: New Texts, New Identities* (London: Routledge, 1996), pp. 3–26; J. E. Richardson, 'News Reports from Press Agency Sources: An Insight on Newspaper Style' (2002), Sheffield Online Papers in Social Research (ShOP), no. 2, 2000.

and automated methods developed in the project to detect and measure text reuse. Finally, Section 4 concludes the chapter with some final remarks and suggestions for future work.

## Text reuse and newspaper production

### The news industry

The narrative of a newspaper communicates daily events to its audience using a particular language and discourse.[6] The manner in which journalists report the news can have a big impact on how a reader will interpret and understand a story; their views are influenced by what the journalist writes. By means of how events and people are portrayed, newspapers and news agencies control what is published based upon editorial decisions and the influence of political and commercial ownership. The production of a newspaper is not the work of just one person, but of many (often referred to as 'newsworkers'). Together they manipulate and revise texts within a continual cycle of editing. Personal style or variation is removed from a news story to leave text whose author is not the individual writers, but one 'meta-author' – the newspaper. Editors work to change and manipulate text into a form which meets specific language requirements as prescribed by the newspaper's house style guide. There are many other constraints on the production of a newspaper story which lead to variation in the reuse of text, affecting both syntax and lexical choice.

The news agency[7] (or newswire) is a media organisation whose primary function is to gather and sell news to media companies (e.g. newspapers, broadcasters and online suppliers), and other organisations (e.g. government, private individuals and business institutions). Most countries have a news agency that covers events at home (e.g. the Press Association, PA, in

---

[6] The way in which journalists create stories is mostly instinctive, from years of practice, but Keeble suggests there are prescriptive structures which news stories follow. For example, journalists are typically encouraged to include the '5 Ws': the who, what, when, where and why near the beginning of a story. For further information see e.g. R. Keeble, *The Newspapers Handbook* (London, Routledge, 1998); D. Reah, *The Language of Newspapers* (London, Routledge, 1998); H. Evans, *Essential English for Journalists, Editors and Writers* (rev. edn, London, Pimlico, 2000); Bell, *Language*; T. van Dijk, *News as Discourse* (Hillsdale, NJ: Lawrence Erlbaum, 1988).

[7] For further information about the role of news agencies, see e.g. T. van Dijk, *News Analysis: Case Studies of International and National News in the Press* (Hillsdale, NJ: Lawrence Erlbaum, 1988) and Bell, 'Text, Time'.

the UK), but larger news agencies will also be international (e.g. Reuters). News organisations such as newspapers use text provided by the news agency (called copy), even when they have their own news production team. It is well known in the newspaper industry that the reuse of news agency text is standard practice and that news agency text will be used for at least the following: (1) the editor may want to verify the facts of a story written by a journalist, (2) a journalist may not have the time to gather their own news because of tight deadlines, therefore they may use agency copy as the basis for their story, (3) the editor may rely on the advisory supplied by the news agency as a summary of the previous day's news, and (4) the journalist may rely on the agency copy to supply background information to a story.

In the UK and Ireland the Press Association[8] (PA) is the national news agency providing a continuous stream of regional, national and international news. On average, the PA outputs 1,500 news, sport and feature stories on a daily basis and consumers of its services include national and international newspapers, regional morning and evening papers and terrestrial radio and television broadcasters. In the UK, all national newspapers pay to use the services provided by the PA; in addition thousands of weeklies, periodicals and magazines also receive various types of PA output. Because of its ongoing supply of both domestic and national news, the PA is in a unique position in the British media industry and is widely regarded as a credible, authoritative and trustworthy journalistic source for the newspaper and broadcast.[9]

## Journalism and text reuse

Prefabricated texts such as the news agency press release are often combined together with other sources[10] during the creation of a newspaper

---

[8] See the Press Association website for further details: www.pa.press.net (site accessed: 1 June 2009).

[9] Hamer describes the role of the PA in the UK news industry in the following: M. Hamer, 'The Press Association at Work: Examination of a News Agency's Contribution to the Media and Public Spheres' (M.Sc. dissertation, Liverpool John Moores University, 2000).

[10] Other sources may include press releases from legislative bodies, committees and organisations, reports from organisations, notes of interviews and phone calls, printed versions of speeches and press conferences (van Dijk, News).

story, especially when reporting 'hard' news which contains just facts with little or no editorial comment or views (this contrasts with 'soft' news – feature stories which deviate from the structure of hard news). Journalists rely heavily upon press agencies as their primary source of prefabricated news material: 'most of what journalists "write" is actually a re-processing of already existing text'[11] and in a busy newsroom news agency text stands a good chance of being reused. Although newswire text may be reused verbatim 'news agencies provide most of the copy on any newspaper ... most agency stories will be run verbatim', it is also common to find the text rewritten to meet specific production constraints[12] and invariably differences will arise. The following short example illustrates how the same newswire text may be rewritten by newspapers from the popular and quality press:

**Newswire version**
A Chief Constable's daughter who assaulted two officers in her father's force after drinking a litre of strong cider was today sentenced to 150 hours' community service.
**Derived version (popular press or tabloid)**
A Top Cop's daughter who assaulted two of her Dad's officers after downing a litre of cider was sentenced to 150 hours' community service yesterday.
**Derived version (quality press or broadsheet)**
The daughter of the Chief Constable of Sussex was sentenced to 150 hours' community service yesterday.

Although short, this example illustrates the kind of editing operations typical within this domain: deletion, word substitution (e.g. 'in the last 10 years' might be replaced by 'in the last decade') and applying or reversing syntactic rules (e.g. changing active to passive voice). Further processes may involve sentence reduction and combination, syntactic transformation, paraphrasing, generalisation and specification and sentence reordering.[13]

---

[11]  Bell, 'Text, Time', 20–2.
[12]  These may include a newspaper's house style, short deadlines, word length limits imposed by physical size during page layout, readability and audience comprehension, editorial bias and the use of prescriptive writing practices. See, e.g. Keeble, *Newspapers Handbook*, for further details.
[13]  These operations are similar to those previously identified as being used by humans to generate text summaries; see K. McKeown and H. Jing, 'The Decomposition of Human-Written Summary Sentences', in *Proceeding of the 22nd International Conference on Information Retrieval SIGIR'99* (1999), pp. 129–36.

## The METER Project

*Manually identifying text reuse*

The METER project focused on investigating automated methods for detecting text reuse in the British press industry. To study text reuse, data was collected from two sources: the real-time repository of PA stories (the same service used by subscribers) and nine daily British newspapers.[14] Stories produced by the PA are classified under a number of categories (e.g. courts, education, entertainment, etc.) and further subdivided into specific stories (called catchlines). Under each catchline, the PA follows the development of an event as it happens and continually releases updated versions of the story (resulting in the duplication of text). For a selected time period, corresponding newspaper stories on the same catchline as the PA version were collected.

To analyse the newswire–newspaper text pairs, a systematic comparison by two trained journalists, with a working knowledge of the British news industry, was carried out: each sentence from the newspaper version of a story was compared with the original PA version to attempt to locate its possible source sentence(s) and to reconcile any differences.[15] In many instances, the differences would come from editing operations used to transform or restyle the text (e.g. the replacement of words with lexical equivalents: 'a youth confronted the 14-year old' to 'a blade-wielding yob confronted the teenage girl' and syntactic editing: 'was due in court today' to 'was due in court yesterday'). This task was often made more difficult because of the varying degree of rewriting carried out by newsworkers and the use of stylised language.[16]

Given the commercial needs of the PA in wanting to quantify and monitor reuse and the practical constraints in manually analysing reuse, a simple classification scheme was developed.[17] Newswire–newspaper

---

[14] Newspaper sources included 'broadsheets' (*Times, Guardian, Independent* and *Daily Telegraph*), 'middle-road tabloids' (*Daily Mail* and *Express*) and 'tabloids' (*Sun, Daily Star* and the *Mirror*).

[15] An approach similar to that described in van Dijk, *News* and J. E. Richardson, 'News Reports from Press Agency Sources: An Insight on Newspaper Style', Sheffield Online Papers in Social Research (ShOP), (2000), no. 2.

[16] For example, the use of 'journalese' in tabloids. See e.g. K. Waterhouse, *Waterhouse on Newspaper Style* (London: Penguin, 1993).

[17] P. D. Clough, R. Gaizauskas and S. L. Piao, 'Building and Annotating a Corpus for the Study of Journalistic Text Re-Use', in *Proceedings of the 3rd International Conference on Language Resources and Evaluation, LREC'02* (2002), pp. 1678–85.

text pairs for each catchline were manually classified using a simple three-way scheme to reflect the degree of text reuse from the PA as a source text.[18] The first category, wholly derived (WD), reflects the situation in which it is likely that the news agency text has been reused and is the only source of information used. The second category, partially derived (PD), reflects the situation in which the news agency text has likely been reused, but is one of many sources used. The final category, non-derived (ND), reflects the situation in which it is unlikely the news agency text has been reused (i.e. the newspaper version is written independently).

Because this categorisation scheme was applied retrospectively (it was impractical to monitor the journalists at work directly due to limited access to the newsworkers), it is impossible to be certain about the derivation relationship between texts. However, trained journalists with knowledge and experience of the UK news industry were employed in the task. Although the decision for whether a newspaper article is derived or not from a PA source text is often intuitive, subjective and reliant on a deep understanding of the news industry, during the course of text analysis a number of general features for distinguishing between derived and non-derived texts did emerge. These included: (1) the presence of factual information and direct quotes in the newspaper version not reported by the newswire would signal the use of multiple sources; (2) the degree of lexical (and syntactic) similarity between texts (i.e. greater similarity indicating possible reuse); (3) the proportion of matching character sequences between texts (i.e. longer matches indicated derivation); (4) the level of detail in reported facts (i.e. more detail in the newspaper version than PA indicating the use of further sources); and (5) similarity in the ordering of events being reported.

To enable the empirical study of text reuse and evaluation of automated approaches of detection, we manually gathered and analysed 1,716 texts to create the METER corpus.[19] The corpus contains a

---

[18] This scheme is similar to those proposed for copy detection, S. Brin, J. Davis and H. Garcia-Molina, 'Copy Detection Mechanisms for Digital Documents', in *Proceedings of the ACM SIGMOD International Conference on Management of Data* (1995), pp. 398–409 and tracking information flow, D. Metzler, Y. Bernstein, B. Croft, A. Moffat and J. Zobel, 'Similarity Measures for Tracking Information Flow', in *Proceedings of the ACM Conference on Information and Knowledge Management CIKM'05* (2005), Bremen, Germany, 517–24.

[19] See e.g. Clough *et al.*, 'Building and Annotating', pp. 1678–85; R. Gaizauskas, J. Foster, Y. Wilks, J. Arundel, P. Clough and S. L. Piao, 'The METER Corpus: A Corpus for

collection of contemporary news between July 1999 and June 2000 in two domains: (1) law and court reporting, and (2) show business and entertainment. These domains were selected for their diversity in reporting, and because they form staple and recurring examples in British media. The selection of newswire–newspaper texts for the corpus was based on several criteria including the following: (1) the type of news story (hard or soft, running or one-off); (2) the period over which stories were considered; (3) the register of newspapers sampled (e.g. tabloid or broadsheet); (4) the length of newspaper article; (5) the degree of reuse; and (6) the number of newspapers reporting the story. This language resource provides examples of derived and non-derived texts from which discriminating features can be identified and facilitates the testing of automated approaches for distinguishing derived from non-derived cases in the UK news domain.

### Automatically identifying text reuse

To automate the detection of text reuse the challenge is being able to capture and quantify suitable features that can reliably be used to discriminate derived from non-derived texts. Typically comparing texts involves the following stages:[20] normalising the input texts (e.g. converting all letters to lowercase), selecting suitable discriminating features, and using statistical inference to compare feature distributions (e.g. to perform document classification). Features can be derived from counting the occurrence of features in a text (e.g. word counts, counts of style markers) or based on measures resulting from comparing the content of texts directly (e.g. the proportion of overlapping words or substrings) reflecting theme or topic, expression or the style/authorship of writing. In a manner similar to addressing other tasks in computational text analysis (e.g. information retrieval, document clustering, document summarisation, sentence alignment, duplicate and copy detection, plagiarism detection, authorship attribution), we simplified the problem of identifying text reuse or derivation by capturing similarities (and differences) between texts.

Analysing Journalistic Text Re-use', in *Proceedings of Corpus Linguistics 2001* (2001), Lancaster, UK, pp. 214–23.
[20] P. Juola, 'Authorship Attribution', *Foundations and Trends in Information Retrieval*, 1(3) (2006), 233–4.

In the METER project we investigated various techniques to automatically identify text reuse including:[21] word overlap, n-gram matching, sequence comparison and sentence alignment. In the first approach, lexical items (words and phrases) between two texts are compared and used to compute some degree of similarity.[22] The second approach (n-gram matching) is very similar except that instead of comparing lexical items, groups of $n$ adjacent characters or words are formed and treated as separate units before comparison (i.e. documents are represented not as words, but as sets of n-grams). For example, the character bi-grams ($n=2$) resulting from the word SUBSTRING are: SU, UB, BS, ST, TR, RI, IN, NG. Because there are many ways to express the same concept, the longer $n$ becomes, the more unlikely it is that the same sequence of $n$ tokens (words or characters) will appear in the same order in independently written texts.[23] Taking advantage of document individuality as captured by n-grams has been successfully applied to plagiarism detection,[24] copy detection[25] and to find revisions of newswire texts on the Internet.[26] When using n-grams the value for $n$ must be decided

---

[21] Clough *et al.*, 'Measuring Text Re-use', 152–9.

[22] This has been used for plagiarism detection by computing the proportion of hapax legomena words – those occurring only once – that overlap between two texts; see Woolls, D. and Coulthard, M., 'Tools for the Trade', *Forensic Linguistics*, 5(1) (1998), 33–57 and detecting reuse in blogs and online news articles, see J. Kim, K. S. Candan, and J. Tatemura, 'Efficient Overlap and Content Reuse Detection in Blogs and Online News Articles', in *Proceedings of the 18th International Conference on World Wide Web WWW'09* (2009), ACM, New York, NY pp. 81–90.

[23] As McEnery and Wilson state about finding the same sentence more than once: 'unless it is a very formulaic sentence (such as those appearing as part of a legal disclaimer at the beginning of a book), it is deeply unlikely that you will find it repeated in its exact form in any book, in any library, anywhere' (*Corpus Linguistics* (Edinburgh textbooks in empirical linguistics, 1996), p. 7).

[24] See e.g. C. Lyon, J. Malcolm and B. Dickerson, 'Detecting Short Passages of Similar Text in Large Document Collections', in *Proceedings of the 2001 Conference on Empirical Methods in Natural Language Processing* (2001), pp. 118–25; W. Kienreich, *et al.*, 'Plagiarism Detection in Large Sets of Press Agency News Articles', in *Proceedings of 17th International Conference on Database and Expert Systems Applications DEXA'06* (2006), pp. 181–8.

[25] See e.g. S. Brin, *et al.*, 'Copy Detection Mechanisms for Digital Documents', in *Proceedings of the ACM SIGMOD International Conference on Management of Data* (1995), pp. 398–409; N. Shivakumar and H. Garcia-Molina, 'Building a Scalable and Accurate Copy Detection Mechanism', in *Proceedings of 1st ACM International Conference on Digital Libraries DL'96* (1996), pp. 160–8; A. Broder, 'On the Resemblance and Containment of Documents', in *Proceedings of the Compression and Complexity of Sequences*, June, pp. 11–13, 1997.

[26] R. Steinberger *et al.*, 'Continuous Multi-Source Information Gathering and Classification', in *Proceedings of the International Conference on Computational*

empirically and in advance: values too small will result in simply matching common words or idioms in the language used by independently written texts; too large and matches between dependent texts will be missed.

In the third approach (sequence comparison), rather than comparing lexical or n-gram representations of the texts, the content (or structure) of the texts is compared directly. We used an existing algorithm called Greedy String Tiling[27] (or GST) to compute, in an efficient way, the longest matching substrings (called *tiles*) between the tokens in two sequences (e.g. the words in a text). It has been successfully applied to various problems including biological sequence comparison and plagiarism.[28] GST computes a 1:1 mapping (or alignment) between the tokens of two sequences (e.g. words in a text) in such a way that as much of one sequence as possible is covered with maximal non-overlapping substrings (tiles) from the other. Unlike some methods of sequence comparison, GST is not affected by the ordering of strings (a problem referred to as *block moves*). GST is 'greedy' because it prefers longer matches to shorter ones and given the choice between two possible matches, it will use the first occurrence.

Figure 1 shows the result of applying GST on a derived newswire–newspaper text pair and the resulting alignment (the matching substrings are linked between the two texts). The underlined matches represent the longest common substrings between the texts (i.e. similarities), which are typically longer and more frequent in derived texts. The differences (represented by gaps between the matches) represent the presence of new information in the newspaper version, trivial word insertions (e.g. 'the'), or the effects of edits (e.g. lexical substitution – 'that' for 'which'). The result of alignment with GST as shown in Figure 1 helps to highlight *where* similarities between the two texts lie. In addition to the alignment, the similarities (or differences) between two texts can also be quantified using measures such as the average length of substring

*Intelligence for Modelling, Control and Automation CIMCA'03* (2003); M. Bendersky and B. Croft, 'Finding Text Reuse on the Web', in *Proceedings of the 2nd ACM International Conference on Web Search and Data Mining WSDM'09* (2009) ACM, New York, NY, 262–71.

[27] M. Wise, 'Running Karp–Rabin Matching and Greedy String Tiling,' Technical Report (1993), 463, Basser Department of Computer Science, Sydney University.

[28] M. Wise, 'YAP3: Improved Detection of Similarities in Computer Programs and Other Texts', in *Proceedings of 27th Technical Symposium on Computer Science Education SIGCSE'96* (1996), pp. 130–4.

**News agency version**
A man accused of <u>nail bomb attacks in London</u> which <u>killed three people</u> and injured more than 100 others <u>made a brief</u> pre-trial <u>appearance</u> today <u>at the Old Bailey.</u> David Copeland, 22, from Cove near Farnborough, Hampshire, was remanded in custody to appear again <u>on</u> September 24. He faces <u>three murder charges</u> and <u>three</u> charges of causing an explosion with intent to endanger life in April this year. . . .

**Re-written version**
A MAN <u>accused of</u> the <u>three nail bomb attacks in London</u> that <u>killed three people</u> <u>made a brief</u> court <u>appearance</u> yesterday <u>at the Old Bailey.</u> David Copeland, 22, from Cove, near Farnborough, Hampshire, was <u>remanded in custody on three murder charges.</u> . . .

**Figure 1**    Example alignment from the GST algorithm (matching substrings underlined)

match, the longest substring match and the proportion of overlapping substrings.[29]

In the final approach (sentence alignment),[30] an attempt is made to automatically align each sentence in a potentially derived text with one or more sentences from a source text.[31] This is achieved by first breaking texts into sentences and then comparing each sentence in the derived text with all sentences in the source text. A similarity score is then computed (based on word and n-gram overlap) for each sentence pair and the most similar selected for alignment.

Figure 2 illustrates the possible sentence alignments between a source and possibly derived text: one sentence in the source text (ST) maps to one sentence in the derived text (DT); one sentence in the source text maps to many sentences in the derived text (i.e. sentences from the source text are split); and many sentences in the source text maps to one sentence in the derived text (i.e. sentences from the source text are combined or merged). The similarity scores of individual sentence alignment scores are then summed to create an overall measure of similarity

[29] More details on the results of applying GST to newswire–newspaper text pairs can be found in P. D. Clough, 'Measuring Text Reuse'.
[30] For further information on sentence alignment, see e.g. Wu, D., 'Alignment', in R. Dale, H. Moisl and H. Somers (eds), *Handbook of Natural Language Processing* (New York: Marcel Dekker, 2003), 415–58.
[31] The METER implementation of sentence alignment deals with situations where sentences are merged or combined, split and reordered as shown in Figure 2. These capture common (sentence-level) editing operations performed by newsworkers.

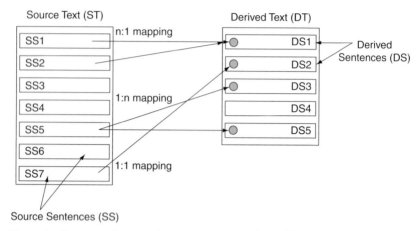

**Figure 2**    Sentence alignment between a source and possibly derived text

between texts and indicate whether a text is likely derived from a source or not.

Based on features derived from the approaches outlined above for comparing newswire–newspaper text pairs, we automatically classified newspaper texts as being derived or not from a given newswire source.[32] Using examples from the METER corpus to train and test automatic classifiers, we are able to classify approximately 71 per cent of newspaper texts correctly as wholly derived (WD), partially derived (PD) or non-derived (ND). Distinguishing only derived (WD+PD) from non-derived cases can be achieved with 80 per cent success and classification of cases entirely dependent on the PA as a source (WD from the rest) with 82 per cent success. The most successful classification is achieved when distinguishing wholly derived from non-derived texts: 92 per cent of cases are classified correctly.

## Concluding thoughts

The reuse of text is a regular occurrence in the news industry, but only more recently have methods from computational text analysis emerged to identify and measure reuse automatically. This has been stimulated

[32] Further information on these approaches and others for identifying text reuse and finding different versions of news articles can be found in Clough and Gaizauskas, 'Corpora', pp. 1249–71.

by the availability of evaluation resources, the development of new algorithms in related areas such as copy detection and information retrieval, and concerns from news organisations over the proliferation of copied material freely available online. The intellectual challenge from this work comes from how best to conceptualise the problem, how best to detect and measure text reuse automatically using discriminators derived from an original and derived text pair, how best to evaluate methods of distinguishing derived from non-derived texts, and how best to construct suitable collections of examples for empirical investigation. Benefits from this work to other members of the academic community include the provision of examples, analysis and tools which may be of particular interest to journalism academics studying the reuse of newswire texts, and academics investigating plagiarism detection strategies. These applications could be applied to any news agency and indeed to any provider of digital content. Because news agencies generate large volumes of text on a daily basis, manually analysing reuse in the news is a complex, time-consuming and largely impractical process. Using computational techniques offers a practical way of generating reuse statistics (i.e. monitoring reuse) for news agencies and publishers.

There is still potential for further work to be carried out, both with utilising computational linguistic methods in the field of text reuse and also for carrying out systematic evaluation of various techniques. This also includes the exploration of more 'semantically-orientated' approaches,[33] the construction of further resources to evaluate proposed techniques, studying the reuse of text through observation (and recording of author actions) rather than retrospective analysis, exploring techniques for detecting copies of newswire material on the Internet, and measuring reuse between translated versions of the original text (particularly pertinent to international news agencies who distribute copy worldwide in English).

---

[33] By 'semantically-orientated' we mean approaches which deal with semantic representations of texts rather than simply lexical or syntactic. For example, see I. Mani and E. Bloedorn, 'Summarising Similarities and Differences among Related Documents', *Information Retrieval*, 1(1–2) (1999), 35–67 and Barzilay, R. and McKeown, K., 'Extracting Paraphrases from a Parallel Corpus', in *Proceedings of ACL'01* 2001, 50–7.

# 13

# Reflections on measuring text reuse from a copyright law perspective

TANYA APLIN

## Introduction

Dr Paul Clough's contribution to this volume (Chapter 12) examines ways of measuring text reuse in respect of material produced by news agency services. It describes the METER project, a project which involved quantifying and measuring the probable reuse of Press Association (PA) material or 'copy' in specific stories by members of the British national press. The project used both manual techniques and computational models of measurement, although clearly the real interest is in developing the latter. These computational or automated methods of measuring text reuse could prove useful not only in the sphere of news agency services, but also in other contexts, such as copy detection.

As a UK copyright academic, I found Dr Clough's research interesting in, broadly speaking, two main ways. First, I was struck by the similarities and differences between the concept of text reuse and that of UK copyright law. Second, I was interested in the role computational models of measuring text reuse might have in the copyright sphere.

## Translating the concept of text reuse into copyright law

I will start by drawing some comparisons and contrasts between text reuse and UK copyright law. The concept of text reuse does not neatly translate into copyright law terms. First of all, text reuse is confined to written works or documents and ignores other types of media, such as film, music and artworks, which do fall within the purview of copyright law.[1] Also, the notion of a 'source text' in text reuse is simply about identifying documents or parts of documents – it is not concerned with whether or not that material is itself protected by copyright (in particular, whether it is original)[2] or, if copyright does subsist, who owns it. It also does not ask whether or not the derived text is capable of copyright protection. Further, the concept of text reuse is neutral as to its lawfulness and is described as 'rewriting', 'paraphrasing' or 'summarizing'. Whereas, a copyright lawyer would characterize such activities in terms of the exclusive acts that are reserved to the copyright owner, including reproduction and adaptation.[3] He/she would then go on to ask whether copying or derivation has occurred and, if so, whether in relation to the whole or substantial part of the work? Despite these differences, there are, however, two areas of similarity or overlap between text reuse and UK copyright law. The first is in terms of derivation; the second relates to the copying of ideas.

## Derivation

In copyright law terms, independently creating the same or similar text will not amount to an infringement. Rather, it is essential to show that the allegedly infringing work has been copied or derived from the relevant copyright work. This is described as the requirement of 'copying' or 'causal connection'.[4] Often this issue is not disputed, the defendant conceding that

---

[1] E.g. Art. 2(1) of the Berne Convention for the Protection of Literary and Artistic Works (Berne Convention) refers to 'literary and artistic works' which include, *inter alia*, books, lectures, dramatic works, musical compositions, cinematographic works, works of drawing, painting, architecture, sculpture, engraving and lithography, and photographic works. See also s. 1 of the UK Copyright Designs and Patents Act 1988 (CDPA) which refers to original literary, dramatic, musical and artistic works, as well as films, sound recordings, broadcasts and typographical arrangements.

[2] Originality is a requirement of almost all copyright systems by virtue of Art. 2(1) of the Berne Convention. For further discussion, see S. Ricketson and J. Ginsburg, *International Copyright and Neighbouring Rights: The Berne Convention and Beyond*, vol. 1 (Oxford University Press, 2006), para. 8.03. The Berne Convention does not, however, provide much guidance on the nature of this requirement and so different jurisdictions reflect different approaches.

[3] See CDPA, ss. 16, 17 and 21.

[4] In *Francis Day & Hunter Ltd* v. *Bron* [1963] Ch 587 the Court of Appeal, refers to 'copying', although note that Diplock LJ, at 624, also refers to causal connection. In *Designers' Guild Ltd* v. *Russell Williams (Textiles) Ltd* [2000] 1 WLR 2416 the Law Lords refer to 'copying'.

he/she copied from the claimant's work, but arguing that it was not a substantial part[5] or that a relevant exception applies.[6] However, sometimes a defendant will argue that the circumstances in which they created their work had absolutely nothing to do with the claimant's copyright work. An example of this is *Designers' Guild v. Russell Williams.*[7] In this case the claimant owned copyright in a painting from which it had produced its 'Ixia' fabric design, which was a design consisting of a vertically striped pattern scattered with flowers. The claimant complained that the defendant had infringed copyright in its painting, by virtue of copying the 'Ixia' design in its own 'Marguerite' fabric design. In other words, this was a case of indirect copying.[8] The defendant vigorously denied this allegation, claiming that it was not aware of the 'Ixia' design at the time of creating its own 'Marguerite' design. The judge at first instance applied the well-established principle that in the absence of direct evidence of copying, proof of access to the allegedly copied work and sufficient similarity between the two works gives rise to prima facie evidence of copying and shifts the evidential burden to the defendant.[9] On the facts, the judge found that copying *had* occurred – he pointed to the marked similarities between the two designs,[10] which went

---

[5] See e.g. *Hawkes* v. *Paramount* [1934] Ch. 593; *Ludlow Music Inc.* v. *Williams* (*No. 1*) [2001] EMLR 7; [2001] FSR 19.

[6] See e.g. *Ashdown* v. *Telegraph Group* [2002] Ch. 149.

[7] [1998] FSR 803 (Ch. D.); [2000] FSR 121 (CA); [2000] 1 WLR 2416 (HL).

[8] s. 16(3)(b) CDPA recognizes the possibility of indirect copying.

[9] *Designers' Guild* v. *Russell Williams Ltd* [1998] FSR 803, 811.

[10] The similarities are these:

1. Each fabric consists of vertical stripes, with spaces between the stripes equal to the width of the stripe, and in each fabric flowers and leaves are scattered over and between the stripes, so as to give the same general effect.

2. Each is painted in a similar neo-Impressionistic style. Each uses a brush-stroke technique, i.e. the use of one brush to create a stripe, showing the brush marks against the texture.

3. In each fabric the stripes are formed by vertical brush strokes, and have rough edges which merge into the background.

4. In each fabric the petals are formed with dryish brushstrokes and are executed in a similar way (somewhat in the form of a comma).

5. In each fabric parts of the colour of the stripes shows through some of the petals.

6. In each case the centres of the flower heads are represented by a strong blob, rather than by a realistic representation.

7. In each fabric the leaves are painted in two distinct shades of green, with similar brush strokes and are scattered over the design.

(*Designers' Guild* v. *Russell Williams Ltd* [1998] FSR 803, at 813
(Deputy Judge Lawrence Collins, QC))

beyond mere coincidence,[11] and the fact that the defendant had had access to the claimant's design (at a trade show and through pre-sale distribution of sample books). The defendant was unable to refute this evidence. Indeed, the judge disbelieved the account given by the defendant's designers as to the provenance of their 'Marguerite' design.[12]

With text reuse it is also essential to show 'copying' or a 'causal connection' since the concept is premised on the notion of reusing or recycling material from a source text in a subsequent (or derived) text. Also similar to copyright law is the need to show *probable* reuse.[13] However, Dr Clough explains in another paper, 'the key distinction between an author being influenced by, or drawing on the work of, another and re-using another's text is whether or not the author *consciously* applies some process of transformation to the form of expression in the source text to arrive at the final text'.[14] In other words, what is required for text reuse is copying that is *conscious*.

By way of contrast, copyright law envisages that copying may be *subconscious* or *unconscious*. This is illustrated by the case of *Francis Day Hunter* v. *Bron*.[15] The case involved alleged infringement of copyright in a musical work, 'In a Little Spanish Town', first published in 1926 and extensively exploited in the US and elsewhere since that time. The plaintiffs alleged that the defendant's work, 'Why', published in 1959, was an infringement because it reproduced the first eight bars of the chorus of the claimant's work. The defendants denied that they had copied the claimant's work, the composer giving evidence that he had not consciously copied the claimant's song and had not heard it (accepting that if he had heard it, it must have been when he was young). The judge (Wilberforce J.) found a considerable degree of similarity between the two songs, but accepted the evidence of the composer of 'Why' that there had been no conscious copying. He also found insufficient evidence to prove unconscious copying. The Court of Appeal held that proof of similarity between the allegedly infringing work and the original,

---

[11] 'it is extremely improbable that the similarities between *Ixia* and *Marguerite* could be the result of coincidence. There are simply too many, and too many obvious, similarities, any one of which could of itself be coincidental, but the combination of which could not' (*ibid.*).

[12] *Ibid.*, at 820.

[13] The aim of the METER project was to quantify or measure the *probable* reuse of PA source text in stories in the British national press. In copyright law, derivation must be shown on the balance of probabilities.

[14] Clough and Gaizauskas, 'Corpora', p. 1251.    [15] [1963] Ch. 587.

coupled with proof of access to the original, creates a prima facie case but not an irrebuttable presumption of copying.[16] As to the issue of subconscious or unconscious copying,[17] Willmer LJ stated that, 'if subconscious copying is to be found, there must be proof (or at least a strong inference) of de facto familiarity with the work alleged to be copied. In the present case, on the findings of Wilberforce J., this element is conspicuously lacking.'[18] Upjohn LJ did not stipulate the same requirement of de facto familiarity with the allegedly copied work, but he did stress that strong evidence would be required in order to draw an inference of unconscious copying and that 'the possibility that the defendant had heard it, or even played it in his early youth, is quite insufficient'.[19] Although the decision of Wilberforce J. was upheld (the Court of Appeal finding it impossible to say that he had reached a wrong conclusion of fact), *Francis Day Hunter* v. *Bron* shows that it *is* possible to infringe copyright through subconscious or unconscious copying.[20]

## Copying of ideas/substantial part

An often-repeated axiom of UK copyright law, indeed copyright law generally, is that it protects expression rather than ideas.[21] In the House of Lords' decision in *Designers' Guild* v. *Russell Williams* Lord Hoffmann attempted to elucidate this axiom. His view was that ideas were not protected either 'because they have no connection with the literary, dramatic, musical or artistic nature of the work' or because the ideas

---

[16] *Francis Day Hunter* v. *Bron* [1963] Ch. 587, 612 *per* Willmer LJ; Upjohn LJ was in agreement.

[17] The terms were used interchangeably. Willmer LJ referred to 'subconscious' copying, while Upjohn LJ referred to 'unconscious' copying, and Diplock LJ referred both to 'subconscious' and 'unconscious' copying.

[18] *Francis Day Hunter* v. *Bron* [1963] Ch. 587, 613 *per* Willmer LJ, at 614. Willmer LJ emphasizes this point again when he states: 'subconscious copying is a possibility which, if it occurs, may amount to an infringement of copyright. But in order to establish liability on this ground, it must be shown that the composer of the offending work was in fact familiar with the work alleged to have been copied.'

[19] *Ibid.*, at 620–1.    [20] Followed in *Baigent* v. *Random House* [2007] FSR 24 (CA).

[21] In the UK see, for example, *Navitaire Inc.* v. *Easyjet Airline Co. Ltd* (*No. 3*) [2006] RPC 3; *Nova Productions Ltd* v. *Mazooma Games Ltd* [2007] RPC 25 (CA); *Baigent* v. *Random House Group Ltd* [2007] FSR 24 (CA); and *Designers' Guild Ltd* v. *Russell Williams* (*Textiles*) *Ltd* [2000] 1 WLR 2416 (HL). In the US see, for example, s. 102(b) US Copyright Act 1976 and *Feist Publications Inc* v. *Rural Telephone Service Co.* (1991) 499 US 340. At the international level, see Art. 2(8) Berne Convention and Art. 9(2) of the Agreement on Trade Related Aspects of Intellectual Property Rights 1994 (TRIPs).

are 'not original, or so commonplace as not to form a substantial part of the work'.[22] The notion of text reuse also recognizes a distinction between ideas and expression.[23] At the same time, text reuse is not restricted to verbatim copying - or what copyright lawyers would describe as 'literal copying' - but includes instances where 'very little, if any, of the original forms of expression are retained'.[24] How, then, to draw the line between what is or is not text reuse? The means of drawing the line according to Dr Clough is down to whether the copying is conscious or intentional. However, this is not the case with UK copyright law where, as discussed above, the consciousness of the copying is relevant only to causal connection. The 'line-drawing' instead occurs at the stage of assessing whether or not the defendant has copied a *substantial part* of the claimant's work.[25] Where it is established that a substantial part of the work has been copied prima facie this will amount to copyright infringement.[26]

What constitutes a substantial part of the claimant's work is difficult to predict but the UK courts have provided general guidance on this issue. The overriding principle is that the assessment is a *qualitative* one and *not* quantitative.[27] In determining whether a qualitatively substantial part has been copied, courts have taken into account various factors.[28] A significant and consistently used factor is the originality - i.e. skill and labour - of the part that has been copied. The more skilful or creative the part that is copied, the more likely it is to be substantial[29] and thus infringing. This link between originality and what constitutes infringement has been reiterated at a European level in the ruling of the European Court of Justice in *Infopaq International A/S* v. *Danske*

---

[22] *Designers' Guild Ltd* v. *Russell Williams (Textiles) Ltd* [2000] 1 WLR 2416 (HL), at 2423.

[23] See Clough and Gaizauskas, 'Corpora', p. 1251: 're-use implies more than the re-use of some content or ideas drawn from the original'.

[24] Clough and Gaizauskas, 'Corpora', p. 1251.

[25] See s. 16(3)(a) CDPA which stipulates that copyright is infringed where a person, without the licence of the copyright owner, does one of the restricted acts in relation to the whole or substantial part of the work.

[26] Unless one or more of the exceptions listed in CDPA, Chapter III are applicable.

[27] *Designers' Guild Ltd* v. *Russell Williams (Textiles) Ltd* [2000] 1 WLR 2416; *Newspaper Licensing Agency* v. *Marks & Spencer Ltd* [2003] 1 AC 551.

[28] Importantly, the intention of the copier (sometimes referred to as *animus furandi*) is irrelevant: *Baigent* v. *Random House* [2007] FSR 24 (CA) *per* Lloyd LJ, at 95–7 and *per* Rix LJ, at 106.

[29] See *Designers' Guild Ltd* v. *Russell Williams (Textiles) Ltd* [2000] 1 WLR 2416, 2423 *per* Lord Hoffmann, at 2423; *Nova Productions Ltd* v. *Mazooma Games Ltd* [2007] RPC 25 (CA) and *Cantor Fitzgerald International* v. *Tradition (UK) Ltd* [2000] RPC 95, at 76.

*Dagblades Forenig.*[30] Infopaq was in the business of electronically scanning in selected newspaper articles from Danish newspapers and producing summaries based on searches of these electronic documents. The summaries included the search word and the five words appearing on either side of this word (i.e. an eleven-word extract). One of the questions referred to the European Court of Justice was whether this activity amounted to a 'reproduction . . . in part' according to Article 2 of the Information Society Directive.[31] The Court ruled that parts of a work enjoy protection under Article 2(a) of the Information Society Directive 'provided they contain elements which are the expression of the intellectual creation of the author of the work', in other words original elements.[32] In the context of Infopaq's activities the Court further noted that:

> the possibility may not be ruled out that certain isolated sentences, or even certain parts of sentences in the text in question, may be suitable for conveying to the reader the originality of a publication such as a newspaper article, by communicating to that reader an element which is, in itself, the expression of the intellectual creation of the author of that article. Such sentences or parts of sentences are, therefore, liable to come within the scope of the protection provided for in Article 2(a) of that directive.[33]

The Court held that it was a matter for the national court to determine whether the eleven-word extracts contained in the summaries produced by Infopaq reflected the author's own intellectual creation, i.e. originality.[34] It also noted that Infopaq's summaries often included several extracts from the same article and this increased the likelihood that reproductions in part would be made.[35] Although UK courts consider originality as part of the infringement analysis, a worrying feature of the ECJ ruling is that it seems to treat the originality of the part taken as determinative of infringement and, in envisaging that isolated sentences, or even parts of sentences may be original, appears to set the originality threshold at a low level.

Finally, it is worth noting that UK courts have at times treated the issue of 'substantial part' as synonymous with whether the idea or expression

---

[30] Case C-5/08 judgment delivered on 16 July 2009.
[31] Directive 2001/29/EC on the harmonization of certain aspects of copyright and related rights in the information society [2001] OJ L167/10. Note that Art. 2 of this directive uses the language of 'part' rather than 'substantial part'.
[32] *Infopaq International A/S v. Danske Dagblades Forenig* (Case C-5/08), at 39.
[33] *Ibid.*, at 47.   [34] *Ibid.*, at 48.   [35] *Ibid.*, at 49–50.

has been copied. More specifically, courts have indicated that the copying of ideas, as opposed to expression, does not amount to a 'substantial part'. Take for example Jacob LJ in *Nova Productions* v. *Mazooma*:[36]

> Accordingly I think the appeal on literary copyright fails on the simple ground that what was found to have inspired some aspects of the defendants' game is just too general to amount to a substantial part of the claimants' game. The judge's evaluation, far from being wrong in principle, was right when he said:
> "They are ideas which have little to do with the skill and effort expended by the programmer and do not constitute the form of expression of the literary works relied upon."

Similarly, in the Court of Appeal decision in *Baigent* v. *Random House* Mummery LJ observed that to establish copying of a substantial part it is not 'sufficient for the alleged infringing work simply to replicate or use items of information, facts, ideas, theories, arguments, themes and so on derived from the original copyright work'.[37]

## The role of measuring text reuse in copyright law

What role could measuring text reuse, according to the types of models explored in the METER project, have for copyright law? Are these modes of detection of reuse, particularly automated ones, of any value to copyright owners?

The digitization of information alongside the development of computer networks, such as the Internet, has heightened the potential for wide-scale piracy of copyright works. This has been a concern for some time, although I would suggest that it has been associated more with creative works of a musical or audiovisual nature, rather than written works. While there have been some controversies regarding digitization of literary works (see e.g. Google books digitization project[38] and the activities of John Eldred, who digitized literary works in which copyright had expired),[39] piracy fears have mainly been raised by the music and film industries. The print industries have been comparatively silent about digital piracy, preferring to focus their efforts on large-scale, commercial photocopying.[40]

---

[36] [2007] RPC 25, at 44. Lloyd LJ and Sir Andrew Morritt were in agreement.
[37] *Baigent* v. *Random House* [2007] FSR, at 146.    [38] See http://books.google.com/.
[39] *Eldred* v. *Ashcroft* 123 S. Ct. 769 (2003) (Sup. Ct.).
[40] E.g. see www.publishers.org/main/IntCopright/intCopyProtect/intCopy_01_04.htm.

Assuming large-scale digital piracy of literary works becomes problematic, will the automated measurement models suggested by Dr Clough
have a role to play? Arguably yes, from the point of view of enforcement
or, more specifically, piracy detection. His model/s could be a useful
starting tool in identifying possible infringements. Should a copyright
owner then decide to pursue infringement proceedings, the model/s may
also have a role to play in proving infringement, particularly as a means
of establishing copying or causal connection. Automated methods for
measuring text reuse could help establish the similarities between two
works and thus give rise to an inference of copying. Would courts be
open to accepting this type of evidence? Courts are certainly open to
receiving expert evidence on this issue,[41] but there may be some scepti-
cism about whether this evidence is as relevant as, say, that from linguistic experts. Dr Clough's model/s could also provide a sense of exactly
how much has been copied. Here, however, it is important to remember
that the issue of substantial part is a *qualitative* one in copyright law and
the automated detection of text reuse may not lend itself readily to this
type of analysis.

Perhaps the greatest relevance to copyright owners of something like
the METER project is in gathering more information about the patterns
of use of copyright material. For example, an organization such as the PA
can find out what stories are being used (and those which are not), how
much of those stories are being used, and the overall reliance on PA
copy. This, in turn, can be fed back into negotiations about appropriate
subscription rates. Having discovered greater details about the usage of
their works, organizations may be able more effectively to value and price
them, offering individualized rather than flat-rate subscriptions.
This might be useful in other fields, such as online journal services and
e-books. In this way, automated measurement of text reuse becomes an
effective tool, not only for enforcement of copyright works, but their
exploitation as well.

---

[41] See Deputy Judge Lawrence Collins, QC in *Designers' Guild* v. *Russell Williams Ltd*
[1998] FSR 803, 811.

# PART VIII

## Literature

# 14

# Unoriginal genius: plagiarism and the construction of 'Romantic' authorship

NICK GROOM*

'Viva La Vida', released on 7 May 2008, was the band Coldplay's first single to top both the UK Singles Chart and the US Billboard Hot 100, and it was subsequently nominated for a Grammy award; it was also allegedly stolen from an obscure Brooklyn-based group called Creaky Boards. Their version, entitled with presumably unwitting irony 'The Songs I Didn't Write', had been written a year before. Creaky Boards argued their case on YouTube and achieved overnight fame, before retracting the allegation and claiming that both songs shared a common source in a video game, 'The Legend of Zelda'.

Then, on 4 December 2008 guitarist Joe Satriani stepped up to the plate and accused Coldplay of plagiarizing 'Viva La Vida' from one of his songs, 'If I Could Fly' (2004). Fifty seconds into 'If I Could Fly' Satriani plays a melody line which does seem to be remarkably similar to/have inspired/been plagiarized for the refrain of the Coldplay hit. He sought 'any and all profits' from 'Viva La Vida'. And at the same time, Yusuf Islam (formerly Cat Stevens) also identified similarities with his 'Foreigner Suite' (1973). Yusuf's allegation was dropped ('I don't think they did it on purpose', he told the *Sun*, 'I'd love to sit down and have a cup of tea with them and let them know it's ok'), but Satriani's case went to court in Los Angeles. Reuters reported that, 'While details of the case remain sealed, legal sources said a financial settlement between the two parties may have been reached. Coldplay will not be required to admit to any

* I would like to thank Isabella Alexander, Lionel Bently, Jane Ginsburg and Joanne Parker who have all generously contributed to this chapter and its ideas.

wrongdoing.'[1] A hostage to fortune perhaps, Coldplay singer Chris Martin had admitted in 2005 to *Rolling Stone* magazine: 'We're definitely good, but I don't think you can say we're that original. I regard us as being incredibly good plagiarists.'[2]

Such rash, or faux naif, or deliberately provocative statements do not impress in every field. Popular British media psychiatrist and consultant Dr Raj Persaud was in June 2008 struck off for three months by the General Medical Council for plagiarizing academic books and articles in his own published work. The GMC decided that his behaviour was 'inappropriate, misleading, dishonest and liable to bring the profession into disrepute'.[3] Even if Coldplay had been successfully sued, it is impossible to imagine anyone could have condemned them in comparable terms. Persaud claimed he was under stress due to publishing deadlines: it was a 'cut-and-paste error' – although one of his victims declared himself to be 'flabbergasted' at the effrontery of Persaud's comprehensive appropriation and went on to describe it as 'blatant' and 'stupid'.[4] There was however no need for further civil proceedings. Having been exposed as a plagiarist, Persaud resigned as consultant psychiatrist at the South London and Maudsley NHS Trust and has all-but disappeared from television and radio.

Proceedings have, however, been launched against J. K. Rowling. Her Harry Potter series is no stranger to zealous litigation brought on her behalf by Bloomsbury (her publishers) and Time-Warner (who hold the rights to the film series), but in June 2009 it was reported that Rowling is herself being sued for £500m. by the estate of Adrian Jacobs for allegedly plagiarizing *The Adventures of Willy the Wizard: Livid Land* (1987). This is not the first time she has attracted such claims: no matter how thin the accusation might be, the vast wealth accrued by Rowling works an irresistible charm. Indeed, in one such case launched against Rowling, the evidence against her had been *forged*.[5]

This blending of plagiarism and literary forgery is not unusual. Both are 'crimes of writing': authorship issues of attribution. Plagiarism is a form of copying that presents the work of someone else as if it were one's

---

[1] *Rolling Stone*, 5 and 8 December 2008; the *Sun*, 15 June 2009; *Reuters*, 16 September 2009. See *Joe Satriani* v. *Christopher Martin and co.* CV08–07987 (2008), USDC for the Central District of California.

[2] *Ibid.*, 16 June 2005.

[3] *Telegraph*, 16 June 2008; see also 'First Daze of the Raj', *Private Eye* (11–24 July 2008), 25.

[4] *Guardian*, 18 June 2009.

[5] This is comparable to William Lauder's activities: see below, n. 37.

own; conversely, literary forgery is presenting one's own work as the work of someone else. Although they are recognizably different activities, plagiarism and forgery are often conflated, and in fact often coexist in the same text. Both are forms of imposture, ways of exploring identity under changing notions of individuality and originality, and it is perhaps no surprise that Sigmund Freud proposed copying or repetition of the self as a prime example of the 'Uncanny'.[6]

Plagiarism also has a legal dimension via its association with copyright or trademark infringement. Copyright originally gave legal protection to booksellers (the producers and distributors of all forms of printed text) by restricting the right to make copies, and in doing so gave authors property in their works. As such, copyright law covers broad ground. Instances of copyright infringement may be individually plagiaristic (again, falsely attributing the work of another to oneself), but might equally acknowledge original authorship and correctly attribute work, as in the case of a book or piece of recorded music being commercially reproduced. These unauthorized copies (pirated books, downloads, samples) would obviously not benefit originating artists or whoever holds the copyright of the work.

Not all copying is bad or requires licensing. Imitation, allusion and quotation are all culturally acceptable forms of copying, and it is at the point where legitimate and illegitimate forms of copying overlap that this chapter is positioned. I argue that contemporary meanings of plagiarism and copyright infringement (piracy) emerged from an eighteenth-century literary context of copyright law and the professionalization of authorship, giving rise to models of creative artistic composition that favoured originality and authenticity. Recent work in eighteenth and nineteenth-century 'fakelit studies', ranging from imposture to plagiarism, has led me to rechart the vexed discourse of originality in the period, developing a new understanding of 'Romantic' models of authorship and the construction of the enduring and evergreen figure of the individual creative genius.[7] More immediately, Isabella Alexander's pointed

---

[6] Susan Stewart, *Crimes of Writing: Problems in the Containment of Representation* (Durham, NC: Duke University Press, 1994); Sigmund Freud, *The Uncanny*, ed. Adam Phillips, tr. David McClintock (London: Penguin, 2003). See my article, 'Forgery or Plagiarism? Unravelling Chatterton's Rowley', *Angelaki* 1(2) (1993), 41–54.

[7] For Romantic impostors, see Debbie Lee, *Romantic Liars: Obscure Women Who Became Impostors and Challenged an Empire* (New York and Basingstoke: Palgrave Macmillan, 2006) and Margaret Russett, *Fictions and Fakes: Forging Romantic Authenticity, 1760–1845* (Cambridge University Press, 2006). Recent studies include Tilar J. Mazzeo,

observation that 'Copyright law always gave the same level of protection to works that showed no inspiration, genius or other authorial qualities, like street directories' has enabled a reconsideration of the model of authorship promulgated by earlier critics such as Martha Woodmansee and Mark Rose.[8] As will become apparent, plagiarism and piracy were not consistently defined or distinguished at this time. They were some-times aligned, sometimes in conflict, and it is through this tempestuous relationship that they influenced the canons of artistic originality. Indeed, it is no exaggeration to say that the emphasis on creativity that emerged at the end of the eighteenth century to define Romanticism would not have developed in the same way without decades of debate over plagiarism and the ensuing cultural anxieties over composition. Put simply, then, it was plagiarism that laid the foundations of literary originality.

Literary composition in the century or so immediately preceding the advent of the Romantic period was characterized by copying. Authors relied on earlier works, whether as models of excellence to aspire to through imitation (classical *mimesis* or *imitatio*) or, somewhat less edifyingly, as examples of risible dross to parody and satirize. The most influential work on composition in the period was undoubtedly Longinus' treatise *On the Sublime*, made widely available after 1739 in William Smith's popular translation, in which imitation was presented as a form of inspiration.[9] Alexander Pope, Joseph Addison and Edmund Burke all referred to and commented on Longinus, who among his discussions of inspiration and classical style also endeavoured to

*Plagiarism and Literary Property in the Romantic Period* (Philadelphia, PA: University of Pennsylvania Press, 2007); Robert Macfarlane, *Original Copy: Plagiarism and Originality in Nineteenth-Century Literature* (Oxford University Press, 2007); and Jack Lynch, *Deception and Detection in Eighteenth-Century Britain* (Aldershot: Ashgate, 2008). It is worth noting three discussions of plagiarism in my own work: *The Forger's Shadow: How Forgery Changed the Course of Literature* (London: Picador, 2002), esp. pp. 25–31; 'Forgery, Plagiarism, Imitation, Pegleggery', in Paulina Kewes (ed.), *Plagiarism in Early Modern England* (London: Palgrave, 2002), pp. 74–89; and 'Romanticism and Forgery', in *Literature Compass Online* (Blackwell's, 2007); the latter discusses impostors in some detail.

[8] Personal communication. See Martha Woodmansee and Peter Jaszi (eds.), *The Construction of Authorship: Textual Appropriation in Law and Literature* (Durham, NC: Duke University Press, 1994); Martha Woodmansee, *The Author, Art, and the Market: Rereading the History of Aesthetics* (New York: Columbia University Press, 1994); and Mark Rose, *Authors and Owners: The Invention of Copyright* (Cambridge, MA: Harvard University Press, 1993).

[9] Other classical theorists of imitation include Plato, Aristotle, Horace, and Quintilian: see Groom, *Forger's Shadow*, pp. 31–44.

distinguish imitation from plagiarism. Imitation for Longinus was both a conscious and inspired response to other writers – a way of seizing the spirit or grasping the profound conception of a work and thereby communing with the sublime – what Quintilian would later call emulation: 'Nor is such Proceeding to be look'd upon as Plagiarism, but in Methods consistent with the nicest Honour, an Imitation of the finest pieces, or copying out those bright Originals.'[10] Artistic genius aimed not at superficial copying, but was essentially a deep reflection of an earlier model writer, an infusion, a form of possession, even while it remained craft or *technê* displaying the productive skill and principles of literary knowledge.

Superficial copying was, however, more than an indication of a poor writer – it was a serious threat to the integrity of literature. The adjective 'plagiary' is derived from the legal Latin term *plagium*, one who falsely acquires a slave, and Martial, possibly Longinus' contemporary, created the neologism *plagiarius* to mean a kidnapper of books:

> I consign my books to you Quintianus – if I can indeed call mine the books that your poet recites. If they complain of a burdensome slavery, may you come as their vindicator and stand security for them; and, when he calls himself their master, may you declare that they are mine and have been set free. If you call this out three or four times, you will make the kidnapper shamed [last line in original: *'impones plagiario pudorem'*].[11]

Martial was actually complaining that although he had already 'freed' his own verses, the plagiarist, by claiming them as his own, had effectively re-enslaved them. Evidently Martial's rights as an author were imagined to extend beyond his own metaphor of slavery: he maintained an interest in their well-being and retained the authority to free them from unauthorized subjugation.

William Fitzgerald notes that Martial's use is the only instance in Latin literature of *plagiarius* being deployed to describe literary theft, and that modern usage comes from Lorenzo Valla's imitation of Martial in the preface to *Elegantiarum latinae linguae* (*libri sex*, composed 1435–44, pub. 1471).[12] So while plagiarism seems to have been a feature of classical literary culture, the word did not appear in Britian until the sixteenth century, and only became prominent in the seventeenth

---

[10] Dionysius Longinus, *On the Sublime*, tr. William Smith (London, 1739), p. 37.
[11] Martial, Epigrams 1.52 [numbering varies]: quoted and translated by William Fitzgerald in *Martial: The World of the Epigram* (University of Chicago Press, 2007), p. 96.
[12] *Ibid.*

century.[13] Early English uses date from 1598 – 'plagiary' (adjective and noun) was for example used by Ben Jonson in *Poetaster* (1602) to mean a literary plagiarist – but it also retained its non-figurative meaning. 'Plagiary' was used by Samuel Purchas in 1613 to mean a kidnapper, the word knotting together the legal and the literary.[14] Later uses became increasingly confined to the literary context rather than the legal, but the relationship between children, slaves and literary works is rich with suggestion and suggests an overlap with 'piracy'.[15] The word 'piracy', as robbery or kidnap at sea, dates from the mid-sixteenth century (England of course being a maritime power), and according to the *OED* 'piracy', like 'plagiary', quickly developed figurative uses for plagiarism and copyright infringement. Hence in 1603 Thomas Dekker attacked plagiarists and possibly nefarious printers as 'Word-pirates', and perhaps the most striking marriage of the two words was made by Thomas Fuller in his *Worthies of England* (1662), in which he criticized John Rider's English–Latin/Latin–English dictionary (1589) for being plagiarized from that published by Thomas Thomas two years earlier: 'Such Plageary-ship ill becometh Authors or Printers.'[16] By the eighteenth century the language of piracy was commonly deployed to describe unauthorized copies or printers of books, but also remained a synonym for plagiarism.[17]

Both the word and concept of plagiarism – 'a literary thief' – came to prominence at the advent of mass print culture, and interestingly,

---

[13] *Oxford Classical Dictionary* (Oxford: Clarendon Press, 1949), 'Plagiarism'; Anthony Grafton, *Forgers and Critics: Creativity and Duplicity in Western Scholarship* (Princeton, NJ: Princeton University Press, 1990), pp. 78–9; Richard Terry, '"Plagiarism": A Literary Concept in England to 1775', *English: The Journal of the English Association*, 57 (2007), 1–16.

[14] Ben Jonson, *Poetaster*, ed. Tom Cain (Manchester University Press, 1996), IV. iii. 96; Samuel Purchas, *Purchas His Pilgrimage. Or Relations of the World and the Religions Observed in all Ages and Places Discovered* . . . (London, 1613), III. 3. 199.

[15] Dates of first use include 1621 ('plagiarisme', noun), 1674 ('plagiarist', noun), 1660 ('plagiarize', verb). *OED* also records the rare and obsolete uses 'plagiator' as a synonym for plagiarist (1889), and 'plagiat' as kidnapping (1809).

[16] *OED*: *Wonderfull Yeare*, sig. A4 – this is a prose memoir of the year 1603. 'Pirate' derives from Old French (1213), originally from Latin *pirata* and ancient Greek; Fuller died in 1661.

[17] *OED*: (1732) F. Hargrave, *Argument in Defence of Literary Property*, 32, 'If the right of printing books should once be declared common by a judicial opinion . . . pirating would then become general'; (1774) A. Donaldson & J. Donaldson, *Case of Appellants*, 5, 'From the Erection of the Stationers Company, Copies were entered as Property, and Pirating was punished.'

plagiarism stands symbolically at the head of the English literary canon.[18] Six years before the first specific usage of the word itself, Robert Greene (1558–92) was criticizing a presumptuous young dramatist for appropriating the work of others, alluding to Aesop's fable of the crow who disguises himself with peacock's feathers:

> there is an vpstart Crow, beautified with our feathers, that with his *Tygers hart wrapt in a Players hyde*, supposes he is as well able to bombast out a blanke verse as the best of you: and beeing an absolute *Iohannes fac totum*, is in his owne conceit the onely Shake-scene in a countrey.[19]

This, of course, is the first literary notice given of William Shakespeare – being criticized for plagiarism. Despite Shakespeare's well-known borrowings from Chapman's *Homer*, North's *Plutarch*, Golding's *Ovid* and Holinshed's *Chronicles*, it is ironic that by the end of Shakespeare's career, he was being celebrated as pioneeringly original. Leonard Digges twice wrote eulogies on Shakespeare: the first for the Folio of 1623, the second appearing after his death and prefixed to Benson's 1640 edition of Shakespeare's *Poems*. In the latter, Digges explicitly rebutted Greene's inaugural accusation:

> Thou shalt find he doth not borrows [*sic*]
> One phrase from the Greekes, nor Latines imitate,
> Nor once from vulgar Languages Translate,
> Nor plagiari-like from others gleane . . .[20]

Digges recognized that the mud of plagiarism was liable to stick: the charge, once levelled, could taint subsequent encounters with the author's texts. It was liable to escalate, or spread like a stain or poison – or a plague.

Shakespeare was however very much the exception in a literary culture that increasingly celebrated classical imitation. As already indicated, by the eighteenth century poets sought in their lines memorable authority rather than individual originality. As Pope succinctly put it in his *Essay on Criticism* (1711):

---

[18] Harold Ogden White, *Plagiarism and Imitation during the English Renaissance* (Cambridge, MA: Harvard University Press, 1935), p. 120ff.
[19] Robert Greene, *Greene's Groatsworth of Witte, bought with a Million of Repentance* (London, 1592), sig. F1v; see Samuel Schoenbaum, *William Shakespeare: A Compact Documentary Life* (Oxford University Press, 1987), 151; '*Tygers hart*' alludes to 3.*Henry VI*, I. iv. 138.
[20] William Shakespeare, *Poems* (London, 1640), f.3$^r$; Digges died in 1635.

What oft was *Thought*, but ne'er so well *Exprest*.[21]

Imitation was an idealistic form of composition that generously recognized cultural heritage, one's place in history and the cousinhood of poets. Conceived in this way, poetry could be read as a series of encounters with the geniuses of the past, made pertinent for a contemporary context, and indeed Pope's own imitations can read like an anthology of poetic models: Horace, Homer, and Virgil; Chaucer, Spenser and Shakespeare; Waller, Cowley and Dryden. Indeed, Samuel Johnson recognized that imitation was Pope's supreme forte:

> This mode of imitation, in which the ancients are familiarised, by adapting their sentiments to modern topicks . . . is a kind of middle composition between translation and original design, which pleases when the thoughts are unexpectedly applicable and the parallels lucky. It seems to have been Pope's favourite amusement; for he has carried it further than any former poet.[22]

Yet the extent of such imitations, allusions, borrowings, and so forth created problems.[23] The boundary between imitation and literary theft was indistinct and unstable. Pope himself had mischievously complicated the matter in satirical works such as *Peri Bathous* (1727) and *The Dunciad* (*Variorum* edition, 1729) by recycling some of the cant that had been published about him and his work, as well as parodying and quoting Grub Street poetasters, hacks, dunces, and even his own juvenilia. *The Dunciad* included imitation, allusion, direct quotation, (pseudo-)academic citation, and, arguably, some sly plagiarism, but the distinctions between these forms was deliberately, playfully obscured.[24]

This blurring of definitions was possible in part because despite its origins in *plagium*, plagiarism was not a criminal offence. It could only realistically be enforced in a civil suit, and such cases had no precedent. Consequently, plagiarism was understood as a cultural transgression

---

[21] Alexander Pope, *Poem*, ed. John Butt (London and New York: Routledge, 1989), 153: l. 298.

[22] Samuel Johnson, *The Lives of the Most Eminent English Poets; with Critical Observations on their Works*, ed. Roger Lonsdale, 4 vols. (Oxford: Clarendon Press, 2006), iv. 45.

[23] Roger Lonsdale, 'Gray and "Allusion": The Poet as Debtor', in R. F. Brissenden and J. C. Eade (eds.), *Studies in the Eighteenth Century IV: Papers Presented at the Fourth David Nichol Smith Memorial Seminar* (Canberra: Australian National University Press, 1979), pp. 31–55, 38.

[24] 'Can we account for Pope's recycling of the works of others without reconsidering the idea of plagiarism (or perhaps proposing Pope as a pioneering eco-poet, recycling rubbish writing)?' (Groom, 'Forgery, Plagiarism', 79).

rather than as an indictable crime. Writers have not been fined for plagiarism, neither have they been stood in the pillory, or whipped, or locked up, or had their ears shorn off, or been hanged. Plenty of writing was deemed dangerous and judged illegal and subjected writers and booksellers to dreadful penalties: William Prynne had his ears cropped (twice), his nose slit and cheeks branded, and was heavily fined for seditious libel for his book *Histriomastix* (1633), an attack on the stage; Daniel Defoe stood in the pillory for three days for seditious libel following his satirical pamphlet, *The Shortest-Way with the Dissenters* (1702); Edmund Curll was fined, pilloried and imprisoned for several months for obscene publications (1725–8). The public has thus been protected from the influence of corrupting writings for a long time. But plagiarism is rather different, and by virtue of its close association with piracy has influenced attitudes towards copyright infringement.

The Queen Anne 'Copyright' Act of 1710 (Statute of Anne) sought to protect the rights of booksellers and authors by outlawing unauthorized publication: that is, piracy.[25] But for the first few years after the Act, writers and printers resorted to other, more traditional means to defend their interests.[26] Piracy was a grey area that overlapped with surreptitious publication – a deliberate tactic enabling writers to publish potentially compromising material apparently without consent as well as with reportage, abridgements, translations, reference works and of course with plagiarism.[27] Edward Cave, for instance, the mastermind behind the *Gentleman's Magazine* (first published in 1731 and from 1741 engaging Samuel Johnson as parliamentary correspondent) regularly courted accusations of piracy in his news digests and poetry columns. But such piracy, like plagiarism, was in the immediate wake of the Queen Anne

---

[25] David Foxon points out that the word 'copyright' was not used in the Act, but that Pope was already referring to 'copy right' in 1727 (*Pope and the Early Eighteenth-Century Book Trade*, rev. and ed. James McLaverty (Oxford: Clarendon Press, 1991), p. 237). The first printed instance appears to be by Francis Wilkinson in *Dr. Burnet's Appendix to the Ninth Chapter of the State of the Dead* (1729), 5: 'to them only the Copy-Right of the *Archælogia* belongs' (for this case, see Isabella Alexander's contribution to this volume, Chapter 15, below, n. 6, p. 301). The Act 'for the encouragement of learning' (8 Ann.c.19) was introduced on 11 January 1709 (Old Style) and became law on 6 April 1710.

[26] A 'bookseller' in the eighteenth century was both a publisher as well as a retailer of books and publishing rights.

[27] The fashionable physician George Cheyne reckoned himself '*no more a* Plagiary' for borrowing and adapting medical practices from other authorities '*than a Lawyer is to be accounted one for quoting his* Code *or* Pandects' (George Cheyne, *A New Theory of Continu'd Fevers* (Edinburgh, 1701), Preface, unpaginated [iii–iv]).

Act treated as a literary malfeasance rather than a potentially indictable criminal offence. It could be dealt with internally and punished culturally through accusations, exposures, threats, embargoes, and so forth.[28]

Much of the hubbub raised by claims of piracy was therefore simply sword rattling, but occasionally things became more serious. In 1716, when Pope discovered that the unscrupulous bookseller Edmund Curll was intending to publish poems by himself, John Gay and Lady Mary Wortley Montagu without permission, he arranged a meeting with the man ostensibly to negotiate an arrangement. Pope then literally dealt with the matter internally. At the meeting, not content with making his case, Pope spiked Curll's drink with an emetic. Curll was violently ill; two days later Pope published *A Full and True Account of a Horrid and Barbarous Revenge by Poison, on the Body of Mr. Edmund Curll, Bookseller; with a Faithful Copy of his Last Will and Testament*, in which 'Curll' confessed his sins as his bodily functions became more and more noxious. Insult was added to injury and Curll was ridiculed. Moreover, this poisoning created a precedent. In the same year Curll visited Westminster School where he was again assaulted for piracy. Curll had been planning to publish a funeral oration given by the headmaster of the school – without permission. He was apparently seized by the students, flogged on his bare buttocks, and tossed in a blanket for 'Copy-stealing': a 'Pirate' and a 'Plagiary'. And again the event was celebrated in a pamphlet:

> The Pirate's frighted from his Trade:
> Tho' vengeful Birch should flea his Thighs,
> Tho' toss'd from Blankets he should rise,
> Or stand fast nail'd to Pillories![29]

---

[28] I am grateful to Jane Ginsburg, who has indicated that proposals for French copyright law in 1791 included exposing the guilty party in a public square for three hours chained to a placard reading 'thief infringer' (see Rideau, *La Formation*, p. 262 and n. 744). Margaret Ezell, however, notes that despite Foucault's 'transhistorical constants in the rules that govern the construction of an author', this formation is determined by specific legal discourses that are necessarily dependent on specific times and places: 'thus, a European model does not necessarily mesh well with the conditions of authorship in Britain' (*Social Authorship and the Advent of Print* (Baltimore, MD and London: Johns Hopkins University Press, 1999), p. 15). Indeed, one could go further and chart the relative rights in the period of English, Scottish and Irish printers.

[29] See Samuel Wesley, *Neck or Nothing: A Consolatory Letter from Mr. D-nt-n to Mr. C-rll Upon his being Tost in a Blanket, &c.* (n.p. [London], 1716), pp. 7 and 8 ('Printers and Stationers undone/A Plagiary in ev'ry one'); Wesley specifically refers to Pope's emetic on p. 11. Gay, meanwhile, was employed by Pope to rough up Colley Cibber after he had

Such perhaps was the rough and tumble of life on Grub Street, but other attacks on the pirates were more ruthless forms of character assassination. Samuel Richardson, author of *Clarissa* (1747–8) and a printer himself, held his Irish printer George Faulkner responsible for allowing *Sir Charles Grandison* (1754) to be pirated in Dublin *before* the authorized text was even published. Richardson published two pamphlets in which he named names, and apparently went so far as to blackball Faulkner when he applied to join the Society for Promoting Arts, Commerce and Manufactures.[30] Richardson should perhaps have followed Swift's example: under the guidance of Pope, Gay and Erasmus Lewis he had spread the publication of *Gulliver's Travels* (1726) between no less than five printers to guard against piracy. Ironically, Richardson had himself published Elizabeth Carter's 'Ode to Wisdom' in *Clarissa* without permission; subsequently unauthorized versions of her poems appeared in Robert Dodsley's *Collection of Poems by Various Hands* (1748, 1755–8) – her only real recourse was to seek an apology (which she received from Richardson) and ensure that only authorized versions were subsequently published.

There is a strong sense here that despite the provisions of the Queen Anne Act, piracy (publishing without consent) was likely to be treated in much the same way as plagiarism: by the victims taking the law into their own hands and seeking redress through a literary 'sentence', such as public humiliation reported in sensational pamphlets. Yet the times were changing. Pope increasingly sought recourse in legal remedies: in 1729 he obtained an injunction against James Watson and other printers who had pirated *The Dunciad*; and in 1737 he again took Watson to court for pirating his *Letters* (settled by arbitration). In 1741, moreover, Pope won a landmark case against the ubiquitous Curll. Although Pope had already effectively published his letters surreptitiously through Curll (encouraging Curll to print unauthorized versions which then allowed Pope himself to publish his own letters accurately), he invoked the Queen Anne Act against Curll in 1741. Curll had published Swift's correspondence, which included letters from Pope. The court upheld Pope's

parodied their play *Three Hours After Marriage* (1717): see Maynard Mack, *Alexander Pope: A Life* (New Haven, CT and London: Yale University Press, 1985), p. 775.

[30] Samuel Richardson, *Case of Samuel Richardson, of London, Printer; with regard to the Invasion of his Property in The History of Sir Charles Grandison, before Publication* (n.p. [London], n.d. [1753]), and *An Address to the Public, on the Treatment of which the Editor of the History of Sir Charles Grandison has met with from certain Booksellers in Dublin* (London, 1753).

contention that the Act extended to protecting letters, and established the rights of the recipients of letters.[31]

Clearly Curll was not a plagiarist: he published without consent – it was piracy rather than plagiarism. And yet he was denounced as a 'Plagiary'. The world of early eighteenth-century letters, rapidly changing from an elite literary manuscript culture into a mass-print marketplace, was evidently liable to conflate these terms and blur their meanings together. The contemporary case of Raj Persaud can provide some retrospective help here in distinguishing this terminology. Plagiarism has specific implications within a specialist, often academic and textual, discourse and the internal policing of plagiarism persists after centuries – from Greene's attempt to discredit Shakespeare to the BMC striking off Persaud. But when plagiarism becomes attacked or defended outside the field in which it is taking place it becomes something else entirely: it is redefined. Discourses such as the legal and the psychological reconfigure plagiarism into piracy or (in Persaud's case) a symptom of stress, respectively. In law, plagiarism shifts into copyright infringement, a form of criminal theft – a text is transformed into something economic – and it is the owner of the copyright who has redress; in psychology, plagiarism becomes an indication of some mental disorder, the sign of something deeper, something sinister, something aberrant.

Following the Queen Anne Act and the recognition of booksellers' rights in printed works, problems in defining plagiarism and defending authors became increasingly acute. Prefaces to eighteenth-century poems, plays, medical and scientific works, travel narratives and memoirs frequently anticipated such accusations, galvanizing writers and readers. The word retained its classical charge – John Kersey's *Dictionary* (1702) defined a 'Plagiary, *or book-thief*' as one '*that sets forth other mens [sic] works, under his own name; properly a man-stealer or kid-napper*' – but now had a further dimension: that of being, of what it was to be human. As Bill Marsh puts it, 'in committing the sin of plagiarism (crime against originality), plagiarists commit an equally egregious sin of "original" betrayal (crime against humanity)'.[32] The plagiarist was like an ape or a parrot – a weird threat to the very definition of the human, or they were imagined to be impostors or uncanny

---

[31] See Foxon, *Pope*, pp. 237–51; Rose, *Authors*, pp. 59–66.
[32] Bill Marsh, *Plagiarism: Alchemy and Remedy* (Albany, NY: State University of New York Press, 2007), p. 14.

doubles.[33] In 1712, John Dennis called a plagiary 'a scandalous Creature, a sort of spiritual Outlaw', and in 1753 Richard Hurd described them as 'those base and abject spirits, who have not the courage or ability to attempt any thing of themselves, and can barely make a shift, as a great poet of our own expresses it, *to creep servilely after the sense of* some other'.[34]

No longer simply enslavers of human property, plagiarists dematerialized and evanesced: they stole expressed thoughts now, took credit for those thoughts, and in doing so eroded humanity itself. Dennis went on to say that:

> 'Tis only a Man's Thoughts and Inventions that are properly his: being alone Things that can never be alienated from him, neither by Force nor Persuasion, nor by Fate it self; and tho' another may basely usurp the Honour of them, yet they must for ever rightfully belong to their first Inventor. Thus even the richest and the happiest of Men have nothing that is truly and really their own but their Thoughts and Inventions. But Authors for the most part, and especially Poets have nothing that can so much be call'd their own but their Thoughts. 'Tis for those alone, and the Glory which they expect from those that they entirely quit their Pretensions to Riches, and renounce the Pomps and Vanities of this wicked World; and therefore to endeavour to deprive them of those is exceedingly inhuman.[35]

The tone here is one of evangelical Lockeanism.[36] Plagiarism not only undermined culture, was not mere stealing – it was identity theft: indeed, it was an evisceration of the soul. The plagiary was barbarous, inhuman, diabolical, irredeemable.

The devilry of plagiarism confused everything, and fatally compromised other, more legitimate literary activities. The biggest and by far the most peculiar plagiarism debate in the eighteenth century concerned

---

[33] Locke, the great eighteenth-century theorist of property, includes parrots in his *Essay concerning Human Understanding*: 'Before a Man makes any Proposition, he is supposed to understand the Terms he uses in it, or else he talks like a Parrot, only making a Noise by Imitation, and framing certain Sounds which he has learnt of others; but not as a rational Creature, using them for Signs of *Ideas* which he has in his Mind' (*Essay concerning Humane Understanding* (5th edn, London, 1706), p. 525; notwithstanding this, see also i. 221–3).

[34] John Dennis, *An Essay on the Genius and Writings of Shakespeare* (London, 1712), p. 59: quoted by Lonsdale, 'Gray and "Allusion"', 37; Richard Hurd, ed. and tr., *Q. Horatii Flacci epistola ad Augustum. With an English Commentary and Notes. To which is added, A Discourse Concerning Poetical Imitation*, 2 vols. (London, 1751–3), ii, pp. 210–11.

[35] Dennis, *Essay*, p. 60.   [36] For Locke, see Rose, *Authors*, pp. 121, 126.

William Lauder's attempts to accuse Milton of plagiarizing *Paradise Lost* – or rather, claiming that Milton had composed lines in his epic by simply translating lines from Latin poets. The claim compounded translation with plagiarism. And yet the lines that Lauder quoted to prove his case were – bizarrely – interpolated by Lauder himself into his sources: they were imitations, forgeries. The case was a 'knot intrinsicate' of plagiarism, translation, imitation and forgery, symptomatic of the textual anxieties surrounding authenticity and originality in the period.[37]

Such Gordian tangles of 'crimes of writing' were a constant in the cultural life of the eighteenth century. It was a practice that risked divine displeasure: *The Christian's Magazine*, for example, was quick to condemn a pamphleteer of the 'meanest plagiarism' as 'an infidel'.[38] It could also embarrass one socially. In *The Merry Philosopher; or, Thoughts on Jesting* (1764) – a particularly unfunny treatise on humour – Georg Friedrich Meier considered at some length the temptation to adopt the jests and witticisms of others:

> To the novelty of a jest, in some measure, is opposed the borrowing of a jest from an other, or giving it out as one's own. In this case a kind of learned plagiarism is committed. As soon as this plagiarism is discovered, the jest loses much of its beauty, being no longer considered as the produce of the plagiary. And even should this plagiarism remain undiscovered, the jest loses in beauty, only with this difference, that the hearers are not apprized of it. Whoever utters stolen wit, must, if not lost to all shame, anxiously dread a discovery by his hearers; and in that case they know the jest, and must consider the relater as a speaking-trumpet only, thro' which the distant inventor of the jest communicates his jocular conceit. When a person utters the ludicrous conceits of another as his own, he can very rarely keep up that decent assurance which is requisite to express a happy jest. Nay, the jest may in the mouth of its inventer [*sic*] have had a great deal of sprightliness, which is lost when realed [*sic*] by another; as both may have happened in different circumstances, which however must always exactly suit, for the jest to succeed. I will admit a case may happen in which none is apprized of the plagiarism; then the borrower retails the jest with the most decent assurance, and it may appear excellent and perfectly suit all the then circumstances. However,

---

[37] See Groom, 'Forgery, Plagiarism', for an unravelling of Lauder's Byzantine textual practices. For a contemporary if less sophisticated example of this activity, see N. K. Stouffer's proceedings against J. K. Rowling: *Scholastic* v. *Stouffer* (2002) (US Dist. LEXIS 17531).

[38] *The Christian's Magazine, or A Treasury of Divine Knowledge* (vol. iv: London, 1760–6), ii. p. 361.

it is undeniable, such a borrowed jest wants a beauty, tho' unobserved in this case; and with respect to the borrower it is known, he being only a bare relater of it. A witty person, who out of a noble pride stands upon his honour, must never steal a jest . . . I would therefore advise each ludicrous facetious person, never to retail the jests of others. If incapable of inventing lucky jests, he would do much better not to jest at all, than to be so inconsiderate as to endanger betraying the barrenness of his wit; or when we repeat the lucky jests of others in a very happy manner, and agreeably entertains our hearers, we should afterwards have the honesty to disclaim any right to the conceit as our property. The same judgment we are to pass on those, who by reading witty and ingenious Authors have collected a store of witty and pleasant conceits, which they retail on all occasions, without mentioning whence they were taken. We cannot oftentimes refuse them the reputation of happy and dexterous imitators. A Bayle, a Fontenelle may be the fathers of many little Bayles and Fontenelles. But such ingenious copiers should have the modesty not to claim the honour of a wit of the first rate till after having distinguished themselves by witty conceits of their own growth. To be a fair copy, is an honour, but to be a fair original is a much greater and a more distinguishing honour.[39]

*The Merry Philosopher* was exactly contemporaneous with *The Christian's Magazine* – both were published in the 1760s. Plagiarism appeared to be everywhere, the literary world being further sensitized to plagiarism and originality by two recent commentators. Richard Hurd in his *Discourse concerning Poetical Imitation* (1753) and Edward Young in *Conjectures on Original Composition* (1759) mark the moment at which the tide turned against imitation, and are therefore crucial in the exegesis of plagiarism in the period.

Hurd's *Discourse*, appended to his edition of Horace, began with a familiar theme: all poetry was imitation:

> every wondrous *original*, which ages have gazed at, as the offspring of creative fancy; and of which poets themselves, do honour to their inventions, have feigned, as of the immortal panoply of their heroes, that it came down from heaven, is itself but a *copy*, a transcript from some brighter page of this vast volume of the universe. Thus all is *derived*; all is *unoriginal*.[40]

Hurd's proposition was that 'primary or original *copying*' – what was commonly described as 'invention' – should really be defined as 'imitation'. It was precisely because the '*objects* of imitation, like the *materials*

[39] Georg Friedrich Meier, *The Merry Philosopher; or, Thoughts on Jesting* (London, 1764), pp. 141–3
[40] Hurd, *Discourse*, ii. p. 118.

of human knowledge, are a common stock, which experience furnishes to
all men' that imitation was the key to invention: 'Here the genius of the
*poet* hath room to shew itself; and from hence alone is the praise of
*originality* to be ascertained.'[41] But switching the terms 'invention' and
'imitation' was not enough to inject new life into the rapidly tiring
practice of imitation. Neither could Hurd escape the question of originality, which occupied him throughout the 1750s. In *A Letter to
Mr. Mason; on the Marks of Imitation* (1757) Hurd presented rules for
discovering imitation, but as Roger Lonsdale has suggested he was
'baffled' by just how much imitation he then exposed, and the likely
effect it would have on the English canon.[42]

Hurd was a reluctant 'originalist', backing out of an era of imitation,
disinclined to acknowledge the direction of literary composition.
Shakespeare's simultaneous emergence as a natural genius and pre-
eminent poet of English letters was a case in point for him. Francis
Beaumont (1584–1616) had written a eulogy to Shakespeare in 1613 or
thereabouts in a letter addressed to their mutual friend Ben Jonson:

> And from all learning keep these lines as clear
> As Shakespeare's best are, which our heirs shall hear
> Preachers apt to their auditors to show
> How far sometimes a mortal man may go
> By the dim light of Nature.[43]

The myth of the unlearned bard had since become a favourite motif of
poetic assessments offered of Shakespeare after his death in 1616. In
addition to Digges' lines noted above, John Milton (1608–74) had for
example in 'L'Allegro' described hearing

> sweetest Shakespeare fancy's child,
> Warble his native wood-notes wild.[44]

Hurd was moreover particularly alive to what he perceived to be the
peculiarly 'English' qualities of Shakespeare's natural genius: he praised
Shakespeare's description of an 'English Spring' and declared his phra-
seology to be 'perfectly English . . . purely English'.[45] Yet Shakespeare

---

[41] *Ibid.*, ii. pp. 118, 175.    [42] Lonsdale, 'Gray and "Allusion"', 43.
[43] *Ben Jonson*, ed. C. H. Herford and Percy and Evelyn Simpson, 11 vols. (Oxford:
    Clarendon Press, 1925–52), xi. pp. 374–7.
[44] John Milton, *Complete Shorter Poems*, ed. John Carey (Harlow: Longman, 1971), p. 138:
    ll. 133–4.
[45] Richard Hurd, *A Letter to Mr. Mason; on the Marks of Imitation* (1757), p. 16 – this is
    also discussed in Hurd's *Discourse* (1753), ii, pp. 128–30; Hurd, *Letter*, pp. 74–5.

also appeared to be an arch-imitator of, alluder to, and borrower from other texts. To prevent such canonical praise being fatally undermined by Shakespeare's inexplicably wide range of imitation, Hurd was consequently compelled to propose a category of justifiable literary copying, tailored to Shakespeare. This was 'learned Allusion' – in which 'even Shakespear himself abounds. How he came by them, is another question'.[46] The canons of criticism were being assiduously recast to ensure that Shakespeare's literary primacy was recognized as the English original.

Two years later Edward Young was on the case, and the climate now changed very rapidly. Young had been a friend of Addison, Swift and Pope, and was the bestselling poet of the decade – indeed, the runaway success of *Night Thoughts* (1742–5) had resulted in his collected works being pirated in 1752 and 1755. He addressed *Conjectures on Original Composition* to Samuel Richardson – specifically with respect to the *Sir Charles Grandison* fiasco of 1753 – and corresponded with Richardson on the subject; indeed, when *Conjectures* eventually appeared it was subtitled 'in a letter to the author of *Sir Charles Grandison*'. The Irish pirates had helped to bring about a paradigm shift in literary values.

*Conjectures on Original Composition* has been credited with setting a new agenda for originality, and certainly the imagery Young used would later become irresistibly associated with Romanticism. He argued passionately for a reassessment of the terms of imitation, and originality was presented as organic, yet magical and divine. Original poetry was like flowers in a 'perpetual Spring' – natural, exotic, mysterious, dreamlike, heavenly – a form of miraculous replenishment inspired by 'a sort of noble Contagion', wildly disorientating:

> we are at the Writer's mercy; on the strong wind of his Imagination, we are snatched from *Britain* to *Italy*, from Climate to Climate, from Pleasure to Pleasure; we have no Home, no Thought, of our own; till the Magician drops his Pen: And then falling down into ourselves, we awake to flat Realities, lamenting the change, like the Beggar who dreamt himself a Prince.[47]

Imitations, in contrast to divine originals, were mechanical, manufactured, retrogressive, impoverishing and against nature: condemned like mules to 'die without issue'.[48] With hindsight, Young appears to be

---

[46] *Ibid.*, 23–4.  [47] Young, *Conjectures*, pp. 9, 41, 13.  [48] *Ibid.*, 68.

writing the manifesto of Romantic authorship over a generation in advance.

The sea change conjectured by Young is exemplified, for example, in Samuel Johnson's wranglings with plagiarism. As a journalist, lexicographer, editor and biographer much of Johnson's literary output was dependent on the work of others. He actually qualified his *Dictionary* definition of plagiarism with the notion of 'adoption' (1755–6), and in *Rambler* 143 (1751) had reminded readers that there is 'a common stock of images, a settled mode of arrangement, and a beaten track of transition . . . So that in books which best deserve the name of originals, there is little new beyond the disposition of materials already provided.'[49] His poetry too was in the neoclassical tradition of imitation, particularly of Horace, yet even he came to question its felicity:

> such imitations cannot give pleasure to common readers; the man of learning may be sometimes surprised and delighted by an unexpected parallel; but the comparison requires knowledge of the original, which will likewise often detect strained applications. Between Roman images and English manners there will be an irreconcilable dissimilitude, and the work will be generally uncouth and party-coloured; neither original nor translated, neither ancient nor modern.[50]

Johnson was well aware that questions of plagiarism and imitation could generate deep if not bottomless complications around the written word. Despite his oft-cited attack on James Macpherson's *Ossian*, which has naively been read as a simple statement of black–white morality in literary practice, Johnson actually wrote in support of divers plagiarists, impostors and forgers – William Lauder (the same), 'Psalmanazaar', and the 'Macaroni Parson' Dr Dodd, respectively – and claimed to be 'surprized to find Young [in his *Conjectures*] receive as novelties, what he thought very common maxims', effectively attacking the high priest of originality for being unoriginal.[51]

---

[49] Robert Burchfield, 'Dictionaries New and Old', *Encounter* (Sept.–Oct. 1984), 10–19; Samuel Johnson, *The Rambler*, 6 vols. (1752), v. pp. 58–67 (17 July 1751); Johnson, *Rambler*, v. p. 59. See also *Rambler* no. 121, *Adventurer* no. 95, and James Boswell, *Boswell's Life of Johnson (Together with Boswell's Journal of a Tour to the Hebrides and Johnson's Diary of a Journey into North Wales)*, ed. George Birkbeck Hill, rev. L. F. Powell, 6 vols. 2nd edn (Oxford: Clarendon Press, 1934–50), i. p. 334.

[50] Johnson, *Lives of the Poets*, ed. Lonsdale, iv. p. 78.

[51] Boswell, *Journal*, in Boswell's *Life*, v. p. 269. For naivety, see Thomas Curley, *Samuel Johnson, the Ossian Fraud, and the Celtic Revival in Great Britain and Ireland* (Cambridge University Press, 2009).

The years following Young's *Conjectures* were characterized by the two major literary forgeries of the period (*Ossian* and Thomas Chatterton's *Rowley*), editorial work (including the founding of the Johnson–Steevens–Malone dynasty of Shakespeare editions, 1765), biography (Johnson's magisterial *Lives of the Poets* 1779–81), history (Thomas Warton's *History of English Poetry*, 1774–81), law (William Blackstone's *Commentaries on the Laws of England*, 1765–69), hymn writing, a handful of Gothic and sentimental novels and comic plays, and Laurence Sterne's uncategorizable *Tristram Shandy* (1760–8), which deployed plagiarism as an ironical mode of composition, winking piracy.[52] But there was little 'original' poetry, and in spite of Roger Lonsdale comprehensively redrawing the map of eighteenth-century poetry in 1987, the period between Thomas Gray and William Blake still lacks definition.[53] Oliver Goldsmith, Christopher Smart, Charles Churchill, George Crabbe, Chatterton's non-Rowley work: is this Young's harvest of original composition? Perhaps another way of thinking about the influence of Young's *Conjectures* would be to argue that it devastated the next generation of writers, and that the new credo was responsible for the dearth of poetry for a quarter of the century after its publication.

While it would doubtless be overstating the case to attribute to the *Conjectures* the apparent collapse of verse from 1760 to 1785 compared with the twenty-five years prior to Young's rhapsodic paean to originality, Young nevertheless does seem to have set impossibly high expectations, bequeathing to the poetic community the most crushing anxiety of influence. Writers certainly discussed Young's essay, but they could not actually live up to it. Instead, they avoided his exhortations on original composition; if anything defines this period, it is an attempt to come to terms with writing as a sustainable professional career, not as the medium of inspiration.[54]

Indeed, the professionalization of writing – writing as an economic activity – was one way of making a sharp distinction between, say,

---

[52] At one point Sterne famously plagiarized Robert Burton's own remarks on plagiarism from the *Anatomy of Melancholy* (1621–51). Jane Ginsburg suggested the delightful phrase 'winking piracy'.

[53] Roger Lonsdale (ed.), *The New Oxford Book of Eighteenth-Century Verse* (Oxford University Press, 1987).

[54] See Nick Groom and Adam Rounce, 'Literature: 1756–1770', in David Womersley (ed.), *Companion to Literature from Milton to Blake* (Oxford: Blackwell's, 2000), pp. 464–80. For a useful chronological table of publications 1740–89, see John Butt, *The Eighteenth Century*, ed. Geoffrey Carnall (Oxford: Clarendon Press, 1979), pp. 516–31.

imitating Homer and stealing from John Dryden. By the 1960s, Homer had been dead for over two thousand years whereas Dryden was very much alive, and Richard Blackmore's apparent plagiarism of Dryden in two Arthurian epics (1695 and 1697) directly threatened his livelihood.[55] As Henry Fielding put it in *Tom Jones* (1749):

> the antients may be considered as a rich common, where every person who hath the smallest tenement in Parnassus has a free right to fatten his muse. Or, to place it in a clearer light, we moderns are to the antients what the poor are to the rich . . . [T]he ancients, such as Homer, Virgil, Horace, Cicero, and the rest, [are] to be esteemed among us writers, as so many wealthy squires, from whom we, the poor of Parnassus, claim an immemorial custom of taking whatever we can come at. This liberty I demand, and this I am as ready to allow again to my poor neighbours in their turn. All I profess, and all I require of my brethren, is to maintain the same strict honesty among ourselves, which the mob shew to one another. To steal from one another, is indeed highly criminal and indecent; for this may be strictly stiled defrauding the poor (sometimes perhaps those who are poorer than ourselves) or, to see it under the most opprobrious colours, robbing the spittal [charity hospital].[56]

The presentation of writing as an economic activity was itself anyway implicit in Young through his language of affluence and trade. But his *Conjectures* were also important for reasons that tie it to wider concerns – concerns that are mirrored in the complex range of literature in this period and evident in Fielding from the passing reference to the 'Mob'. Much of the writing of the time was driven, at least in part, by the need to identify the nation – particularly Britain, but also within the Union to distinguish England and Scotland. Enormous efforts went into establishing the canon and the cultural history of the country, producing library editions of the great poets, and analysing national taste and national character. Young's contribution to this trend was to claim that originality itself was peculiarly British:

> Something new may be expected from *Britons* particularly; who seem not to be more sever'd from the rest of mankind by the surrounding sea, than by the current in their veins; and of whom little more appears to be required, in order to give us *Originals*, than a consistency of character, and making their compositions of a piece with their lives.[57]

---

[55] See Richard Terry, 'Pope and Plagiarism', *Modern Language Review*, 100 (2005), 593–608.
[56] Henry Fielding, *The History of Tom Jones*, ed. R. P. Mutter (Harmondsworth: Penguin, 1985), p. 552. See Rose, *Authors*, pp. 118–19.
[57] Young, *Conjectures*, 76.

Moreover, he argued that originality was tied not only to Britain as an island and the British national character, but was also a crucial defining feature of Britain as a Protestant nation.[58] Hence Alexander Pope, as a Roman Catholic, had failed to realize his poetic genius because:

> His taste partook the error of his Religion ... True Poesy, like True Religion, abhors idolatry; and though it honours the memory of the exemplary, and takes them willingly (yet cautiously) as guides in the way to glory; real, though unexampled, excellence is its only aim; nor looks it for any inspiration less than divine.[59]

Originality did not merely give identity to the individual; it was the keynote of Great Britain – and hence an impossible poetic burden to bear. This crippling equation – that originality was not merely the business of the poet but was vital for national cultural wellbeing – would take a generation to be accommodated, whereupon there was an outbreak of epic poetry encompassing everything from William Cowper's *The Task* (1785), to Henry Pye's *Alfred* (1801), to William Wordsworth's *Prelude* (commenced 1798, finally published 1850), and so on throughout the nineteenth century. Originality had by then become the very definition of English poetry.

But things might not be so straightforward. Plagiarism cannot simply be contained as the dead end of literary imitation, and thereby dismissed. Imitation expects recognition – indeed, imitation is *defined* by the reader's recognition and knowledge of the source. Recognition informs the processes of poetic recasting of lines, sources and typologies. Imitation in other words demands a cultural community, a canon: it has textual expectations for readers as well as writers, and, as Johnson noted, the collapse or failure of these relationships causes the imitative model of composition to break down. But plagiarism is covert – it must travel incognito, or rather it must appear to the plagiarism-spotter to be covert usage. If allusion or imitation derives from some arcane or inaccessible source and is therefore not easily recognized, it becomes plagiarism. There is a further twist here: plagiarism feigns and claims originality, but does not practise originality. Plagiarized lines are presented as original effusions that are activated by the reader's ignorance of the source, and so plagiarism can therefore be seen as a side-effect of the turn to originality. Imitation therefore becomes less effective as a

---

[58] This would concur with one of Linda Colley's points on Britishness and Protestantism in *Britons: Forging the Nation 1707–1837* (London: Random House, 1994), pp. 11–54.

[59] Young, *Conjectures*, pp. 67–8.

compositional theory when canonical familiarity is recoded, as higher levels of literacy generate different communities of readers, and when there is a greater focus on contemporary living authors fostered by these new reading communities and the emergent profession of writing than on the society of dead poets. Although imitation remains, it is at best rarefied as echo or, for the Romantics, the *haunting* of past writings.

'Constructivist' critics such as Martha Woodmansee and Peter Jaszi historicize plagiarism in a similar way, linking it to the rise of printing, an ideological consequence of the mass availability of texts and the relative ease of theft.[60] In chirographic or scribal manuscript culture, copying was positively encouraged – or rather, there was little distinction made between composition, copying and editing. It was the advent of print that delineated these activities more clearly: the press assumed the job of copying, the bookseller (who during this period usually doubled as the publisher) took over the roles of editor and disseminator.

Historicizing plagiarism means that critics today are unlikely to accuse the upstart crow Shakespeare of plagiarizing Chapman, North, Golding or Holinshed, or to censure Pope by uncovering his multifarious sources. These accusations of plagiarism were evidently contemporary and short-lived. And yet the charge of plagiarism levelled at Samuel Taylor Coleridge, for example, first made by Thomas De Quincey, does continue to rumble on. Attempts to clear Coleridge's name by reading his use of German metaphysical philosophy as a continuation of the Augustan context of imitation and allusive satire have proved difficult to sustain because the ideology of Romantic authorship – the individual artist seen as an organically creative, divinely inspired genius – looms large in Coleridge's own work. In a sense, Coleridge has become a victim of the very myth of the imagination he laboured to promote. In helping to create the figure of the Romantic artist, Coleridge's own historical in-debtedness and ultimate inability to live up to that model have been exposed. Or perhaps he never did intend to live up to that figure – perhaps Romantic authorship is a more retrospective construction, a reaction to a different sort of literary development, an unintended consequence . . .'[61]

---

[60] See Martha Woodmansee, *The Author, Art, and the Market: Rereading the History of Aesthetics* (New York: Columbia University Press, 1994), and Martha Woodmansee and Peter Jaszi (eds.), *The Construction of Authorship: Textual Appropriation in Law and Literature* (Durham, NC: Duke University Press, 1994).

[61] For an interesting discussion of 'Romantic authorship', see Macfarlane, *Original Copy: Plagiarism and Originality in Nineteenth-Century Literature* (Oxford University Press, 2007).

One way of rethinking the nature of copying then would be to reposition plagiarism. If Romantic poets frequently imitated, quoted, alluded to, echoed and were haunted by earlier works, then the advocacy of Romantic originality by constructivist critics is at the least overstated. Could the growing desire for originality and creativity have been instead a response to a growing obsession with plagiarism? In other words, did a plagiarized text not only function under the same cultural laws of originality and authenticity underwriting Romantic authorship, but actually constitute those very cultural laws? In such a scenario, plagiarism would not simply be an inversion of the Romantic valorization of origin; it would be precisely because plagiarism presented such a threat to potential authorial earnings that theories of originality could gain precedence in order to confirm the economic viability of professional authorship.

To put it another way, plagiarism increasingly became a literary obsession when authors began to identify their originality – particularly originality in voice – with earnings.[62] But what was gradually identified as literature was perhaps less the *originality* and more the *origination* of a text: it was origination that conferred Lockean property rights that could be ideologically identified and legally defended, thus:

> Though the Earth, and all inferior Creatures be common to all Men, yet every Man has a *Property* in his own *Person*. This no Body has any Right to but himself. The *Labour* of his Body, and the *Work* of his Hands, we may say, are properly his. Whatsoever then he removes out of the State that Nature hath provided, and left it in, he hath mixed his *Labour* with, and joyned to it something that is his own, and thereby makes it his *Property*.[63]

In the aftermath of Young's *Conjectures*, then, plagiary-hunting became a favourite activity of antiquarian sleuths. Accusations of plagiarism were not only made against canonical pillars such as Gray and Johnson, but against experimental authors such as Sterne, and also against Macpherson and Chatterton – those writers who can be understood as challenging definitions of literature and composition and engaging with Young's ideas most radically.[64] Critically, all had distinctive, originating

---

[62] On whether voice and thereby Romantic subjectivity could be plagiarized, see Russett, *Fictions and Fakes*, pp. 72–82.

[63] John Locke, *Two Treatises of Government*, ed. Peter Laslett (Cambridge University Press, 1990), pp. 287–8 (II s. 27).

[64] Françoise Meltzer, *Hot Property: The Stakes and Claims of Literary Originality* (University of Chicago Press, 1994), p. 2.

voices and energetically pursued financial independence through their works.

If the relationship of literary originality is dependent on plagiarism, this might explain the tenacity of plagiarism issues since Young's *Conjectures*, from Coleridge to Oscar Wilde to T. S. Eliot.[65] Eliot famously revived the legal terminology of property theft in verse by declaring that poets 'steal', although his remarks were insistently framed by considerations of the value of literature – what makes good poetry good and bad poetry bad:

> One of the surest of tests is the way in which a poet borrows. Immature poets imitate; mature poets steal; bad poets deface what they take, and good poets make it into something better, or at least something different. The good poet welds his theft into a whole of feeling which is unique, utterly different from that from which it was torn; the bad poet throws it into something which has no cohesion. A good poet will usually borrow from authors remote in time, or alien in language, or diverse in interest. Chapman borrowed from Seneca; Shakespeare and Webster from Montaigne. The two great followers of Shakespeare, Webster and Tourneur, in their mature work do not borrow from him; he is too close to them to be of use to them in this way.[66]

Eliot blends neoclassical techniques of borrowing from ancient or otherwise distant authors with a belief in the integrity of Romantic organicism. He dismisses the term 'imitation', and hints at the kidnap associations of plagiarism by describing bad poets as defacers of what they take – as gypsies were popularly supposed to deface the children they stole to prevent them being immediately recognized.

Eliot's recommendation to 'steal' is therefore rather melodramatic, a deliberately provocative term beneath the familiar umbrella of 'borrowing', yet it has caught the imagination and twentieth-century 'neoplagiarisms' lie under the long shadow of Eliot's apparent modernist endorsement of artistic theft. What is really happening here is calculated copyright infringement, but invoking the term 'plagiarism' adds a spurious postmodern glamour to the activity: plagiarism as the paramilitary wing of postmodern 'bricolage', a form of artistic terrorism attempting to demolish serious culture. As Hillel Schwartz portentously declares, 'plagiarism must be a thoughtful assault upon privilege, retaking that which

---

[65] See Macfarlane, *Original Copy*.

[66] T. S. Eliot, 'Philip Massinger', *The Sacred Wood: Essays on Poetry and Criticism* (London: Methuen & Co., 1934), pp. 123–43, p. 125.

should belong to everyone'.[67] Such overt strategies are evident in the work of the conceptual artists Jeff Koons and Damien Hirst (both successfully sued or threatened with proceedings for breach of copyright), and in recordings by the KLF (a.k.a. The JAMs) and Negativland (again, successfully sued).[68] In such examples, the right to 'artistic freedom' is demanded and expressed as a deliberate breach of copyright resulting in legal action. The work is not complete until it has at least been threatened with legal action, and so the ensuing controversy constitutes part of the artwork. As suggested by Schwartz, this is anti-capitalist politics pursued by artistic means – KLF standing for 'Kopyright Liberation Front'.[69] The comment made by Coldplay's singer as the band being 'incredibly good plagiarists' may have been an attempt to scrape acquaintance with such activities.

In these contexts, copyright infringement and plagiarism have effloresced into 'Appropriation Art', sampling, 'plunderphonics', 'mashups', and so forth. These 'new' definitions of plagiarism are explicit and easily recognized, and it is difficult to reconcile them with earlier, covert forms – they might more accurately be dubbed 'neo-imitation'. Nevertheless, 'neo-plagiarism' has had some literary influence: Kathy Acker developed William Burroughs's cut-up technique into a style of appropriation literature, and Stewart Home, a 'Neoist' writer heavily influenced by Situationism and the most garrulous of the new plagiarists, has tried to shift literary plagiarism into a form of freedom fighting, declaring authenticity as its target.[70] Acker, however, has obviously not been sued for reusing material by, for example, Charles Dickens (whose work is now in the public domain) or, more controversially, William Gibson, and neither has Home – despite, one feels, his best efforts. So although Eliot's remarks appear to be a modernist retrenchment of the legal discourse in defining literary terms, his analogy doesn't really go very far. Good (or bad) poets are not going to be sued for stealing words or images, particularly if they trumpet their thefts at every opportunity.

---

[67] Hillel Schwartz, *The Culture of the Copy: Striking Likenesses, Unreasonable Facsimiles* (New York: Zone Books, 1996), p. 314.

[68] Hirst has however since changed sides in trying to defend his diamond-encrusted platinum skull 'For the Love of God' from unauthorized copies made from a 16-year-old collage artist: see Robert Preece, 'Reality Check: When Appropriation Becomes Copyright Infringement', *Sculpture*, 28.5 (June 2009).

[69] This has neither been confirmed nor denied.

[70] See Stewart Home, *Neoism, Plagiarism and Praxis* (Edinburgh: AK Press, 1995).

Realistically, they are more likely to be prosecuted for copyright infringement by excessive use of the library photocopier.

Plagiaristic writers who don't deliberately court controversy through premeditated copyright infringement might still, however, be demonized, as in the Persaud case. Here, plagiarism was considered an inexcusable ethical transgression within an academic discourse. The discourse enforces its values rigorously by having the right to expel transgressors – in reality, by excluding them from the institution that authorizes the discourse. Such an internally regulated model of plagiarism forms the basis of university plagiarism policies. Plagiarism statements are specific to each university, and sometimes even to certain disciplines: they are non-universal in definition, application, and penalty, uniform only in treating plagiarism as an internal matter. Some statements include such draconian clauses as the condemnation of unintentional plagiarism, drawn from copyright law. To quote the University of Oxford's 'Educational Policy and Standards':

> Not all cases of plagiarism arise from a deliberate intention to cheat. Sometimes students may omit to take down citation details when copying and pasting, or they may be genuinely ignorant of referencing conventions. However, these excuses offer no protection against a charge of plagiarism. Even in cases where the plagiarism is found to have been unintentional, there may still be a penalty.[71]

In essence, this is a comparable form of regulation to that brandished by Robert Greene against William Shakespeare, and a century or so later in Grub Street to deal with piracy. But as I have argued elsewhere, it is perhaps counterproductive to glamorize cheating in academic examinations (or indeed in academic publications) by calling it 'plagiarism'.[72] It is cheating; plagiarism in literature is more complex, more nuanced and has a history that entangles it with copyright, and embeds it deep within the genealogies of originality, identity and Romantic subjectivity. Literary criticism should be wary when its terminology is being made to pay lip-service to institutional morality and other forms of judgement.

Aside from the self-styled and largely ignored avant-garde of the Ackers and the Homes, though, what are the real implications of copying literary texts today? An unnamed novelist reported in the *Independent on Sunday* his 'long waking nightmare that all his works have been written

---

[71] www.admin.ox.ac.uk/epsc/plagiarism/plagfaqs.shtml.
[72] Groom, 'Forgery, Plagiarism'

before, by others, creating just a dread form of unwitting plagiary'.[73] This selfsame fear that a writer's creativity may just be a repetition of what has gone before is itself derived (if not plagiarized) from Jorge-Luis Borges's renowned short story 'Pierre Menard, Author of the *Quixote*', in which a writer attempts to reproduce the Cervantes novel word for word. Borges's story is an outlandish, uncanny and astute response to the anxiety of influence mentioned above, a twisted reworking of the Oedipus myth in which the founding novel of the Spanish tradition is blindly cloned as a way of dissolving its authority.

Pierre Menard does not reread the *Quixote* in preparing to achieve this mind-boggling feat – in fact, he dies after having completed what appear to be two disconnected chapters and a fragment of a third – but of course for the anonymous author this dream is simply an anxiety brought about by a literary culture that now fetishizes originality and origination. But what happens when a literary work is plagiarized today? In 1980 *The Observer* printed Martin Amis's review of Jacob Epstein's *Wild Oats*. *Wild Oats* was a highly anticipated first novel, by a hotly tipped first-time novelist whose parents were the vice-president of Random House and an editor on the *New York Review of Books*. Amis, however, recognized various parallels with his own debut, *The Rachel Papers* (1973). Both books have, for instance, ageing, balding men as lovers. The character in *Wild Oats* has 'two gray-colored wiry wings on either side of his otherwise hairless head'; in contrast, Amis's had 'two grey-coloured wirey wings on either side of his hairfree head'. 'Well, at least Epstein changed the spelling', Amis observed wryly – going on to note, disarmingly perhaps, that: 'That bit about "wiry wings," for example, was stolen by me from Dickens.' Stealing from Dickens, a dead author out of copyright, was acceptable – at least for post-Acker Amis – although it is unlikely that any reader would have recognized the allusion. But Epstein's usage was rather different:

> The boundary between influence and plagiarism will always be vague. Reading *Wild Oats*, it soon became clear to me that the boundary, however hazy, had been decisively breached.

It had been decisively breached because Amis found over fifty parallels between *The Rachel Papers* and *Wild Oats*.[74]

---

[73] *OED*: 1993 *Independent on Sunday* 12 Sept. (review suppl.) 29/3.
[74] See Susan Heller Anderson, 'New Novelist is Called a Plagiarist', *New York Times*, 21 October 1980; and Thomas Mallon, *Stolen Words: Forays into the Origins and Ravages of Plagiarism* (New York: Ticknor and Fields, 1989), pp. 89–143.

Isabella Alexander has suggested that if Amis had brought infringement of copyright proceedings against Epstein, he would have been likely
to succeed.[75] But he did not sue, and it is moreover impossible to imagine
him doing so. Instead, the plagiarism was dealt with by ideological
mechanisms that disclose the values of the literary establishment; comparable, if infinitely more subtle than those used to discipline Raj Persaud
or a cheating student. There was no General Literary Council or dis-
ciplinary board to oversee Epstein's expulsion, but his book was with-
drawn from sale and has not been republished (hardback copies can be
bought second hand for as little as 15¢). He has been wholly excluded
from the literary world – indeed, the *New York* magazine noted a couple
of years ago, 'he's served a 26-year sentence for his youthful crime'.[76]
Epstein has all-but disappeared from high literary culture – been made to
disappear – and perhaps this low profile has helped him to elude
Wikipedia and similar sites. Information is sketchy, but it transpires
that since his 'youthful crime', Jacob Epstein now writes and produces
for television, apparently specializing in legal dramas such as *L.A. Law*
(1986–8) – which as Thomas Mallon notes in *Stolen Words*, neatly sums
up conservative highbrow attitudes towards TV: at best derivative, at
worst plagiaristic. It is certainly a strange form of justice that finds him
working successfully in television, dramatizing the process of the law;
in 1999 Epstein shared a Satellite Award with his co-writers for the
screenplay for a TV film with the very title *Strange Justice*.

The plagiarist is an impostor, someone in the wrong place, and the
disappearance of the author Joseph Epstein and his metempsychosis into
a TV producer is a reminder of the threats to identity posed by plagiarism. Unlike television series, novels and stories, essays and articles are
nearly always sealed with a single name, like a signature this is a form of
corroboration that enacts its own authenticity – and it is a powerful,
talismanic remnant of the persistent ideology of Romantic authorship. I
had hoped to sign off this chapter with such an authenticating mechanism: my name, Nick Groom. Except that that very name is itself a
proverbial nickname, used in the sixteenth and seventeenth centuries
to denote labouring-class rebels. It is really no name at all. And further
investigation into the name Groom reveals a complex of imposture. One
namesake, Charles Ottley Groom (1839–94), is described in the *Oxford*

---

[75] Response paper at 'Inspiration, Interpretation or Infringement? Interdisciplinary Approaches
to Creativity and Copyright', Emmanuel College, Cambridge, UK, 1 July 2008.
[76] Kurt Andersen, 'Generation Xerox', *New York*, 6 May 2006.

*Dictionary of National Biography* simply as an 'impostor' – someone in the wrong place. This Groom, both my precursor and historical *Doppelgänger*, promoted radical vegetarianism as a cure for alcoholism, and advocated drinking curry champagne (curry powder dissolved in ginger beer) – but his notoriety as an impostor actually stems, appropriately enough, from fabricating his pedigree. He was obsessed with genealogy. Across 700 calligraphic pages he traced his descent back to King David of Israel, discovering along the way that he was heir to the title Prince of Mantua and Montferrat, as well as Prince of Ferrera, Nevers, Rethel and Alençon; Baron de Tobago; and Master of Lennox, Kilmahew and Merchiston. Groom's dynasty had moreover in their time allegedly acted as artistic patrons by awarding medals to Raphael, Michelangelo, Dante, Galileo, Columbus, Cervantes, Lope de Vega, Erasmus, Milton, Molière, Rubens and Shakespeare – Shakespeare even proposed writing a play about this remarkable family of Grooms. This practice of awarding medals of Mantua was revived by Groom, and during his tenure at the head of the clan grateful recipients included John Ruskin and Alfred, Lord Tennyson.[77] So much for the impostor Charles Ottley Groom? Further investigation reveals that he was as avid a collector of plants, minerals and fossils as he was of minor aristocratic titles, and that moreover his collections were sufficiently respected for his herbarium, for instance, to find its way into Bolton Museum, where it is currently being analysed for a project on ecological conservation. Charles Ottley Groom has achieved a certain legitimation. And yet it transpires that I have a smaller claim to his illustrious, if faked, lineage than I had hoped. Shortly after I encountered Charles Ottley Groom, I discovered that my own surname was taken from my great-grandmother. Through the male line I am a Wilsher (or some variant thereof). The impostor Charles Ottley Groom is effectively a more authentic Groom than I, but whether that imposture has laid the foundations of an original individual subjectivity is not for me to answer.[78]

---

[77] Richard Davenport-Hines, 'Charles Ottley Groom', *ODNB*.
[78] I have since changed my name by deed poll.

15

# The genius and the labourer: authorship in eighteenth- and nineteenth-century copyright law

ISABELLA ALEXANDER

The idea of originality has long engaged the attention of literary scholars. It also attracts the scrutiny of lawyers through its central role in copyright law. Consequently, it provides fertile ground for interdisciplinary study and significant and influential work has been done in this area by Martha Woodmansee, Peter Jaszi and Mark Rose.[1] This work links the emergence of the proprietary model of authorship with the construction of Romantic authorship, the link being forged in the fire of the literary property debates which culminated in the cases of *Millar* v. *Taylor*[2] and *Donaldson* v. *Becket*.[3] The focus of such work is thus on the similarities to be found in the fields of law and literature in this period, the shared rhetoric and the players found in both camps. But concentrating attention on the cases relating to the question of common law copyright and the debates they engendered has obscured the fact that the courts were also required to deal with other disputes relating to the printing and selling of books in this period and, in such cases, aesthetic theories of creative originality were distinctly absent.

Nick Groom in his contribution to this volume (Chapter 14) seeks to reposition the concept of originality by viewing it as a response to plagiarism, itself acquiring a new significance when the rise of professional authorship meant it posed a threat to authorial earnings. He locates the moment at which 'problems in defining and defending against plagiarism became

---

[1] Martha Woodmansee and Peter Jaszi (eds.), *The Construction of Authorship* (Durham, NC: Duke University Press 1994), Mark Rose, *Authors and Owners: The Invention of Copyright* (Cambridge, MA: Harvard University Press, 1993), Peter Jaszi, 'Toward a Theory of Copyright: The Metamorphoses of "Authorship"', *Duke Law Journal* (1991), 455.

[2] *Millar* v. *Taylor* (1769) 4 Burr. 2303; 98 ER 201.

[3] *Donaldson* v. *Becket* (1774) 2 Bro. PC 129; 1 ER 837.

increasingly acute'[4] as the date of the passing of the Statute of Anne.[5] Does this mean we should start to see authors reconfiguring their plagiarism grievances into legal suits following the passing of the Statute of Anne? Nothing of the sort occurs and, indeed, the law of infringement, as it stood at the time, would have meant such suits were highly unlikely to succeed. The Statute of Anne was essentially a law aimed at unauthorized reprinting, or piracy, of books. Plagiarism, in the sense of copying phrases or ideas, or imitating another author, was something different and the Statute gave no guidance on how to treat copying of something less than an entire book, or copying which altered what it took. The matter was therefore left to the courts of law and equity and, although no authors brought their complaints of plagiarism to the courts, booksellers did begin bringing actions in respect of partial and altered taking.

The first such case to be reported arose when the son of the theologian Dr Thomas Burnet sought an injunction to prevent the publication in English of Burnet's book, *Archaeologica Philosophica*, originally written in Latin.[6] The defendant argued:

> A translation of a book was not within the intent of the act, which being intended to encourage learning by giving the advantage of the book to the author, could be intended only to restrain the mechanical art of printing, and that others should not pirate the copy and gain an advantage to themselves by reprinting it; but not to hinder a translation of a book into another language, which in some respects might be called a different book and the translator may be said to be an author, in as much as some skill in language is requisite thereto, and not barely a mechanic art, as in the case of reprinting in the same language; and that the translator dresses it up and clothes the sense in his own style and expression, and at least puts it into a different form from the original, and *forma dat esse rei*; and therefore should rather seem to be within the encouragement than the prohibition of the act.[7]

Lord Chancellor Macclesfield accepted this argument. Indeed, it was consistent with the pre-Statute of Anne cases which had also sought to identify if the book complained of was the same as the plaintiff's book, or different and, if the latter, no infringement would have occurred.[8]

---

[4] Groom, Chapter 14 in this volume, 'Unoriginal Genius: Plagiarism and the Construction of "Romantic" Authorship', above p. 282.

[5] An Act for the Encouragement of Learning by Vesting the Copies of Printed Books in the Authors or Purchasers of such Copies (1710) 8 Anne c.19.

[6] *Burnett* v. *Chetwood* (1720) 2 Mer. 441.    [7] *Ibid.*

[8] In the 1681 case of *Chiswell* v. *Lee*, the Court ordered that the author, again Dr Burnet, should read the book complained of and ascertain whether or not it was the same book as his book, *History of the Reformation of the Church of England*: *Chiswell* v. *Lee* (1681)

Nineteen years later, Edward Cave, proprietor of the hugely successful *Gentleman's Magazine*, was less successful in defending a case of partial copying. Cave was frequently accused of plagiarism by his competitors in the magazine market[9] but the action was brought against him for publishing extracts from a book of four sermons by Dr Trapp. Samuel Johnson, Cave's editor and friend, wrote in his defence: 'Every single book, so sold by the proprietor, becomes the property of the buyer, who purchases with the book the right to make such use of it as he shall think most convenient, either for his own improvement or amusement, or the benefit or entertainment of mankind.'[10] Johnson's particular argument here was that 'every book, when it falls into the hands of the reader, is liable to be examined, confuted, censured, translated and *abridged*; any of which may destroy the credit of the author, or hinder the sale of the book.'[11] Johnson's statements regarding the law were more aspirational than descriptive; his claim that Bishop Burnet made no appeal to the Court of Chancery when he heard his 'History of the Reformation' was to be abridged may have been correct as regards the author, but Burnet's publisher did complain to that Court about the abridgment.[12]

Notwithstanding his unreliability regarding the actual state of the law, Johnson's eloquence may have suggested the strategy of characterizing their books as abridgments in order to escape liability to subsequent defendants. While this was not always a successful ploy, it did result in the courts accepting that a 'fair abridgment' would not fall foul of the Statute of Anne.[13] In 1774, Lord Apsley LC held in the case of *Strahan* v. *Newbery*, 'an abridgment where the understanding is employed in retrenching unnecessary and uninteresting circumstances, which rather deaden the narration, is not an act of plagiarism upon the original work,

C33/257/112. Similarly, in the 1709 case *Wellington* v. *Levi*, the defendant argued that his book 'differed in substance as well as title' from the plaintiff's book. The court ordered a Master to compare the two books in question to see if they were the same book, or whether they differed materially: *Wellington* v. *Levi* (1709) C33/314/54–5.

[9] See the discussions in Titia Ram, *Magnitude in Marginalia: Edward Cave and the Gentleman's Magazine 1731–1754* (Utrecht: Gottmann & Fainsilber Katz, 1999), ch. 4; C. Lennart Carlson, *The First Magazine: A History of the Gentleman's Magazine* (Providence, RI: Brown University, 1938), pp. 80–1.

[10] Samuel Johnson, 'Considerations [by the late Dr Samuel Johnson] on the Case of Dr T[rapp]'s Sermons', abridged by Mr Cave, 1739, *The Gentleman's Magazine*, 57(2) (1787), 555.

[11] *Ibid.*, 556. Original italics.   [12] *Chiswell* v. *Lee* (1681) c.33/257/112.

[13] *Read* v. *Hodges* (1740) c.11 538/36, c.33/374/153, 250, 255, 275, 276; *Gyles* v. *Wilcox* (1740) c.33/375/274, 275; 2 Atk. 141; Barn. C. 368; 2 Eq. Ca. Abr. 697; *Cogan* v. *Cave* (1743) c.12/2204/24; *Tonson* v. *Walker* (1752) 3 Swans. 672; *Dodsley* v. *Kinnersley* (1761) Amb. 403.

nor against the property of the author in it, but an allowable and meritorious work'.[14] Towards the end of the century, the rule allowing fair abridgments was applied to other kinds of works that could also be characterized as 'new' works. The first case in which such reasoning was applied was *Sayre* v. *Moore*.[15] The great jurist Lord Mansfield, who had been intimately involved in arguing in favour of common law copyright earlier in the century, held that a sea-chart which copied from the plaintiff's map but also made alterations and improvements would be no infringement.

The language used in some of these cases might seem to bear some similarity to that used in discussions of plagiarism. Groom quotes Richard Hurd's indictment of those who 'creep servilely after the sense of some other'[16] and, in the case just mentioned, Lord Mansfield instructed the jury to decide whether the defendant's work was a 'mere servile imitation, and pirated from the other'.[17] But it is also clear that, for the legal players involved, the flip side of servile imitation was not novelty in the sense of creativity, but novelty in the sense of difference. While the courts welcomed constructive uses of existing books, such uses were not required to be imaginative or aesthetic improvements. All that was required in *Burnett* v. *Chetwood*, for example, was 'some skill in language'.[18] In *Sayre* v. *Moore*, Lord Mansfield recognized that the conflict inherent in such cases was not between imitative plagiarist and genius first creator, but between the economic claims of the first author and the public interest in more accurate maps. He observed:

> we must take care to guard against two extremes equally prejudicial; the one, that men of ability, who have employed their time for the service of the community, may not be deprived of their just merits, and the reward of ingenuity and labour; the other, that the world may not be deprived of improvements, nor the progress of the arts be retarded. The Act that secures copy-right to authors guards against the piracy of the words and sentiments; but does not prohibit writing on the same subject.[19]

While the reference to 'progress to the arts' could be read as suggesting aesthetic merit was a relevant criterion, on reading further it becomes apparent that the object was improvement for the sake of the community: 'if an erroneous chart be made, God forbid it should not be

---

[14] *Strahan* v. *Newbery* (1774) Lofft 775, 775.
[15] *Sayre* v. *Moore* (1785) 1 East 361n; 102 ER 139n.
[16] Groom, 'Unoriginal Genius', p. 283.    [17] 1 East 361n, 362n; 102 ER 139n, 140n.
[18] See above n. 7.    [19] 1 East. 361n, 362n; 102 ER 139n, 140n.

corrected even in a small degree, if it thereby become more serviceable and useful for the purposes to which it is applied.'[20]

This observation links to a second strand of Groom's suggestion that plagiarism took on a new importance with the rise of professional authorship: the claim that originality was not so much about creativity as about identifying the person entitled to payment.[21] This is reflected in the treatment of originality by the courts, which made no distinction between works of high authorship, such as poems, novels or songs, and those of a more factual or derivative nature, such as almanacs and maps. In 1789 when the publisher John Murray (later to become one of the wealthiest and most conservative of London publishers) argued before the Court of Chancery that in a book of chronology 'there was no originality, and that it was not on the whole, such a kind of work as merited the protection of the court',[22] Sir Thomas Sewell MR did not accept this argument. He 'admitted that every man might publish a Chronology, but made the following distinction; that a chronology, like other subject-matter of books, was a work of labour, of course, it came under the denomination of property, and merited protection.'[23]

Again, however, this approach was not new to the eighteenth century. Under the old guild rules of the Stationers' Company, any book could be protected, regardless of content, so long as the bookseller in question was a member of the Company. Likewise, under the royal prerogative, a patent could be granted for any book which was not already under patent to someone else. Notwithstanding, the protection granted to Trusler's chronology was clearly not welcomed in all quarters. On 7 December 1789, five days after the case was reported, an article appeared in *The Times* in which 'Mr Alpha and Omega' presented their compliments to Dr Trusler and asked whether he would prosecute them for their 'Hornbook', because in that book:

> as they will find in that hornbook there are exactly the TWENTY FOUR LETTERS, which the Doctor not only used in the sermon burned behind St Clement's Church, but likewise in that incorrect stuff for which his Reverence brought his Puffing action the other day against a bookseller in Fleet-Street.
>
> Alpha and Omega wish to be informed whether the whole alphabet is the exclusive literary property of his reverence.[24]

---

[20] *Ibid.*    [21] Groom, 'Unoriginal Genius', p. 290.
[22] J. Trusler, *An Essay on Literary Property Containing Comments on the Statute of Queen Anne and Animadversion on that Statute* (London, 1798), p. 16.
[23] *Ibid.*    [24] *The Times*, 7 December 1789, p. 3d

The courts' tethering of copyright subsistence to labour, rather than inventiveness, novelty, genius or creativity, continued throughout the nineteenth century, culminating in the well-known case of *Walter* v. *Lane* in 1899.[25] In this case the House of Lords held that a reporter who copied down a speech in shorthand could be held to be the 'author' of that speech within the meaning of the 1842 Copyright Act. The reasons given by the Lords differed, but Lord Halsbury, Lord Davey and Lord Brampton all held that literary merit had nothing to do with copyright law,[26] and Lord James of Hereford considered that an 'author' might come into existence without producing any original matter at all.[27] The dissenting judge, Lord Robertson, would have conferred some greater content upon the word 'author', considering it presented 'a criterion consistent with the widest application of the Act to all who can claim as embodying their own thought, whether humble or lofty, the letterpress of which they assert the authorship'.[28]

The low threshold applied to confer copyright protection might have met with resistance over the course of two hundred years, but it continued to be applied. By contrast, the courts' treatment of those who copied only part of a book, or altered what they had copied, did change during the nineteenth century. The latitude granted to those who could establish that their book was 'new' or different to the book they had copied flourished in the early decades of the century.[29] However, the courts soon began to place greater emphasis on whether the new book would compete in any way with the old.[30] This seems to dovetail with Groom's proposition that, in literature, theories of originality gained precedence in order to confirm the economic viability of professional authorship. The law, with its inevitable focus on markets and competition, could be seen as reinforcing, or helping to constitute, such economic interests.

It is also worth noting that, in moving away from applying the fair abridgment or new-work principle, the courts also began to denigrate the authorial quality of the labour expended by the second author. In *D'Almaine* v. *Boosey*, which related to adaptations of airs from an opera for dancing purposes, Lord Abinger CB observed: 'The original

---

[25] *Walter* v. *Lane* (1899) 2 Ch. 749; [1900] AC 539.    [26] [1900] AC 539, 548, 552, 558.
[27] *Ibid.*, 554.    [28] *Ibid.*, 562.
[29] See *Cary* v. *Kearsley* (1802) 4 Esp. 168; *Wilkins* v. *Aikin* (1810) 17 Ves. Jun. 422;.
[30] For further discussion, see I. Alexander, *Copyright and the Public Interest in the Nineteenth Century* (Oxford: Hart Publishing, 2010), ch. 6.

air requires the aid of genius for its construction, but a mere mechanic in music can make the adaptation or accompaniment.'[31] A further example can be found when the author Charles Dickens brought a case to Chancery in 1844 complaining of the serial publication of a work intriguingly entitled 'A Christmas Ghost Story, re-originated from the original, by Charles Dickens Esq.'[32] Knight Bruce VC found in Dickens' favour, rejecting the defendant's claim that his work was a 'fair abridgment', and observed that it appeared to him 'a mere borrowing, with alterations and departures merely colourable'.[33]

An interpretation that aligns the economic considerations of authors, theories of originality and the law becomes more complicated when we move to the latter part of the nineteenth century and consider the interesting case of Charles Reade. Robert Macfarlane includes Reade among the six authors he studies in his re-examination of originality and plagiarism in the late Victorian period.[34] As Macfarlane notes, 'Reade's stance on originality and literary property appears to be categorically inconsistent.'[35] Reade certainly had a schizophrenic relationship with originality: on the one hand, he shamelessly plundered newspapers like *The Times* for material, as well as translating and adapting French plays for the English stage, as well as some English works; on the other hand, he wrote openly and often about his own genius and invention. At the same time, he was a vigorous campaigner for reform of copyright laws, both domestic and international. He appeared before a Select Committee of 1866 to complain about the prevalence of French stage adaptations, which he claimed were debasing the state of English drama,[36] and brought several legal actions seeking to prevent other people from turning his novels into plays.[37] However, the courts drew the line at preventing novels from being turned into plays. Harking back to the 'new work' principle, they held that dramatizing a novel did not amount to infringement, as the author who published a novel had given it to the world, to make whatever use anyone wished of it, subject only to reprinting it.[38]

[31] *D'Almaine* v. *Boosey* (1835) 1 Y. & C. Ex. 288, 302.     [32] *Dickens* v. *Lee* (1844) 8 Jur. 183.
[33] *Ibid.*, 184.     [34] Robert Macfarlane, *Original Copy* (Oxford University Press, 2007).
[35] *Ibid.*, p. 136.
[36] Select Committee on Theatrical Licences and Regulation (373) (1866) 16 Parliamentary Papers 351, pp. 237–41.
[37] *Reade* v. *Conquest* (*No.1*) (1861) 9 CB (NS) 755; *Reade* v. *Lacy* (1861) 1 J. & H. 524; *Reade* v. *Conquest* (*No. 2*) (1862) 11 CB (NS) 479.
[38] See also *Toole* v. *Young* (1874) LR 9 QB 523; *Tinsley* v. *Lacy* (1862) 32 LJ (Ch.) 537; 1 H. & M. 747.

For Reade, who had begun his career as a lawyer, it seems that the disjunction between law and literature was complete, at least in relation to his own practices. It is worth noting that in his notebooks, he referred to the adaptation of French plays as 'plagiarism', while before the Select Committee of 1866 he used the word 'piracy'.[39] Both words are metaphors, and, as Groom points out, the etymological roots of both lie in the law. Piracy, however, has come to take on a more direct role in copyright law as the commonly accepted term for the unauthorized printing of books. It designates the economic harm caused by copying, while 'plagiarism' remains a more complex textual phenomenon, indicating a wider range of effects, literary, moral and aesthetic.

The law relating to piracy, or copyright infringement, changed over the course of the two centuries and was not always expressed coherently or with a high degree of precision. However, its status as 'law', rendered as a binding judgment with economic consequences, and its publication in written form as a decision accompanied by reasoning, means that its transformation can be tracked with some degree of objectivity. Plagiarism, while also evaluative, is more difficult to pin down. As Macfarlane has pointed out, 'Attempts to describe plagiarism transhistorically, for example, find themselves consistently thwarted by inconsistency – one person's plagiarism is discovered to be another's originality.'[40] Even when it is policed in academic circles, the elements of the 'offence' of plagiarism are uncertain. Groom describes the University of Oxford's educational policy as covering unintentional plagiarism, thus rendering it a strict liability offence.[41] By contrast, in a recent decision, the University of Cambridge found that the mental elements of the 'crime' of plagiarism were intention or negligence.[42]

There is considerable scope for more interdisciplinary work to be done on literature and the law of copyright. Such work highlights the sharing of language and ideas between the legal and literary discourses – particularly pertinent in the field of copyright law where many of the players were both lawyers and authors.[43] However, it is important not to overemphasize the similarities. Contrary to Mark Rose's assertion that the common law copyright debates of the eighteenth century blended legal

---

[39] Macfarlane, *Original Copy*, pp. 148–9; 1866 Select Committee, pp. 253–4.
[40] *Ibid.*, p. 13. [41] Groom, 'Unoriginal Genius', p. 296.
[42] 'Court of Discipline: Notice', *Cambridge University Reporter*, 138(15) (16 January 2008).
[43] James Boswell, William Blackstone, Thomas Noon Talfourd and Charles Reade are but a few.

and literary discourses in such a way as to crystallize the concept of author as original creator and economic owner of literary property, such a merging of discourses was far from complete.[44] While recognizing the roles played by the concerns of literature and literary men in the development of copyright law, it is equally important to be aware of the other sources of influence, such as the continuing application of pre-Statute of Anne approaches to partial and altered copying. For the same reasons, copyright law cannot be so easily presented as influencing the development of literary theory and practice. Examining the infringement cases in more detail demonstrates some areas in which the literary and the legal corresponded, and the concerns of one informed the other, but it also reveals divergences. By uncovering a more complex view of originality in the pre-Romantic and Romantic period, Groom assists in the construction of a more nuanced history of copyright law, a fuller understanding of the literary construct of originality in the period and a richer account of the interactions between them.

[44] Rose, *Authors*, p. 6.

# PART IX

---

## Art

# 16

# Piracy and authorship in contemporary art and the artistic commonwealth

DANIEL MCCLEAN[*]

## Introduction

This chapter is about the tension between concepts of authorship and piracy in contemporary art and in copyright law. On the one hand, it questions how far copyright (which regulates the reproduction of cultural media) applies to the contemporary art system (which is based upon the production and distribution of unique, 'original' artefacts) either as an incentive for artists to create artworks or as a source of authorial protection.

It suggests that the 'high' art system, which emphasises the authenticity and provenance of unique artefacts, has generated an alternative system of authorship and enforcement for artists to that found within copyright law where infringement actions best suit authors whose work is linked to reproductive cultural media, such as music, literature and film. Discussing movements such as Pop art, Minimalism, Conceptual art, Appropriation art and their descendants, it considers key aspects of artistic authorship, including the authority of artists to designate an apparently limitless array of objects as artworks (including copies) and to delegate control to others in the artwork's creation and execution. It argues that the institution of authorship within contemporary art (and in particular, the desire of artists to control their work after sale) has created its own system of 'administrating aesthetics'[1] in which authorisation by the artist and his or her estate of the work is fundamental, rather than

---

[*] The author would like to express his thanks to Jane C. Ginsburg, Morton L. Janklow, Professor of Literary and Artistic Property Law, Columbia School and Anna Blest, solicitor, Withers LLP (London) for their assistance with this chapter.
[1] See, Benjamin Buchloh, 'Conceptual Art 1962–1969: From the Aesthetics of Administration to the Critique of Institutions', *October*, 55 (1999), 105–43.

enforcement of exclusive rights to copy. This system makes other legal rights of authorship more relevant to artists than copyright, in particular contractual rights and moral rights when the artwork as object is at stake. However, copyright is a relevant source of protection for artists when artworks are exploited through reproduction, as in merchandising, such as in posters, postcards, coffee-table books, clothing and packaging and in advertising and in film.

On the other hand, the chapter links the problem of copyright infringement by artists to the question of what in the art world would (or, more often, would not) be considered 'piracy'. It suggests that the peculiarities of the institution of artistic authorship have enabled a shared culture of copying among artists or 'artistic commonwealth' of images, forms and styles to flourish, some of which potentially conflict with copyright norms. It would appear to be an unwritten convention of the artistic commonwealth that artists do not sue one another for copyright infringement, hence the apparent absence of any relevant precedents in UK case law of such infringement claims[2] – though this position may change when artists' estates become owners of artistic copyright.[3]

The chapter argues that the artistic commonwealth is disrupted when artists come into conflict with other authors and owners protected by copyright law, particularly 'commercial' photographers, who do not share the same authorial and economic interests. Copyright facilitates these conflicts because its 'aesthetically neutral' conception of artistic work and authorial originality diverges radically from the criteria adopted to judge art within the art world. In particular, copyright law does not prima facie distinguish between 'high' and 'low' artistic works[4]

---

[2] The norms of the artistic commonwealth have not prevented Damien Hirst from threatening to sue other artists for copying his work, see: 'Damien Hirst threatened to sue teenager over alleged copyright threat', *Daily Mail* (12 December 2008). However, this must be regarded as an exception to the norm.

[3] For example, the artist Glenn Brown experienced difficulties from the Salvador Dalí Estate when copying works by Salvador Dalí in his paintings. See Michael Wilson, 'Glenn Brown: Gagosian Gallery', *Art Forum International* (22 June 2004), New York.

[4] In the UK for example, s. 4(1)(a) of the Copyright, Designs and Patents Act 1988 (CDPA), states that 'artistic works', including graphic works, photographs, sculptures and collages are protected 'irrespective of artistic quality', though this differs with works of 'artistic craftsmanship' under s. 4(1)(c) CPDA. The traditional tests for 'originality' in UK copyright law, is a minimum degree of independent skill, judgement and effort, *per* Peterson J. in *University of London Press Ltd* v. *University Tutorial Press Ltd* [1916] 2 Ch. 601 and copyright can protect basic visual forms, *Kenwrick* v. *Lawrence* [1890] LR25, QBD 99.

and therefore protects a far wider array of artistic works – fine artworks, mass reproductions, industrial designs – and with this, authors. The exercise of artistic copyright would, therefore, seem to fall almost too neatly across a 'high–low' axis, revealing fine artists to be willing to enforce copyright when the (commercial) mechanical reproduction of their work is involved and for photographers aligned with mechanical reproduction willing to sue fine artists for the unauthorised and unattributed use of their images. Thus if we look at the main artistic copyright infringement disputes in recent American case law, we find that it is 'commercial' photographers, such as Patrick Cariou[5] (documentary), Thomas Hoepker[6] (documentary), Andrea Blanch (advertising)[7] and Art Rogers (portrait commissions)[8] who have been claimants against 'Appropriation' artist defendants acclaimed by the art establishment such as Richard Prince, Barbara Kruger and Jeff Koons. Companies who have been assigned photographic copyright can also be litigious as seen in the recent high-profile dispute in the US between Associated Press and Shepherd Fairey concerning Fairey's use of an image of President Obama.[9] Likewise in the UK, the illustrator Anthony Roberts publicly alleged that the painter, Glenn Brown[10] had infringed copyright

---

[5] *Patrick Cariou* v. *Richard Prince et al.* (SDNY) (claim filed 30 Dec. 2008). Cariou alleges that Prince has infringed his copyright in photographs published in the book, *Yes Rasta* (2000) and reproduced by Prince in a series of collage paintings exhibited at Gagosian Gallery, New York (2008) in the Canal Zone Exhibition (see myartspace.com/blog/200901/Patrick-cariou-versus-richardprince).

[6] *Hoepker* v. *Kruger* 200 F. Supp. 2d 340 (SDNY 2002). See also, Martha Buskirk, 'Creative Intent: The Recent Fortunes of Appropriation in the United States', in Daniel McClean (ed.), *The Trials of Art* (London: Ridinghouse, 2007), pp. 241–4.

[7] *Blanch* v. *Koons*, Docket No. 05–6433-cv (2nd Cir. 2006). See Buskirk, 'Creative Intent', pp. 244–9. Jeff Koons copied a part of the photograph, *Silk Sandals* (2000) by Andrea Blanch and published in *Allure* magazine. The image showed the legs of a woman wearing a pair of Gucci sandals. The painting was used in Koons' collage painting *Niagara* (2000). Koons successfully defended Blanch's copyright infringement action under the US fair use exemption.

[8] *Rogers* v. *Koons*, 960 F.2d 301, 310 (2nd Cir. 1992).

[9] See *Fairey* v. *Associated Press*, Case NO: 09–01123 (AKH) (filed, SDNY, 9 Feb. 2009). Fairey sought a declaratory judgment of non-infringement of the copyright in a photograph of President (then Senator) Obama taken by Mannie Garcia for the Associated Press. Fairey had created an iconic poster of President Obama, which had sold thousands of copies. It is, however, uncertain whether the case will proceed to a judgment on the merits, since Fairey has admitted to lying to the court regarding which AP photograph he used to create the poster.

[10] Glenn Brown also faced copyright infringement proceedings when he copied Anthony Roberts' cover jacket for the 1974 Robert A. Heinlein novel, *Double Star*. See Stuart Lockyear, 'Copyright and the Visual Arts: Questions and Answers', in Daniel McClean

by reproducing his science-fiction book illustration in the painting, *The Love of Shepherds* (*After Anthony Roberts*) in 2000.

Conversely, artists have also been willing to enforce their artistic copyright outside of the artistic commonwealth where it has been exploited commercially as in advertising and film. In *Lebbeus Woods* v. *Universal Pictures* (2005)[11] for example, the claimant, an avant-garde architect, successfully sued for copyright infringement when his drawings were adapted in a sequence in the film, *The Twelve Monkeys* (1995) produced by the defendant. Artists are also willing through artists' copyright collection societies such as DACS (UK), ADAGP (France) and ARS (US) to enforce their copyright interests, particularly in relation to merchandising, publishing and advertising.

The social and cultural position of authors is often neglected in discussions of artistic copyright infringement, which tend to focus instead on the structure of copyright law, in particular its 'fair use' exemptions.[12] While the structure of copyright law is undoubtedly important we need to analyse artists' practices and why conventions of borrowing in one context come to be seen as acts of piracy or plagiarism in another.

It is not the purpose of this chapter to propose normative solutions to the problems caused by the application of copyright law to art; if anything, some of the difficulties caused by movements such as Appropriation art would appear to be intractable from a copyright perspective. Nor is it to argue that copyright does not have a place for fine artists. When economies of reproduction have been at stake, artists have been only too willing to urge that the law redress new kinds of infringements where reproduction is concerned. For example, the passage of the Engraving Copyright Act 1734 (UK) which extended copyright protection to artists' original engravings was heavily promoted by the English painter and printmaker, William Hogarth and is known as 'Hogarth's Act'.[13]

Copyright is often justified as an incentive for authors to create cultural works by bestowing upon them property rights of a finite duration to control particular types of third-party uses of their works,

---

and Karsten Schubert (eds.), *Dear Images: Art, Copyright and Culture* (London: Ridinghouse, 2002), pp. 164–5.

[11] *Woods* v. *Universal Studios, Inc.* 920. F. Supp, 62 (1996).

[12] See Barton Beebe, 'An Empirical Study of US Copyright Fair Use Opinions, 1978–2005', *University of Pennsylvania Law Review*, 156(1) (2008), 549–624.

[13] Mark Rose, 'Technology and Copyright in 1735: The Engraver's Act', *The Information Society*, 21(1) (January–March, 2005), 63–6 and Kathy Bowery, 'Who's Painting Copyright's History', in McClean and Schubert, *Dear Images*, pp. 265–7.

including acts of reproduction and distribution.[14] The US Constitution explicitly enshrines this justification in Article 1, s. 8, cl. 8, the so-called, 'Copyright Clause' by stating that copyright's function is '[t]o promote the Progress of Science and useful Arts, by securing for limited Times to Authors and Inventors exclusive Right to their respective Writings and Discoveries'. Copyright is justified in other legal systems as in the UK and civil law jurisdictions on deontological grounds as protecting the economic and moral interests of authors.[15] I wish to query how far the economic rationale explains why contemporary artists create artworks and in particular are rewarded economically through copyright.

An examination of some statistics of the global art market reveals that at its height in 2007, this market was valued at $6.4 billion USD.[16] It is clear that only a fraction of this market's value derives from the exploitation by artists of copyright and that the value of this market instead derives from the sale of art works as unique, exclusive and precious commodities. At the Christie's New York auction in November 2007, Jeff Koons' *Hanging Heart* (1994–6) (a bright magenta heart with gold undulating bow) was sold for $23.6 million dollars[17] establishing an auction record for a living artist. Almost a year later in September 2008, during the start of the global economic recession, Damien Hirst in an unprecedented auction at Sotheby's London, sold a whole body of artworks directly to the 'public' making $200.7 million (USD) in the process.[18] While auction records are not an entirely accurate reflection of the market values of contemporary art works (and Hirst has been accused of forcing his dealers, Larry Gagosian and Jay Jopling to purchase many of his works at auction thereby keeping their prices artificially high)[19] they are an indication of the high value that artworks by such artists attain.

Compare these figures to the total copyright royalties collected by the Designers and Artists Copyright Society[20] (DACS) in 2007–8 in the UK.

---

[14] Spence, 'Justifying Copyright', in McClean and Schubert, *Dear Images*, pp. 389–92.

[15] *Ibid.*, pp. 393–402. Spence distinguishes between different types of deontological justification for copyright, including justifications based on desert (as reflected in the UK copyright system) and notions of personal autonomy (as reflected in civil law copyright regimes such as Germany and France).

[16] The Global Fine Art Market, *Reuters*, 22 March 2007.

[17] www.culturekiosque.com/art/artmrkt/koons.html.

[18] 'Bull Market for Hirst in Sotheby's 2-Day Sale', *New York Times*, 16 September 2008.

[19] Ben Lewis, 'Why I was Banned from Damien Hirst's £120m gamble', *London Evening Standard*, 15 September 2008.

[20] www.dacs.org.uk/pdfs/royalties.pdf.

In 2007, DACS collected a total of £3 million sterling (in pay-back royalties)[21] for 12,734 UK and international artists and visual creators and a total of £700,000 in copyright management royalties to 1,000 UK and international artists. Interestingly, the top ten UK and top ten international beneficiaries of DACS's collection of copyright royalties were artists' estates rather than living artists, an indication perhaps that copyright benefits artists more after death than during their lifetime.

No doubt Hirst and Koons represent the extreme spectrum of success for contemporary artists, and the vast majority of artists earn far less than they do. However, with a few exceptions, it is difficult to imagine the majority of artists deriving anything like an equivalent income stream from the exploitation of copyright compared to the sale of their individual artworks, unless their work is primarily connected to reproduction. In this sense, cheap and unauthorised reproductions of artworks by Hirst and Koons cannot be said to compete with or harm their primary markets.

The fact that artists' primary income derives from the sale of artworks (paintings, sculptures, installations, etc.) as unique artefacts and not from reproduction, may explain perhaps, in part, the anomaly of the artists' droit de suite or resale royalty right. The droit de suite provides artists or their heirs or beneficiaries with a fixed percentage of the income derived from the resale of an artwork.[22] Typically, the sale has to involve one or more 'art market professionals'.[23] The right, which has now been harmonised across the EU[24] and exists in other countries as well as under Californian law,[25] is from an intellectual property perspective a strange or impure right, attaching to the resale of the artwork *qua object*, rather than through the exploitation of the intangible aspects of the work protected by copyright law. The rationale for the droit de suite[26] when it was first introduced into French law in 1920 was to ameliorate the hardship caused to artists and particularly their heirs, by giving them a

---

[21] www.dacs.org.uk/pdfs/paybackrelease.pdf.

[22] See ss. (1)–3(3) of the Artist's Resale Right Regulations, 2006 (UK) (Regs.). A sliding scale of the amount remunerated to artists or their beneficiaries is set out in sched. 1 to the Regs.

[23] *Ibid.* s. 12(3).

[24] The Artists' Resale Rights Directive 2001/184/EC 27 September 2001, stipulated that it was to be transposed into national law across the EC member states before 1 January 2006.

[25] Californian Resale Royalties Act 1976.

[26] Simon Stokes, 'Moral Rights and Droit de Suite', in *Art and Copyright* (Oxford: Hart Publishing, 2001), pp. 78–9.

share of the benefits of the resale of the artwork over time precisely because artists benefited less from the market for reproductions and public performances of their work than did authors of other kinds of works. This would reduce the asymmetry caused when an artwork which might be sold for very little at an early stage in the artist's career is sold for a much greater sum later on. This rationale persists and was also one of the motives for the introduction and harmonisation of the right across the EU as contained in the EU Directive in 2001.[27]

## The institution of authorship in art

Although this chapter concerns the art world's and the legal world's different concepts of wrongful copying, it is necessary first to consider the affirmative side: what are legal or artistic norms endeavouring to protect? Foucault's analysis of authorship in *What is an Author?*[28] is frequently adopted as a starting point in discussions of authorship in copyright law[29] as well as in cultural theory. An obvious reason for this is that Foucault highlights the important role copyright law plays from the eighteenth century onwards in helping to construct and solidify the figure of the author, binding a particular work or text to a specific individual creator.[30] Aside from historicising the author function, Foucault points out how it varies greatly between discourses: certain discourses (for example, literature) require authors, he stresses, in comparison to other discourses (for example, science), which do not.

Authorship as analysed by Foucault is clearly critical to the way in which the art system classifies and values artworks. However, while there are some parallels between how authorship is defined within copyright law and within the art system (both systems have, for example, arguably drawn upon Romantic notions of the author as a solitary, creative genius),[31] there are also important differences. Fine art objects are valued because of their attribution both to a particular artist and because of their

---

[27] *Ibid.*, 76–81.

[28] Michel Foucault, 'What is an Author?', in Donald Bouchard (ed.), *Language, Counter-Memory, Practice* (Ithaca, New York: Cornell University Press, 1977), pp. 24–127.

[29] Mark Rose, 'The Author as Proprietor', in Brad Sherman and Alain Strowel (eds.), *Of Authors and Origins* (Oxford: Clarendon Press, 1996), pp. 23–55, esp. p. 27 ('the principal institutional embodiment of the author–work relation is copyright').

[30] Foucault, 'What is an Author?'.

[31] Peter Jaszi, 'Towards a Theory of Copyright: The Metamorphosis of "Authorship"', *Duke Law Journal* (1991), 445.

uniqueness and scarcity.[32] The authorial function in art therefore links, in contrast to copyright law, to two distinct notions of originality.

The first is an evaluative notion of originality, that an artwork is by an artist whose authorship is *novel* in art historical terms and has accordingly been ascribed recognition within art discourse (art criticism, history, etc.) and by art institutions (exhibitions in museums, galleries, etc.). These structures help to shape a historical narrative of significant artists, schools, styles and movements, thereby also validating the market for particular artists and artworks. Ironically, art history might be said to have a 'legislative' function, with art historians and critics making a *case* for particular artists and artworks (including their authenticity), thereby establishing precedents within the history of art. Richard Schiff[33] identifies three main paradigms of artistic originality underpinning the authorship function in art: classical, modernist and postmodernist. The classical paradigm (ascendant from the Renaissance to the mid-nineteenth century) he argues is founded upon the *imitation* as opposed to the mere copying of earlier artistic precedents. Central to the classical paradigm is the notion that to achieve artistic originality, an artist must place himself within a tradition and emulate the genius of past masters such as Raphael (it is this link to copying and tradition within the classical paradigm that explains the emergence of the artistic commonwealth, discussed below).

In contrast, the modernist paradigm which is heavily indebted to Romanticism, emphasises artistic *origination*, individual genius and self-expression. Here the notion of a past is rejected by artists and nature (without social rules) is valorised as opposed to culture.

Finally, in the postmodern paradigm, authorship is constructed by artists out of images and texts drawn from other authors, thus calling into question the validity of modernist notions of originality in which acts of copying and repetition are repressed. Here, the notion of the artist designating the artwork as art is key. Whilst the term 'postmodern' is arguably now redundant in contemporary cultural discourse, Schiff's typology is useful. The second is a notion of originality that is tied to the trace of the author as creator, in other words, the authenticity of the

---

[32] Walter Benjamin, 'The Work of Art in the Age of Mechanical Reproduction', in Hannah Arendt (ed.), *Walter Benjamin: Illuminations* (New York: Schoken Books, 1968), pp. 217–52, esp. pp. 220–5.

[33] Richard Schiff, 'Originality', in Richard Schiff and Robert Nelson (eds.), *Critical Terms for Art History* (2nd edn, University of Chicago Press, 2003), pp. 145–59.

artwork. Historically, authenticity describes the creation of artworks as unique or 'original' artefacts and their physical link to a particular artist, which guarantees their art historical and economic value. Walter Benjamin argued[34] that it is the artwork's unique existence in time and space and its connection to a specific history of ownership and creation (provenance) that bestows upon the contemplated artwork, its 'auratic' qualities, i.e. a sense of reverence or awe. According to Benjamin, the artwork's auratic quality enables the artwork to be integrated into religious and secular ritual, in particular, into the cult of beauty.[35] For Benjamin mechanical reproduction could undermine the auratic qualities of the art object in a positive, politically radical way.[36]

The authenticity of artworks is conventionally underpinned by the artist's signature, which registers the artist's 'umbilical' connection to the artwork and verifies that it is finished and ready for exhibition – the artist's signature is typically inserted directly onto the bottom (right-hand) corner of a painting or drawing. In many contemporary artworks however, particularly works of Conceptual art, which can exist as linguistic descriptions and instructions, it is no longer possible for authenticity to be guaranteed directly through the artist's signature and certificates (and even contracts) function as alternative sources of authentication.

A persistent feature of the art system would seem to be that no matter how authorship is critiqued by artists and how the artwork is dispersed through multiplication, reproduction and dematerialisation, the fetish for the auratic art object remains. Susan Lambert for example,[37] illustrates how in the nineteenth century, artists' prints, which were previously excluded from the canon of artistic originality, came to be codified by artists as original artworks with artists such as Whistler signing them, thereby marking their authenticity. Patrick Elliot[38]

---

[34] Benjamin, 'Work of Art', 220–5.    [35] Ibid., 223–4.

[36] Ibid. Benjamin argued that with mechanical reproduction the work of art would be freed from its dependence upon ritual and brought under the gaze of the masses, leading to the destruction of its aura. This would have radical political consequences particularly when expressed in film, to which the masses unlike with singular works of art would be able to collectively respond to avant-garde innovations in a progressive manner.

[37] Susan Lambert, The Image Multiplied: Five Centuries of Printed Reproductions of Paintings and Drawings (London: Trefoil Publications, 1987), p. 33.

[38] Patrick Elliot, Sculpture in France: 1900–1940 (New Haven, CT: Yale University Press, 2010, forthcoming). The author has kindly advanced a copy of his manuscript in which he establishes this evidence. In 1972, a year before his death, Guino successfully established before the French courts that he was joint author of the copyright in Renoir's

discusses how bronze sculptures attributed to Renoir were in fact created by the sculptor Richard Guino based on drawings made by Renoir and how bronze sculptures of Daumier were all made posthumously under the authorisation of the artist's estate.

It is hardly surprising then, that the greatest threat to the art system derives less from the unauthorised reproduction of the artwork than from its wrongful attribution. As Hillel Schwartz points out,[39] a fake may or may not be an errant and 'deceitful' copy of a lost or an existing original, it may, for example, be an artist's imaginary work in the style of another more famous artist, such as the forger, Hans Van Meegeren's copies of Vermeer.[40] However, fakes threaten the regime of authenticity that underpins the value of the art market. The legal sanctions applied to this offence are accordingly severe, but lie outside the regime of copyright law which does not regulate authenticity in other civil and criminal sanctions such as fraud. The misattribution of the authorship of artworks is also a problem inherent within the art system that affects the authenticity and market value of particular artworks over time, leading some artworks to dramatically increase in value and others to dramatically decrease in value as attribution shifts.

## Contemporary art and copyright

The art of the last four decades has led to the startling proposition that almost anything can be called art. Theorists have grappled with the extraordinary heterogeneity of artistic media, objects, methods and movements (Pop, Minimalism, Conceptual art, Institutional Critique, Installation art, Relational Aesthetics, Appropriation art), which characterise contemporary art. This heterogeneity and the apparent, self-validating authority of the art system to judge itself, are described by Jacques Rancière as aspects of an 'aesthetic regime' of the visible[41] no

---

sculpture. Accordingly, his descendants enjoy copyright royalties in relation to the reproduction of Renoir's sculptures.

[39] Hillel Schwartz, *The Culture of the Copy: Striking Likenesses, Unreasonable Facsimiles* (New York: Zone Books, 1996), p. 248.

[40] See, Dennis Dutton, 'Artistic Crimes: The Problem of Forgery in the Arts', *British Journal of Aesthetics*, 19 (1979), 302–24.

[41] Jacques Rancière, *The Politics of Aesthetics* (London: Continuum Press, 2006), esp. pp. 20–30 and 23 ('[t]he aesthetic regime [33] of the arts is the regime that strictly identifies art in the singular and frees it from any specific rule, from any hierarchy of the arts, subject matter and genre').

longer bounded by genre/medium-based differences and boundaries. Boris Groys[42] identifies the 'regime of equal aesthetic rights for all artworks' as defining art today, and also paradoxically (in the absence of aesthetic judgment) of guaranteeing art's autonomy.[43] These developments can be ascribed to different causes. The gesture of Marcel Duchamp's ready-made *Fountain* (1917) in which the artist selected and designated an everyday mass-produced object (a urinal) as an artwork (a designation later accepted within the art system) is typically identified as a generative cause of this paradigm – this complex enunciation gesture also revealing the conditions of art's circulation.[44]

However, it is clear that many contemporary artworks since Duchamp's ready-made can be said to be *productive* of situations (phenomenological, discursive, etc.), which directly involve their audiences. In this sense much of contemporary art aspires to what Michael Fried (the arch-modernist critic) decried as 'theatricality' in art.[45] By this he meant the collapse of distinctions between artistic media, for example, between painting and sculpture (whose self-reflexive purity, modernist critics such as Fried and Clement Greenberg sought to preserve) and the co-presence of the audience with the artwork in real space and time: a phenomenon which Rosalind Krauss has termed the 'post-medium condition'[46] and Groys, the art of

---

[42]  Boris Groys, *Art Power* (Cambridge, MA: MIT Press, 2008), esp. pp. 13–22, and 13–14 ('[t]hus the autonomy of art implies not an autonomous hierarchy of taste – but abolishing every such hierarchy and establishing the regime of equal aesthetic rights for all artworks. The art world should be seen as the socially codified manifestation of the fundamental equality between all visual forms, objects and media').

[43]  *Ibid.*, p. 13 ('[t]he territory of art is organized around the lack or, rather, the rejection of any aesthetic judgment', and at p. 16, 'One might say that today's art operates in the gap between the formal equality of all art forms and their factual inequality. That is why there can be and is "good art" – even if all artworks have equal aesthetic rights. The good artwork is precisely that work which affirms the formal equality of all images under the conditions of their factual inequality').

[44]  Thierry De Duve, *Kant After Duchamp* (Cambridge, MA: MIT Press, 1996), pp. 373–462.

[45]  Michael Fried, 'Art and Objecthood', in Gregory Battock (ed.), *Minimal Art: A Critical Anthology* (New York: E. P. Dutton, 1968), pp. 116–47. Fried criticised the 'theatricality' of Minimalist art arguing that whenever a consciousness of viewing exists among spectators of the artwork (as with Minimalist artworks) absorption in the artwork is sacrificed and theatricality results. For Fried, theatricality had negative associations with entertainment, kitsch and mass culture. By contrast, Fried like Greenberg praised modernist artworks for their self-reflexive concentration on the formal properties of their artistic medium.

[46]  Rosalind Krauss, *A Voyage on Art in the Age of the North Sea: Post Medium Condition* (London: Thames & Hudson, 1999).

'installation'.[47] Paradoxically, the co-presence and involvement of curators and audiences in the production and reception of many contemporary artworks has not prevented the ascription of their authorship to single, individual artists and their circulation as artworks within the art market. I do not want to get bogged down in the question of whether copyright law does or can protect many of these types of artistic works, though this is undoubtedly an important question which has been discussed by various critics, including Anne Barron.[48] Criticism has been levelled at the defini-tion of copyrighted artistic works contained in certain statutes, for example, the CDPA 1988, and its narrow, medium-based categories of 'graphic works', 'photographs', 'sculpture, 'collage' and 'works of artistic craftsman-ship' which are said to potentially exclude 'post-medium' artworks, particu-larly artworks which lack permanence or 'fixation'.[49] Further criticism has been levelled at the potential inability of copyright to protect the 'origi-nality' of basic artistic forms, for example, monochrome paintings; and to provide insufficient protection to 'ideas' as opposed to 'expressions' thereby excluding Conceptual artworks, for example, from the scope of copyright protection.[50] As Sol LeWitt famously said, 'in conceptual art the idea or concept is the most important part of the work'. [51] It has been argued by Celia Lury[52] accordingly, that other species of intellectual property law,

---

[47] Groys, *Art Power*, p. 94 ('[t]he elementary unit of art today is therefore no longer an artwork as object but an art space in which objects are exhibited: the space of an exhibition, of an installation').

[48] Anne Barron, 'Copyright, Art and Objecthood', in McClean and Schubert, *Dear Images*, pp. 277–311. Barron argues that UK copyright law appears to be unable to accommodate many forms of contemporary artistic expression, which are ephemeral, not 'original' in a copyright sense, and involve 'basic' components of cultural production. She ascribes this not to copyright's internalisation of Romantic conceptions of authorship, but to its incorporation of outdated, medium-specific categories of artistic work deriving from eighteenth-century aesthetic theory and modernist definitions of artistic work.

[49] The recent UK case of *Lucas* v. *Ainsworth* [2008] EWHC 1878 (Ch.) concerning the definition of works of sculpture under s. 4(1)(a) CDPA, however, might suggest other-wise. Mann J. said *obiter* at 118 that copyright protection would extend in his view to Carl Andre's bricks as works of 'sculpture' under CDPA, s. 4(1)(a).

[50] Nadia Walravens, 'The Concept of Originality and Contemporary Art', in McClean and Schubert, *Dear Images*, pp. 171–95. Walravens argues in relation to French copyright law that many of copyright's features preclude the protection of contemporary artworks; in particular, the requirements that an artwork be personally executed by its author and the protection of 'expressions' rather than ideas.

[51] Sol LeWitt, 'Paragraphs on Conceptual Art (1967)', in Charles Harrison and Paul Wood (ed.), *Art in Theory 1900–1990: An Anthology of Changing Ideas* (Oxford: Blackwell, 1992), pp. 834–37.

[52] See, Celia Lury, 'Portrait of the Artist as a Brand', in McClean and Schubert, *Dear Images*, pp. 310–28.

in particular, the Anglo-American common law action of passing off, might protect the trademark, 'branded' elements of an artist's work, such as an artist's visual style, in contrast to copyright law.

A question which is less often addressed is of what relevance copyright law is to protecting the type of authorial interests that are at stake in the production of many types of contemporary artworks? I wish to argue that these authorial interests are connected with the artwork as a unique artefact (even in artworks which challenge traditional notions of the artwork's construction and the artist's indexical link to the work) so that other mechanisms – legal and aesthetically juridical – are more relevant. In the words of Benjamin Buchloh:[53]

> [i]n the absence of any specifically visual qualities and due to the manifest lack of any (artistic) manual competence as a criterion of distinction, all the traditional criteria of aesthetic judgment – of taste and connoisseurship – have been programmatically voided. The result of this is that the definition of aesthetic becomes on the one hand a matter of linguistic convention and on the other the function of both a legal contract and an institutional discourse (a discourse of power rather than taste).

This can be illustrated with reference to works of Conceptual and Minimalist art. As Martha Buskirk highlights, the question of authorial control over the artwork is central to both artistic movements because in different ways they propose a separation between artistic ideas, as recorded in drawings, diagrams and written instructions, and their material expression or execution.[54] Minimalist and Conceptual artists sought to control the way in which their artworks are owned and displayed after sale, requiring collectors, through certificates and contracts to consult with them on a whole range of issues from the execution and placement of the work, to its conservation and resale. The key notion here is the artist's authorisation of the work rather than his or her physical trace or imprint on the object. The issue of the artist controlling the placement or site-specificity of the artwork becomes critical, particularly in Minimalism.

For Minimalists like Carl Andre, Donald Judd and Dan Flavin who created serial compositions out of industrially manufactured material

---

[53] Buchloh, 'Conceptual Art', 117–18.
[54] Martha Buskirk, 'Authorship and Authority', *The Contingent Object of Contemporary Art* (Cambridge, MA: MIT Press, 2005), pp. 21–56, esp. 34–45, where Buskirk discusses the importance of artists' certificates for the influential art collector, Count Panza and the disputes between Count Panza and Donald Judd and Carl Andre regarding the fabrication and placement of their artworks.

elements (including bricks, metal plates, wooden and metal boxes and lighting fixtures), the 'relatively disembodied realms of written words and diagrams are enmeshed with work that is about a particular kind of physical experience':[55] the issue is about the placement of the object in a specific way in physical space. Buskirk illustrates how the certificate of authenticity along with plans and drawings became the most important site of ownership for Minimalist artists in seeking to regulate the rules of the artwork and its control.

Likewise, the certificate of authenticity plays an equally significant role in Conceptual art. Artists including Joseph Kosuth, Sol LeWitt and Lawrence Weiner take the process of separation between idea and execution one step further, 'dematerialising' the artwork so that it consists of linguistic propositions or statements that may or may not be installed on a surface (Weiner) or wall drawings (LeWitt) where the only object that is actually transferred is a certificate, accompanied by a diagram with instructions for the realisation of the drawing.[56]

Developments in Minimalism and Conceptual art have in a sense led to a need for artists from these movements to create aesthetic systems organised and administered on a quasi-legal basis. The importance assigned to artistic ideas and the basic elements generally used by these artists mean that their artworks can potentially be easily replicated and forged. Yet the primary way for artists to deal with this threat has not been to rely on copyright but rather to rely upon certificates of authenticity, as Buskirk shows. Indeed, artists have even appointed lawyers to organise the issuing and maintenance of their certificates. Carl Andre, for example,[57] has created a system of registration whereby he requires that every time one of his works is sold, the new owner must notify him of the sale and that owner will be provided with a new certificate of authenticity. If a purchaser of an Andre sculpture has failed to notify the artist of his interest, then he or she will not own an up-to-date certificate and from the point of view of the art market he or she will be unable to demonstrate ownership of an authentic Andre work, despite there being in legal terms a possible line of provenance linking the owner back to Carl Andre. In Andre's case, the artist seems to have developed a system, which at times runs parallel to the law and exhibits a quasi-judicial character.

---

[55] *Ibid.*, p. 27.   [56] *Ibid.*, pp. 45–7.
[57] See, 'Certificates and Policies' (at: www.carlandre.net).

In *The Artist's Contract* (1971)[58] the legendary Conceptual art dealer and curator, Seth Siegelaub and lawyer, Bob Projansky, would seek to create a paradigm for the assertion of artists' rights and control over the artwork through the sale agreement with buyers.[59] Most commonly associated with the economic right (akin to the droit de suite) for artists to benefit in the resale of the artwork (a 15 per cent share of each sale), *The Artist's Contract* also contains important authorial rights, including control over the exhibition and maintenance of the artwork after sale.[60] Though not widely adopted by artists (for fear this would antagonise collectors),[61] *The Artist's Contract* nevertheless marks an important historical moment in the codification of aesthetic relations between artist, collector and work. Furthermore, as Alexander Alberro argues,[62] *The Artist's Contract* would also become another tool in the fixation and authentication of the dematerialised artwork, thereby also paradoxically partaking in its commodification in contradiction with the expressed aims of early Conceptual art.

It is easy to see why moral rights of authorship might have more relevance to artists than copyright: in particular, the paternity right (the right to be recognised as author of the work); the right to object to the false attribution of the work; and the so-called 'integrity right': the

---

[58] The full name of the Artist's Contract is the 'Artist's Reserved Rights Transfer and Sale Agreement', (1971). The Artist's Contract was commissioned by the legendary Conceptual art dealer and curator, Seth Siegelaub and drafted by a New York attorney, Bob Projansky. A copy of the agreement is published in Maria Eichhorn (ed.), *The Artist's Contract* (Köln: Walter König, 2009), pp. 58–65, and her book discusses the legacy of the contract and the general failure of artists to use it.

[59] *Ibid.* The Artist's Contract obliged collectors to agree to a whole range of conditions protecting the artist's economic and authorial rights. Upon the transfer of the artwork, the collector would, under the Artist's Contract, ensure that the new buyer of the artwork would contract with it according to the same conditions.

[60] *Ibid.* Article Two provides that the collector must pay the artist a 15 per cent share of the appreciated value of the artwork upon resale, and Article Seven gives the artist exhibition rights over the artwork and under Article Nine the collector agrees not to destroy or modify the artwork intentionally.

[61] Eichhorn, *The Artist's Contract*, pp. 67–81 and 179–85. Only Hans Haacke has continued to use the agreement and Jackie Windsor made limited use of it.

[62] Alexander Alberro, 'Artists' Rights And Product Management', in *Conceptual Art and the Politics of Publicity* (Cambridge, MA: MIT Press, 2003), p. 169 ('Although the Agreement, drafted to help destabilize the calcified art industry, may have been politically progressive in its intention, it had the opposite effect, leading conceptual art into what Lippard condemns as "the tyranny of a commodity status and market orientation"').

right to object to the derogatory treatment of the work.[63] This is because moral rights capture the artist's relationship to the original work as well as to its reproduction, giving artists some measure of control over the exhibition of their artworks after sale. In the landmark trial of *Serra* v. *US General Services Administration* (1986),[64] the Minimalist artist, Richard Serra was unable to rely upon the provisions of his commissioning contract with the GSA to prevent the removal of his site-specific sculpture, *Tilted Arc* (1981) conceived for Federal Plaza, New York. Serra argued to no avail that to remove his sculpture from Federal Plaza would amount to destruction of his work.[65] Serra's trial preceded the incorporation into US law of moral rights for artists, in the Visual Artists Rights Act (1990) (VARA). Had Serra created *Tilted Arc* after VARA's incorporation into US law, it is possible that he would have been able to prevent its removal on the grounds that this would have amounted to destruction.[66] The protection afforded to artists by moral rights legislation varies greatly between jurisdictions. Civil law countries like France have historically offered authors and artists far greater protection than common law jurisdictions such as the UK and US,[67] although ironically, it is not clear whether they prevent the destruction of artworks.[68]

---

[63] For example, CDPA, ss. 77, 80 and 84, and US Copyright Act (1976), s. 106A (the rights of attribution and integrity) as amended by the Visual Artists' Rights Act 1990 (US) (VARA).

[64] *Serra* v. *US General Services Administration* 847 F 2d 1045 (2nd Cir 1988), 1047.

[65] Richard Serrra said that '[i]t is a site-specific work and as such is not to be relocated. To remove the work is to destroy the work'. See letter from Richard Serra to Donald Thalacker, Director of GSA Art in Architecture Program, 1 January 1985, in Clara Weyegraf-Serra and Martha Buskirk (ed.), *The Destruction of Tilted Arc: Documents* (Cambridge, MA: MIT Press, 1991), p. 38.

[66] VARA, s. 106A(3)(b) grants the right 'to prevent the destruction of a work of recognized stature'. However, works of art are precluded from protection if they were installed before the Act came into force or if the artist has signed an agreement to that effect. For a discussion of the limitations of VARA in relation to the destruction of artworks, see Christina Michalos, 'Murdering Art', in McClean, *Trials*, pp. 184–7.

[67] For example, Article. L.121 of the French Intellectual Property Code contains a wider number of authors' moral rights than found in common law jurisdictions, including the right to withdraw the artwork from publication or to make modifications (*droit de retrait ou de repentir*) and the right of disclosure (*droit de divulgation*). In addition, the rights of attribution and integrity have historically been construed more widely. See Ruth Redmond-Cooper, 'Moral Rights', in McClean and Schubert, *Dear Images*, pp. 69–79.

[68] *Ibid.* 69.

## The artistic commonwealth

I wish to argue that there is a strong historical relationship between the institution of authorship operative within the art world and an artistic commonwealth where artists share common artistic forms, images, styles and ideas as set out below. In the art world and in the artistic commonwealth, concepts of 'piracy' have less relevance. As I have suggested above, this can be ascribed in part to the economy of the art system, which is predicated on the production of original and scarce objects as opposed to reproduction. The artistic commonwealth has parallels with the Creative Commons copyright licensing system adopted by many artists, cultural creators and organisations who seek to provide an open model for legally sharing and developing cultural works subject to important limitations being imposed upon users under the licensing system.[69] Creative Commons was established in order to challenge the domination of contemporary culture by traditional content distributors who misuse copyright in order to strengthen and maintain their monopolies on cultural goods such as popular music and cinema, and therefore to create a 'richer public domain' in the words of one of its co-founders, Lawrence Lessig.[70] There are six main types of Creative Commons' licence.[71] Important restrictions include the author of the copyright work being attributed in subsequent uses of the work (common to all licences) and constraints on the creation of derivative works and the commercial exploitation of a right-holder's work. Violation of these terms of use has led holders licensing content under Creative Commons to take legal action against third parties, including companies such as Virgin Mobile.[72]

With its emphasis on the importance of sharing cultural content, but also on authorial attribution and the non-commercial exploitation of the

---

[69] See the Creative Commons website and licence options (at: http://creativecommons/about/licences).

[70] 'Lawrence Lessig on Creative Commons and the Remix Culture' (mp3), *Talking with Talis*, 17 December 2007.

[71] Creative Commons. The six main types of Creative Commons' licences are: attribution, attribution share alike, attribution no derivatives, attribution non-commercial, attribution non-commercial share alike, attribution non-commercial no derivatives.

[72] See the report in *New York Times*, 1 October 2007, of the legal dispute between Alison Chang, a 15-year-old student from Dallas (US) and Virgin Mobile (US) and (Australia) following the use in a Virgin mobile advertisement of an image of the claimant uploaded onto Flickr by a photographer using a Creative Commons' attribution non-commercial no-derivative licence.

licensed work, Creative Commons resembles in some respects the artistic commonwealth with its own corpus of unwritten rules and conventions. However, there are also important differences between both systems. Not only is consent expressly (rather than impliedly) granted in the Creative Commons system, licensors do not generally allow for the free sharing and remixing of their content.[73] This is seen for example on Flickr (the world's largest photographic repository of Creative Commons-licensed images). Thus in some respects the artistic commonwealth would seem to be more resistant to considering some uses 'piratical' than Creative Commons.

The conventions of attribution between both systems also differ. When canonical artworks are used within the artistic commonwealth, authorial attribution is often implied rather than expressed – an audience is expected to be familiar with an artwork's underlying visual sources, which often will not be named. This becomes problematic (as discussed below) when 'high' and 'low' visual sources are hybridised in many contemporary artworks, as the authorship of the photographer or 'low' artist is often non-attributed (again in marked contrast to the Creative Commons position).

The notions of 'derivative work' and 'commercial exploitation' have, it would seem, different comparative meanings: the conventions of the artistic commonwealth generally do not rule out artists making derivative artworks, which can compete with earlier artworks in the marketplace, providing that their authorship is clearly distinguished (i.e. they are not fakes). However, this position changes (as with Creative Commons) when an artwork is exploited commercially through reproduction as in advertising, film or in merchandising.

A good example is the complaint of the Swiss artist duo, Fischli & Weiss[74] in 2003 against the advertising agency, Wieden & Kennedy for the alleged misuse of the artists' film, *The Way Things Go* (1987) in the advertisement 'Cog' created to promote a car manufactured by Honda. Fischli & Weiss' film depicts in real time (lasting 15 minutes) a complex chain reaction of interacting mechanical and combustive parts

---

[73] See Creative Commons on Flickr: 'Users Prefer Restrictive Licenses', on Read Write Web, 26 March 2009 (www.readwriteweb.com/archives/) which reports that only 12 per cent of users choose the BY licence which allows for free sharing and remixing as long as the author is attributed.

[74] See 'Acclaimed Honda Ad in Copycat Row', *Guardian*, 27 May 2003. Both Fischli & Weiss' film *The Way Things Go* (1987) and Wieden & Kennedey's film, 'Cog' (1983) can be viewed on YouTube.

(including tyres, boots, a kettle and bottles). The makers of 'Cog' copied this idea and certain choreographic sequences from the original film, translating it into a short (2-minute film) using elements from the Honda Accord car. For Fischli & Weiss, who ultimately decided not to bring copyright infringement proceedings, the offence caused by the advertisement was the commercialisation and simplification of the film's content and the false impression that they might have endorsed this use. The artists had been asked on numerous occasions[75] prior to the making of 'Cog' to license the intellectual property rights attached to the film and for significant sums, but had always declined.

The artistic commonwealth is built around traditions and conventions of copying, in particular homage. As noted, Richard Schiff[76] shows how 'originality' from the Renaissance to the nineteenth century was predicated upon the 'imitation' of the works of earlier masters (as opposed to copies) rather than Romantic/modernist notions of the artist as 'genius' originator. To imitate Raphael successfully was, as Joshua Reynolds[77] stated in his *Discourses*, to attain the highest level of artistic self-expression. Within the classical tradition, young artists were instructed to copy master artists from the past as the foundation of their practice and for successful artists to emulate and surpass their achievements was a sign of success: Picasso famously said: '[i]t is better to copy a drawing or painting than to try to be inspired by it, to make something similar'.[78] Though this statement is somewhat disingenuous because Picasso's series of variations on past masterpieces don't just copy, they substantially rework the original image.

A classic example is the sequence of copying that originates from Raphael's lost painting, *The Last Judgement of Paris* (1576) and continues via Marcantonio Raimondi's engraving to Manet's *Le déjeuner sur l'herbe* (1863) and to Picasso's repeated reworkings of Manet's iconic painting.[79] This sequence of copying rotates around the central motif of a group of reclining figures sitting in a pastoral setting, which is translated ironically, from Raimondi's engraving into Manet's painting as fully

---

[75] In conversation with the author who was instructed by the artists to advise them on bringing copyright infringement proceedings against Wieden & Kennedy and Honda under UK copyright law.

[76] Schiff, 'Originality', pp. 145–59.     [77] *Ibid.*, p. 149.

[78] Quoted in Dore Ashton, 'The Atelier of La Californie', in *Picasso: Les Grandes Series* (exh. cat.: Madrid: Nacional Reina Sofia. 2000), p. 253.

[79] See Karsten Schubert's discussion, 'Raphael's Shadow: On Copying and Creativity', in McClean and Schubert, *Dear Images*, pp. 361–73.

clothed male figures sat next to a naked female. Manet's *Déjeuner* like *Olympia* (1865) provoked a social scandal: the coupling of antimonies, classical–modern, pastoral–urban, clothed–naked, along with the flatness of the painting, outraging its contemporary bourgeois audience. Manet's *Dejeuner* was subsequently reworked by Picasso in a series of drawings and paintings, including in *Le déjeuner sur l'herbe, after Manet* (1961). It is clear that for both Manet and Picasso paying homage and establishing artistic identity in relation to artistic tradition through acts of copying was, and still remains, a vital motive in asserting artistic authorship.

It is important to grasp how earlier conventions of the artistic commonwealth have persisted under modernist and so-called postmodernist artistic practices. In particular, while practices based upon reproduction, as seen in so-called Appropriation art, in one sense challenge modernist notions of authorship and originality, they also affirm and enlarge the field of authorship within art extending the conventions of copying and citation among artists. According to Sherri Irvin,[80] 'responsibility is constitutive of authorship and accounts for the interpretability of artworks'. In other words, the author of the deconstructionist or appropriated artwork assumes responsibility for and is validated (in contrast to the forger) as the author of an artwork as much as the author of the original artwork that is subject to appropriation.

In one sense, modernism seems to disrupt the paradigm of the artistic commonwealth. Modernist notions of originality of authorship are founded upon Romantic notions asserting the primacy of individual experience (in contrast with classicism's notion of community) and the self as the source of origination: the fetishism of the 'new' in contrast to tradition comes to define modernism. Yet as Rosalind Krauss argues,[81] modernism itself is founded upon a blindness towards or repression of copying. Krauss points to the paradox of modernist artists' obsession (from Mondrian to Agnes Martin) with the figure of the grid. The figure is referred to as a template for purity and origination, yet is underscored by repetition and points to the very absence of a unifying, originating authorial presence.

[80] Sherri Irvin, 'Appropriation and Authorship in Contemporary Art', *British Journal of Aesthetics*, 45(2) (2005), pp. 123–37.

[81] Rosalind Krauss, 'The Originality of the Avant-Garde', in *The Originality of the Avant-Garde and Other Modernist Myths* (Cambridge, MA: MIT Press, 1986), pp. 50–61.

In opposition to modernism we find counter artistic practices affirming the importance of reproduction, and questioning the relationship between the original and copy. These practices, which again can be linked to Marcel Duchamp and in particular his replicas and framing of his earlier artworks (as seen in his *Box in a Valise* (1941))[82] and which emerge in Pop art and Appropriation art, enlarge the artistic commonwealth. An important example of this is the Pop art practice of Andy Warhol (discussed below) whose work is explicitly premised upon reproduction and serial repetition.[83] In particular, Warhol adopted photographic images derived from mass culture (generally of iconic celebrities and products) and reprinted these in the form of silkscreen paintings and prints. At the same time, Warhol shifted artistic production from the artist's studio to a factory system whereby authorial decision making and production was delegated to a network of assistants, including Gerard Malanga, though the ultimate authorisation of Warhol works, remained with Warhol.[84]

Buskirk describes this shift in practices of authorship:[85]

> [a]uthorship isolates, frames, and provides the context within which the copy or even the found object can be designated an honorary original. While categorizing works of art according to author is a mode particularly associated with the rise of the museum, recent trends allow the artist's act of making to be replaced by an act of designation, such that selecting and categorizing can become the act of authorship itself.

### High and low, photography and copyright law

As Thomas Crow illustrates,[86] the recycling of images and forms from mass culture, including advertising, consumption, popular entertainment and fashion into avant-garde artistic practices and then back into mass culture has been a staple feature of twentieth-century art. Avant-garde movements such as Cubism, Dada, Surrealism and Pop art have all participated in this changing of registers between 'high' and 'low', incorporating and reproducing imagery taken from the everyday world – only

---

[82] Buskirk, *Contingent Object*, pp. 68–72.
[83] *Ibid.*, for a discussion of Warhol's practice see, pp. 74–80.
[84] Andrew Wilson, '"This is Not by Me." Andy Warhol and the Question of Authorship', in McClean and Schubert, *Dear Images*, pp. 375–85.
[85] Buskirk, *Contingent Object*, pp. 102–5.
[86] Thomas Crow, 'Modernism and Mass Culture in the Visual Arts', in *Modern Art in a Common Culture* (New Haven, CT: Yale University Press 1996), pp. 9–11.

for many of their innovations to be absorbed back into mass culture. This changing of registers has continued through the work of Appropriation artists into twenty-first-century contemporary artistic practices and is often a source of friction when photographers' works outside the domain of high art are used, as it is photography that is the primary visual medium of mass culture.

It is useful to contextualise copyright infringement disputes between photographers and appropriation artists within Crow's 'high–low' typology. It is interesting to note that the photographers at the centre of these disputes have often seen themselves as artists and have wished to have been accorded artistic status. A continuous dilemma for photographers throughout the history of photography has been their lack of recognition as artists in their own right.[87] While copyright law was in the late nineteenth century relatively quick to protect the new medium of photography and to provide protection to photographers as authors, with correspondingly low levels of 'originality' being required,[88] the reception of photography within the realm of fine art was mixed. In particular, photography was seen as an objective, mechanical medium ('nature's pencil' in the words of Fox Talbot), impersonally transcribing the natural world and lacking the necessary imprint of authorial subjectivity that is required of art.[89] This position would become increasingly entrenched in the art world in the twentieth century, as modern art retreated into abstraction in resistance to photography which displaced its function for mimetically recording the world.

An important response of photographers to this exclusion by the fine art community was to emphasise the artistic authorship of the photograph as opposed to its archival or documentary features. The artistic features of photographs were emphasised through strategies, including the pictorial stylisation of the image, to emphasise qualities of mood and composition (the late nineteenth-century and early twentieth-century US photographers Edward Steichen and Alfred Stieglitz were masters of this approach) as well as the hand printing and the touching-up of

---

[87] Liz Wells, 'On and Beyond the White Walls', in Liz Wells (ed.), 'Photography as Art' in *Photography: A Critical Introduction* (3rd edn, London: Routledge, 2004), pp. 247–94, esp. 248–62.

[88] See Simon Stokes' discussion of the protection afforded to photographs under the Fine Arts Copyright Act 1862 (UK) in *Graves'* case (1869) in '*Graves'* Case and Copyright in Photographs: *Bridgeman* v. *Corel* (US)', in McClean and Schubert, *Dear Images*, pp. 109–12.

[89] Wells, *Photography as Art*, pp. 248–62.

photographs.[90] Significantly, photographers who had artistic aspirations would create limited editions of their photographs to affirm their artistic uniqueness and originality.

The ambivalent relationship between photography and fine art and this sense of exclusion by photographers from the institution of authorship is, I would like to suggest, at the heart of infringement disputes between 'photographers' and 'artists' involving artistic copyright. Furthermore, it is an important reason for ruptures in the artistic commonwealth where photographers do not share the same norms of copying as artists. These tensions can be illustrated if we look at some of the main disputes involving photographers and contemporary artists over the last fifty years.

In 1964, Patricia Caulfield published her photograph of hibiscus flowers in an article about colour processing in the US magazine, *Modern Photography*.[91] Caulfield was executive editor of the magazine at the time. *Modern Photography* is and was a publication dedicated to examining and promoting the technical and artistic elements of modern photography. Caulfield had come across the vase of hibiscus flowers in a restaurant in Barbados, where it was set off by a play of light so striking that she decided to photograph it. Caulfield's photograph (further cropped in the magazine) would be appropriated by Andy Warhol and transformed into one of his most famous early images, *Flowers* (1964). In Warhol's treatment, Caulfield's image is reinterpreted (without attribution) in a series of silk-screen images printed onto canvas where it is further cropped (to show four flowers only) and the flowers are overpainted. As with many of his screen images, Warhol's *Flowers* was produced with heavy studio assistance, through his delegated system of authorship discussed above.

Warhol's *Flowers* sparked a copyright infringement dispute when Caulfield saw a poster of Warhol's work in the window of a New York bookstore in 1965. While Warhol had transformed Caulfield's image into a highly successful artwork, Caulfield could claim copyright authorship and thus legal ownership over the underlying image. It is revealing to see how Warhol, who undoubtedly had a strong eye for selecting culturally resonant images, downplayed Caulfield's authorship in the making of his work, failing to attribute its source. Likewise, defenders of Warhol's use of Caulfield's image would misleadingly downplay Caulfield's status as an amateur photographer suggesting the image to have been taken from a

---

[90] *Ibid.*    [91] Buskirk, *Contingent Object*, pp. 84–7.

woman's magazine.[92] In Caulfield's words: 'What's irritating is to have someone like an image enough to use it, but then denigrate the original talent.'[93] Caulfield's action against Warhol would eventually be settled out of court, like other actions brought against Warhol by photographers for copyright infringement including Charles Moore in response to Warhol's appropriation of his photography of Jackie Kennedy in his *Jackie* series (1963–4).[94] While no doubt the large profits Warhol derived from sale of the work would have been an incentive for Caulfield to sue Warhol, the lack of authorial attribution by Warhol was also clearly an important factor.

It is illuminating to compare Warhol's use of Caulfield's image with Sturtevant's use of Warhol's *Flowers*.[95] Sturtevant (who some commentators regard as the first 'appropriation artist')[96] had, with Warhol's consent, copied *Flowers* using screens that Warhol had given her, deploying the same techniques of silkscreen printing applied by Warhol's assistants. Placed alongside replicas of works by Jasper Johns, Claes Oldenburg and Frank Stella, Sturtevant's copy is materially indistinguishable from Warhol's work, save for its title *Warhol Flowers*, which announces that that it is a copy of Warhol and its authorial attribution which declares it to be a work not by Warhol but by Sturtevant instead. In contrast to Warhol's appropriation of Caulfield's image we can see how Sturtevant's *Warhol Flowers* falls within the copying conventions of the artistic commonwealth and if it challenges notions of authorial originality, it does not threaten Warhol's authorship.

If we fast forward almost thirty years, we find that similar issues arise in another copyright infringement dispute between the photographer, Art Rogers and the well-known appropriation artist, Jeff Koons.[97] In *Rogers v. Koons* (1994),[98] Jeff Koons used Art Rogers' black and white

---

[92] *Ibid.*, 86; see Ivan Karp, a member of Leo Castelli's gallery who represented Warhol at the time. According to Karp: 'Warhol was very innocent of doing a disservice to the photographer because this photograph was not what you might call a "remarkable photograph". It was not an earthshaking photograph, but Warhol made a remarkable series of paintings out of it.'

[93] *Ibid.*, p. 87.

[94] *Ibid.* See also discussion of the claims brought by the photographer Charles Moore relating to Warhol's use of the image taken from *Life* magazine by Charles Moore and used in Warhol's 'Race Riot' series (1963–4).

[95] *Ibid.*, pp. 82–4.    [96] See for example, Crow, *Modern Art*, p. 70.

[97] See the discussion of Johnson Okpaluba in McClean and Schubert, *Dear Images*, pp. 202–7.

[98] *Rogers v. Koons* 960 F.2d 301 (2d. Cir.1992).

photograph, *Puppies* (1980) depicting a smiling suburban couple holding a litter of nine German puppies as the basis for his sculpture, *String of Puppies* (1986). Koons had discovered the photograph reproduced on a postcard. In Koons' rendition the central characters and puppies in Rogers' photograph are reproduced in the form of a garishly coloured, wooden sculpture executed in a baroque style by Italian craftsman. A *String of Puppies* (sold as an edition of three) was included in Koons' notorious *Banality Show* held at the Sonnabend Gallery, New York in 1986, commenting on the relationship between art, consumerism and kitsch.

On being alerted to Koons' work, Rogers sued Koons for copyright infringement and for damages, claiming $367,000 (USD) – the value of one of the editions of Koons' sculpture. Part of Rogers' anger was the way in which he was not credited as the author of the original image; in fact Koons had removed the attribution and copyright notice attached to the postcard when instructing the fabrication. During the trial, Koons sought to rely upon the parody defence developed within US case law under the fair use provisions of s.107 of the US Copyright Act 1979.[99] In particular, Koons argued that he wanted the *Banality Show* to 'provide a critique of the conspicuous consumption, greed, and self-indulgence of modern consumer society', and that he selected Rogers' image in order to comment upon 'the degradation of the artistic tradition'.[100] What is striking again in Koons' testimony is the way in which Roger's identity as the creator of the photographic image is unimportant because the image is of a 'type' conveying particular cultural or social content, rather than an authored work in its own right, once again expressing the high–low divide.

Koons' parody defence was rejected by the court on the grounds that it did not target the original image (as parody should), but general social values and that Koons' audience lacked the requisite recognition of the work's source to 'conjure up the original' as is required of parody,[101] i.e. it

---

[99] Section 107 of the US Copyright Act 1976, provides that: '[i]n determining whether the use made of a work in any particular case is a fair use the factors to be considered shall include – 1. the purpose and character of the use, including whether such use is of a commercial nature or is for non-profit educational purposes; 2. The nature of the copyright work; 3. the amount and substantiality of the portion used in relation to the copyrighted work as a whole; and 4. the effect of the use upon the potential market for or value of the copyrighted work'.

[100] *Rogers* v. *Koons* 751 F.Supp. 474–6 (SDNY 1990).

[101] *Rogers* v. *Koons* 960 F.2d 301 (2d. Cir. 1992), at 309.

was a 'weapon' not a 'target'. Parody is a genre, which, as Michael Spence points out,[102] is notoriously difficult to define, but which is linked, it would seem, to audience recognition of an authorial source (in contrast to pastiche which attaches to more general cultural forms and styles). For this reason, parody as a genre flourishes when artworks are referred to within the artistic commonwealth but not when they are taken from outside.

Compare, for example, the Neo-Conceptual artist, Jonathan Monk's recent parodies of Jeff Koons' iconic metallic *Rabbit* (1986) (modelled on an inflatable toy) in his exhibition *The Deflated Inflated* (2009)[103] with Koons' use of Rogers' *Puppies*. Monk arranged apparently without Koons' authorisation for five variations of Koons' *Rabbit* to be recast, representing the Rabbit comically in various stages of deflation – a comment on Koons' work as well as on the current economic recession. Koons' underlying authorship is never in question in Monk's work; indeed it depends upon its audience recognition which can be assumed. It would clearly be ironic and, I would also suggest, transgressive of the artistic commonwealth for Koons to sue Monk for copyright infringement of his artistic work. Koons' move would be seen as transgressive and hypocritical within the artistic community because it would violate the shared norms of copying.

## Conclusion

I have argued that a rich commonwealth of shared forms and images flourishes among fine artists in much the same way as *dōjinshi* – an offshoot of Japanese animation or manga flourishes in Japan[104] – because authors do not view artists' copying of their work as 'piracy', and therefore choose not to exercise their copyright against one another working within the same field. I do not wish to suggest that artists are adverse to enforcing their copyright, particularly when the commercial exploitation of their work is at stake as in advertising and merchandising. However, in respect to other artists working within the artistic commonwealth their position differs. I have also argued that the artistic commonwealth is

---

[102] Spence, 'Justifying Copyright', pp. 226–8. In particular, see Spence's discussion of the problems of defining parody, p. 218, and the distinction between 'target' and 'weapon' parodies.
[103] www.artrabbit.com/uk/events/event/12266/jonathan_monk_the_deflated_inflated.
[104] See Lawrence Lessig, *Free Culture* (New York: Penguin Press, 2004), pp. 25–7.

shaped by the peculiarities of the art system and its economy, which valorises the uniqueness and authenticity of objects, and in which copyright (a property right originating with the protection of literary, not artistic property)[105] applies imperfectly. It is the mixture of 'high' and 'low' art forms, in particular, fine art and commercial photography, that leads to the collapse of the artistic commonwealth and to copyright infringement disputes. In addition, owners who are not authors (e.g. artists' estates like the Walker Evans estate) are also more willing to enforce copyright interests against artists and the artistic commonwealth.[106]

What conclusions might we draw about the assumptions and structure of copyright law from this analysis? It is tempting to castigate copyright law and argue that its foundations are built upon archaic Romantic notions of authorship, which 'postmodern' practices such as appropriation question and that it must adapt to new formations of authorship. Yet as Brad Sherman has warned[107] this position ignores the 'postmodern' features of copyright law, that copyright law with its de minimis notions of originality, protects both 'high' and 'low' cultural works and with it a wide class of authors. Indeed, it is copyright's democratic features, which arguably facilitates such conflicts. If appropriation artists use images taken from low culture, without authorisation or attribution, why should copyright law accommodate these practices?

It is difficult to discern how the current structure of copyright law can accommodate conflicts between appropriation artists and photographers. The US courts have in cases such as Blanch v. Koons (2006)[108] developed a flexible notion of transformative copying built upon the fair use doctrine contained in s. 107, US Copyright Act 1976 – which appears to allow for the limited recontextualisation of copyright protected images in the production of new artworks and the consideration of aesthetic

---

[105] Rose, 'Author as Proprietor'. See Rose's discussion of the protection of literary property for booksellers and printers in eighteenth-century England.

[106] Artists' estates can also be litigious in the enforcement of copyright interests against artists using copyright protected artistic works. Sherrie Levine, for example, stopped using the photographs of Walker Evans after Evan's estate legally challenged this; see Irvin, 'Appropriation and Authorship', 16.

[107] Brad Sherman, 'Appropriating the Postmodern', in McClean and Schubert, Dear Images, pp. 405–19, esp. p. 415.

[108] Blanch v. Koons, Docket No. 05–6433-cv (2nd Cir. 2006). See Buskirk's discussion in McClean, Trials, pp. 244–9.

intentionality as part of an appropriation artist's defence.[109] Yet it is difficult to see how this type of defence can extend to the wholesale appropriation of images.

A radical (if unlikely) direction that copyright law could take is to seek consciously to arbitrate between 'high' and 'low' artistic works in order to *protect* artistic expression of fine artists in particular, art's capacity to reflect upon and question mass media dominated culture.[110] If copyright law does not apply to cultural artefacts in a unified way, why can't it recognise differences in value between cultural artefacts? If society values the promotion of artistic expression (above other forms of cultural expression) why can't this be reflected in copyright law? A possible direction identified by lawyers, such as Judith Bresler and Ralph Lerner[111] would be to create a compulsory licensing system, allowing appropriation artists to use copyrighted works for artistic purposes only subject to reasonable remuneration. This is problematic, not least because it is hard to police the borders between art and merchandising and 'high artists' may claim that merchandising (e.g. coffee mugs with the relevant image) is part of their artistic message. Another would be to create an entirely different statutory regime for fine artistic works separating them from visual works based on reproduction.[112] It is beyond the scope of this chapter to discuss such directions, but clearly they would amount to a radical rehauling of the whole copyright

---

[109] *Ibid.*, the Second Circuit Appeals Court (Sack J.) accepted Koons' testimony that he had 'by his own undisputed description, used Blanch's image as fodder for his commentary on the social and aesthetic consequences of the mass media'.

[110] For example, in the jurisprudence of the European Court of Human Rights, artistic freedom of expression is given greater weight than commercial speech, though lesser weight than political speech, when Article 10 (the right to freedom of expression) is balanced against other competing rights; see the case of *Vereinigung Blidender Künstler v. Austria* ECHR Application 68354/01, 25 January 2007. However, there is no case law on the relationship between artistic expression and copyright law.

[111] Judith Bresler and Ralph Lerner, *All About Rights for Visual Artists* (New York: Practising Law Institute, 2006), pp. 162–70. Bresler and Lerner advocate a compulsory 'Fine Art License' applying to artworks made and published in the US which incorporate copyright protected works. A subsequent work would be a single, original work of fine art, e.g. painting or sculpture or a multiple of no more than 500 copies. The Fine Art License would be administered by a central collective administration service and protected works would be licensed according to fixed and reasonable thresholds payable on income generated through the sale of the subsequent work. The Fine Art License would not allow for wider commercial exploitation, e.g. in merchandising.

[112] For example, fine artworks were protected under UK copyright law under the separate statute of the Fine Arts Copyright Act 1862, until their codification and inclusion with other copyright works in the Copyright Act 1911.

system[113] contradicting also the cardinal principle of aesthetic neutrality[114] enshrined by national legislatures and courts.

Paradoxically, just as hierarchies between visual media disappear within the context of artistic production and exhibition in Groy's regime of 'equal aesthetic rights', so inequalities within the authorial chain between categories of artists (and artists and curators)[115] become increasingly visible. Just as the art system and the art market require 'sovereign authors', the realities of cultural production today (including within the art system) mean that the authorship of artworks is increasingly multiplied and the potential for copyright disputes is magnified. The question then becomes: should copyright law continue to adopt a 'neutral', transcendent position in relation to such disputes or should it and can it intervene within the cultural domain to protect the autonomy of art and how might this be done?

---

[113] See Okpaluba, in McClean and Schubert, *Dear Images*, pp. 214–16. Okpaluba points out, p. 216, that '[w]hilst there may be some advantages to a system of compulsory licensing for images, it is unlikely that such a system could be currently adopted, as it runs contrary to U.K. and U.S. obligations to the Berne Convention, is contrary to copyright's overall free market philosophy and deprives the right-holder of the right to strike a bargain for the use of his work'.

[114] See the discussion of Daniel McClean and Armen Avanessian, 'The Trials of the Title', in McClean, *Trials*, pp. 42–8 and the well-known *dicta* of Holmes J. in *Bleistein* v. *Donaldson Lithographic* (1903) 188 US 239–51: '[i]t would be a dangerous undertaking for persons trained only to the law to constitute themselves final judges of the worth of pictorial illustrations, outside of the narrowest and most obvious limits'.

[115] See Groys, *Art Power*, pp. 43–52.

# 17

# Copyright's imperfect republic and the artistic commonwealth

JONATHAN GRIFFITHS

Daniel McClean's contribution to this volume (Chapter 16) considers the norms of authorship and infringement in the culture of 'high' art.[1] He suggests that this culture – even in its postmodern variants – is shaped by a predominant concern with the unique artefact and, as a result, obeys norms that differ significantly from those underpinning copyright law. He explains that, as a result of the fundamental discrepancies between these two systems, artists have been obliged to employ mechanisms outside copyright law to secure their interests and that copyright infringement proceedings involving 'high' artists sometimes fail to protect the conventions of the 'artistic commonwealth'. He concludes by suggesting ways in which this gulf may be bridged. The chapter is a valuable addition to the literature on the relationship between art and copyright law, particularly because, while other scholars have explored issues relating to the subsistence[2] and infringement[3] of copyright in contemporary art in great detail, McClean reveals a fundamental conflict of preoccupation between the two cultures affecting all aspects of their relationship.

---

[1] For the purpose of this chapter, McClean's distinction between 'high' and 'low' art forms is accepted.

[2] See, for example, A. Barron, 'Copyright Law and the Claims of Art', IPQ (2002), 368; D. Booton, 'Framing Pictures: Defining Art in UK Copyright Law', IPQ [2003], 38; J. Pila, 'An Intentional View of the Copyright Work', MLR (2008), 535; B. Sherman, 'Appropriating the Postmodern: Copyright and the Challenge of the New', *Social and Legal Studies* [1995], 31; N. Walravens, 'The Concept of Originality and Contemporary Art', RIDA (1999), 181.

[3] See, for example, L. Greenberg, 'The Art of Appropriation: Puppies, Piracy and Post-Modernism', *Cardozo Arts and Entertainment Law Journal* (1992), 1; E. Ames, 'Beyond *Rogers* v. *Koons*: A Fair Use Standard for Appropriation', *Columbia Law Review* (1993), 1473; J. Okpaluba, 'Appropriation Art: Fair Use or Foul?', in McClean and Schubert, *Dear Images*.

He claims that the institution of authorship in 'high' art culture is concerned with the 'authorisation' of unique artefacts. Such 'authorisation' confirms the existence of a physical link between artwork and creator. Surprisingly, this concern is as much a feature of postmodern artistic practice as of earlier movements in art:

> A persistent feature of the art system would seem to be that no matter how authorship is critiqued by artists and how the artwork is dispersed through multiplication, reproduction and dematerialisation, the fetish for the auratic art object remains.[4]

However, while the author's trace (his or her 'authorisation') would traditionally have been recorded physically (typically in the form of a signature), this is unlikely to be the case in postmodern artistic practices such as minimalism or conceptual art, where an author may have no direct physical involvement with a particular object. Accordingly, while the persistent relationship between artist and artefact is maintained, the institution of authorship is modified; both to accommodate practices of designation and to encompass the ongoing control of the location of 'authorised' artefacts:

> The key notion . . . is the artist's authorisation of the work rather than his or her physical trace or imprint on the object. The issue of the artist controlling the placement or site-specificity of the artwork becomes critical particularly in Minimalism . . .[5]

These conceptions of authorship lead directly, as McClean explains, to the establishment of an 'artistic commonwealth' within which the borrowing and reuse of artistic works assumes positive cultural value.

By contrast, he ascribes two predominant features to the law of copyright. First, he describes it as a form of legal protection originating with the protection of literary works rather than artistic works and suggests that, as a result, it is more closely attuned to the needs of media exploited through reproduction than to the needs of 'high' art culture. He thus establishes a dichotomy between the 'material' underpinnings of 'high' art culture and a law that focuses on the 'immaterial' or 'intangible'. The second predominant feature of the model of copyright law that he identifies is its 'aesthetic neutrality'; that is, its 'democratic' unwillingness to distinguish between 'high' and 'low' artistic forms. In this response, I

---

[4] See D. McClean, Chapter 16 in this volume, 'Piracy and Authorship in Contemporary Art and the Artistic Commonwealth', p. 319.
[5] *Ibid.*, p. 323.

argue that, although his characterisation of copyright law is certainly accurate in general terms, the distinction that he draws between material artistic practice and intangible legal right is too stark. While copyright law has indeed 'closed' to a great extent on a model identifying intangible essence rather than material artefact as its object of regulation, this closure is far from complete. I claim here that copyright both continues to display features capable of securing interests in material cultural forms and – to some extent – remains 'open' to alternative norms – particularly to norms deriving from the cultural practices falling within the scope of its sphere of regulation. As a result, it is more capable of accommodating materially focused 'high' art culture than might initially appear likely. The law's 'aesthetic neutrality', however, presents a much more serious impediment to its recognition of the 'autonomy of art'.[6]

## Copyright – between the artefact and its essence

The history of copyright law in the United Kingdom has indeed been marked by the steady development of a model of intangible property organised around the need to convert cultural endeavour into a marketable and defensible form of property. This model has, over time, evolved to allow a copyright owner to control not just exact copies of his or her work, but also versions (translations, dramatisations, etc.) reproducing the 'expression' or 'essence' of the work. In this form, the protected intangible essence (the 'work') can be followed from form to form, assuming greater significance than any particular carrier of that 'work'. As a consequence, distinctions between media diminish and the model is more readily able to assimilate new creative forms. The law has come to accept a Japanese translation as a 'reproduction' of a novel in English, a dramatisation as a 'reproduction' of an epic poem and a sound recording as a reproduction of a musical work.[7] The identification of the protected 'essence' of a work facilitates the treatment of cultural works as property. In this 'intangible property' model of copyright law, the task of determining whether or not an infringement of copyright has occurred is presented as a relatively straightforward, almost scientific process. A court's role is first to examine the material carrier within which the

---

[6] This chapter focuses upon United Kingdom copyright law, governed by the Copyright, Designs and Patents Act 1988 (CDPA).
[7] Under the law in the United Kingdom, some of these activities are formally defined as 'adaptations'. See CDPA 1988, s. 21.

claimant's work is recorded in order to identify the protected essence and then, second, to determine whether the defendant has reproduced[8] a 'substantial part' of that property.[9]

This model has developed over a long period. Writing of intellectual property in general, Sherman and Bently place the origins of the model in the eighteenth century:

> Because it was necessary for the intangible to be both identifiable and at the same time malleable enough to move from work to work, it was forced to take on a transcendental quality. With this single gesture, which was perhaps the most important that took place in this area in the eighteenth century, intellectual property law was set on a course from which it has been unable to escape.[10]

The dominance of this generalised model continues to be reinforced. Courts are increasingly keen to identify generalised principles applying across the range of forms of 'work' protected under the Copyright, Designs and Patents Act 1988 (CDPA). For example, in *Sawkins* v. *Hyperion*,[11] which concerned a question of subsistence of copyright in 'high' culture musical works, the Court of Appeal generalised the principle of 'originality' by reference to a perceived need to ensure consistency with *Walter* v. *Lane*,[12] a case concerning 'low' literary work. In *Newspaper Licensing Agency* v. *Marks & Spencer*,[13] the quasi-scientific approach to infringement described above was applied to 'published edition' copyright, a form of protection for entrepreneurial works for which there is no prerequisite of originality under the Act. Both examples demonstrate a consolidation of an approach that self-consciously identifies intangible 'work' rather than material carrier as the focus of protection. At the same time, the House of Lords has reinforced the authority of this approach to infringement[14] and courts have begun to accept that the protected 'essence' of a work (identified as 'information')[15] is capable of

---

[8] Or committed one of the other infringing acts listed under CDPA 1988, s. 16, in relation to the work.

[9] See *Designers' Guild Ltd* v. *Russell Williams Textiles Ltd* [2000] 1 WLR 2416 (HL).

[10] B. Sherman and L. Bently, *The Making of Modern Intellectual Property Law: The British Experience 1760–1911* (Cambridge University Press, 1999), p. 56.

[11] *Sawkins* v. *Hyperion* [2005] 1 WLR 3281, at [33]–[36]; [78]–[86].     [12] [1900] AC 539.

[13] *Newspaper Licensing Agency Ltd* v. *Marks & Spencer plc* [2003] 1 AC 551 (HL).

[14] *Designers' Guild Ltd* v. *Russell Williams Textiles Ltd* [2000] 1 WLR 2416 (HL).

[15] '[I]n my judgment ... the defendants ... reproduced the information which is the literary work contained in the circuit diagram' (*Anacon Corporation* v. *Environmental Research Technology* [1994] FSR 659, 663 (*per* Jacob J.)).

travelling further across different forms of carrier than had previously been considered possible.[16] All this suggests that McClean is right in emphasising copyright law's preoccupation with the intangible or immaterial and that he is likely to become even more right in future. Nevertheless, despite the time it has taken for this intangible property model to evolve, it can be suggested that the process is incomplete. While the attractions of a consistent organising principle are great, law makers are also driven by a competing impulse to ensure that the law functions as an appropriate system of regulation of 'real-world' cultural activities. These impulses are not always easily reconciled and, while striving for the transcendental, copyright law remains in some respects a mixed and inconsistent system stubbornly grounded in the material. While the proper subject of copyright's attention may be the intangible 'work', that work is not protected unless and until it is given material form[17] that is recognised in existing cultural practice.[18]

Interestingly, the greatest resistance to the development of a fully transcendent, intangible model of copyright law in the United Kingdom appears to be found in the law's treatment of artistic works.[19] McClean himself raises one of the most striking examples of this phenomenon – the 'droit de suite'[20] – a form of protection allied to copyright, but attaching to the sale of certain material artistic works. This 'strange and impure'[21] right, introduced in recognition of the way in which the art market functions, is out of keeping with a fully intangible model of copyright law.[22] This resistance to 'purification' in the case of 'artistic works' is, however, also apparent in a number of other respects.

---

[16]  Ibid.; Sandman v. Panasonic UK Ltd [1998] FSR 651.

[17]  CDPA 1988, ss. 3(2); 4–5B, 8. Although cf. 'broadcasts' (s. 6).

[18]  A 'closed-list' system of copyright operates under the CDPA 1988. That is, in order to be protected under copyright law, a 'work' must fall within the definition of one of the categories listed at CDPA 1988, s. 1(1).

[19]  'Fine art' was not protected under the copyright law of the United Kingdom until about 150 years after the introduction of the first statutory protection of literary property (see Fine Arts Copyright Act 1862). Note, however, that the first copyright statute offering explicit protection to altered versions of a work was the Engraving Copyright Act 1734 (sometimes known as 'Hogarth's Act').

[20]  Or 'resale right'. See Artist's Resale Right Regulations 2006, implementing Directive 2001/84/EC of the European Parliament and of the Council of 27 September 2001 on the resale right for the benefit of an author of an original work of art.

[21]  See McClean, 'Piracy and Authorship', p. 316.

[22]  In a sense, the 'impurity' of the resale right is recognised by the fact that it has not been implemented through an amendment of the CDPA 1988, but through a separate set of statutory regulations, the Artists' Resale Right Regulations 2006.

One clear example is provided by the recording requirement under the CDPA 1988. As noted above, a literary, dramatic or musical work will not be protected 'unless and until it is recorded, in writing or otherwise'.[23] As suggested above, this requirement evidences the incomplete evolution of the intangible model of copyright. However, it also bears witness to a perceived distinction between the protected intangible 'work' and its recording in material form.[24] The recording is not the protected work, but only a precondition for its protection. There is a distinction between protected form and material carrier in the case of literary, dramatic and musical works. In the case of artistic works, the situation is different. The Act contains no explicit recording requirement for such works. On the face of it, the absence of such a requirement might suggest that the protection of 'artistic' works is more fully aligned with a 'pure' intangible model. However, the opposite is true. The Act has no explicit requirement for recording because the artistic work in question – the 'painting', 'sculpture' or 'work of artistic craftsmanship' – necessarily takes a material form. There is no 'gap' between tangible sculpture or painting and 'work'.

A further example of copyright law's recognition that artistic works are less easily separated from their material form than other forms of work can also be observed in the provisions of the CDPA 1988 governing moral rights.[25] The right to be acknowledged as the author of a work arises only when asserted.[26] Generally, the Act envisages that such assertion will be documentary.[27] However, in the case of some forms of artistic work, the significance of the unique material artefact is recognised by specific provisions allowing assertion to be made for certain purposes on the artefact itself.[28] Indeed, it can be suggested that the fact that the United Kingdom's attribution and integrity rights allow authors to control activities relating to an original material artefact as well as to control the making of copies is further evidence of the law's accommodation of the interest of 'high' art's material culture. While these rights

---

[23] CDPA 1988, s. 3(2).

[24] On this, see E. Adeney, 'Unfixed Works, Performers' Protection and Beyond: Does the Australian Copyright Act Always Require Material Form?', IPQ (2009), 77.

[25] McClean identifies moral rights as an alternative form of protection to copyright. There are undoubted distinctions of nature between the two rights. However, under the CDPA 1988, the two forms of right are so connected (e.g., moral rights arise only in respect of 'works' protected for the purposes of copyright and the rules on authorship are shared) that it seems reasonable to regard them as part of the same system.

[26] CDPA, 1988, s. 77(1).     [27] Ibid., s. 78 (2).     [28] Ibid., s. 78(3)(a).

are also granted to authors other than artists, it can be suggested that the primary intended beneficiaries of this extension of the right to 'originals' are 'high' artists.

My aim here has not been to deny the validity of the basic distinction between 'high' art culture's concern with material artefact and copyright law's focus upon the 'pure' intangible. Rather, it has been to suggest that copyright law in the United Kingdom is not perfectly aligned with a norm of intangible property primarily designed for the regulation of symbolic forms such as literary and musical works. The law has a more mixed and inconsistent form. The tendency to maintain its core model – its 'legal aesthetics' – has to some extent been thwarted by the conflicting impulse to regulate the real world of artistic practice and art markets appropriately. In the second part of this response, I seek to apply this model of copyright as a mixed and inconsistent system to McClean's discussion of the contrasting cultures of copying/infringement within 'high' art and copyright law.

## Infringement in art and copyright

McClean supports his argument that the law fails to deal sensitively with 'high' art by reference to infringement conflicts of different types. I want to look a little more closely at these conflicts and to suggest that the system of copyright sketched above retains a degree of flexibility that, to some extent, may allow it to accommodate the norms of 'high' art culture to a greater extent than one might at first assume.

### The 'artistic commonwealth' – accommodating transgression

In McClean's description, 'high' art culture functions as a form of 'artistic commonwealth', within which artists share 'common artistic forms, images, styles and ideas'[29] and within which there is considerable

---

[29] McClean draws a parallel between the artistic commonwealth's tolerance of copying and (a) the arrangements established under Creative Commons licences and (b) *dōjinshi*, an offshoot of Japanese manga ('Piracy and Authorship', pp. 327–38, 326). There are also other cultures in which, within certain conventions, copying is either tolerated or encouraged. See, for example: fan fiction (A. Chander and M. Sunder, 'Everyone's a Superhero: A Cultural Theory of "Mary Sue" Fan Fiction as Fair Use', *California Law Review*, 9 (2007), 597; R. Tushnet, 'Payment in Credit: Copyright Law and Subcultural Creativity', *Law and Contemporary Problems*, 70 (2007), 135, 153); academia (R. Tushnet, 'Payment in Credit: Copyright Law and Subcultural Creativity', *Law and Contemporary Problems*, 70 (2007), 135, 153); folk music (R. Jones and E. Cameron,

tolerance of copying.[30] To some extent, this culture derives from the art market's focus upon tangible artefacts. As the primary market for 'high' art does not depend upon reproduction, copying is not an economic threat. However, there are also aesthetic reasons for the flourishing of this 'commonwealth'. 'High' art's conception of authorship is not threatened by the copying of the work of one recognised member of the artistic commonwealth by another. The copier creates, and 'authorises', a new material artefact. The 'authorisation' of the original work is not thrown into question by those actions (cf., for example, forgery). Indeed, within the 'artistic commonwealth', the copied work is not perceived as a 'copy' at all.[31] At least by implication, McClean contrasts this culture with the norms of the copyright system. Activities which would be regarded as acceptable – even as homage – in 'high' art would be regarded as infringements under copyright law.

In practical terms, of course, copyright does not challenge this conception of the 'artistic commonwealth'. Nobody is obliged to sue when such copying occurs.[32] Nevertheless, it is instructive to consider this apparent conflict of cultures more closely. Is the mixed, imperfectly intangible model of copyright described above capable of recognising the embedded values of 'high' art culture? McClean himself presents an interesting test case. He describes *The Deflated Inflated*, Jonathan Monk's sculptural parody of Jeff Koons' metal *Rabbit* and argues that it would be 'ironic and ... transgressive of the artistic commonwealth' if Koons were to sue over the reproduction of his work in *The Deflated Inflated*.[33] What, then, would be the position under copyright law if Koons were to bring proceedings against Monk? Would copyright law be sufficiently responsive to the norms of the 'artistic commonwealth' to recognise the transgressive nature of that claim?

Could it, for example, be argued that, in a case such as this, Monk would not infringe the copyright in Koons' work? Alternatively, even if

---

'Full Fat, Semi-Skimmed or No Milk Today – Creative Commons Licences and English Folk Music', *International Review of Law, Computers and Technology* (2005), 1).

[30] Although, cf. C. Brooker 'What Do Lord Mandelson, Damien Hirst and the Music Industry Have in Common?', *Guardian*, 14 September 2009, G2, 5.

[31] See J. S. G. Boggs, 'Who Owns This?', *Chicago-Kent Law Review*, 68 (1993), 889 (discussing *Rogers* v. *Koons*, Boggs writes: 'Sculpture is a different discipline from photography', 900); F Macmillan, 'Artistic Practice and the Integrity of Copyright Law', in M. Rosenmeier and S. Teilmann (eds.), *Art and Law: The Copyright Debate* (DJØF Publishing, 2005), pp. 49, 66–71.

[32] The idea of Creative Commons, as discussed by McClean, is of course dependent upon the existence of copyright protection.

[33] See McClean, 'Piracy and Authorship', p. 336.

this argument were unsuccessful, would Monk be able to claim the benefit of one of the defences to an infringement claim under the CDPA 1988? Let us consider, first, a claim that the parody of *Rabbit* does not even *infringe* the copyright in that work.[34] At first sight, there may appear to be two ways to frame such an argument. First, Monk could argue that – within the 'artistic commonwealth' – the work in question would not be regarded as a 'copy' of Koons' work at all, but as a separate, properly authorised artefact in its own right and, therefore, that the law should not regard it as a copy. This argument reflects the norms of the artistic commonwealth. Second, it could be claimed that the improper or transgressive nature of the proceedings brought by Koons ought to be recognised in considering whether an infringement had taken place. Under current United Kingdom copyright law, neither of these arguments looks very promising. The first ('not a copy') argument seems incompatible with the quasi-scientific approach to infringement endorsed in the decision of the House of Lords in *Designers' Guild*.[35] This approach is premised on the need only to identify whether the defendant has reproduced a 'substantial part' of the protected essence of the protected work. If so, the appearance of the defendant's work becomes irrelevant.[36] Any possibility of the development of a more discriminating approach to the question of copying – perhaps taking greater account of the material nature of the carrier of the works in question – would appear to have been foreclosed.[37] A similar fate is also likely to await the second argument outlined above. At an earlier date in copyright's history, an argument that a court ought to take account of the propriety of the defendant's actions in determining whether an infringement had taken place may have been better received.[38] Now, however, it is equally difficult to reconcile such an approach with the prevalent quasi-scientific, property-based analysis, which leaves little, if any,[39]

---

[34] Such an argument would be tenable in some other jurisdictions. See, for example, the German 'free use' provision (Copyright Act 1965, s. 24). For application in the context of parody, see *Bild-Kunst* v. *Focus* [2005] ECDR 6 (BGH, Federal Supreme Court, Germany).

[35] *Designers' Guild Ltd* v. *Russell Williams Textiles Ltd* [2000] 1 WLR 2416 (HL).

[36] *Ibid.*, at 2420–1, 2425–6; cf. 2430–3.

[37] Cf., for example, the speech of Lord Griffiths in *British Leyland Motor Corporation Ltd* v. *Armstrong Patents Co. Ltd* [1986] AC 577, 645–55.

[38] See K. Garnett, G. Davies and G. Harbottle, *Copinger and Skone James on Copyright* (15th edn, London: Sweet & Maxwell, 2005), pp. 7–28. *Baigent* v. *Random House* [2008] EMLR 7 (CA), at 95–8.

[39] In *Ravenscroft* v. *Herbert* [1980] RPC 193, Brightman J. accepted that historical works were not to be judged by precisely the same standards as works of fiction. However, in the

space for questions of fairness, plagiarism or compliance with common practice.

In relation to the question of infringement, then, copyright doctrine appears to have closed fairly comprehensively around the intangible property right model described earlier in this response. Do the defences available under the CDPA 1988 offer a more promising means of accommodating the norms of the 'high' art world?[40] In this respect, the fair dealing defences, although not as open-ended as the fair use defence under United States law, preserve a degree of flexibility.[41] Would a work such as Monk's fall within the defence of fair dealing for the purpose of criticism or review?[42] In order to satisfy this provision, he would have to satisfy three conditions. First, he would have to demonstrate that *The Inflated Deflated* reproduced *Rabbit* for the purpose of 'criticism' or 'review' of that or of other works. According to the Court of Appeal, the concepts of 'criticism' and 'review' are to be interpreted liberally.[43] On this basis, it is certainly possible that Monk's knowing reference to *Rabbit* would be regarded as a form of 'criticism' or 'review' of that work or of Koons' œuvre more generally.[44] Second, Monk would have to demonstrate that he had made a 'sufficient acknowledgement' of *Rabbit* and its author.[45] As noted by McClean, implicit attribution is the norm within the 'artistic commonwealth'. By contrast, it is possible that a copyright court would conclude that some explicit acknowledgement is necessary

recent decision of *Baigent* v. *Random House* [2008] EMLR 7 (CA), such a differential approach, based upon the implicit expectations of authors, was not approved, the Court of Appeal preferring to reiterate a single set of principles applying in all infringement cases.

[40] If a custom or practice is universal in a particular sector, it may be possible to argue that use of a work within the conventions of that custom or practice is impliedly licensed (see, for example, *Express Newspapers plc* v. *News UK Ltd* [1990] 1 WLR 1320). However, courts have been reluctant to hold that an alleged custom or practice of prima facie infringement is universal and certain. See *Walter* v. *Steinkopff* [1892] 3 Ch. 489; *Banier* v. *News Group Newspapers Ltd* [1997] FSR 812.

[41] I have argued elsewhere that courts have sought (either consciously or subconsciously) to retain this flexibility (see J. Griffiths, 'Preserving Judicial Freedom of Movement – Interpreting Fair Dealing in Copyright Law', IPQ (2000), 164. Cf. however, R. Burrell, 'Reining in Copyright Law: Is Fair Use the Answer?', IPQ (2001), 361.

[42] CDPA 1988, s. 30(1).

[43] *Pro Sieben Media AG* v. *Carlton UK Television Ltd* [1999] 1 WLR 605, 614. Although, cf. now *Infopaq International AS* v. *Danske Dagblades Forening* (C-5/08) [2009] ECDR 16 (ECJ), at 56–8 and, in the case of parody, cf. *Cie générale des établissements Michelin – Michelin & Cie* v. *National Automobile, Aerospace, Transportation and General Workers Union of Canada (CAW – Canada)* [1997] 2 FC 306 (Canada), at [63]–[68].

[44] See *Pro Sieben Media AG* v. *Carlton UK Television Ltd* [1999] 1 WLR 605, 615–16.

[45] CDPA 1988, s. 30(1), 178.

under s. 30(1). Nevertheless, this point has been left open by the Court of Appeal[46] and there is support for an argument that implicit acknowledgement, relying on an average viewer's prior awareness of the reproduced work, could be effective.[47] Finally, Monk would also have to demonstrate that his activities constituted 'fair dealing'. Judicial approaches to 'fairness' have varied. Often, courts have applied this notion in a manner that favours property-owning right-holders.[48] However, such an approach has not been universal and there are many cases which have been decided more liberally.[49] Indeed, it can plausibly be argued that the inconsistency and imprecision of the factor-based jurisprudence on 'fairness' leave considerable flexibility for courts in cases in which a defendant is deemed to be meritorious.[50] As a result, while there is no guarantee that Monk's parody would be regarded as 'fair', the fact that he had acted in accordance with the usual norms of the relevant cultural sector – here the 'artistic commonwealth' – might well militate in favour of a finding of 'fairness',[51] particularly because market harm – as understood within the 'artistic commonwealth' – would not arise.

### Aesthetic neutrality and the artistic commonwealth

This hypothetical analysis demonstrates that copyright law retains a degree of flexibility – through the operation of the defence of fair dealing – that may permit it to accommodate the norms of the 'artistic commonwealth' to some extent. However, such accommodation is likely to prove much harder to achieve in another form of copyright dispute

---

[46] See *Pro Sieben Media AG* v. *Carlton UK Television Ltd* [1999] 1 WLR 605, 618. Cf. *Cie générale des établissements Michelin – Michelin & Cie* v. *National Automobile, Aerospace, Transportation and General Workers Union of Canada (CAW – Canada)* [1997] 2 FC 306 (Canada), at [73]–[74].

[47] *Fraser-Woodward Ltd* v. *British Broadcasting Corporation* [2005] EMLR 22, at [71]–[78].

[48] See, for example, *Hyde Park Residence Ltd* v. *Yelland* [2000] EMLR 363 (CA); *Ashdown* v. *Telegraph Group Ltd* [2002] Ch. 149 (CA). For a strong argument to this effect, see R. Burrell, 'Reining in Copyright Law: Is Fair Use the Answer?', IPQ (2007), 368.

[49] See, for example, *Time Warner* v. *Channel Four* [1994] EMLR 1 (CA); *Pro Sieben Media AG* v. *Carlton UK Television Ltd* [1999] 1 WLR 605.

[50] See Griffiths, 'Preserving Judicial Freedom'.

[51] See, for example, *British Broadcasting Corporation* v. *British Satellite Broadcasting Ltd* [1992] Ch. 141. For the potential danger of deciding questions of 'fairness' by reference to customary standards within a particular cultural sector, see J. Rothman, 'The Questionable Use of Custom in Intellectual Property', *Virginia LR*, 93 (2007), 1899.

considered in detail by McClean. He argues convincingly that difficulties (and litigation) tend to arise when 'high' artists reproduce images from 'low' art forms such as commercial photography. He cites the notorious *Rogers* v. *Koons*[52] dispute as an archetype of such claims. From the perspective of 'high' art, the problem with such cases is that copyright insists on treating commercial photography and 'high' art artefact as equivalent. By contrast, the artistic commonwealth places little significance on works of 'low' art:

> What is striking again in Koons' testimony is the way in which Rogers's identity as the creator of the photographic image is unimportant because the image is of a 'type' conveying particular cultural or social content, rather than an authored work in its own right . . .[53]

Again, the focus on the unique 'authorised' artefact is vital. Works falling outside this tradition are simply not recognised and, accordingly: (a) it is unnecessary to obtain permission from the creators of such works for their reproduction within 'high' artistic artefacts; and (b) attribution of authorship to the creator of such works is irrelevant. Viewed from within the 'artistic commonwealth', Koons ought not to have been held liable for his use of Rogers' photograph.

To what extent, then, can 'high' art's perception of this dispute be accommodated within the copyright system? While *Rogers* v. *Koons* was decided under United States law, there is reason to believe that courts in the United Kingdom would be likely to be even less sympathetic to the defendant than the Court of Appeals of the Second Circuit if the facts of that case were to be tried in this jurisdiction.[54] A number of the points made above in relation to the hypothetical dispute between Koons and Monk would apply equally in such a case. It would be futile to argue that Koons' sculpture did not 'copy' the photograph and there would be even less mileage in the argument that the assessment of infringement should take into account the propriety of the defendant's actions than in the case of the hypothetical dispute between Monk and Koons. Rogers' decision to bring proceedings could not easily be described as improper or transgressive as he is

---

[52] 960 F 2d 301 (1992). For discussion, see Greenberg, 'Art of Appropriation'; Ames, 'Beyond Rogers'; Okpaluba, 'Appropriation Art'.
[53] McClean, 'Piracy and Authorship', p. 335.
[54] See also Okpaluba, 'Appropriation Art', 196, 207–8. It should be noted that a court's response to artist defendants who 'appropriate' images may have liberalised in any event in the United States since *Rogers* v. *Koons*. See, for example, *Blanch* v. *Koons* 467 F 3d 244 (2d Cir., 2006).

not himself a member of the 'artistic commonwealth'. What then about potential defences?[55] Section 30(1) CDPA 1988 seems less likely to excuse Koons than Monk in the situation discussed above. While Koons' sculpture could certainly be interpreted as a form of criticism or review of the photograph, or of similar works,[56] he would have greater difficulties in establishing, first, that his dealing with the photograph was 'fair' and, second, that he had made 'sufficient acknowledgement' of Rogers and his photograph. In respect of 'fair dealing', by contrast with the *Rogers* v. *Monk* hypothetical discussed above, the parties do not share a customary borrowing norm militating in favour of fairness. An even greater difficulty is presented by Koons' failure to acknowledge the photograph's authorship. In this case, the sculpture's viewers' familiarity with the artistic tradition would not even permit them implicitly to identify Rogers. A claim that the photographer's identity is unimportant because the image is purely generic is unlikely to recommend itself to a court.

It can be suggested that the likely failure of the defence in this case reveals the most deep-seated difficulty in accommodating the norms of 'high' art within copyright law. Courts will be very reluctant to accept distinctions of entitlement determined by a self-validating institution such as the 'artistic commonwealth'.[57] Ultimately, I would argue, it is not 'high' art culture's 'fetish for the auratic object' that impedes copyright law's reception of its values, but rather the 'evaluative' conception of originality or authorship that McClean also identifies as a feature of that culture. This is a conception of authorship deriving from the fact:

> that an artwork is by an artist whose authorship is novel in art historical terms and has accordingly been ascribed recognition within art discourse (art criticism, history etc.) and by art institutions (exhibitions in museums, galleries, etc.).[58]

This description reveals the self-referential and self-validating aspects of 'high' art. McClean's words, in explaining 'evaluative' originality, are also revealing:

---

[55] In such circumstances, an argument based upon an alleged implied licence will clearly be unavailing (see n. 40 above).

[56] *Pro Sieben Media AG* v. *Carlton UK Television Ltd* [1999] 1 WLR 605, 615–16.

[57] Ambivalence about the role of experts in art is apparent in the United Kingdom case law on the application of copyright to 'works of artistic craftsmanship' (see, now, CDPA 1988, s. 4(1)(c)). See, for example, *George Hensher Ltd* v. *Restawile Upholstery* (*Lancs*) *Ltd* [1976] AC 64, 78, 97.

[58] McClean, 'Piracy and Authorship', p. 318.

[A]rt history might be said to have a 'legislative' function, with art historians and critics making a case for particular artists and artworks (including their authenticity), thereby establishing precedents within the history of art.[59]

The decisions of this alternative system of regulation establish distinctions in accordance with forms of reasoning that cannot readily be accommodated within legal discourse. McClean himself recognises the important role of copyright's 'aesthetic neutrality' as a cause of its resistance to the norms of the 'artistic commonwealth'. In his analysis, it is the law's failure to distinguish between 'low' art forms and 'high' art's unique material artefacts that leads it to treat both alike. However, it seems to me that the 'aesthetic neutrality' principle is independent of any preference for the intangible over the material and, although it is sometimes explained as a response to a lack of judicial qualification in aesthetics, it actually reflects a much more fundamental commitment to the authority of recognised decision-making institutions and processes. In the United Kingdom, copyright courts are reluctant to delegate the task of making decisions affecting entitlements to individual artists or to experts in art.[60] To a very great extent, I would suggest, this reluctance arises because those artists and/or experts make judgements in accordance with a culture and methodology (sometimes designated as 'subjective') that is quite different from that employed in legal reasoning (which must always be 'objective').

## Conclusion

Viewed in this light, it is copyright's 'aesthetic neutrality' that is likely to present an obstacle to the smooth reception of McClean's two tentative proposals for the more sensitive protection of the 'autonomy of art' under copyright law. Both are premised on the assumption that 'creative expression' could be better protected if 'high' artists were to receive more favourable treatment (either through a compulsory licence scheme or through an entirely separate legal regime for fine artistic works) than the creators of other forms of 'artistic work' recognised under copyright law. These solutions would clearly have some advantages and the latter, in

---

[59] Ibid., p. 318.
[60] See, for example, Tidy v. Trustees of the Natural History Museum (1995) 39 IPR 501; George Hensher Ltd v. Restawile Upholstery (Lancs) Ltd [1976] AC 64, 78 (per Lord Reid); 97 (per Lord Kilbrandon).

particular, would allow the law to accommodate 'high' art's predominant concern with the tangible artefact to an even greater extent than it currently does. However, ultimately, both are based upon aesthetic distinctions drawn by the 'artistic commonwealth' itself and, as a result, are unlikely to be accepted within the culture of copyright law.

# PART X

Sociology/music

# 18

# Reggae open source: how the absence of copyright enabled the emergence of popular music in Jamaica

JASON TOYNBEE

Since 1960 a highly innovative form of music making has developed in Jamaica in the effective absence of copyright. Over the first two-thirds of the chapter I argue that in fact reggae music[1] would never have emerged had copyright been implemented on the island. Quite simply, local forms of creativity and the nature of the musical labour process were inimical to intellectual property (IP). In the last section, I go a step further by suggesting there are wider lessons to be learned here. Creative practice in Jamaica has been based on principles which may well apply in other territories and to other forms of culture choked by the constrictions of the contemporary copyright regime. A comparison with open-source software reinforces this case.

## On Orange street: political economy at the birth of reggae

In 1960 the music industry in Kingston, Jamaica was still at an embryonic stage. The main form of music entertainment, however, was distinctly modern. Across the city black working-class people danced to recorded music. This was provided by mobile sound systems, consisting of a record deck, amplifier and large loudspeaker boxes, together with oper-ating crew and truck to carry the equipment. The sound systems con-stituted a highly competitive market, where what counted was the playing of new and exclusive rhythm and blues records from the US. Audiences provided immediate feedback in the form of getting up to

---

[1] Reggae is used here as the generic term for Jamaican popular music after around 1962.

dance – or not – and the fortunes of a sound depended on its ability to keep audiences moving.[2]

In order to ensure exclusivity sound system operators often scratched out the labels on new records to prevent competitors from finding out their provenance, and thus acquiring copies for themselves.[3] Significantly, the practice has some of the same functions as copyright. Both institutions represent the imperative to exert monopoly control over new products in cultural markets where innovation is at a premium. However in Jamaica copyright proper was never enforced in relation to the commercial exploitation of music. True, UK copyright law did apply in name across the British West Indies. And after Independence in 1962, the British Copyright Act of 1911 and a local statute for implementing it from 1913, were received into Jamaican law.[4] But, quite unlike the case of the core states of the world system, no infrastructure for the exploitation of music rights developed in this period.

The explanation lies in the first place with the leading role taken by the sound systems in the early Jamaican music business. This initial orientation of the Jamaican music scene, shaped by intense competition in the highly innovative primary market of the dancehall, persisted even after domestically produced records replaced US repertoire. That is, a specialised form of end use, public performance of records for dancers, has strongly determined the organisation of the industry and forms of innovation. It is perhaps worth sketching the history of the 'sounds', then, and their role in the political economy of Jamaican music.

By 1960 sound system operators were encountering a repertoire shortage. As gospel-influenced styles came to the fore in the American R&B market, the sound system operators, or their scouts who were sent over to the US to scour record shops, found it increasingly difficult to find new recordings in the older 'jump' style that had remained popular in Jamaican dancehalls. So the operators began to turn to local musicians in order to replicate this style on record. In 1960 there were two studios. RJR was a commercial radio station which

---

[2] N. Stolzoff, *Wake the Town and Tell the People: Dancehall Culture in Jamaica* (Durham, NC: Duke University Press, 2000), pp. 52–3.

[3] *Ibid.*, 51.

[4] D. Daley, and N. Foga, 'Jamaica: Beyond the TRIPs agreement', *Managing IP*, Americas IP Focus (3rd edn, 2007) (accessed 28 March 2008, at: www.managingip.com/Article.aspx?ArticleID=1450368).

incorporated a small studio. A local entrepreneur, Ken Khouri, owned the other one. From the mid-1950s he recorded, pressed and released mostly mento, the national 'folk' music style related to calypso, at his Federal studio. By the start of the new decade the sound system operators, Khouri himself, and a handful of independent producers including Chris Blackwell and Edward Seaga were recording tunes in a local variant of jump R&B.[5] Two years later, at the time of independence, making records for the dance hall had expanded exponentially. In terms of style, the music had taken on a distinct local inflection and been given a name – ska. By mid-decade, labels, recording studios and record shops were starting to spread along the Orange Street corridor at the Western edge of downtown Kingston.[6]

There are parallels here with the emergence of rock music in Britain and the US, as well as significant divergences. In both cases new musical forms were built upon thriving new markets and ways of consuming music. In both, recording took a much more important and autonomous role than previously when its function had been merely to document live performance. And in both rock and reggae, musical sources beyond the home culture were hugely important. The divergences have to do with the way in which economics and aesthetics intersected quite differently in each case around problems of creativity and innovation. Whereas copyright, a corporatist industrial structure and the cult of the *auteur* governed innovation in rock, reggae was characterised by a dynamic blend of competition and cooperation, and the absence of effective IP.

## Social authorship (1): intensification and the division of labour

We can hear this right from the start of domestic recording for the sound systems. What was at stake was a form of social authorship[7] where continuity between recordings was much more important than originality. Yet this did not prevent innovation; far from it. The transformation in style between 1960 and 1962 which led to the

---

[5] G. White, 'The Evolution of Jamaican Music pt. 1: "proto-ska" to ska', *Social and Economic Studies*, 57(1) (1998), 5–19.

[6] M. Cooke, 'No Preservatives On Reggae History', *Jamaica Gleaner*, 25 February 2007 (accessed 19 March 2008, at: www.jamaica-gleaner.com/gleaner/20070225/ent/ent1.html).

[7] J. Toynbee, 'Copyright, the Work and Phonographic Orality in Music', *Social and Legal Studies*, 15(1) (2006), 77–99.

'birth of reggae', was both radical and coherent. Its single most important element was a change in rhythmic accent. Built on a 4/4 rhythm, the favoured jump R&B idiom featured a 'walking' bass line and snare drum 'backbeats' on beats 2 and 4. Many of the most popular tunes in the dancehall also featured an accent on the offbeat voiced by piano or guitar; namely, '1 and 2 and 3 and 4 and', where the offbeat is represented by 'and'. What Jamaican musicians then did as they started recording in this idiom at the end of the 1950s was to slightly emphasise the offbeat.

If we jump forward to early 1962 and 'Judge Not', the first recording by a 16-year-old Bob Marley (1996), we can hear ska almost fully formed. There is still the walking 4/4 bass line and snare backbeat as heard in jump R&B, but the accent on the offbeat, voiced by piano and saxophone, dominates the rhythm completely: '1 **ska** 2 **ska** 3 **ska** 4 **ska**'. By the time of 'Don't Throws Tones' [sic] by Prince Buster (2000), probably from 1965, the style has been consolidated. The core musicians on this recording are the Skatelites, the leading group of session musicians in Jamaica. They deliver what might be called high ska. The offbeat accent is now voiced by piano, guitar, brass section and harmonica, but with an articulation that is both complex and highly evocative of groove.[8] Key here is a slight sustain on the harmonica such that it can be heard immediately after the other instruments have stopped playing in a reedy echo of the tight ensemble sound.

Let's call the process at stake in the development of ska, *intensification*.[9] By this is meant collective production of change through the identification of an aesthetic zone – here, the accent on the offbeat – and then the making of this zone more and more salient over a cycle of recordings. For the present argument the significance of intensification lies in its essentially collective nature. Change was generated collectively in that the whole cohort of musicians in Kingston was involved as a group in the research and development of the new sound. Certainly, there was intense competition too, particularly among producers and sound system operators. Nevertheless, music makers contributed to stylistic innovation as artisans rather than heroic individuals as in the

---

[8] Groove refers to the dimension of rhythmic propulsion in music. See C. Keil, 'Motion and Feeling through Music', in C. Keil and S. Feld (eds.), *Music Grooves: Essays and Dialogues* (University of Chicago Press, 1990).

[9] J. Toynbee, *Bob Marley: Herald of a Postcolonial World?* (Cambridge: Polity, 2007), pp. 87–94.

case of rock. Across all roles – musicians, vocalists, engineers, producers – and notwithstanding different interests and contractual relations, there was in effect a common culture and practice of making new: taking things a little further than last time, picking up on a trope used on that record, copying but varying what someone else has been doing . . .

The fluid, collaborative yet competitive structure in which this kind of innovation flourished depended on a particular kind of economic organisation. At the top of the hierarchy producers (the most powerful of whom owned sound system operations too) called the shots, arranging recording sessions, hiring musicians and named artists, and then organising distribution. At first distribution simply meant record play at sound systems – the primary commodity was a whole evening's selection of records played in the dancehall. Then during the early 1960s a retail record market began to take off, though one which was always dependent on the dancehall for the presentation of new tunes and the consecration of successful ones.

This was 'primitive accumulation'[10] – tough, small-scale capitalism based on the charismatic power (sometimes backed by violent coercion) of the producers. Nevertheless, the labour process was shaped very much by labour market conditions. Most significantly, session players in Kingston were able to work for different producers with impunity. So although the Skatalites have sometimes been described as a house band for Coxsone Dodd's Studio One operation, they actually made many recordings for others, for instance Buster in the example just described. Coxsone himself testifies to this mobility of labour in an account of the way his rival Duke Reid would often outbid him.

> Whatever it costs, Duke would find the money. Even if I had a contracted artist, Duke would still insist and use them, like Don Drummond and Roland [Alphonso – both from the Skatalites] was contracted to me, but after a while you realise the man is a musician and that's the only way he could really earn, so you let him play, which is different from vocalists.[11]

Dodd emphasises his own altruism here. But probably what counted much more was the nature of the labour market. Voracious demand for new recordings for the sound systems, and by the mid-1960s the developing retail singles market, gave the relatively small number of

---

[10] K. Marx, *Capital, Volume 1* (Harmondsworth: Penguin Books Marx, 1976), pp. 873–940.

[11] Quoted in D. Katz, *Solid Foundation: An Oral History of Reggae* (London: Bloomsbury, 2003), p. 61.

skilled session musicians a strong bargaining position. Singers, on the other hand, even extremely successful ones like the Wailers at Studio One, could be contracted on the basis of a small retainer.[12] Quite simply, demand uncertainty in respect of the recordings of 'name' solo artists or vocal groups, together with oversupply of singers themselves, made them weaker as labour market players. As for the role of 'songwriter', this was much less important in reggae than in rock. But to the extent that there were songwriters, they tended to come from the ranks of the singers. Writing was simply another duty to be performed. Producers paid no royalties and generally claimed writing credits for themselves when work was issued overseas.[13]

As for the function of producer, s/he (there was one female producer in the 1960s and 1970s – Sonia Pottinger) was not just a hirer of labour, but also took on the function of marque. That is to say Jamaican producers became publicly identified with a certain quality of sound, stable of singers or stylistic inflection. Producer-artists like Prince Buster, and later on Lee Perry, even released records under their own names.

Perhaps the general conclusion to draw is that in the Jamaican system the division of labour meant that creative input, and just as important the *attribution* of creative input, were spread across the various roles. In other words authorship was profoundly social even though it was far from being organised on a mutual basis. In this context copyright was simply beside the point. For the petty capitalist producers at the top of the chain, the priority was to ensure a constant supply of new records for the sound system, not to stop others from

---

[12] T. White, *Catch a Fire: The Life of Bob Marley* (London: Omnibus Press, 2000), p. 160.
[13] For instance, see the account by singer and song writer Bob Andy of his dealings with Coxsone Dodd at Studio One, B. Andy (1983), 'Interview with Ray Hurford and Colin Moore', *Small Axe* (accessed 31 March 2008, at: www.bobandy.com/int-smaxe2.htm). It might seem that this dual system of copyright abroad/no copyright at home was iniquitous: producers benefited while songwriters and performers were denied the full fruits of their labour. But there is no reason to believe that formal attribution of rights to artists would have reduced the economic exploitation at stake here. For copyright hardly changes the nature of cultural labour markets where oversupply (many want to become symbol makers) is combined with uncertainty of demand, R. Towse, 'Copyright and Artists: A View From Cultural Economics', *Journal of Economic Surveys*, 20(4) (2006), 567–85. This combination radically reduces the bargaining power that can be brought to the table by artists (see the discussion above of singers, songwriters and session musicians in Kingston). And that in turn means that cultural intermediaries are able to demand the assignment of artists' rights on terms favourable to themselves. To put it succinctly, what counts in the cultural economy is not initial ownership of rights but rather the power to exploit them.

exploiting their product over the long term. Crucially, to be the first with a new sound gave producers competitive advantage. In other words, speed was of the essence. Even when the retail record market grew during the 1960s, the economic imperative remained the same: to come first to market. The point is that, brutal and exploitative though the system could be, it worked extremely efficiently to generate a high rate of musical innovation in the absence of IP.

### Social authorship (2): translation, origination and reuse

The process of intensification which we have been examining in the development of ska was a key part of the social authorship which flourished in Kingston during the 1960s. Critically, it became important again in the emergence of later styles such as rocksteady, reggae and dub. However, there was another significant aspect of Jamaican social authorship which, although complementary to intensification, involved quite a different creative principle.

Intensification is an endogenous process of innovation. It depends on identifying a salient zone within a larger musical code, and then research and development of the aesthetic possibilities which emerge from this initial step. As we have heard, in the case of ska such possibilities centred on the accented offbeat. Conversely, in what might be called *translation*, the animating principle is lateral reference to that which is notionally outside a given musical code, rather than vertical reference to what precedes it. Translation involves broadening, rather than deepening, musical signification through the reframing of musical materials. No doubt there was an aesthetic of hybridity at play here (for the significance of hybridity in Caribbean culture, see Shalina Puri's important work).[14] But translation was also a response to hyper-innovation – the need to constantly produce new 'record-texts' for the 45 rpm singles which were reggae music's staple medium of reproduction. Reuse of existing texts, or the production of same-but-different ones, represented a highly efficient means of solving the problem.

Actually, we have already examined one instance of reggae translation, namely the importation of R&B. Effectively what initiated the cycle of intensification that culminated in ska was a lateral move; the

---

[14] S. Puri, *The Caribbean Postcolonial: Social Equality, Post-Nationalism and Cultural Hybridity* (New York: Palgrave Macmillan, 2004).

bringing across of the popular music of African-America. This was a relatively gross form of translation in that a whole genre – jump blues – provided the source code. However translation in reggae music occurred across a broad spectrum; not just genre but also œuvre (where the source was the music of a single artist or group) and the version (the basis of which was a specific recording).

Let's consider some examples; first, from somewhere in the middle of spectrum, the extensive use made by reggae artists during the 1960s of the work of US soul group, the Impressions. The characteristic tenor-to-falsetto voice of many Jamaican singers in this period is clearly copied from the Impressions' lead singer and guitarist, Curtis Mayfield.[15] This is not only a matter of vocal register though. It also has to do with the quality of voice, accompaniment and production values. Critically, such translation is not at all a static or unresponsive form of copying. Rather it represents a sideways development of musical codes into new areas of semiotic possibility. Many aspects of the work of Bob Marley and the Wailers between 1964 and 1967 demonstrate this. Indeed, translation of a whole variety of traits from the Impressions' œuvre arguably provided the most important means by which the Wailers extended their signifying range in this period, enabling the production of a sophisticated yet earthy, tough but tender, local while also cosmopolitan musical style.[16]

Translation of this kind is of course perfectly permissible under copyright law, probably everywhere around the world. Timbres and textures, patterns of antiphony, phrasing, a characteristic guitar sound – all of which were at stake in the Wailers' appropriation of the Impressions – do not reach the threshold of what may be protected in the musical work.[17] Melody and lyrics, on the other hand, are commonly agreed to be at the core of the musical work as it is constituted by copyright statutes and case law. Yet in respect of these elements, as much as with the idiomatic traits and tropes we have just been

---

[15] Apart from the evidence provided by recordings, Jamaican music makers have themselves pointed out the near ubiquitous influence of Curtis Mayfield, for instance Derrick Harriott (2005 personal communication) and Pat Kelly, quoted in Katz, *Solid Foundation*, p. 88.

[16] Toynbee, *Bob Marley*, pp. 94–8.

[17] For discussion of which musical parameters are protected in law, see L. Bently, 'Authorship of Popular Music under UK Copyright Law', *E-Journal of IP Rights*, Oxford IP Research Centre (2005) (accessed 28 March 2008, at: www.oiprc.ox.ac.uk/EJWP1005.pdf), and A. Barron, 'Introduction: Harmony or Dissonance? Copyright Concepts and Musical Practice', *Social and Legal Studies*, 15(1) (2006), 25–51.

discussing, Jamaican musicians were profligate copiers. What's more, they were quite open about their imitation, and understood it to be a perfectly legitimate method for the generation of new recordings.

This point is critical for the present argument. There was, and indeed still is, little distinction within the musical culture between licit and illicit translation, between, at one end of our spectrum, the bringing across of generic traits and at the other end, the importation of melodies, lyrics, substantial motifs or even whole songs made by others – in other words, work elements whose reuse would constitute infringement of copyright law. This is not at all to suggest that translation was an indiscriminate process. But it does mean that it took place without recognition of norms of copyright, or of codes of authorship (as in rock culture) which converged with these norms. In what kinds of way, then, are copyrighted work elements translated into reggae in the 1960s?

First, there is the reuse of an existing song – what would be termed in rock, the cover version. Derrick Harriot's 'Do I Worry?' (1998) from 1966 is a good example. This is a recording of the song written by Stanley Cowan and Bobby Worth in 1940. It was a big hit for African-American vocal group, the Ink Spots, in 1941, and it is probably in this form that Harriott first heard the song. His own rendition is pure rocksteady, that is to say in the much slower and sparer style which succeeded ska in the summer of 1966. In copyright terms, of course, it is simply a version of a work written by others and whose rights were owned (at the time and place of issue of my CD copy) by Peer Music (UK) Ltd. However it is reasonably safe to assume that no publisher information would have been shown on the original Jamaican release, nor that there would have been any recovery of royalties in respect of mechanical reproduction of the work at that time.[18]

A second type of translation of a work element is the cover version which uses the same title, but then deviates far from the musical form of the original. An example is the Wailers' (1991) recording of 'Rolling Stone' from early 1966. Clearly inspired by the Bob Dylan song, the Wailers' version nevertheless has a completely different harmonic and

---

[18] Jamaican singles from the 1960s invariably show song title and artist. Sometimes composer information is included, but the present author has not seen any reference to publishers or to copyright among the fifty or so such pressings he has examined. The fact that Jamaica was not a signatory to international copyright conventions provides the overarching explanation here. For a collection of images of Jamaican record labels from the 1960s see, J. Collingwood, *Bob Marley: His Musical Legacy* (London: Cassell, 2005).

melodic shape. The Skatalites play the 'Hang On Sloopy' chord changes, using a relaxed and funky ska rhythm that owes much more to New Orleans R&B than it does to Dylan's organ-based, rock angst. On the verses Bunny Livingstone doesn't just sing a different melody, he has written different words, and while the lyrics of the chorus remain the same, the melody only approximates Dylan's. In any event, the unvarying three-chord pattern undermines the verse–chorus structure of the original based as it is on different chord changes across verse and chorus. This is, in effect, another song; re-engineered for another context – the dancehall.

In a third type of copying, a different title is used from the original. However, either the whole song or its melody are adopted. 'Don't Throws Tones' by Prince Buster (2000) discussed earlier is a good example. It features a spoken word introduction by Buster, a warning to rude boys, and then an instrumental version of the tune, 'Quizás, Quizás, Quizás', written by the Cuban songwriter Osvaldo Farrés in 1947. Buster and the Skatalites would almost certainly have heard Doris Day's version from that singer's very popular *Latin for Lovers* album, released in the US in March 1965. Entitled 'Perhaps, Perhaps, Perhaps', this used English lyrics by Joe Davis. On my CD copy of the Buster track, however, writing credits are shown as 'C. Campbell' (Cecil Campbell is Buster's birth name), and the publisher is given as 'Prince Buster Music (BMI)'. There is, to put it mildly, something of a contradiction here. Still, at the time it was released the absence of a copyright regime in Jamaica suggests that the use of an alternative title (very likely 'Don't Throw Stones' on the original single) was not motivated by intent to deceive so much as Buster's desire to rejoin the ongoing rude boy controversy. The 'Quizás … / Perhaps …' melody and chord changes simply provided a vehicle, albeit a sublimely ska-able vehicle, for doing this.

Another example of a cover with a different title to the original is 'Darker Shade of Black', released as a Studio One single in 1967. The artists credited on the original single are Sound Dimension, the group of session musicians led by Jackie Mittoo at that time. The composer, very typically on Studio One releases, is shown as the producer; 'C. [for Clement] Dodd'.[19] However, the melody taken by Mittoo's organ consists in the verse part of the Lennon and McCartney tune, 'Norwegian Wood'. This is repeated over an extraordinary 'riddim'

---

[19] An image of the label can be seen at: www.soundsoftheuniverse.com/releases/?id=9442.

which was to become a standard in Jamaican music, being rerecorded by Mittoo himself in the late 1970s, and then revived by Frankie Paul for his hit, 'Pass the Tu-Sheng Peng' in 1983 (this version also included the 'Norwegian Wood' motif, but now voiced by a brass section). As recently as 2007 Chuck Fender employed the riddim on the single, 'So Many Girls'. Indeed, the online directory ReggaeID lists a total of 183 recordings up to that date based on 'Darker Shade of Black'.[20]

In the case of 'Darker Shade of Black', although the keyboard melody is derivative and would undoubtedly be considered to infringe copyright in any court, the most significant aspect of the recording, and what has given it such enormous longevity, are the bass line and guitar riff. These each consist of a three-note pattern. Notwithstanding their extraordinarily effective combination in the riddim, this would be very unlikely to reach any threshold of substantiality currently being used in a copyright court.[21]

## Riddims, open source and coming first to market

The institution of the riddim is perhaps the most graphic example of the way that social authorship in Jamaican popular music operates at a complete tangent to the norms of copyright law. As Peter Manuel and Wayne Marshall explain:

> [f]rom the early 1970s reggae music – whose most popular form since around 1980 has been called 'dancehall' – has relied upon the phenomenon of the 'riddim', that is, an autonomous accompanimental track, typically based on an ostinato (which often includes melodic instrumentation as well as percussion). While a dancehall song consists of a deejay singing (or 'voicing') over a riddim, the riddim is not exclusive to that song, but is typically used in many other songs.[22]

In an important sense, the riddim represents a synthesis of those processes of intensification and translation which we have been examining over the previous two sections. It involves intensification in that the repetition of a melodic/percussive pattern over many recordings

---

[20] See: www.reggaeid.co.uk/riddims.php?show_letter=D&PHPSESSID=0f92e1db4965be5a1018 8aa0cbbaa983, accessed 1 April 2008.

[21] For the US, see Toynbee, 'Copyright, the Work', and A. Korn, 'Issues Facing Legal Practitioners in Measuring Substantiality of Contemporary Musical Expression', *John Marshall Review of IP Law*, 6(3) (2007), 489–500.

[22] P. Manuel and W. Marshall, 'The Riddim Method: Aesthetics, Practice, and Ownership in Jamaican Dancehall', *Popular Music*, 25(3) (2006), 447.

provides a medium for the micro-phonic development of sonority; an aesthetic exploration in *depth*. Equally, though, the successive manifestations of a riddim can signify in *breadth*, with each one a translation of some or all of the others by dint of the different words and delivery used by each deejay or singer. This is a profoundly dialogical form of music making.

But in all cases what is surely at stake is music-*ing*, in other words the continuous and always unfinished performance of a tradition, rather than the production of the individual works/recordings that are the object of copyright law. So, the 'Darker Shade of Black' riddim doesn't belong to Jackie Mitto, the Sound Dimension – or even Clement Dodd despite the fact that his name is shown as composer on that Studio One single from forty years ago. And it clearly doesn't belong to the writers or publishers of 'Norwegian Wood' either, despite its provenance.

Perhaps it might be said to belong to the Jamaican people. Arguably, the de facto common ownership at stake in the 'riddim method'[23] derives as much from long established folklore as it does from recording for the dance hall. As we heard above, a national style, mento, was popular in Jamaica during the 1950s. But its origins go back much further. Ken Bilby suggests that mento encapsulates strong African retentions yet also 'elements of a variety of European social-dance musics'.[24] It seems highly likely that its offbeat accents contributed to the development of ska. Another older form of people's music that has fed reggae is nyabinghi. This is the drumming used at Rasta rituals. It seems to have emerged as a specific style, and with a particular set of drums, towards the end of the 1950s. The most notable practitioner was Count Ossie whose group was based in a Rasta camp in the Wareika hills above Kingston. Nyabinghi was itself built on rural drumming idioms with strong African retentions.[25] Significantly for the present chapter, it has been constantly translated into reggae. The original 'Darker Shade of Black' riddim, for instance, has hand drumming which is strongly influenced by nyabingi.

These examples of 'folk continuity' in reggae bring out a key point about the hybridity at stake in Jamaican music making. Little heed is

---

[23] *Ibid.*

[24] K. Bilby, 'Jamaica', in P. Manuel, with K. Bilby and M. Largey, *Caribbean Currents: From Rumba to Reggae* (Philadelphia, PA: Temple University Press, 1993), p. 193

[25] *Ibid.*

paid to precepts of originality. Whether a musical trope derives from a notionally domestic or foreign culture is less important than the fact that it is woven into something which becomes 'ours' through the synthetic act of translation. However this suggests that the concept of collective indigenous ownership of reggae music by the Jamaican people is ultimately as unsustainable as the ownership of individual rights in specific reggae 'works'. The point is that the radically diverse provenance of reggae's sources, both oral *and* phonographic, simply doesn't fit current conceptions of 'indigenous culture'. In any event, as Joseph Githaiga argues,[26] enormous problems arise when one attempts to map existing forms of copyright law on to indigenous cultures, even when such a culture is clearly defined.

It appears, then, that reggae exists outside any recognisable political economic context. Its codes of social authorship, and the continuity between recordings and songs seem on the face of it to make this music a pariah form. Of course, institutions of copyright can perfectly well handle it when it is exported to the core of the world system. The huge revenues earned by Bob Marley's songs and recordings testify to this, not to mention the court cases in which ownership of the rights has been contested.[27] Still, the key point for the present argument is that in Jamaica, reggae's system of production has continued to break not only with principles of copyright, but also the economic logic which underlies it. The question is, then, if copyright is supposed to prevent free-riders from exploiting the all too copyable work of others, if it generates an incentive where none would otherwise exist, how can we account for the vitality of Jamaican music making?

A comparison with the production of open-source software may provide some answers. Here sophisticated computer programs (like Linux) are developed by geographically and organisationally separated programmers. These software designers not only work without a hierarchical structure of coordination, they use IP rights to invert notions of property so as 'to protect distribution and access rather than restrict access'.[28] Consequently, developers receive no remuneration in respect

---

[26] J. Githaiga, 'IP Law and the Protection of Indigenous Folklore and Knowledge', *Murdoch University Electronic Journal of Law*, 5(2) (1998) (accessed 28 March 2008, at: www.murdoch.edu.au/elaw/issues/v5n2/githaiga52nf.html).

[27] See for example, *Barrett* v. *Universal Island Records* [2006] EWHC 1009 (Ch.) [2006] EMLR (21) 567.

[28] T. Jordan, *Hacking: Digital Media and Technological Determinism* (Cambridge: Polity, 2008), p. 107.

of rights. As Steven Weber notes in an influential paper,[29] this raises three problems from the perspective of orthodox business models.

First is the issue of what might motivate individual programmers. Weber suggests it is the intrinsic interest and enjoyment in solving software design problems. This is supplemented by the desire to enhance one's reputation since a good piece of work will be acclaimed by other programmers in the software community. Lastly, there is a shared altruistic culture which helps to motivate individuals.[30] Overall, the economic logic is one where software becomes an 'anti-rival good'. Even ostensible free-riders contribute by reporting bugs, and the more people involved the greater their interest in achieving good software design.[31]

These motivational factors all apply to reggae, including the fact that reggae music can be seen as an 'anti-rival good'. Competing musicians and producers tend not to object to others using 'their' songs, sounds or riddims because they understand the result will be better music and a bigger market for everyone. That is to say, the more translators the better. We shouldn't take this argument too far though. There *have* been plenty of disputes over the ownership and use of musical materials from the early years of ska[32] to today when (probably as a result of Jamaica's new more vigorous copyright regime) disputes over riddims sometimes take a litigious turn.[33] What's more, whereas open-source programmers tend to have day jobs which sustain their 'hacking',[34] reggae music makers are often impoverished, belonging to the marginalised 'precariat'.[35] These caveats noted, the fact remains that, the parallels between reggae and open source regarding motivation are strong indeed. In each case, economic actors not only tolerate the open nature of the system, they recognise its centrality for their *modus operandi*.

The second problem raised by open source has to do with coordination. Weber reflects on why, at any given moment individual

[29] S. Weber, 'The Political Economy of Open Source Software', BRIE Working Paper 140 (2000), 5 (accessed 2 April 2008, at: http://economy.berkeley.edu/publications/wp/wp140.pdf).
[30] *Ibid.*, 25–7.   [31] *Ibid.*, 28–9.
[32] D. Katz, *Solid Foundation: An Oral History of Reggae* (London: Bloomsbury, 2003), pp. 41–3.
[33] Manuel and Marshall, 'The Riddim Method', 447–70.   [34] Jordan, *Hacking*, pp. 112–17.
[35] L. Wacquant, 'Territorial Stigmatization in the Age of Advanced Marginality', *Thesis Eleven*, 91 (2007), 66–77.

programmers, do not work on their own and pursue developments which lead away from the collectively produced code. One answer is that such 'forking' leads to a smaller audience and therefore lower potential acclaim. Another is that cultural norms of responsibility and leadership reinforce a congruent understanding of technical excellence.[36] Forking isn't such a critical issue in reggae because sideways moves (usually deriving from translation rather than intensification) are not merely tolerated, they may sometimes lead to successful aesthetic developments. Nonetheless, the factors Weber describes do have considerable force, and as a consequence reggae is an extremely coherent, well coordinated genre. In the terms we have been using here, reggae depends on strong 'social authorship'.

Third, Weber discusses the received wisdom according to which increases in the division of labour lead to decreases in efficiency as communication becomes more complex, and organisational structures have to be built in order to compensate for this. In open-source software development, however, 'modular design' tends to obviate these problems. As he puts it, '[a] large program works by calling on relatively small and relatively self-contained modules'.[37] Once again, there are uncanny parallels in reggae. Riddims are small units of musical code. Likewise vocal timbres, characteristic patterns of phrasing, metres ... All may be developed relatively discretely, yet easily combined in the meta-module that is the reggae record.[38]

The model of open-source software thus offers a highly illuminating way of conceiving the reggae mode of production. Nevertheless, it cannot account for the way the music realises exchange value at point of sale. Open-source products are sold on the basis of the consumer support that is provided for them rather than the software itself (the copyright protection of the GPL licence used by open-source programmers specifically precludes restrictions on copying). But reggae records are sold on 'their own'. How can this be so given the absence of copyright which might prevent those who are not the

---

[36] These values are enshrined in the GPL licence which specifically prohibits forking, Jordan, *Hacking*, pp. 107–12.
[37] Weber, 'The Political Economy of Open Source Software', 33.
[38] Interestingly, in one way copyright with its privileging of expression over function offers a higher level of proprietorial control over musical 'modules' rather than those found in software. That said, 'click-wrap' or 'shrink-wrap' agreements can effectively restore the copyright owner's grip over software functionality. Where copyright fails, contract steps in.

producers of a new record selling copies on free-ride terms?[39] One
answer is that producers often acquire proprietary control through
custom and convention, backed up by force or the threat of it. But
another factor is the sheer competitive advantage derived from coming
first to market.

We have already hinted at this. But the work of Michele Boldrin
and David Levine can help to explain what's at stake here.[40] The main
thrust of their argument is that all kinds of symbolic goods – the
objects of IP law – are actually much less different from non-symbolic
ones than is normally suggested. The writers confront the free-rider
argument by suggesting that in most markets significant 'first-mover'
advantages apply before IP is factored in. In effect, the original creator
is a monopolist up to the point that resellers are able to get their
hands on a copy of the artefact, tool up for replication and then
enter the market. Certainly, there will be competition at this point,
but – absent IP – sufficient returns over and above the 'opportunity
cost' of creation will already have been achieved on the part of the
originator.[41] This factor certainly applies in reggae, whose political
economy has been shaped by the imperative to be first in delivering
new sounds to the dancehall audience. More research is needed to
show distribution of revenue over the period of a record's release,
but it seems highly probable that most money is made in the very
early stages as a tune becomes acclaimed in the dancehall.[42]

As a corollary to first-mover advantage Boldrin and Levine point
to the negative effects of IP on innovation. What happens when
copyright is enforced is that costly and sometimes lengthy processes
of rights clearance have to be negotiated with damaging consequences
for innovation.[43] Imagine a situation in which clearances had to be
obtained for all riddims. This might not wipe out the riddim method,

---

[39] In fact, the new, and strengthening, copyright regime in Jamaica is now beginning to
result in the prosecution of piracy, Daley and Foga, 'Jamaica Beyond the TRIPs'.

[40] M. Boldrin and D. Levine, 'The Economics of Ideas and Intellectual Property',
*Proceedings of the National Academy of Sciences*, 102 (2005), 1252–6.

[41] *Ibid.*, 1254.

[42] True, in a digital environment of almost instantaneous copying and redissemination
first-mover advantage is reduced. But in such an environment copyright hardly works
either, or at least only for mainstream cultural products where makers and (sometimes
users too) opt into the copyright system. Increasingly the norm is one of free entitlement
to music in the digital domain.

[43] Boldrin and Levine, 'Economics of Ideas', 1255.

but it would almost certainly lead to atrophy.[44] Over the longer term, Boldrin and Levine highlight the problem of rent seeking which is endemic under any IP system. 'Monopoly creep' occurs as governments tend to respond to the lobbies of rights-owners and increase 'the scope and duration of monopoly power'.[45] In Jamaica the 1993 Copyright Act and the post-2000 creation of a state and para-statal copyright regime[46] indicate the international power of this lobby, given expression most recently through TRIPs. Arguably, and only time will tell, this new regime threatens the political economy of music in Kingston on which the extraordinary achievements of reggae music makers have been built.[47]

## Conclusion

I began by arguing that reggae music was premised on social authorship and the absence of copyright, albeit in a context of vigorous, petty-capitalist competition. In the last section I went further, suggesting that if reggae has flourished absent copyright, then perhaps there is something about it which is not merely idiosyncratic. Could it be that principles of the political economy of reggae have wider application? Research on open-source software,[48] and modelling of markets for symbolic goods without IP law[49] suggest that this is the case. In the reggae system of production strong collaboration, efficient coordination and complex creative processes – all features of open source – seem to be combined with a competitive market system. This is encouraging. It suggests that copyright's grant of monopoly might not be a necessity in market economies after all. Or to put it more facetiously: the pirates of the Caribbean turn out to be good neighbours and role models.

---

[44] In a similar situation, the free use of samples in hip-hop music in the US was controlled through a clearance system in the late 1980s. This drastically curtailed the use of samples by small-scale producers as well as leading to a shift towards 'softer' aesthetic norms, Toynbee, 'Copyright, the Work', 96.

[45] Ibid.    [46] Daley and Foga, 'Jamaica Beyond the TRIPs'.

[47] Though for an argument which makes the opposite case, in other words for the benefits of introducing a comprehensive IP regime in Jamaica, see D. Power and D. Hallenkreutz, 'Profiting from Creativity? The Music Industry in Stockholm, Sweden and Kingston, Jamaica', Environment and Planning (A), 34 (2002), 1833–54.

[48] Weber, 'The Political Economy of Open Source Software'.

[49] Boldrin and Levine, Proceedings.

# 19

## 'Free-riding on the riddim'? Open source, copyright law and reggae music in Jamaica

JOHNSON OKPALUBA*

Jason Toynbee asserts that reggae music would never have emerged had 'copyright proper' been enforced in relation to the commercial exploitation of music in Jamaica.[1]

Our starting point is the Imperial Copyright Act of 1911 ('the 1911 Act') which applied to colonies of the UK and was adopted in Jamaica in 1913.[2] A brief background to the 1911 Act in relation to the exploitation of music in the UK will serve to put that Act in context.

In the UK, in the nineteenth and early twentieth centuries, music publishing was an industry of small family businesses whose revenue centred on the sale of sheet music. Sheet music and live performances were the predominant mode of dissemination of music. At this time, music publishers 'showed little enthusiasm for the bothersome, costly, unfamiliar, and unpopular business of collecting fees for performances'.[3] In the late nineteenth century, the recording industry was in its infancy and its business was based upon the mechanical reproduction of music. Music publishers challenged this practice in a test case, and Stirling J. held that the unauthorised reproduction of musical works by mechanical instruments was not an infringement of copyright.[4] The subsequent

---

* The author would like to thank Professor Lionel Bently, Deadly Dragon Sound, Winston Francis, Steve Golding, Professor Jane Ginsburg, David Katz and Dr Jason Toynbee.
[1] See similarly, J. Boyle, *The Public Domain: Enclosing the Commons of The Mind* (New Haven, CT: Yale University Press, 2008) pp. 124–59, where Boyle questions whether jazz, blues, R&B, gospel and soul would have been possible as musical styles, if from their inception they had been covered by the strong property rights applied today.
[2] The administrative structure of Orders in Council allowed UK copyright law to be extended to the dominions and colonies, see ss. 25–28 of the 1911 Act.
[3] C. Ehrlich, *Harmonious Alliance: A History of the Performing Right Society* (Oxford University Press, 1989), p. 6.
[4] See *Boosey* v. *Whight* [1900] 1 Ch. 122.

boom in the recording industry, combined with sheet music piracy, left music publishers experiencing a serious downturn in sales of sheet music, which music publishers sought to redress by collecting fees for public performance of music which led to the establishment in 1914 of the Performing Right Society (PRS).

Following the Berlin Revision of the Berne Convention in 1908, rights-holders were granted control over the mechanical reproduction of their literary and musical works and this was adopted in the 1911 Act.[5] However, through effective lobbying, the recording industry among other things, managed to secure for itself a statutory exemption which enabled it to continue reproducing music mechanically without infringing copyright, by giving a prescribed notice and payment of a royalty to the right-holder. So once a work had been issued to the public, another version could be made of it, as long as royalties were paid and notice formalities were complied with.[6] In anticipation of the 1911 Act, the Mechanical Copyright Licensing Company Ltd was established in 1910, to collect and distribute mechanical royalties due from the new record companies. The UK music industry was sufficiently well organised to respond to changes in the consumption of music and relied on copyright to protect its interests.

Toynbee's suggestion that the reason that no infrastructure for the exploitation of music rights developed in Jamaica until relatively recently, lies in the leading role taken by Jamaican sound system operators in the early Jamaican music business, needs to be qualified. There was an infrastructure of sorts. The PRS had set up a local office in Jamaica in the 1930s. Its main task was to collect public performance fees, and return them to London for distribution. As well as collecting on behalf of UK members, it accepted local members and collected royalties on their behalf both locally and internationally.[7] Beyond the influence of the sound system operators, perhaps other reasons exist to explain the lack of a comprehensive infrastructure for exploitation of music rights.[8] First,

---

[5] For further background to the 1911 Act see, *Report of the Committee on the Law of Copyright* (1909) Cd. 4976. See also W. Boosey, *Fifty Years of Music* (London: Ernest Benn Limited, 1931),pp. 145–57.

[6] See Copyright Act 1911, s. 19(2).

[7] R. Wallis and K. Malm 1984, *Big Sounds from Small Peoples: The Music Industry in Small Countries* (London: Constable, 1984), pp. 163–215.

[8] Ironically, the lack of an adequate copyright environment and the lack of any direct involvement of the major record companies in Jamaica has meant that the vast majority of pre-1990s recordings and rights have been entirely appropriated by the global major

in the UK, copyright was necessary to encourage publishers to invest in music and record companies to invest in the manufacture and distribution of records.[9] Whereas, in Jamaica, musical traditions remained orally based until the era of sound recording and did not pass through the intermediate stage of printed music that was fundamental to the establishment of copyright norms in the UK.[10] Second, enforcing local copyright law was a low priority for a government struggling to maintain basic law and order.[11] Linked to this, is the fact that the domestic music industry in Jamaica with its roots in the ghettoes of Kingston, has traditionally been a part of the subculture of the Jamaican society previously associated with drugs, violence and anti-establishment counterculture, and this contributed to it not being accepted by mainstream Jamaican society.[12] Third, it could not have helped that the 1911 Act was directly imposed upon Jamaica and was thus not shaped or influenced by cultural traditions or lobbying interests.

When sound system operators began to record local musicians, they booked studio time, chose the performers and the songs and kept the resulting recordings as they had paid all the bills. When Coxsone Dodd set up his own recording studio in 1963, he recruited a nucleus of studio musicians and paid them a wage rather than paying them per tune recorded.[13] As for vocalists, where Coxsone entered into agreements, he would take an assignment of copyright in the vocalist's songs and be granted the right to exploit those songs, subject to a royalty payment.[14]

---

record companies with little or no revenue finding its way back to the original artistes or producers, see D. Power and D. Hallencreutz, 'Profiting from Creativity? The Music Industry in Stockholm, Sweden and Kingston, Jamaica', 34(10) (2002) *Environment and Planning (A)*, 1833, 1844.

[9] Under section 24(b) of the 1911 Act, any person who had before the 26 July 1910 incurred any expenditure or liability in respect of the reproduction or performance of a work which was lawful at the time, did not have to pay royalties.

[10] M. E. Veal, *Dub: Soundscapes and Shattered Songs in Jamaican Reggae* (Connecticut, CT: Wesleyan University Press, 2007), p. 91

[11] See P. Manuel and W. Marshall, 'The Riddim Method: Aesthetics, Practice, and Ownership in Jamaican Dancehall', *Popular Music*, 25(3) (2006), 447–70, 463, citing L. Mann, 'Intellectual property and the Jamaican music industry' (unpublished Master's thesis, London School of Economics, 2000).

[12] Despite Edward Seaga being one of the pioneers in the recording industry in Jamaica, when he became first a cabinet minister and later Prime Minister, he did nothing to further the development of the recording industry; see Z. Kozul-Wright and L. Stanbury, 'Becoming A Globally Competitive Player: The Case of the Music Industry in Jamaica' (1998) (at: www.unctad.org/en/docs/dp_138.en.pdf, last accessed 6 June 2009), 17–18.

[13] L. Bradley, *Bass Culture: When Reggae Was King* (London: Viking, 2000), pp. 99–100.

[14] A copy of a Studio One contract from 1969 is on file with the author.

Under Jamaican music industry practice, neither the original musicians nor even the song's composer had any further rights to their work once they had been paid for the original session.[15] Singers would be paid a one-off fee of between £10 and £20, and would not receive statements, regardless of whether the record made money or not.[16]

Under the 1911 Act, the author of the 'record' was the person who was the owner of the original plate at the time when such plate was made,[17] and this would be the financier of the recording session. As for the works contained within the record, the author was deemed to be the first owner of copyright therein, provided that where the author of a work was under a contract of employment or apprenticeship to some other person and the work was made in the course of his employment by that person, the person by whom the author was employed, owned copyright in the work unless there was an agreement to the contrary.[18] So, assuming the studio musicians were employees of Coxsone, he would own the copyright. If they were not employees, it is possible that he could have obtained assignments in writing.[19]

Under the 1911 Act, Jamaican authors would not have been able to avail themselves of moral rights because there were no moral rights provisions.[20]

---

[15] Bradley, *Bass Culture*, pp. 41–2. Coxsone set up one of the first music publishing companies in Jamaica, Jamrec Music.

[16] As Toynbee has noted artists often struggled to receive royalties. Deejay, U Brown who started recording in the mid-1970s, has said in relation to royalties, 'If you don't know nothing about those things, sometime you do a song for someone an' after they give you some money it's like you never go back to get any more. It's not until late, about late seventies going into the eighties that I start to realize that there should be a thing called "royalties". Some form of returns supposed to be coming from the song, from the sales of the record' (see I, P. Interview with U Brown, 'Mr Brown Somet'ing' (2005) (at: www.reggae-vibes.com/, last accessed 1 October 2009)). So producers would not only take advantage of artists by securing copyrights that they were not entitled to, they would also avoid paying artists. Unfortunately, such practices are not common to the Jamaican record industry. See S. Clarke, *Jah Music: The Evolution of the Popular Jamaican Song* (London: Heinemann Educational Books Ltd, 1980), pp. 73 and 159–72 for an account of the potential earnings and sources of revenue for reggae artists.

[17] Copyright Act 1911, s. 19(1).    [18] *Ibid.*, s. 5(1)(b).

[19] Pursuant to s. 5(2) of the 1911 Act, an assignment of copyright was not valid unless it was in writing.

[20] In 1977 there was an attempt to update Jamaican copyright law but the draft Copyright Act was deemed to be unsatisfactory, because it 'was silent on the rights of performers and the issue of moral right was never brought into force', see V. James (ed.), 'The Caribbean Music Industry Database 2000' (at: www.wipo.int/about-ip/en/studies/pdf/study_v_james.pdf, last accessed 6 June 2009), citing Dianne Daley, 'Legislation and Administration of Copyright and related Rights in Developing Countries', WIPO/CRR, 17 August 2000.

The Jamaican Copyright Act 1993 provides for the moral right to be identified as the author of one's work[21] and the moral right to object to derogatory treatment of one's work.[22] 'Derogatory treatment' in relation to a work means any addition to, deletion from, alteration to or adaptation of the work (not being a translation of a literary or dramatic work or an arrangement or transcription of a musical work involving no more than a change of key or register) which amounts to a distortion or mutilation of the work, or is otherwise prejudicial to the honour or reputation of the author.[23] In the context of the reuse of a riddim without consent – it is hard to see how this would be considered a derogatory treatment.[24] In any event, it is standard practice in recording/publishing agreements, to require artists to waive their moral rights. Assuming moral rights had been in force in Jamaica in the 1960s, it is submitted that they would not have had a material effect on the production of reggae music.

Toynbee states that 'translation' was a response to the need to constantly produce new 'record texts' and reuse of existing texts solved the problem.[25] Toynbee's examples of how copyrighted work elements were incorporated into reggae in the 1960s mirror musical practices from the earliest of times. Even the most celebrated classical musicians such as Beethoven, J. S. Bach, Handel and Brahms, were not averse to using themes, melodies, motifs and parts of earlier works, to create new works.[26] The very fact that musicologists use a number of terms to

---

[21] Copyright Act 1993, s. 14.

[22] These rights were introduced in the UK under the Copyright, Designs and Patents Act 1988.

[23] Copyright Act 1993, s. 15(4)(a).

[24] See though in the UK, *Confetti Records* v. *Warner Music UK Ltd* [2003] EMLR 790, where a moral rights claim was brought after a rhythm track had been licensed for use and a rap had been laid down on top of it. The author of the rhythm track claimed that his moral right of integrity had been infringed because the rap contained references to violence and drugs. The words of the rap were very difficult to decipher and there was no evidence of the honour or reputation of the author, which counted against the author and the judge dismissed the claim. Given the popularity in Jamaica of lyrics that involve sex, violence and drugs, a similar issue might arise.

[25] Between the mid-1950s and 2000, Jamaica produced over 100,000 recordings. With more than one new recording each year per thousand people, Jamaica could be, per capita, the world's most prolific generator of recorded music, see J. McMillan, 'Trench Town Rock: The Creation of Jamaica's Music Industry' (2005) (at: http://faculty-gsb.stanford.edu/mcmillan/personal_page/documents/Jamaica%20music%20paper.pdf, last accessed 26 June 2009), 2.

[26] See Clarke, *Jah Music*, pp. 20–1, for an account of how African slaves adopted an African and European tradition into their music and how this relates to contemporary Jamaican musical styles.

describe composers' use of existing works, such as borrowing, transformative, imitation, quotation, allusion, homage, influence and indebtedness, indicates the widespread nature of borrowing within music.[27]

The different types of translation that Toynbee describes have different implications for copyright law. The translation of stylistic traits as Toynbee acknowledges is generally acceptable under copyright law.[28] The 'cover version' which uses the same title but deviates far from the musical form of the original, may constitute an infringement of copyright, but the further it deviates from the original, the less likely it is to be an infringement. In the third type of copying that Toynbee illustrates, namely adoption of a whole song or melody, there could have been copyright infringement issues if no mechanical royalties were paid and no formalities complied with. However, as Jamaica was not a signatory to any international copyright conventions, Jamaican producers could freely copy songs.[29] Clearly not all reggae music produced in Jamaica was an illicit translation, and as Toynbee notes, institutions of copyright were able to handle reggae music when it was exported. This would have been critical, as Jamaican entrepreneurs as early as 1960, began to license tunes from Jamaica's top producers to sell in the UK.[30] Thus it is hard to

---

[27] O. Arewa, 'From J. C. Bach to Hip Hop: Musical Borrowing, Copyright and Cultural Context', NCL Rev., 84 (2006) , 547–645, 600–1. See generally, P. Burkholder, 'Borrowing', in *Grove Music Online. Oxford Music Online*(at: www.oxfordmusiconline. com/subscriber/article/grove/music/52918pg1, last accessed 23 August 2009).

[28] In the UK, see *Coffey* v. *Warner/Chappell Music Ltd* [2005] FSR 34, where the claimant claimed that the allegedly infringing work had copied the vocal expression, pitch contour and syncopation of or around the words of the lyrical hook 'does it really matter', in her song. The court decided that these performance aspects were not sufficiently separable from the song so as to be a musical work in their own right, and taken as a whole they did not amount to a substantial part of the claimant's work.

[29] Although Toynbee correctly points out that label copy on Jamaican singles in the 1960s was minimal in terms of information, Studio One recordings invariably always featured the name of the publisher, Jamrec Music on the label. For scanned images of Jamaican record labels from the 1960s see generally www.dancecrasher.co.uk/blog (last accessed 1 October 2009). Veteran reggae artist, Winston Francis, states that initially label copy in Jamaica was based on copying US record labels without any real understanding of publishing (personal interview July 2009). See also R. Nelson, Transcript of interview with Clinton Fearon (1999) (at: www.niceup.com/interviews/clinton_fearon_KRCL, last accessed 26 June 2009), where Clinton Fearon suggests that writing credits were simply included on label copy to make the records look legal and important, but producers didn't really register the rights.

[30] See generally M. De Koningh and M. Griffiths, *Tighten Up: The History of Reggae in the UK* (London: Sanctuary, 1989), for an account of the history of reggae music in the UK.

support Toynbee's contention that reggae would not have emerged had copyright been enforced.

Toynbee describes the 'riddim' as 'perhaps the most graphic example of the way that social authorship operates at a complete tangent to the norms of copyright law' and is, according to Toynbee, a response to the need to continually produce records for the Jamaican market. Indeed, it seems that economic necessity was one of the reasons which helped the emergence of the riddim in Jamaica. In late 1971 or early 1972, the Jamaican government put a restriction on the price a record producer could sell a pre-release record for and passed a law stating that the maximum price a record could sell in the shops for was seven shillings and sixpence, the price of a normally released record.[31] As session musicians were able to command higher fees, some producers did not find it economical to record new music and as they did not have to pay additional session fees, reused riddims with a different vocal over the top. Record producer Rupie Edwards contends that the downturn in the record business stopped creativity because no money was being put back into making music and nobody could afford to experiment too much.[32]

The most common form of 'illicit translation' of a domestic record, would most likely take the form of reuse of another person's riddim, a practice which started in the early 1970s, after the emergence of reggae both locally and internationally. The reaction of local producers suggests that they were far from tolerant of others using their songs. For instance, in the early 1970s when Coxsone was made aware that Channel One studios were using his old riddims and giving them a thoroughly contemporary make-over, to keep up, he resorted to redoing his own riddims in a more modern contemporary style.[33] Coxsone would also record his own version of Channel One songs and release them before Channel One.[34] It is noteworthy that Coxsone wholeheartedly endorsed the

---

[31] Bradley, *Bass Culture*, p. 334. See Clarke, *Jah Music*, p. 61 where the author explains in detail the retail of records in Jamaica.

[32] Bradley, *Bass Culture*, p. 334. Producer, Bunny Lee, has said that he could not afford to pay musicians and made minor adjustments to old rhythms to make them new: see S. Brooks, 'Striker Gets His Due', *Jamaica Gleaner*,26 October 2008 (at: www.jamaica-gleaner.com/gleaner/20081026/ent/ent5.html, last accessed 23 August 2009).

[33] D. Katz, *Solid Foundation: An Oral History of Reggae* (London: Bloomsbury Publishing plc, 2003), p. 217.

[34] *Ibid.*, pp. 163–7, 226–7.

introduction of the Copyright Act 1993,[35] and thereafter began to pursue vigorously those who had used his riddims without permission.[36]

The model of open-source software production has been offered as an alternative to the copyright paradigm by those who critique what is in their view, the overarching reach of copyright and its negative effects on innovation and creativity.[37]

Toynbee considers that the production of open-source software offers a highly illuminating way of conceiving the reggae mode of production. While the production of both open-source software and reggae music challenges the romantic notion of a solitary author of an artistic artefact, they are not alone in this and it has been apparent for some time that the 'romantic' notion of the author does not equate with creative practice. We need to take care though, because the widespread circulation of riddims has given rise to a number of superficial impressions, one of which is that of a pool of riddims serving as a creative commons, supported by an anti-materialistic Jamaican willingness to share.[38] According to Toynbee, the willingness to share is derived from recognition that openness is central to the political economy of reggae. However, this is contradicted by the views of many musicians and producers, who appear only willing to share if compensated and bemoan the lack of creativity involved in the reuse of riddims.[39]

The claim that creators of open-source software do it for reasons contrary to normal markets has been questioned, as many of the

---

[35] Coxsone Dodd interviewed in B. Jahn and T. Weber, *Reggae Island: Jamaican Music in the Digital Age* (New York: Da Capo Press, 1998), p. 235.

[36] See 'Time to Pay', *Jamaica Gleaner*, 23 July 2000 (at: www.jamaica-gleaner.com/gleaner/20000723/Ent/Ent1.html, last accessed 23 August 2009). It has been suggested that Coxsone allowed infringement of his works because he was aware of the disquiet among vocalists and musicians who accused him of not paying advances or regular royalties; see D. Howard, 'Copyright and the Music Business in Jamaica: Protection for Whom' (2008) (at: www.revistabrasileiradocaribe.org/DennisHoward.pdf) (last accessed 6 August 2009), 11.

[37] See e.g., S. Weber, 'The Political Economy of Open Source', *Berkeley Roundtable on the International Economy* (2000). Paper BRIEWP140 (at: http://repositories.cdlib.org/brie/BRIEWP140) (last accessed 26 June 2009); E. Moglen, 'Anarchism Triumphant: Free Software and the Death of Copyright', *First Monday*, 4(8) (August 1999) (at: http://firstmonday.org/htbin/cgiwrap/bin/ojs/index.php/fm/article/view/684/594) (last accessed 6 October 2009) and L. Liang, 'Copyright, Cultural Production and Open-Content Licensing', *Indian Journal of Law and Technology*, 1 (2006), 96–157.

[38] P. Manuel and W. Marshall, 'The Riddim Method: Aesthetics, Practice, and Ownership in Jamaican Dancehall', *Popular Music*, 25(3) (2006), 447–70, 462.

[39] See e.g., interviews with Judy Mowatt, Chalice, Sly Dunbar, Jah Screw and Gussie Clarke in Jahn and Weber, *Reggae Island*, pp. 98–231.

individuals providing the bulk of the work are supposedly paid to do so by large corporations.[40] These large corporations may benefit from the possibility of selling complementary goods, such as hardware, support contracts or advertising.[41] Consequently, it is not so clear that the parallels between open source and reggae regarding motivation are strong at all. The motives are myriad and perhaps more involved and complex than Toynbee portrays.[42]

Toynbee states that in open-source software development, the problem of increases in the division of labour leading to decreases in efficiency can be obviated by modular design. For Toynbee, there are uncanny parallels with reggae, as he perceives riddims to be small units of musical code. This parallel is not convincing for several reasons: first, music is not put together in the same manner as software; second, these small units of musical code may be too basic to be protected by copyright; and third, elements such as vocal timbres, phrasing and metre are not of themselves copyright subject matter.[43]

Toynbee's suggestion of first-mover advantage being the mechanism by which music would realise exchange value at point of sale is problematic, as records are uniformly priced and can be almost instantly copied, thus providing very little lead time at all.[44] In Jamaica, one day is not an uncommon time for new riddims to be widely copied by other artists and made available to the market.[45] While Toynbee accepts that first-mover advantage is reduced in the digital environment, he argues that in the digital domain copyright hardly works as the norm is one of

---

[40] Large corporations such as Hewlett Packard, IBM and Sun have launched projects to use and develop open-source software; see J. Lerner and J. Tirole, 'The Scope of Open Source Licensing' (2006) (at: www.people.hbs.edu/jlerner/OSLicense.pdf) (last accessed 6 October 2009).

[41] S. Liebowitz and R. Watt, 'How to Best Ensure Remuneration for Creators in the Market for Music? Copyright and its Alternatives', *Journal of Economic Surveys*, 20 (4) (2006), 513–45, 529.

[42] For an indication of what motivates programmers, see J. Lerner and J. Tirole, 'The Simple Economics of Open Source' (2000) (at: www.hbs.edu/research/facpubs/workingpapers/papers2/9900/00-059.pdf ) (last accessed 6 October 2009), 14–20.

[43] See *Coffey* v. *Warner/Chappell Music Ltd* [2005] FSR 34 discussed above at n. 28.

[44] First-mover advantage was originally considered by Arnold Plant specifically in relation to book publishing, where he questioned the need for any type of legal protection system; see A. Plant, 'The Economic Aspects of Copyright in Books', *Economica*, 1 (1934), 167–95. In relation to riddims, it would be interesting to test the so-called competitive advantage of coming first to market, with evidence of the success or otherwise of later versions that have reused an original riddim.

[45] Power and Hallencreutz, 'Profiting', 1845.

free entitlement to music.[46] Toynbee endorses the view that the corollary of this is that if copyright is enforced, it will lead to a situation of costly rights clearances which negatively impact on innovation, and if applied to riddims, would lead to atrophy. As support for his thesis, Toynbee refers to the clearance of digital samples in the US,[47] however, the two situations are readily distinguishable.

While hip-hop music was still an underground phenomenon, artists didn't really clear samples, except where obvious.[48] When, in 1991, a US Federal court found against a hip-hop artist who had used an unauthorised sample,[49] it was thought that the decision would 'kill hip-hop music and culture'.[50] Hip-hop artists wanting to use samples, risked being sued for copyright infringement if they failed to clear the samples. The limitation on hip-hop artists' use of samples is neatly exemplified by the group Public Enemy. Public Enemy's second and third albums, *It Takes A Nation of Millions to Hold Us Back* and *Fear of a Black Planet*, released in 1988 and 1990 respectively, are widely regarded as two of hip-hop music's greatest albums. Both albums heavily utilise sampling. Chuck D, of Public Enemy, also part of Public Enemy's production team, the Bomb Squad, describes their attitude towards recording tracks:

> We approach every record like it was a painting . . . We used about 150, maybe 200 samples on 'Fear of a Black Planet'. 'Fight the Power' has, like, 17 samples in the first ten seconds . . . Our music is all about samples in the right area, layers that pile on each other. We put loops on top of loops, but then in the mix we cut things away.[51]

---

[46] This does not provide an adequate explanation as to how music would realise exchange value at point of sale.

[47] See generally, P. DiCola and K. McLeod, *Creative License: The Law and Culture of Digital Sampling* (Duke University Press, NC, forthcoming 2010) for an interdisciplinary approach to the problems of sample licensing which pays close attention to history, culture, technology, media, the law and the economy.

[48] Hank Shocklee, a member of Public Enemy's production team said that in 1987 when he was producing the album *It Takes a Nation of Millions to Hold Us Back* that '[t]he only time copyright was an issue was if you actually took the entire rhythm of a song, as in looping'; see K. McLeod, 'How Copyright Law Changed Hip Hop', *Stay Free*, 20 (2002) (at: www.stayfreemagazine.org/archives/20/public_enemy.html, last accessed 6 June 2008).

[49] *Grand Upright Music Ltd* v. *Warner Bros. Records, Inc.* 780 F. Supp. 182 (SDNY 1991). See the more recent decision of *Bridgeport Music, Inc.* v. *Dimension Films* 383 F.3d 390 (6th Cir. 2004) where the court stated 'Get a license or do not sample'.

[50] S. Vaidhyanathan, *Copyrights and Copywrongs: The Rise of Intellectual Property and How It Threatens Creativity* (New York University Press, 2003), p. 143.

[51] See M. Dery, 'Public Enemy Confrontation', *Keyboard* (1990), 81, 92. Cultural critic, Greg Tate, has described the Bomb Squad's reconstructive composition of new works from archival bites as advancing sampling to the level of microsurgery ('The Devil Made

By the time, Public Enemy's fourth album, *Apocalypse 91* was released in 1991, their sound had radically changed. This change was a direct result of the fact that it would have proved too costly to sample as they had done on their previous albums.

So, strict enforcement of copyright law has not stopped the production of hip-hop music, it merely changed the sound of hip-hop and altered creative opportunities for some artists by making it more expensive to produce using samples. In some instances though, it has caused artists to become more innovative and can lead to interesting artistic opportunities.[52]

In contrast to this ad hoc sample clearance process, Jamaica has a compulsory licence system for music, which is broadly similar to the compulsory licence in the US, and makes the reuse of riddims possible without needing clearance.[53] Since 1999, the Jamaican Association of Composers, Authors & Publishers Limited (JACAP) has administered mechanical royalties. Currently, where an artist wants to reuse a riddim, the practice is that the author of the riddim will receive a share in the publishing of any derivative work. This share is usually a minimum of 25 per cent, but can be negotiated in excess of this figure, to a maximum of around 33 per cent. JACAP has yet to start collecting mechanical royalties in Jamaica, but due to arrangements with other collecting societies, the copyright owner of the riddim will be paid mechanical royalties in other territories.[54] Although it seems that the mechanics of this compulsory licence are still being fine-tuned, it goes some way to making works freely available at what may eventually be a statutorily regulated rate. Of recent times, many more artists and producers in Jamaica have become aware of the benefits for them of copyright and now take greater care to

---

'Em Do It: Public Enemy', in G. Tate, *Flyboy in the Buttermilk* (New York: Simon & Schuster, 1992), p. 126).

[52] DiCola and McLeod, *Creative License*, pp. 207–8. See generally at pp. 152–3, where it is suggested that a digital divide has been created between those who can afford to sample and those who cannot; see also K. McLeod, *Freedom of Expression: Overzealous Copyright Bozos and other Enemies of Creativity*(New York: Doubleday, 2005), pp. 62–113; D. K. Henning, 'Rappers Sorrow, or How Copyright's Restriction on Digital Sampling Inhibits African-American Participation in Societal Discourse' (2008) (at: http://works.bepress.com/darrin_henning/2, last accessed 6 June 2009); and E. Steuer, 'The Remix Masters' (2004) (at: wired.com/wired/archive/12.11/beastie.html, last accessed 1 October 2009) where Mike Diamond of the Beastie Boys explains the difference in making sample-based music in 2004 as opposed to in the 1980s.

[53] Copyright Act 1993, s. 77.

[54] Telephone interview with Steve Golding, Chairman of JACAP, 5 October 2009.

negotiate royalties and to register their works with the relevant collecting societies.[55]

The relationship between copyright and innovation is at the very heart of Toynbee's chapter. Copyright is said to provide incentives to create and disseminate the expression of ideas. Toynbee highlights the fact that copyright played no role as an economic incentive in encouraging the production of reggae music in Jamaica. We should not be surprised by this, as even in the core states of the world system authors were creating works long before any system of intellectual property rights was in place. It is evident that copyright could not act as an incentive to those that were not aware of it,[56] but if there had been an effective copyright regime in Jamaica, we do not know that it would not have acted as an incentive. It has been suggested that recent generations of those involved in the music business in Jamaica are overwhelmingly in favour of the international model of musical production and copyright as it tends to secure much higher rewards for them.[57] Absent copyright, it is not disputed that music will still be created, but given the capitalist base of the music industry, questions remain as to what incentive there would be to fund, market and promote new works.

Open-source software is distributed under a series of public licences, and although reliant on copyright law, open source is promoted as an alternative to the copyright paradigm. The GNU Public Licence or GPL is one of the most well known of the open-source licences and was designed to limit the ability of software developers to commercialise modifications to the code by: (a) insuring that any derivative works remain subject to the same licence and; (b) by prohibiting the mixing of open- and closed-source software in any distributed works. If the author of a piece of open-source software were to relinquish their copyright, it would mean that anyone could use their code and create a derivative work and then license it as a proprietary piece of code, thereby

---

[55] Manuel and Marshall, 'Riddim Method', 464. When the PRS closed its office in Jamaica in 1998 it had 1,100 members; membership of JACAP currently stands at just under 1,800 (personal interview with Steve Golding 5 October 2009).

[56] Not enough is known of the general awareness of copyright law of those involved in the recording industry, although it is clear that producers became more aware of copyright than the artists who recorded for them and were able to exploit this. For instance, singer Max Romeo started off in the music business in Jamaica in 1965 and despite having a number two hit in England in 1969, and touring the UK and Europe on the strength of that hit, knew nothing about publishing until he became a member of the PRS in Jamaica in 1970 or 1971, see I P., 'It Sipple Out Deh' (2005).

[57] Power and Hallencreutz, 'Profiting', 1845.

preventing others from using the software in a free manner.[58] Clearly, enforceable rights in the form of copyright are vital to maintaining the integrity of open-source works.[59]

While the open-source model has made a significant impact on the computer software industry, it would be fair to say that it has not caught on in the same way in the production of music. This may be for a number of reasons. First, as the model of open-source software rests, among other things, on the assumption that the original work becomes far more valuable as many add their own contributions, it may be that production of music using the open-source model is suited to certain types of artists, and not to others, equally it may well be suited to certain types of music and not to others.[60] Second, from the authors' perspective, one has to question the desirability of not having the right to prevent or authorise derivative works, which in turn raises issues of moral rights, and the unauthorised distortion of works. Finally, it may simply be that many artists are reluctant to subscribe to the open-source model because of the lack of any direct monetary reward.

As portrayed by Toynbee, the production of reggae music in Jamaica and open-source software raise interesting questions concerning copyright law as it is and copyright law as it should ideally be. However, the economics of the production of music is not the same as the economics of the production of software – and it does not readily fit into the open-source model. Even if the production of reggae music did at one time provide a paradigm example of collective innovation and social authorship, what else we can learn from it in terms of copyright law and market economies, remains an open question.

---

[58] L. Liang, 'A Guide to Open Content Licences' (2004) (at: http://pzwart.wdka.hro.nl/mdr/research/lliang/open_content_guide, last accessed 26 June 2009), 30.

[59] Where the rights under a licence are violated, authors will still have to rely upon copyright law to enforce their rights, as exemplified in *Jacobsen* v. *Katzer* 535 F.3D 1373 (Fed. Cir. 2008) where a copyright holder's claim for copyright infringement was upheld when he sued the defendant for non-compliance with the terms of the GPL Artistic Licence.

[60] See Liang, 'Guide to Open Content', 71–6 for detail on open music licences.

# PART XI

Criminology

# 20

# Copyright infringement: a criminological perspective

LORAINE GELSTHORPE

## Introduction

This chapter explores copyright infringement via Internet piracy as a new 'crime'[1] of the twenty-first century, it outlines some of the limitations of traditional criminological theorizing about the causes of crime, and suggests that this new 'crime' has to be seen in the context of late modernity. Late modernity has brought with it new technology and a whole host of social transitions which perhaps blur conventional moralities, thus making Internet piracy much less of a 'crime' (in some people's eyes) than it would hitherto have been seen.

As David Wall and others have suggested, the introduction and extension of the Internet represents a seismic shift in social life.[2] Criminologists have perhaps been slow to recognize that new forms of computer-mediated communication may be contemporary vehicles for criminality. Moreover, where there has been interest, the critical gaze of criminologists and socio-legalists has generally been directed

---

[1] I should at once make it clear that I am referring to 'crime' in its broadest sense here and not exclusively to criminal liability for copyright infringement. I am thus referring to 'crime' in a non-technical legal sense, to mean unlawful act. At the same time, elements of the chapter refer to 'crime' as a social construction. My intention is to convey here that 'crime' is an ideological category, a violation of moral codes, sometimes a social harm, and not just an act punishable by law (i.e. criminal law violation). For further discussion of the concept of 'crime' from a criminological perspective, see J. Muncie, 'The Construction and Deconstruction of Crime', in J. Muncie and E. McLaughlin (eds.), *The Problem of Crime* (2nd edn, London: Sage, in assoc. with the Open University 2001).

[2] D. Wall (ed.), *Crime and the Internet* (London: Routledge, 2001), D. Wall, *Cybercrime. The Transformation of Crime in the Information Age* (Cambridge: Polity, 2007), M. Yar, *Cybercrime and Society* (London: Sage, 2006), and Y. Jewkes (ed.), *Crime Online* (Cullompton: Willan Publishing, 2007).

towards the creation of hyper-criminal networks,[3] fraud (including 'phishing'),[4] the dissemination of hate-related propaganda,[5] stolen identities,[6] cyber stalking[7] and the extension of paedophile networks,[8] with the latter tending to dominate media interest. Wall[9] has suggested that there are now three generations of cybercrime: first, *traditional or ordinary crimes using computers*, second, *hybrid cybercrimes* whereby computer technology has created entirely new global opportunities, and third, *true* cybercrimes which are solely the product of the Internet. I am concerned with the second and third category of crimes, and I take music piracy as my prime example of copyright infringement in this chapter. I do this not least because it is one of the most common forms of Internet-related crime, and in light of recent publicity and debates about the effect of Internet piracy on music sales[10] and debates about effective forms of intervention.[11]

In order to understand why copying and distributing music downloaded from the Internet may be considered a form not only of illegal but also of *criminal* activity, it is of course important to establish what is meant by such terms as 'piracy', 'intellectual property' and 'copyright'. Other chapters in this volume explore such concepts in depth; suffice to say here that although settling on a precise definition of piracy is difficult,[12] IP laws concern 'intangibles' such as ideas, inventions, signs, information and expression, as opposed to laws covering 'real' property concern rights over 'tangibles'. 'Piracy' thus amounts to

---

[3] D. Mann and M. Sutton, 'Netcrime: More Change in the Organisation of Thieving', *British Journal of Criminology*, 38(2) (1998), pp. 210–29.

[4] See D. Wall, *Cybercrime. The Transformation of Crime in the Information Age* (Cambridge: Polity, 2007).

[5] Wall, *Cybercrime*.

[6] E. Finch, 'The Problem of Stolen Identity and the Internet', in Y. Jewkes (ed.), *Crime Online* (Cullompton: Willan Publishing, 2007), pp. 95–108.

[7] M. Wykes, 'Constructing Crime: Stalking, Celebrity, "Cyber" and Media', in Jewkes, *Crime Online*, pp. 128–43.

[8] M. Taylor and E. Quayle, *Child Pornography: An Internet Crime* (London: Brunner-Routledge, 2003), and Jewkes, *Crime Online*.

[9] Wall, *Cybercrime*.

[10] See, for instance, M. Peitz and P. Waelbroeck, 'The Effect of Internet Piracy on Music Sales: Cross-Section Evidence', *Review of Economic Research on Copyright Issues*, 1(2) (2004), 71–9, and International Federation of the Phonographic Industry (ifpi), *Recording Industry in Numbers 2009* ([place of publ. not indicated], 2009) (see: www.ifpi.org/content/section_news/20100428.html).

[11] Wall, *Crime and the Internet*, Wall, *Cybercrime*; K. Tagaris, 'UK Says Illegal Downloaders May Lose Web Access' (Associated Press, 2009).

[12] Bently and Sherman, *Intellectual Property*.

the unauthorized copying and distribution of copyrighted content. As the IP Crime Group point out: 'Piracy involves the illegal copying of content such as music, film, sports events, literary works, broadcasts, computer games and software for commercial gain. Copyright infringement also includes illegal copying and downloading of digital content.'[13]

Having set out the issues in this way, I now discuss the expansion in the illegal downloading of material in terms of the activity being perceived to be 'free and easy'. I then turn to the limitations of traditional criminological perspectives, and argue, instead, that we need to recognize the moral ambiguity surrounding the activity of music piracy in late modern culture. This leads to two conclusions. The first concerns a perceived need to take an educative approach; the second concerns the need to question why it is that music piracy is so 'demonized' and 'criminalized' and whose interests are being protected and promoted in the initiatives taken.

### Free-and-easy crimes

Notwithstanding that crime has undoubtedly increased in advanced industrial countries since the 1950s, it is clear that in England and Wales there are notable dips too.[14] This said, crime in western societies remains unacceptably high. Indeed, the music industry appears to be faced with an unprecedented crime wave since the technological advances of recent years have brought with them capacity to copy from CDs, and obtain protection-free copies of music from the Internet.

MP3 technology[15] has been heralded as the music lover's dream; it has grown in popularity and is alleged to now compete with 'sex' as the most queried keyword on search engines across the World Wide Web – in 2000.[16] The ifpa[17] annual report points out that music companies have embraced technological change and that new services

---

[13] IP Crime Group, *2008–2009 IP Crime Report* (Newport: IP Crime Group, 2009), p. 6.

[14] M. Maguire, 'Crime Data and Statistics', in M. Maguire, R. Morgan and R. Reiner (eds.), *The Oxford Handbook of Criminology* (Oxford University Press, 2007), pp. 241–301.

[15] MP3 audio files are the most popular form of digital music compression technology. Other forms include: Windows Media Audio (.wma), and Free Audio Lossless Codec (.flac), itunes (.m4a, m4p) and Ogg Vorbis (.ogg), but for purposes of simplicity, MP3 technology is used here as a shorthand to refer to all digital music.

[16] S. Hinduja, *Music Piracy and Crime Theory* (New York: LFB Scholarly Publishing LLC, 2000).

[17] ifpi, *Recording Industry*; see above, n. 10.

to users are being created: à la carte downloads, listen to free streamed music, and access to music videos or music as part of ISP subscription or mobile phone purchase. New technology has granted free, unrestricted access to songs by huge numbers of musicians, past and present. It has allowed individuals to amass enormous collections of digital music files, provide these files to others, make custom audio CDs of favourite tracks, and transfer them onto portable players. The technology has also spawned massive virtual communities in Internet chat rooms, message boards, newsgroups and other cyber-venues – in existence solely for the purpose of distributing MP3s. It has also facilitated burgeoning dot.com businesses in terms of capitalizing on the profitability and marketability of this method of distributing audio over the Internet.

However, it seems that until recently, illegal MP3s have been uploaded and downloaded with relative impunity. According to the Recording Industry Association of America[18] music piracy in the form of counterfeit and bootlegged recordings on physical media cost the record industry $5 billion a year in the mid-1990s, with $1million lost each day in the USA. More recently, the International Intellectual Property Alliance reported that piracy of US-copyrighted materials results in $420–22 billion in losses to rights-holders.[19] Illegal exchanges of digital music files over the Internet are exponentially more difficult to track, though we might imagine the amount of revenue lost to musicians and record companies if their music is repeatedly circulated over the Internet without their consent. Jupiter Research 2007[20] suggests that in the UK market alone, the music industry lost £180 million and will lose more than a £1 billion pounds by 2012 if nothing is done. Putting this another way, it can be argued that digital businesses are an important part of Britain's economy both in terms of gross domestic product (GDP) and as an employer. Figures from UK Trade and Investment suggest that the creative industries generated 8.2 per cent of the UK GDP in 2007. Support for the importance of the industry comes from the Digital Britain Interim Report[21] which

---

[18] RIAA (Recording Industry Association of America) '531 more file sharers targeted in latest RIAA efforts' (at: www.riaa.com/news/newsletter/021704.asp) (2004).

[19] IIPA (International Intellectual Property Alliance) 'Statistics' (at: www.iipa.com/copytighttrade_issues.html) (2006).

[20] Cited in ifpi, *Recording Industry*; see above, n. 10.

[21] Department for Culture, Media and Sport and Department for Business, Enterprise and Regulatory Reform *Digital Britain Interim Report* (London: Department for Culture, Media and Sport, January 2009).

indicates that it accounts for over 1.9 million jobs in the UK. Indeed, even in 2006 the annual British software Alliance and International Data Corporation Global Software Report stated that a 10 per cent reduction in piracy in the UK would generate 30,000 jobs and contribute £11 billion to the economy.[22] (See also the IP Crime Group Report, 2009 for further discussion of costs and job losses.)

This said, it is possible that any figures on costs and lost revenue should be treated with some suspicion, not least because they may be based on the assumption that every time someone illegally downloads music the record company has lost a sale. Ben Goldacre, noted *Guardian* critic of 'bad science' has certainly drawn attention to wildly exaggerated figures about costs, and errors in the arithmetic employed by journalists if not in the original research.[23] There is certainly strong suggestion of a 'spiral of amplification' in all of this.

Who are the 'offenders'? Recent statistics suggest that peer-to-peer file sharing (P2P, which produces the most Internet traffic) accounts for a good deal of illegal downloading. In the US 18 per cent of users aged 13 and over used P2P services in 2008; in Japan, 10 per cent of Internet users file-shared in 2008; in Europe, 16 per cent of Internet users regularly swap music on P2P, while in the UK 15 per cent of users frequently file-share.[24] Unlawful file sharing is seemingly most popular among young consumers. As the IFPI annual report[25] indicates, 'While 16% of the general internet population in Europe file-share on a regular basis, among the 15–24 year olds this figure jumps to 34%. This is three times the proportion of 15–24s consuming music via legitimate a la carte services'.[26] In the UK 37 per cent of file-sharers are aged 16–24 and more than 70 per cent are aged under 35 (Harris Interactive/BPI).[27]

The findings of a UK Government Crime and Justice Survey in 2003 reported that 9 per cent of people over 18 years old had admitted to committing 'technology offences'.[28] More recently, a Home Office compendium of statistics on fraud and technology crimes drawn from

---

[22] See also IP Crime Group, *2008–2009 Report*, for further discussion of costs and job losses.

[23] B. Goldacre, 'Illegal Downloads and Dodgy Figures', *Guardian*, 5 June 2009.

[24] ifpi, *Recording Industry*; see above, n. 10.     [25] *Ibid.*     [26] *Ibid.*, at p. 14.

[27] Cited in *ibid.*

[28] T. Budd, C. Sharpe, G. Weir, D. Wilson and N. Owen, *Young People and Crime: Findings from the 2004 Offending, Crime and Justice Survey*, Home Office Statistical Bulletin 20/05 (London: Home Office, 2005).

the British Crime Survey (an annual survey of some 45,000 house-
holds), the 2004 Offending, Crime and Justice Survey and administrative sources, suggests that 26 per cent of 10–25-year-old Internet users
had illegally downloaded software, music or films in the previous
twelve months.[29] Moreover, just over one-third (36 per cent) of those
who committed illegal downloading had done so on three or more
occasions. Male Internet users were more likely to report having
illegally downloaded software, music or films (33 per cent) compared
with females (19 per cent).[30] Young adult Internet users were more
likely than children to report this activity (31 per cent compared with
20 per cent).

A major factor in explaining the growth in Internet piracy is of
course the rapid expansion in the Internet itself. In 2003 there were an
estimated 605 million Internet users.[31] In June 2008, the figure was
estimated to be over 1 billion,[32] with over 400 million users in Europe
alone.[33] The growth of broadband Internet access in particular enables
users to download quickly large quantities of digital content in com-
pressed format. In the UK alone over 50 per cent of all adults had
broadband at home in 2007 (39 per cent in 2006).[34]

There have been recent moves to make 'offenders' who are illegally
downloading material to settle upfront and out of court or to otherwise
take out civil law suits against them. The Recording Industry
Association of America (RIAA), for example, began legal actions
against US citizens in June 2003[35] targeting university campuses in
particular where peer-to-peer file sharing is perhaps rife. Once
revealed, individuals are offered a discounted settlement at an RIAA
website P2P Lawsuits.com – failure to comply at that stage means that
the case goes forward. In one case which reached the national press in

---

[29] D. Wilson, A. Patterson, G. Powell, R. Hembury, *Fraud and Technology Crimes. Findings
from the 2003/04 British Crime Survey, the 2004 Offending, Crime and Justice Survey and
administrative sources*, Home Office Online Report 09/06 (London, Home Office, 2006).
[30] *Ibid.*
[31] NUA Internet Statistics 'How Many Online?' (at: www.nua.ie/surveys/how_many_online/)
(2003).
[32] Pingdom statistics (at: www.pingdom.com/services/-) (2008).
[33] World Internet Usage Statistics News and World Population Statistics 2008, dated
17 Aug, 2009 (at: www.internetworldstats.com/internet.htm).
[34] Ofcom, *Prosecution Statistics 2006–2007* (at: www.ofcom.org.uk/media/new/2007/04/
nt_20070401 (2007).
[35] A. Webb, 'Can Filesharers Be Made to Pay?', *Guardian*, 22 March 2007.

the UK, in 2007, single mother Jammie Thomas had damages of $220,000 (£108,000) awarded against her following her reluctance to settle out of court, and her challenge to large record companies in the USA.[36] Indeed, at the retrial on 19 June 2009 the jury awarded $1.92 million in statutory damages against Thomas.[37] In June 2009 another mother faced a £4,000 request for compensation from solicitors acting for the music industry after her 14-year-old daughter was caught illegally downloading songs by her favourite artists.[38] Moreover, there are now active debates in the UK about the possibility of denying Internet access to those who repeatedly download copyrighted music and films. Other countries have already enacted similar laws.[39] There is governmental recognition that plans to restrict users' broadband speed would not go far enough to deter music piracy and that tougher measures are needed.[40]

Whatever the precise dimensions of the problem of illegal downloading and file sharing (and perhaps the true dimensions remain as a dark figure of crime), the phenomenon has caused and is causing great consternation. How can these illegal actions best be explained? That it is 'free and easy' is perhaps only a partial answer. Traditional criminological perspectives appear to be rather limited in helping us understand the phenomenon, however.

### A criminological perspective: 'piracy' and theories of crime

What motivates or impels individuals to do this? Do certain dispositions or inclinations differentiate participants from non-participants? Put simply, are offenders acting entirely out of choice or free will and thus culpable and rightly called to account for their actions, or are offenders less volitional in that their choices are shaped by contemporary notions of crime and morality? Certainly, definitions of crime are problematic and crime cannot be extricated from its social, political

---

[36] 'Single Mother Jammie Thomas Fined $220,000 for Music File Sharing', *Guardian*, 5 October 2007. (It should be noted that the reference to a 'fine' is inaccurate; as above, strictly speaking the matter concerned 'damages' awarded against her.)

[37] See, e.g., http://artsbeat.blogs.nytimes.com/2009/06/19/woman-fined-192-million-for-music-piracy/?scp=1&sq=jammie%20Thomas%20damages%202009&st=cse.

[38] 'Mother Faces Music for Girl's Illegal Downloads', *Guardian*, 21 June 2009 (at: www.guardian.co.uk/technology/2009/jub/21/arts.netmusic).

[39] See David Lefranc's contribution to this volume (Chapter 4).

[40] Tagaris, 'UK Says Illegal Downloaders May Lose Web Access'.

and cultural context.[41] Is the theft of intellectual property a crime? A sin? Injurious activity? Harmful? Morally wrong? Is the language of 'crime' even appropriate to describe the phenomenon of music piracy? For the moment I take four examples to explore the potential and limitations of criminological theorizing to explain music piracy[42]:

> Example 1: Individual theories (psychological or biological theories) range from consideration of genetics, physical factors, biochemical factors, personality (and personality disorder or dysfunctioning), intelligence and mental disorder. Essentially, the theories revolve around individual characteristics or qualities that might explain criminal tendencies. But while these theories have been seen to be important in the history of the development of criminology as a discipline, it is now widely recognized that the complexities of definitions of crime are matched by the complexities of attributing crime to a matter of individual factors. The more serious crimes, of course, may be accounted for by biomedical imbalances and mental disorder, but for the most part it is acknowledged that individual characteristics may only trigger offending behaviour in interaction with environmental factors. In sum, biological theories as a general theory of crime have been out of vogue for some time. In regard to genetics it is unclear as to the importance of 'nature' as opposed to 'nurture'-based factors. Moreover, it is accepted that while everyone has a 'personality', it is difficult to predict criminal behaviour by studying psychology and personality.[43] Music 'piracy' is evident in all age groups (though more popular in younger age groups), in diverse social groupings, and more generally in all walks of life where there is access to technological developments. There is no evidence at all to suggest that those who engage in music 'piracy' have any particular individual characteristics that would help explain 'piracy'.
>
> Example 2: Strain theory (a sociological theory) essentially argues that people are more likely to engage in crime if they cannot get what they want via legitimate channels. Put simply, they become frustrated or angry, strike out at others in anger or try to gain what they want through illegitimate means. Robert Merton[44] developed the first theory of strain in his attempt to understand crime in the USA as a response to individuals' frustration in not being able to achieve the culturally approved goals of material wealth. Do feelings of strain or dissonance play a role in music

---

[41] N. Christie, A Suitable Amount of Crime (London: Routledge, 2004).

[42] They are presented in simplistic form since I am using them as heuristic devices in this context to point to the limitations of theories of crime. More sophisticated versions of these and other theories may be found in R. Hopkins Burke, An Introduction to Criminological Theory (Cullompton: Willan Publishing, 2001), and T. Newburn, Criminology (Cullompton: Willan Publishing, 2007).

[43] K. S. Williams, Textbook on Criminology (Oxford University Press, 2004).

[44] R. K. Merton, Social Theory and Social Structure (New York: Free Press, 1949).

piracy as a 'crime'? It would be hard to sustain this argument perhaps since the commonplace response is that 'everyone does it' or because you can do it with little chance of getting caught.[45] Apart from the evidence to suggest that music piracy is a youthful phenomenon, there is little to suggest that it is engaged in by particular social classes or occupational groups more than others, and nothing to suggest that educational qualifications or geographical area or employment rates demarcate differences between those who do illegally download and those who do not. (That said, one has to be well-enough off to have the proper equipment and broadband access to engage in significant levels of P2P copying.)

*Example 3: Social learning theory* (a social–psychology theory linking individuals with their environment) maintains that to understand behaviour it is necessary to account for the reciprocal relationship between the person and his or her surroundings or context. Social learning theorists incorporate the role of cognition into explanations of behaviour (going beyond mere observations of how people interact with their environment).[46] Again, put simply, it is thought that behaviour can be shaped through an individual's experience of the rewarding or punishing consequences, contingent on their actions that are delivered by the environment. Thus the question here is whether individuals engage in music piracy because others do and because in some way their (illegal) actions are reinforced or rewarded. The problem here, however, is that although there may be peer-to-peer sharing of music files (thus interaction and reinforcement), this does not explain the downloading in the first place which may be a very private act. This said, social learning theory holds at least some interest for us here because offenders usually need to be in a particular frame of mind for offending to take place. This involves elements such as attitude, moral standards, feelings for and about other people and ideas of responsibility. It is arguable that if attitude is learned from others (parents in particular, but peers too), then an attitude which accepts illegal activity (including music piracy) may be absorbed. It is very likely that young people know more about downloading music than their parents, however, and that peers may lie either in mutual ignorance or see the practice of illegal downloading as a widespread cultural practice which they do for 'kicks',[47] a point to which I shall return in due course. There is also the issue of comparative moral reasoning insofar as people may excuse their own behaviour if they are aware of more heinous acts by others and which remain unpunished (or seemingly lightly punished). Linked to this is

[45] S. Furnell, *Cybercrime: Vandalizing the Information Society* (Boston, MA: Addison-Wesley, 2002).

[46] A. Bandura, *Social Learning Theory* (New York: General Learning Press, 1977).

[47] M. Yar, 'Teenage Kicks or Virtual Villainy? Internet Piracy, Moral Entrepreneurship and the Social Construction of a Crime Problem', in Jewkes, *Crime Online*, pp. 95–108.

a desire to believe that their acts are not very harmful by saying that the victim can do well without the goods illegitimately taken from them; this is particularly easy if it is a large corporation or a rich individual, or someone covered by insurance.[48]

*Example 4: Critical criminology.* Other criminologists would be more critical and would question what counts as 'crime' anyway; at least, what counts as crime beyond the legal definition of an illegal act – which is in any case arguably limited in telling us what matters to people in terms of 'public harm'. Critical criminologists are far more interested in who has the power to label 'this' behaviour rather than 'that' as crime, and how behaviours and activities have come to be seen as 'crime' over time. The 'New Criminologists' for example,[49] inspired by Marxist thinking, argued that crime was a response to state oppression through capitalism. Thus 'crime' in this perspective is to be found less in particular individual circumstances and environmental conditions, but more through relations of power and selective processes of criminalization. This means that we need to look at crime at particular social, political and historical junctures, and at who is doing the labelling of any set of people as 'criminals'. This perspective also has resonance for our understanding of music piracy in that an emphasis on power relations endorses the idea that 'offenders' may not empathize with victims perceived to be 'rich' (such as music companies). It also has resonance in the way that music piracy itself has over the past few years become 'criminalized' (that is, socially constructed as a 'crime').[50]

But none of these explanations on their own provide an adequate understanding of music piracy.

*Example 5: A general theory of crime.* Even the much vaunted 'general theory of crime' which strives to explain all criminal actions has its limitations. In Gottfredson and Hirschi's model[51] it is stable, underlying

---

[48] K. S. Williams, *Textbook on Criminology* (Oxford University Press, 2004).

[49] I. Taylor, *et al.*, *The New Criminology: For a Social Theory of Deviance* (London: Routledge & Kegan Paul, 1973).

[50] That is, seen to be an ideological category of censure *as well as* an illegal act in this context. Elsewhere in this chapter of course I suggest that music piracy is *not* seen as a crime, and that that is perhaps part of the problem, but here, in consideration of any contribution that 'critical criminology' might make to our understanding of the phenomenon of music piracy, there is emphasis on power relations, the power of one group over another to denote certain behaviours as 'crime'. One perception is that powerful music companies have created 'music piracy' to protect their own interests. Needless to say, matters are more complex than this, and music piracy has an impact on all creators and producers of music, large companies and individuals, rich and poor. This is why any 'critical criminology' perspective is limited in its contribution.

[51] M. R. Gottfredson and T. Hirschi, *A General Theory of Crime* (Palo Alto, CA: Stanford University Press, 1990).

individual differences – 'persistent heterogeneity' – that provides the basis for explaining offending over the life course. At the heart of their 'general theory' of crime is self-control and concern for the long-term consequences of one's acts.[52] It is self-control that allows us to resist temptation, including the temptation of criminal opportunity. (Their theory covers a range of behaviours, including smoking, promiscuity and alcohol misuse, as well as criminal behaviour.) But this theory not only focuses on males who offend rather than females and thus misses out half the population,[53] it does not explain *all crimes* at all. Heralded as one of the most important contributions to criminology in years, later critics have questioned whether or not Gottfredson and Hirschi's[54] contribution really helps explain white-collar (or corporate) crime. Moreover, what helps explain crime among the young may not be relevant to an understanding of the same crime among older offenders.

While some criminologists would undoubtedly be interested to test various hypotheses relating to the relevance of these theories to an understanding of music piracy – since that is de rigueur within the field – it is not at all clear that this is the appropriate direction in which to go. Rather, and drawing on the insights of Yar,[55] I want now to first outline particular challenges which I think music piracy poses for criminologists, and then, second, to examine music piracy as a 'grey area crime'.

## Challenges to criminologists

The emergence of technological crimes such as music piracy arguably poses particular challenges to existing criminological perspectives insofar as the familiar problems of measuring crime are exacerbated.[56] Limited police resources and the prioritization of both public and private policing on other illegal activities means that intellectual property theft is left for the music industries and other rights-holders to pursue. Offenders remain anonymous and hidden, with massive under-reporting, under-detection and under-recording. Rapid technological developments also lead to circumvention or evasion of the law.

---

[52] T. Hirschi and M. R. Gottfredson, 'In Defense of Self-Control', *Theoretical Criminology*, 4(1) (2000), 55–69, 64.

[53] F. Heidensohn, 'Gender and Crime', in M. Maguire, R. Morgan and R. Reiner (eds.), *The Oxford Handbook of Criminology* (2nd edn, Oxford University Press, 1997).

[54] Gottfredson and Hirschi, *General Theory*.     [55] Yar, *Cybercrime*.

[56] M. Maguire, 'Crime Data and Statistics', in Maguire *et al.*, *Oxford Handbook*, pp. 241–301.

The 'crime' of music piracy also exhibits structural and social features that diverge considerably from conventional settings. As indicated, the first such challenge is the challenge of 'who' is actually doing it. Conventional criminological theories have sought to understand why it is that some individuals engage in criminological behaviour and others do not. Official statistics (based on police returns to central government alongside volumes of research evidence)[57] demonstrate that crime is both spatially and *socially* located. In other words, notwithstanding general observations about the limitations of criminological perspectives regarding understandings of music piracy, the profile of offenders in general shows a preponderance of those with certain shared characteristics. One such characteristic has been the overrepresentation among known offenders from socially, economically, culturally and educationally marginalized backgrounds. There are clearly intergenerational factors also which can compound matters for some in these circumstances who might be considered to be at risk of offending.[58] However, when it comes to music piracy, our understanding of who the offenders are breaks down.

The third challenge for criminologists concerns the problem of 'where'. A good deal of criminological theorizing has been based on ecological assumptions. That is, criminologists have viewed crimes as being associated with particular places: disorganized communities,[59] 'slums', the 'city', the neighbourhood, the large-scale, run-down housing estate.[60] Moreover, 'routine-activities' approaches focus on how potential offenders are able to identify target crimes by converging space and time, thereby creating the conditions for offending.[61] Music piracy can perhaps be viewed as anti-spatial. It can take place anywhere as long as there is access to the Internet.

---

[57] See, for example, the successive volumes of M. Maguire, R. Morgan, R. Reiner (eds.), *The Oxford Handbook of Criminology* (Oxford University Press, 1994, 1997, 2004 and 2007, 1st, 2nd, 3rd and 4th edns).

[58] D. P. Farrington, 'Childhood Risk Factors and Risk-Focused Prevention', in Maguire *et al.*, *Oxford Handbook*, pp. 602–40.

[59] C. R. Shaw and H. D. McKay, *Juvenile Delinquency and Urban Areas* (University of Chicago Press, 1942).

[60] A. E. Bottoms, 'Place, Space, Crime And Disorder', in Maguire *et al.*, *Oxford Handbook*, pp. 528–74.

[61] L. E. Cohen and M. Felson, 'Social Change And Crime Rate Trends: A Routine Activity Approach', *American Sociological Review*, 44 (1979), 488–608.

## Music piracy as a grey area 'crime'

It would seem obvious to most people that crime, unlawfulness and morality are closely linked. The criminal statistics of any given country are often described as its 'moral barometer' and indeed, echoes of that view can be clearly discerned in the political and media responses whenever governments publish their latest crime figures.

Needless to say, there have been some critical questions in this area. Criminal law textbooks rightly caution against forging oversimplistic conceptual links between crime and morality. There are a number of acts that might be regarded as immoral, for example, but which are not illegal. Equally, it may not be immoral for a starving person to steal food, but it is certainly illegal. Such caveats are important perhaps, but they do not limit the assertion that crime and morality are linked.

Thus the key question of when a 'crime' may not be perceived to be a crime reflects the moral ambiguity surrounding the activity of music piracy. As Yar reports,[62] a number of studies worldwide have found very high levels of what is known as 'soft lifting' (downloaded copyrighted software from the Internet) among college and university students. Little weight has been attached to legal and moral objections.[63] A Canadian study of young people in 2004 found that 47 per cent of 12–21-year-olds intended to 'download music, video or software from the internet over the next six months'.[64] The common argument here was that music companies are rich and would not be harmed by downloading material. (There is a parallel argument which is often used in relation to stealing (shoplifting) from major supermarket chains such as Sainsbury and Tesco where 'offenders' can see no harm.)

As well as posing questions about why people might engage in music piracy (and how they might justify this to themselves and others), it is useful to take a different approach and to consider why it is that people obey the law. Anthony Bottoms,[65] among others, has written

---

[62] Yar, *Cybercrime*.

[63] R. Kini, H. Pamakrishna and B. Vijayaraman 'An Exploratory Study of Moral Intensity Regarding Software Piracy of Students in Thailand', *Behaviour and Information Technology*, 22(1) (2003), 63–70.

[64] J. Jedwab, 'The Lowdown on Music Downloading in Canada: Youth Regard Internet Downloading of Music, Video and Software as Acceptable: Only Threat of Legal Action is Effective Deterrent' (at: www.acs-aec.ca/Polls/18–10–2004–1.pdf (2004), 1.

[65] A. E. Bottoms, 'Compliance and Community Penalties', in A. E. Bottoms, L. Gelsthorpe and S. Rex (eds.), *Community Penalties. Change and Challenges* (Cullompton: Willan Publishing, 2001), pp. 87–116.

extensively about compliance and under what circumstances people obey the law.[66] *Normative compliance* (compliance linked to moral factors) is often seen to be the ideal form of compliance (as opposed to *instrumental compliance* for example which relies on threats of punishment or punishment itself, or *constraint-based compliance* – which relies on physical limits to participation in crime, neither of which are particularly effective in the long term).[67] As Bottoms[68] suggests, there are perhaps three types of normative compliance: (a) compliance resulting from acceptance of or a belief in a social norm; (b) compliance resulting from a social bond (attachment to a significant other or group); and (c) legitimacy (compliance resulting from obedience to the wishes of a recognized legal or social authority, that person or body being recognized as legitimate). It is arguable that the extensive and pervasive social changes of the last half-century have probably, in Britain, weakened all three sub-types of normative compliance as a result of increased moral individualism). Finally, what has been described as the 'democratisation of social and cultural life' (or the decline of deference) means that contemporary authority figures must typically work much harder than their predecessors to achieve legitimacy.[69] I expand on some of these points below in order to move us closer to a contemporary criminological understanding of music piracy.

## Copyright infringement in late modernity: the importance of culture

Indeed, in an attempt to understand music piracy it is useful to put this 'new crime' in context and to pose some questions as to whether the activity is perceived to be 'crime' at all. This leads to critical observations which revolve around the social transformations which have taken place in the past fifty years or so, the period which is commonly referred to as 'late modernity'. [70]

---

[66] See also T. R. Tyler, *Why People Obey the Law* (New Haven, CT: Yale University Press, 1990).

[67] See A. von Hirsch, P.-O. Wikström and E. Burney, *Criminal Deterrence and Sentence Severity* (Oxford: Hart Publishing, 1999).

[68] Bottoms, 'Compliance'.

[69] R. Sennett, *Respect. The Formation of Character in an Age of Inequality* (London: Allen Lane, 2003).

[70] 'Modernity' might be taken to mean the social transformation which emerged out of industrialization. 'Late modernity', by contrast, might be taken to mean the period since

The social transformations that we have witnessed in Britain (and indeed other industrialised countries) since the 1950s include economic, technological and 'social' (family- and community-related) changes. The decline of manufacturing and the rise of the service industry, and the emergence of a technologically driven society, increased mobility and changes in the structure of the family all feature here.[71] In similar vein, sociological analyses of late modernity include consideration of changes in the sources of 'trust' and the growth of 'ontological insecurity' in society (i.e. fundamental insecurity).[72] At the risk of oversimplification, sociologists note that a 'risk society' has emerged in response to the erosion of localized trust which was previously embedded in kinship relations in settled communities. For Ulrich Beck:

> Risk may be defined as a systematic way of dealing with hazards and insecurities induced and introduced by modernization itself. Risks, as opposed to older dangers, are consequences which relate to the threatening force of modernization and its globalization of doubt.[73]

While the focus of key sociological authors in this area lies primarily on 'high consequences risks' of environmental degradation, nuclear proliferation, and so on, the 'risk thesis', as such, is that as societies have become more fragmented, there is a need to work harder to calculate risks in order to deal with life's contingencies. There is a notable pursuit of security.[74] Mary Douglas, for example, has argued that in contemporary culture it is the language of risk that provides a 'common forensic vocabulary with which to hold persons

---

the 1950s – as we move towards postmodernity (a state in which all certainties, concepts and practices become open to scrutiny and change). Postmodern architecture, for example, represents an inversion of the expected – with service pipes exposed on the outside of a building rather than inside and hidden (as in the Pompidou Centre in Paris). Postmodernity has connections with a position of relativism, however, and we are not there yet, as a culture. Hence the term 'late modernity' is used in the context of this introduction to denote a focus on some of the empirical (and observable) transformations presently taking place.

[71] A. H. Halsey (ed.) with J. Webb, *Twentieth-century British Social Trends* (Basingstoke: Macmillan, 2000).

[72] A. Giddens, *The Consequences of Modernity* (Oxford: Polity Press, 1990).

[73] U. Beck, *Risk Society: Towards a New Modernity* (London: Sage, 1992), p. 21.

[74] L. Zedner, 'The Pursuit of Security', in T. Hope and R. Sparks (eds.), *Crime, Risk and Insecurity* (London: Routledge, 2000), pp. 200–14, and L. Zedner, 'Securing Liberty in the Face of Terror: Reflections from Criminal Justice', *Journal of Law and Society*, 32 (2005), 507–33.

accountable'.[75] In this process the notion of risk is 'prised away' from its moorings within probability calculations, and becomes a cultural keyword with much wider reference to debates about social life, accountability, crime, punishment, and so on.

In other words, moments of intense controversy or recrimination crystallize societal anxieties and expose lines of division about the competence, trustworthiness and legitimacy of the authorities. The culture of risk is thus transposed into a 'culture of blame'.

The emphasis on blame here is perhaps mirrored in the rise of individualism, with its associated hedonism, consumerism and emphasis on 'individual rights'. While modernity might be said to have opened up what Giddens[76] calls the 'project of the self', this extends to the way in which market economies promote individualism and individual rights. Self-identity, Giddens[77] suggests, has to be created and more or less continually reordered against a background of shifting day-to-day life experiences and the fragmentary tendencies of modern institutions. Email, video links and other technological changes, for example, serve to unify the experience of individuals. By contrast, our experience is dislocated by the diversifying contexts of human interaction (way beyond families and communities). Moreover, feelings of powerlessness are engendered by the increasing scale of the social universe, the deskilling effects of abstract systems[78] and concerns about the sources of authority. Tradition (reflected in religion and local community and kinship systems, for example) as a prime source of authority has been replaced by an indefinite pluralism of expertise.

Finally, there is the issue of personalized versus commodified experience.[79] Here the narrative of the self is constructed in a context of consumption (all shaped by capitalist market economies). Market-governed freedom of choice (in relation to the use of key services – hospitals, schools, and so on – as well as commercial purchases) becomes an enveloping framework for individual self-expression and from this we see the emergence of a rights-based culture. Writing about the new stakeholding society in Britain for instance, Will Hutton[80] describes

---

[75] M. Douglas, *Risk and Blame: Essays in Cultural Theory* (London: Routledge, 1992), p. 22.
[76] A. Giddens, *Modernity and Self-Identity* (Cambridge: Polity Press, 1991).   [77] *Ibid.*
[78] That is, the negation of local knowledge and control in favour of expert systems, which leads to alienation.
[79] S. Strasser (ed.), *Commodifying Everything* (London: Routledge, 2003).
[80] W. Hutton, *The Stakeholding Society. Writings on Politics and Economics* (Cambridge: Polity Press, 1999).

how the politicians have succeeded in creating a new language in which choice and individual rights have become the overwhelmingly dominant values, rather than responsibility, mutuality or obligation and social duty. Even without this political framing of the issue, there is a need to recognize that people have become vocal in asserting their rights. Beyond the assumed importance of choice such thinking is epitomized in 'me first' thinking and in the 'compensation' or 'personal injury' culture.

Even without sociological analyses, many of us can probably identify with something that Robert Putnam[81] has described as the 'decline of social capital'. In *Bowling Alone* he describes how we have become increasingly disconnected from one another; informal connections of civil society (through churches, social clubs and local political activism) have largely disintegrated (though there are notable exceptions of course).[82] Other social commentators have observed similar trends (see, for example, Richard Sennett's *Corrosion of Character*[83] and Zygmund Bauman's *Liquid Love*);[84] the very titles give clue to the erosion of commitment, loyalty in the job market, and our fastening onto short-term relationships instead.

Late modernity then is arguably 'a distinctive pattern of social, economic and cultural relations' which has 'brought with it a cluster of risks, insecurities and control problems that have played a crucial role in shaping our changing response to crime'.[85] There are 'distinctive problems of social order that late modernity brings in its wake'.[86] These macro-level changes in society have arguably not only profoundly affected social and cultural life, but have shaped crime and morality (and crime policies also). While policies are not the subject of discussion here, it is nevertheless relevant to refer to the neglected aspect of the 'return of the victim' in political criminal justice

---

[81] R. Putnam, *Bowling Alone: The Collapse and Revival of American Community* (New York: Simon & Schuster, 2000).

[82] Internet chat rooms suggest quite the opposite, but perhaps it is important to distinguish between 'Internet' links, conversations and attachments, and other more direct social interactions.

[83] R. Sennett, *Corrosion of Character. The Personal Consequences of Work in the New Capitalism* (New York: W. W. Norton, 1999).

[84] Z. Bauman, *Liquid Love* (Oxford: Polity, 2003).

[85] D. Garland, *The Culture of Control. Crime and Social Order in Contemporary Society* (Oxford University Press, 2001), p. viii.

[86] *Ibid.*, p. ix.

discourse. Hans Boutellier,[87] moves us on from the description of the emergence of the victim-based movement found in Garland's[88] analysis to suggest that a focus on the victim in political and public arenas is becoming a key component of contemporary morality. That is, 'the victim' is presented as someone we can all identify with and thus serves as a touchstone for morality – a value base. But if the 'victims' are multinational companies (music companies included) there is much less identification. Indeed, analyses of late modernity would suggest that as 'the rich get richer and the poor get poorer'[89] and with the prospect or the uncertain threat of the humiliation of poverty and social exclusion, there is 'late modern vertigo'[90] and a profound fear of falling, and thus the way is cleared for brute individualism and shifting moralities (notwithstanding the fact that peer-to-peer networks may actually create communities). The idea of music on the Internet, as intellectual property, neither has legitimacy nor commands respect. The dizzying heights of late modernity, set individuals in free fall, 'living for the moment' and taking what is accessible and seemingly free. The many challenges of late modernity or 'liquid life', as sociologist Zygmunt Bauman[91] has put it, thus include a flow of crime and transgression as it seeps across traditional categories of crime and morality. In this sense, it is not just crime and morality which are inextricable, but crime, morality and culture.[92]

Social transformations and the coming of late modernity challenge traditional conceptions of crime; the traditional questions are perhaps an irrelevance. There is no one story to be told of crime. Stories of crime are now fragmented or 'pot-pourried'. The late modern world is altogether a much less certain world, a provisional world. It is a world much less dominated by generalities and 'master narratives' than hitherto.

Constituent criminologists argue that crime is 'co-produced' by individuals and the society in which they live.[93] In late modern

---

[87] H. Boutellier, *Crime and Morality. The Significance of Criminal Justice in Post-modern Culture* (Dordrecht: Kluwer Academic Publishers, 2000).

[88] Garland, *Culture.*

[89] Halsey, *Twentieth-century British Social Trends.*

[90] J. Young, *The Vertigo of Late Modernity* (London: Sage, 2007), p. 13.

[91] Bauman, *Liquid Love.*

[92] J. Ferrell, K. Hayward, W. Morrison and M. Presdee, *Cultural Criminology Unleashed* (London: Glasshouse, 2004) and J. Ferrell and C. R. Sanders, *Cultural Criminology* (Boston, MA: Northeastern University Press, 1995).

[93] S. Henry and D. Milanovanovich, *Constitutive Criminology* (London: Sage, 1996).

society – this means that 'grey area' offenders are rational consumers ... just like us. Crime is a normal, common aspect of modern living.[94] Copyright infringement reflects technological developments and changing patterns of social interactions and participation in social life, as well as a new culture of rights, consumerism, choice, and so on. In this sense, music piracy is a 'crime' which has become a risk to be calculated by offender and potential victim, rather than a deviation from civilised conduct caused by individual pathology or faulty socialization – the hallmark of traditional criminology. Instead, it is an outcome of normal social interaction.

## Concluding reflections

One of the most notable features of Internet piracy is its seeming ubiquity; it spans all social classes and walks of life (with a preponderance of young people being involved). And as a number of consumer surveys points out, there is little stigma to music piracy or indeed other forms of Internet piracy.[95] But this is changing. Yar[96] offers some interesting insights here in noting how the language of copyright violations is changing. The very use of the term 'piracy' he argues, serves as a rhetorical device to moralize copyright infringement as a 'serious crime'. Moreover, forging a link between copyright violations and 'organized crime' enhances the moral and emotional case against the activity. The increasing involvement of national policy bodies and reference to Internet violations as 'fraud' legitimate the conception and perception of the activity as 'crime'.[97] Indeed, Yar[98] suggests that the process of labelling Internet violations as 'crime' parallels other (and earlier) sociocultural processes of criminalizing activity driven by 'moral entrepreneurs' (most notably in Cohen's 1972 influential study *Folk Devils and Moral Panics*).[99] Thus the recasting of illegal copying reflects an attempt to create a normative consensus that it is harmful, in contrast to the ubiquity which has suggested that it is socially acceptable. Tough measures to enforce a

---

[94] J. Lea, *Crime and Modernity* (London: Sage, 2002).
[95] See IPSOS Online software piracy poll (at: www.ipsos-na.com?news/pressrelease.cfm?id=2452 (2004), and I. Thomson, 'Britain Becoming a Nation of Pirates' (at: www.crn.vnunet.com/news/1157189) (2004)).
[96] Yar, *Cybercrime*.  [97] Yar, 'Teenage Kicks', p. 102.  [98] Yar, 'Teenage Kicks'.
[99] S. Cohen, *Folk Devils and Moral Panics. The Creation of the Mods and Rockers* (London: MacGibbon and Kee, 1972).

new normative consensus will play their (limited) part, but insights drawn from work on why people obey the law lead us to the need for an educational approach as well. There is much evidence that music companies and copyright industries are already aware of this however and there are various campaigns aimed at schoolchildren ('Play It Cybersafe' and 'Copyright Kids' included) which emphasize the moral meanings and effects of music piracy. But there is also at least some evidence of cultural resistance (with musicians lauding pirate fans and wishing their music to be distributed as widely as possible, whatever the means or legitimacy of those means).[100]

In this chapter I have raised some questions about the potential contribution of conventional criminology to an understanding of the phenomenon of music piracy. Having found conventional criminological theories wanting, I turned to the insights to be drawn from analyses of the impact of late modernity, and the importance of recognizing connections between 'crime', morality and culture. There are other questions to ask, of course: how 'piracy' has come to be criminalized and how 'piracy statistics' on losses are calculated for instance (and whose interests are being protected in those calculations). While the emergence of Internet piracy as a 'crime problem' depends very fundamentally upon the assumption behind the legal facts that people can, and ought, to have property rights in relation to the expression of ideas, it is no longer clear whether the public still subscribes to it. But this may be based on the false understanding that it is only 'large and powerful' music companies who are affected by infringement, when this is not the case. Moreover, the substantial jury awards made by ordinary citizens in the USA P2P civil actions suggest that the 'disconnect' between the legal conclusion and social sentiment may be less extensive than the popular press has sometimes

---

[100] I. Escolar (2003) 'Please Pirate My Songs', in *WSIS World Information: Knowledge of Future Culture* (Vienna: Institut für Neue Kulturtechnologien). Since developing an interest in this area, I have monitored daily 'Google alerts' regarding music piracy on the Internet. While this source of information cannot be said to be reliable, there is at least a suggestion that some artists are in favour of piracy because it advertises their music. Musicians such as Radiohead, Blur and Pink Floyd have all been referred to as 'complacent' in relation to illegal file sharing, if not active supporters of it. They have also been criticized for this, having made their money in a climate where illegal file sharing was significantly more difficult. But it should be acknowledged that the music world is fast changing, and arguments which seem in favour of piracy one day, may amount to mild ambivalence the next.

imagined. There is thus a clear role for an educational campaign which emphasizes that 'victims' are not necessarily large multinational companies, but that they include the solo composer and musician whose livelihood depends on royalties, and in this way the modern moral maze of music piracy may be clarified.

# 21

# Towards a clearer understanding of the file-sharing phenomenon? Comments on a criminological perspective

SHIRA PERLMUTTER*

Loraine Gelsthorpe in her contribution to this volume (Chapter 20) explores copyright infringement on the Internet as 'a new crime of the twenty-first century'. She notes the pervasiveness of the phenomenon, and seeks to apply theories of criminology to explain what motivates it. She concludes that conventional criminological theories cannot provide a satisfactory explanation for the phenomenon, which she characterises as a 'grey area crime', one marked by moral ambiguity. Instead, she turns to the insights to be drawn from analyses of the impact of late modernity, or the social transformations that have taken place since the 1950s.

In her view, the normative compliance that ideally provides reasons to obey the law (based on the acceptance of social norms, social bonds or the legitimacy of authority), has been weakened in the UK and elsewhere in the last fifty years. She sees an increased moral individualism and relativism, and the 'democratization of social and cultural life', or a decline of deference. As a result, authority figures today must work harder to achieve legitimacy. In addition, the emergence of a 'risk society' in late modernity has led to an environment where tradition is replaced by a pluralism of expertise, and the emergence of a rights-based culture where the dominant values are choice and individual rights. She describes as a key component of contemporary morality a strong focus on 'the victim' – and the problem is that there may be little sympathy for the victim here, perceived as rich multinational corporations.

---

* Executive Vice President, IFPI, London. The views expressed in this article are those of the author and do not necessarily represent those of IFPI.

Gelsthorpe's analysis indicates that many of the factors at play extend well beyond the copyright realm, and that illegal behaviour is generally more likely to thrive in the modern world's relative absence of traditional constraints founded on normative compliance and respect for authority. She outlines the dimensions of online infringement, based on data from multiple sources,[1] and examines how it is perceived by members of the public in an effort to find more satisfactory explanations for the prevalence of this behaviour.

My comments will start with some observations from a technical legal perspective, and then seek to evaluate the motivations behind this consumer behaviour and the implications for an appropriate societal response. I will keep to the same ground as Gelsthorpe's chapter in exploring the reasons for mass online infringement, as conduct that is clearly illegal under current law. While as she indicates, there are broader policy questions that may arise, relating to the continued acceptance of copyright as a property right and whether the law should change to make the behaviour permissible, these questions go beyond the scope of her thesis and I will not address them here.

## General observations

As a preliminary matter, one factor that may contribute to the misfit of conventional criminological theories is that copyright infringement is not necessarily a crime, and is not likely to be perceived as criminal in nature by private actors engaged in non-commercial activity. While Gelsthorpe refers to 'crime' in a broad non-technical sense to mean 'unlawful act', copyright infringement may not fully lend itself to the same analysis as other forms of illegality typically addressed by these theories.

In most cases, copyright infringement is a tort, involving harm to another person's legal rights (economic and/or moral). A closer analogy therefore may be to trespass, misappropriation or libel – and it could be difficult to explain by criminological theories why perpetrators are impelled to engage in such conduct. On the other hand, infringement may be seen as similar in some respects to burglary or theft, as conduct that society has defined as a violation of law because of the damage

---

[1] In doing so, she raises questions about how 'piracy statistics' are calculated, but these questions relate more to the reliability of measurements of the impact of online infringement than to its prevalence.

caused to rights defined as property.[2] And unlike most acts of trespass or libel, unauthorised file sharing tends to be an ongoing activity – almost a conscious lifestyle choice – rather than a single event. From this perspective, a criminological approach to understanding the phenomenon, such as the 'late modernity' analysis proposed by Gelsthorpe, may help shed some light.

An additional legal wrinkle is the distinction between downloading and uploading as forms of copyright infringement. Gelsthorpe does not draw this distinction, using the term 'downloading' to refer to all online infringement, including the use of unauthorised file-sharing networks generally. The users of these networks are themselves likely to focus on the 'sharing' concept rather than exactly how the sharing is accomplished. Nevertheless, it is worth pointing out that most of their standard justifications relate primarily to their own downloading – behaviour that is much less damaging to right-holders' markets than uploading. It is uploading – the making available of copyright works to the public – that has triggered lawsuits and could in appropriate circumstances lead to criminal as well as civil liability.[3] To the extent that file-sharers are aware that it is possible to choose one without the other (through changing the default setting in the P2P software), their motivations may not be equally applicable to both. It seems plausible that they would find it easier to justify downloading as an essentially private act.

In her concluding reflections, Gelsthorpe refers to: 'the recasting of illegal copying' as reflecting an attempt to create a normative consensus that this conduct is harmful, and raises the question of 'how "piracy" has come to be criminalized.' Although the right to control the making of copies has always been at the core of copyright, it is true that individual acts of copying for private purposes in the past were generally either permitted by the law or ignored by right-holders. (Arguably, the primary significance of the illegality of copying by individuals was that it could

---

[2] It is this analogy that has led to the use of the term 'piracy' to describe large-scale infringement. Such terminology, as with other colourful rhetoric used on all sides of the copyright debates, has been controversial, especially when applied to non-commercial conduct (as noted by Gelsthorpe), and I will instead use the more neutral technical term 'infringement' in these comments. See C. Seville's contribution in to this volume, Chapter 2, 'Nineteenth-Century Anglo–US Copyright Relations: The Language of Piracy Versus the Moral High Ground'.

[3] See, e.g., UK Copyright, Designs and Patents Act 1988, s. 107(2A). It should be noted, however, that the cases mentioned by Gelsthorpe that were brought by record companies against individual file-sharers (all uploaders of large numbers of files, not solely downloaders) were civil lawsuits, not criminal prosecutions.

form the basis for a secondary liability claim against businesses that contributed to the infringement.) Other types of infringement by individuals, however, were more threatening – those that interfered with markets by moving out of the private sphere and potentially satisfying a wider public demand. What has changed in recent years are the facts – the volume of infringement by individuals, their ability to distribute as well as copy, and the damage they can cause, all enabled by newly developed technologies.[4] Thus, although illegal copying has long been technically infringing, the case for deeming it harmful has become much stronger. It is unclear how a normative consensus should be evaluated in light of these evolving circumstances (or a decision made as to whether any such consensus should be accepted or challenged). To the extent there is a consensus in favour of unauthorised file sharing,[5] it is the product of only the past few years, since the development of file-sharing and other digital network technologies, and presumably could change again.

This is one manifestation of the reality that the facts in this area are in constant flux (whether relating to technology, market offerings or consumer attitudes). It is dangerous to draw overly firm conclusions from such rapidly evolving normative contexts. One interesting aspect that deserves further exploration, for example, is the extent to which individuals may change their perspectives on these issues as their life circumstances change – as their relative access to money versus time shifts, and as they become more active participants in the world of market transactions.

In seeking an explanation for these illegal actions, Gelsthorpe notes that the fact that online infringement is 'free and easy' is only a partial answer, and puts forth several additional motivations. I will examine these motivations, and others often cited for illegal file sharing, looking at

---

[4] On the other hand, the ability to identify infringement by individuals may in some contexts be easier online than in analogue contexts. Unlike copying in the privacy of a home or office, those who participate in P2P networks normally reveal to other participants the IP addresses assigned to their accounts.

[5] It is not clear this is the case. A 2009 study by Harris Research in the UK, for example, found that 73 per cent of the public believed more should be done to reduce the level of illegal file sharing. Harris Interactive, *Research on the Effectiveness of Deterring Illegal Music Filesharing on P2P Sites and Networks in the UK* (2009). And as pointed out by Gelsthorpe, the large damages awards against Jammie Thomas (set by a jury of her peers after having the opportunity to assess her credibility at a trial) suggest that public sentiment may in fact be more consistent with the law than commonly reported in the popular press.

three questions: (a) to what extent are these actual motivating factors rather than rationalisations? (b) apart from their motivating force, to what extent are they based on a full and fair assessment of the facts? and (c) most importantly, what are the implications for what can or should be done to respond to the epidemic of illegal behaviour?

## Motivation versus rationalisation

The primary motivations for illegal file sharing identified by Gelsthorpe may be summarised as: (a) the victim is not sympathetic and in any event rich so not really harmed; (b) it is a widespread cultural practice, or 'everyone does it'; and (c) some musicians are happy with unauthorised file sharing of their works. A range of related justifications proliferate on blogs, in press reports, and in consumer surveys. Other common variations include the assertions that (d) producers treat performers badly; and (e) prices for legal music are too high. In addition, the younger age groups that are disproportionately involved may simply enjoy the thrill of challenging authority and the status quo.

Whatever their theoretical explanatory power, all of these proffered explanations also serve as rationalisations for what is undeniably in a user's economic self-interest. Given the obvious incentive to obtain something desired free of cost, it is difficult to assess the extent to which each rationale, no matter how sincere, contributes to the behaviour. Most of the same rationales would also justify shoplifting CDs, yet this activity has not resulted in the same epidemic of illegality – the difference perhaps lying in a combination of the perception of a greater risk of being caught and a more instinctive respect for ownership in tangible goods. Finally, to the extent these rationales are in fact motivating, the question remains whether they are based on an accurate and informed assessment. If not, they may be more easily subject to reconsideration.

## Validity of rationales

While these rationales may reflect deeply held convictions, each one mistakes or omits significant points. In part they appear based on a lack of information or an incomplete understanding of how the industry and markets work. A fuller perspective would be more complex.

First, to the extent users focus on the unsympathetic identity of the victims of online infringement, they are missing a bigger picture. As

Gelsthorpe recognises, the victims are not solely multinational corporations. They encompass the entire spectrum of individual creators, performers and right-holders of all sizes, from sole proprietorships to family
businesses and other small and medium-sized enterprises (SMEs) operating at local levels. In some of the largest national markets, the majority
of record sales are made by local independent labels.[6]

As to large corporations, harm to their interests too can ultimately
impact on consumers. These corporations are major investors in new
talent and local cultural content. Their music evidently appeals to file-
sharers, as it still represents the bulk of what is shared most actively on
P2P networks. While it is in the public interest to have a wide variety of
works from diverse sources available to choose from, the music-loving
public will not benefit from major record companies cutting back on
their Artists & Repertoire (A&R) spend.

Second, the belief that file sharing causes no harm is counter-intuitive
and demonstrably wrong. The majority of third-party studies have concluded that the impact of unauthorised file sharing on sales is significant.[7] While the exact degree of the losses caused can be hard to measure,
and some techniques and studies are doubtless more reliable than others,
the weight of the evidence shows a meaningful negative impact. Globally,
the record industry has shrunk by about one-third since file sharing
became a widespread phenomenon less than ten years ago. One need
not believe that file sharing is the sole cause, or that every illegal

[6] See, e.g., www.riaj.org, describing Japan Gold Disc Award 2009 (7 of the top 10 bestselling
new domestic acts, 8 out of the top 10 best selling singles, and 7 of the top 10 albums were
from local indie labels). The percentages in India are reportedly even higher.

[7] See studies by Jupiter Research, *Analysis of the European Online Music Market
Development and Assessment of Future Opportunities* (2007, 2009); Norbert Michel,
'The Impact of Digital File Sharing on the Music Industry: An Empirical Analysis',
*Topics in Economic Analysis and Policy*, 6(1) (2006), Art. 18; Rafael Rob and Joel
Waldfogel, 'Piracy on the High C's: Music Downloading, Sales Displacement, and
Social Welfare in a Sample of College Students', *Journal of Law and Economics*, 49( 1)
(2006), 29–72; Alejandro Zentner, 'Measuring the Effect of Online Music Piracy on Music
Sales' (University of Chicago, 2003) (at: http://economics.uchicago.edu/download/music
industryoct12.pdf); Alejandro Zentner, 'File Sharing and International Sales of
Copyrighted Music: An Empirical Analysis with a Panel of Countries', *Topics in
Economic Analysis and Policy*, 5(1) (2005), Art. 21; Alejandro Zentner, 'Measuring the
Effect of File-Sharing on Music Purchases', *Journal of Law and Economics*, 49(1) (2006),
63–90; Stan J. Liebowitz, 'File-Sharing: Creative Destruction or Just Plain Destruction?',
December 2004, School of Management, University of Texas, Dallas (at: http://som.
utdallas.edu/centers/capri/documents/destruction.pdf); cf. Felix Oberholzer-Gee and
Koleman Strumpf, 'The Effect of File Sharing on Record Sales – An Empirical Analysis'
(2004) (at: www.unc.edu/~cigar/papers/FileSharing_March2004.pdf).

download corresponds to a lost sale, to conclude that this sharp decline during this exact time period is not coincidental.

It is true that file sharing is widespread and widely accepted, particularly in certain circles. In that sense, 'everyone (at least of a certain age) does it'. Arguably, they do it because they can, and because so far they can usually get away with it. But it is circular to rely on this as a justification for the activity. One might as well say that because everyone speeds, there is no reason to comply with speed limits.

It is likewise true that a number of musicians have publicly stated their support for file sharing, and their willingness to allow their works to be shared over unauthorised P2P services. Many other musicians, however, are not happy about it, and have spoken out about the need to curb this behaviour.[8] Their community is divided in its views, depending on each artist's perception of his career goals and relationship with his audience, as well as the particular stage he is at in his career. At the outset of a career, the broadest possible audience may be the most important goal; once established, the artist typically becomes more focused on generating income.

As to the rationale that performers are treated badly, most public concern seems to emanate from a lack of understanding of how the royalty system works. Consumers focus on complaints that performers do not receive royalties. They may not be aware, however, that artists are in part compensated through advances, with royalties payable once the advances are recouped; that the vast majority of recordings never make a profit and therefore never pay back the advances; and that the artists keep advances that haven't been recouped.[9] In other words, many artists do not get royalties because most records are not profitable, and the record company bears the risk of loss.[10] Most fundamentally, however, issues

---

[8] See, e.g., latest position of UK Featured Artists Coalition (at: www.featuredartists coalition.com/showscreen.php?site_id=161&screentype=site&screenid=161&loginreq= 0&blogaction= showitem&bloginfo=800); Sir Elton John (at: www.timesonline.co.uk/ tol/news/uk/article6843437.ece); James Blunt (at: www.timesonline.co.uk/tol/comment/ letters/article6841788.ece); Patrick Wolf (at: www.nme.com/news/patrick-wolf/47316).

[9] See generally M. William Krasilovsky and Sidney Shemel, *This Business of Music* (10th edn, New York: Watson-Guptill Publications, 2007), ch. 2, pp. 19–22. See D. Lefranc's contribution to this volume, Chapter 4, 'The Metamorphosis of *Contrefaçon* in French Copyright Law'.

[10] Nevertheless, artists still should have an economic interest in preventing infringement and promoting sales, either because their recordings may become profitable and earn royalties or because they may be able to negotiate better terms in the next contract due to a better sales track record.

between performers and producers should not justify third parties using their works without permission or payment in violation of existing law.

Finally, the argument that music costs too much is strikingly out of date. Prices for music have declined markedly in the past few years, both for online purchases and for physical sales. Today there is little that can be bought so cheaply – music in many markets costs less than a cup of coffee or a bus ticket. Indeed, legal services now exist that provide music free to the consumer (usually paid for by advertising). Nor is dissatisfaction with price usually considered an acceptable excuse for taking market products without paying for them.

## What can and should be done?

As Gelsthorpe's analysis suggests, there is a multiplying effect from the interaction of the centrifugal conditions of post-1950s society and today's sheer technological capabilities.

The last fifty years are the first time individual consumers have been given the power to infringe in economically meaningful ways. This began with the photocopier – allowing fast, easy, cheap wholesale copying, done in anonymity. Digital network technology may be seen as the latest version of the same phenomenon, but exponentially more powerful, with copies indistinguishable from originals and virtually instantaneous mass dissemination. In these circumstances, if nothing is done, infringement is almost inevitable. Many find it hard to resist getting something of value for free, easily and without consequences. If this result is to be avoided,[11] meaningful constraints on behaviour are needed. And as Gelsthorpe points out, many of those that used to exist are no longer being provided by society.

What alternative sources of constraints are available and appropriate? Gelsthorpe's conclusion of the need for an educational approach seems irrefutable. Surely educating the public will be key. If normative compliance is a goal, consumers must have an understanding of the reasons to comply. Part of the problem is that their newfound powers to use copyright content have outstripped their awareness of the impact of exercising them. Numerous commentators and policy makers have noted the current gap between need to know and actual knowledge.

[11] Some will argue that this result should not be avoided, and that instead the law should change to accept the 'facts on the ground' of such widespread consumer conduct. As noted above, for purposes of this comment I will not address this far-reaching policy debate.

To the extent file-sharing behaviour can be shaped by normative compliance, it is crucial to improve this understanding. Education should include an explanation of the basic purpose of copyright and the larger societal benefit it is intended to serve, above and beyond the economic interests of individual right-holders. Consumers' perception of themselves as passive users, essentially recipients of works provided by others, should also be broadened – their self-image updated to reflect their current role as creators (whether of entirely original works or 'mash-ups' of various kinds) and distributors in the online environment. Their potential stake in all sides of the copyright system stands to enhance their ability to recognise its value.

More specifically, there is a need to communicate better to the public a fuller range of facts with respect to the standard justifications provided for infringement. The misunderstandings and incomplete information noted above should be corrected – in Gelsthorpe's words, helping to clarify 'the modern moral maze of music piracy'. Consumers may still choose to infringe, but at least the facts should be available to be taken into account in making those choices. The challenge, of course, is how to convey the information effectively in an objective and balanced way. Unfortunately this is not a task that the mainstream press is likely to take on – their interest more often lies in reporting controversy and conflict. The responsibility may therefore need to be shared by the public and private sectors.

Finally, re-establishing some version of lost authority could be a major element in enforcing social norms. If traditional entities and institutions no longer play a normative role, alternative sources may be able to fill the gap. As one step in this direction, clear consequences for violation of the law, whether implemented through industry or government action, may be internalised and respected as part of social reality. The message would be that society as a whole values creativity and will take steps to protect it.

In Gelsthorpe's words, 'the commonplace response [to why do you infringe?] is that "everyone does it" or because you can do it with little chance of getting caught'. This calculus may be changed by enforcement measures of various kinds. I agree that these measures should not be the sole approach, but they can play an important and necessary part. Experience so far has indicated that education alone is not sufficient (as many who are fully aware of the illegality continue to infringe),[12] but needs to be combined with meaningful disincentives.

[12] See for example, Harris, *Research*.

Various enforcement measures have been utilised in the past or are under discussion. Lawsuits against individual file-sharers have substantially raised public awareness of illegality, but would in most countries need to be brought in greatly increased volumes to create a high enough perception of real risk. An alternative currently gaining ground internationally is the possibility of ISPs taking action to curb infringement, such as through a 'graduated response' system of warnings leading to ultimate sanctions for those who refuse to stop.[13] Several studies have indicated that such systems are likely to have a significant deterrent effect.[14]

An additional piece of the behavioural puzzle is the availability of attractive legal alternatives. Consumers must have other appealing options to weigh in the mix. While the music industry has been criticised in the past for being slow to develop online offerings, today there is a wide variety for consumers to choose from. More than 400 legal services worldwide are offering access to music in many different ways, including various download, subscription and streaming models with a range of price structures. If the impact and potential risks of illegal uses are well understood, the consumer is more likely to opt for one of these services.

One other alternative is worth mentioning: the possibility of returning to some extent to a world where individuals no longer infringe in harmful ways, not by retreating to pre-digital times, but by using technology to minimise the opportunities for illegal uses. This could involve technological measures such as filtering of unauthorised content.[15] Such measures may yet prove to be part of a solution to rampant online infringement, if they can be implemented in a way that appropriately accommodates technical, economic and policy concerns.

---

[13] Over the past two years, 'graduated response' systems have been the topic of much discussion around the world, and have been adopted in some jurisdictions through legislation or private agreement. The advisability of 'graduated response' or the pros and cons of any particular version thereof are beyond the scope of this comment, which focuses only on the potential role of such a system as an element in influencing consumer behaviour. It should be noted, however, that none of the systems adopted so far have included as an ultimate sanction the complete denial of Internet access – as opposed to the temporary suspension of an Internet account.

[14] See for example, IPSOS, 'The Opinion of French People Regarding Illegal Music Downloading on the Internet' (2008); Harris, *Research*.

[15] See for example, *SCRL Société Belge des Auteurs* v. *SA Scarlet*, Case No. 04/8975/A, District Court of Brussels (28/6/2007).

## Conclusion

Affecting consumer behaviour in the area of online copyright infringement is likely to involve numerous factors, not necessarily taken into
account in traditional criminological theory. The current reality of the
modern world, including both its social and technological parameters,
suggests that decisions will be formed through a combination of inputs
(in contrast to the more centralised authority sources of the past).
As Gelsthorpe puts it, '"grey area" offenders are rational consumers',
and 'music piracy is a "crime" which has become a risk to be calculated by
offender and potential victim'. A rational consumer will weigh as factors
the availability of attractive legal alternatives (in terms of flexibility of
use, price and security), her level of respect for copyright and understanding of the impact of online infringement, and the perceived level of
risk of meaningful consequences for illegal conduct.

It seems likely that a change in any of these factors will lead to some
degree of change in consumer behaviour. There is of course no way of
knowing how much any particular change will be effective in reducing
overall online infringement. But the steps described above are worth the
effort, if we are not to abandon existing law. A reduction in the current
epidemic of illegality is important not only to preserving the copyright
system's fundamental goals but also to the broader public policy issue of
how to maintain societal values in the brave new digital world.

# BIBLIOGRAPHY

Adeney, E. *The Moral Rights of Authors and Performers: An International and Comparative Analysis* (Oxford University Press, 2006)
'Unfixed Works, Performers' Protection and Beyond: Does the Australian Copyright Act Always Require Material Form?', *Intellectual Property Quarterly* (2009), 77

Aderman, R. M., L. Kleinfield and J. S. Banks (eds.), *Washington Irving, Letters*, 4 vols. (Boston: Twayne Publishers, 1978–1982), vol. I, 554

Aitchison, J. *Words in the Mind: An Introduction to the Mental Lexicon* (Oxford: Blackwell, 1994)

Alberro, A., *Conceptual Art and the Politics of Publicity* (Cambridge, MA: MIT Press, 2003)

Alexander, I., *Copyright and the Public Interest in the Nineteenth Century* (Oxford: Hart Publishing, 2010)

Ames, E., 'Beyond *Rogers* v. *Koons*: A Fair Use Standard for Appropriation', *Columbia Law Review* (1993), 1473

Andersen, B., R. Kozul-Wright and Z. Kozul-Wright, 'Rents, Rights n' Rhythm: Conflict and Cooperation in the Music Industry', *Industry and Innovation*, 14(5) (2007), 513–40

Andersen, K. 'Generation Xerox', *New York*, 6 May 2006

Anderson, R. J. 'Security in Open Versus Closed Systems – The Dance of Boltzmann, Coase and Moore', Presented at Open Source Software Economics, 2007 (at: www.cl.cam.ac.uk/~rja14/Papers/toulouse.pdf)

Andy, B. (1983) 'Interview with Ray Hurford and Colin Moore', *Small Axe* (accessed at www.bobandy.com/int-smaxe2.htm on 31 March 2008)

Aplin, T., *Copyright Law in the Digital Society: The Challenges Of Multimedia* (Oxford: Hart, 2005)

Aplin, T. and J. Davis *Intellectual Property Law: Text, Cases, and Materials* (Oxford University Press, 2009)

Arendt, Hannah (ed.) *Walter Benjamin: Illuminations* (New York: Schoken Books, 1968)

Arewa, O., 'From J. C. Bach to Hip Hop: Musical Borrowing, Copyright and Cultural Context', *NCL Rev.*, 84 (2006), 547–645
'The Freedom to Copy: Copyright, Creation and Context', *UC Davis Law Review*, 41 (2007), 477–588

Arner, R. D., *Dobson's* Encyclopaedia *the Publisher, Text and Publication of America's First* Britannica, 1789–1803 (University of Pennsylvania Press, 1991)

Arnold, R., 'Infringement of Copyright in Computer Software by Non-textual Copying: First Decision at Trial by an English Court', *European Intellectual Property Review* (1993), 250

Ashton, D. 'The Atelier of La Californie', in *Picasso: Les Grandes Series*, exh. cat.: Madrid: Nacional Reina Sofia, 2000

Ashworth, A. *Principles of Criminal Law* (6th edn, Oxford University Press, 2009)

Attridge, D. *The Rhythms of English Poetry* (London: Longman, 1982)

Bader, A.L., 'Frederick Saunders and the Early History of the International Copyright Movement', *Library Quarterly*, 8 (1938), 25–39

Bandura, A. *Social Learning Theory* (New York: General Learning Press, 1977)

Banner, S. 'Transitions Between Property Regimes', *Journal of Legal Studies*, 31 (2002), 359

Barker, J. C. 'Grossly Excessive Penalties in the Battle Against Illegal File-Sharing: The Troubling Effects of Aggregating Minimum Statutory Damages for Copyright Infringement', *Texas Law Review*, 83 (2004), 525.

Barron, A., 'Copyright Law and the Claims of Art', *Intellectual Property Quarterly* (2002), 368

'Introduction: Harmony or Dissonance? Copyright Concepts and Musical Practice', *Social and Legal Studies*, 15(1) (2006), 25

Barrow, S. and P. Dalton, *The Rough Guide to Reggae* (3rd edn, London: Rough Guides Limited, 2004)

Barzel, Y., *Economic Analysis of Property Rights* (Cambridge University Press, 1989)

Barzilay, R. and K. McKeown, 'Extracting Paraphrases from a Parallel Corpus', *Proceedings of ACL'01* (2001), 50–7

Bauman, Z., *Liquid Love* (Oxford: Polity, 2003)

Beard, J. F. (ed.), *James Fenimore Cooper, Letters and Journals*, 6 vols. (Cambridge, MA: Harvard University Press, 1960–8), vol. VI, 178

Beck, U., *Risk Society: Towards a New Modernity* (London: Sage, 1992)

Beebe, B., 'An Empirical Study of US Copyright Fair Use Opinions, 1978–2005', *University of Pennsylvania Law Review*, 156(3) (January 2008), 549

Bell, A., *The Language of News Media*, (Oxford: Blackwell, 1991)

'Text, Time and Technology in News English', in S. Goodman and D. Graddol (eds.), *Redesigning English: New Texts, New Identities* (London: Routledge, 1996), pp. 3–26

Bendersky, M. and B. Croft, 'Finding Text Reuse on the Web', *Proceedings of the 2nd ACM International Conference on Web Search and Data Mining WSDM'09* (2009) ACM, New York, NY, 262–71

Bently, L., 'Authorship of Popular Music under UK Copyright Law', *E-Journal of IP Rights* (2005), Oxford IP Research Centre (accessed 28 March 2008, at: www.oiprc.ox.ac.uk/EJWP1005.pdf)

'Authorship of Popular Music in UK Copyright Law', *Information, Communication and Society*, 12(2009), 179

Bently, L. and M. Kretschmer, *Primary Sources on Copyright in Five Jurisdictions, 1550–1900* (at: www.copyrighthistory.org)

Bently, L. and B. Sherman, *Intellectual Property Law* (3rd edn, Oxford University Press, 2009)

Berg, S., 'Remedying the Statutory Damages Remedy for Secondary Copyright Infringement Liability: Balancing Copyright and Innovation in the Digital Age', *Journal of the Copyright Society of the USA*, 56 (2009), 265–333

Bergne, J.H.G., 'Anglo-American Copyright', *Quarterly Review*, 172 (1891), 380–98

Biber, D., S. Conrad and R. Reppen, *Corpus Linguistics: Investigating Language Structure and Use* (Cambridge University Press, 1998)

Bilby, K., 'Jamaica', in P. Manuel, with K. Bilby and M. Largey, *Caribbean Currents: From Rumba to Reggae* (Philadelphia, PA: Temple University Press, 1993)

Birrell, A., *Seven Lectures on the Law and History of Copyright in Books* (London: Cassell & Co. Ltd, 1899)

Blanc, A. F and E. Vivien, *Traité de la législation des théâtres ou Exposé complet et méthodique des lois et de la jurisprudence relativement aux théâtres et spectacles publics* (Paris: Brissot-Thivars, 1830)

Blanc, É., *Traité de la contrefaçon en tous genres et de sa poursuite en justice* (Paris: Plon, 1855)

Bloomer, A., P. Griffiths and A. Merrison, *Introducing Language in Use: A Coursebook* (London: Routledge, 2005)

Blunt, J., *Blunt Message – British Musicians Should Galvanise to Save Our Music Businesses*, Times Online, 21 September 2009 (at: www.timesonline.co.uk/tol/comment/letters/article6841788.ece)

Boggs, J. S. G., 'Who Owns This?', *Chicago-Kent Law Review*, 68 (1993), 889

Boldrin, M. and D. K. Levine, 'The Economics of Ideas and Intellectual Property', *Proceedings of the National Academy of Sciences*, 102 (2005), 1252–6

Boldrin, M. and D.K. Levine, *Against Intellectual Monopoly* (Cambridge University Press, 2008)

Boncompain, J., *La Révolution des auteurs. Naissance de la propriété intellectuelle (1773–1815)* (Paris: Fayard, 2001)

Boosey, W., *Fifty Years of Music* (London: Ernest Benn Limited, 1931)

Booth, S. (ed.), *Shakespeare's Sonnets* (New Haven, CT: Yale University Press, 1977)

Booton, D., 'Framing Pictures: Defining Art in UK Copyright Law', *Intellectual Property Quarterly*, 1 (2003), 38–68

Borges, J.-L., 'Pierre Menard, Author of the Quixote', in J.-L. Borges, *Labyrinths* (London: Penguin Classics, 2000)

Bornat, R., *et al.*, 'Mental Models, Consistency and Programming Aptitude', *Proceedings of the Tenth Conference on Australasian Computing Education*, 78 (2008), 53–61

Boswell, J., *Boswell's Life of Johnson (Together with Boswell's Journal of a Tour to the Hebrides and Johnson's Diary of a Journey into North Wales)*, ed. G. Birkbeck Hill, rev. L. F. Powell, 6 vols. (2nd edn, Oxford: Clarendon Press, 1934–50)

Bottoms, A. E., 'Compliance and Community Penalties', in A. E. Bottoms, L. Gelsthorpe and S. Rex (eds), *Community Penalties. Change and Challenges* (Cullompton: Willan Publishing, 2001), pp. 87–116

'Place, Space, Crime and Disorder', in M. Maguire, R. Morgan and R. Reiner (eds), *The Oxford Handbook of Criminology* (4th edn, Oxford University Press, 2007), pp. 528–74

Bourdon, W., 'Le droit pénal est-il un instrument efficace face à la criminalisation croissante de la contrefaçon?', D. 2008, 729–34

Boutellier, H., *Crime and Morality. The Significance of Criminal Justice in Postmodern Culture* (Dordrecht: Kluwer Academic Publishers, 2000)

Boyle, J., *The Public Domain: Enclosing the Commons of the Mind* (New Haven, CT: Yale University Press, 2008)

Bradley, L., *Bass Culture: When Reggae Was King* (London: Viking, 2000)

Bresler, J. and Lerner, R., *All About Rights for Visual Artists* (New York: Practising Law Institute, 2006)

Breyer, S., 'The Uneasy Case for Copyright: A Study of Copyright in Books, Photocopies, and Computer Programs', *Harvard Law Review*, 84 (1970), 281

Brin, S., J. Davis and H. Garcia-Molina, 'Copy Detection Mechanisms for Digital Documents', *Proceedings of the ACM SIGMOD International Conference on Management of Data* (1995), 398–409

Broder, A., 'On the Resemblance and Containment of Documents', *Proceedings of the Compression and Complexity of Sequences*, 11–13 June 1997

Brooker, C., *The Seven Basic Plots: Why We Tell Stories* (London: Continuum, 2005)

'What do Lord Mandelson, Damien Hirst and the Music Industry Have in Common? . . .', *Guardian*, 14 September 2009

Brooks, S., 'Striker Gets His Due', *Jamaica Gleaner*, 26 October 2008 (at: www.jamaica-gleaner.com/gleaner/20081026/ent/ent5.html, last accessed 23 August 2009)

Brown, D., *The Da Vinci Code* (New York: Doubleday, 2003)

Buchloh, B., 'Conceptual Art 1962–1969: From the Aesthetics of Administration to the Critique of Institutions', *October*, 55 (1999), 105–43

Budd, T., C. Sharpe, G. Weir, D. Wilson and N. Owen, *Young People and Crime: Findings from the 2004 Offending, Crime and Justice Survey*, Home Office Statistical Bulletin 20/05 (London: Home Office, 2005).

Burchfield, R., 'Dictionaries New and Old', *Encounter* (Sept.–Oct. 1984), 10–19

Burkholder, P., 'Borrowing', in *Grove Music Online. Oxford Music Online* (at: www.oxfordmusiconline.com/subscriber/article/grove/music/52918pg1, last accessed 23 August 2009)

Burrell, R., 'Reining in Copyright Law: Is Fair Use the Answer?', *Intellectual Property Quarterly*, (2001) 361.

Burrell, R. and A. Coleman, *Copyright Exceptions: The Digital Impact* (Cambridge University Press, 2005)

Buskirk, M., *The Contingent Object of Contemporary Art* (Cambridge, MA: MIT Press, 2005)

Butt, J., *The Eighteenth Century*, ed. Geoffrey Carnall (Oxford: Clarendon Press, 1979)

Carey, M., *A Short Account of Algiers* (2nd edn, Philadelphia, for M. Carey, 1794)
*Vindiciae Hibernicae* (Philadelphia, PA: M. Carey and Son, 1819)
*Autobiography* (New York: E.L. Schwaab, 1942)

Caron, C., 'Droit pénal de la contrefaçon. Bilan des acteurs sur le terrain', CCE, July–August 2006, chron. no. 1

Carrier, J. G., (ed.), *Meanings of the Market: The Free Market in Western Culture* (Oxford: Berg, 1997)

Carte, *A Second Letter from an Author to a Member of Parliament* (London: n.p., 23 April 1735)

*Cases of the appellants and respondents in the cause of literary property, The* (London: for J. Bew, W. Clarke, P. Brett, C. Wilkins, 1774)

Castells, M., 'Innovation, Information Technology, and the Culture of Freedom' (2009) (at: choike.org/nuevo_eng/informes/2623.html, last accessed 26 June 2009)

Chacksfield, M., 'The Hedgehog and the Fox: A Substantial Part of the Law of Copyright', *European Intellectual Property Review*, 23 (2001), 259

Chander, A. and M. Sunder, 'Everyone's a Superhero: A Cultural Theory of "Mary Sue" Fan Fiction as Fair Use', *California Law Review*, 95 (2007), 597

Chang, K. O. and W. Chen, *Reggae Routes: The Story of Jamaican Music* (Philadelphia, PA :Temple University Press, 1998)

Chartier, Roger, and Henri-Jean Martin, *Histoire de l'édition française, Le livre triomphant* (Paris: Fayard 1990)

Cheng, T. S. L., 'Copyright Protection of Haute Cuisine: Recipe for Disaster?', *European Intellectual Property Review* (2008), 93–101

Cheyne, G., *A New Theory of Continu'd Fevers* (Edinburgh, 1701)

Chomsky, N., *Syntactic Structures* (The Hague: Mouton, 1957)

*Christian's Magazine, or A Treasury of Divine Knowledge*, vol. iv (London, 1760–6)

Christie, A., 'Designing Appropriate Protection for Computer Programs', *European Intellectual Property Review*, 11 (1994), 486–93

Christie, N., *A Suitable Amount of Crime* (London: Routledge, 2004)

Clarke, S., *Jah Music: The Evolution of the Popular Jamaican Song* (London: Heinemann Educational Books Ltd, 1980)

Clough, P. D., 'Measuring text reuse', Ph.D. thesis, University of Sheffield , 2003

Clough, P. D. and R. Gaizauskas, 'Corpora and Text Re-use', in A. Lüdeling and M. Kytö (eds.), *Corpus Linguistics: An International Handbook* (Berlin: Mouton de Gruyter, 2009), 1249–71

Clough, P. D., R. Gaizauskas, S. L. Piao and Y. Wilks, 'Measuring Text Re-use', *Proceedings of the 40th Anniversary Meeting for the Association for Computational Linguistics ACL'02* (2002)

Clough, P. D., R. Gaizauskas and S. L. Piao, 'Building and Annotating a Corpus for the Study of Journalistic Text Re-use', *Proceedings of the 3rd International Conference on Language Resources and Evaluation, LREC'02* (2002), 1678–85

Cohen, J., 'Lochner in Cyberspace: The New Economic Orthodoxy of Rights Management', *Michigan Law Review*, 97 (1998), 462

Cohen, L. E. and M. Felson, 'Social Change and Crime Rate Trends: A Routine Activity Approach', *American Sociological Review*, 44 (1979), 488–608

Cohen, S., *Folk Devils and Moral Panics. The Creation of the Mods and Rockers* (London: MacGibbon and Kee, 1972)

Colley, L., 'Britishness and Protestantism', in *Britons: Forging the Nation 1707–1837* (London: Random House, 1994)

Collingwood, J., *Bob Marley: His Musical Legacy* (London: Cassell, 2005)

Cooke, M., 'No Preservatives on Reggae History', *Jamaica Gleaner*, 25 February 2007 (accessed 19 March 2008, at: www.jamaica-gleaner.com/gleaner/20070225/ent/ent1.html)

Cope, J., 'The Experience of Survival During the 1641 Irish Rebellion', *Historical Journal*, 46 (2003), 295–316

Couhin, C., *La propriété industrielle, artistique et littéraire* (Paris: Librairie de la Société du Recueil Général des Lois et des Arrêts, Larose 1894)

Coulthard, M. and A. Johnson, *An Introduction to Forensic Linguistics: Language in Evidence* (London: Routledge, 2007)

Croft, W. and D. A. Cruse, *Cognitive Linguistics* (Cambridge University Press, 2004)

Crow, T., *Modern Art in a Common Culture* (New Haven, CT: Yale University Press, 1996)

cummings, e.e., *Complete Poems, 1904–1962* (New York: Norton, 1994)

Curley, T., *Samuel Johnson, the Ossian Fraud, and the Celtic Revival in Great Britain and Ireland* (Cambridge University Press, 2009)

Curtis, G. T., *A Treatise on the Law of Copyright* (3rd prtg., 1847) (Clark, NJ: Lawbook Exchange, 2005)

Daley, D. and N. Foga, 'Jamaica: Beyond the TRIPs Agreement', *Managing Intellectual Property* (2007), Americas IP Focus, 3rd edn (accessed 28 March 2008 at: www.managingip.com/Article.aspx?ArticleID=1450368)

Dalhuijsen, L., 'Reggae Riddims in Prosperity'(at: www.waks.nl/mt/cr/, last accessed 1 August 2009)

Davenport-Hines, R., 'Charles Ottley Groom', *ODNB*.

Davies, G. *Copyright and the Public Interest* (London: Sweet & Maxwell, 2002)

Davis, J., *Intellectual Property Law* (3rd edn, Oxford University Press, 2008)

Davis, M., *The Undecidable, Basic Papers on Undecidable Propositions, Unsolvable Problems And Computable Functions* (New York: Raven Press, 1965)

Deazley, R., M. Kretschmer and L. Bently (eds.), *From Privilege to Property* (Cambridge: Open Book, 2010)

Deci, E., R. Koestner and R. Ryan, 'A Meta-Analytic Review of Experiments Examining the Effect of Extrinsic Rewards on Intrinsic Motivation', *Psychological Bulletin*, 125(3) (1999), 627–8

De Duve, T., *Kant After Duchamp* (Cambridge, MA: MIT Press, 1996)

De Koningh, M. and M. Griffiths, *Tighten Up: The History of Reggae in the UK* (London: Sanctuary, 1989)

Demsetz, H., 'Toward a Theory of Property Rights', *American Economic Review*, 57(2) (1967), 347–59

  'Frischmann's View of "Toward a Theory of Property Rights"', *Review of Law and Economics*, 4(1) (2008), 127

Dennis, J., *An Essay on the Genius and Writings of Shakespeare* (London, 1712)

Department for Culture, Media and Sport and Department for Business, Enterprise and Regulatory Reform, *Digital Britain Interim Report* (London: Department for Culture, Media and Sport, January 2009)

Depoorter, B., 'The Several Lives of Mickey Mouse: The Expanding Boundaries of Intellectual Property Law', *Virginia Journal of Law and Technology*, 9(4) (2004), 14–15

Dery, M., 'Public Enemy Confrontation', *Keyboard* (1990), 81–96

Desbois, H., *Le droit d'auteur. Droit français. Convention de Berne révisée* (Paris: Dalloz 1950)

  *Le droit d'auteur en France* (Paris: Dalloz, 1966)

Di Cataldo, V., 'Nuove tecnologie e nuovi problemi – Chi inventa le nuove regole e come?', in S. Rossi and C. Storti (eds.), *Le matrici del diritto commerciale tra storia e tendenze evolutive* (Varise: Insubria University Press, 2009), pp. 135–52

DiCola, P. and K. McLeod, *Creative License: The Law and Culture of Digital Sampling* (Duke University Press, NC, forthcoming 2010)

Dixit, A., 'Incentives and Organizations in the Public Sector', *Journal of Human Resources*, 37 (2002), 696–727

Douglas, M., *Risk and Blame: Essays in Cultural Theory* (London: Routledge, 1992)

Dreyer, E., 'La protection pénale du droit de l'auteur' (Communication Commerce-Electronique) (CCE), September 2007

Duffy, J. P., 'Intellectual Property Isolationism and the Average Cost Thesis', *Texas Law Review*, 83 (2005), 1077

Duncan-Jones, K. (ed.), *Shakespeare's Sonnets*, Arden (3rd edn, London: Thomson Learning, 2010)

Durant, A., *Meaning in the Media: Discourse, Controversy and Debate* (Cambridge University Press, 2010)

Durant, A. and N. Fabb, *Literary Studies in Action* (London: Routledge, 1990)

Durant, A., and M. Lambrou, *Language and Media* (London: Routledge, 2009)

Dutton, D., 'Artistic Crimes: The Problem of Forgery in the Arts', *British Journal of Aesthetics*, 19(4) (1979), 302–14

Duvenage, P., *Habermas and Aesthetics* (Cambridge: Polity, 2003)

Dionysius Longinus, *On the Sublime*, tr. William Smith (London, 1739)

Eaton, A. J., 'The American Movement for International Copyright, 1837–60', *Library Quarterly*, 11 (1945), 99

Edelman, B., *Le sacre de l'auteur* (Paris: Seuil, coll. Essai, 2004)

Ehrlich, C., *Harmonious Alliance: A History of the Performing Right Society* (Oxford University Press, 1989)

Eichhorn, M., *The Artist's Contract* (Köln: Walter König, 2009)

Eliot, T. S, 'Philip Massinger', *The Sacred Wood: Essays on Poetry and Criticism* (4th edn, London: Methuen & Co., 1934)

Elliot, P., *Sculpture in France: 1900–1940* (New Haven, CT: Yale University Press, forthcoming 2010)

Escolar, I., 'Please Pirate My Songs', in *WSIS World Information* (Vienna: Institut für Neue Kulturtechnologien, 2003)

Evans, H., *Essential English for Journalists, Editors and Writers* (rev. edn, London: Pimlico, 2000)

Evanson, B., Note, 'Due Process in Statutory Damages', *Georgetown Journal of Law and Public Policy*, 3 (2005), 601–38

Ezell, M., *Social Authorship and the Advent of Print* (Baltimore, MD and London: Johns Hopkins University Press, 1999)

Fabb, N., *Linguistics and Literature* (Oxford: Blackwell, 1997)

Farrington, D. P., 'Childhood Risk Factors and Risk-focused Prevention', in Maguire *et al.*, *Oxford Handbook of Criminology*, 4th edn, pp. 602–40

Fatout, P. (ed.), *Mark Twain Speaking* (University of Iowa Press, 1976)

Ferrell, J., K. Hayward, W. Morrison and M. Presdee, *Cultural Criminology Unleashed* (London: Glasshouse, 2004)

Ferrell, J. K. and C. R. Sanders, *Cultural Criminology* (Boston, MA: Northeastern University Press, 1995)

Fielding, H., *The History of Tom Jones*, ed. R. P. Mutter (Harmondsworth: Penguin, 1985)

Fielding, K. J. (ed.), *The Speeches of Charles Dickens: A Complete Edition* (Brighton: Harvester Wheatsheaf, 1988)

Fitzgerald, W., *Martial: The World of the Epigram* (University of Chicago Press, 2007)

Fodor, J., *The Modularity of Mind* (Cambridge, MA: MIT Press, 1983)

Foucault, M., 'What is an Author?', in Bouchard, D. (ed.), *Language, Counter-Memory, Practice* (Ithaca, NY: Cornell University Press, 1977)

Foxon, D., *Pope and the Early Eighteenth-Century Book Trade*, rev. and ed. James McLaverty (Oxford: Clarendon Press, 1991)

Françon, A., 'Les sanctions pénale de la violation du droit moral' (Paris: Litec, 1997)

Freud, S., *The Uncanny*, ed. Adam Phillips, tr. David McClintock (London: Penguin, 2003)

Frey, B. and R. Jegen, 'Motivation Crowding Theory', *Journal of Economic Surveys*, 15(5) (2001), 589–611

Fried, M., 'Art and Objecthood', in Battock, G. (ed.), *Minimal Art: A Critical Anthology* (New York: E. P. Dutton, 1968)

Frischmann, B. M., 'Evaluating the Demsetzian Trend in Copyright Law', *Review of Law and Economics*, 3(3) (2007), 649–77

'Speech, Spillovers, and the First Amendment', *University of Chicago Legal Forum*, 301 (2008), 301

Frischmann, B. M., and M. A. Lemley, 'Spillovers', *Columbia Law Review*, 107 (2007), 257–301

Furnell, S., *Cybercrime: Vandalizing the Information Society* (Boston, MA: Addison-Wesley, 2002)

Gaizauskas, R., J. Foster, Y. Wilks, J. Arundel, P. Clough and S. L. Piao, 'The METER Corpus: A Corpus for Analysing Journalistic Text Re-use', *Proceedings of Corpus Linguistics 2001* (2001), Lancaster, UK, 214–23

Garland, D. *The Culture of Control. Crime and Social Order in Contemporary Society* (Oxford University Press, 2001)

Garnett, K., G. Davies and G. Harbottle, *Copinger and Skone James on Copyright* (15th edn, London: Sweet & Maxwell, 2005)

Gastambide, J.-A., *Traité théorique et pratique des contrefaçons en tous genres, ou De la propriété en matière de littérature, théâtre, musique, peinture, dessin, gravure, dessins de manufactures, sculpture, sculptures industrielles, marques, etc.* (Paris: Legrand et Descauriet, 1837)

Gherman, S., 'Harmony and Its Functionality: A Gloss on the Substantial Similarity Test in Music Copyrights', *Fordham Intellectual Property Media and Ent. L.J.*, 19 (2009), 483–517

Ghidini, G. and E. Arezzo, 'Patent and Copyright Paradigms vis a vis Derivative Innovation: The Case of Computer Programs', *IIC*, 2 (2005), 159–278

Gibbs, R. W., *Intentions in the Experience of Meaning* (Cambridge University Press, 1999)

Giddens, A., *The Consequences of Modernity* (Cambridge: Polity Press, 1990)

*Modernity and Self-Identity* (Cambridge: Polity Press, 1991)

Ginsburg, J. C., 'A Tale of Two Copyrights: Literary Property in Revolutionary France and America', *Tulane Law Review*, 46 (1990), 991

'Moral Rights in a Common Law System', *Entertainment Law Review* (1990), 121

'No "Sweat"? Copyright and Other Protection of Works of Information After *Feist* v. *Rural Telephone*', *Columbia Law Review*, 92 (1992), 338

'L'avenir du droit d'auteur: un droit sans auteur?', CCE, May 2009, study no. 10

Ginsburg, J. and Y. Gaubiac, 'Contrefaçon, fourniture de moyens et faute: per-spectives dans les systèmes de common law et civilistes à la suite des arrêts Grokster et Kazaa', RIDA, 2006, no. 2007

Githaiga, J., 'IP Law and the Protection of Indigenous Folklore and Knowledge', *Murdoch University Electronic Journal of Law*, 5(2) (1998) (at: www. murdoch.edu.au/elaw/issues/v5n2/githaiga52nf.html, accessed 28 March 2008)

Goldacre, B., 'Illegal Downloads and Dodgy Figures', *Guardian*, 5 June 2009

Goldstein, P., *Copyright's Highway: From Gutenberg to the Celestial Jukebox* (2nd edn, Stanford: Stanford Law and Politics, 2003)

Goodrich, S. G., *Recollections of a Lifetime*, 2 vols. (New York: Auburn, Miller, Orton and Mulligan, 1857), vol. II

Gordon, W. J., 'Authors, Publishers and Public Goods', *Loyola of Los Angeles Law Review*, 36 (2002), 139

   'Intellectual Property', in P. Cane and M. Tushnet (eds.), *The Oxford Handbook of Legal Studies* (Oxford University Press, 2003), pp. 617–46

   'Introduction', in W. J. Gordon and R. Watt (eds.), *The Economics of Copyright* (Cheltenham: Edward Elgar, 2003), pp. xiv–xxii

Gordon, W. J. and R. G. Bone, 'Copyright', in B. Bouckaert and G. Degeest (eds.), *Encyclopedia of Law and Economics*, vol. 2 (Cheltenham: Edward Elgar, 2000), pp. 189–223

Gottfredson, M. R. and T. Hirschi, *A General Theory of Crime* (Palo Alto, CA: Stanford University Press, 1990)

Gowers, A., *The Gowers Review of Intellectual Property* (London: HM Treasury on behalf of HMSO, 2006)

Gracyk, T., *Rhythm and Noise: An Aesthetics of Rock* (London: I.B. Tauris & Co. Ltd, 1996)

Grafton, A., *Forgers and Critics: Creativity and Duplicity in Western Scholarship* (Princeton, NJ: Princeton University Press, 1990)

Green, S. P., 'Plagiarism, Norms and the Limits of Theft Law: Some Observations on the Use of Criminal Sanctions in Enforcing Intellectual Property Rights', *Hastings Law Journal*, 54 (2002–3), 167

Greenberg, L., 'The Art of Appropriation: Puppies, Piracy and Post-Modernism', *Cardozo Arts and Entertainment Law Journal*, 11(1) (1992), 1–33

Greene, R., *Greene's Groatsworth of Witte, Bought with a Million of Repentance* (London, 1592)

Grierson, H. J. C. (ed.), *The Letters of Sir Walter Scott 1826–1828* (London: Constable, 1936)

Griffiths, J., 'Preserving Judicial Freedom of Movement – Interpreting Fair Dealing in Copyright Law', *Intellectual Property Quarterly* (2000), 164

   'Misattribution and Misrepresentation – The Claim for Reverse Passing off as "Paternity" Right', *Intellectual Property Quarterly*, 10 (2006), 34–54

Groom, N., 'Forgery or Plagiarism? Unravelling Chatterton's Rowley', *Angelaki*,
   1(2) (1993), 41–54

*The Forger's Shadow: How Forgery Changed the Course of Literature* (London:
   Picador, 2002)

'Forgery, Plagiarism, Imitation, Pegleggery', in P. Kewes (ed.), *Plagiarism in
   Early Modern England* (London: Palgrave, 2002), 74–89

'Romanticism and Forgery', in *Literature Compass Online* (Blackwell, 2007)

Groom, N., and A. Rounce, '*Literature: 1756–1770*', in D. Womersley (ed.),
   *Companion to Literature from Milton to Blake* (Oxford: Blackwell, 2000)

Groys, B., *Art Power* (Cambridge, MA: MIT Press, 2008)

*Guardian*, 'Mother Faces Music for Girl's Illegal Downloads', 21 June 2009 (at:
   www.guardian.co.uk/technology/2009/jub/21/arts.netmusic)

Gumperz, J., and S. Levinson (eds.), *Rethinking Linguistic Relativity* (Cambridge
   University Press, 1996)

Gupta, A., 'Are Open Standards a Prerequisite to Open Source? A Perspective in Light
   of Technical and Legal Developments', *Computer and Telecommunications
   Law Review*, 15(1) (2009), 3

Habermas, J., 'Remarks on the Concept of Communicative Action', in G. Seebass
   and R. Tuomela (eds.), *Social Action* (Dordrecht: Kluwer, 1985), 151–78

*The Theory of Communicative Action*, vol. 2 (Cambridge: Polity Press, 1987)

*Between Facts and Norms* (Cambridge: Polity 1996)

Halliday, M. A. K., *System and Function in Language* (Oxford University Press,
   1976)

*An Introduction to Functional Grammar* (London: Hodder Arnold, 2004)

Halsey, A. H. (ed.) with J. Webb, *Twentieth-century British Social Trends*
   (Basingstoke: Macmillan, 2000)

Hamer, M., 'The Press Association at work: examination of a news agency's
   contribution to the media and public spheres', M.Sc. dissertation,
   Liverpool John Moores University 2000

Harris, E. T., 'Integrity and Improvisation in the Music of Handel', *Journal of
   Musicology*, 8(3) (1990), 301

Harris Interactive, *Research on the Effectiveness of Deterring Illegal Music
   Filesharing on P2P Sites and Networks in the UK*, 2009

Heidensohn, F., 'Gender and Crime', in Maguire *et al.*, *Oxford Handbook of
   Criminology* (2nd edn)

Henning, D. K., 'Rappers Sorrow, or How Copyright's Restriction on Digital
   Sampling Inhibits African-American Participation in Societal Discourse'
   (2008) (last accessed 6 June 2009, at: http://works.bepress.com/darrin_hen-
   ning/2)

Henry, S. and D. Milanovanovich, *Constitutive Criminology* (London: Sage, 1996)

Herford, C. H. and P and E. Simpson (eds.), *Ben Jonson*, 11 vols. (Oxford:
   Clarendon Press, 1925–52)

Heritage, M., 'The End of "Look and Feel" and the Invasion of the Little Green Men? UK Copyright and Patent Protection for Software after 2005', *Computer and Telecommunications Law Review*, 12(3) (2006), 67

Hill, A. G., (ed.), *The Letters of William and Dorothy Wordsworth*, 8 vols. (2nd edn, Oxford: Clarendon Press, 1967–93), vol. vi, p. 493

Hinduja, S., *Music Piracy and Crime Theory* (New York: LFB Scholarly Publishing LLC, 2000)

Hirschi, T. and M. R. Gottfredson, 'In Defense of Self-control', *Theoretical Criminology*, 4(1) (2000), 55–69

Holt, H., 'The Recoil of Piracy', *Forum*, 5 (1888), 27–37

Home, S. *Neoism, Plagiarism and Praxis* (Edinburgh: AK Press, 1995)

Honneth, A., *Critique of Power* (Cambridge, MA: MIT Press, 1991)

Hope, J., *The Authorship of Shakespeare's Plays: A Socio-Linguistic Study* (Cambridge University Press, 2008)

Hopkins Burke, R., *An Introduction to Criminological Theory* (Cullompton: Willan Publishing, 2001)

Horth, L. (ed.), *Herman Melville, Correspondence* (Evanston and Chicago, IL: Northwestern University Press, 1993)

House, M., G. Storey and K. Tillotson (eds.), *The Letters of Charles Dickens*, 12 vols. (Oxford: Clarendon Press, 1965–2002), vol. III, p. 60, n. 1

Howard, D., 'Copyright and the Music Business in Jamaica: Protection for Whom' (2008) (last accessed 6 August 2009, at: www.revistabrasileiradocaribe.org/DennisHoward.pdf)

Hurd, R., ed. and tr., *Q. Horatii Flacci epistola ad Augustum. With an English Commentary and Notes. To which is added, A Discourse Concerning Poetical Imitation*, 2 vols. (London, 1751–3)

*A Letter to Mr. Mason; on the Marks of Imitation* (1757)

Hutton, W., *The Stakeholding Society. Writings on Politics and Economics* (Cambridge: Polity Press, 1999)

Hymes, D., *Foundations in Sociolinguistics: An Ethnographic Approach* (Philadelphia, PA: University of Pennsylvania Press, 1977)

I, P., 'It Sipple Out Deh' (2005) (last accessed 1 October 2009, at: www.reggae-vibes.com/concert/maxromeo/maxromeo3.htm)

I, P., Interview with U Brown, 'Mr Brown Somet'ing' (2005) (last accessed 1 October 2009, at: www.reggae-vibes.com/)

IIPA (International Intellectual Property Alliance) 'Statistics' (at: www.iipa.com/copytighttrade_issues.html, 2006)

International Federation of the Phonographic Industry (ifpi), *Recording Industry in Numbers 2009* (London, 2009)

IP Crime Group, (2009) *2008–2009 IP Crime Report* (Newport: IP Crime Group)

IPSOS, 'Online Software Piracy Poll' (at: www.ipsos-na.com?news/pressrelease.cfm?id=2452, 2004)

'The Opinion of French People Regarding Illegal Music Downloading on the Internet', 2008

Irvin, S., 'Appropriation and Authorship in Contemporary Art', *British Journal of Aesthetics* (2005)

Jackson, H., *Lexicography: An Introduction* (London: Routledge, 2002)

Jahn, B. and T. Weber, *Reggae Island: Jamaican Music in the Digital Age* (New York: Da Capo Press, 1998)

Jakobson, R., '*Closing Statement: Linguistics and Poetics*', in T. Sebeok (ed.), *Style in Language* (Cambridge, MA: MIT Press, 1960)

Jamaica, G., 'Time to Pay', *Jamaica Gleaner*, 23 July 2000 (at: www.jamaica-gleaner. com/gleaner/20000723/Ent/Ent1.html, last accessed 23 August 2009)

Jaszi, P., 'Toward a Theory of Copyright: The Metamorphosis of "Authorship"', *Duke Law Journal* (1991), 455

Jedwab, J., 'The Lowdown on Music Downloading in Canada: Youth Regard Internet Downloading of Music, Video and Software as Acceptable: Only Threat of Legal Action is Effective Deterrent'( at www.acs-aec.ca/Polls/ 18-10-2004-1.pdf, 2004)

Jewkes, Y., (ed.), *Crime Online* (Cullompton: Willan Publishing, 2007)

John, Sir Elton, Times Online, 'Elton John Backs Lord Mandelson's Move to Disconnect Illegal File Sharers', 22 September 2009 (at www.timesonline. co.uk/tol/news/uk/article6843437.ece)

Johns, A., *The Nature of the Book: Print and Knowledge in the Making* (University of Chicago Press, 1998)

*Piracy: The Intellectual Property Wars from Gutenberg to Gates* (University of Chicago Press, 2010)

Johnson, R. U., *Remembered Yesterdays* (London: Allen & Unwin, 1924)

Johnson, S., 'Considerations [by the late Dr Samuel Johnson] on the Case of Dr T [rapp]'s Sermons, abridged by Mr Cave, 1739', *The Gentleman's Magazine*, 57(2), 555

*The Lives of the Most Eminent English Poets; with Critical Observations on their Works*, ed. R. Lonsdale, 4 vols. (Oxford: Clarendon Press, 2006)

Jones, R., 'Technology, the Cultural Appropriation of Music and the Creative Commons', *International Review of Law, Computers and Technology*, 23 (2009), 109

Jones, R. and E. Cameron, 'Full Fat, Semi-skimmed or No Milk Today – Creative Commons Licences and English Folk Music', *International Review of Law, Computers and Technology*, 1 (2005)

Jonson, B., *Poetaster*, ed. T. Cain (Manchester University Press, 1996)

Jordan, T., *Hacking: Digital Media and Technological Determinism* (Cambridge: Polity, 2008)

Juola, P., 'Authorship Attribution', *Foundations and Trends in Information Retrieval*, 1(3) (2006), 233–334

Jupiter Research, *Music Industry Losses*, 2007

*Analysis of the European Online Music Market Development and Assessment of Future Opportunities*, 2009

Katz, D., *Solid Foundation: An Oral History of Reggae* (London: Bloomsbury Publishing plc, 2003)

Keeble, R., *The Newspapers Handbook* (London: Routledge, 1998)

Keil, C., 'Motion and Feeling through Music', in C. Keil and S. Feld (eds.), *Music Grooves: Essays and Dialogues* (University of Chicago Press, 1990)

Kennedy, D. M., 'A Primer on Open Source Licensing Legal Issues: Copyright, Copyleft and Copyfuture' (last accessed 1 August 2009, at: www.denniskennedy.com/opensourcedmk.pdf)

Kienreich, W., M. Granitzer, V. Sabol and W. Klieber, 'Plagiarism Detection in Large Sets of Press Agency News Articles', *Proceedings of 17th International Conference on Database and Expert Systems Applications DEXA'06* (2006), 181–8

Kim, J. K., S. Candan, and J. Tatemura, 'Efficient Overlap and Content Reuse Detection in Blogs and Online News Articles', *Proceedings of the 18th International Conference on World Wide Web WWW'09*, (2009), ACM, New York, NY, 81–90

Kini, R., H. Pamakrishna and B. Vijayaraman, 'An Exploratory Study of Moral Intensity Regarding Software Piracy of Students in Thailand', *Behaviour and Information Technology*, 22 (2003), 63–70

Kintsch, W., *Comprehension: A Paradigm for Cognition* (Cambridge University Press, 1998)

Kitch, E. W., 'The Nature and Function of the Patent System', *Journal of Law and Economics*, 20 (1977), 265

Knowles, Elizabeth (ed.), *The Oxford Dictionary of Quotations* (Oxford University Press, 2004)

Kompridis, N., *Critique and Disclosure* (Cambridge, MA: MIT Press, 2006)

Korn, A., 'Issues Facing Legal Practitioners in Measuring Substantiality of Contemporary Musical Expression', *John Marshall Review of IP*, 6(3) (2007), 489–500

Kozul-Wright, Z. and L. Stanbury, 'Becoming A Globally Competitive Player: The Case of The Music Industry in Jamaica', (1998) (last accessed 6 June 2009, at: www.unctad.org/en/docs/dp_138.en.pdf)

Krasilovsky, M. W. and S. Shemel, *This Business of Music* (New York: Watson-Guptill Publications, 2007)

Krauss, R., *The Originality of the Avant-Garde and Other Modernist Myths* (Cambridge, MA: MIT Press, 1986)

*A Voyage on Art in the Age of the North Sea: Post Medium Condition* (London: Thames & Hudson, 1999)

Laboulaye, E. and G. Guiffrey, *La propriété littéraire au XVIIIe siècle. Recueil de pièces et de documents* (Paris: Librairie Louis Hachette, 1859)

Lacan, J., *Four Fundamental Concepts of Psycho-analysis*, trans. A. Sheridan (London: Hogarth Press and the Institute of Psycho-analysis, 1977)

Lakoff, G., *Don't Think of an Elephant: Know Your Values and Frame the Debate* (Vermont: Chelsea Green Publishers, 2004)

Lakoff, G., and M. Johnson, *Metaphors We Live By* (University of Chicago Press, 1980)

Lambert, S., *The Image Multiplied: Five Centuries of Printed Reproductions of Paintings and Drawings* (London: Trefoil Publications, 1987)

Lancaster, K., *Consumer Demand: A New Approach* (New York: Columbia UP, 1971)

Landes, W. M. and R. A. Posner, *The Economic Structure of Intellectual Property Law* (Cambridge, MA: Harvard University Press, 2003)

Lathrop, G. P., 'Should Foreign Authors Be Protected?', *Forum*, 1 (1886), 495–500

Latman, A., '"Probative" Similarity as Proof of Copying: Toward Dispelling Some Myths in Copyright Infringement', *Columbia Law Review*, 90 (1990), 1187

Lawrence, K. F., 'The web of community trust – amateur fiction online: a case study in community focused design for the semantic web', Ph.D. thesis, University of Southampton, 2007 (at: http://eprints.ecs.soton.ac.uk/14704/)

Lea, J., *Crime and Modernity* (London: Sage, 2002)

Lebel, R., *Marcel Duchamp* (New York: Grove Press, 1959)

Lee, D., *Romantic Liars: Obscure Women who became Impostors and Challenged an Empire* (New York and Basingstoke: Palgrave Macmillan, 2006)

Lefranc, D., *La renommée en droit privé* (Paris: LGDJ, 2004)

'Le piratage déraciné', *Omnidroit newsletter*, 27 August 2008, no. 14, p. 2; D. 2008, 2087–8

'Téléchargement illégal: que faire?', *Gaz. Pal.*, 119–20 (29–30 April 2009), 2

Lemley, M. A., 'The Economics of Improvement in Intellectual Property Law', *Texas Law Review*, 75 (1997), 989

'Romantic Authorship and the Rhetoric of Property', *Texas Law Review*, 75 (1997), 873

'Ex Ante versus Ex Post Justifications for Intellectual Property', *University of Chicago Law Review*, 71 (2004), 129

'Property, Intellectual Property, and Free Riding', *Texas Law Review*, 83 (2005), 1031

Lennart Carlson, C., *The First Magazine: A History of the Gentleman's Magazine* (Providence, RI: Brown University, 1938)

Lerner, J. and Tirole, J., 'The Simple Economics of Open Source' (2000) (last accessed 6 October 2009, at: www.hbs.edu/research/facpubs/workingpapers/papers2/9900/00–059.pdf)

Lerner, J. and Tirole, J., 'The Scope of Open Source Licensing' (2006) (last accessed 6 October 2009, at: www.people.hbs.edu/jlerner/OSLicense.pdf)

Lessig, L., *Code* (New York: Doubleday, 2003)

*Free Culture* (New York: Penguin Press, 2004)

Levinson, S., *Pragmatics* (Cambridge University Press, 1983)

Levy, D., 'Document Re-use and Document Systems', *Electronic Publishing*, 6(4) (1993), 339–48

LeWitt, S., 'Paragraphs on Conceptual Art', (1967), in C. Harrison and P. Wood (eds.), *Art in Theory 1900–1990: An Anthology of Changing Ideas* (Cambridge, MA: Blackwell, 1992)

Liang, L., 'A Guide to Open Content Licences' (2004) (last accessed 26 June 2009, at: http://pzwart.wdka.hro.nl/mdr/research/lliang/open_content_guide)

'Copyright, Cultural Production and Open-Content Licensing', *Indian Journal of Law and Technology*, 1 (2006), 96–157

Liebowitz, S. J., 'File-Sharing: Creative Destruction or Just Plain Destruction?', December 2004, School of Management, University of Texas at Dallas (at: http://som.utdallas.edu/centers/capri/documents/destruction.pdf)

Liebowitz, S. J. and R. Watt, 'How to Best Ensure Remuneration for Creators in the Market For Music? Copyright and its Alternatives', *Journal of Economic Surveys*, 20(4) (2006), 513–45

Litman, J., *Digital Copyright* (Amherst, NY: Prometheus, 2001)

Locke, J., *Essay Concerning Humane Understanding* (5th edn, London, 1706)

*Two Treatises of Government*, ed. P. Laslett (Cambridge University Press, 1990)

Lonsdale, R., 'Gray and "Allusion": The Poet as Debtor', in R. F. Brissenden and J. C. Eade (eds.), *Studies in the Eighteenth Century IV: Papers Presented at the Fourth David Nichol Smith Memorial Seminar* (Canberra: Australian National University Press, 1979)

Lonsdale, R. (ed.), *The New Oxford Book of Eighteenth-Century Verse* (Oxford University Press, 1987)

Loughlan, P., 'You Wouldn't Steal a Car … : Intellectual Property and the Language of Theft', *European Intellectual Property Review*, 29 (2007), 401

Loughran, T., *The Republic in Print: Print Culture in the Age of US Nation Building, 1770–1870* (New York: Columbia University Press, 2007)

Love, Harold, *Attributing Authorship: An Introduction* (Cambridge University Press, 2002)

Lucas, A., and H.-J. Lucas, *Traité de la propriété littéraire et artistique* (3rd edn, Paris: Litec, 2006)

Lunney, G. S., 'Reexamining Copyright's Incentives–Access Paradigm', *Vanderbilt Law Review*, 49(3) (1996), 48

Lynch, J., *Deception and Detection in Eighteenth-Century Britain* (Aldershot: Ashgate, 2008)

Lyon, C. J. Malcolm and B. Dickerson, 'Detecting Short Passages of Similar Text in Large Document Collections', *Proceedings of the 2001 Conference on Empirical Methods in Natural Language Processing* (2001), 118–25

Macfarlane, R., *Original Copy: Plagiarism and Originality in Nineteenth-Century Literature* (Oxford University Press, 2007)

Mack, M., *Alexander Pope: A Life* (New Haven, CT and London: Yale University Press, 1985)

Mackaay, E., 'Economic Incentives in Markets for Information and Innovation', *Harvard Journal of Law and Public Policy* (1990), 867

Macmillan, F., 'Artistic Practice and the Integrity of Copyright Law', in M. Rosenmeier and S. Teilmann (eds.), *Art and Law: The Copyright Debate* (DJØF Publishing, 2005), p. 49

MacQueen, H., C. Waelde and G. Laurie, *Contemporary Intellectual Property: Law and Policy* (Oxford University Press, 2008)

Maguire, M., 'Crime Data and Statistics', in Maguire *et al.*, *Oxford Handbook of Criminology*, 4th edn, pp. 241–301

Maguire, M., R. Morgan, R. Reiner (eds.), *The Oxford Handbook of Criminology* (1st, 2nd, 3rd and 4th edns, Oxford University Press, 1994, 1997, 2004 and 2007)

Mallon, T., *Stolen Words: Forays into the Origins and Ravages of Plagiarism* (New York: Ticknor and Fields, 1989)

Mani, I. and E. Bloedorn, 'Summarising Similarities and Differences Among Related Documents', *Information Retrieval*, 1(1–2) (1999), 35–67

Mann, D. and M. Sutton, 'Netcrime: More Change in the Organisation of Thieving', *British Journal of Criminology*, 38(2) (1998), 210–29

Manuel, P. and W. Marshall, 'The Riddim Method: Aesthetics, Practice, and Ownership in Jamaican Dancehall', *Popular Music*, 25(3) (2006), 447–70

Marsh, B., *Plagiarism: Alchemy and Remedy* (Albany, NY: State University of New York Press, 2007)

Martin, A., *The Undecidable: Basic Papers on Undecidable Propositions, Unsolvable Problems and Computable Functions* (New York: Raven Press, 1965)

Marx, K., *Capital, Volume 1* (Harmondsworth: Penguin Books, 1976)

Masiyakurima, P., 'The Futility of the Idea/Expression Dichotomy in UK Copyright', IIC (2007), 548

Matthews, B., 'American Authors and British Pirates', *Princeton Review*, 5(4) (1877), 201–12

'Memories of Mark Twain', in *The Tocsin of Revolt and Other Essays* (New York: Charles Scribner's Sons, 1922), pp. 255–9

Maugham, R., *Treatise on the Laws of Literary Property* (London, 1828)

Mazzeo, T. J., *Plagiarism and Literary Property in the Romantic Period* (Philadelphia, PA: University of Pennsylvania Press, 2007)

McClean, D. (ed.), *The Trials of Art* (London: Ridinghouse, 2007)

McClean, D. and K. Schubert, (eds.), *Dear Images: Art, Copyright and Culture* (London: Ridinghouse, 2002)

McEnery, A. M. and A. Wilson, *Corpus Linguistics* (Edinburgh Textbooks in Empirical Linguistics, 1996)

McKeown, K. and H. Jing, 'The Decomposition of Human-Written Summary Sentences', *Proceeding of the 22nd International Conference on Information Retrieval SIGIR'99* (1999) 129–36

McLeod, K., 'How Copyright Law Changed Hip Hop', *Stay Free*, 20 (2002) (at: www.stayfreemagazine.org/archives/20/public_enemy.html, last accessed 6 June 2008)

 *Freedom of Expression: Overzealous Copyright Bozos and other Enemies of Creativity* (New York: Doubleday, 2005)

McMillan, J., 'Trench Town Rock: The Creation of Jamaica's Music Industry' (2005) (last accessed 26 June 2009, at:http://faculty-gsb.stanford.edu/mcmillan/personal_page/documents/Jamaica%20music%20paper.pdf)

Meeker, H., 'Origins and Development of Open Source and GPL Licencing', *Communications and Technology Law Review*, 41 (2008)

Meier, G. F., *The Merry Philosopher; or, Thoughts on Jesting* (London, 1764)

Meltzer, F., *Hot Property: The Stakes and Claims of Literary Originality* (University of Chicago Press, 1994)

Mercuro, N. and S. G. Medema, *Economics and the Law* (2nd edn, Princeton, NJ: Princeton University Press, 2006)

Merges, R. P., 'Of Property Rules, Coase, and Intellectual Property', *Columbia Law Review*, 94 (1994), 2655–95

 'One Hundred Years of Solicitude', *California Law Review*, 88 (2000), 2187

 'A New Dynamism in the Public Domain', *University of Chicago Law Review*, 71 (2004), 183

Merlin, Ph.-A., *Contrefaçon in Répertoire universel et raisonné de jurisprudence* (Brussels: H. Tarlier, 1825) (available at: www.copyrighthistory.org/cgi-bin/kleioc/0010/exec/ausgabe/"f_1825")

Merrill, T. W., 'The Demsetz Thesis and the Evolution of Property Rights', *Journal of Legal Studies*, 31 (2002), 331

Merton, R. K., *Social Theory and Social Structure* (New York: Free Press, 1949)

Metzler, D. and Y. Bernstein, B. Croft, A. Moffat and J. Zobel, 'Similarity Measures for Tracking Information Flow', *Proceedings of the ACM Conference on Information and Knowledge Management CIKM'05* (2005) Bremen, Germany, 517–24

Michel, N. J., 'The Impact of Digital File Sharing on the Music Industry: An Empirical Analysis', *Topics in Economic Analysis and Policy*, 6(1) (2006), Article 18

Miles, S. and E. Stoker, '*Nova Productions Limited* v. *Mazooma Games Ltd*', Ent. LR (2006), 181

Milton, J., *Complete Shorter Poems*, ed. John Carey (Harlow: Longman, 1971)

Moglen, E., 'Anarchism triumphant: Free software and the death of copyright', *First Monday* 4(8) (August 1999) (last accessed 6 October 2009, at:http://firstmonday.org/htbin/cgiwrap/bin/ojs/index.php/fm/article/view/684/594)

Muncie, J., 'The Construction and Deconstruction of Crime', in J. Muncie and E. McLaouglin (eds.), *The Problem of Crime* (2nd edn, London: Sage, in assoc. with the Open University, 2001)

Nagappan, N. *et al.*, 'The Influence of Organizational Structure on Software Quality: An Empirical Case Study', *ICSE* (2008), 521–30

Nelson, R., Transcript of interview with Clinton Fearon, (1999) (last accessed 26 June 2009, at: www.niceup.com/interviews/clinton_fearon_KRCL)

Netanel, N. W., 'Copyright and a Democratic Civil Society', *Yale Law Journal*, 106(2) (1996), 283

Newburn, T., *Criminology* (Cullompton: Willan Publishing, 2007)

Nimmer, D., 'A Riff on Fair Use in the Digital Millennium Copyright Act', *University of Pennsylvania Law Review*, 148 (2000), 673–742

Nimmer, David, 'Access Denied', *Utah Law Review*, (2007), 769

NUA Internet Statistics, 'How Many Online?', (2003) (at:www.nua.ie/surveys/how_many_online/)

Nuyts, J., and E. Pedersen, *Language and Conceptualization* (Cambridge University Press, 1997)

Oberholzer, F. and K. Strumpf, 'The Effect of File Sharing on Record Sales: An Empirical Analysis', *Journal of Political Economy*, 115(1) (2007), 1–42

Oberholzer-Gee, F. and K. Strumpf, 'The Effect of File Sharing on Record Sales – An Empirical Analysis' (2004) (at: www.unc.edu/~cigar/papers/FileSharing_March2004.pdf)

Ofcom, *Prosecution Statistics 2006–2007*, (2007) (at:www.ofcom.org.uk/media/new/2007/04/nt_20070401)

Okpaluba, J., 'Digitisation, culture and copyright law: digital sampling, a case study', Ph.D. thesis, King's College London, 2000

'Appropriation Art: Fair Use or Foul?', in McClean and Schubert, *Dear Images*

O'Neill, J., *The Market: Ethics, Knowledge and Politics* (London: Routledge, 1998)

Ormerod, D., 'The Fraud Act 2006 – Criminalising Lying?', *Criminal Law Review* (2007), 193–219

*Oxford Classical Dictionary* (Oxford: Clarendon Press, 1949)

Palmer, T., 'Intellectual Property: A Non-Posnerian Law and Economics Approach', *Hamline Law Review* (1989), 261

Peitz, M. and P. Waelbroeck, 'The Effect of Internet Piracy on Music Sales: Cross-Section Evidence', *Review of Economic Research on Copyright Issues*, 1(2) (2004), 71–9

Pfister, L., 'L'auteur, propriétaire de son œuvre ?: la formation du droit d'auteur du XVIe siècle à la loi de 1957', thesis, Université Robert Schuman : Strasbourg, 1999

Pila, J., 'An Intentional View of the Copyright Work', *Modern Law Review*, 71(4) (2008), 535–58

Pincus, S., *1688: The First Modern Revolution* (New Haven, CT: Yale University Press, 2009)

Plant, A., 'The Economic Aspects of Copyright in Books', *Economica*, 1 (1934), 167–95

*Pleading of the counsel before the House of Lords, in the great cause concerning literary property, The* (London: for C. Wilkin, S. Axtell, J. Axtell and J. Browne, [1774])

Pope, A., *Poem*, ed. John Butt (London and New York: Routledge, 1989)

Posner, R. A., *Economic Analysis of Law* (4th edn, Boston, MA: Little, Brown, 1992)

*Economic Analysis of Law* (6th edn, New York: Aspen, 2002)

Pouillet, E., *Traité théorique et pratique de la propriété littéraire et artistique et du droit de représentation* (Paris: Imprimerie et Librairie Générale de Jurisprudence, 1908)

Power, D. and D. Hallencreutz, 'Profiting from Creativity? The Music Industry in Stockholm, Sweden and Kingston, Jamaica', *Environment and Planning* (A), 34(10) (2002), 1833–54

Preece, R., 'Reality Check: When Appropriation becomes Copyright Infringement', *Sculpture*, 28(5) (June 2009)

Propp, V., *The Morphology of the Folktale* (Austin, TX: University of Texas Press, 1968)

Purchas, S., *Purchas His Pilgrimage. Or Relations of the World and the Religions Observed in all Ages and Places Discovered . . .* (London, 1613)

Puri, S., *The Caribbean Postcolonial: Social Equality, Post-Nationalism and Cultural Hybridity* (New York: Palgrave Macmillan, 2004)

Putnam, R., *Bowling Alone: The Collapse and Revival of American Community* (New York: Simon & Schuster, 2000)

Ram, T., *Magnitude in Marginalia: Edward Cave and the Gentleman's Magazine 1731–1754* (Utrecht: Gottmann & Fainsilber Katz, 1999)

Rancière, J., *The Politics of Aesthetics* (London: Continuum Press, 2006)

Randall, M., *Pragmatic Plagiarism: Authorship, Profit and Power* (University of Toronto Press, 2001)

Rawley, J. A., 'An Early History of the International Copyright Movement', *Library Quarterly*, 11 (1941), 202–6

Rawson, Hugh and Miner, Margaret (eds.), *The Oxford Dictionary of American Quotations* (Oxford University Press, 2006)

Reah, D., *The Language of Newspapers* (London: Routledge, 1998)

Reichman, J. H., 'A Manifesto Concerning the Legal Protection of Computer Programs', *Columbia Law Review*, 94 (1994), 2308–2431

'Legal Hybrids between Patent and Copyright Paradigms', *Columbia Law Review*, 94 (1994), 2434

Remer, R., *Printers and Men of Capital: Philadelphia Book Publishers in the New Republic* (Philadelphia, PA: Pennsylvania University Press, 1996)

Renouard, A.-C., *Traité des droits d'auteurs dans la littéraire et artistique et du droit de representation* (Paris: Jules Renouard et Cie., 1838–9)

Report of the Committee on the Law of Copyright (1909) Cd. 4976

RIAA (Recording Industry Association of America) (2004), '531 more file sharers targeted in latest RIAA efforts' (at:www.riaa.com/news/newsletter/021704.asp)

Richardson, J. E., 'News Reports from Press Agency Sources: An Insight on Newspaper Style', Sheffield Online Papers in Social Research (ShOP), (2000), no. 2

Richardson, S., *An Address to the Public, on the Treatment of which the Editor of the History of Sir Charles Grandison has met with from certain Booksellers in Dublin* (London, 1753)

    *Case of Samuel Richardson, of London, Printer; with regard to the Invasion of his Property in The History of Sir Charles Grandison, before Publication* (n.p. [London], n.d. [1753])

Ricketson, S. and J. Ginsburg, *International Copyright and Neighbouring Rights: The Berne Convention and Beyond*, vol. 1 (Oxford University Press, 2006)

Rideau, F., *La formation du droit de la propriété littéraire en France et en Grande Bretagne. Une convergence oubliée* (Aix en Provence: Presses Universitaires d'Aix-Marseille, 2004)

Rob, R. and J. Waldfogel, 'Piracy on the High C's: Music Downloading, Sales Displacement, and Social Welfare in a Sample of College Students', *Journal of Law and Economics*, 49(1) (2006), 29–62

Rose, M., *Authors and Owners: The Invention of Copyright* (Cambridge, MA: Harvard University Press, 1993)

    'The Author in Court: *Pope v. Curll* (1741)', in M. Woodmansee and P. Jaszi (eds.), *The Construction of Authorship: Textual Appropriation in Law and Literature* (Durham, NC: Duke University Press, 1994)

    'The Author as Proprietor', in B. Sherman and A. Strowel (eds.), *Of Authors and Origins* (Oxford: Clarendon Press, 1996), pp. 23–55

    'Technology and Copyright in 1735: The Engraver's Act', *Information Society*, 21(1) (January–March 2005), 63–6

Rosenberg, M., 'Note, Do You Hear What I Hear? Expert Testimony in Music Infringement Cases in the Ninth Circuit', UC Davis L. Rev., 39 (2006), 1669

Rossi, S. and C. Storti (eds.), *Le matrici del diritto commerciale tra storia e tendenze evolutive* (Insubria University Press 2009), pp. 147–8

Rothman, J., 'The Questionable Use of Custom in Intellectual Property', *Virginia LR*, 93 (2007), 1899

Russett, M., *Fictions and Fakes: Forging Romantic Authenticity, 1760–1845* (Cambridge University Press, 2006)

Saeed, J., *Semantics* (Oxford: Blackwell, 1997)

Sag, M., 'Beyond Abstraction: the Law and Economics of Copyright Scope and Doctrinal Efficiency', *Tulane Law Review*, 81 (2006), 187–250

St Clair, W., 'Metaphors of intellectual property'. Unpublished paper presented at 'Inspiration, Innovation, or Infringement: multidisciplinary perspectives on piracy and copyright', a seminar held at Emanuel College, University of Cambridge, 1 July 2008

'Metaphors of Intellectual Property', in Deazley *et al.*, *From Privilege to Property*, pp. 365–95

Samuelson, P., 'Why Copyright Law Excludes Systems and Processes from the Scope of Its Protection', *Texas Law Review*, 85 (2006–7), 1921

Samuelson, P., R. Davis, M. D. Kapor and J. H. Reichman, 'A Manifesto Concerning the Legal Protection of Computer Programs', *Columbia Law Review*, 94 (1994), 2308

Samuelson, P. and T. Wheatland, 'Statutory Damages in Copyright: A Remedy in Need of Reform' (2009) (at: http://papers.ssrn.com/sol3/papers.cfm? abstract_id=1375604)

Saunders, F., *The Early History of the International Copyright in America* (1888) *Saunders Mss.*

Saussure, F. de, *Course in General Linguistics*, trans. and annot. R. Harris (London: Duckworth, 1983)

Schiff, R. and R. Nelson (eds.), *Critical Terms for Art History* (2nd edn, University of Chicago Press, 2003)

Schoenbaum, S., *William Shakespeare: A Compact Documentary Life* (New York and Oxford: Oxford University Press, 1987)

School of Mathematics and Statistics, University of St Andrews *The MacTutor History of Mathematics archive* (1998) (available at: www-gap.dcs.st-and.ac. uk/~history/Mathematicians/Babbage.html)

Schwartz, H., *The Culture of the Copy: Striking Likenesses, Unreasonable Facsimiles* (New York: Zone Books, 1996)

Seager, R. II (ed.), *The Papers of Henry Clay*, 11 vols. (Lexington, KY: University of Kentucky Press, 1959–92), vol. IX, 22

Sennett, R., *Corrosion of Character. The Personal Consequences of Work in the New Capitalism* (New York: W. W. Norton, 1999)

  *Respect. The Formation of Character in an Age of Inequality* (London: Allen Lane, 2003)

Shadbolt, M., *The New Zealand Wars Trilogy: The House of Strife* (Auckland, NZ: David Ling Publishing, 2005)

Shagan, E., 'Constructing discord: Ideology, Propaganda, and English Responses to the Irish Rebellion in 1641', *Journal of British Studies*, 36 (1997), 4–34

Shakespeare, W., *Poems* (London, 1640)

  *Twelfth Night*, Oxford World's Classics (New York: Oxford University Press, 1994)

Shavell, S., *Foundations of Economic Analysis of Law* (Cambridge, MA: Harvard University Press, 2004)

Shaw, C. R. and H. D. McKay, *Juvenile Delinquency and Urban Areas* (University of Chicago Press, 1942)

Sherman, B., 'Appropriating the Postmodern: Copyright and the Challenge of the New', *Social and Legal Studies*, 4 (1995), 31–54

Sherman, B., and L. Bently, *The Making of Modern Intellectual Property Law: The British Experience* 1760–1911 (Cambridge University Press, 1999)

Shivakumar, N. and H. Garcia-Molina, 'Building a Scalable and Accurate Copy Detection Mechanism' (1996), *Proceedings of 1st ACM International Conference on Digital Libraries DL'96*, 160–68

Shuy, R., *Fighting over Words: Language and Civil Law Cases* (Oxford University Press, 2008)

Slater, D. and F. Tonkiss, *Market Society: Markets and Modern Social Theory* (Cambridge: Polity, 2001)

Slater, J. H. *The law relating to copyright and trade marks, treated more particularly with reference to infringement: forming a digest of the more important English and American decisions, together with the practice of the English courts and forms of informations, notices, pleadings and injunctions* (London: Stevens and Sons, 1884)

Smiles, S., *A publisher and his friends: Memoir and correspondence of the late John Murray*, 2 vols. (London: Murray, 1891), vol. I, 27

*Speech of Mr Jacob Ilive to his brethren the master-Printers, the* (London: n.p.n.d. [1750])

Sperber, D., and D. Wilson, *Relevance: Communication and Cognition* (2nd edn, Oxford: Blackwell, 1995)

Spiller, Michael, *The Development of the Sonnet: An Introduction* (London: Routledge, 1992)

Springer, R., 'Folklore, Commercialism and Exploitation: Copyright in the Blues', *Popular Music*, 26(1) (2007), 33–45

Steinberger, R., B. Pouliquen, S. Scheer and A. Ribeiro, 'Continuous Multi-Source Information Gathering and Classification' (2003) *Proceedings of the International Conference on Computational Intelligence for Modelling, Control and Automation CIMCA'03*

Sterns, L., 'Copy Wrong: Plagiarism, Process, Property and the Law', *California Law Review*, 80 (1992), 513

Steuer, E., 'The Remix Masters' (2004) (last accessed, 1 October 2009, at:wired. com/wired/archive/12.11/beastie.html)

Stewart, S., *Crimes of Writing: Problems in the Containment of Representation* (Durham, NC: Duke University Press, 1994)

Stich, S., and T. Warfield (eds.), *Mental Representation: A Reader* (Oxford: Blackwell, 1994)

Stigler, G. and G. Becker, 'De Gustibus Non Est Disputandum', *American Economic Review*, 67 (1977), 76–90

Stokes, S., *Art and Copyright*, (Oxford: Hart Press, 2001)

'The Development of UK Software Copyright Law: From John Richardson Computers to Navitaire', *Communications and Technology Law Review*, 11(7) (2005), 129–33

Stolzoff, N. C., *Wake The Town and Tell The People: Dancehall Culture in Jamaica* (Durham, NC: Duke University Press, 2000)

Strasser, S. (ed.), *Commodifying Everything* (London: Routledge, 2003)

Stubbs, M., *Words and Phrases: Corpus Studies of Lexical Semantics* (Oxford: Blackwell, 2002)

Tagaris, K., 'UK Says Illegal Downloaders May Lose Web Access', Associated Press, 2009

Tanenbaum, A. S., *et al.*, 'Guidelines for Software Portability', *Software: Practice and Experience*, 8(6) (1978), 681–98

Tate, G., 'The Devil Made 'Em Do It: Public Enemy', in G. Tate, *Flyboy in the Buttermilk* (New York: Simon & Schuster, 1992)

Taylor, I., P. Walton and J. Young, *The New Criminology: For a Social Theory of Deviance* (London: Routledge & Kegan Paul, 1973)

Taylor, M. and E. Quayle, *Child Pornography: An Internet Crime* (London: Brunner–Routledge, 2003)

Tebbel, J., *A History of Book Publishing in the United States, vol. I: The Creation of an Industry 1630–1865* (New York: Bowker, 1975)

Tehranian, J., 'Infringement Nation: Copyright Reform and the Law/Norm Gap', *Utah Law Review*, 3 (2007), 537

Terry, R., '"Plagiarism": A Literary Concept in England to 1775', *English: Journal of the English Association*, 57 (2007), 1–16

'Pope and Plagiarism', *Modern Language Review*, 100 (2005), 593–608

Thompson, D., *Reggae and Caribbean Music* (San Francisco: Backbeat Books, 2002)

Thomson, I., 'Britain Becoming a Nation of Pirates' (2004) (at: www.crn.vnunet.com/news/1157189)

Towse, R., *Creativity, Incentive, and Reward: An Economic Analysis of Copyright and Culture in the Information Age* (Cheltenham: Edward Elgar, 2001)

'Copyright and Artists: A View from Cultural Economics', *Journal of Economic Surveys*, 20(4) (2006), 567–85

Toynbee, J., 'Copyright, the Work and Phonographic Orality in Music', *Social and Legal Studies*, 15(1) (2006), 77–99

*Bob Marley: Herald of a Postcolonial World?* (Cambridge: Polity, 2007)

Trusler, J., *An Essay on Literary Property containing comments on the Statute of Queen Anne and Animadversion on that Statute* (London, 1798)

Turing, A. M., 'On Computable Numbers, with an Application to the *Entscheidungsproblem*', *Proceedings of the London Mathematical Society*, 2 (42) (1937), 230–65

Tushnet, R., 'Payment in Credit: Copyright Law and Subcultural Creativity', *Law and Contemporary Problems*, 70 (2007), 135

Tyler, T. R., *Why People Obey the Law* (New Haven, CT: Yale University Press, 1990)

Udupa, S. K. *et al.*, 'Deobfuscation: Reverse Engineering Obfuscated Code', *12th Working Conference on Reverse Engineering*, 7–11 November 2005

Umbeck, J., 'Might Makes Rights: A Theory of the Foundation and Initial Distribution of Property Rights', *Economic Inquiry*, 19 (1981), 38

Vaidhyanathan, S., *Copyrights and Copywrongs: The Rise of Intellectual Property and How It Threatens Creativity* (New York University Press, 2003)

van Dijk, T., *Text and Context: Explorations in the Semantics and Pragmatics of Discourse* (London: Longman, 1977)

   *News Analysis: Case Studies of International and National News in the Press* (Hillsdale, NJ: Lawrence Erlbaum, 1988)

van Dyke, H., *The National Sin of Literary Piracy* (New York: Scribner's, 1888)

van Schijndel, M. and J. Smiers, 'Imagining a World without Copyright' (2002) (last accessed 26 June 2009, at:www.deburen.eu/uploads/documents/Artikel_Smiers_Van_Schijndel.pdf)

Veal, M. E., *Dub: Soundscapes and Shattered Songs in Jamaican Reggae* (Connecticut, CT: Wesleyan University Press, 2007)

Vincent, D., *Literacy and Popular Culture* (Cambridge University Press, 1989)

von Hirsch, A., P.-O. Wikström and E. Burney, *Criminal Deterrence and Sentence Severity* (Oxford: Hart Publishing, 1999)

Wacquant, L., 'Territorial Stigmatization in the Age of Advanced Marginality', *Thesis Eleven*, 91 (2007), 66–77

Wadlow, C., *The Law of Passing Off: Unfair Competition by Misrepresentation* (London: Sweet & Maxwell, 2004)

Wagner, R. P., 'Information Wants to be Free: IP and the Mythologies of Control', *Columbia Law Review*, 103 (2003), 995

Wall, D. (ed.), *Crime and the Internet* (London: Routledge, 2001)

   'Maintaining Order and Law on the Internet', in Wall, *Crime and the Internet Cybercrime. The Transformation of Crime in the Information Age* (Cambridge: Polity, 2007)

Wallis, R. and K. Malm, *Big Sounds from Small Peoples: The Music Industry in Small Countries* (London: Constable, 1984)

Walravens, N. 'The Concept of Originality and Contemporary Art', RIDA, 181 (1999), 96–167

Wanat, D. A., 'Copyright Law: Infringement of Musical Works and the Appropriateness of Summary Judgment under Federal Rules of Civil Procedure, Rule 56(c)', *University of Memphis Law Review*, 39 (2009), 1037

[Ward, E.], *A Journey to Hell: Or, a Visit paid to the Devil* (2nd edn, London: printed, and are to be sold by the Booksellers of London and Westminster, 1700)

Warfel, H. R. (ed.), *Letters of Noah Webster* (New York: Library Publishers, 1953)

Waterhouse, K., *Waterhouse on Newspaper Style* (London: Penguin, 1993)

Watt, R., *Copyright and Economic Theory* (Cheltenham: Edward Elgar, 2000)

Weaver, C. A., S. Mannes, and C. Fletcher (eds.), *Discourse Comprehension: Essays in Honor of Walter Kintsch* (Hillsdale, NJ: Lawrence Erlbaum Associates, 1995)

Webb, A., 'Can Filesharers Be Made to Pay?', *Guardian*, 22 March 2007

Weber, S., 'The Political Economy of Open Source Software' (2000) BRIE Working Paper 140 (accessed 2 April 2008, at: http://e-conomy.berkeley.edu/publications/wp/wp140.pdf)

'The Political Economy of Open Source' (2000) *Berkeley Roundtable on the International Economy*. Paper BRIEWP140 (accessed 26 June 2009, at: http://repositories.cdlib.org/brie/BRIEWP140)

Webster, N., 'On Education', *American Magazine* (December 1787–May 1788), 22–374

Wells, L. (ed.), 'Photography as Art', in *Photography: A Critical Introduction* (3rd edn, London and New York: Routledge: 2004)

Wesley, S., *Neck or Nothing: A Consolatory Letter from Mr. D-nt-n to Mr. C - rll Upon his being Tost in a Blanket, &c.* (n.p. [London], 1716)

Weyergraf-Serra, C. and M. Buskirk (ed.), *The Destruction of Tilted Arc: Documents* (Cambridge, MA: MIT Press, 1991)

White, G., 'The Evolution of Jamaican Music pt. 1: "Proto-ska" to Ska', *Social and Economic Studies*, 57(1) (1998), 5–19

White, H. O., *Plagiarism and Imitation during the English Renaissance* (Cambridge, MA: Harvard University Press, 1935)

White, T., *Catch a Fire: The Life of Bob Marley* (London: Omnibus Press, 2000)

Wilks, Y., 'On the Ownership of Text', *Computers and the Humanities*, 38(2) (2004), 115–27

Williams, K. S., *Textbook on Criminology* (Oxford University Press, 2004)

Wilson, D., A. Patterson, G. Powell and R. Hembury, *Fraud and technology crimes. Findings from the 2003/04 British Crime Survey, the 2004 Offending, Crime and Justice Survey and administrative sources*, Home Office Online Report 09/06 (London, Home Office, 2006)

Wilson, M., 'Glenn Brown: Gagosian Gallery', *Art Forum International* (22 June 2004), New York

Wise, M., 'Running Karp–Rabin Matching and Greedy String Tiling', Technical Report 463 (1993), Basser Department of Computer Science, Sydney University

'YAP3: Improved Detection of Similarities in Computer Programs and Other Texts' *Proceedings of 27th Technical Symposium on Computer Science Education SIGCSE'96*, (1996), pp. 130–4

Witter, M., 'Music and the Jamaican Economy' (2004) Prepared for UNCTAD/WIPO (last accessed 19 June 2008, at: www.wipo.int/export/sites/www/about-ip/en/studies/pdf/study_m_witter.pdf)

Wolf, M., *Proust and the Squid: The Story and Science of the Reading Brain* (New York: HarperCollins, 2007)

Wolf, P., on NME.com, 'Patrick Wolf backs Lily Allen over illegal music download stance', 15 September 2009 (at: www.nme.com/news/patrick-wolf/47316)

Woodmansee, M., *The Author, Art, and the Market: Rereading the History of Aesthetics* (New York: Columbia University Press, 1994)

Woodmansee, M. and P. Jaszi (eds.), *The Construction of Authorship: Textual Appropriation in Law and Literature* (Durham NC: Duke University Press, 1994)

Woolls, D. and M. Coulthard, 'Tools for the Trade', *Forensic Linguistics*, 5(1) (1998), 33–57

World Internet Usage Statistics News and World Population Statistics 2008, dated 17 August 2009 (at: www.internetworldstats.com/internet.htm)

Wu, D., 'Alignment', in Robert Dale, Hermann Moisl and Harold Somers (eds.), *Handbook of Natural Language Processing* (New York: Marcel Dekker, 2003), pp. 415–58

Yar, M., *Cybercrime and Society* (London: Sage, 2006)

Young, Y., *The Vertigo of Late Modernity* (London: Sage, 2007)

Zboray, R. J., *A Fictive People: Antebellum Economic Development and the American Reading Public* (Oxford University Press, 1993)

Zedner, L., 'The Pursuit of Security', in T. Hope and R. Sparks (eds.), *Crime, Risk and Insecurity* (London: Routledge, 2000), pp. 200–14

    'Securing Liberty in the Face of Terror: Reflections from Criminal Justice', *Journal of Law and Society*, 32 (2005), 507–33

Zentner, Alejandro, 'Measuring the Effect of Online Music Piracy on Music Sales', preliminary version, 2003, University of Chicago (at: http://economics.uchicago.edu/download/musicindustryoct12.pdf)

    'File Sharing and International Sales of Copyrighted Music: An Empirical Analysis with a Panel of Countries', *Topics in Economic Analysis and Policy*, 5(1) (2005), Article 21

    'Measuring the Effect of File-Sharing on Music Purchases', *Journal of Law and Economics*, 49(1) (2006), 63–90

## Discography

Beastie Boys (1989) 'Paul's Boutique', Capitol Records EST 2102
    (2004) 'To The 5 Boroughs', Capitol Records 7243 4 73397 1 4

Buster, Prince (1966) 'Don't Throw Stones/Prince of Peace', Blue Beat 45/BB 343
    (2000) 'Don't Throws Tones', *King of Ska*. Jet Star PBCD 11

Harriott, D. (1998) 'Do I Worry', *Trojan Rocksteady Box Set*. Trojan TRBCD 003

Minott, Sugar (1977) 'Live Loving', Studio One PSOL 001

Mittoo, J. (2000) 'A Darker Shade of Black', *The Keyboard King at Studio One*. Universal Sounds USCD 8

Public Enemy (1988) 'It Takes A Nation of Millions to Hold Us Back', Def Jam Recordings FC 44303

(1990) 'Fear of A Black Planet', Def Jam Recordings 466281 1

(1991) 'Apocalypse 91 . . . The Enemy Strikes Black', Def Jam Recordings C2 47374

Various Artists (1983) 'Best of Studio One', Heartbeat Records HB 007

(1985) 'Best of Studio One Vol. 2 – Full Up', Heartbeat Records HB 014

(1985) 'Master Mega Hits – Sleng Teng Extravaganza Vol. 1', Jammy's Records JM002

(1985) 'Master Mega Hits – Sleng Teng Extravaganza Vol. 2', Jammy's Records J003

(1988) 'Downbeat The Ruler: Killer Instrumentals, Best of Studio One Vol. 3', Heartbeat Records HB 038

(2004) 'Reggae Anthology The Channel One Story', VP Records VPRL–1678

(2004) 'Studio One Ska', Soul Jazz Records SJR CD85

Wailers, The (1991) 'Rolling Stone', *One Love at Studio One.* Heartbeat 617611

# INDEX

social welfare
  economic aspects of copyright 96
  meaning, economic theory 96
  overpricing, effect 104
software 211–12, 221
  ability to write 211
  abstraction 211
  algorithms *see* algorithms
  alteration 213
  applications 210
  attributed use 226
  binary *see* executables *below*
  binary code 212
  bugs, fixing 212–13, 222
  bundled 215–16, 256–7
  change, pace of 216–17, 258–9
  Church–Turing thesis 221, 283
  compilers 210
  component market 214
  computer games 225–6
  content of chapter 209–10
  continual innovation 216–17, 258–9
  copying
    detection 222, 228
    ease of 216, 240–1, 257–8
    legitimate needs 222
    non-literal copying, cases 233–6
    plagiarism detection programs,
      use 222
  copyright
    adequacy 239–40
    application of 218–23
    attitudes to, compared with music
      225–6
    cases 231–6
    concerns 230
    different approach needed 228
    disregard 225
    equivalence to other copyright
      works 230–8
    idea–expression dichotomy 231–6
    infringement 223–6
    level of protection 223
    open source 241–3
    protection 195
    *sui generis* right 238–43
    traditional models, applicability
      221, 283

creation 210–11
decompilation 210, 226
difference to other protected works
  209, 225
distinct characteristics 209
distribution, networks 215–16,
  217–18
downloading *see* downloading
'draft-excluder' analogy 235–6
education for writing 211–12
embedded 216, 258
encryption 227
enhancement 222–3
executables
  copying 223
  generally 210, 212
  licensing 218
Features 213
free software 215, 255
hardware as 217–18
hardware specifying by 217
impermanence 209
interaction 211
investment in, protection 222–3,
  239–40
licences *see* licences
'look and feel' concept 233–6
maintenance of 212–13, 222–3
meaning 210
mobile phones 216, 257–8
modularization 211
networking *see* networking
obfuscation 214, 227
obsolescence 224
open source *see* open source
operating systems, compatibility 214
ownership rights, approaches 209
piracy
  aspects 223
  China 224–5
  ease 240–1
  extent 224–5, 226
  wholesale 223–4
'plot or pudding' analogy 235
pricing for obsolescence 224
programming, newness of 212
programming languages 210, 211–12
protection technology 227